After the Black Death

After the Black Death

Economy, Society, and the Law in Fourteenth-Century England,

The Ford Lectures for 2019

MARK BAILEY

OXFORD

UNIVERSITY PRESS

OXFORD
UNIVERSITY PRESS

Great Clarendon Street, Oxford, OX2 6DP,
United Kingdom

Oxford University Press is a department of the University of Oxford.
It furthers the University's objective of excellence in research, scholarship,
and education by publishing worldwide. Oxford is a registered trade mark of
Oxford University Press in the UK and in certain other countries

First Edition published in 2021

Impression: 5

Published in the United States of America by Oxford University Press
198 Madison Avenue, New York, NY 10016, United States of America

British Library Cataloguing in Publication Data
Data available

Library of Congress Control Number: 2020952083

ISBN 978-0-19-885788-4

DOI: 10.1093/oso/9780198857884.001.0001

Printed and bound in the UK by
TJ Books Limited

Preface

In 1991 I wrote an article documenting a dramatic rise in storminess in the North Sea basin between the 1280s and 1340s, which resulted in extensive damage to English coastal communities between the Humber and Sussex (the storminess, not the article) and pointed to an unusual period of sustained, severe, weather conditions.[1] I had neither the courage nor the conviction to draw the obvious conclusion: something significant was happening to the climate, which in turn was driving major economic change. Even if I had, the academic community would have received the argument with polite but deep scepticism. The prevailing intellectual paradigm within economic and social history promoted a binary separation between human agency in long-term change ('endogenous' factors) and the agency of the environment and microbes ('exogenous'). Not only were the two regarded as autonomous and independent variables but exogenous factors were deemed to be subordinate to endogenous. Since then, however, global society's preoccupation with climate change, and the advances in our knowledge about past climates gained through scientific research, have comprehensively shifted the paradigm. In 2020 it is now obvious that the storminess in the North Sea was one manifestation of monumental long-term changes in the climate of the Northern hemisphere, which unleashed forces that no human agency on earth could control. Environmental history is now taken very seriously, and climate and human agency are understood to be complex and interdependent variables.

Similar observations hold for our changing interpretation of disease in general, and the Black Death in particular. Nineteenth-century historians were convinced of its primacy in driving social, economic, and cultural change, but views changed during the twentieth century when historians relentlessly downplayed its long-term influence. This downplaying was based in part upon on empirical research into original documents, but it also drew upon a growing societal scepticism about the importance of exogenous factors such as disease. Thirty appalling years of conflict and suffering between 1914 and 1945—two world wars, and a global influenza pandemic—had generated the highest aggregate level of mortality in the history of humanity, but even these unprecedented catastrophes had not prevented miraculous advances in science and medicine, or subsequent exponential growth in technology and wealth generation. The lesson of the twentieth century seemed to be that neither the human capacity for self-destruction nor the devastation wrought by invisible microbes could trump the creative forces of endogenous change: necessity inexorably stimulated humanity to invent. At the end of the twentieth century, however, two new and terrifying diseases shook this confidence and complacency. AIDS and Ebola reminded society of the capacity of pathogens to jump species and to mutate in ways that can outstrip the medical community's ability to cope. It cannot be coincidental that, from the 1990s, historians have been much more receptive about the transformative power of epidemic diseases and, as Chapter 1 shows, the scholarship on the Black Death changed accordingly.

This preface was written during the UK's lockdown period at the height of the Covid-19 pandemic in May 2020. The experience of watching medical science and support structures stretching to breaking point; governments intervening drastically to protect the welfare of their peoples, without necessarily defining exactly what that meant; the introduction of draconian quarantining measures; the emergence of conspiracy theories about the origins of the disease; pointing the finger of blame for its spread; and the appreciation and admiration for frontline carers during the pandemic, all provide partial insights into what coping with the Black Death must have been like in the late 1340s. In the eerie quiet and isolation of lockdown, we wonder about the likelihood of infection. The very real sense of uncertainty about what society and the economy might look like in twelve months' time—let alone years—is pervasive, powerful, and unsettling. Both provide a pertinent context for understanding the responses of survivors and the decisions they made in the 1350s and 1360s, which I have tried to do in Chapters 3 and 4, written some while before Covid-19 struck.

In 1991 the evidence for heightened storm activity between the 1280s and 1340s was overwhelming, yet my immaturity and timidity prevented me from drawing the obvious conclusions about climate and human agency in long-term economic wchange. In 2020 I am less immature and more emboldened by the wider acknowledgement of the influence of the environment and disease. What follows is an exercise in diminished timidity and increased confidence. It addresses head-on the discrepancies, contradictions, paradoxes, shortcomings, and residual strengths of the traditional narrative and the explanatory framework for the English economy and society in the fourteenth century. It explores the merits of a revised narrative and an alternative explanatory framework. It is not bold in the sense of possessing the conviction that the proposed narrative and framework are definitive, but in the sense of believing there is real merit in them and in further exploring their possibilities.

Waldringfield,
May 2020

Note

1. Mark Bailey, '*Per impetum maris*: natural disaster and economic decline in eastern England, 1275–1350', in Bruce M.S. Campbell, ed., *Before the Black Death: essays in the crisis of the early fourteenth century* (Manchester, 1991).

Acknowledgements

This book began life as the James Ford Lectures in British History, delivered in the Hilary term 2019 at the University of Oxford. The six central chapters (2 to 7), and their themes, are still readily identifiable as the six lectures in the series. The latter were carefully constructed, but they were not tightly scripted with the intention of enabling a good deal of extemporization suited to the lecture format . . . which, at times, must have showed. In converting the lectures into book format, the weak jokes have been removed and a few lines of argument have been refined, but most of the latter have been developed, illustrated, and integrated in ways that were not possible within the restrictions of the lecture format. In particular, Chapter 7 has been improved and sharpened, aided by an opportunity to re-work it and to discuss the ideas at the Economic History Seminar, University of Oxford, in November 2019.

I am most grateful to the electors to the James Ford Lectureship for the opportunity to develop some long-ruminating thoughts about fourteenth-century England. The prospect of addressing a mixed audience comprised of both eminent academics and members of the public for six weeks on successive Friday evenings in midwinter, coupled with the challenge of maintaining the right pitch for such an eclectic group, helped keep the mind focused and anxiety at bay (partially). Steven Gunn and Stephen Baxter on behalf of the electors were warm hosts. The associated Visiting Fellowship at All Souls, Oxford, in Michaelmas 2018 provided the ideal environment to prepare for the lectures. I am most grateful to the Warden and Fellows. Whilst in Oxford, Ros Faith, Ian Forrest, Jane Humphries, Colin Kidd, Pamela Nightingale, Deb Oxley, Robert Peberdy, the late Richard Sharpe, Julia Smith, Benjamin Thompson, and John Watts were all kind, supportive, and willing sources of advice and ideas. Rowena Archer, Steve Broadberry, Peter Coss, Richard Hoyle, and Hannah Skoda were especially helpful and generous. I have always admired the work of Paul Brand and Paul Hyams in the field of medieval legal history, and both shared a good deal of their time and expertise during my Oxford sojourn.

Preparing and delivering the lectures were not straightforward for someone whose day job did not involve academic history. The chair and the governors of St Paul's School granted half a term's sabbatical leave from my role as High Master to coincide with the Fellowship at All Souls, and the Master and Court of Assistants of the Mercers' Company awarded a research grant. For all this, I am especially grateful to Fred Hohler, Johnny Robertson, and Rob Abernethy. The funding enabled me to secure the services of Nick Amor, himself a fine medieval historian, as a research assistant, and his work in the legal sources opened up a number of interesting new lines of argument. David Addy and Harry Bailey helped prepare the slides, graphs, and maps for the lectures and the book, and Julie Noy-Bailey helped with the bibliography. Julie and our daughter Katie's wider domestic and organizational brilliance has carved the time and space for me indulgently to research, read, think, opine, and write. Various local historians have readily placed information and digital copies of manuscripts at my disposal, notably Rosemary Hoppitt, John Walker, and Diana Maywhort: Diana's knowledge of the Redgrave material provided the striking example of Roger le Reve and John Docke. The late Mark Ormrod highlighted some specialist research on fourteenth-century justice. Bruce Campbell offered stimulating feedback on the third lecture, which has improved Chapter 4. Anthony Musson read and commented upon an early draft of Chapter 5, and likewise David Stone on Chapters 3 and 4, and Louisa Foroughi on Chapter 6. I benefited from sharing ideas with Deborah Boucoyannis, whose research from a very different starting point appears to be heading in the same direction as mine.

Duncan Bythell has read all of the drafts, and provided wise counsel from the perspective of a non-medievalist economic historian. John Hatcher has listened, argued, debated, and encouraged as the ideas in this book were formulated then refined. Steve Rigby was a ferociously fast, sharp, direct, and informed commentator on and editor of various drafts, capable of spotting at many paces a weak argument and thin evidence. All three have provided intellectual stimulus and challenge, sometimes uncompromising, but always in a spirit of support, advancement, and improvement. The book is immeasurably better as a consequence.

Contents

List of Tables

List of Figures

List of Abbreviations

BL	British Library
CCR	*Calendar of Close Rolls*
CFR	*Calendar of Fine Rolls*
CIM	*Calendar of Inquisitions Miscellaneous*
CPR	*Calendar of Patent Rolls*
CUL	Cambridge University Library
PROME	*The Parliament rolls of medieval England, 1275–1504*, ed. Chris Given-Wilson (16 volumes; Woodbridge, 2005)
SROB	Suffolk Record Office, Bury St Edmunds
SROI	Suffolk Record Office, Ipswich
Statutes of the Realm	*Statutes of the Realm, volume I and II* (Record Commission, 1810, 1816)
TNA	The National Archives, Kew
UC Bacon	University of Chicago, Joseph Regenstein Library, Bacon manuscript collection.

1

Introduction

The Black Death

The Black Death raged across Europe between 1347 and 1353, killing a far higher proportion of the population than any global epidemic or warfare in modern times, and then returned frequently over the next four centuries. Contemporaries named this terrifying and seemingly new disease 'pestilence', while generations of modern schoolchildren know it as bubonic and pneumonic plague. It coincided with a phase of momentous ecological, demographic, economic, and social changes across Europe. The tenth to the thirteenth centuries represented a sustained period of efflorescence and expansion, which first slowed, then halted and decisively reversed, during the first half of the fourteenth century due to an exceptional combination of catastrophic events: famine, warfare, bovine disease, human disease, and an unstable climate.[1] Population levels across Europe collapsed in the mid-fourteenth century, and did not recover for two to three centuries. By one recent estimate, the English population fell from a peak of around five million on the eve of the Black Death to 2.25 million in the mid-fifteenth century, and it did not return to its former level until the early eighteenth century.[2] Furthermore, the pestilential fourteenth and fifteenth centuries were a transitional age between the 'medieval' and 'early modern' eras, when social and economic structures in some parts of Europe evolved from 'feudalism' to 'proto-capitalism'.[3] This period also marked the opening of a wage and wealth gap between, on the one hand, north-west Europe (including England) and, on the other hand, the rest of the continent: the so-called 'Little Divergence'.[4] The superior economic performance of north-west Europe became even more pronounced in the seventeenth and eighteenth centuries.[5]

The Black Death thus stands unchallenged as the greatest catastrophe in human history, and this pestilential scourge was omnipresent throughout the transitional period from the middle to the modern age. As a result, it has attracted intense attention from countless historians as well as rafts of economists and theorists from many disciplines. Key questions here have been whether the Black Death was central or incidental to these monumental social and economic changes; whether we should regard this chance exogenous event as radically altering the course of history; or, instead, we should focus on the role played by human responses and actions. Most attempts to answer these questions have sought to fit the Black

After the Black Death: Economy, Society, and the Law in Fourteenth-Century England. Mark Bailey, Oxford University Press (2021). © Mark Bailey. DOI: 10.1093/oso/9780198857884.003.0001

Death into long-term economic and social trends, and into overarching theories of development, rather than carrying out detailed investigations of what actually happened in the second half of the fourteenth century as a prelude to explaining why they happened. Unsurprisingly, such broad-brush approaches have failed to generate much consensus on the influence and importance of the Black Death. Two recent studies, for example, have reached very different conclusions, with Gregory Clark claiming that it 'effected no significant long run economic changes in Europe', whereas Chavas and Bromley suggest that it marked 'the most important transition period in European economic history'.[6]

Demographic disasters create stresses that reveal much to the historian about a society's institutions, habits of mind, and behaviour.[7] They also create stresses, tensions, and disagreements between historians. In the late nineteenth and early twentieth centuries, most historians were convinced that the Black Death marked a major turning point in English history. Thus Seebohm, writing in the 1860s, argued that it caused a great social revolution that changed the whole course of English history, as falling land values and rising wage rates after the epidemic forced lords to bargain away serfdom.[8] For Gasquet, the Black Death was the turning point in English national life, triggering a crisis of faith and the decline of the late-medieval church.[9] As William Page stated, 'it may be said that the Black Death gave a blow to the old system from which it never recovered'.[10] Yet even as Gasquet published his classic work, other historians were beginning to downplay the epidemic's importance and effects. In 1907, for example, Lodge concluded that 'the effects of the Black Death in Berkshire were severe rather than lasting', Frances Page regarded it as 'a great episode...but it would be incautious to ascribe to it per se any far-reaching influence upon subsequent events', and Levett noted 'its effects were short-lived'.[11] By the eve of World War II, the cumulative effects of this relentless downplaying were such that Putman observed how 'unfashionable it is today to attribute significance or lasting effects to the plague'.[12]

The downgrading of the Black Death drew upon a series of pioneering case studies of particular localities, based upon detailed archival evidence. They revealed that the key socio-economic changes initially attributed to the Black Death—such as the decline in labour services and in the direct exploitation of manorial demesnes by their lords—were already in motion before its arrival, and that the plague's impact did not conform to any consistent pattern, but instead varied markedly from place to place.[13] Consequently, the attention of scholars drifted away from the events of 1348–9 towards an earlier and wider 'crisis of feudalism' that had first become apparent in the late thirteenth century.[14] Some explained this crisis along Malthusian lines, as the inevitable correction to a widening and unsustainable imbalance between rising population and inelastic resources during the European efflorescence, and saw the Black Death simply as one of a number of positive demographic checks. Others explained it along

Marxist lines, whereby the crisis of agrarian productivity was the function of excessive exploitation of peasant surpluses through feudal rent, which again relegated the Black Death to a secondary cause of long-term socio-economic change. Throughout the second half of the twentieth century, these two classic supermodels dominated the historiography of the medieval economy. Proponents of each agreed broadly on the chronology and symptoms of the early fourteenth-century crisis, though they differed violently and ideologically on its causes. Both are essentially anthropocentric and deterministic models of long-term development, in which human agency triggered production crises that in turn generated major and predictable structural changes.[15] External or chance events, such as epidemic disease, do not fit comfortably within such models, except as catalysts or accelerators of trends already in motion. From the perspective of these two supermodels, 'to admit a [major] role to autonomous disease is to threaten to reduce the aspiring scientific historian to a mere chronicler of the random and bizarre'.[16]

Throughout the second half of the twentieth century, a succession of local studies appeared to confirm the remarkable resilience of social structures and the unexpected buoyancy of the economy in the 1350s and 1360s, prompting Platt to comment on 'the strikingly rapid social and economic recovery' following the initial impact.[17] In a similar vein, DeWindt concluded that the Black Death's 'immediate results are not observable, and what is observable is a mild and minor disruption of manorial operation, not a dramatic upheaval', whilst Bridbury marvelled at 'how little effect it seems to have had on the social and economic life of the country'.[18] Such studies emphasized that the main anticipated consequences of demographic collapse—falling grain prices and land values, contracting occupation of the land, rising living standards of ordinary people, and the dissolution of serfdom—did not actually materialize until the last quarter of the fourteenth century. It seemed that the Black Death could not possibly have been the primary driver of social and economic change when there was no consistent or obvious pattern to its initial impact, and when the anticipated consequences took so long to emerge.[19] The role of plague continued to be cut down to size.[20]

The reputation of plague as a destructive force was tarnished further through demographic studies suggesting that earlier historians had exaggerated the mortality rate in 1348–9.[21] In 1970 Shrewsbury, a bacteriologist, advocated the immutability of plague's epidemiology and pathology over time, and so, extrapolating backwards from the known characteristics of modern plague, estimated that it could only have caused a 5 per cent mortality rate in the first epidemic.[22] He argued that if the death rate in 1348–9 really did exceed 25 per cent, then the Black Death must have comprised a medley of diseases, such as typhus and smallpox, acting in tandem with plague. Shrewsbury's work highlighted a conundrum that subsequently attracted intense scrutiny: namely, that the reconstructed speed, seasonality, and mortality rates of the disease that struck between 1346 and 1353 were incompatible with the observed behaviour and the known epidemiology of modern plague. If the higher death rates claimed for 1348–9 were correct, and if the Black Death really did spread so quickly and completely, then plague was unlikely to have been the cause. This so-called 'diagnosis debate' raged well into the first decade of this century.[23]

Just as the reputation of the Black Death had reached its lowest ebb in the 1990s, so waves of new research and exciting methodological advances revived interest in the subject and, in the process, restored the disease as a major force in world history. There is now little debate over its mortality rate, characteristics, or identity.[24] The epidemic reached southern England during the late summer of 1348, spread during the winter months, and became especially active throughout the country during the spring and summer of 1349. The disease moved primarily along the coast and arterial route ways, and was remarkably complete in its spread: hardly anywhere evaded its grip in 1348–9.[25] Death rates are calculable from three main categories of source material: tenant deaths, appointments of beneficed clergy to parishes, and, exceptionally, deaths of males in tithings. The first two categories are the most voluminous, with a good spread across England, and indicate local death rates ranging from 19 per cent to 80 per cent.[26] Various allowances have to be made for the typicality of the evidence, and for regional variations in mortality, but there is widespread acceptance that 40 per cent to 50 per cent of the population of England died in the first epidemic.[27] Around Europe, estimates of mortality rates vary between 30 per cent and 50 per cent.[28] Thereafter, the same disease returned repeatedly, with epidemics in England in 1361–2, 1368–9, 1373–5, 1390–3, and on a dozen more occasions in the fifteenth century.[29] As a result, while the population of England stood at an estimated 5.5 million in the 1340s, it had fallen to 2.8 million in the early 1350s, 2.5 million in 1377, 2.3 million in the 1520s, and had recovered only slightly to 2.8 million by the mid sixteenth century.[30]

We also now know the identity of the Black Death definitively, following DNA analysis of dental pulp extracted from the skeletons of victims buried in mass graves during the epidemic.[31] This technology identified *Yersinia pestis* as the offending pathogen, although of a different strain from the modern form. Medieval plague behaved differently from modern plague, probably acting through direct transmission between humans via droplet infection and/or fleas and ectoparasites.[32] This was the same disease that had struck Latin Christendom in the 530s, which means that it has been afflicting humanity for at least 1,500 years.[33] Indeed, *Y. pestis* remains present across the globe, with exception of Australasia and Antarctica, and so still poses a serious threat, especially in a world where antibiotics are increasingly ineffective.[34]

The notion that an epidemic killing around a half of the English population did not trigger any immediate economic and social changes of significance, and its effects delayed until the 1370s, is barely credible.[35] Consequently, the tide of historical opinion began to turn once again, and historians and econometricians increasingly portrayed the Black Death as the watershed event of the last 1,000 years of European history. For Miller and Hatcher, 'demographic attrition on so massive a scale inevitably had social and economic consequences of the first importance'.[36] Dobson stated that the Black Death 'was unquestionably the most significant turning point in late medieval British urban history'.[37] Palmer regarded the government's legislative response to the Black Death as bringing 'a lasting change to governance in England' and as constituting the turning point when relations between lords and peasants became more 'economic' than 'feudal'.[38] Judith Bennett has argued that the influence of the labour legislation which was introduced in response to the plague 'has echoed through centuries of class and gender relations...shaping employment law throughout the British Empire and touching by one estimate about a quarter of the world's population'.[39] Benedictow believes that combating 'plague gave a strong impetus to the notion that governments had responsibilities for the welfare of their peoples'.[40]

Furthermore, the belief that the origins of the Little Divergence are to be found in this period has gathered momentum among econometricians, elevating the Black Death once more to the status of a major watershed in world history.[41] As Broadberry states, 'the catching-up process of the North Sea area with Mediterranean Europe and with China started with the arrival of the Black Death in the mid-fourteenth century'.[42] From this date, estimates of GDP per head rose more sharply in England and Holland than in areas of southern Europe, such as Spain and Italy.[43] Likewise, during the course of the fifteenth century a gap in the average level of real wages first becomes apparent between north-west Europe and central and southern Europe.[44] Greif identifies 'a late-medieval institutional revolution', in which many of the modern, Western-style institutions and cultural beliefs become clearly identifiable for the first time: 'individualism, corporatism, the legitimacy of man-made formal law, a voice and influence among those subject to law, and the development of the centralized state'.[45] More specifically, Voigtlander and Voth argue that the Black Death triggered a fundamental change in the dominant marriage pattern in north-west Europe, delaying the age of women at first marriage and increasing the proportion who never married (discussed below, pp. 286–9).[46] Similarly, Foreman-Peck and Zhou regard the persistence of the disease as 'a vital characteristic of English economic history' because of its long-term impact on demographic structures and household formation.[47] The resultant decline in fertility rates meant that future upswings in population translated into higher incomes and consumption per capita, propelling north-west Europe in general and England in particular to precocious riches through the Industrial Revolution, in contrast to other parts of Europe where future upward swings in population led to declining real incomes.[48] The origins of the Little Divergence are to be found in the age of plague.

Recent research has also revealed one other intriguing characteristic of the Black Death, one which it shared with the first pandemic of the 530s: both coincided with a sharp deterioration in the global climate.[49] The period between the 1280s and the 1350s was a period of significant environmental disturbance. Cooler, wetter, stormier, and more unpredictable weather, due mainly to reduced solar irradiance, contributed to a succession of harvest failures and led to the spread of a pan-European bovine epidemic during the 1310s and 1320s.[50] According to Campbell, these hazards struck a society severely impoverished through overpopulation, high taxation, and endemic warfare, and so by the 1340s this 'cascading process of contingent chaotic development' had brought Europe to a tipping point. The Black Death arrived at the back end of this process, creating a perfect storm of adverse socio-ecological conditions.[51] Here the crisis of the early fourteenth century is portrayed as an exceptional combination of exogenous environmental shocks and endogenously generated socio-economic stresses, interacting in highly complex and unpredictable ways, following which the Black Death led to irreversible regime change.

Social and Economic Change in Fourteenth-Century England

The recent, extraordinary surge of interdisciplinary research has breathed new life into the study of the Black Death. Yet there have been few attempts to reconcile the current enthusiasm for depicting the Black Death as a major turning point with the findings of the raft of earlier local studies, which had suggested that it had little immediate impact on the English economy and society. Furthermore, we are still struggling to understand why the long-term response to the catastrophe in England and parts of north-west Europe was so different from that in most areas of southern and central Europe. Why did the same biological shock and demographic trend—sudden collapse, then sustained decline—result in very different social, political, and cultural outcomes across Europe?[52] Why did demographic decline result in the decline of serfdom in some areas, but its preservation or even strengthening in others?[53] Why was it associated with a major rise in wealth per head in some places, a modest rise in others, but a decline elsewhere?

The English response to the Black Death was unquestionably distinctive by European standards. It has attracted especial attention from historians, sociologists, and economists for four main reasons. First, England was the first nation to industrialize, so its journey from medieval to modern, and the motors driving its development, both acquire a special significance. Second, the nature and extent of institutional change in late medieval England were marked, and contrast with the experience of some other areas of Europe where changes were less pronounced: whereas Grantham has observed that 'in 1500 much of France looked very much like it did in 1300', the same could not be said of England's economy and society.[54]

Third, GDP per head rose in England after the Black Death, and during the fifteenth century wage rates in English towns rose above those paid in urban centres in southern and central Europe, suggesting that its economic performance was already diverging from other parts of Europe.[55] Finally, medieval England is exceptionally blessed with extant local and central records, which present the historian with an opportunity to explore and analyse what was distinctive about its institutional structure and, by extension, the origins of the modern world economic system.

All existing narratives and explanations for economic and social change in fourteenth-century England proceed from three fundamental assumptions about the country's characteristics on the eve of the Black Death. The first is that it represented a laggard by European standards. Certainly, in c.1300 England was backward when compared with the likes of the Low Countries and northern Italy by all the main measures of economic development. For example, estimates of GDP per capita in 1340 place England well behind Holland and Spain, and at half the level of northern Italy.[56] Likewise, its level of urbanization was far below that achieved in Italy, Spain, and Flanders, and, indeed, was even below the European average.[57] On the eve of the Black Death 'there was nothing to indicate that England would one day achieve world or even European economic hegemony'.[58]

The second assumption is that in the 1340s economic growth in England had faltered, and that its society was suffering from extreme pressures of overpopulation and impoverishment. Living standards were falling from the middle of the thirteenth century and by the early fourteenth century had become perilously low for the majority of the populace. Historians usually assume that a holding of ten acres was necessary to cover the bare subsistence needs of the average family, yet across England mean landholding size had fallen well below that level. This was especially characteristic of many parts of south-east England, where the combination of a high occupancy rate of peasant land with very active free and villein land markets drove down the mean landholding size among all tenants to below the level of subsistence.[59] For example, in the 1330s at Hunstanton (Norfolk) the average holding size was just four acres, 67 per cent of all tenants held less than four acres, and only 17 per cent held more than 6.2 acres of land.[60] The inexorable fall in mean landholding size forced a majority of peasants to seek supplementary income from wage labour, but a combination of high prices for foodstuffs and modest wages meant that their purchasing power was pitifully low.[61] One recent estimate suggests that a landless labourer had to work most of the available days in the year to obtain enough cash to feed a family.[62] Yet, in practice, it is highly unlikely that enough work was available for all those seeking it. Much of the day work was seasonal, weather dependent, sporadic, and low skilled, especially in regions dominated by grain production. Competition was fierce and pre-plague towns were awash with waves of underemployed and poor labourers rippling in from the countryside.[63] Labourers entered the market on very unfavourable terms.[64] On the eve of the Black Death, England was flush with unemployed and underemployed labourers who were hungry for work but trapped in a makeshift world of uncertainty and poverty.[65] Gregory Clark estimates that the marginal productivity of agricultural labour declined 60 per cent between the early thirteenth and early fourteenth centuries, at which date it had fallen to the lowest level in the whole of the last millennium.[66] The strain of persistently high taxation and purveyance for the royal armies exacerbated these problems, imposing upon ordinary people a burden they could scarcely bear.[67] Such poverty and undernourishment help to explain the extreme mortality in 1348–9.[68]

The underemployed hordes of impoverished smallholders and landless had no option but to eke whatever sustenance they could from common rights, charity, or the produce of whatever land they could access. Somehow, they survived in all but the most extreme conditions.[69] A major element in their survival strategy must have been lavishing as much of their spare labour as possible on their smallholdings and gardens, while the landless might exploit tiny illegal encroachments on common land and perhaps worked on the land of family and friends in return for morsels of food and fuel.[70] The application of vast amounts of labour to smallholdings might have caused labour productivity to plummet, but the payback was in maximizing the output of food per acre. We have no sources that will ever provide reliable measures of the productivity of medieval peasant holdings. The standard assumption has been that yields per acre on peasant holdings were broadly comparable to those on the 'demesne' lands of landlords, for which we have abundant and reliable evidence.[71] However, the application of significant inputs of otherwise idle labour to these smallholdings and gardens must have raised gross output, even without much capital equipment, which meant that on the eve of the Black Death peasant land productivity may well have been at least 50 per cent higher than on demesnes.[72] Heavy applications of underemployed family labour in digging, spreading manure, weeding, and bird scaring would have raised land productivity, irrespective of the falling returns to labour.

The two widespread assumptions about the character of pre-plague England sketched so far—that England was economically backward, and that living standards were low for the majority of the populace—are securely documented and uncontentious. The third and final assumption is that society and the economy remained heavily constrained by its underlying 'feudal' structures and social relations, and that these were the principal source of its poor performance on the eve of plague. While this assumption is also widely held, its evidentiary base is less secure and deserves much closer critical scrutiny. The term 'feudalism' is the label given to a wide variety of systems of social and economic organization across medieval Europe, whose unifying characteristic was the allocation and exchange of key resources through personal services and obligations, and a system of enforcement through seigniorial impositions and coercion. It includes 'serfdom', whereby a high proportion of peasants were personally and tenurially bonded and subjected to private lordship. Historians assume that feudalism and serfdom stifled the development of factor markets (in land, labour, and capital) and commodity markets (even in basic foodstuffs and household goods), because much of the produce of the peasantry's land and labour was diverted to support the activities of a tiny military and religious elite. Consequently, the structure of rent tied peasant labour to the agricultural holdings of the lord and their own family, and facilitated the non-economic extraction of peasant 'surplus', both of which imposed tight restrictions on peasant enterprise.[73] In contrast, in proto-capitalism the market is the major influence upon the allocation and exchange of resources, with prices and tasks being determined primarily through the forces of supply and demand, monetary transactions, and contractual arrangements. Proto-capitalism also implies a culture whereby buyers and sellers will seek to maximize either profits or their own utility.

The use of the label 'feudalism' to describe the institutional structure of medieval Europe is controversial and so here we will use the phrase manorial lordship to describe the social arrangements between English lords and peasants on the eve of the Black Death, and deploy 'villeinage' to refer to the English form of serfdom.[74] It is widely assumed that at this date manorial lordship remained the most powerful influence on the allocation of resources in England, as a result of which property relations and the structure of rent remained at best economically inefficient and at worst extractive and coercive. The combination of the stifling effects of the structure of manorial lordship and the intense population pressure on the resource base explain both the impoverishment of the mass of the populace, and England's modest economic performance. Commerce and towns had undoubtedly grown during the twelfth and thirteenth centuries, and the state had increased its influence in raising taxes and providing justice, and, as a consequence, rudimentary factor and commodity markets had emerged.[75] In this viewpoint, however, on the eve of plague they remained small and under close seigniorial control, in contrast to areas of Italy and Holland where factor markets were both larger and less subject to the control of manorial lordship.[76] Indeed, after c.1200 the emergence of the common law appears to have strengthened the power of manorial lordship in England, because it clarified lordly rights over villein land and labour, excluding the latter from accessing the royal courts and so denying them any formal legal protection from capricious and arbitrary seigniorial behaviour. Hence historians have commonly depicted the 'common law of villeinage' as reinforcing the capacity of lords to extract peasant surpluses at will and, by extension, to tighten their grip over English society.[77]

Thus, in this interpretation, manorial lordship is seen as reaching its apogee on the eve of the Black Death and, by extension, as the dominant influence upon the allocation of resources and shaping social relations in England.[78] At best, its impact upon economic development was constraining, inefficient, and inequitable, resulting in economic stagnation and structural poverty: at worst, it was coercive, demeaning, and exploitative.[79] Seigniorial controls over villein land and labour could extract the surplus produce of the peasantry and inhibit the growth of factor and commodity markets, causing productivity in the peasant sector to fall inexorably as population rose, triggering a 'crisis of feudalism'.[80] This general view is widely shared among historians of different backgrounds and persuasions. For example, Evans commented that 'the essence of a manorial lord's relationship with his tenants . . . was exploitation', and so 'lordship may have left little room for a free economic market in land, labour, or produce'.[81] Palmer states that 'manorial lords . . . were immensely powerful over the whole of their tenantry', and Braid argues that manor courts 'controlled the mobility of and forced labour on both free tenants and bondmen'.[82] Even those historians who acknowledge the commercial and technical advances of the age deploy similar arguments to explain the limits to those advances. For example, Ghosh documents the spread of commercial forces, but still concludes that England operated within 'the feudal mode of production' where 'some surpluses were extracted by extra-economic means' and where 'the locus of the class struggle was the extraction of rents and services', rather than the market. For him, the 'constraints of feudal social-property relations' remained the dominant force, and, as such, 'extra economic coercion operated on those who cultivated the land'.[83] Kitsikopoulos states explicitly that 'the main cause of the feudal crisis in England' was the inefficiencies of its institutional structure, foremost among which was the 'heavy reliance on seigniorial extractions . . . [that] drained capital resources' away from the peasantry—he estimates one-third of their revenues—and therefore 'seigniorial prerogatives were a zero-sum game'.[84]

In a similar vein, European scholars tend to explain the modest economic performance of England on the eve of the Black Death compared with the performance of the continent's most precocious regions—such as parts of the Low Countries, north Germany, and north Italy—in terms of the differential strengths of manorial lordship.[85] Van Zanden and van Bavel contrast the dissolution of manorialism and the corresponding growth of markets in the Netherlands in the thirteenth and early fourteenth centuries under the pressure of high population with the rigidity and relative power of the 'feudal' structure in England.[86] Van Bavel attributes the stunted development, inefficiencies, and inequalities of English markets to the 'institutional sclerosis' created by the extreme polarization of wealth and by the political and legal powers of the mercantile and ruling elites, which enabled them to manipulate factor and commodity markets to further their own interests at the expense of the many.[87]

The assumption that manorial lordship had reached its apogee on the eve of the Black Death in England also explains why its lords were able to clamp down heavily on the peasantry after the Black Death had struck in 1348–9, according to the orthodox view. The sudden shortages of tenants and labourers posed an urgent and cogent threat to the economic well-being and the social standing of

English lordship, whose response was to mobilize their existing and extensive powers under villeinage to attempt to coerce peasants to hold land and to work on terms favourable to the lords, as if nothing had happened. This belief is reflected in the arguments of some historians that in the third quarter of the century the ruling class applied 'non-economic compulsion' to prevent rents, 'especially those of a feudal type', from falling.[88] In addition, the shortages of labour prompted the government to intervene in the labour market with sweeping new legislation to force labourers to work on terms that were beneficial to the lords. In these ways, manorial lords and the state forged a new alliance against the lower orders of society to stem the contrary economic and social tide, a novel combination of feudal power and statute law that constituted a widespread 'seigniorial reaction' (see pp. 83–5).[89] Bolton captures this view when he writes 'the decades after the Black Death saw exploitation of the peasants in excess even of the bad days of the thirteenth century'.[90] Meanwhile, commodity prices, and especially those of basic foodstuffs, leaped upwards and remained high until the mid-1370s. The combination of high prices and seigniorial reaction protected the economic position of landlords, so that initially their social relations with the peasantry changed little. Overall, life appears to have returned to normality and the lower orders gained little material benefit from the shortages of labour and abundance of land.[91]

In this orthodox narrative, the anticipated effects of plague only became apparent during the final quarter of the fourteenth century. In the words of Bridbury, 'if the Black Death is to be regarded as a dynamic force in the history of the fourteenth century, then we must look to the 1370s'.[92] Lords now had to contend with two reinforcing yet contrary forces. First, the oppressive seigniorial reaction triggered a mounting wave of peasant resistance along class lines, culminating in the Peasants' Revolt of 1381 (this is considered in Chapter 5). Thereafter, both the state and manorial lords relaxed their coercive policies in the land and labour markets and offered major concessions on rents and wages to an increasingly confident and assertive peasantry. Second, the prices of staple goods fell sharply from the mid-1370s and remained low, while wages rose, eating into the profits of agriculture and forcing lords to abandon the direct exploitation of their manors (see Chapter 6). Trapped in an inexorable pincer movement, lords bargained away the old servile rents and labour services, and greatly eased their restrictions upon the movement of labour. As a result, villeinage largely disappeared between the 1380s and 1430s and, as it dissolved, so the land, labour, and commodity markets expanded in relative terms, and contractual arrangements displaced the old personal ties and bonded forms of labour.[93] This chronology and narrative is widely accepted within the existing scholarship.[94] Indeed, some literary scholars even argue that commercialization itself was a novelty of the late fourteenth century.[95] Similarly, continental scholars reproduce this conventional narrative as a verity of the English experience. For example, van Bavel argues that a seigniorial reaction was one of the main causes of the Peasants'

Revolt, and then the revolt itself 'hastened the decline of manorialism while strengthening the confidence and assertiveness of the peasant elites . . . [thereafter] the disappearance of arbitrary and lordly dues extended the opportunities for the market exchange of land and labour'.[96]

Thus, the existing narrative of how English society responded to the arrival of the Black Death proceeds from the presumption that manorial lordship was the dominant, and a severely constraining, force on economic development in pre-plague England. Its relative strength explains why in the 1340s England was an economic laggard by European standards.[97] The residual strength of English manorial lordship when plague struck also explains how it was capable of mounting a vigorous seigniorial reaction in the aftermath, why English life returned swiftly to normality, and why peasant living standards did not improve immediately. The clear implication is that after 1349 market forces alone could not shake the grip of English manorialism, which instead had to be overthrown through passive and active peasant resistance, and rising class consciousness, leading to social conflict and revolt.[98] This viewpoint conforms to a wider orthodoxy in which conflict, peasant resistance, and armed struggle were a systemic component of a pan-European feudal crisis and an essential precondition to the redistribution of wealth after the Black Death.[99] When a rising tide of resistance and the Peasants' Revolt caused villeinage to decline, so from the 1380s factor and commodity markets began to grow in relative importance, which in turn triggered further institutional changes that improved their operational efficiency.[100] These profound changes created the foundations for England's future emergence as a leader of European economic development.[101] The cogent and compelling simplicity of this narrative, and indeed the absence of any coherent alternative, explains its persistence and its dominance of our understanding of England's unique response to plague and its route to modernity.

There are, however, three major objections to this widespread assumption, which, when taken together, gravely damage its credibility. The first objection is that manorial lordship in the 1340s was not as dominant or as powerful as portrayed. Seigniorial power over the peasantry varied markedly even within particular English regions, depending upon the size and composition of manors, and the status of the lord.[102] Manorial lordship was not some constant and cogent force exercised equally throughout England. Furthermore, half the rural peasantry were legally free, and in reality lords exercised few controls over their activities (see below, pp. 28–38). Even for the other half of the rural peasantry bound by servility, the actual practice and experience of villeinage on the ground were not nearly as harsh as its legal theory would suggest, because the force of custom fixed the rent packages of villeins and protected them against extremes of arbitrary lordly behaviour.[103] Some lords manifestly did not employ their authority to thwart the productive capacity, or to exploit the commercial acumen, of their customary tenants, and instead encouraged their activities in the expectation that such a relationship would bring mutual benefits.[104] Villeinage was not some fixed, absolute, or abstract concept but comprised a variety of local practices and relationships delimited from freedom by a thin legal line drawn in the common law. The practices of villeinage were essentially concerned to establish subordination and conditional access to rights, not to establish powers of compulsion in some uniform and absolute form.[105]

As a result, on the eve of the Black Death the vast majority of English peasants possessed greater freedom of time and action than conventionally portrayed. They did not conform to the stereotype of immobile, subsistence-orientated, family units associated with traditional peasant societies.[106] Furthermore, research in the last two decades has confirmed that earlier historians had underestimated the development of factor and commodity markets, and overestimated the ability of lords to control what markets did exist.[107] Nearly one-fifth of the population lived in around 600 (mainly small) towns, and were largely dependent upon commerce for their livelihoods.[108] The development of commerce alongside the existence of high levels of personal freedom weakened the coercive power of manorial lordship. After all, if the latter really had been so strong and exploitative when plague struck, and if lords' powers to determine the labour of their whole tenantry were so wide-ranging, the government would not have had to intervene at all after 1349 with radical new legislation in the labour market. Since, however, the government *did* intervene, why did it not legislate to impose a harsher and wider form of villeinage? Why did it introduce a system to regulate voluntary contractual arrangements within the labour market, instead of simply compelling peasants to work for their lord (see Chapter 3)?

The second objection to the orthodox narrative is that it imposes far too neat a pattern upon the events of the third quarter of the fourteenth century, when in reality this was a highly complex and contradictory period. The weather was highly variable, plague returned with devastating force in 1361–2 and 1369, and epidemics of livestock created severe problems (see Chapter 4). The old narrative of rapid and widespread recovery draws heavily upon the twentieth-century scholarship that sought to downplay the effects of plague, a good deal of which, in fact, offers superficial or loose generalizations about this period.[109] A more careful re-reading of the published studies, together with new original research, suggests a much more varied and contradictory picture, where evidence for devastation and hardship sits alongside evidence for rapid recovery and new opportunities. Similarly, upon closer scrutiny, it is apparent that many lowly-paid workers did enjoy sharp improvements in their material welfare in the 1350s and 1360s.[110] How was this possible, if manorial lordship was so dominant at this time and so determined to prevent the lower orders from benefiting from the disaster? The succession of extreme events in this period—from plagues and poxes to extreme weather conditions—and the uncertainty they generated have been seriously overlooked.

The final objection is that, in direct contrast to the orthodox view that villeinage dissolved between 1380 and 1430, recent research shows it to have been in headlong retreat on many manors from as early as the 1350s, and absent from some by the 1380s.[111] Powerful forces were dissolving the glue of serfdom long before the Peasants' Revolt (Chapters 3 and 6). Even the notion of a widespread seigniorial reaction between the first epidemic and the Peasants' Revolt is now subject to serious challenge (see Chapter 3).[112] So, if the chain reaction of seigniorial oppression, peasant resistance, and then the dissolution of serfdom did not materialize, what *did* cause English serfdom to decline? The absence of a coherent alternative explanatory framework adds to the difficulty of answering this question, but the evidence points to decisive changes in the immediate aftermath of the first epidemic. Indeed, this is consistent with the observations of some historians that hardly any fundamental structural and economic changes are discernible in the fifteenth and early sixteenth centuries. As Yates remarks, 'the fifteenth century saw little that was decisive or unprecedented'.[113] If this was indeed the case, then the major changes in English society and economy must have occurred in the second half of the fourteenth century, perhaps before 1381, and not in the half century between the 1380s and 1430s.

What follows throughout the rest of this book is an attempt to provide an alternative framework for what happened in the wake of plague. It is argued that, although manorial lordship on the eve of plague was still a significant influence in determining the allocation and control of resources, the forces of custom, family, commerce, markets, and the common law had combined to dilute its strength. Consequently, factor and output markets were already larger than the orthodoxy allows, and their operation was less subject to seigniorial control and interference. This does not mean that these markets were efficient or equitable, or that they were comparable to markets in modern England, or, indeed, that villeinage was irrelevant.[114] It does imply, however, that factor markets were inefficient under the pressure of population before the Black Death, but then operated with greater efficiency after 1349 under very different demographic conditions and aided by some important institutional changes.

This alternative framework ascribes a greater and immediate role to competition between lords for scarce tenants and labourers, and to the rapid spread of contractual arrangements in the land and labour markets. It rejects the notion that lords had exercised considerable control over peasant labour, and instead argues that the pre-plague labour market was open, sizeable, and scarcely regulated by either manorial lordship or government. Thus the government's rapid intervention in the labour market in 1349 was a desperate and tardy attempt to exert some form of control, which heightened resentment in the run-up to 1381. It better explains why villeinage began to decline rapidly and widely from the 1350s, and relies less heavily upon social conflict to explain that process. It identifies the third quarter of the fourteenth century as a pivotal period characterized by complexity, volatility, uncertainty, and opportunity, when 'profound and irreversible change occurred in both environmental and human conditions'.[115] The extent of that change and the importance of this period have been seriously overlooked, partly because of the conviction throughout the twentieth century that not much happened, and partly because our gaze has been transfixed by the collapse of prices and land values from the mid-1370s and the social upheaval of 1381. The third quarter of the fourteenth century is one of the most fascinating and important periods in English history, but it has not attracted the attention it deserves.

Notes

1. Bruce M.S. Campbell, *The great transition: climate, disease and society in the late-medieval world* (Cambridge, 2016).
2. Jim L. Bolton, 'Looking for *Yersinia pestis*: scientists, historians, and the Black Death', in Linda Clark and Carole Rawcliffe, eds., *The fifteenth century XII: society in an age of plague* (Woodbridge, 2013), p. 37.
3. Ole J. Benedictow, *The Black Death 1346-1353: the complete history* (Woodbridge, 2004), pp. 387–94; Richard H. Britnell, *Britain and Ireland, 1050-1530: economy and society* (Oxford, 2004), pp. 516–20; Christopher Dyer, *An age of transition?: economy and society in England in the later Middle Ages* (Oxford, 2005), pp. 1–6, 42–4, 242–6.
4. The Great Divergence is the growing gap in economic performance between Europe and the Orient.
5. Sevket Pamuk, 'The Black Death and the origins of the Great Divergence across Europe, 1300–1600', *European Review of Economic History*, 11 (2007), p. 292; Campbell, *Great transition*, fig. 5.14, p. 375; Mattia Fochesato, 'Origins of Europe's north–south divide: population changes, real wages and the "little divergence" in early modern Europe', *Explorations in Economic History*, 70 (2018), pp. 94, 100–11.
6. Gregory Clark, 'Microbes and markets: was the Black Death an economic revolution?', *Journal of Demographic Economics*, 82 (2016), p. 139; John-Paul Chavas and Daniel W. Bromley, 'Modelling population and resource scarcity in fourteenth-century England', *Journal of Agricultural Economics*, 56 (2005), p. 217.
7. Paul Slack, *The impact of plague in Tudor and Stuart England* (Oxford, 1990), pp. 4–5.
8. Frederic Seebohm, 'The Black Death and its place in history: part I', *The Fortnightly Review*, 2 (1865), pp. 149–60, and 'The Black Death and its place in history: part II', *The Fortnightly Review*, 4 (1866), pp. 268–79. For summaries, see Nils Hybel, *Crisis or change: the concept of crisis in the light of agrarian structural reorganisation in late medieval England* (Aarhus, 1989), pp. 4–16; John Hatcher, 'England in the aftermath of the Black Death', *Past and Present*, 144 (1994), p. 3.
9. Francis A. Gasquet, *The Black Death of 1348 and 1349* (London, 1908), p. 227.
10. T. William Page, *The end of villeinage in England*, American Economic Association, 3rd series, I (New York, 1901), p. 58.

11. Eleanor C. Lodge, 'Economic and social history', in *Victoria County History of Berkshire, volume 2* (London, 1907), p. 189; Frances M. Page, *The estates of Crowland abbey* (Cambridge, 1934), p. 125; Ada E. Levett, *The Black Death on the estates of the see of Winchester* (Oxford, 1916), p. 140.

12. Bertha H. Putnam, *Proceedings before the justices of the peace in the fourteenth and fifteenth centuries* (London, 1938), p. xliii.

13. Levett, *Black Death*, p. 142.

14. Anthony R. Bridbury, *The English economy from Bede to the Reformation* (Woodbridge, 1992), p. 203.

15. For useful summaries of the models and their proponents, see Stephen H. Rigby, *English society in the later Middle Ages: class, status and gender* (Basingstoke, 1995), pp. 45–59, 76–95; John Hatcher and Mark Bailey, *Modelling the Middle Ages: the history and theory of England's economic development* (Oxford, 2001), pp. 21–120; Margaret Yates, *Town and countryside on west Berkshire 1327–1600: social and economic change* (Woodbridge, 2007), pp. 1–19.

16. John Hatcher, 'English serfdom and villeinage: towards a reassessment', *Past and Present*, 90 (1981), pp. 5–6.

17. Colin Platt, *King Death: the Black Death and its aftermath in late-medieval England* (London, 1996), p. 10.

18. Edwin B. DeWindt, *Land and people in Holywell-cum-Needingworth: structures of tenure and patterns of social organization in an East Midlands village 1252–1457* (Toronto, 1972), p. 65; Bridbury, *English economy*, pp. 212–13. Also Jim L. Bolton, *The medieval English economy 1150–1500* (London, 1980), pp. 210–11. For summaries of these and similar views, see Hatcher, 'England in the aftermath', p. 3 and Rosemary Horrox, ed., *The Black Death* (Manchester, 1994), p. 232.

19. As suggested by Levett, *Black Death*, pp. 142, 146, and Eugene Robo, 'The Black Death in the hundred of Farnham', *English Historical Review*, 45 (1929), pp. 571–2. This approach is summarized by David Stone, 'The Black Death and its immediate aftermath: crisis and change in the Fenland economy', in Mark Bailey and Stephen H. Rigby, eds., *Town and countryside in the age of the Black Death: essays in honour of John Hatcher* (Turnhout, 2012), p. 214.

20. Horrox, *Black Death*, p. 234.

21. Horrox, *Black Death*, p. 231.

22. J.D.F. Shrewsbury, *A history of bubonic plague in the British Isles* (Cambridge, 1970), pp. 36, 123.

23. See, for example, John Theilmann and Frances Cate, 'A plague of plagues: the problem of plague diagnosis in medieval England', *Journal of Interdisciplinary History*, 37 (2007), pp. 371–93; Karl Birkelbach, 'Plague debate: methodology and meaning in the retrospective diagnosis of the Black Death' (PhD dissertation, University of Western Australia, 2009), pp. 201–65.

24. For a recent summary, see Sharon N. Dewitte and Maryanne Kowaleski, 'Black Death bodies', *Fragments*, 6 (2017), pp. 1–11.

25. Benedictow, *Black Death*, pp. 130–42.

26. Jim L. Bolton, 'World turned upside down', in W. Mark Ormrod and Philip Lindley, eds., *The Black Death in England* (Stamford, 1996), pp. 22–4. See the discussion in Zvi

Razi, *Life, marriage and death in a medieval parish: economy, society and demography in Halesowen 1270–1400* (Cambridge, 1980), pp. 99–109.

27. John Hatcher, *Plague population and the English economy 1348–1530* (London, 1977), p. 71; Richard M. Smith, 'Human resources', in Grenville Astill and Annie Grant, eds., *The medieval countryside* (Oxford, 1988), pp. 190, 208–9; Benedictow, *Black Death*, pp. 342–79; Horrox, *Black Death*, pp. 234–5; Bolton, 'Looking for *Yersinia pestis*', pp. 31–2; Stephen Broadberry, Bruce M.S. Campbell, Alexander Klein, Mark Overton, and Bas van Leeuwen, *British economic growth 1270–1870* (Cambridge, 2015), p. 20, table 1.06.

28. Monica H. Green, 'Editor's introduction', in Monica H. Green, ed., *Pandemic disease in the medieval world: rethinking the Black Death* (Kalamazoo, 2015), p. 9; Benedictow, *Black Death*, pp. 342–79; Campbell, *Great transition*, pp. 306–10.

29. Smith, 'Human resources', pp. 208–11; Bolton, 'Looking for *Yersinia pestis*', p. 33; John Hatcher, 'Understanding the population history of England 1450–1750', *Past and Present*, 180 (2003), pp. 95–9.

30. Other estimates broadly concur: the most secure are Hatcher, *Plague, population*, p. 78; Smith, 'Human resources', pp. 190–1; Rigby, *English society*, p. 70; Britnell, *Britain*, p. 81; Broadberry et al., *British economic growth*, p. 20, table 1.06; Phillipp R. Schofield, *Peasants and historians: debating the medieval English peasantry* (Manchester, 2016), pp. 156–8.

31. Bolton, 'Looking for *Yersinia pestis*', pp. 15–38; Campbell, *Great transition*, pp. 289–94. Also see Samuel K. Cohn, 'The historian and the laboratory: the Black Death disease', in Clark and Rawcliffe, eds., *Fifteenth century XII*, pp. 195–212.

32. Lester K. Little, 'Plague historians in lab coats', *Past and Present*, 213 (2011), pp. 267–90; Campbell, *Great transition*, pp. 227–52.

33. Green, 'Editor's introduction', p. 10.

34. Sharon N. Dewitte, 'The anthropology of plague: insights from bioarchaeological analyses of epidemic cemeteries', in Green, ed., *Pandemic disease*, pp. 97–8.

35. Horrox, *Black Death*, p. 236.

36. Edward Miller and John Hatcher, *Medieval England: towns, commerce and crafts 1066–1348* (London, 1995), p. 429.

37. R. Barrie Dobson, 'General survey 1300–1500', in David Palliser, ed., *The Cambridge Urban History of Britain: volume I* (Cambridge, 2000), p. 276.

38. Robert C. Palmer, *English law in the age of the Black Death, 1348–1381: a transformation of governance and law* (Chapel Hill, 1993), pp. 11–12, 17–20. In a similar vein, 'under the long shadow of the BD some of the most distinctive features of English constitutional and legal system came to be firmly set in place', Michael Bennett, 'The impact of the Black Death on English legal history', *Australian Journal of Law and Society*, 11 (1995), p. 203.

39. Judith M. Bennett, 'Compulsory service in late medieval England', *Past and Present*, 209 (2010), p. 7; Jane Whittle, *The development of agrarian capitalism: land and labour in Norfolk 1440–1580* (Oxford, 2000), pp. 275–301;; Bruce M.S. Campbell, 'Factor markets in England before the Black Death', *Continuity and Change*, 24 (2009), p. 98.

40. Benedictow, *Black Death*, p. 394.

41. Pamuk, *Black Death*, pp. 306–11.

42. Stephen Broadberry, 'Accounting for the Great Divergence' (Working Paper, 2015), p. 19.

43. Campbell, *Great transition*, fig. 5.1, p. 378; Alexandra de Pleijt and Jan Luiten van Zanden, 'Accounting for the "Little Divergence": what drove economic growth in pre-industrial Europe, 1300–1800?', *European Review of Economic History*, 20 (2016), fig. 2, p. 390; Bruce M.S. Campbell, 'The European mortality crisis of 1346–52 and the advent of the Little Ice Age', in Dominik Collet and Maximilian Schuh, eds., *Famines during the Little Ice Age, 1300–1800: socionatural entanglements in premodern societies* (Cern, 2018), fig. 2.8. A similar conclusion is drawn in Paolo Malanima, 'Italy in the Renaissance: a leading economy in the European context, 1300–1550', *Economic History Review*, 71 (2018), table 6, p. 19.

44. Campbell, *Great transition*, fig. 5.14, p. 375; Fochesato, 'Origins', pp. 94, 100–11.

45. Avner Greif, *Institutions and the path to the modern economy. lessons from medieval trade* (Cambridge, 2006), pp. 379, 388–99, quote at 399.

46. Nico Voigtlander and Hans-Joachim Voth, 'How the West "invented" fertility restriction', *American Economic Review*, 103 (2013), pp. 2,227–30.

47. James Foreman-Peck and Peng Zhou, 'Late marriage as a contributor to the industrial revolution in England', *Economic History Review*, 71 (2018), p. 1075.

48. This argument is expertly summarized and critiqued in Judith M. Bennett, 'Wretched girls, wretched boys, and the European marriage pattern in England (c. 1250–1350)', *Continuity and Change*, 34 (2019), pp. 315–20.

49. Campbell, *Great transition*, pp. 229–30.

50. Campbell, *Great transition*, pp. 36–58, 198–227.

51. Campbell, *Great transition*, pp. 328–9, 399; Campbell, *European mortality crisis*, pp. 19–42.

52. Robert Brenner, 'Agrarian roots', in Trevor H. Aston and Charles H.E. Philpin, eds., *The Brenner Debate: agrarian class structure and economic development in pre-industrial Europe* (Cambridge, 1985), p. 219; Whittle, *Agrarian capitalism*, p. 309; Pamuk, *Black Death*, p. 312; Campbell, *Great transition*, p. 15.

53. The most influential framework for addressing this question is the Brenner debate: see Aston and Philpin, eds., *The Brenner Debate*. For useful critiques and commentaries, see Henry French and Richard H. Hoyle, *The character of English rural society: Earls Colne, 1550–1750* (Manchester, 2007), pp. 3–12; Rigby, *English society*, pp. 127–43; Whittle, *Agrarian capitalism*, pp. 305–16; Bruce M.S. Campbell, 'The agrarian problem in the early fourteenth century', *Past and Present*, 188 (2005), pp. 5–6; Bas van Bavel, 'Land lease and agriculture: the transition of the economy in the Dutch river area from the fourteenth to the sixteenth century', *Past and Present*, 172 (2001), pp. 16–18; Shami Ghosh, 'Rural economies and transitions to capitalism: Germany and England compared (c.1200–c.1800)', *Journal of Agrarian Change*, 16 (2016), pp. 255–90.

54. George Grantham, 'France', in Harry Kitsikopoulos, ed., *Agrarian change and crisis in Europe, 1200–1500* (Abingdon, 2012), p. 79.

55. Pamuk, 'Black Death', p. 292; Fochesato, 'Origins', pp. 92–106.

56. Campbell, *Great transition*, p. 378, has England at $777 (based on 1990 prices), Holland at $876, Spain at $1,030, and Italy at $1,376. A similar conclusion is drawn in Malanima, 'Italy in the Renaissance', table 6, p. 19.

57. Campbell, *Great transition*, fig. 5.1, p. 378; Malanima, 'Italy in the Renaissance', table 2, p. 8.
58. Campbell, 'Factor markets', p. 80.
59. Summarized in Miller and Hatcher, *Medieval England: towns*, pp. 394–02; Hatcher and Bailey, *Modelling the Middle Ages*, pp. 43–49; Junichi Kanzaka, 'Villein rents in thirteenth-century England: an analysis of the Hundred Rolls of 1279–1280', *Economic History Review*, 55 (2002), p. 598; Campbell, *Great transition*, pp. 182–91.
60. Jane Whittle, 'The food economy of lords, tenants and workers in a medieval village: Hunstanton, Norfolk, 1328–48', in Maryanne Kowaleski, John Langdon, and Phillipp R. Schofield, eds., *Peasants and lords in the medieval English economy: essays in honour of Bruce M.S. Campbell* (Turnhout, 2015), pp. 41–2.
61. Campbell, *Great transition*, pp. 160–72.
62. Edward Miller and John Hatcher, *Medieval England. Rural society and economic change 1086-1349* (London, 1978), pp. 49–53; Robert C. Allen, 'The Great Divergence in European wages and prices from the Middle Ages to the First World War', *Explorations in Economic History*, 38 (2001), p. 430; Robert C. Allen and Jacob L. Weisdorf, 'Was there an "industrious revolution" before the industrial revolution?: an empirical exercise for England, c. 1300–1830', *Economic History Review*, 64 (2011), fig. 1 and p. 721.
63. Campbell, 'Agrarian problem', p. 62; Elizabeth Routledge, 'Immigration and population growth in early fourteenth century Norwich: evidence from the tithing rolls', *Urban History Yearbook* (1988), pp. 25–6.
64. Ghosh, 'Rural economies', pp. 280–1. This was especially true of single women, Judith M. Bennett, 'Women and poverty: girls on their own in England before 1348', in Kowaleski et al., eds., *Peasants and lords*, pp. 299–323.
65. Richard H. Britnell, 'Specialization of work in England, 1100–1300', *Economic History Review*, 54 (2001), pp. 8, 14; Mavis E. Mate, 'Work and leisure', in Rosemary Horrox and W. Mark Ormrod, eds., *A social history of England 1200-1500* (Cambridge, 2006), p. 280; Campbell, 'Agrarian problem', p. 65.
66. Gregory Clark, 'The long march of history: farm wages, population, and economic growth, England 1209-1869', *Economic History Review*, 60 (2007), fig. 8.
67. John R. Maddicott, 'The English peasantry and the demands of the Crown, 1294–1341', *Past and Present*, Supplement 1 (1975); Bridbury, *English economy*, pp. 189–99.
68. Dewitte and Kowaleski, 'Black Death bodies', pp. 7–11.
69. Mark Bailey, 'Peasant welfare in England, 1290–1348', *Economic History Review*, 51 (1998), pp. 228–30; Mark Page, 'The smallholders of Southampton water: the peasant land market on a Hampshire manor before the Black Death', in Sam Turner and Bob Silvester, eds., *Life in medieval landscapes: people and places in the Middle Ages* (Oxford, 2012), pp. 181–97; Susan Kilby, 'Struggle and enterprise: the experience of servile peasants in Wellingborough, 1258-1322', *Midland History*, 35 (2010), pp. 18–25; Hugo J.P. La Poutre, 'The contribution of legumes to the diet of English peasants and farm servants, c.1300', *Agricultural History Review*, 63 (2015), pp. 19–38; Campbell, *Great transition*, pp. 166–8.
70. For the value and output of gardens, see Christopher Dyer, *Everyday life in medieval England* (London, 1994), pp. 116–31.

71. Bruce M.S. Campbell, *English seigniorial agriculture 1250–1450* (Cambridge, 2000), pp. 391, 396; Bridbury, *English economy*, p. 186.

72. Bailey, 'Peasant welfare', pp. 228–9; Erin Karakacili, 'English agrarian labour productivity rates before the Black Death: a case study', *Journal of Economic History*, 64 (2004), pp. 24–60; David J. Stone, *Decision-making in medieval agriculture* (Oxford, 2005), pp. 263–72; David J. Stone, 'The consumption of field crops in late medieval England', in Christopher M. Woolgar, Dale Serjeantson, and Tom Waldron, eds., *Food in medieval England. Diet and nutrition* (Oxford, 2006), pp. 19–20; Kilby, 'Struggle and enterprise', p. 20; La Poutre, 'Contribution of legumes', p. 37; Jan Myrdal and Alexandra Sapoznik, 'Technology, labour, and productivity potential in peasant agriculture: England c.1000 to 1348', *Agricultural History Review*, 65 (2017), pp. 194–12; Hugo J.P. La Poutre, 'Fertilisation by manure: a manor model comparing English demesne and peasant land, c.1300', *Agricultural History Review*, 65 (2017), pp. 20–48; Whittle, 'Food economy', pp. 38–9, 53–4. For a cautionary view, see John Langdon, 'Bare ruined farms?: extents for debt as a source for landlord versus non-landlord agricultural performance in fourteenth-century England', in Kowaleski et al., eds., *Peasants and landlord*, pp. 59–82.

73. See, for example, Richard H. Britnell, 'Commerce and capitalism in late medieval England: problems of description and theory', *Journal of Historical Sociology*, 6 (1993), pp. 359–76; Robert Brenner, 'Property and progress: where Adam Smith went wrong', in Chris Wickham, ed., *Marxist history-writing for the twenty-first century* (Oxford, 2007), pp. 59–95.

74. Susan Reynolds, *Fiefs and vassals: the medieval evidence reinterpreted* (Oxford, 1994).

75. Hatcher and Bailey, *Modelling the Middle Ages*, pp. 121–73; Ghosh, 'Rural economies', pp. 257–61; Schofield, *Peasants and historians*, pp. 125–41.

76. Bridbury, *English economy*, pp. 258–61; van Bavel, 'Land, lease', pp. 24–5; Bas van Bavel, *Manors and markets: economy and society in the Low Countries, 500–1600* (Oxford, 2010), pp. 74–90; Jan Luiten van Zanden, '"Revolt of the Early Modernists" and the "First Modern Economy": an assessment', *Economic History Review*, 55 (2002), pp. 635–8; Ghosh, 'Rural economies', pp. 258–61.

77. For a summary of the views, see Schofield, *Peasants and historians*, pp. 91–9, 118–23. See, for example, Brenner, 'Agrarian roots', pp. 222–4, 228–42, 246–53, 257–8, 261–4; Brenner, 'Property and progress', pp. 83, 95–7; Rodney H. Hilton, 'A crisis of feudalism', in Aston and Philpin, eds., *Brenner Debate*, pp. 121–8; Robert Brenner, 'The rises and falls of serfdom in medieval and early modern Europe', in Michael L. Bush, ed., *Serfdom and slavery: studies in legal bondage* (London, 1996), pp. 262–3; Kitsikopoulos, 'England', pp. 46–7; Christopher Dyer, 'Villeins, bondsmen, neifs and serfs: new serfdom in England c.1200–1600', in Paul Freedman and Monique Bourin, eds., *Forms of servitude in north and east Europe: decline resistance and expansion* (Turnhout, 2005), pp. 419–24.

78. Ghosh, 'Rural economies', p. 258; Gerald L. Harriss, *Shaping the nation: England 1360–1461* (Oxford, 2005), pp. 216–17. English serfdom at its peak was associated with 'strong landlord oppression', Whittle, *Agrarian capitalism*, p. 312.

79. Such views are surveyed in Bruce M.S. Campbell, 'People and land in the Middle Ages, 1066–1500', in Robert A. Dodgshon and Robin A. Butlin, eds., *An historical geography*

of England and Wales (2nd edition, London, 1990), pp. 98–100; Rigby, *English society*, pp. 69–80, 104–9, 127–44; Hatcher and Bailey, *Modelling the Middle Ages*, pp. 21–173; Dyer, 'Villeins, bondsmen', pp. 424–7; Stephen H. Rigby, 'Introduction: social structure and economic change in late-medieval England', in Horrox and Ormrod, eds., *Social history*, pp. 1–30; Campbell, *Great transition*, pp. 160–98.

80. Brenner, 'Agrarian class structure', p. 26, 31–5; Hilton, 'Crisis of feudalism', pp. 131–2; Brenner, 'Property and progress', p. 83. For a summary, see Hatcher and Bailey, *Modelling the Middle Ages*, pp. 71–91.

81. Ralph Evans, 'Whose was the manorial court', in Ralph Evans, ed., *Lordship and learning: studies in memory of Trevor Aston* (Woodbridge, 2004), p. 155.

82. Palmer, *English law*, p. 16; Robert Braid, 'Behind the ordinance of labourers: economic regulation and market control in London before the Black Death', *Journal of Legal History*, 34 (2013), p. 28.

83. Ghosh, 'Rural economies', pp. 260–1.

84. Harry Kitsikopoulos, 'England', in Kitsikopoulos, ed., *Agrarian change*, pp. 45–7, 335, quotes from pp. 45–6. See also: 'the economy did not necessarily operate by the laws of supply and demand', John Aberth, *From the brink of the apocalypse: confronting famine, war, plague and death in the later Middle Ages* (London, 2001), p. 136.

85. Van Bavel, *Manors and markets*, pp. 86–93; van Bavel, *Invisible hand*, pp. 19–21; Ghosh, 'Rural economies', pp. 258–61; Paolo Malanima, 'Italy', in Kitsikopoulos, ed., *Agrarian change*, pp. 99–110; Whittle, *Agrarian capitalism*, p. 309.

86. Van Zanden, 'Revolt', pp. 635–8; van Bavel, *Manors and markets*, pp. 74–93.

87. Van Bavel, *Invisible hand*, pp. 2, 5–6, 19–22.

88. Hilton, 'Crisis of feudalism', p. 132. Summarized in Schofield, *Peasants and historians*, pp. 102–4.

89. Dyer, 'Villeins, bondsmen', pp. 428–33.

90. Bolton, *Medieval English economy*, p. 213.

91. This line of argument is summarized in Hatcher, 'England in the aftermath', pp. 3–9.

92. Bridbury, *English economy*, p. 217. See also John A.F. Thomson, *Transformation of medieval England 1370–1529* (Harlow, 1983), p. 18.

93. Brenner, 'Agrarian roots', pp. 31–5, 46–7; Hilton, 'Crisis of feudalism', p. 133; Zvi Razi, 'The myth of the immutable English family', *Past and Present*, 140 (1993), pp. 33–40; Yates, *Town and countryside*, p. 232. Andrew Dunn, *The Peasants' Revolt* (Stroud, 2004), pp. 35–6 argues that 'the early beginnings of a peasant land market' are discernible in the decades after 1348–9.

94. See, for example, Thompson, *Transformation*, pp. 32–3; Bolton, *Medieval English economy*, pp. 214–15; P. Jeremy and P. Goldberg, *Medieval England: a social history 1250–1550* (London, 2004), pp. 161–73, 186–99; Harriss, *Shaping the nation*, pp. 225–9; van Bavel, *Manors and markets*, p. 87; Pamuk, 'Black Death', p. 309; Kitsokopolous, 'England', pp. 34–5.

95. Ethan Knapp, 'John Gower: Balzac of the fourteenth century', in Ana Saez-Hidalgo and Robert F. Yeager, eds., *John Gower in England and Iberia: manuscripts, influences, reception* (Cambridge, 2014), pp. 216–18, 227.

96. van Bavel, *Manors and markets*, p. 87, 273; Bas van Bavel, *The invisible hand?: how market economies have emerged and declined since AD500* (Oxford, 2016), pp. 211–12.

97. Campbell, 'Factor markets', pp. 80, 96; de Pleijt and van Zanden, 'Accounting', figs. 1 and 2; van Bavel, 'Land, lease', p. 24–5; van Bavel, *Manors and markets*, pp. 74–90; Ghosh, 'Rural economies', pp. 258–61.

98. van Bavel, *Manors and markets*, p. 273.

99. Jan Myrdal, 'Scandanavia', in Kitsikopoulos, ed., *Agrarian change*, pp. 231–7; Kitsikopoulos, 'Epilogue', pp. 348–52.

100. van Bavel, *Manors and markets*, pp. 86–7; van Bavel et al., 'Factor markets', p. 16; van Bavel, *Invisible hand*, pp. 6, 20–1, 211–14; Kitsikopoulos, 'Epilogue', in Kitsikopoulos, ed. *Agrarian change*, pp. 350–1.

101. van Bavel, *Invisible hand*, pp. 215–18.

102. Mark Bailey, *The English manor c.1200–c.1500* (Manchester, 2002), pp. 2–10; Bruce M.S. Campbell, 'The land', in Horrox and Ormrod, eds., *Social history*, pp. 190–5; Mark Bailey, 'Villeinage in England: a regional case study c.1250–1349', *Economic History Review*, 62 (2009), pp. 430–57; Junichi Kanzaka, 'Manorialisation and demographic pressure in medieval England: an analysis of the Hundred Rolls of 1279–80', *Journal of Historical Geography*, 60 (2018), pp. 11–23.

103. Hatcher, 'English serfdom', pp. 6–26; Kanzaka, 'Villein rents', p. 617; Christopher Dyer, 'The ineffectiveness of lordship in England, 1200–1400', in Christopher Dyer, Peter Coss, and Chris Wickham, eds., *Rodney Hilton's Middle Ages: an exploration of historical themes* (Past and Present Society, 2007), pp. 69–86; Bailey, 'Villeinage in England', pp. 437–57; John Hatcher, 'Lordship and villeinage before the Black Death: from Karl Marx to the Marxists and back again', in Kowaleski et al., eds., *Peasants and lords*, pp. 113–45.

104. J. Ambrose Raftis, *Peasant economic development within the English manorial system* (Stroud, 1996), pp. 10, 118–31.

105. Alice Rio, *Slavery after Rome 500–1100* (Oxford, 2017), pp. 243–9.

106. Campbell, 'Agrarian problem', pp. 46–7; Henry French and Richard H. Hoyle, *The Character of English Rural Society: Earls Colne, 1550–1750* (Manchester, 2007), pp. 12–16.

107. This approach develops and refines the monumental work of a productive and influential generation of scholars. See, for example, Richard H. Britnell, *The commercialisation of English society 1000–1500* (1st edition, Cambridge, 1993), pp. 79–127; Miller and Hatcher, *Medieval England: towns*; Richard H. Britnell, 'Commercialisation and economic development in England 1000–1300', in Richard H. Britnell and Bruce M.S. Campbell, eds., *A commercialising economy: England 1086 to 1300* (Manchester, 1995), pp. 7–26; Bruce M.S. Campbell, 'Measuring the commercialisation of seigniorial agriculture in c.1300', in Britnell and Campbell, eds., *A commercialising economy*, pp. 132–93; Dyer, *An age of transition*, pp. 7–45; John Langdon and James Masschaele, 'Population growth and commercial activity in medieval England', *Past and Present*, 190 (2006), pp. 35–81; Langdon and Masschaele, 'Commercial activity', pp. 37–77; and Campbell, *Great transition*, pp. 96–121.

108. Britnell, *Commercialisation*, p. 115; Richard Holt, 'Society and population 600–1300', in Palliser, ed., *Urban history*, pp. 103–4; Britnell, *Britain*, p. 74; Christopher Dyer, 'Small towns', in Palliser, ed., *Urban history*, pp. 505–8. This was not, however,

a peculiarly English phenomenon, because small towns proliferated throughout the continent after 1000 and, if their populations are also admitted, the average urbanization ratio across Europe was comparable to that of England, Campbell, *Great transition*, pp. 122–3.

109. Chavas and Bromley, 'Modelling population', pp. 230–2.
110. Hatcher, 'England in the aftermath', pp. 3–32.
111. Mark Bailey, *The decline of serfdom in late-medieval England: from bondage to freedom* (Woodbridge, 2014), pp. 16–61, 285–337.
112. John Munro, 'The late medieval decline of English demesne agriculture: demographic, monetary and political-fiscal factors', in Bailey and Rigby, eds., *Town and countryside*, p. 301; Mark Bailey, 'The myth of the seigniorial reaction in England after the Black Death', in Kowaleski et al., eds., *Peasants and lords*, pp. 147–72.
113. Summarized in Yates, *Town and countryside*, pp. 4–5, 23.
114. The suggestion that markets in medieval and modern England were comparable in many ways is made in Gregory Clark, *A farewell to alms: a brief economic history of the world* (Princeton, 2007), pp. 147–8, 162–3. Cf. van Bavel, *Manors and markets*, pp. 162–6.
115. As suggested by Campbell, *Great transition*, pp. 10–15, quote at p. 2; and Peter L. Larson, *Conflict and compromise in the late medieval countryside: lords and peasants in Durham 1349–1400* (London, 2006), pp. 199–200, 212, 222, 237–8.

2

Old Problems, New Approaches

Introduction

As we saw in Chapter 1, there is no dispute that on the eve of the Black Death England was in the grip of a chronic socio-economic crisis or that its economic performance was modest by European standards. The conventional explanation for this general state of over-population and impoverishment is that the society and economy were in the grip of either a Malthusian crisis of subsistence or a Marxist crisis of feudalism.[1] While these two competing models of pre-industrial economic development provide different explanations for the crisis, they both proceed from similar assumptions about the structure of society. Both attribute the petering out of growth to structural inefficiencies of various kinds emanating from the unequal distribution of land; the overwhelmingly subsistence-based nature of peasant production; the tight bonds between lord, land, and family; and the extensive seigniorial powers of extra-economic coercion through villeinage. Consequently, both models assume that the size of factor and commodity markets, and the extent of urbanization, were limited, and that 'feudalism' (what we will call manorial lordship) continued to exert considerable influence over their operation. Indeed, scholars who contrast the precociousness of the Low Countries in the pre-plague era with the immaturity of England point to the constraints imposed by the strength of English manorial lordship as the differentiating factor.[2]

Over the course of the past three decades, detailed research into pre-plague England has portrayed a rather different picture of English society and economy on the eve of the Black Death. The nature of villeinage, the extent of commercial activity, and the operation of the law have all been subject to careful analysis, and the findings are often at odds with the assumptions and assertions described above. Cumulatively, they indicate that manorial lordship was less powerful than conventionally depicted. Yet the implications of these findings have yet to be accommodated effectively into a revised explanatory framework for the early fourteenth-century economy and, by extension, for assessing the economic and social consequences of the Black Death. This chapter summarizes this recent research and attempts to reconstruct the nature of the main factor and commodity markets in pre-plague England, how they operated, and the forces influencing the allocation of resources. This provides a clearer insight into their constraints and inefficiencies on the eve of plague, and how they changed in its wake.

After the Black Death: Economy, Society, and the Law in Fourteenth-Century England. Mark Bailey, Oxford University Press (2021). © Mark Bailey. DOI: 10.1093/oso/9780198857884.003.0002

The Institutional Framework on the Eve of the Black Death

A feature of many of the recent econometric approaches to the era of the Black Death is their determination to identify the principal processes driving economic growth and divergence over many centuries, and, in particular, the forces behind the development of markets, which are deemed essential to economic growth.[3] The latter involves reconstructing the size of markets at any given time and place, and how they operated, because their operation differed markedly depending upon the particular institutional framework in which they were embedded. Institutions are the humanly derived arrangements that shape decision-making, and comprise both formal and observable elements (laws, organizations, franchises), and informal and non-observable ones (beliefs, culture).[4] Differences in institutional arrangements meant that the English labour market in the 1340s operated differently, say, from that in Russia, and indeed from that of England in the 1840s. Likewise, a different institutional framework meant that commerce in medieval Europe was very different from commerce in modern Europe both operationally and culturally.[5] Such differences meant that the operation of markets could stimulate economic growth in some places while retarding it in others.[6]

Institutions are context-specific, which requires their reconstruction for each particular time and place.[7] This is neither a straightforward nor a simple task, and the ability to undertake it reliably depends upon the survival of sufficient contemporary sources. Historians are best placed to undertake context-specific reconstructions of institutional arrangements because of their detailed knowledge of time and place, and their command and understanding of the local source material.[8] Indeed, econometric analysis can too readily overlook the non-observable elements of institutions.[9] The onus is upon the historian to reconstruct—essentially through description—the observable and non-observable institutional arrangements at a given time and place accurately and fully because, without it, there can be no effective or reliable comparisons with the arrangements that existed at other times and places.[10] This is especially true for factor markets in land, labour, and capital, which until recently have received limited attention from historians.[11] Only detailed studies of this type are capable of revealing how demographic collapse filtered through, and interacted with, different institutional frameworks to create divergent socio-economic outcomes.

Thus, the purpose of this section is to establish the size of the main markets in the 1340s and the broad institutional arrangements governing their operation. This analysis will enable an assessment of how effective they were under the sustained pressure of a high population, and then to explore how the same framework adapted to the sudden and dramatically different land/labour ratio of the 1350s and 1360s. This approach also lays a firm foundation for identifying the main institutional changes in the wake of plague, and for considering their significance, if any, for England's future economic precocity (Chapter 7). This narrow and focused approach enables the interplay between the Black Death, society, economy, and institutional change to be explored in detail within a tight chronology. In doing so, it avoids the trap of resorting to broad generalizations about large areas of territory over long periods, where the significance of specific and detailed interactions, and by extension the precision about causation, is apt to become lost. The scholarship on the Black Death in England has tended to offer, or simply to recite, broad-brush generalizations about its impact. For example, some econometricians portray the whole of the period between the fourteenth and eighteenth centuries as the age of the Black Death, without any tighter periodization, and even medieval historians are prone to generalizing about 1350 to 1500 as if it was a single and undifferentiated period.[12] Without more detailed analysis, whereby key institutional changes are carefully reconstructed over shorter time-frames, econometric approaches to the big question of the Little Divergence will ultimately struggle to progress beyond high-level generalizations (see Chapter 7).

Few scholars would dispute Campbell's observation that the institutional response to plague in England was highly distinctive, causing a fundamental change in the nature of property relations and 'shaping labour markets and informing decisions about household formation for centuries to come'.[13] Equally, however, few would agree about exactly what those changes were, why they came about, and when they acquired significance for England's long-term economic development. The objective of this book is to discuss, clarify, and attempt to resolve those issues for the period between c.1340 and c.1400. The purpose of this section is to reconstruct the key institutional arrangements in England on the eve of the Black Death by focusing upon the size and the operation of the factor and commodity markets.[14] We will draw upon recent research into the commercialization of English society, but also develop the analysis further by addressing the extent to which manorial lordship influenced the workings of the land, labour, capital, and commodity markets. This will then provide a benchmark for assessing the impact of the Black Death and for measuring subsequent changes.

The land market

There were three basic categories of land in medieval England: demesne, free, and unfree. On the eve of the Black Death demesne land comprised around 30 per cent of the arable, free c.35 per cent, and unfree c.35 per cent.[15] Its social distribution was highly inequitable, because c.20,000 lords held the demesne land, around three million free peasants and townsfolk shared free tenure, and two million villeins the remainder.[16] None of this land was owned outright and exclusive of the rights of others in the modern sense, reflecting its origins as a gift from one individual to another that created a personal bond of reciprocity between them, usually involving some form of service.[17] Furthermore, various rules and customs determined and restricted its use and disposal, such as common rights, inheritance customs, and seigniorial privileges.[18]

Lords could choose either to exploit their demesne land directly or to lease it to third parties either in many small parcels or as a single unit. Very occasionally, they might transfer some parcels of demesne permanently over to the peasant sector in order to augment the land available to their tenantry. In the 1340s perhaps 40 per cent of all demesne land was leased and the rest was exploited directly.

Peasants held their land from a lord through the administrative unit of the manor.[19] Most free and unfree (also known as customary or villein) tenure did not render a commercial head rent but instead the rent package comprised a range of payments and obligations, such as a notional cash rent, labour services, attendance at the manorial court, renders in kind, suit of mill, and personal dues of various types (such as merchet, a marriage fine, and heriot, a death duty). The lord granted the tenant seisin (possession) of the land, providing the latter with some defensible rights, and local custom influenced inheritance patterns. Most free and unfree land was held heritably—whether partible (shared among heirs) or impartible (a single heir)—while a minority was held for a stipulated number of lives (usually one or three). Life tenancies are recorded throughout England, but tended to be more common in the west and less so in East Anglia and the south-east.[20] These 'service' tenancies were non-commercial, in the sense that their head rents were not adjusted or renegotiated in line with the prevailing market value of land. In the 1340s the overwhelming proportion of peasant land—perhaps 90 per cent—was held on some form of non-commercial tenancy.

The remaining c.10 per cent of peasant land in the 1340s was held on a form of contractual tenancy, i.e. for a cash head rent fixed at a commercial or quasi-commercial rate.[21] These were usually grants of either newly-colonized land on free or unfree tenure, or where lords had bought up freeholds then re-granted them to a new tenant.[22] There were three basic forms of contractual tenancies. The first was a grant of land on either a heritable tenancy or for a stipulated term of lives for a cash rent fixed at the time of the first grant close to a commercial rate. An entry fine on the admission of the heir, a heriot on the death of the tenant, and suit of court were usually the only other components of the rent package. This form of contractual tenancy passed under a variety of names, such as 'ad censum', 'arrentata', and 'fee farms'. The head rent could not be changed until either the end of the term of lives or the failure of an heir to take up the holding, in which case the lord could grant the land to a third party and change the terms of the tenancy. Hence the cash rent might become a 'quasi-commercial' rent, meaning that the head rent had been originally set and fixed at a commercial rent, but the value of land had risen or fallen subsequently.

The second type of contractual tenure was a lease for a term, which involved the grant of land to a named tenant in a contractual relationship for a limited and specified period at a fixed annual rent, the latter reflecting the negotiated value between the two voluntary parties.[23] The land reverted to the lord at the expiry of the term, and the lessee possessed no automatic rights to renew, assign, or inherit.[24] Leases were fixed, usually for a stipulated number of years, and in many ways resembled the modern form of economic lease.[25] Regularly renewed, short-term leases would most closely reflect the prevailing market value of land. Leases in this form began to emerge in the most agriculturally progressive areas of north-west Europe at the beginning of the thirteenth century.[26] As leases did not involve the transfer of seisin, the typical formula of conveyance in the manor court roll was styled simply and often called a 'farm'.[27] Most were short-term, owing a fixed money rent set at or close to the commercial rate and suit of court. They seldom attracted entry fines, and, where they did, the fines were nominal.[28]

The final form of contractual tenure was tenure-at-will. This was the least secure form of contractual tenancy because it was held for no stipulated period in return for a fixed annual money rent and could literally be seized at the will of the lord at any time.[29] No entry fine or other servile incident was payable. It was sometimes described as a payment 'of issue' [de exitus]. Landlords deployed tenure-at-will to find tenants for vacant customary land immediately and temporarily, often in the wake of some emergency until conventional terms could be settled with a permanent replacement.[30] Usually tenure-at-will is recorded in the manorial account, or occasionally the court roll, with little more than the name of the tenant and the annual payment. Tenure-at-will existed throughout England without becoming a significant form of tenure anywhere.[31]

The development of the common law from the late twelfth century was instrumental in clarifying the obligations and rules surrounding the tenure of land, and in increasing the security of free tenure and the ability of the free tenant to alienate land without seigniorial interference.[32] A freeman could establish and defend the title to free tenure in the royal courts of common law on the basis of written proof. This did not necessarily prevent landlords from seizing a free tenure or attempting to hike up its rent, but it greatly discouraged such behaviour and provided the tenant with a means of redress if they did. The emergence of these relatively secure property rights transformed freehold land from a frozen to a liquid asset, as a result of which a market in freehold land—largely independent of seigniorial control—emerged during the course of the thirteenth century.[33] This process also contributed to changing cultural perceptions of land, from the concept of a gift involving personal service towards a more impersonal contract between two parties, and the gradual replacement of rents payable in kind or services with monetary rents. On the eve of the Black Death the free land market was very active, featuring a high volume of transfers of many small parcels of land. It is impossible to reconstruct the dynamics of this market locally because the transfers of free land did not have to be registered with the lord. Manorial surveys, however, reveal graphically how the combination of high demographic pressure, strong demand for land, rising land values, and the operation of a free land market had caused holdings to splinter and the average holding size to fall.[34]

Lords retained a tighter grip on the disposal of villein land. Late twelfth- and thirteenth-century lawyers stressed that 'the very essence of villeinage is uncertainty... serfs hold only from day to day at the will of their lords and for no certain services'.[35] In theory, lords could vary rent levels as they pleased, and villeins could not transmit property either in their lifetime (*inter vivos*) or, indeed, after their death (*post mortem*), because they did not own the land and because their heir was the lord.[36] Nor did the villein have any effective legal mechanism for redress in the event of any such arbitrary lordly intervention because the courts of common law had no jurisdiction over pleas relating to villein tenure.[37] The title to villein land could only be pleaded in the landlord's own manorial court, which by definition could not guarantee an independent hearing for the tenant. Without any guarantee of independent legal redress in the event of dispute, the villein tenant was theoretically vulnerable to exploitation and seizure entirely on a seigniorial whim.[38] Lords possessed the legal power to force unwilling serfs to hold land, or to impose harsh terms against the tenant's will; to override inheritance customs or eject tenants on a whim or a minor pretext; and to consolidate servile holdings into the lord's own demesne rather than allowing heirs to enter them.

This strict legal theory explains the traditional belief that lords could and did exercise arbitrary and coercive powers over villein tenure whenever it suited them and that, on the eve of plague, the villein rent package was essentially exploitative.[39] Medieval historians now accept, however, that the gap between this legal theory and the actual reality on the ground was considerable.[40] Custom created a good deal of protection to the holders of villein land.[41] First, lords did not evict tenants at will or remove them in favour of others who were prepared to pay more rent, and evidence from manorial courts shows that eviction only occurred following a proven breach of the terms of the tenancy.[42] Even then, immediate seizure was rare and usually occurred only when the formal legal procedures of distraint and seizure had been exhausted.[43] Second, villeins routinely transmitted property either to their heirs or within their lifetime to their chosen recipients (who might be non-kin), subject to following the correct procedures and recording the transfer of seisin in the manorial court.[44] This relative security meant that a customary land market followed the development of the free land market.[45] At Coltishall (Norfolk) in the 1330s and 1340s 21 per cent of all customary land exchanged hands each year, mainly through commercial sales of small parcels of half an acre.[46] Rather than prohibiting exchanges of villein land, lords opted to formalize the system of transfer in order to track and profit from it.[47]

Finally, during the thirteenth century the twin forces of custom and codification had the effect of freezing the rent packages attached to most villein tenancies, which prevented lords from increasing rent levels in line with market forces.[48]

Even the two most flexible incidents of villein tenure offering the greatest scope for landlords to squeeze more cash from their villeins—entry fines (charged when land changed hands) and tallage-at-will (a prerogative seigniorial tax on villeins)—were governed by custom and so used with restraint. Levels of entry fines generally followed the direction of market conditions, but they seldom matched commercial rates because they were often set according to customary formulae that protected heirs.[49] Similarly, tallage was not a universal charge upon villeins, and, even where levied, it was largely fixed in frequency and size, and was not used to recoup a commercial rent.[50] Landlords who attempted to increase the rent package on customary holdings, usually by increasing the number of labour services, faced the prospect of strident and well-organized opposition from their villeins, who often combined local protests with coordinated legal action.[51] The combined effects of these forces meant that, in reality, few lords were capable of extorting exorbitant rents from their tenants.[52] On the contrary, on the eve of the Black Death head rents on servile, and especially free, holdings were well below the prevailing market rate for land.[53]

Thus the force of custom had diluted the legal powers of manorial lordship over villein land, it had caused head rents to become fixed on service tenancies, and contributed to the growth of a villein land market. The relationship between lord and villein had become more contractual and less personal, which is reflected in the widespread use of the noun 'tenant' [*tenens*] to describe the latter.[54] Strictly speaking, a distinction should have been carefully maintained between the personal status of the serf (a 'neif' or 'a serf of the lord by blood', *nativus domini de sanguine*], which was hereditary through the male line, and the tenurial status of the landholder, which was determined by the tenancy of the land. In the pre-plague era, however, manorial documents seldom maintained this distinction because of the presumption that personal status and tenurial status were synonymous.[55] It should be stressed, however, that for all the villein's *de facto* rights over villein tenure, and the benefits it bestowed upon the tenant, villein tenure was still a good deal more disadvantaged than free tenure. The levels of rent were usually higher than those enjoyed by free tenants.[56] The villein had to register all transfers of villein land in the lord's manorial court, the associated entry fine was invariably far higher than anything the free tenant had to pay, and the overall rent burden was higher and less predictable than on freehold. A free person could acquire a villein holding, but a serf could not obtain free tenure without seigniorial permission. The choices available to villein tenants were restricted in various ways, and to a greater degree than free tenants, and attempts to evade seigniorial prerogatives over their land carried greater risks and costs.

Research in the past three decades has shown conclusively that free and unfree peasants possessed relatively secure property rights, and that a peasant land market was sizeable and vibrant in many areas of England. Its size and its operation varied from place to place, however, depending upon the relative importance locally of manorial structures, custom, and demography. Manorial lords could still play an influential role in restricting the extent to which a market emerged on any given manor. In a few places, they retained a customary right to regulate the transfer of free tenures.[57] In other places, they sought to preserve the integrity of standardized villein holding ('virgates', 'bovates', 'full-lands', etc.) by restricting or prohibiting permanent alienations of small parcels of villein land. A villein land market of sorts still existed in such places, because the complete holdings were transferred to third parties and even sold to non-kin, and some temporary subletting of small parcels was permitted, but the volume of transfers was relatively small.[58] Where lords adopted a much more permissive approach to the sales of villein land, such as in most parts of eastern and south-east England, the action of a very active land market fragmented the original standardized holdings and a sizeable proportion of villein land was sold to non-kin.[59]

Thus the size and the operation of peasant land markets varied from place to place on the eve of the Black Death. In general, a high population pressure, a proliferation of free tenures, partible inheritance, and a permissive seigniorial attitude to villein transfers resulted in a large and active land market, whereas low population pressure, a proliferation of villein tenures, impartible inheritance, and lordly resistance inhibited its development and dynamism.[60] Manorial lordship was no longer the primary influence over allocation of land, but it was one factor within a complex mix that included custom, family, tenurial arrangements, the market, and the law, and the mix varied regionally.[61]

Furthermore, the market was not the primary determinant of the levels of head rents, because on c.90 per cent of peasant land these were frozen by custom at levels well below the market value of land. Market forces dominated just two aspects of the peasant land market: the sale price of peasant land and the levels of rent on fixed-term sub-leases from head- to sub-tenant.[62] Hence an institutional structure with a peculiar mix of market and non-market forces determined the operation of peasant land market, and consequently landlords were unable to extract the full commercial yield from their tenants: instead, they could only raise their rental income by increasing tenant numbers and the land available to rent through reclamations.[63] The same institutional structure also created a powerful incentive for the larger landholding peasants either to sub-tenant land to other peasants for a commercial rent (while they themselves paid a nominal head rent to their lord), or to sell slivers of land to other peasants for a commercial sum and pocket the proceeds. It did not encourage the construction of large holdings for the purposes of commercial production.

The combination of these institutional arrangements and high population pressure resulted in the splintering of larger holdings (especially freeholdings), which in turn led to a very low mean landholding size and mounting impoverishment. Hence in the 1340s the majority of the English population comprised an underclass of smallholders and the landless living in chronic rural congestion and poverty.[64] The land market was also very sensitive to high grain prices and harvest failures, as starving peasants sold land in order to survive.[65] The combination had created a tenurial tangle inimical to long-term growth or to the creation of larger, more efficient, farming units. At best, it had proved capable only of supporting a larger population at lower levels of welfare. Campbell has dubbed this institutional sclerosis as 'the agrarian problem' of the early fourteenth century.[66]

The labour market

The development of any market in wage labour is predicated upon the presence of sufficient demand for such labour, and upon the ability and willingness of people to participate in it. The institution of serfdom is widely assumed to inhibit the development of a hired labour market because it ties manual labour to work on self-sufficient family farms and to the service of the lord. As a result, a large proportion of the workforce is committed to unpaid work either for the lord or on subsistence holdings. Furthermore, the restrictions upon movement under systems of serfdom and the small size of the commercial and industrial sectors greatly constrain the economic mobility of labour. Conversely, as serfdom dissolves, and as markets expand, so the ability of individuals to offer their labour for hire, and the availability of paid work, increase.[67]

These general assumptions have shaped the conventional view that the pre-plague labour market in England was small, that urban authorities and manorial lordship heavily regulated what market did exist, and that the restrictions of villeinage greatly restricted the ability of a large proportion of rural labour to access the market. Under the common law, the villein was the lord's chattel and therefore, according to the contemporary legal authority known as Bracton, 'is bound to do whatever is commanded of him, and does not know in the evening what he must do in the morning'.[68] In theory, then, the villein could not work or migrate, whether temporarily or permanently, without the lord's permission, and could be called upon to perform labour services on the manorial demesne at the lord's will. A strict and literal reading of the legal position of the villein under the common law informed the work of early twentieth-century historians, who regarded labour services as the central component of English villeinage: indeed, they believed that villeinage existed primarily to maintain and coerce a workforce for manorial lords.[69] This perspective continues to be highly influential, despite having been criticized by Kosminsky as early as the 1930s. For example, Michael Bennett states that on the eve of plague 'England still had some of the features of a caste society, and the great majority of men, let alone women and children, were in some sense bound to the soil or in some form of service in which their freedom was very constrained'.[70]

Recent research indicates a very different reality to this traditional view because on the eve of the Black Death villeins enjoyed considerable economic freedom and labour services were relatively light and fixed. Labour services were unquestionably one of the most resented and irksome aspects of serfdom, but they were actually 'one of the least common components of rent, [and] they were also the least valuable'.[71] They were either non-existent or light on many estates and in many areas of the country. Hatcher has estimated that in *c*.1300 fewer than one-third of all villein households in England actually owed works, and Campbell reckons that a mere *c*.15 per cent of villein rent was paid as labour services.[72] By another estimate labour services accounted for just *c*.8 per cent of all seigniorial production, and landlords overwhelmingly worked their demesnes with hired labourers, who were more industrious, productive, and easier to manage than forced labour.[73] By *c*.1300 labour services had become fixed, just like the other elements of rent packages, and so were seldom varied at the will of the lord. This was partly a function of the gradual codification in writing of the frequency and duration of services during the course of thirteenth century, although ironically the very process of creating a formal record of works owed eroded the principle that they were determined at the will of the lord and rendered subsequent increases much less likely.[74] Furthermore, the codification and ossification of labour services meant that villeins were able to anticipate lordly demands reliably, leaving them at liberty to participate in the wage labour market once they had discharged their known and fixed works.

The conventional view also overstates the cogency of seigniorial controls over the mobility of servile labour. The prohibition on the movement of villeins under the common law was never absolute.[75] Neither lords nor borough officials were under any legal requirement to return flown serfs to their rightful lord, which further weakened their powers of retrieval, as did the law of 'borough privilege', which enabled any villein who resided in a royal borough or on royal demesne for a year and a day to obtain legal freedom from his lord and condition.[76] As a consequence, any landlord determined to control servile migration had few effective options through the royal courts and so had to rely instead on self-help and force.[77] The most direct method of self-help was to make manorial officials responsible for fugitive serfs and sometimes to direct them to launch an expedition against, and physically retrieve, a serf.[78] Yet, in general, 'there is little evidence for physical coercion' and forcible recovery.[79] Indeed, a lord was theoretically given four days in which to retrieve a flown serf through his own agency, after which the recommended legal course of action was to issue a common-law writ for recovery.[80] Few lords or their officials were sufficiently watchful or proactive to respond within such a short timeframe.

The most common and pragmatic way of dealing with flown serfs was to maintain track of them through the formal licensing of departures or, where this did not prove possible, to exert pressure upon unlicensed migrants through the device of presenting them for absence in the manorial court, then following this up through the processes of distraint and pledging. During the thirteenth century chevage developed as a generic licensing system to recognize the reality that large numbers of villeins left their home manors temporally or permanently.[81] In this system, the serf was granted leave, year by year, on payment of a fee, but had to return once each year to the manorial view of frankpledge in order to acknowledge servile status and to retain the tithing affiliation: any sons were also required to return following their twelfth birthday to acknowledge their status as hereditary serfs.[82] The fee was usually low and affordable enough—a few pennies or a chicken or two a year—to encourage villeins to self-register, although large lump sums were occasionally levied.[83] Chevage was informal and pragmatic in the sense that it was developed and recorded in manorial court rolls, not in the courts of the common law, but its legal purpose was to enable lords to retain seisin of their serfs while permitting them to leave their manor of origin.[84] Although its use spread during the course of the thirteenth century, even in c.1300 it was still not deployed on many manors.[85] A lack of consistency even within the same estate and within the same manor is evident.[86] Variations in managerial priorities and administrative effectiveness on seigniorial estates had a demonstrable effect on the record of servile migrations.[87] Nevertheless, the general slackness in the management of flown serfs before the Black Death is striking, and relatively few were recorded, pursued, or harassed. Consequently, the hazards and risks of detection, and the costs of evading the lord's attention, were too low to discourage serfs from migrating. Economic circumstances—not lords—compelled serfs to work.

Thus, while English landlords possessed extensive theoretical legal powers over servile labour, in practice their powers were much restricted and consequently serfs exercised a great deal of choice over the deployment of their labour.[88] Lords possessed even fewer controls over the time and action of the free peasantry, who comprised around one-half of the rural population. They might owe a few light seasonal labour services, but otherwise disposed of their labour without lordly interference. Therefore the majority of peasants exercised considerable discretion over how to deploy their own labour for most of the time, whether on the landholding of family or friends, or in paid employment. The growth in the population and commercialization of the economy in the late twelfth and thirteenth centuries had greatly increased the demand for and supply of waged employment.[89] Seigniorial demesnes were heavily dependent upon hired labour for their operation, and peasants holding more than 20 acres of arable land also needed additional seasonal labour to work the holding.[90] Opportunities for paid work were greatest in urban centres because of the concentration of demand and greater specialization in the division of labour. Rural areas endowed with a diverse resource base—fenland, woodland, heathland, coast—presented wider opportunities for work than arable regions.[91]

We can never know definitively how large this labour market had become on the eve of the Black Death, and consequently estimates of its size and significance vary.[92] Nearly one-fifth of the population lived in towns, and over half of the rural population were either smallholders or landless, all of whom had to seek paid employment to varying degrees to bolster their household incomes.[93] Britnell, for example, estimated that at least one-quarter of all economic output was generated by wage labour, whereas Wood suggests between one-third and one-half of the population found paid employment of some form or another.[94] The main difficulty in constructing such estimates is that we can deduce that most peasants needed some paid employment, but we can never know how much they actually secured.

Figure 2.1 attempts to provide a basic estimate of the main areas of expenditure of productive peasant labour. The majority (c.60 per cent) was committed to the holding, whether on the arable, in the garden, tending livestock, or in various domestic activities. Labour services were insignificant in the grand scheme of things. Around 30 per cent of labour was absorbed by the hired labour market. Possibly just over one-half of this market comprised day-, task-, and piece-workers, and the remainder comprised individuals on half- or full-year contracts.[95] The latter were either working as permanent labourers on manorial demesnes or as single servants working in the households of others, especially in towns and pastoral districts.[96] Most individuals who entered the labour market were not wholly dependent upon wages for their livelihoods because they were members of household with some access to land, so there was not yet a permanent waged proletariat.[97]

What were the transactional arrangements and the institutions that shaped the operation of this labour market?[98] Thirteenth-century theologians accepted that wage levels were to be determined through honest bargaining according to market forces of supply, demand, need, and utility, although they also believed that

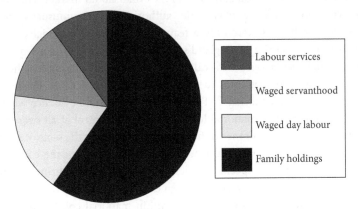

Figure 2.1 Estimated expenditure of productive labour in England, c.1340

behaviour in the hired labour market should serve the common good. Consequently, they formulated the idea of a 'just wage' to ensure a fair and balanced reward for work contracted between two parties.[99] The just wage should be high enough to provide a level of subsistence appropriate to the skill and status of the worker; it should be the product of fair bargaining, freely entered into; and it should be paid expeditiously.[100] In other words, before the Black Death the concept of the just wage remained an ideal, never enshrined in any government legislation, and its object was to prevent wages from falling rather than rising.

In the absence of any government intervention in the pre-plague labour market, historians have supposed that borough and manorial authorities regulated local wage levels, restricted economic mobility, and directed some recalcitrant labourers to work.[101] This viewpoint derives partly from traditional notions of powerful manorial lordship, but also from some evidence that municipal authorities and seigniorial courts regulated aspects of their local labour market.[102] For example, urban craft gilds imposed a system of apprenticeships upon certain trades, which included wage fixing, and the London civic authorities sometimes capped seasonal wages for construction workers and for those working in the grain trade.[103] Similarly, some rural manors issued community ordinances and by-laws to place restrictions on the movement of labour during the harvest period and to cap day wage rates for reapers.[104] Such evidence encouraged Elaine Clark to suggest that 'village by-laws, even in the thirteenth century, commonly gave priority in the hiring of labour to manorial lords', and Braid to state that village courts 'controlled the mobility [of] and forced labour upon both free tenants and bondmen'.[105]

Clark and Braid capture the widespread view that civic and manorial authorities closely controlled the pre-plague labour market, but the evidentiary base has not been subject to close analysis and, in fact, it does not withstand careful scrutiny. Although civic authorities did control the wages and movement of workers within the building trades and the system of craft gilds, they exercised no control over the operation of the rest of the urban labour market. This was even in the case in London, where the authorities were unusually active.[106] Furthermore, craft gilds were only a feature of the largest boroughs, and were absent from the majority of England's 600 towns where, as a consequence, no controls existed over labour.[107] In reality, towns simply did not possess the powers or the administrative structures to regulate the vast majority of the semi- and unskilled urban labour market.[108] Furthermore, there is no evidence whatsoever that the vast majority of manorial lords wielded any control at all over the rural labour market. Every one of the confident statements about the scale of seigniorial control over the pre-plague rural labour market derives from the early work of Ault, who identified a few specific restrictions upon labourers during the 'harvest' period, the six weeks or so every year when demand for labour was at its peak.[109] Ault cited community by-laws contained within manorial courts from the early fourteenth century seeking to maximize the number of available workers and to punish anyone attempting to extort high wages during the harvest period. The examples were derived from a dozen manors operating commonfield agriculture. Ault did not demonstrate whether or how effectively these by-laws were enforced within the communities for which he had evidence.[110] In reality, presentments for infractions of rural labour regulations are exceptionally rare in pre-plague manorial court rolls. Nor did he establish that such by-laws were typical of other communities. In fact, the types of by-laws and ordinances cited by Ault are rare before 1400, and were entirely absent from the many communities where communal controls over agriculture were weaker, such as regions of irregular open fields and enclosures.[111] Finally, Ault provided little evidence for regulating labour outside the harvest period.

Once the evidence has been carefully scrutinized, it is apparent that the only evidence for seigniorial controls over the rural labour market relate exclusively to ordinances restricting the movement of the able-bodied and to setting day rates for reaping during the six weeks of the harvest in a handful of commonfield communities. This is no basis whatsoever for arguing that before the Black Death manorial lordship exercised close control over rural labour throughout England.[112] Neither manorial nor borough authorities exercised much control over the labour market, and consequently wage-labourers, servants, and craft workers were free to strike contracts and to move from one employer to another with minimal interference. The prevailing conditions of over-supply and the severe under-employment of labour strengthened the position of employers by ensuring a ready supply of cheap labour, which meant that local authorities— whether rural or urban—had little incentive to regulate the market. The size of this hired labour market indicates its relative efficiency, and its presence undermined the viability and cost effectiveness of coerced labour.[113]

The main historical consequence of the lack of official regulation of the labour market is that we have very little information about how it operated. It is highly unlikely that individuals created, let alone kept, written records of work contracts. Many agreements would have been informal and cashless, consisting of swap arrangements between individuals and families known to one another.[114] Daily hirings or contracting for annual servanthood between loosely connected parties or strangers involved the striking of an oral bargain or covenant, preferably in front of witnesses to provide proof of the terms and conditions, and sealing by a pledge or an earnest.[115] Servants were free to negotiate their contracts for a fixed term (usually between six months and one year), and they were under no obligation to work if they did not like the proposed terms or duties.[116] Shortages of ready cash in small denominations meant that many payments to servants and *famuli* (demesne workers on annual contracts) were paid in a combination of food, lodgings, clothing, and cash: day-labourers received some cash, but many were paid in kind, on credit or through customary entitlements.[117] The availability of work was discontinuous and seasonal, and information flows about opportunities were poor. Consequently, it was less stable, controllable, and predictable as a source of livelihood than acquiring land and working one's own holding.

Contracts bestowed obligations on the employer, as well as on the employee, and both parties could litigate privately if anything went wrong.[118] Most disputes over these oral contracts must have been resolved informally through arbitration by mutually acquainted third parties. An individual seeking a more formal route for redress could do so by initiating a private plea of debt or breach of covenant in any one of a variety of legal tribunals, including borough and manorial courts.[119] Local courts handled private pleas relating to disputes over employment.[120] For a number of reasons, it is unlikely that many ended up in common-law courts: disputes over oral covenants were seldom heard in these courts, the cost of litigating there was higher than in local courts, and villeins did not have access to the king's courts.[121] Unfortunately, the written record of personal plaints in seigniorial and borough courts are terse and seldom include much detail about the source of the dispute, so it is impossible to reconstruct the extent to which labour issues featured among them. On the very rare occasions when one of these plaints does relate to a dispute over labour, the prevalence of informal contracts for waged labour is evident.[122]

Hence, on the eve of the Black Death, the hired labour market—comprised of day-labourers and servants on annual contracts—was larger than once supposed, absorbing perhaps 30 per cent of expended labour. Peasants enjoyed largely unobstructed access to this market, where the forces of supply and demand, and free bargaining, determined the levels of most wage rates: indeed, a wage was defined as a contract for a service.[123] Contrary to the accepted wisdom, urban and manorial authorities exercised few controls over the market's operation. Most disputes over labour contracts were resolved privately, either through informal agreements or private pleas in various legal tribunals. Furthermore, the government played no role in regulating labour. This was to change dramatically after 1349 (see pp. 77–83).

The capital market

The capital market was relatively well developed on the eve of the Black Death.[124] Credit was widely available at all levels of medieval society, although interest payments were disguised as either gifts, compensation, or an artificially enlarged loan in order to avoid the church's prohibition of usury. English kings borrowed on a grand scale to wage war, the ruling elite borrowed to build lavishly and pay taxes, and the mercantile community needed credit to speculate and to ease their cash flows. One estimate suggests that the scale of debt in the early fourteenth century was equivalent to at least 3 per cent of the taxable wealth of England.[125] Less obvious than the borrowings of kings and merchants, though no less important, was the large number of small credit and debt transactions at the lower levels of urban and rural society.[126] Briggs has shown that lending was practised by 'virtually everyone within a rural community who had the capacity or the opportunity, rather than being the preserve of a specialist few'.[127] Most petty credit agreements were based on oral contracts, and the thousands of cases of debt litigation recorded annually in hundreds of manorial, borough, market, and fair courts prove that such lesser tribunals had become reasonably effective at determining cases and enforcing their decisions on behalf of creditors.[128]

Thus, as Campbell states, credit was 'all-pervasive, at least in the most populous and commercialized parts of the country in the south and east'.[129] Capital markets were not yet very efficient, however, and they neither changed the basic contours of the economy nor eased the chronic impoverishment of most of the lower orders of society. Instead, they reinforced the wealth and the social influence of the urban and peasant elites who were the main sources of credit within local communities, and tended to compound the vulnerability of the poorer elements within them.[130] Furthermore, credit came at a price. Interest rates on private loans in c.1300 have been calculated at around 10 per cent to 12 per cent, which were almost double the rates prevailing in northern Italy, where cheaper credit reflected higher levels of wealth and greater institutional development. English interest rates fell after 1348–9, perhaps as low as 6 per cent, but in c.1400 they were still double those of Italian city states and were prone to wilder fluctuations.[131] The volatility and high level of English interest rates must also reflect a higher incidence of default experienced by creditors.

The commodities market

The conventional view of peasant societies in general and of pre-plague England in particular is that commodity markets were not especially large, because subsistence requirements and seigniorial expropriation absorbed most of the product of peasant land and labour, leaving few surpluses for sale. Where peasants did engage with commodity markets, their involvement was usually sporadic and small-scale, and driven by the compulsion to obtain cash to pay rents, fines, and taxes. Seigniorial demand for goods and services was therefore the engine driving the development of commodity markets.[132]

Research over the past two decades, however, has revealed that commodity markets on the eve of the Black Death had developed to a greater extent than the conventional depiction. One crude indicator of their development is the size and proportion of the urban sector. One estimate suggests that by c.1300 the proportion of people living in towns larger than 5,000 people averaged 8 per cent across Europe as a whole, peaking at around 20 per cent in the Low Countries and Italy. England's ratio was 7 per cent, just below the European average, broadly on a par with the Germanic states and just ahead of much of eastern Europe.[133] London was one of the greatest cities in Europe, with a population of perhaps 80,000 people, but the size of the other English towns quickly tailed away. Major provincial centres such as York, Norwich, and Bristol may have possessed populations of up to 20,000, but the town ranked eighteenth on the list of wealthiest English towns in 1334—Gloucester—had an estimated population of just 4,000 people.[134] The overwhelming majority of England's 600 towns were small, with populations of less—usually much less—than 4,000 people.[135] If the populations of these smaller towns are included in calculations of the urbanization ratio, then it rises to between 15 per cent and 20 per cent.[136]

The consensus that around one-fifth of the English population lived in towns on the eve of the Black Death undermines the old view that commodity markets were small and driven by seigniorial demand. It is undermined further by estimates of GDP that reveal the decline in the seigniorial share of national income, and the rapid growth of non-elite wealth and consumption, during the twelfth and thirteenth centuries. Mayhew and Campbell have both estimated independently that GDP expanded around tenfold between 1086 and 1300, while the seigniorial share declined from around 25 per cent to 15 per cent.[137] The absolute and relative growth in non-elite wealth, and the size of the urban sector, both indicate that the peasantry routinely engaged in sizeable markets for basic foodstuffs, clothing, fuel, and household goods.[138] Indeed, Ghosh suggests that by the early fourteenth century the size and value of the mass market in non-elite goods was now larger than the market for elite goods.[139] By one estimate, at least a quarter of the population was dependent upon the market for their consumption needs.[140] By another, nearly one-half of all agricultural produce was sold, especially animal produce and grains such as wheat, dredge, and barley.[141] Careful analysis of local sources has revealed that peasants themselves were the main source of supply of raw materials and processed foodstuffs for both markets.[142] The greatest cash crop was wool, the produce of both seigniorial and peasant flocks, much of it exported abroad.[143] Sheep constituted about one-fifth of the pastoral sector of both peasants and demesnes even though they were not essential to the working of the farm.[144] Livestock could walk to market, saving on the costs of transport, and cattle and horses reared on the English uplands were sold in south-east England. Peasant producers formed the bedrock of the horse trade, and their pastoral activities tended to be more commercialized than those of demesnes.[145] Fuel was produced and sold commercially, though the high bulk and low value of coal, faggots, and turves meant that markets tended to be local.[146]

It is one thing to recognize the commercial developments of the high Middle Ages, and another to evaluate their exact extent and significance. The majority of agricultural produce was not destined for the market but instead was consumed within the unit of production. Urban demand remained relatively weak, and even the largest towns obtained their food supplies from sources within a few miles.[147]

Most local marketing was discontinuous and sporadic.[148] People did not routinely buy ready-made consumables and agricultural equipment from the market but instead obtained essential components and materials as necessary, and re-used old clothes, utensils, and parts as best they could.[149] Information flows about prices and local shortages were slow, knowledge about distant markets was limited, contracts could be vague, and many sales were based more on trust through established personal contacts and networks than on impersonal exchange.[150] The instability of coin values and the variability of coin in circulation meant that many purchases were valued in price but not paid in cash: instead, extensive use was made of tallies, payments in kind, and exchanges for other goods or services.[151]

The characteristics of the grain market provide a useful exemplification of the nature of commodity markets on the eve of the Black Death.[152] Around one-third of all grain was sold, most of it wheat (for bread), and dredge and barley (for malt): meanwhile rye and oats were usually consumed as fodder or within the household.[153] Around one-third of all grain was retained as seed. This was especially true of the commercialized areas of the Home Counties, East Anglia, and places with easy access to water transportation, where managers on some demesnes were adapting production strategies to urban markets and responding to local price fluctuations.[154] Conversely, perhaps only 10 per cent of grain in the far north and in south-west England entered commercial markets.[155] These estimates derive from the reliable information about sales from seigniorial demesnes contained in manorial accounts, but no peasant accounts are extant to determine whether they followed similar strategies. Indirect indicators suggest that they did because on the eve of the Black Death well over half of the grain sold in England originated from the peasant sector.[156] Some historians suggest that the market for grain was relatively well integrated and efficient, based on the 'coalescence of towns and rural markets into a series of integrated regional networks of trade' throughout England.[157] This might have been a characteristic of some areas close to London and the handful of other large towns, and of the coastal trade in grain in south-east England, but otherwise the grain market remained fragmented and poorly integrated.[158] Limited market integration is indicated by the volatile swings in grain prices from year to year (25 per cent variation per annum in the early fourteenth century), and from region to region, and by the low aggregate price elasticities for grains, especially when compared to those in modern developing economies.[159]

The operation of pre-plague commodity markets was subject to a variety of constraints and rigidities from non-market forces. For example, a handful of major landlords possessed some privileges over the sale of peasant produce, such as the levy of a charge on the sale of villein livestock or first refusal on sales of peasant grain.[160] Likewise, burgesses enjoyed a privileged position for trading goods within their own town, while non-burgesses and non-residents contended with tolls and discriminatory practices.[161] All peasants were subject to purveyance, the prerogative right of the king to purchase foodstuffs and to requisition transport from his subjects to feed his own household and to support his armies. Although the royal household was often itinerant, and therefore purveyance could fall upon anyone within the realm, it was based mainly upon various royal residences within the Thames valley so most household purveying was borne by residents within a 30-mile radius of London.[162] Military purveyance was less frequent, but was undertaken on a far grander scale, and fell disproportionately upon the peasantry in the grain belt of the eastern counties, whose navigable river systems also enabled the goods to be transported readily and cheaply via Lynn (Norfolk) and Boston (Lincs.) to wherever the English army was situated.[163] The prices for compulsory purchases might be artificially low, and delays in payments required peasants to absorb the uncertainty and the pressure on their cash flow for an indeterminate length of time.[164]

The final, and most pervasive, example of interference in pre-plague commodity markets was the involvement of the government in regulating the sale price and the profit levels in the retail of key foodstuffs, notably grain, fish, bread, and ale. Indeed, the English government's regulation of these markets was unusually strict by European standards.[165] Since the late twelfth century it had established the national assizes of bread, ale, and fish, which introduced some price-setting and profit-capping to every market in the land, drawing upon the theoretical concepts of a 'just price' and a 'reasonable profit'. These recognized that free bargaining among traders was the primary determinant of market prices, yet sought to moderate prices through some communal estimation of what represented a fair price to ensure both affordability to ordinary people and to counter the effects of any commercial dishonesty, fraud, deception, or collusion.[166] Theologians feared that a desire for wealth and personal profit rendered merchants and traders especially vulnerable to the sins of avarice, covetousness, and greed, and so were liable to lose sight of their collective obligation to the common good. The corrective mechanisms of the 'just price' and 'reasonable profit' would counteract monopolistic and dishonest practices that inflated the 'natural' market price and boosted profits, such as wholesale hoarding (engrossing), forestalling (intercepting goods on their way to market) and regrating (buying and then reselling at a higher price within the market), and enabling public authorities to punish such practices. In effect, the freely negotiated market price was subject to the imposed social check of the just price in order to protect the humble consumer against commercial excesses and to hold all traders to private virtue and to their public moral obligations. Such legislation 'regarded what we now consider legitimate speculation as a crime'.[167] As such, it provides a reminder of how belief systems can result in behaviour or legislation that distorts the operation of markets.[168]

Contemporaries accepted that just prices and reasonable profits could not be calculated or fixed absolutely for all occasions and situations because of the almost infinite permutations of time, locations, and personnel.[169] Therefore borough and manorial authorities appointed local officials to calculate and proclaim them in the light of local conditions, and then to enforce them within their market. These officials also determined which 'essential' goods would be subject to the price and profit controls within their jurisdiction. The London authorities routinely applied a just price to a wide range of goods, setting prices for poultry, fish, and even various categories of livestock according to season and the quality of the animal.[170] Yet London was exceptional, and price setting in most boroughs and markets was usually restricted to a much narrower range of essential foodstuffs and to transactions within the market place during official market hours. In general the just price was applied routinely to 'public' sales of bread, ale, fish, and wine, and sometimes to sales of grain, meat, candles, eggs, and 'victuals', whereas sales of any foodstuffs outside market hours, including those in shops and inns, and sales of luxury commodities at any time, were excluded.[171] The same principles applied to calculations of excess profit. This was defined as the gains made by individuals who simply bought goods at one price then exploited or manipulated market conditions to sell the same good later at a higher price, with such profits deemed unreasonable because they had neither added value to nor changed the nature of the product.[172]

The assizes of bread and ale codified these principles by pegging the price of these commodities to the prevailing price of grain, thus restricting inflation and protecting public supplies of essential foodstuffs against profiteering. They also regulated the quality of these essential foodstuffs and guarded against deceit by insisting upon the use of standardized weights and measures.[173] The government devolved responsibility for enforcing the assizes to local officials through leet, borough, market, and fair courts, although occasionally it took direct supplementary action either by the king's itinerant justices or through the dispatch of royal commissions to targeted localities for that sole purpose.[174] Most offenders against the assize were small-time operators desperately trying to making ends meet, whose activities were far too modest to have any detrimental impact on overall market price.[175] Officials recognized this reality, plus the impossibility of making a detailed assessment of every single case, by imposing nominal fines on the regular bakers and brewers as *de facto* licences to trade.[176] They would only investigate the specific details of the most flagrant or damaging breaches of the assize. While pragmatism prevailed in most cases, local practice varied and officials possessed considerable discretion. As the definitions of a just price and reasonable profit, along with the judgements about who to fine and how much, were left to local initiative, it followed that the application of the assize to specific situations in the marketplace was variable, vague, and vulnerable to manipulation and prejudice (see below, pp. 206–18).[177]

Thus, by the eve of the Black Death, the institutional framework of the English economy was far more conducive to market participation than had been the case at the start of the thirteenth century.[178] It is now indisputable that markets in land and labour had developed to a greater degree than assumed in the conventional narrative and explanatory framework, and that the influence of manorial lordship on their operation had substantially diminished. Villeinage was not a barrier to participation in these markets (see below, pp. 48–50).[179] Commercialization had created a new economic geography, new ways of making a living, and new social institutions, which cumulatively constituted an enduring achievement and a notable phase in the complex story of how the market economy of the modern world came into being.[180]

Nevertheless, despite all these achievements, the market was not yet the dominant mode of exchange in the allocation of key resources, and many 'commercial' transactions were not between complete strangers through monetarized trade. Peasants bought land to store wealth, to enhance status, and to provide for progeny, not to provide a source of working capital or to increase financial yields.[181] The development of factor markets in England remained well behind the economic leaders in the 1340s, such as Italy and Holland. The high interest rates in English capital markets reflected greater risks, rigidities, and inefficiencies than in, say, northern Italy. The size and efficiency of factor and commodity markets also varied markedly within England, and they had developed furthest around London, East Anglia, and the south-east, but least in the north and west. Furthermore, even in the most commercialized areas, many peasants sold grain because they had to raise cash for rents and other disbursements, not because they were choosing to enter the market on terms favourable to them.[182] In short, factor and commodity markets operated within institutional arrangements that were ultimately deleterious to the welfare of the majority of the peasantry under the prevailing conditions of high demographic pressure. Soaring prices, stagnant wages, and splintering land holdings had created widespread congestion and poverty. Climate change, famine, disease of livestock, taxation, and warfare added to the stresses.[183] This semi-commercial, highly precarious, yet subsistence economy had created a social and economic bottleneck in dire need of relief, reform, or both.[184]

The Law and Legal Culture

One obvious paradox exists within the institutional framework of early fourteenth century England. On the one hand, it would seem that English landlords had considerable potential to exploit their peasants aggressively and arbitrarily, given the legal means available to them under the common law and given the prevailing conditions of land scarcity and labour abundance. On the other hand, all the evidence available to us shows that, in practice, the lords seldom took full advantage of their legal powers or their economic muscle in order to impose commercial rents on peasant holdings, either to evict peasants in favour of others who were prepared to pay more, or to restrict the movement of labour, or to force it to work.[185] Even villeins possessed effective property rights in land, and in their goods and chattels: they could transfer land, travel to market with few restrictions, they could choose how to deploy most of their own labour free of seigniorial interference, and they could make enforceable contracts and recover goods through a system of local courts.[186] They were even taxed by the state through lay subsidies.

The main explanations offered by historians for this paradox is that a combination of the protective power of custom, the inadvertent effects of codifying rents, and persistent peasant resistance to excessive seigniorial demands diluted the considerable theoretical legal powers of lords. There is no doubt that these were significant influences. One other important influence has been underexplored, however, namely the emergence of a pervasive English legal culture which promoted respect for the authority of written documents and a commitment to standardized processes of dispute resolution, both of which served as strong deterrents to arbitrary lordly behaviour. This argument is contentious, given the widely held belief that the implications and perhaps also the effects of the common law were largely deleterious to the welfare of the lower orders.[187] Dyer argues that the growing power of the royal courts around 1200 cast the servile population into the jaws of private seigniorial jurisdiction.[188] The manorial court was the primary locus for the exercise of this jurisdiction, and Marxist-influenced historians depict it as a powerful instrument for the extraction of rents and dues from the peasantry in general and villeins in particular.[189] Evans states explicitly that the manorial court was primarily an instrument of seigniorial will.[190] In other words, the common law not only excluded villeins but also strengthened the powers of private lordship over them.

A raft of recent research has shown that this conventional depiction of the common law and understanding of manor courts are no longer tenable. In reality, by c.1300 many manorial courts were handling a much wider range of business than the lord's own interests, and their operation and decision-making followed standardized procedures, not the personal whim and will of the lord. As a result, the peasantry had acquired a vested interest in the business of the manor court, as reflected in the significant volume of communal, commercial, and private business transacted there.[191] For example, the lord's rights and interests comprised just c.20 per cent of all court business at Sutton (Cambs.) between 1308 and 1345.[192] Many manorial courts now handled inter-personal plaints between peasants, which in places absorbed around one-third of their business.[193] Indeed, manorial courts held in areas where minor lay lordship and personal freedom predominated contained hardly any seigniorial business, but instead were dominated by petty personal pleas between peasant litigants.[194] These private plaints had nothing to do with the lord: the lord was simply allowing the machinery of his court to be used (for a fee, of course) to settle disputes between peasants. Manorial courts were in some ways competing for business with other local tribunals, such as leet, hundred, market, fair, and ecclesiastical courts, and even other manor courts. Those local courts deemed most efficient at dealing with such business even attracted peasants who were not tenants of the manor but were locals seeking a tribunal capable of resolving their disputes cheaply and effectively.[195] The benefits to the lord of a more eclectic range of business lay in the revenues it could generate: for example, between 1289 and 1364 there were nearly 3,000 cases of inter-personal litigation and 1,000 cases of dispute in the manorial court rolls of Redgrave and Hinderclay (Suffolk), which raised 38 per cent of all court income for the lord at the former and 19 per cent at the latter.[196]

Clearly, by the 1340s the manor court had become far more than an instrument of seigniorial will. First, its business extended well beyond the narrow confines of the lord's interests and dealt with a variety of communal and private matters. Second, peasants largely chose whether to pursue their private business there. Freemen certainly exercised wide choice over which court to use when acting as plaintiffs in personal pleas, but villeins also enjoyed a good deal of discretion in this regard.[197] Briggs argued that 'it was possible for both free and unfree villagers to engage in market transactions with people living at a distance safe in the knowledge that one's own lord would not seek to restrict the choice of civil jurisdictions that might be used to bring an opponent to justice'.[198] In Hyams' words, 'the manor lacked monopoly jurisdiction over its inhabitants'.[199] Finally, the procedures of the manor court had become largely standardized, partly reflecting customary practices and partly replicating those used in the royal courts.[200]

The inter-personal plaints described above—mainly relating to debt, trespass, and covenant disputes—originated in the royal courts of common law, and, as they spread into manorial courts during the second half of the thirteenth century, they replicated closely the same processes and procedures.[201] Consequently, they provide a powerful example of the ways in which common-law processes, influences, and some of its business spread into the many private and non-common-law courts in England during the course of the thirteenth century. Furthermore, these general common-law procedures and associated culture came to influence and regulate the relationship between lord and villein. This is illustrated by the evolution of the record of the transfer of individual parcels of villein land in manorial court rolls, which by c.1300 followed a highly consistent format using carefully chosen language in the conveyance, both of which were based directly on the livery of seisin in the common law.[202] This adaption of common-law process strengthened villein property rights. Likewise, the staged process of summons, attachment, and distraint, which was used in the common law to force those accused of wrongdoing to engage in the legal process, was now used routinely in private courts, including when lords sought to enforce their rights under villeinage.[203]

The usual explanations for the spread of common-law processes into local— manorial, borough, and market—courts are the growing professionalization of estate management, the determination of lords to document their legal rights, and their desire to extract rent and to exert social control over their tenantry.[204] All three developments were certainly influential to varying degrees in promoting a greater reliance upon written records and a higher degree of standardization of administrative practices throughout England. But they do not fully explain the extent of the spread, or indeed the extraordinary level of consistency in the format, business, and procedures of manorial courts in c.1300 right across England, from Shropshire to Suffolk, and from one estate to another. The shift from an oral to a written culture on this scale, and to this degree of standardization, was a peculiarly English phenomenon, with no continental parallels.[205] The fundamental difference between the English and continental experience was the emergence of the common law from c.1200. Its creation and operation required a strong central government. Its very nature, based on precedent, case law, and consistency of practice, meant that it was heavily reliant upon written records and judgements, procedural formalization, and bureaucratic centralization.[206] The early successes of the royal courts in attracting a large volume of business from thousands of humble freemen—much of it private and petty dispute resolution—encouraged the spread of its business and the copying of its procedures in non-common-law courts.[207] The provision of system of royal justice from the late twelfth century had generated endogenously a greater desire among all levels of English society for access to such justice, and for social relations to be guided by its principles. Indeed, it is likely that this development was a major driver behind the emergence of representative institutions such as parliaments.[208]

Thus an inadvertent, but major, consequence of the development of the English common law was the spread of its procedures and business far beyond the confines of the royal courts, permeating the whole of society. While this development is well documented in recent research, its wider implications for the operation of markets on the eve of the Black Death have been largely overlooked. The more rigorous documentation of peasant dues and customs during the thirteenth century contributed materially to the ossification of rents of assize, services, and rental values (see above, pp. 26-30), and this was as much a function of the spread of common-law culture relating to written documents and precedents as of the professional management of estates.[209] The breadth of business in manor courts provided all peasants—including villeins—with a relatively accessible, cheap, sophisticated, and effective process of dispute resolution and contract enforcement, which therefore reduced the risks of market participation.[210] The growth of record-keeping, of standardized procedures, and of a roughly overlapping system of central and local courts constituted a cluster of innovations that aided the process of commercialization and the development of markets in England.[211] As common-law principles and practices spread far beyond the royal courts, so they promoted rule-governed behaviour and dispute resolution.

Furthermore, the spread of common-law practices promoted a new, if as yet hazy, culture of law.[212] It engendered greater trust in, and engagement with, legal processes, and conditioned expectations and behaviour throughout society. It promoted decision-making based on written precedents and rules, rational thought, and standardized procedures; it promoted a commitment to due process and a respect for contracts; and it promoted consistency in treatment of similar wrongs. These attitudes and behaviours resonate with 'modern' belief systems, although, of course, on the eve of the Black Death they were still imperfectly developed. Yet they were already strong enough to act as a countervailing force to the arbitrary judgements and the personal discretion in matters of justice associated with traditional manorial lordship. The ways in which manor courts now operated, the nature of their business, and the expectations of how they should operate all limited the scope for seigniorial discretion, and, in doing so, diluted the coercive power of manorial lordship and conditioned the relationship between lord and villein.[213] As Musson observes, 'the ability of the lower orders to obtain legal advice and use the judicial system to their advantage has long been underestimated'.[214] Of course, major inequalities before the law still existed, and many peasants could not afford to indulge in legal activity.[215] Juries could be stacked and fixed. A determined and unscrupulous lord could manipulate justice. But such occasions were increasingly rare, and they attracted disapprobation. A peculiarly English legal culture—the origins of the 'Western Legal Tradition'—was already established on the eve of the Black Death, and its existence helps to explain the weakness of lordship and the resilience of markets in its aftermath.

The endogenous interplay of developments in the law, villeinage, custom, and markets during the thirteenth century had diluted the powers of manorial lordship, enabling peasants—even villeins—to participate in markets. The implications of this for ordinary people have not been fully grasped, but they are usefully illustrated through the activities of two villeins, who were also hereditary serfs, in Redgrave (Suffolk). John Docke was from a family of villeins who in the late thirteenth century had built up a sizeable portfolio of customary land and some free land locally. John extended the portfolio in the 1310s to include stalls and other property in the market of Botesdale, a thriving commercial centre within Redgrave manor.[216] In the 1320s and 1330s he continued to acquire small market properties.[217] His son, John junior, served in a number of manorial offices from the 1330s, mainly as an ale taster, but also as an affeeror and messor.[218] Roger le Reve was another prominent villein landholder, who served as an ale taster intermittently from the 1320s, including alongside John Docke junior in 1336,[219] and he was twice elected as reeve.[220] In the mid-1340s he was also described as 'the alderman of the gild of Corpus Christi in Botesdale'.[221] The elections of both men as ale tasters indicate that they were regular brewers themselves, and Roger's other commercial interests are implied by his role as a pledge for a man who in 1342 had been amerced for a trading infraction in the market and for litigating for debt in other local courts.[222] Roger's son, John, was also a prominent holder of villein land who was later described explicitly as a 'serf by blood' (i.e. a hereditary serf), and who just before his death in 1392 purchased a charter of personal freedom (a 'manumission') for his son, Henry.[223]

John Docke and Roger le Reve were members of the small elite of Redgrave residents who held a portfolio of land, houses, and commercial properties, and who engaged in a variety of trading activities. Both were very active in the local credit market, as both borrowers and lenders.[224] Their careers show how villeins could immerse themselves deeply in factor and commodity markets, occupy a variety of manorial offices, and were not particularly constrained by their unfree status, but rather enjoyed a relative economic freedom. Indeed, they paid among the highest levels of tax in their community.[225] One aspect of their wheeling and dealing was, however, very remarkable: they leased Botesdale market from their own lord, the abbot of Bury St Edmunds. Botesdale was a small but bustling town whose weekly market at the end of the thirteenth century generated over £3 in rents and £5 6s. 8d. in tolls per annum.[226] During the 1320s and 1330s the abbot's own officials ran the market directly, but after 1342 the franchise was leased each year.[227] Between 1342 and 1345 John and Roger were the co-lessees, who rendered the sizeable rent of £5 13s. 4d. each year for the tolls, while Roger continued as sole lessee in 1345–6 on the same terms after John's death.[228] Roger's son (or grandson), John le Reve, maintained his father's business interests, leasing the market every year from 1372 to 1389.[229]

This case is extremely significant for how we understand the economic opportunities available to peasants, and their wide scope for action within the expanding legal system and culture, even to those of unfree status. The practice of leasing commercial franchises meant that the lessee was fully responsible for administering the market, including collecting tolls; policing its rules; monitoring weights, measures, and quality against the statutory assizes of bread and ale; maintaining a safe, orderly, and hygienic marketplace; and resolving disputes between traders.[230] The entry in the account roll for 1344–5 notes that the lease included responsibility for implementing the assize of bread and ale in Botesdale.[231] The lessee, or his agent, would have featured prominently during the hours of the market's operation, being on hand to adjudicate issues personally and to dispense justice as the authorized market official. In the case of Botesdale, the abbot of Bury St Edmunds was delegating full authority to a succession of serfs to administer the market, including the option to convene a formal market court.[232] Docke and le Reve were responsible for enforcing mercantile, and aspects of statute and the common law, including—if necessary—punishing freemen and resolving disputes involving other lords. The better they were at doing this, the more likely traders would return here and the more profit could be made from the lease of the franchise. The activities of Docke and le Reve illustrate that villein tenants and hereditary serfs dispensed justice locally and enforced the law relating to commercial activities, irrespective of status.

In the accounting year 1348–9 (i.e. from 28 September 1348) the manor of Redgrave received no income at all from Botesdale market.[233] It must have functioned during the winter of 1348–9, but then ceased to operate from March as the Black Death swept through the locality.[234] The manor received no income because the lessee—Roger le Reve—succumbed to the epidemic in April 1349, although his four sons survived to inherit some of his land in May 1349.[235] As plague continued to rage, however, it claimed the lives of three of them between May and July, leaving just John le Reve as the sole surviving heir.[236] The devastating passage of this first epidemic throughout England, and the responses of the survivors such as John over the next half century, are the focus of the rest of this book.

Conclusion

There is no dispute among historians and economists that the growth of the English economy in the twelfth and thirteenth centuries eventually petered out, so that by the early fourteenth century it could hardly support a population of around 5.5m people. By this date, an estimated 40 per cent of the population eked a perilous existence around the level of bare subsistence, most labour was underemployed, unemployed, or devoted to a smallholding, real wage rates were at a long-term low, many people could not obtain any land, and mean holding size in many areas of the country was pitifully small. A large substratum of very poor people underpinned both urban and rural society, who by c.1300 had become highly sensitive to harvest failures and vulnerable to extreme weather events. Society had now reached a tipping point because previous subsistence crises had caused neither sustained distress nor population to stop growing.[237] Whatever the extent of technical, commercial, and productivity gains during the high Middle Ages, they had provided means of survival for a larger population, but not prosperity for the majority. In the 1340s England was not in the vanguard of European economic development.

Most scholars have explained England's modest economic performance, its productivity crisis, and the impoverishment of its people in terms of the structure of manorial lordship, which, bolstered by the development of the common law, was sufficiently powerful to restrict the freedom of action of the peasantry and to restrict the growth of factor and commodity markets. Its strength also explains how the ruling elite were capable of increasing its exploitation of the peasantry after the Black Death and why peasant resistance and social conflict was essential to its overthrow. As manorialism and serfdom crumbled in the last two decades of the fourteenth century, so factor and commodity markets began to expand.

The approach adopted here has been to review the recent specialist research to reconstruct—at the current state of our knowledge—the size, nature, and institutional arrangements governing the operation of the main factor and commodity markets on the eve of the Black Death. This provides a clearer understanding of the inefficiencies and constraints within the English economy as well as a more secure base for evaluating the impact of the Black Death. Research over the past two decades or so has demonstrated incontrovertibly the growth of factor and commodity markets within the interstices of the English system long before the Black Death. Lords had lost control of the land market in free tenures, and villeins enjoyed *de facto* property rights in land. Only around one tenth of peasant labour was coerced to work on manorial demesnes through labour services, and most villeins were able to move around and to obtain work with limited or no interference from their lord. An estimated 30 per cent of all expended peasant labour was hired, most of which was rewarded through either day or piece wages, and a sizeable minority through annual contracts as live-in servants. Peasants routinely engaged with the market for basic foodstuffs and household goods, and on the eve of plague the mass market in non-elite goods was now larger than the niche market for elite goods.[238] It is probable that around 30 per cent of all grain was sold commercially, the majority supplied from the peasant sector. These commercial developments were most prominent in East Anglia and south-east England, and much less advanced in the north and west, although markets were poorly integrated and inefficient even in the most commercialized regions. A combination of custom and the spread of common-law procedures beyond the confines of the royal courts and into wider society had combined to reduce the arbitrary, unpredictable, and oppressive elements of manorial lordship, even for villeins. Legal developments had contributed to the growth of commerce by reducing the transaction costs of peasant engagement in factor and commodity markets.

This is not to argue that the market was the main influence over the allocation of key resources on the eve of the Black Death. Non-market forces—custom, family, and manorial lordship—still exerted the greatest influence over the allocation of key resources. Nor does it mean that lords were powerless to direct their peasantry, or that they behaved benignly towards them. Lords could and did behave capriciously and high-handedly towards their social inferiors, and they had greater influence under the law. They exercised a range of powers over villein tenure and status, villeins had no right of appeal on such matters in the courts of common law, and lords did ride rough shod over custom. But, overwhelmingly, they did not dictate or obstruct villein choices at will, and the importance of villeinage in restricting economic development has been persistently overstated.

Consequently, we must seek alternative explanations for the congestion and distress of English society, and its entrapment in a cul-de-sac of low productivity. A complex mix of forces had created an institutional mosaic that was incapable of absorbing the rise in population pressure without a serious diminution in levels of welfare.[239] Effective demand had reached a ceiling due to low and flat incomes per capita, and to structural poverty.[240] The social and geographical unevenness of economic development exacerbated the problem, because most population and wealth were concentrated in the south and east where dependence on the market was greatest yet existence was most precarious. Most demand was rural, not urban, and therefore fragmented and dispersed, which meant there was insufficient incentive to specialize in agriculture, or to raise rates of production and sales per unit area.[241] Further obstacles to growth existed on the supply side: limited savings and investment, non-commercial head rents (and subletting at rack rents), piecemeal adaptation of agrarian techniques to commercial opportunities, no state or seigniorial intervention for reform, and no institutions to disseminate knowledge.[242] Lords might have lost control of the land market, but this did not mean that it had become fully commercialized or had much in common with later land markets: for example, it did not promote the creation of larger farming units and few tenures were commercial.[243] Credit was widely available, but interest rates were high and the operation of the capital market tended to compound the vulnerability of the poorer elements within those communities.[244] When these institutional inefficiencies combined with a series of extreme events in the early fourteenth century—persistently high taxation, sustained warfare, extreme weather, and epidemic disease—they brewed up a perfect storm of 'contingent chaotic development'.[245]

The back end of that storm—the catastrophe of the Black Death—finally released society from its choking congestion. Although England's institutional structure in the 1340s was ill-suited to a high demographic regime, after 1349—under a radically different labour/land regime—it harnessed market forces in ways that rapidly reduced wealth inequality and triggered irreversible institutional changes. The limitations of seigniorial and state power on the eve of the Black Death also conditioned and weakened their short- and medium-term responses to demographic collapse. It was the catastrophe of the Black Death, and the ensuing institutional changes, which were to release English society from this structural poverty and to provide a route out of future cycles of the Malthusian trap.[246]

Notes

1. Hatcher and Bailey, *Modelling the Middle Ages*, pp. 55–65, 95–106, 208–42; Campbell, *Great transition*, pp. 395–401.
2. Van Bavel, *Manors and markets*, pp. 86–93; Kitsikopoulos, 'England', pp. 45–7, 335; van Bavel, *Invisible hand*, pp. 19–21; Ghosh, 'Rural economies', pp. 258–61.
3. Bas van Bavel, Tina de Moor, and Jan Luiten van Zuiten, 'Introduction: factor markets in global economic history', *Continuity and Change*, 24 (2009), pp. 9–21; van Bavel, *Manors and markets*, pp. 3–8, 162–241, 372–409; Victoria Bateman, 'The evolution of markets in early modern Europe, 1350–1800: a study of wheat prices', *Economic History Review*, 64 (2011), pp. 447–9.

4. Greif, *Institutions*, pp. 5–53; Shelagh Ogilvie, 'Whatever is, is right', *Economic History Review*, 60 (2007), pp. 649–84.

5. Martha C. Howell, *Commerce before capitalism in Europe 1300–1600* (Cambridge, 2010), pp. 8–9.

6. van Bavel, *Manors and markets*, pp. 3–8.

7. Greif, *Institutions*, pp. 30, 350–1; Ogilvie, 'Whatever is', pp. 650, 677; van Bavel, *Invisible hand*, pp. 13–14.

8. Greif, *Institutions*, pp. 350–5.

9. Greif, *Institutions*, p. 387.

10. Chris Briggs, 'Introduction: law courts, contracts and rural society in Europe, 1200–1600', *Continuity and Change* (2014), pp. 4–5.

11. van Bavel et al., 'Factor markets', pp. 9–14; Campbell, 'Factor markets', pp. 79–106; van Bavel, *Manors and markets*, p. 5.

12. For an example of the former, see Pamuk, 'Black Death', pp. 307–13. For an example of the latter, see the innovative attempt to model the impact of the Black Death on the household budget of a typical middling peasant family using a single calculation to cover the whole of the period 1350–1500, Harry Kitsikopoulos, 'The impact of the Black Death on peasant economy in England 1350–1500', *Journal of Peasant Studies*, 29 (2002), pp. 71–90.

13. Campbell, 'The land', p. 237; Campbell, *Great transition*, p. 328.

14. For an outline of the fortunes of the English economy on the eve of the Black Death, see Miller and Hatcher, *Medieval England: towns*, pp. 418–29.

15. Campbell, 'Agrarian problem', p. 36. Unfree land is also known as customary, villein, bond, and servile land. For a slightly different estimate—25% demesne, 38% customary, and 37% free—see Jane Whittle, 'Leasehold tenure in England c.1300–1600: its forms and incidence', in Bas van Bavel and Phillipp R. Schofield, eds., *The development of leasehold in north western Europe, c. 1200–1600* (Turnhout, 2008), p. 140.

16. Campbell, 'Agrarian problem', tables 1 and 3, pp. 12, 19.

17. Campbell, 'Factor markets', p. 82; David Ibbetson, *An historical introduction to the law of obligations* (Oxford, 2001), p. 3.

18. Whittle, *Agrarian capitalism*, pp. 92–100; van Bavel, *Manors and markets*, pp. 161–3.

19. Bailey, *English manor*, fig. 1 and pp. 1–5.

20. For examples in Durham, see Larson, *Conflict and compromise*, p. 163; Shropshire, see Una Rees, 'The leases of Haughmond abbey, Shropshire', *Midland History*, 8 (1983), pp. 17–20; Ann J. Kettle, '1300–1540', in G.C. Baugh, ed., *VCH Shropshire, volume IV* (London, 1989), pp. 110–11, 117–18, 123; for Oxfordshire, see R.W. Jeffrey, ed., *The manors and advowson of Great Rollright*, Oxfordshire Records Society, 9 (1927), pp. 14, 77; for Berkshire, see Larry R. Poos and Lloyd Bonfield, eds., *Select cases in manorial court 1250–1550: property and family law*, Selden Society, 114 (1997), p. 18; and for Gloucestershire, see Rodney H. Hilton, *A medieval society: the west Midlands at the end of the thirteenth century* (Cambridge, 1967), pp. 137–8.

21. Cash tenancies usually included the payment of an entry fine upon admission to the holding and suit of court, and on villein holdings sometimes heriot and perhaps some nominal seasonal labour services. They are sometimes described as rents '*ad censum*', '*arrentata*', and customary fee farms.

22. For freeholds on cash leases, see, for example, Kettle, '1300–1540', p. 81, and Abigail Stevenson, 'From Domesday Book to the Hundred Rolls: lordship, landholding and local society in three English hundreds, 1086 to 1280' (PhD dissertation, University of London, 2014), p. 182. For villein tenure at commercial cash rents, Christopher Dyer, 'The Midland economy and society 1314–1348: insights from changes in the landscape', *Midland History*, 42 (2017), pp. 54–5. For examples of both, Edmund B. Fryde, *Peasants and landlords in late medieval England 1380–1525* (Stroud, 1996), pp. 27–8.

23. van Bavel, 'Land lease', p. 23; Bas van Bavel and Phillipp Schofield, 'The emergence of lease and leasehold in a comparative perspective: definitions, causes and consequences', in van Bavel and Schofield, eds., *Development of leasehold*, pp. 12–13.

24. Leasing for a term must be distinguished from subleasing of customary land from an existing head tenant to a subtenant for a term, which required a seigniorial licence and was widespread throughout East Anglia and the south-east around 1300. These inter-peasant subleases largely disappeared after 1348–9 as lordly grants at lease increased, Miriam Muller, 'Peasants, lords and developments in leasing in late medieval England', in van Bavel and Schofield, eds., *Development of leasehold*, p. 167.

25. Van Bavel, *Manors and markets*, pp. 175–6.

26. van Bavel, *Manors and markets*, p. 171; van Basel, 'Land lease', pp. 24–5.

27. For example, 'he/she holds at farm for the term of X years paying Y shillings per annum': '*dominus concessit ad firmam*' or '*de firma tenementi dimissa*' or '*X dimissit*'...'*ad firmam et terminum X annorum*'. Poos and Bonfield, *Select cases*, pp. lxxxiv–v.

28. Barbara Harvey, *Westminster abbey and its estates in the Middle Ages* (Oxford, 1977), pp. 250–1; Larson, *Conflict and compromise*, pp. 163–5; Muller, 'Peasants, lords', pp. 172–4; Mark Bailey, 'The transformation of customary tenure in southern England c.1350 to 1500', *Agricultural History Review*, 62 (2014), p. 214; Michael J. Thornton, 'Rural society in the manor courts of Northamptonshire, 1350–1500' (PhD dissertation, University of Leicester, 2004), p. 163.

29. Tenure-at-will is usually described as '*ad voluntatem domini*'. Strictly speaking *all* customary land was held at the will of the lord, but this was only literally true of tenure-at-will. Bailey, 'Transformation', pp. 212, 219.

30. For example, it was used to tenant land abandoned immediately after Scottish raids in Cumberland in the 1320s and after the great famine of 1315–16 in Essex, Edward Miller, 'Social structure: northern England', in Edward Miller, ed., *The agrarian history of England and Wales, volume III: 1348–1500* (Cambridge, 1991), p. 686; Phillipp R. Schofield, 'Tenurial developments and the availability of customary land in a later medieval community', *Economic History Review*, 49 (1996), p. 255, fn. 3.

31. Levett, *Black Death*, p. 83; Edward Miller, 'Tenant farming and farmers: Lancashire and Yorkshire', in Miller, ed., *Agrarian history, volume III*, p. 597.

32. Robert C. Palmer, 'The economic and cultural impact of the origins of property: 1180–1220', *Law and History Review*, 3 (1985), pp. 375–96.

33. Palmer, 'Economic and cultural', pp. 385–9; Campbell, 'Factor markets', pp. 88–90.

34. M.A. Barg, 'The social structure of manorial freeholders: an analysis of the Hundred Rolls of 1279', *Agricultural History Review*, 39 (1989), pp. 111–15; Kanzaka, 'Villein

rents', p. 599; Cliff T. Bekar and Clyde G. Reed, 'Land markets and inequality: evidence from medieval England', *European Review of Economic History*, 17 (2013), pp. 294–317.

35. Hatcher, 'English serfdom', p. 8; Hatcher, 'Lordship and villeinage', p. 115.
36. Paul R. Hyams, *King, lords, and peasants in medieval England: the common law of villeinage in the twelfth and thirteenth centuries* (Oxford, 1980), pp. 38, 66–7.
37. Hyams, *King, lords, and peasants*, p. 65.
38. Paul Vinogradoff, *Villeinage in England* (Oxford, 1892), pp. 44–58; Hyams, *King, lords, and peasants*, pp. 2–69.
39. Ghosh, 'Rural economies', pp. 260–2.
40. Hatcher, 'English serfdom', pp. 3–21; Richard M. Smith, 'Some thoughts on hereditary and proprietary rights in land under customary law in thirteenth and early fourteenth century England', *Law and History Review*, 1 (1983), pp. 96–128; Campbell, Factor markets', pp. 88–92; Chris Briggs, 'English serfdom, c.1200–c.1350: towards an institutionalist analysis', in Silvia Cavaciocchi, ed., *Serfdom and slavery in the European economy 11th – 18th centuries* (Florence, 2014), pp. 23–8.
41. Vinogradoff, *Villeinage*, pp. 172–7; Hyams, *King, lords and peasants*, pp. 49, 184–5; Hatcher, 'English serfdom', pp. 8–14; Lloyd Bonfield, 'The nature of customary law in the manor courts of medieval England', *Comparative Study of Society and History*, 31 (1989), 514–33; Campbell, 'Agrarian problem', pp. 5–6; Campbell, 'Factor markets', pp. 90–2.
42. Smith, 'Some thoughts', p. 114; Poos and Bonfield, eds., *Select cases*, pp. xxxiv, lxxxvi–cvii.
43. The common-law process of distraint and seizure were used at all levels of medieval English society for redress, so its routine use in breaches of villein tenure in private courts is significant: Paul Brand, *Kings, barons, and justices: the making and enforcement of legislation in thirteenth-century England* (Cambridge, 2003), pp. 42–3, 94–6.
44. Hyams, *King, lords, and peasants*, pp. 68–77; Smith, 'Some thoughts', pp. 106–12; Richard M. Smith, 'Some issues concerning peasants and their property in rural England 1250–1800', in Richard M. Smith, ed., *Land, kinship and life cycle* (Cambridge, 1984), pp. 38–59, 62–8; Leon A. Slota, 'Law, land transfer and lordship on the estates of St Albans abbey in the thirteenth and fourteenth centuries', *Law and History Review*, 6 (1988), pp. 121–3; Zvi Razi and Richard M. Smith, 'The origins of the English manor courts as a written record', in Zvi Razi and Richard M. Smith, eds., *Medieval society and the manor court* (Oxford, 1996), pp. 53–4; Paul R. Hyams, 'What did Edwardian villagers mean by law?', in Razi and Smith, eds., *Medieval society*, pp. 81–2; Poos and Bonfield, *Select cases*, pp. lxxvi–lxxxv, cliv–v; Campbell, 'Factor markets', pp. 90–2; Mark Page, 'The peasant land market on the estates of the Bishop of Winchester before the Black Death', in Richard H. Britnell, ed., *The Winchester pipe rolls and medieval English society* (Woodbridge, 2003), pp. 61–80.
45. Phillipp R. Schofield, 'Lordship and the early history of peasant land transfer on the estates of the abbey of Bury St Edmunds', in Kowaleski et al. eds., *Peasants and landlords*, pp. 210–20.

46. The manor contained *c.*200 acres of customary land. Between 1330 and 1348 there are ten years (1332–6, 1340, 1345–8) for which the records of more than one court session have survived, and therefore are likely to yield a more accurate indication of the amount of land transacted in a calendar year. In these ten years a total of 420 acres were transacted, or 42 acres per annum, or 21% turnover of all customary land, Bruce M.S. Campbell, 'Population pressure, inheritance and the land market in a fourteenth century peasant community', in Smith, ed., *Land, kinship*, pp. 94, 131–3.

47. Jane Whittle, 'Individualism and the family-land bond: a reassessment of land transfer patterns among the English peasantry c.1270–1580', *Past and Present*, 160 (1998), pp. 49–55; Schofield, 'Lordship and early history', p. 220. In the early fourteenth century, transfers of villein land *inter vivos* outnumbered *post mortem* transfers 3 to 1 at Hinderclay (Suffolk) and 4 to 1 at Redgrave (Suffolk), Jennifer Phillips, 'Collaboration and litigation in two Suffolk manor courts 1289–1360' (PhD dissertation, University of Cambridge, 2005), p. 100.

48. Kanzaka, 'Villein rents', pp. 593–618; Britnell, *Britain*, p. 309; Campbell, 'The land', pp. 228–30.

49. Jan Z. Titow, *English rural society 1200–50* (London, 1969), p. 76; Kanzaka, 'Villein rents', pp. 613–14; Campbell, 'Agrarian problem', p. 41; Bailey, 'Villeinage in England', pp. 444–5; Page, 'Peasant land market', pp. 78–9; David Postles, 'Migration and mobility in a less mature economy: English internal migration, c. 1200–1350', *Social History*, 23 (2000), p. 293; Whittle, *Agrarian capitalism*, p. 82.

50. Kanzaka, 'Villein rents', p. 613; Mark Bailey, 'Tallage-at-will in medieval England', *English Historical Review*, 134 no. 566 (2019), pp. 25–58.

51. Dyer, 'Villeins, bondmen', pp. 424–8; Jean Birrell, 'Manorial custumals reconsidered', *Past and Present*, 224 (2014), pp. 17–25.

52. Campbell, 'Agrarian problem', p. 43.

53. Rigby, *English society*, p. 56. See also Campbell, 'Agrarian problem', p. 69.

54. Miller and Hatcher, *Rural society*, pp. 111–12; Kathleen Biddick, 'People and things: power in early English development', *Comparative Studies in Society and History*, 32 (1990), pp. 9–13; Tracy K. Dennison, 'The institutional context of serfdom in England and Russia', in Chris Briggs, Peter T. Kitson, and Stephen J. Thompson, eds., *Population, welfare and economic change in Britain, 1290–1834* (Woodbridge, 2014), p. 265.

55. Vinogradoff, *Villeinage*, 128–37; Rodney H. Hilton, *The decline of serfdom in late medieval England* (second edition, London, 1983), pp. 10–17; Miller and Hatcher, *Medieval England: rural society*, p. 116; Hyams, *King, lords and peasants*, pp. 1–2, 29–37; Peter Coss, 'Neifs and villeins in later medieval England', *Reading Medieval Studies*, 40 (2014), pp. 197–8.

56. Briggs, 'English serfdom', pp. 25–8.

57. Ralph Evans, 'Merton College's control of its tenants at Thorncroft, 1270–1349', in Razi and Smith, eds., *Medieval society*, pp. 206–7, 212–14.

58. Whittle, 'Individualism', pp. 51–5; J. Ambrose Raftis, *Tenure and mobility. Studies in the social history of the medieval village* (Toronto, 1964), pp. 63–81. Only five of a sample of fourteen manors in Northamptonshire had developed an active villein land market, Thornton, 'Rural society', p. 154.

59. Whittle, 'Individualism', pp. 33–5, 49–54; Phillips, 'Collaboration and litigation', pp. 60–2.
60. For the contrast between the active villein land market south-east England/East Anglia and the less active Midlands, see Whittle, 'Individualism', pp. 49–54.
61. See, for example, James P. Bowen and Alex T. Brown, 'Introduction', in James P. Bowen and Alex T. Brown, eds., *Custom and commercialisation in English rural society. Revisiting Tawney and Postan* (Hatfield, 2016), pp. 5–11, 14–19; John Broad, 'English agrarian structures in a European context, 1300–1925', in Bowen and Brown, eds., *Custom and commercialisation*, pp. 53–5.
62. Kanzaka, 'Villein rents', p. 612; Campbell, 'Agrarian problem', pp. 52, esp. fn. 153, 55–9; Bailey, 'Villeinage in England', pp. 444–5.
63. Campbell, 'Agrarian problem', pp. 52–3; Campbell, 'The land', pp. 228–30; Campbell, *Great transition*, pp. 183–8. The lord could only convert a holding to a commercial cash rent if there was a failure of heirs.
64. Harold S.A. Fox, 'Exploitation of the landless by lords and tenants in early medieval England', in Razi and Smith, eds., *Medieval society*, pp. 522–33; Campbell, 'Agrarian problem', pp. 60–70; Bekar and Reed, 'Land markets and inequality', pp. 294–317; S. Kilby, 'Struggle and enterprise', pp. 7–27.
65. Phillipp R. Schofield, 'Dearth, debt and the local land market in a late thirteenth-century village community', *Agricultural History Review*, 45 (1997), pp. 1–17; Bekar and Reed, 'Land markets and inequality', pp. 294–317.
66. Campbell, 'Agrarian problem', pp. 60–70.
67. George Grantham, 'Economic history and the history of labour markets', in George Grantham and Mary McKinnon, eds., *Labour market evolution: the economic history of market integration, wage flexibility and the employment relation* (London, 1994), pp. 1–26; Jan de Vries, 'How did pre-industrial labour markets function?', in Grantham and McKinnon, eds., *Labour market*, pp. 39–63; van Bavel, *Manors and markets*, pp. 200–3.
68. Frederick Pollock and F. William Maitland, *The history of English law before the time of Edward I*, volume I (Cambridge, 1896), p. 391.
69. Page, *Villeinage*, pp. 18–24, 31–40; Edward P. Cheyney, 'The disappearance of serfdom in England', *English Historical Review*, 15 (1900), pp. 32–4.
70. Evgeny A. Kosminsky, *Studies in the agrarian history of England in the thirteenth century* (Oxford, 1956), pp. 283–318; Bennett, 'Impact of the Black Death', p. 199. For similar sentiments, see Chris Given-Wilson, 'Service, serfdom and English labour legislation, 1350–1500', in Anne Curry and Elizabeth Matthew, eds., *Concepts and patterns of service in the later Middle Ages* (Woodbridge, 2000), p. 22; Palmer, *English law*, pp. 14–15; Kitsikopoulos, 'England', pp. 46–7.
71. Bruce M.S. Campbell and Ken Bartley, *England on the eve of the Black Death: an atlas of lay lordship, land and wealth, 1300–49* (Manchester, 2006), p. 253 and map 14.2.
72. Hatcher, 'English serfdom', pp. 10–12; Campbell, 'Agrarian problem', pp. 36–7; Harriss, *Shaping the nation*, p. 225.
73. Campbell, 'Factor markets', p. 84; Campbell, *Seigniorial agriculture*, pp. 55–6, 357, 420–1; Richard H. Britnell, 'Minor landlords in England and medieval agrarian capitalism', *Past and Present*, 89 (1980), p. 10; Campbell, 'The land', p. 213; Bridget Wells Furby, *The Berkeley estate 1281–1417: its economy and development*, Bristol and

Gloucestershire Archaeological Society Monographs, 1 (2012), pp. 113–15; Whittle, 'Food economy', pp. 42–6.

74. Edward Miller, *The abbey and bishopric of Ely* (Cambridge, 1951), p. 103; J. Ambrose Raftis, *The estates of Ramsey abbey: a study in growth and organisation* (Toronto, 1957), p. 193; Harvey, *Westminster abbey*, p. 223; Birrell, 'Manorial custumals', pp. 6, 29–30.

75. Hyams, *King, lords, and peasants*, p. 31.

76. Hyams, *King, lords, and peasants*, pp. 167–9.

77. Hyams, *King, lords, and peasants*, p. 182.

78. Hyams, *King, lords, and peasants*, pp. 234–5; Raftis, *Tenure and mobility*, pp. 95–7.

79. Raftis, *Tenure and mobility*, pp. 95–6, 141.

80. Pollock and Maitland, *History of English law*, I, pp. 418, 424; Henry S. Bennett, *Life on the English manor: a study of peasant conditions 1150–1400* (Cambridge, 1937), pp. 309–10.

81. Vinogradoff, *Villeinage*, pp. 157–9; Bailey, *Decline of serfdom*, pp. 41–6; Briggs. 'English serfdom', pp. 28–31.

82. Page, *Crowland abbey*, p. 137; David Noy, ed., *Winslow manor court books, Part I: 1327–1377; Part II: 1423–1460* (Buckinghamshire Records Society Publications, 35 and 36 (2011), part I, p. 97.

83. Page, *Villeinage*, p. 36; DeWindt, *Land and people*, p. 176; Raftis, *Tenure and mobility*, p. 139; Briggs, 'English serfdom', p. 29.

84. Hyams, *King, lords, and peasants*, pp. 34–7.

85. See Christopher Dyer, 'Were late medieval English villages self contained?', in Chistopher Dyer, ed., *The self contained village: the social history of rural communities 1250–1900* (Hatfield, 2007), p. 11. For evidence that chevage was unusual, see Page, *Crowland abbey*, p. 149; Paul D.A. Harvey, 'Tenant farming: Home Counties', in Miller, ed., *Agrarian History III*, p. 675; Bailey, 'Villeinage in England', pp. 448–9; Bailey, *Decline of serfdom*, pp. 111, 116, 124, 129, 141, 161, 188–9, 204, 226; Postles, 'Migration', p. 290; Briggs, 'English serfdom', pp. 29–31; Margaret Woods, *Medieval Hadleigh* (Layham, 2018), p. 119.

86. In the first half of the fourteenth century chevage was charged regularly on the abbey of Bury St Edmunds' manor of Hinderclay (Suffolk), but only one case is recorded on its neighbouring manor of Redgrave, Phillips, 'Collaboration and litigation', p. 62. At Sutton (Cambs.) between 1308 and 1319 presentments for absence were recorded regularly and chevage occasionally, but then between 1335 and 1345 they disappeared entirely and chevage payments collapsed Erin McGibbon Smith, 'Reflections of reality in the manor court: Sutton-in-the-Isle, 1308–1391' (PhD dissertation, University of Cambridge, 2005), pp. 95–7.

87. Bailey, *Decline of serfdom*, pp. 267–71.

88. Hence, for example, villeins owned their own fishing boats and became wealthy from the produce of the sea, Maryanne Kowaleski, 'Peasants and the sea in medieval England', in Kowaleski et al. eds., *Peasants and lords*, p. 356.

89. For useful summaries see Britnell, 'Specialization of work', pp. 1–16; Campbell, 'Factor markets', pp. 84–8; Briggs, 'English serfdom', pp. 28–31.

90. Miller and Hatcher, *Medieval England: rural society*, pp. 219–24.

91. Anne DeWindt, 'Redefining the peasant community in medieval England: the regional perspective', *Journal of British Studies*, 26 (1987), pp. 194–5; Mark Bailey, *A marginal economy?: East Anglian Breckland in the later Middle Ages* (Cambridge, 1989), pp. 115–90; Larry R. Poos, *A rural society after the Black Death: Essex 1350–1525* (Cambridge, 1991), pp. 17–24; Rigby, *English society*, pp. 39–40; Simon A.C Penn and Christopher Dyer, 'Wages and earnings in late medieval England: evidence from enforcement of the labour laws', in Christopher Dyer, *Everyday life in medieval England* (London, 1994), pp. 172–3; Mark Bailey, *Medieval Suffolk: an economic and social history 1200 to 1500* (Woodbridge, 2007), pp. 158–90; Kowaleski, 'Peasants and the sea', pp. 353–76.
92. Penn and Dyer, 'Wages and earnings', p. 186.
93. Estimates of the proportion of landless as a percentage of the population vary from *c.*25% to 40%. See, for example, Britnell, 'Specialisation of work', p. 7; Marjorie K. McIntosh, *Autonomy and community: the royal manor of Havering 1200–1500* (Cambridge, 1986), pp. 160–6; James Masschaele, *Peasants, merchants, and markets: inland trade in medieval England, 1150–1350* (Basingstoke, 1997), pp. 14–18; Fox, 'Exploitation' pp. 551–4; Campbell, 'Agrarian problem', pp. 64–5; Campbell, 'The land', pp. 208, 219; Bekar and Reid, 'Land markets', p. 306.
94. Britnell, 'Commerce and capitalism', p. 364; Diana Wood, *Medieval economic thought* (Cambridge, 2002), p. 155; Penn and Dyer, 'Wages and earnings', p. 167; Dyer, *Age of transition*, p. 220; Campbell, *Great transition*, table 3.4, p. 262; Whittle, 'Food economy', pp. 53–4.
95. Jane Humphries and Jacob L. Weisdorf, 'Unreal wages?: Real income and economic growth in England, 1260–1850', *The Economic Journal*, 129 no. 623 (2019), p. 16, estimate that 46% of the waged labour market was on annual contracts. Hence the percentages in fig. 2.1 are 60% family holdings, 10% labour services, 17% waged labour, 13% annual contracts.
96. Rigby, *English society*, pp. 37–40; Mate, 'Work and leisure', pp. 279–82; P. Jeremy and P. Goldberg, 'Life and death: the ages of man', in Horrox and Ormrod, eds., *Social history*, pp. 419–21, 425–6; Jordan Claridge and John Langdon, 'The composition of *famuli* labour on English demesnes', *Agricultural History Review*, 63 (2015), pp. 187–220.
97. Campbell, 'The land', pp. 215–19; Ghosh, 'Rural economies', pp. 268–9.
98. Joyce P. Jacobsen and Gilbert L. Skillman, 'Introduction', in Joyce P. Jacobsen and Gilbert L. Skillman, eds., *Labour markets and employment relationships: a comprehensive approach* (Oxford, 2004), pp. 9–11.
99. Wood, *Medieval economic thought*, pp. 132, 144, 152–5; Stephan A. Epstein, 'The theory and practice of the just wage', *Journal of Medieval History*, 17 (1991), pp. 53–70; A. Lee Beier, 'A new serfdom: labour laws, vagrancy statutes and labour discipline in England 1350–1800', in A. Lee Beier and Paul Ocobock, eds., *Cast out. Vagrancy and homelessness in global and historical perspectives* (Athens, Ohio, 2008), pp. 36–7.
100. Wood, *Medieval economic thought*, pp. 144, 152–5.
101. Elaine Clark, 'Medieval labour law and English local courts', *American Journal of Legal History*, 27 (1983), p. 332; Larry R. Poos, 'The social context of the Statute of

Labourers enforcement', *Law and History Review*, 1 (1983), p. 36; Edmund B. and Natalie Fryde, 'Peasant rebellion and peasant discontents', in Miller, ed., *Agrarian history III*, pp. 755–6; Bennett, 'Impact of the Black Death', p. 199; Anthony J. Musson, 'New labour laws, new remedies? Legal reaction to the Black Death crisis', in Nigel Saul, ed., *Fourteenth-century England* (Woodbridge, 2000), pp. 75–6; Anthony J. Musson, 'Reconstructing English labour laws: a medieval perspective', in Kellie Robertson and Michael Uebel, eds., *The Middle Ages at work: practising labour in late medieval England* (Basingstoke, 2004), p. 114; Dyer, 'Work ethics', pp. 31–32; Kellie Robertson, *Labourer's two bodies. Literary and legal productions in Britain 1350–1500* (Basingstoke, 2006), pp. 14–15; Campbell, 'Factor markets', p. 88; Briggs, 'English serfdom', p. 23; Bennett, 'Compulsory service', p. 13; Catharina Lis and Hugo Soly, *Worthy efforts: attitudes to work and workers in pre-industrial Europe* (Leiden, 2012), pp. 301–2.

102. Hilton, *Medieval society*, p. 155; Warren O. Ault, *Open-field farming in medieval England: a study of village by-laws* (London, 1972), pp. 81–6, 89, and 93; Fryde, 'Peasant rebellion', p. 756; Larson, *Conflict and compromise*, p. 156.

103. Heather Swanson, *Medieval artisans* (Oxford, 1989), pp. 110–15; Sarah Rees Jones, 'Household, work and the problem of mobile labour: the regulation of labour in medieval English towns', in James Bothwell, P. Jeremy, P. Goldberg, and W. Mark Ormrod, eds., *The problem of labour in fourteenth-century England* (Woodbridge, 2000), pp. 133–53; Braid, 'Behind the Ordinance', pp. 17–20; Musson, 'Reconstructing', p. 124.

104. Clark, 'Labour laws', p. 332, and Musson, 'New labour laws', p. 75, but almost all these examples derive from Ault, *Open-field farming*, and Warren O. Ault, 'Some early village by-laws', *English Historical Review*, 178 (1930), pp. 210–17, 226.

105. Clark, 'Labour laws', p. 332; Braid, 'Behind the ordinance', p. 28.

106. Braid, 'Behind the ordinance', pp. 17–20, 27–28, esp. fn. 187; Musson, 'Reconstructing', p. 124; Rees Jones, 'Regulation of labour', pp. 138–9 is explicit that pre-plague urban controls over labour were confined to the building trades.

107. Helen Swanson, *Medieval British towns* (Basingstoke, 1999), pp. 96–102.

108. Susan Reynolds, *An introduction to the history of English medieval towns* (Oxford, 1977), pp. 164–8; Dyer, 'Small towns', pp. 526–32; Mark Bailey, 'Self-government in the small towns of medieval England', in Ben Dodds and Christian D. Liddy, eds., *Commercial activity, markets and entrepreneurs in medieval England: essays in honour of Richard Britnell* (Woodbridge, 2011), pp. 107–28. Craft gilds were neither prominent nor powerful, even a large provincial capital such as Exeter, Maryanne Kowaleski, *Local markets and regional trade in medieval Exeter* (Cambridge, 1995), pp. 99–100.

109. Ault, 'Early village by-laws', pp. 210–17, 226; Ault, *Open-field farming*, pp. 81–6, 89, and 93, are cited as the sole source for wider claims about the temporal and spatial extent of labour control in Clark, 'Labour laws', p. 332 and Dyer, 'Work ethics', pp. 31–2.

110. Ault, *Open-field farming*, pp. 81–6, 89, and 93; Ault, 'Early village by-laws', pp. 208–31; Braid, 'Behind the Ordinance', pp. 27–8.

111. For ordinances in general in commonfield communities, see Christopher Dyer, *Lords and peasants in a changing society: the estates of the bishopric of Worcester, 680–1540* (Cambridge, 1980), p. 269; David Hall, *The open fields of England* (Oxford, 2014), pp. 9–15; and Thornton, 'Rural society', pp. 243–5. They are even rarer in the many areas of the country where communal regulations over agriculture were weak, Mark Bailey, 'The form, function and evolution of irregular field systems in Suffolk, c.1300–c.1550', *Agricultural History Review*, 57 (2009), pp. 15–36. Communal by-laws could only be promulgated and enforced in communities with a strong institutional framework, Mark Bailey, 'Beyond the Midland field system: the determinants of common rights over the arable in medieval England', *Agricultural History Review*, 58 (2010), pp. 151–69.
112. There is, however, a basis for arguing that elements of the new labour legislation in 1349/51 drew upon precedents in customary law, as argued by Musson, 'New labour laws', pp. 75–8; Dyer, 'Work ethics', pp. 32–3.
113. van Bavel et al., 'Factor markets', pp. 15–17.
114. John Hatcher, 'Seven centuries of unreal wages', in John Hatcher and Judy Z. Stephenson, eds., *Seven centuries of unreal wages: the unreliable data, sources and methods that have been used for measuring standards of living in the past* (Basingstoke, 2018), pp. 39–41.
115. Cause paper evidence from the later Middle Ages occasionally casts light on these processes. For example, in 1374 the family of a young female servant from rural Yorkshire witnessed her servant contract with a resident of York, P. Jeremy P. Goldberg, 'What was a servant?', in Curry and Matthew, eds., *Concepts and patterns of service*, p. 11.
116. Goldberg, 'What was a servant?', pp. 9–11.
117. Wood, *Medieval economic thought*, p. 153; Goldberg, 'What was a servant', p. 10. The Statute of Labourers in 1351 noted that may harvest hirings in the countryside used payments in wheat rather than cash, *Statutes of the Realm*, I, p. 311.
118. Goldberg, 'What was a servant?', pp. 9–11.
119. McIntosh, *Autonomy*, p. 162; Clark, 'Labour laws', pp. 331, 335–6, 340–1, 347–9; Briggs, 'English serfdom', p. 23; Musson 'Reconstructing', p. 120.
120. Clark, 'Labour laws', pp. 334–5, 340–1.
121. Palmer, *English law*, pp. 14–15.
122. Bailey, *Medieval Suffolk*, pp. 154–5; Thornton, 'Rural society', p. 74.
123. Epstein, 'Just wage', p. 58.
124. Gregory Clark, 'The cost of capital and medieval agricultural technique', *Explorations in Economic History*, 25 (1988), pp. 265–94; Adrian R. Bell, Chris Brooks, and Tony K. Moore, 'Interest in medieval accounts: example from England 1272–1340', *History*, 92 (2009), pp. 411–33; Campbell, 'Factor markets', pp. 93–6; Briggs, 'English serfdom', p. 31.
125. Campbell, *Great transition*, pp. 100–3.
126. Phillipp R. Schofield, 'Introduction', in Phillipp R. Schofield and Nicholas Mayhew, eds., *Credit and debt in medieval England c.1180–c.1350* (Oxford, 2002), p. 9; Chris Briggs, *Credit and village society in fourteenth-century England* (Oxford, 2009), pp. 1–18, 29–64.

127. Briggs, *Credit and village society*, p. 216.
128. Paul Brand, 'Aspects of the law of debt, 1189–1307', in Schofield and Mayhew, eds., *Credit and debt*, pp. 19–41; Briggs, *Credit and village society*, p. 219.
129. Campbell, 'Factor markets', p. 93.
130. Briggs, *Credit and village society*, pp. 217, 222–3.
131. Clark, 'Cost of capital', pp. 265–6, 273–4, tables 3 and 4; Pamuk, 'Black Death', pp. 308–9; Campbell 'Factor markets', pp. 83, 93; Campbell, *Great transition*, pp. 102–3; 358–60; Adrian R. Bell, Chris Brooks and Tony K. Moore, '*Cambium non est mutuum*: exchange and interest rates in medieval Europe', *Economic History Review*, 70 (2017), pp. 388–9.
132. This view is surveyed and summarized in Schofield, *Peasants and historians*, pp. 118–23.
133. Campbell, *Great transition*, pp. 121–5; Dyer, 'Small towns', p. 506.
134. Dobson, 'General survey', p. 275; Britnell, *Britain*, pp. 120, 144.
135. Dyer, 'Small towns', pp. 505–8.
136. Britnell, *Commercialisation*, p. 115; Heather Swanson, *Medieval British towns* (Abingdon, 1999), pp. 14–15; Holt, 'Society and population'; Richard H. Britnell, 'Town life', in Horrox and Ormrod, eds., *Social history*, pp. 145–6; Britnell, *Britain*, p. 74. This was not, however, a peculiarly English phenomenon because small towns proliferated throughout the continent after 1000 and, if their populations are also admitted, the average urbanization ratio across Europe was comparable to that of England, Campbell, *Great transition*, pp. 122–3.
137. Nicholas Mayhew, 'Modelling medieval monetarisation', in Britnell and Campbell, eds., *Commercialising economy*, pp. 57–62; Campbell, 'Agrarian problem', table 2, p. 15. Mayhew and Campbell estimate GDP in 1086 at £0.4m and *c*.£4m in 1300, see Campbell, 'Agrarian problem', pp. 15, 69. Cf. the estimate of GDP at £5.43m in the 1300s in Broadberry et al., *British economic growth*, p. 205.
138. The best general summaries are Britnell, *Commercialisation*, pp. 79–127; Miller and Hatcher, *Medieval England: towns*, pp. 135–8, 413; and Christopher Dyer, *Making a living in the Middle Ages: the people of Britain 850–1520* (New Haven, 2002), pp. 163–78. See also Ghosh, 'Rural economies', pp. 260–1, 278.
139. Ghosh, 'Rural economies', p. 278.
140. Campbell, 'Measuring', pp. 192–3.
141. David L. Farmer, 'Woodland and pasture sales on the Winchester manors: disposing of a surplus or producing for the market?', in Britnell and Campbell, eds., *A commercialising economy*, pp. 104–5; Campbell, 'Measuring', pp. 156–61, 172–4, 189.
142. Dyer, *Making a living*, pp. 164–9.
143. Nicholas R. Amor, *From wool to cloth: the triumph of the Suffolk clothier* (Bungay, 2016), pp. 91–116.
144. Philip Slavin, 'Peasant livestock husbandry in late thirteenth-century Suffolk: economy, environment, and society', in Kowaleski, et al., eds., *Peasants and lords*, p. 9.
145. Bailey, *Medieval Suffolk*, pp. 172–3; Jordan Claridge, 'The role of demesnes in the trade of agricultural horses in late medieval England', *Agricultural History Review*, 65 (2017), pp. 37–66; Slavin, 'Peasant livestock', pp. 3–23.

146. James A. Galloway, Derek Keene and Margaret Murphy, 'Fuelling the city: production and distribution of firewood and fuel in London's region, 1290–1400', *Economic History Review*, 49 (1996), pp. 447–72; Bailey, *Medieval Suffolk*, pp. 172–3.

147. Bruce M.S. Campbell, James A. Galloway, Derek Keene, and Margaret Murphy, *A medieval capital and its grain supply: agrarian production and distribution in the London region c.1300* (Historical Geography Research Series, 30, 1993), p. 173.

148. Mark Bailey, 'Historiographical essay: the commercialisation of the English economy 1086–1500', *Journal of Medieval History*, 24 (1998), pp. 302–7; James Davis, 'A reassessment of village markets in late medieval England', in Kowaleski et al., eds., *Peasants and lords*, pp. 287–91.

149. Richard H. Britnell, 'Making or buying? Maintaining farm equipment and buildings, 1250–1350', in Kowaleski et al., eds., *Peasants and lords*, pp. 241–2.

150. Greif, *Institutions*, pp. 85–6.

151. Howell, *Commerce*, pp. 12–19.

152. Bateman, 'Evolution', pp. 450–2.

153. And at least one-third of all grain was retained as seed corn. Miller and Hatcher, *Medieval England: towns*, p. 413; Campbell et al., *Medieval capital*, pp. 147, 154–5; Campbell, 'Measuring', pp. 155–61; Richard H. Britnell, 'Urban demand in the English economy 1300–1600', in James A. Galloway, ed., *Trade, urban hinterlands and market integration c.1300–1600* (Centre for Metropolitan History, Institute of Historical Research, 2000), p. 5; Britnell, *Britain*, pp. 198–9.

154. Campbell et al., *Medieval capital*, pp. 53–60, 91–8, 111–44; David J. Stone, 'Medieval farm management and technological mentalities: Hinderclay before the Black Death', *Economic History Review*, 51 (2003), pp. 1–22.

155. Britnell, *Britain*, pp. 198–9.

156. Britnell, *Britain*, pp. 198, 403.

157. Masschaele, *Peasants, markets*, p. 231.

158. See, for example, Britnell, *Commercialisation*, p. 100; Campbell et al., *Medieval capital*, pp. 171–83; Britnell, 'Urban demand', pp. 2–4, 7–9; James A. Galloway, 'One market or many?: London and the grain trade of England', in James A. Galloway, ed., *Trade, urban hinterlands, and market integration* (London, 2000), pp. 23–42; Bailey, *Medieval Suffolk*, pp. 168–71; Harry Kitsikopoulos, 'Manorial estates as business firms', *Agricultural History Review*, 56 (2008), pp. 142–66; Whittle, 'Food economy', pp. 33–5.

159. Bailey, 'Peasant welfare', pp. 235–40; Bateman, 'Evolution', p. 452; Eric B. Schneider, 'Prices and production in agricultural supply response in fourteenth-century England', *Economic History Review*, 67 (2014), p. 86.

160. Miller, *Ely*, p. 139; Bailey, *English manor*, p. 52; Britnell, *Commercialisation*, p. 97.

161. Britnell, *Commercialisation*, p. 92; Campbell et al., *Medieval capital*, pp. 104–7; Mark Bailey, ed., *The bailiff's minute book of Dunwich, 1404–1430*, Suffolk Records Society, 34 (1992), p. 19.

162. Chris Given-Wilson, 'Purveyance for the royal household 1362–1413', *Bulletin of the Institute of Historical Research*, 56 (1983), pp. 147–53; Jennifer Hole. 'The justification of wealth and lordship versus rulers' exploitation in medieval England', *Parergon*, 27 (2017), pp. 39–43.

163. Maddicott, 'English peasantry', pp. 17–19, 24–8; Masschaele, *Peasants, markets,* pp. 36–42, 220–3; Phillips, 'Collaboration and litigation', pp. 117–18.

164. Maddicott, 'English peasantry', pp. 24–8; Masschaele, *Peasants, markets,* pp. 36–42.

165. Britnell, *Commercialisation,* p. 90.

166. This summary draws upon the following key works: Raymond de Roover, 'The concept of the just price and economic policy', *Journal of Economic History,* 18 (1958), pp. 218–34; John W. Baldwin, 'Medieval theories of the just price. Romanists, canonists and theologians in the twelfth and thirteenth centuries', *Transactions of the American Philosophical Society,* 49, 4 (1959), pp. 1–92; Richard H. Britnell, 'Forestall, forestalling and the Statute of Forestallers', *English Historical Review,* 102 (1987), pp. 89–102; Britnell, *Commercialisation,* pp. 90–7; Wood, *Medieval economic thought,* pp. 89–109, 132–59; Richard H. Britnell, 'Price setting in English borough markets, 1349–1500', *Canadian Journal of History,* 31 (1996), pp. 1–15; Gwen Seabourne, *Royal regulation of loans and sales in medieval England* (Woodbridge, 2004), pp. 125–59; James Davis, 'Baking for the common good: a reassessment of the assize of bread in medieval England', *Economic History Review,* 57 (2004), pp. 465–502; James Davis, *Medieval market morality. Life, law and ethics in the English marketplace, 1200–1500* (Cambridge, 2012), pp. 1–64; Hole, 'Justification of wealth', pp. 23–47; Joel Kaye, *A history of balance 1250–1375: the emergence of a new model of equilibrium and its impact on thought* (Cambridge, 2014), pp. 58–125.

167. Charles Gross, *The Gild Merchant,* volume I (Oxford, 1890), p. 51, quoted in Stephen H. Rigby, *Medieval Grimsby. Growth and decline* (Hull, 1993), p. 11.

168. Britnell, 'Price setting', pp. 2, 15.

169. De Roover, 'Just price', p. 422; Wood, *Medieval economic thought,* pp. 149–50.

170. Wood, *Medieval economic thought,* p. 144; Braid, 'Behind the Ordinance', pp. 12–16.

171. Britnell, 'Price setting', pp. 3–5; Richard H. Britnell, *Growth and decline in Colchester 1300–1525* (Cambridge, 1986), pp. 133–4; Seabourne, *Royal regulation,* pp. 74–5, 80; Davis, *Medieval market mortality,* pp. 323–8, 395.

172. For example, resident merchants might intercept fishing boats approaching a port and strike private bargains for sizeable consignments of fish, greatly enhancing their capacity to dictate its supply to the market and therefore its price when the market opened, Britnell, *Colchester,* pp. 133–4.

173. Wood, *Medieval economic thought,* pp. 89–109.

174. Britnell, 'Forestalling', pp. 96–100; Seabourne, *Royal regulation,* pp. 96–7, 131–8, 141–2; Wood, *Medieval economic thought,* pp. 96–7, 143–4; Davis, 'Selling food and drink', pp. 358–60; Davis, *Medieval market morality,* p. 60; Braid, 'Behind the Statute', pp. 3–10; Buchanan Sharp, 'Royal paternalism and the moral economy in the reign of Edward II: the response to the Great Famine', *Economic History Review,* 66 (2013), pp. 628–47.

175. Davis, *Medieval market morality,* pp. 297–322, 330–1, 380–1; Bailey, *Medieval Suffolk,* p. 143.

176. Judith M. Bennett, *Ale, beer, and brewsters in England. Women's work in a changing world 1300–1600* (Oxford, 1999), p. 101; Britnell, *Commercialisation,* p. 175; Kowaleski, *Local markets,* p. 186; Braid. 'Behind the Ordinance', p. 11; Davis, *Medieval market morality,* pp. 297–300; Davis, 'Selling food and drink', p. 360.

177. Britnell, 'Forestalling', pp. 100–2; Britnell, 'Price-setting', p. 13; Seabourne, *Royal regulation*, pp. 86–9.
178. Campbell, 'Measuring', p. 193.
179. For example, Miller, *Ely*, pp. 143–51; Briggs, 'English serfdom', pp. 13–32.
180. Britnell, 'Commercialisation and economic development', pp. 25–6; Miller and Hatcher, *Medieval England: towns*, p. 180.
181. Howell, *Commerce*, p. 12.
182. Bailey, 'Peasant welfare', pp. 233–8.
183. Dyer, *Making a living*, pp. 228–63; Campbell, *Great transition*, pp. 191–8.
184. Campbell, 'Agrarian problem', pp. 7–24, 64–70; Campbell, 'The land', pp. 228–30, 235–7.
185. Campbell, 'The land', pp. 228–30.
186. Kilby, 'Struggle and enterprise', pp. 7–27; Briggs, 'English serfdom', pp. 19–20, 23.
187. Brenner, 'Agrarian roots', pp. 257–8; Bridbury, *English economy*, pp. 261–2; Brenner, 'Rises and declines', pp. 262–3; Kitsikopoulos, 'England', p. 47.
188. Christopher Dyer, 'Memories of freedom: attitudes towards serfdom in England, 1200–1350', in Michael L. Bush, ed., *Serfdom and slavery. Studies in legal bondage* (London, 1996), pp. 277, 295; Dyer, 'Villeins, bondsmen', pp. 419–24.
189. Dyer, *Lords and peasants*, p. 265; Rodney H. Hilton, *The English peasantry in the later Middle Ages: the Ford Lectures and related studies*, (Oxford, 1975), pp. 231–7; 'private jurisdiction was the prop of landlord power, over the free as well as over the unfree', Rodney H. Hilton, 'The English Rising of 1381', *Marxism Today*, June 1981, p. 18.
190. Evans, 'Manorial lordship', pp. 155–6.
191. For example, Bonfield, 'Nature of customary law', pp. 517–21; John S. Beckerman, 'Procedural innovation and institutional change in medieval English manorial courts', *Law and History Review*, 10 (1992), pp. 197–252; Sherri Olson, *A chronicle of all that happens: voices from the village court in medieval England* (Toronto, 1996); Chris Briggs, 'Manor court procedures, debt litigation levels, and rural credit provision in England, c.1290–c.1380', *Law and History Review*, 24 (2006), pp. 519–58; Phillipp R. Schofield, 'Peasants and the manor court: gossip and litigation in a Suffolk village at the close of the thirteenth century', *Past and Present*, 159 (1998), pp. 3–42; Peter L. Larson, 'Village voice or village oligarchy?: The jurors of the Durham Halmote court, 1349 to1424', *Law and History Review*, 28 (2010), pp. 675–85, 701–7.
192. Erin McGibbon Smith, 'Court rolls as evidence for village society: Sutton-in-the-Isle in the fourteenth century', in Bailey and Rigby, eds., *Town and countryside*, fig. 30, p. 255. Evans does concede that peasants had good reason to consider the manorial court as their own, 'Manorial lordship', p. 156–8; Evans, 'Merton College', p. 254.
193. Janet Williamson, 'Dispute in the manorial court: Lakenheath in the early fourteenth century', *Reading Medieval Studies*, 11 (1985), p. 136; McGribbon Smith, 'Reflections', p. 43; Briggs, 'Manor court procedures', pp. 527–35; McGribbon Smith, 'Court rolls', fig. 30, p. 255. Not all manorial courts contained much private business, Evans, 'Merton College', pp. 226–46.
194. Records from such courts have seldom survived, unfortunately, but for one example from the mid-fourteenth century, see SROI HA30/50/22/20.9 (1).

195. Zvi Razi, 'Manorial court rolls and local population: an East Anglian case study', *Economic History Review*, 49 (1996), pp. 761–2; Briggs, 'Manor court procedures', pp. 550–5; Thornton, 'Rural society', pp. 42–4.
196. Phillips, 'Collaboration and litigation', p. 58.
197. Chris Briggs, 'Seigniorial control of villagers' litigation beyond the manor in later medieval England', *Historical Research*, 213 (2008), pp. 399–422; Briggs, 'Manor court procedures', pp. 535–7; Briggs, 'Introduction', pp. 11–12.
198. Briggs, 'Seigniorial control', p. 422.
199. Hyams, 'Edwardian villagers', p. 74.
200. Bonfield, 'Nature of customary law', pp. 514–33; John S. Beckerman, 'Toward a theory of medieval manorial adjudication: the nature of communal judgements in a system of customary law', *Law and History Review*, 13 (1995), pp. 1–22; Hyams, 'Edwardian villagers', pp. 80–8; Lloyd Bonfield, 'The role of seigniorial jurisdiction after the Norman Conquest, and the nature of customary law, in England', in Lloyd Bonfield, ed., *Seigniorial jurisdiction* (Berlin, 2000), pp. 177–94; Larry R. Poos, 'Medieval English manorial courts: their records and their jurisdiction', in Bonfield, ed., *Seigniorial jurisdiction*, pp. 195–214; Richard H. Helmholz, 'Independence and uniformity in England's manorial courts', in Bonfield, ed., *Seigniorial jurisdiction*, pp. 215–36; Briggs, 'Manor court procedures', pp. 519–58.
201. Elaine Clark, 'Debt litigation in a late medieval English vill', in J. Ambrose Raftis, ed., *Pathways to medieval peasants* (Toronto, 1981), pp. 247–79; Razi and Smith, 'Origins', pp. 46–9; Hyams, 'Edwardian villagers', p. 82; Dyer, *Lords and peasants*, p. 266; Britnell, *Commercialisation*, pp. 142–3; Briggs, 'Manor court procedures', pp. 519–58; Judith M. Bennett, *Women in the medieval English countryside. Gender and household in Brigstock before the plague* (Oxford, 1987), pp. 31, 107–10.
202. Hyams, *King, lords, and peasants*, pp. 69, 198, 240–1; Smith, 'Some thoughts', pp. 108–10; Campbell, 'The land', pp. 210–12, 228–30. Poos and Bonfield, *Select cases*, pp. lxxvi–lxxxv, cliv–v; Slota, 'Law, land transfer, and lordship', pp. 121–3; Beckerman, 'Toward a theory', pp. 11–12; Hyams, 'Edwardian villagers', pp. 81–2.
203. Paul Brand, *The making of the common law* (London, 1992), pp. 303–6; Hyams, 'Edwardian villagers', pp. 79–81, 84–6; Slota, 'Law, land transfer, and lordship', pp. 125–6; Beckerman, 'Toward a theory', pp. 15–16.
204. Slota, 'Law, land transfer and lordship', p. 119; Poos and Bonfield, *Select cases*, p. xxi; Dyer, 'Memories of serfdom', pp. 277, 295; Evans, 'Manorial court', pp. 155–8; Britnell, *Britain*, p. 279.
205. Razi and Smith, 'Origins', p. 36; Paul D.A. Harvey, 'English estate records', in Richard H. Britnell, ed., *Pragmatic literacy, east and west 1200–1330* (Woodbridge, 1997), p. 118.
206. Robert C. Palmer, 'England: law, society and the state', in Rigby, ed., *Companion*, pp. 245–7.
207. Beckerman, 'Procedural innovation', pp. 222–4; John Hudson, *The formation of English common law: law and society in England from the Norman Conquest to Magna Carta* (London, 1996), pp. 142–4.
208. Deborah Boucoyannis, *From roving to stationary judges: power, land and the origins of representative institutions* (Cambridge, forthcoming), chapter 1.

209. Vinogradoff, *Villeinage*, pp. 375–6; Smith, 'Some reflections', pp. 100, 126; Hyams, 'Edwardian villagers', p. 82; Bailey, 'Historiographical essay', pp. 301–2.

210. Briggs, 'Introduction', pp. 5–14.

211. Britnell, *Britain*, pp. 275–8.

212. Bonfield, 'Nature of customary law', p. 520.

213. Stephen F.C. Milsom, *The legal framework of English feudalism* (Cambridge, 1977), pp. 36–7. See also the discussion in Tom Johnson, *Law in common: legal cultures in late-medieval England* (Oxford, 2020), pp. 1–16.

214. Anthony J. Musson, *Medieval law in context: the growth of legal consciousness from Magna Carta to the Peasants' Revolt* (Manchester, 2001), p. 169.

215. Evans, 'Manorial court', pp. 165, 159–60.

216. The abbot of Bury St Edmunds acquired a market charter for Botesdale in 1227, and by the 1340s it had become a sizeable commercial centre on the road between Bury St Edmunds and Diss (Norfolk), Richard M. Smith, 'A periodic market and its impact upon a manorial community: Botesdale Suffolk and the manor of Redgrave', in Razi and Smith, eds., *Medieval society*, pp. 464, 472.

217. UC Bacon Ms 18, mm. 1 and 3.

218. He was ale taster in 1330, 1331, and 1336, UC Bacon Mss. 17, m.15, 18, m.2, and 19, m.2; affeeror in 1340, Bacon Ms 19, m. 27; and messor in 1341, Bacon Ms 19, m.29.

219. He was explicitly described as ale taster in Botesdale on one occasion, UC Bacon Ms 16 m.6; he appears with Docke in Bacon Ms 19, m.4.

220. He was elected reeve in 1325, UC Bacon Ms 16 m.16, and again in 1339, Bacon MS. 19 m. 23.

221. UC Bacon Ms 20, m. 15.

222. UC Bacon Ms 19 m. 35, court held January 1342. Villeins were theoretically supposed to litigate as plaintiffs only in the court of their own lord.

223. UC Bacon Ms 26 mm. 1, 3, 5, and 6 for his land and office holding. The manumission and death are recorded in UC Bacon Ms 28.

224. Smith, 'Periodic market', pp. 471–9.

225. S.H.A. Hervey, ed., *Suffolk in 1327, being a subsidy return* (Woodbridge, 1906), p. 39.

226. Smith, 'Periodic market', pp. 464–5.

227. In six extant accounts between 1323 and 1342 the market franchise was leased just once (in 1336–7), UC Bacon Mss. 325–30. The lease of 1342–3, and thereafter, are documented in Bacon Mss. 331 to 363.

228. UC Bacon Mss. 331, 332, and BL Add. Roll 63374. John Docke ceased to be co-lessee after Michaelmas 1345, Bacon Ms 333. The death of John son of John Docke is recorded in a court held on 2 October 1345, Bacon Ms 20 m. 5.

229. UC Bacon Mss. 353 to 368.

230. Bailey, 'Self-government', pp. 111–16; Davis, *Medieval market mortality*, pp. 368–70.

231. BL Add. Roll 63374.

232. The Crown occasionally held one-off inquests into the regulation of markets, James Davis, 'Market regulation in fifteenth-century England', in Dodds and Liddy, eds., *Commercial activity*, pp. 87–8, 91–2, 95–6. According to one justice on the Northamptonshire eyre in the late 1320s, 'the lord of the market must do justice to everyone in the market for matters which concern the market. A market cannot be

held unless the assize of bread and ale is duly enforced and cannot be if the corporeal penalties cannot be imposed', quoted in Buchanan Sharp, *Famine and scarcity in late medieval and early modern England: the regulation of grain marketing 1256–1631* (Cambridge, 2016), p. 20.

233. UC Bacon Ms 334.
234. Bailey, *Medieval Suffolk*, pp. 176–9.
235. UC Bacon Ms 21, m. 23.
236. UC Bacon Ms 21, m. 24.
237. Campbell, 'European mortality', pp. 19–42; Campbell, *Great transition*, pp. 328–9; 396–7.
238. Ghosh, 'Rural economies', p. 278.
239. Britnell, *Britain*, pp. 84–90; Campbell, 'Factor markets', pp. 96–9; French and Hoyle, *English rural society*, pp. 22–3; Kitsikopoulos, 'England', p. 45; Kitsikopoulos, 'Epilogue', pp. 341–7.
240. Campbell, 'People and land', pp. 92–102; Campbell, *Great transition*, p. 168.
241. Campbell et al., *A medieval capital*, pp. 182–3; Campbell, 'Measuring', pp. 192–3.
242. Richard H. Britnell, 'Commercialisation, stagnation and crisis 1250–1350', in John Drendel, ed., *Crisis in the later Middle Ages: beyond the Postan-Duby paradigm* (Turnhout, 2015), pp. 15–34. Britnell, 'Urban demand', p. 3; Campbell, *Great transition*, pp. 168–72.
243. As implied in Alan Macfarlane, *The origins of English individualism* (London, 1978), chapter 5 and p. 167; Clark, *Farewell to alms*, pp. 147–8.
244. Briggs, *Credit and village society*, pp. 217, 222–3.
245. Campbell, *Great transition*, pp. 253–77, 399–400, quote at p. 396. Or, put another way, 'it is true that exogenous factors dealt the decisive blow to English feudalism, but this admission should not be used to deny that the system resembled a train bound for derailment, sooner or later', Kitsikopoulos, 'England', p. 42.
246. Campbell, *Great transition*, p. 168.

3

Reaction and Regulation, 1349 to 1380

Introduction

Detailed reconstructions of the immediate impact of the plague outbreak in 1348–9 upon local communities are still relatively uncommon, although a handful of recent case studies has revealed the richness of English manorial sources for such research.[1] Most studies of English society are based on the estate of a particular lord, but these cover such a long span of history that the events of the 1350s and 1360s are treated fleetingly. As a result, the nature of the crisis and its short- to medium-term impact have received too little attention, although this inattentiveness also owes something to the widespread belief that social relations and factor markets changed little before the late 1370s. The next three chapters will explore in detail the social, economic, cultural, and legal responses to successive plague outbreaks during the third quarter of the fourteenth century. Only such careful and detailed scrutiny of changes over a short timeframe can reveal the subtle interplay between the loss of half the population and the key social and economic responses. They expose the notion that little changed in this period as too neat and tidy because it obscures the extraordinary turmoil and upheaval, and the complexity of events, in the generation after the arrival of plague.

This chapter begins with a review of the immediate impact of the first epidemic of 1348–9, which combined with extreme weather conditions to generate a crisis lasting until 1353. The nature of that crisis, and the difficulties of coping with the challenges it posed, help to explain the shortages of grain—the key commodity in fourteenth-century England—in its wake. The chapter then explores the response of the ruling elite to these shortages, and those of tenants and workers, analysing separately the reaction of the government and manorial lords. Their reaction was a predictable combination of repression and concession, but historians have tended to overemphasize the former and to underestimate the latter. In the 1350s government and seigniorial activity in the sphere of social control was significant and inequitable, and unquestionably heightened tensions. Indeed, a revolt of the peasantry would have made more sense anytime in the 1350s than it did in 1381. The evidence for coercion diminishes markedly after the 1350s, however, and there is no compelling evidence for a widespread and sustained seigniorial reaction in the 1360s and 1370s. Instead, this period represented a watershed in the history of tenure of England, comprising a major swing to

After the Black Death: Economy, Society, and the Law in Fourteenth-Century England. Mark Bailey, Oxford University Press (2021). © Mark Bailey. DOI: 10.1093/oso/9780198857884.003.0003

monetarized and commercial rents, and the decisive separation of tenurial unfreedom from personal unfreedom. These developments increased the mobility of land and people, and represented an irreversible shift towards simpler and more commercial contractual forms that dealt the fatal blow to villeinage and unpicked much of the tenurial tangle of the pre-plague era.

The Anatomy of a Crisis, 1348 to 1353

The human anguish, trauma, and hardship caused through the loss of half the population—family, friends, loved ones—in the twelve months between August 1348 and August 1349 is simple to express but hard to comprehend. Whole families were wiped out at Halesowen (Warks.).[2] Little Peter Clevehog of Walsham (Suffolk) lost his parents and all his siblings.[3] Yet historians, blessed with the benefit and detachment of hindsight, portray this catastrophe as possessing a silver lining because at a stroke it removed the choking overpopulation and acute land deficiency of the pre-plague period.[4] In time, this profound reconfiguration of the land/labour ratio would present major social and economic opportunities for the survivors of the plague, but it is important to emphasize that these benefits were neither immediately apparent to survivors nor equally shared among them. One reason for this time lag is that the arrival of the Black Death in the summer of 1348 triggered a widespread crisis that did not abate until 1353, which created a good deal of hardship and delayed the process of recovery. Another reason is that the plague was accompanied by inflationary forces that increased the costs of essential foodstuffs, fuel, and equipment. Its scale and duration is still not fully grasped.[5] The crisis was the function of an exceptional combination of factors: mass mortality, empty landholdings, acute labour shortages, successive harvest failures, major disruption to markets, and the poverty of many survivors.

The death of around one-quarter of all noble landholders and nearly one-half of all peasant landholders resulted in the greatest turnover of land in any year in the last millennium. In 1349 64 per cent of villein land at Coltishall (Norfolk) changed hands.[6] In the 1340s an average of 570 parcels of customary land were transferred each year on the estate of the bishop of Winchester, but in 1348–9 there were 2,653 transactions.[7] The evidence of a high volume of post-mortem transfers on manor after manor throughout 1348–9 reflects the survival and rapid admittance of known heirs, together with an impressive administrative resilience.[8] Sometimes more distant heirs to land had to be traced and contacted, which usually resulted in some delay in admission to the holding. If no heir survived, or if surviving heirs declined to take up their inheritance, then the lord could offer the holding to any willing tenant and, if necessary, vary the rent and tenure to make it more attractive. In May 1349 74 per cent of tenants admitted to 368 customary holdings on six manors held by St Albans abbey were heirs and 18 per cent were strangers or unrelated to the deceased.[9] Transfers to kin declined on the estate of the bishopric of Winchester, reflecting the thinning out of established families and the influx of immigrants.[10] Rent reductions introduced to entice new tenants at Rudheath (Cheshire) were to remain in place 'until the world is put right'.[11] The scale of the turnover in 1348–9 even resulted in subsequent confusion on some manors about who held what land.[12] Some manorial courts called for new rentals to be drawn up to document the new order of tenantry, as at Merton (Norfolk) in 1350 and at Tottington (Norfolk) in the following year.[13] Confusion over the contributions owed by new tenants to the upkeep of sea banks and fen dykes following the epidemic caused the degradation of defences in the early 1350s and contributed to heavy flooding in parts of the East Anglian fenland.[14]

The pace and scale of the recovery of the land market varied from manor to manor. Historians have been surprised and impressed by the speed and extent of recovery in some places.[15] For example, by the end of 1349 new tenants had reoccupied well over 80 per cent of villein land relinquished by victims of plague during the spring and summer at Walsham (Suffolk) and at Halesowen (Warks.).[16] However, the pace of recovery was much slower elsewhere. At the end of December 1349 only four out of sixty customary tenements at Hanbury (Worcs.) were occupied, five of the seventeen customary holdings at Isaac Hall, Beckham (Norfolk) languished in the lord's hands, and just two customary tenants remained at Woodend (Oxon).[17] In September 1350 two-thirds of the customary holdings at Helston-in-Kirrier (Cornwall) were unoccupied.[18] In late 1350 the majority of villein virgates at Cuddington (Surrey) were unoccupied, while in 1353 one-third of customary virgates were still unoccupied at Witney (Oxon.) and the same proportion in 1356 at Lakenheath (Suffolk).[19] In the mid-1350s thousands of acres of arable land were still unoccupied on the bishop of Winchester's estate.[20] The differences in response rates from place to place reflect differences in the ability of local communities to react rather than differential rates of mortality.[21] Those with a high proportion of resident smallholders contained a wide pool of prospective landholders willing to increase their landholdings, whereas communities with a low proportion of smallholders and landless struggled to fill holdings from within their community and so had to attract new tenants from outside.[22] Many areas of County Durham were already impoverished through warfare and poor weather when plague struck in 1349, which further delayed recovery and explains why vacant land endured throughout the 1350s.[23] Overall, a recent estimate has suggested that one-quarter of the land under cultivation in England in the 1300s was no longer cultivated in the 1350s.[24]

Mass deaths of tenants in 1348–9 generated a one-off financial bonanza for many landlords through the payment of heriots from the estate of deceased tenants and of entry fines by new tenants. These produced sums up to ten times their normal annual levels around Farnham (Hants), and between two- and fourfold at Witney (Oxon), Downton (Wilts.), and Brightwell (Berks.).[25] They explain why income from manorial courts jumped in many places in the year of plague.[26] Yet these immediate gains in curial income from post-mortem land transfers have also to be weighed against losses in income resulting from the non-payment of rents and from the disruption of many economic activities, which invariably extended well into the early 1350s.[27] In 1348–9 many mills reported a severe fall in business, and the number of grain mills in England probably fell 10 per cent in the 1350s.[28] The watermill at Oakington (Cambs.) was disused, and between 1347 and 1350 income from mills and fisheries fell by one-half at Wisbech (Cambs.).[29] In the early 1350s the profits of arable production on the Berkeley estate in Gloucestershire were 'miserable'.[30] Sales of parkland pasture on four Cornish manors fell by more than half in the plague year.[31] Arrears of income jumped on the bishopric of Winchester's manors around Farnham (Surrey) in 1349 and remained stubbornly high over the next few years.[32]

Many sources of seigniorial revenue slumped. Income from land rents fell c.40 per cent between 1347 and 1350 on the Cornish manors of the Duchy of Cornwall, and by c.25 per cent on the bishopric of Winchester.[33] The bishopric of Worcester yielded £250 for the Crown when vacant for five months in 1317, but only £137 for nearly four months during the second half of 1349: no annual tallage was collected across the estate in the plague year, and the £1 8s. 8d. paid as recognition to the incoming bishop in November 1349 was merely 6 per cent of the amount that had been paid in 1337.[34] Recovery was very slow across most of the Worcester estate before 1353, and is only really apparent from the early 1360s.[35] The disruption to trade reduced income from commercial franchises. The weekly market and seasonal fair at Wisbech (Cambs.) were largely inactive in 1349 and did not pick up until 1351, and between 1349 and 1354 inter-peasant debt and contract litigation collapsed at Redgrave (Suffolk).[36] Two-thirds of the regular brewers and regraters of ale in the market town of Clare (Suffolk) disappeared after 1349, and over the next four years tension between the new generation of brewers/tapsters and the manorial authorities rose sharply. The explanation for this sudden surge in the number of petty disputes is unclear, but it probably reflected the poor-quality work of inexperienced newcomers or an enforcement wave in line with new government legislation (see below): or both.[37] The combination of declining manorial revenues and soaring administrative costs (see below) placed some lordly households in financial peril. In 1350–1 Durham priory reported arrears and losses of rent of £290, and by 1360 the figure had reached £454, and in the mid-1350s cash flows around the estate of the abbot of Westminster were still disrupted.[38]

From late 1349 sharp rises in the prices of many goods, and especially fuel and essential foodstuffs, exacerbated the adverse effects of falling revenues on living standards (see fig. 3.1).[39] In 1351 grain prices were more than double and salt prices more than triple their level in 1345. In 1350 one chronicler observed that 'crops were scanty, barns empty', and two years later auditors commented upon a

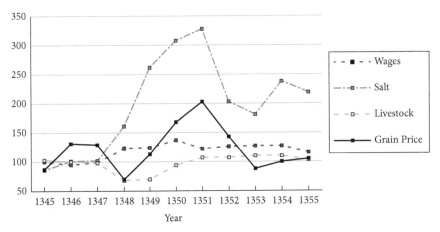

Figure 3.1 Index of basic prices and wages in England, 1345 to 1355
(100 = 1330/1 to 1346/7)
Source: Farmer 1988, 1991

lack of food in Wisbech (Cambs.).[40] In January 1351 the government imposed quotas of grain upon certain counties to supply English garrisons in France, although these had to be halved due to the scarcity of grain and collecting even these reduced quotas still proved impossible.[41] In February 1351 petitions to parliament expressed concern about depopulated communities, uncultivated arable land, and the resultant grain shortages.[42] The fall in grain output in the dominant peasant sector is revealed directly by tithe receipts, which in the north-east fell by one-half.[43] No grain tithes were collected at Kingston (Suffolk) in 1350–1—almost certainly as a charitable gesture from the parish rector given the prevailing hardship—but those collected in 1352–3 were valued at one-third the average value of receipts in the 1340s.[44] The shortages prevailed throughout England until the bountiful harvest of 1353 brought relief and a temporary fall in grain prices. A spate of refusals to perform seasonal labour services that summer on a variety of manors probably reflects a determination among peasants everywhere to make the most of this harvest after four lean years rather than a sudden outburst of rebelliousness.[45] In general, however, it was not until the late 1350s that peasant grain production showed signs of sustained recovery.[46]

   Grain shortages and sustained high prices in the early 1350s seem incongruous given the loss of half the population, so they must have reflected severe disruption to supply. The lack of labourers to perform essential agricultural work during key seasons was undoubtedly a factor in explaining grain shortages: the harvest of 1349 was an outright failure, in part because standing crops rotted in the field.[47] Nevertheless, labour shortages alone cannot explain the succession of poor harvests in 1350, 1351, and again in 1352, each of which was at least 30 per cent below the long-term average: this constitutes the sole example of a four-in-a-row yield failure on medieval record.[48] The weather was exceptionally cold between 1349 and 1352, and a lack of solar radiation would also explain the disruption to salt production (which was mainly produced in sun-dried salt pans).[49] The years from 1348 to 1351 were also very wet with severe flooding recorded in the Severn and Thames valleys.[50] According to Campbell, 'these years mark the culmination of a hundred years of global cooling' and by one estimate global temperatures in 1352–3 sank to their lowest level in the last millennium.[51] The weather was also highly variable because the general conditions of heavy rainfall gave way to drought in the spring and summer of 1352.[52]

The mass mortality resulted in acute shortages of labour, which meant that in 1350 and 1351 wages were nearly double those of the 1340s.[53] This was not just a function of the demographic collapse but of a selective self-withdrawal of survivors from the hired labour market, who were now more choosy about whether and where to work, and who enjoyed the option to acquire their own landholding. Production in activities requiring large inputs of arduous and seasonal labour was severely curtailed, as evidenced by the collapse of Fenland sedge and turf production.[54] Between 1348 and 1350 the cost of producing firewood at Hargrave (Suffolk) jumped by 60 per cent.[55] Tin mining in Cornwall and stone quarrying in Cheshire virtually collapsed.[56] Casual work in unpleasant agricultural tasks was especially unpopular, yet lords were highly dependent upon such labour to work their large arable demesnes, and so the concerns of lords about the workforce are reflected in contemporary comments attributing the shortages more to malice than mortality. A royal order dating from November 1349 claimed that labourers mocked and extorted money from their lords, and in 1350 the Rochester chronicler noted the unwillingness of workers to accept orders and those who did work displayed an 'ill will and a malicious spirit'.[57] Hard evidence from manorial accounts confirms such impressions, conveying the sense of a shell-shocked and lackadaisical workforce, lacking motivation. Between 1347 and 1353 the work productivity of labour services performed on the demesnes of Wisbech and Downham (Cambs.) fell, whilst at Esher (Surrey) manorial officials had to incentivize workers with the provision of extra food and drink, and probably by tolerating a shorter working day.[58]

The outraged views of the ruling elite at what they saw as the sloth and recalcitrance of manual workers paid little heed to the genuine difficulties faced by ordinary people in addressing their own immediate needs. Many survivors were themselves struggling to work their own holdings due to losses of family labour, and probably felt duty-bound to help struggling friends and neighbours before seeking casual work in the pay of lords.[59] The labour market had been bounteously oversupplied in the 1340s, when its contours and rhythms were well settled, but the shock of the Black Death not only reduced the supply of labour but also caused it to be reprioritized and reallocated, upsetting the equilibrium in various sectors of production. Ordinary people reacted and fared differently under the onslaught of the first epidemic: some seized the opportunities, while others were fatalistic and struggled to cope. Contrast, for example, the energy of William Hunte of Esher, who in 1349 inherited 30 acres of arable from his mother, acquired additional parcels of land, then served for eight years consecutively as the manorial reeve, with the despondency of John Derling, who had also inherited land but later forfeited it on two occasions due to impoverishment.[60]

The case of John Derling illustrates how many ordinary people in the 1350s were struggling to rebuild their lives after the trauma of the Black Death and to overcome the effects of hardship and poverty. Even sceptical auditors confirmed problems with poverty on estates from Durham to Cornwall, whose records document the remission of rents and labour services in an attempt to ease the difficulties. Peasants who were described as poor ('*quia pauper*') were not necessarily destitute, 'but at a tipping point ... [so that] without some relief they might not be able to maintain their tenuous grip on subsistence. For them the situation was not yet hopeless, but it was dire'.[61] In November 1349 29 per cent of tenants admitted to villein holdings at Codicote (Herts.) were pardoned their entry fines because of impoverishment.[62] In 1350 the jurors of Boldon (Co. Durham) confirmed that some within their community were too weak to take on a new holding, and in the early 1350s statements of poverty were commonplace across the estate of the bishopric of Durham.[63] In 1351 officials on the Cornish lands of the Duchy of Cornwall recognized that without temporary remissions of rent the poverty of many tenants meant they 'might otherwise have been forced to flee from their holdings'.[64] In 1352 'numerous examples' are recorded of tenants abandoning their landholdings or receiving allowances of rent on the grounds of their poverty on the bishop of Winchester's estate.[65]

The existence of so much poverty among the survivors of plague appears counter-intuitive, given that this powerful pathogenic strike had eradicated at a stroke the pre-existing congestion on the land. But the exceptional combination of events between 1348 and 1353 posed severe short-term challenges for many survivors of plague, which exacerbated their difficulties in dealing with the effects of the epidemic and took several years to overcome. Recovery from four back-to-back harvest failures—the most prolonged sequence of crop failure in recorded history—was inevitably slow.[66] In the early 1350s the cost of essential foodstuffs, salt, and fuel soared far above wages. Salt prices between 1350 and 1352 were three times the pre-plague mean, and thereafter remained at least double.[67] Fuel was especially scarce, due to the extreme cold as well as the lack of workers to prepare it, and consequently its price rose sharply and remained expensive. The price of peat turves tripled between 1348 and 1352 at Downham (Cambs.).[68] The price of firewood at Hadleigh (Suffolk) rose 33 per cent between 1348 and the late 1350s, and in the 1360s was 66 per cent higher than the price in 1348.[69] The price of faggots sold on four Suffolk manors rose from 17d. per hundred in the 1330s to 41d. per hundred in the 1350s, and they were still fetching 35d. per hundred in the early 1370s.[70] The cost of producing them had risen from around 3d. per hundred in the 1330s to 12d. per hundred in the 1370s, so the profits had escalated too.[71]

These examples of sharp then sustained price rises of essential produce under-line the point that after 1349 the cost of living for those dependent upon the market rose and remained high. By one estimate the living costs of a farm labourer jumped 25 per cent between the 1340s and 1350s.[72] Braid argues that for most of the 1350s labourers had to work as long as, if not longer than, in the 1340s to obtain a comparable standard of living.[73] Government taxation depressed living standards further because the lay subsidy of 1352–4 was levied upon a vastly reduced population with few remissions, so that the tax burden per head in the early 1350s was nearly three time higher than it had been in the 1340s.[74] In 1351 some royal officials noted that many workers were unable to pay the fines imposed upon them for breaches of the Statute of Labourers, a reflection of their increased outgoings rather of their recalcitrance.[75]

In addition, many of the new landholders after 1348–9 had been landless and impoverished before plague struck, meaning that they were initially lacking in both farming equipment and experience. Many widows and children were among those acquiring land, comprising, for example, 37 per cent of all entrants to customary holdings during the plague year at Oakington and Dry Drayton (Cambs.).[76] Contemporaries commented explicitly that the lack of animals and equipment, and a lack of cash reserves and agrarian expertise, hampered the capacity and willingness of some survivors to take on larger holdings.[77] Hence many new entrants into the land market struggled to undertake the necessary investment in their holdings, at the very time when vital equipment had become very expensive to acquire. Even before the plague a heavy plough might cost anything between 6s. and 11s., and at least 5s. per annum to maintain, which represented hefty sums for the formerly landless or land deficient.[78] After 1349 the shortages of iron and labour caused the cost of a new plough to double between 1347 and 1352, to the equivalent of the gross wages from forty days of labour.[79] The price of lath nails—essential for repairing and maintaining timber buildings—quadrupled between 1346 and 1352.[80] Even the cost of a humble wheelbarrow doubled across the same period.[81] Such challenges were exacerbated by a sharp contraction in the availability of credit in the 1350s in many village communities.[82] So, although many ordinary people had established a toehold on the property ladder, the extreme conditions they faced meant that their footing was initially precarious and that they were in no position to continue from exactly where their successors had left off.

The bountiful harvest of 1353 and the consequential dip in grain prices signalled the end of the immediate crisis. The corresponding fall in salt prices also implies an end to the very cold weather. Signs of a return to some form of normality are apparent across southern England.[83] The process of structural readjustment to the loss of population had begun, although it was to take many years to complete.

Government Reaction and Regulation

Traditional social ideology envisaged a fixed, hierarchical, and divinely ordained structure of three estates: the clergy, the seigneury, and the peasantry (with merchants and traders grouped loosely alongside the peasantry). The varied functions of the three estates (praying, fighting, labouring) were deemed to be inter-dependent and mutually obligated, irrespective of the manifest inequalities in worldly material wealth within and between them. Harmony between the estates and the preservation of the social order depended upon each member of each estate performing his or her prescribed social duties, and behaving in ways that served the common good ahead of personal interests. Morally good individual acts, no less than good law and good governance, were defined as any behaviour directed to promote the common profit. On occasions of national crisis, when order and justice were threatened, the government could intervene with emergency legislation to protect the common good and to ensure social stability.[84] After late 1349 the sudden and steep inflation of prices of essential foodstuffs and goods, the shortages of workers, and the rise in wages generated among contemporaries a crisis of confidence in the capacity of the economy to order itself. It also inflamed their fears and prejudices that retailers and workers were profiteering and abandoning moral restraint, thus posing a clear and persistent threat to the social order.[85]

The response of the government was immediate, energetic, ambitious, wide-ranging, and unprecedented. On 18 June 1349, with plague still raging across most of England, the King's Council issued the Ordinance of Labourers, which was soon refined and converted into a statute by parliament when it next met in February 1351. The main priority was to control the cost and supply of labour—or, as the ordinance put it, to address 'the lack especially of ploughmen and such labourers hereafter might come'—while the secondary objective was to counter high prices and possible profiteering amid the disruption.[86] Central government had not previously intervened in the labour market. The scale of its intervention in price legislation in the early 1350s was unsurpassed.

The preambles to both the Ordinance and the Statute of Labourers are explicit in claiming that the scarcity of labour and escalating wages were a direct consequence of personal greed and covetousness among the lower orders, reflecting the underlying belief that their behaviour and sudden economic gains were self-interested and therefore damaging to the common good.[87] The shortage of labour was presented as a moral problem, an affront to the natural and divine social order, irrespective of its underlying economic causes. The legislation was highly ambitious in its determination to turn back the clock to the mid-1340s and to reset the labour market as if plague had never happened.[88] It comprised four core elements: a wage clause, a compulsory service cause, a contract clause, and a new judicial function.[89] Wages were fixed at the rates prevailing in 1346-7 (the wage clause); any able body person without sufficient work or land was compelled to accept work from the first employer to offer (the compulsory service clause); hiring was to take place in public not private, annual contracts were preferred to day contracts, and contracts of employment were to be enforced and breaches punishable by a new range of sanctions (the contract clause); and the legislation was to be enforced by a new category of royal justice—the justices of labourers (later justices of the peace)—who were to hold sessions four times a year in each county.[90]

The implications of this novel and far-reaching legislation were considerable. For Palmer it represented nothing less than a new social policy 'directed to the problem of retaining traditional society in the wake of the demographic collapse' through 'the coercion of the people to stand to their duties'.[91] The ambition and resolve of the English government in this sphere certainly contrasts with the situation on the continent, where labour legislation was usually short-lived, ineffective, and largely confined to towns.[92] Palmer also claimed that the English legislation forced a fundamental shift from labour relations based on status (whether a person was free or unfree) to those based on contracts and economic status (whether in work or not), and therefore represented a watershed in the history of serfdom.[93] This is, however, unconvincing because it implies that a hired labour market scarcely existed before 1348-9, yet, as we have seen, this was not the case. The novelty lay in the government's attempts to control that market rather than in its creation of a new set of labour relations.

The government's legislative agenda in 1349-53 is as instructive for its omissions as for its provisions. It conspicuously avoided any attempt to intervene in the land market or to strengthen seigniorial controls over villeinage. There were just two references in the legislation to villeinage, a clause in the ordinance of 1349 confirming that lords had first call on the labour of their own servile tenants, although qualified by a statement that they were to retain no more than they needed, and a similar clause in the Statute of Labourers.[94] Crucially, there was no attempt whatsoever to compel lords to return the flown serfs of other lords who had settled within their jurisdiction. The government continued to ignore the weakened position of landlords in the customary land market, despite six parliamentary petitions between 1376 and 1402 complaining about villeins leaving their holdings.[95] These omissions reinforce the point that lords had long since lost effective control over their servile labour force, and that they were already used to competing for hired workers, irrespective of the latter's personal status. They also reflect that, under the common law, jurisdiction over villeinage was a matter for the individual lord not for the government.

The labour legislation favoured employers in its unstated redefinition of the existing theological concept of the 'just wage' (p. 36). In the thirteenth- and early fourteenth- century this concept encouraged employers not to exploit vulnerable and impoverished workers in an oversupplied labour market, by reminding them of their duties to the common good and to exercise moral restraint. After 1349, however, the ruling elite now believed that it was the workers—not their employers—who needed to be held to their duty to the wider society, and were now ready to legislate to enforce it. The labour laws codified a different interpretation of the just wage that sought to prevent labourers from profiteering. The new laws protected the employer and the existing social hierarchy through the provision of a maximum wage, rather than protecting the worker with a just subsistence wage. Likewise, the original meaning of 'fair and free bargaining' had been recast to mean bargains struck openly rather than privately, a change most likely to benefit employers in the post-1349 world. This legalized prejudice against workers was deeply inequitable, but contemporary political and moral thought was more concerned with social instability than economic equity, and it was contemptuous of the base self-interest of the lower orders.[96]

The Ordinance of Labourers brought about a sudden and profound change in the operation of the hired labour market. In the first half of 1348 wages had been market-determined in conditions highly favourable to employers, and contracts were private matters between two parties. By the second half of 1349 the government had pegged wages below the market rate in conditions highly favourable to employees; it punished workers who did not honour private contracts; and it had redefined a 'just wage' to defend the interests of employers in accordance with new social and political imperatives.[97] Surviving documentary evidence is fragmentary, but historians agree that during the 1350s the new legislation was enforced with considerable energy and success.[98] Powerful lords with a strong regional presence and enhanced legal powers—such as the Black Prince in Cheshire and the bishop of Durham in north-east England—were especially active.[99] In 1352 perhaps 15 per cent of the total adult population of Essex were fined under the statute, rising to 80 per cent in a few places, which represented a sizeable proportion of the labouring population.[100] Tax breaks incentivized the initial enforcement of the legislation, because fines charged for violations were used to offset the liability of county communities for the triennial lay subsidy of 1348–50, and again for the subsidy of 1352–4. From November 1349 to 1354 special royal commissioners were appointed for the express purpose of collecting the labour fines to offset the taxation, some of whom used highly aggressive tactics.[101] The success of such measures is reflected in the behaviour of wage rates, which did not rise in line with market forces: in the late 1350s reaping wages, for example, were just c.10 per cent above those for the early 1340s.[102]

The effectiveness of the legislation declined after the second plague epidemic in 1361.[103] The tax breaks were closed and the volume of cases coming before the justices fell.[104] National wage rates rose sharply: for example, those paid to reapers in 1361–5 were 33 per cent higher than they had been in 1341–5 (table 4.1).[105] Hatcher has shown how many employers in the 1360s and 1370s tolerated daily or weekly contracts rather than insisting that they be by the year, openly paid cash wages in excess of the unrealistic maxima specified by the labour laws, and generously supplemented the stipulated pay with side bonuses and inducements of food and drink. Consequently, the formal wage data compiled by historians seriously understate the real rise in wages and incomes.[106] Britnell's analysis of the economy of Colchester (Essex) concluded that 'the statute affected wage rates in the borough only indirectly, if at all'.[107] Many justices of the peace found contract-based disputes troublesome and often adjourned such cases.[108] By the late 1360s contemporaries began to voice and document concerns about the shortcomings of the legislation.[109] Musson and Ormrod describe the legislation as 'at best a temporary and modest success', while Bridbury observes that 'for all its panoply of enforcement, [it] was virtually a dead letter'.[110]

The reasons for the declining effectiveness of the legislation from the early 1360s were various. The first and most influential was the failure of the population to recover and the cogency of the underlying market forces. Another factor was the willingness of many employers to break the legislation in overt and covert ways in their desperation to secure workers at key times of the year, allied with the failure of the authorities to prosecute them under the statute for doing so (see pp. 214–15). The lack of a professional and standing royal bureaucracy exacerbated the difficulties of enforcement, and instead the government relied mainly upon small numbers of unpaid elected and appointed officials: it simply 'lacked the apparatus required to act as a police state'.[111] Furthermore, the main category of offenders—migrant, perambulating, and landless workers—were also the most difficult to regulate because of their mobility, their readiness to cross county boundaries (and therefore to move into a different legal jurisdiction), and their lack of possessions to seize for effective distraint.[112] Thus by the late 1360s the ruling elite was painfully aware that the labour laws had failed to turn the clock back to the conditions of the 1340s, which over the next two decades resulted in an evolving national debate on how else to grapple with the problem of labour.[113]

The other main focus of government legislation in the decade after 1349 was the high prices of essential goods and the possible profiteering behind them. The approach took three basic forms: prohibiting grain exports without royal licence; setting the prices of key goods below the market price; and capping the profits of retailers. All three interventions had been deployed before 1349, but the scale and persistence of the government's activity after the plague were unprecedented.[114] Prohibiting the export of grain without first obtaining a royal licence had been used very occasionally as a short-term tactic to protect domestic supplies, but became commonplace in the generation after 1349. Between 1350 and 1376 the Crown issued eighteen proclamations prohibiting the export of grain without a licence, five of them between 1350 and 1353.[115] Their main purpose was to protect the supply of grain to major cities, especially London and Bristol, and their frequency underlines the persistent shortages of marketable grain and the authorities' concern about the possible implications for social stability.[116]

The authorities attributed the sudden and sustained inflation of the prices of essential goods in the aftermath of the Black Death to collusion and restrictive practices among suppliers and retailers, which justified the intervention of the government to maintain the social and moral order for the common good.[117] This attitude is essential to understanding the nature and novelty of the government's actions after 1349, which sought to tackle the inflation by gripping the existing system and directing local policy more firmly from the centre through a mixture of new powers and greater use of existing ones. Between 1349 and 1363 six parliamentary statutes extended existing price-setting and profit-capping to a much wider range of commodities, and switched the routine supervision of local market officials from borough and manorial authorities to royal justices. For example, the Ordinance of Labourers in 1349 had extended the principle of the just price to potentially all victuals, and directed that all victuallers should enjoy 'a moderate profit and not excessive'.[118] Soon afterwards, additional statutes were passed to target on-going concerns about the persistently high prices of commodities such as iron (1354), herring and salt-fish (1357), and poultry (1363).[119] In 1351 the Statute of Forestallers gave the newly created justices of labourers power to oversee the sale of all victuals and merchandise in markets and fairs, and was backed by special commissions which were sent to individual counties with the power to summon jurors to name and arrest transgressors.[120] In the early 1350s royal commissions were dispatched on an unprecedented scale to twenty-one counties with the sole purpose of punishing those retailers selling bread and ale at extortionate prices and making excessive profits.[121] In 1351 the new office of justices of labourers became responsible as the standing royal authority for supervising the price- and profit-setting legislation in the shires, and in 1361 this post was combined with that of keeper of the peace into a single office (justice of the peace), and from 1368 sessions of the justices of the peace permanently acquired responsibility for these statutes.[122] In the early 1360s, for example, one-quarter of all cases handled by the Suffolk justices of the peace concerned excessive prices or profits.[123] Furthermore, throughout the 1350s and early 1360s urban elites in London and many other provincial towns actively supported the government initiatives by zealous implementation of the legislation in their own courts.[124]

The main target of this impressive enforcement wave in the 1350s and 1360s was ale, which had quickly become a staple element in the diet of ordinary people and whose consumption per head had increased rapidly.[125] The surge in ale consumption was not due to some national alcoholic binge after the catastrophe, but reflects its status as the primary source of fluid and carbohydrates. As the consumption of ale rose sharply so the structure of the brewing industry changed rapidly from a multitude of casual and episodic brewers producing poor quality ale, who had dominated the pre-plague market, to lower numbers of professional brewers producing higher-quality fare, many of whom were also serving tipples from their own ale houses.[126] These new consumption and behavioural habits are captured in an amendment in 1365 to the statutes of a charity in Chesterfield (Derbys.), which noted piously that 'where the ordinances state that the chaplain shall totally abstain from visiting taverns, this is [now] to be understood as meaning that he shall not visit them habitually'.[127] The changing complexion of the market for ale in the 1350s and 1360s epitomizes many of the economic and social order issues facing the government and local authorities in the aftermath of plague: fast-changing consumption preferences, stubbornly high prices, and concerns that suppliers were profiteering and undermining the common profit.[128]

After the early 1360s the government's general interest in price-setting and profit-capping diminished. Royal commissions and new legislation dried up, and the attentiveness of justices of the peace to economic offences waned. For example, whereas in the sessions in Suffolk in the early 1360s one-quarter of the business had involved excessive prices and profits, in those held in Norfolk in the 1370s only 7 per cent of the business related to the same.[129] Similarly, during the 1360s the zealous enforcement of the assizes of bread and ale in borough and local market courts diminished. The harsher punishments—such as the stocks and imprisonment—were seldom used, and the volume of presentments against the statute fell.[130] From the mid-1370s general concerns about prices and profiteering declined even further when grain prices fell then remained low.

Thus long before the Black Death the government, together with urban and manorial authorities, had been active in regulating prices and profits in local markets for bread, ale, and (occasionally) other essential foodstuffs. The novelty of the government's response in the immediate aftermath of the Black Death lay in the extension of this regulation to a much wider range of commodities, the extent and speed of the enforcement, and in the requirement that local officials be accountable to royal justices—rather than to the communities who had elected them—when implementing the legislation.[131] The enforcement campaign involved greater and more energetic use of established mechanisms (royal commissions, local courts), supplemented by a new jurisdiction (the sessions of the justices of the peace). While the scale of this intervention was impressive, it was also problematic, because the base concepts of 'just price' and 'reasonable profit' were intrinsically vague and left a great deal to local discretion. They were impossible to implement objectively, consistently, and fairly over both time and place, and so the government's new energy in this sphere generated considerable resentment among the lower orders, which was to fuel a mounting sense of injustice in the run-up to the Peasants' Revolt of 1381 (see pp. 206–17).

The government also introduced new sumptuary legislation in 1363, geared primarily to regulating the dress of the lower orders according to their social rank or degree. It also sought to discourage excessive eating and to promote the consumption of food according to social rank. For example, live-in servants and craft workers were to eat meat or fish just once a day, to consume food appropriate to their estate (such as milk, butter, and cheese), and to clothe themselves in cheaper blanket or woollen cloth.[132] The very fact that the government was seeking to address such issues in the early 1360s provides unequivocal confirmation of the rapid and sizeable improvements to the living standards of the lower orders over the previous decade.[133] It also reflects the concerns of the ruling elite about the continuing price inflation, the manifest assertiveness of the peasantry, and the underlying threat to the social order. Yet the most telling aspect of this legislation is that it was unenforceable, and was withdrawn as such in 1364.[134] No evidence of its implementation in royal courts during 1363–4 has survived. The scale of its failure implies that the legislators themselves must have recognized the huge challenges—if not the impossibility—of enforcing this statute, even as they drafted its provisions for parliament to consider. As such, while the sumptuary legislation of 1363 confirms the contemporary belief that government should intervene in social policy to protect the common good, it also exposes the ruling elite's anxieties about identity and status, and, especially, their uncertainty about how to determine rank in the immediate post-plague world.[135] The rank failure of the sumptuary legislation reveals graphically that the government was still fumbling for a definition of its role, at a time when it possessed limited means to enforce its will.

A Seigniorial Reaction?

The traditional interpretation of the third quarter of the fourteenth century proposes that landlords reinforced the coercive effects of the government's labour legislation by using their own legal powers under the common law of villeinage to force their peasants to work and to hold land on terms that took little heed of the radically changed circumstances.[136] This view is captured in Keen's statement that 'the initial reaction of landlords was therefore to assert their rights over their bond tenants with renewed vigour' and Bolton's assertion that lords forced villeins 'to work vacant holdings or pay fines for the privilege of not doing so'.[137] According to Muller, this 'seigniorial reaction' involved lords strengthening their hold on tenants and reasserting their authority by 'attempting to increase their threatened incomes, fining offenders against the labour legislation and trying to crack down on the increasing number of runaways from their manors in search of brighter futures'.[138] As a result, from the mid-1350s many of the revenues from land rents returned to their pre-plague level, which implied that lords were now extracting a larger slice from the shrinking cake of wealth.[139] This line of argument appears to receive support from evidence that by the late 1350s headline rental income on the estate of Canterbury Cathedral Priory had returned to within 4 per cent of its pre-plague level, while on Merton College's manor of Cuxham (Oxon) money rent from peasant holdings actually soared from 45s. per annum in the mid-1340s to over £7 in 1359.[140] Income from some manorial courts also increased, and this is attributed to the harsher exploitation of legal rights and tightening of servile dues.[141] Lords are supposed to have enserfed the free, increased labour services, and restricted the mobility of their own serfs, and bound them to special working conditions.[142] In short, between the 1350s and 1370s 'peasants were made to pay for the demographic, political and economic crisis' in this era of the so-called 'seigniorial reaction', resulting in exploitation 'in excess of even the bad old days of the thirteenth century'.[143]

While lords all over Europe reacted to the scarcity of tenants and workers with various forms and degrees of repression to protect their weakened economic position, in England the seigniorial reaction supposedly triggered peasant resistance then rebellion, which eventually forced lords to abandon repressive policies and to bargain away serfdom. Freedman and Bourin argue that 'assertions of seigniorial right [and] the re-imposition of villeinage obligations after the Black Death ... provoked tremendous resistance' of all kinds: direct, indirect, large, and small-scale.[144] Likewise, Britnell states that 'the effect of landlords using their powers to impose new burdens was to encourage serfs to question the justice of the system under which they lived'.[145] By the 1370s the resistance against this 'ruthless exploitation' and 'overt seigniorial oppression' had become 'widespread ... and all classes of the peasantry were involved', culminating in the Peasants' Revolt of 1381.[146] Thereafter, English lords conceded on villeinage, enabling factor markets in land and labour to expand rapidly.

Despite the widespread acceptance of this neat and powerful narrative of lordly reaction provoking peasant resistance, it is open to challenge on a number of grounds. First, even if we accept the narrative as an accurate reflection of lord–peasant relations in this period, the seigniorial reaction on the manor could only apply to the c.40 per cent of the population who were villeins, and not to the 60 per cent of the population who were either free or lived in towns. Second, there are powerful grounds for doubting the narrative itself.[147] Its evidentiary basis is questionable because on closer inspection the confident assertions about the harsh exploitation of villeins and the coercive tactics of landlords are based upon a handful of anecdotal, or exceptional, examples.[148] In fact, manor after manor yields no evidence of any reaction, especially on the numerically dominant gentry manors.[149] Finally, a seigniorial reaction is only credible if one accepts that on the eve of the Black Death social relations under common law villeinage were restrictive and exploitative, so that an already firm seigniorial grip upon villein land and labour could be immediately tightened. Yet, as we saw in Chapter 2, by the 1340s lords had largely lost control of both the villein land and labour markets, and their actual powers fell a long way short of legal theory, which makes a seigniorial reaction on any scale thereafter improbable.

If the concept of the 'seigniorial reaction' does not offer an accurate representation of social relations between the Black Death and the Peasants' Revolt, and if it no longer serves as a credible explanatory framework for the decline of serfdom and the growth of factor markets in England, then how should we characterize this period and how can we explain the 1381 revolt? The following section argues that a seigniorial reaction did not occur on any scale, and certainly not after the end of the 1350s, and summarizes the evidence for the rapid expansion of contractual relations within the labour and land markets. The build up to, and causes of, the Peasants' Revolt are considered in Chapter 5.

Villein landholdings and tenurial change

(i) Coercion to hold villein land

Doubts about the evidentiary basis for a seigniorial reaction are readily illustrated by a close consideration of changes within the villein land market. The confident assertions that villeins were now forced to hold land, and on terms favourable to lords, find little empirical support. Only the estates of the bishops of Durham and Winchester offer evidence of any systematic attempts to coerce villeins to hold land after 1349 on those of their manors suffering chronic shortages of tenants. In Durham such impositions were initially intended as a short-term arrangement until permanent and committed tenants could be found, but continuing difficulties in the early 1350s meant that the policy hardened.[150] Stoical or grudging acceptance of the impositions among the Durham peasantry soon turned to resentment and resistance, until in 1358 the bishop's administration abandoned the policy as unworkable and inflammatory.[151] In the early 1350s a few manors on the Winchester estate recorded some examples of compulsion: for example, in 1349 c.25 per cent of all new entrants into customary land at Downton (Wilts.), and c.75 per cent in 1354, had been compelled to take on their holdings.[152] The practice ceased soon afterwards, but, in any event, 'compulsion was not a device called upon a great deal' elsewhere on the estate.[153] Indeed, many of the bishop's customary tenants were refusing to hold land, and there was little that estate officials could do about it.[154] If these two exceptionally powerful lords could not sustain a policy of coercion in the servile land market for long, then it is highly unlikely that any others could do so.[155] Not surprisingly, then, evidence for compulsion across the rest of England is either exceptionally rare and largely confined to the 1350s, or non-existent.[156] For example, there is not a single example of coercion between 1349 and 1367 at Bishop's Ichington, Tachbrook and Gaydon (Warks.), despite thirteen virgates still lying abandoned as late as

1361.[157] In 1363 Eynsham abbey granted at leasehold a bond virgate in Little Rollright (Oxon) to one of its own hereditary serfs, unequivocal proof that the abbey did not compel its serfs to hold villein land on the old terms.[158]

So, in reality, during the 1350s coercion was highly atypical within the servile land market, and it was actually much more common for heirs to refuse to enter an unoccupied holding with impunity, for many villein holdings to remain unoccupied, and for prospective tenants to demand and receive concessions.[159] Similarly, estate officials usually went to considerable lengths to find and admit the rightful heirs, even when no heirs immediately presented themselves and even if the land lay unoccupied for many months, rather than compel another villein to occupy the empty land. In other words, landlords were respectful of the customary rights of heirs over a vacant holding. For example, officials on the estate of St Albans abbey dutifully observed the customary practice of making public proclamations in three successive courts for the rightful heirs to present themselves for an empty holding before seeking alternative (non-compelled) tenants.[160] Even when a non-heir finally entered an empty holding, the rights of heirs could still be protected. For example, in May 1351 Reynald Balston entered a croft in Norton (Herts.) on condition that if the rightful heir succeeded in any future claim to the land then Reynald would forfeit it, but would nonetheless receive compensation 'for all his outlay and expenses for the said croft by the consideration of the homage'.[161] The significance of this is worth underlining because it reveals clearly the nature of a major monastic landlord's response when faced with a shortage of tenants after the Black Death: the abbey forced hardly any serfs to hold customary land, but instead actively protected the rights of heirs to inherit even when the heirs were unknown and customary land remained vacant. The rules and customs of the peasant land market were overwhelmingly respected.

(ii) Non-commercial tenancies

The orthodox view is that rents and tenures changed little in the third quarter of the fourteenth century. For example, according to Bridbury, despite the pestilence survivors 'took the places of those who had perished in an orderly succession that left the world of markets and land tenure virtually undisturbed by the losses the community had sustained'.[162] While we would agree that the take-up of land was impressively full for the scale of the demographic losses, the world of land tenancies—and in particular customary tenancies—had been greatly disturbed. The harsh reality was that manorial lords had to treat existing tenants with care for fear of losing them and they had to compete with each other for new tenants. Even officials of a lord as powerful as the bishop of Winchester had no effective means of redress when 'experiencing difficulties with retaining unwilling tenants'.[163] Prior to the Black Death the vast majority of villein land was held on non-commercial 'service' tenure, which meant that custom and the law of villeinage determined how it might be transferred and that the rent package comprised an archaic mixture of payments in kind, nominal cash payments, labour services, and various customary incidents, such as tallage and millsuit.[164] No historian doubts that service tenure continued to be the dominant form of tenure on villein land for many years after the Black Death, but too little attention has been paid to the piecemeal, yet widespread, dilution of the terms of service tenure. This inattentiveness is understandable because the changes are not immediately apparent from a superficial reading of the sources, and, furthermore, we have not really looked for them due to the widespread acceptance of the narrative of the 'seigniorial reaction'.

From the 1350s the dilution of the rent package on villein holdings is readily illustrated, and it was a direct consequence of the increased competition between lords for tenants of customary land. The sums rendered as entry fines—the capital payments paid on accession to villein holdings—fell after the Black Death by anything from 20 per cent to 50 per cent on manors as far apart as Lincolnshire and Gloucestershire.[165] Entry fines even dwindled to the point of extinction on some manors across the Midland counties.[166] Similarly, in the 1350s and 1360s the sums paid as tallage—an annual tax on villein holdings in additional to the fixed annual rent—declined quickly and markedly on many manors, and on some it disappeared entirely.[167] For example, the amount of annual tallage collected from the estate of bishop of Worcester in 1364 was two-thirds lower than in 1302, and likewise recognition payments on the election of a new bishop were down 88 per cent.[168] The advent of plague resulted in the rapid and widespread abandonment of many demesne mills, so the enforcement of milling monopolies—the requirement that villeins and some free tenants mill their grain at lord's mill, and pay a higher toll for the privilege—was no longer possible, although a few lords insisted upon a commuted cash payment to compensate.[169] The incidence of millsuit declined sharply after 1349 even on manors where demesne mills continued to operate, scarcely surviving beyond the 1370s.[170] Merchet ceased to be an incident of tenure in many places, becoming a personal due from hereditary serfs, and so its incidence fell much further than the fall in population.[171] The dilution of the rent package is even evident in the west Midlands, a region usually associated with entrenched and conservative lordship.[172] As Fryde observed of the bishop of Lichfield's estates, 'the one enduring casualty of the epidemic of 1348–9 was the yield of various customary servile renders, which went into permanent decline'.[173]

The management of labour services in the generation after the Black Death was a source of lively debate among historians in the early twentieth century, but this debate seems trivial now that we now know labour services were one of the least common and least valuable components of the customary rent package.[174] In the mid-fourteenth century less than one-third of villein households owed labour services, accounting for just 8 per cent of demesne output.[175] The general shortages of labour after the arrival of plague must have tempted lords to insist upon the completion of all services, and a handful (mainly ecclesiastical) attempted unsuccessfully to impose new labour services in response to plague.[176] In general, however, any lordly desire to have their tenants perform all due works was countered by the reluctance of tenants, whose preference was undoubtedly to commute the works for a cash payment either on an ad hoc basis or through a negotiated agreement for a fixed term. Some lords detected this aversion and accepted reality by increasing commutations-at-will, although they probably also recognized the genuine difficulties their tenants faced in finding the requisite labour.[177] The chronicler Henry Knighton observed that landlords 'had to release and remit labour services, and either pardon rents completely or levy them on easier terms', or face abandoned holdings and tenant shortages.[178] In 1353–4 38 per cent of labour services at Sutton (Hants) were unavailable because the holdings had been converted to cash tenancies.[179] Around 40 per cent of week works and 80 per cent of harvest works had been used in the 1340s at Brandon (Suffolk), but from the 1350s week works were no longer used and just c.10 per cent of harvest works continued to be performed.[180] In general, the scale of commutations-at-will and permanent commutations of labour services increased in the 1350s, as landlords diluted the old service rent package in an attempt to attract or retain customary tenants.[181] Manors on the Berkeley estate (Gloucs.) ceased using any labour services after 1363.[182] By the mid-1370s, it is likely that less than 20 per cent of all villein households in England owed labour services, and that the latter now accounted for less than 5 per cent of demesne output.

In the 1350s the costs to tenants of traditional villein tenure increased in just two areas: fines for the wastage of villein holdings and for not having to perform a major manorial office, such as reeve and harvest reeve, became more frequent and more onerous. The loss of half of the population combined with the engrossment of some holdings meant that many hovels, houses, and agricultural buildings used in the 1340s were now surplus to requirements. While it made sense for tenants to remove these, or simply to allow them to fall down, their decay represented a degradation of a seigniorial asset and so those responsible were liable to be fined. Warnings, presentments, and amercements for wastage increased after 1348–9, and could involve sizeable fines of a few shillings in the 1350s and 1360s either to remove single buildings or for having removed them without permission: although the level of fines quickly fell thereafter, presentments and fines for wastage on customary tenements remained an enduring feature of late-medieval court rolls.[183] Very occasionally, a failure to pay a fine led to eviction from the holding after suitable warnings.[184] Similarly, customary tenants were required on many manors to serve in a manorial office for a year, usually a compulsory 'election' on rotation, and after 1349 tenants paid a fine more frequently to be exonerated. This was costly on some estates, set at around 30s. for the role of reeve, but tolerated without charge on others.[185]

A parallel development to the dilution and disappearance of servile incidents on villein service tenures was the use of more explicit contractual terms and more dignified language in conveyances in order to make them appear less demeaning and more attractive to potential tenants. Historians have tended to believe that such changes were rare before the fifteenth century, but a recent study has revealed that in the 1350s and 1360s phrases such as 'in bondage' and 'in villeinage' were being dropped from conveyances of service tenancies on some East Anglian manors, and replaced with phrases such as 'held at will' or 'by the rod'.[186] Similar developments are also evident in various parts of the east Midlands.[187] For example, in 1383 a court at Willington (Beds.) noted that former tenants 'in bondage' now held by copyholds for lives.[188] Furthermore, the practice of issuing an incoming tenant of villein land with a copy of the court roll entry recording their admission became more common, another move designed to improve the dignity of servile land and also to tighten the terms of the tenure.[189] The grant of such copies emulated the charters issued with freehold tenure, and the written terms provided additional proof and protection against possible arbitrary seigniorial behaviour. This was, of course, the genesis of copy-hold tenure.

One brief case study illustrates the argument that concessions on service tenures occurred soon after plague struck and were widespread. On the cellarer of the abbey of St Albans' manor of Norton (Herts.) grants of villein land after 1349 continued to be dominated by service tenures, with no compulsions to hold villein land.[190] The language of conveyances did not change and very few abandoned holdings lay untenanted for any length of time, so, at first glance, little had changed. Closer analysis of the court rolls, however, reveals considerable dilution of the rent package. The mean level of entry fines charged for tenants entering the standard customary half-virgate fell by two-thirds between 1330–48 and 1350–69.[191] Individuals requiring specific help or encouragement were enticed by the waiving of entry fines or the offer of special deals. For example, when in 1364 John Jecob succeeded his deceased father into a half-virgate, both the heriot of one horse was returned to him and the entry fine waived: a spate of other waived entry fines are also recorded in the mid-1360s.[192] No annual tallage was payable, and after 1350 recognition payments (due on the election of a new abbot) also ceased.[193] The frequency of merchet collapsed from thirty-one cases in the 1340s to just six in the 1350s, and the average fine for women fell by over half (figs. 3.2 and 3.3): merchet was now a levy on hereditary serfs rather than on all villein landholders. Between the 1340s and 1350s fines for millsuit violations fell by nearly two-thirds (fig. 3.2), and the mean fine fell. The last amercement for evading millsuit was paid in 1355, and in 1372 the court noted that no tenants were grinding at the lord's mill and a general penalty of 20s. was threatened for any subsequent failure to grind there.[194] Nothing followed. An absence of manorial accounts prevents any understanding of the management of labour services, although they continued to be liable and their non-performance was unusual. Overall, then, the example of Norton illustrates how a closer analysis of court rolls

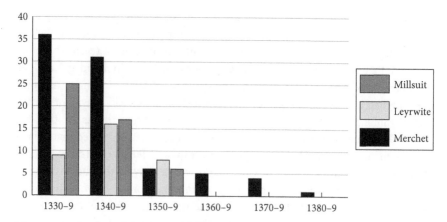

Figure 3.2 Number of fines for merchet, leyrwite, and millsuit at Norton (Herts.) 1330 to 1389, by decade
Source: Foden 2013

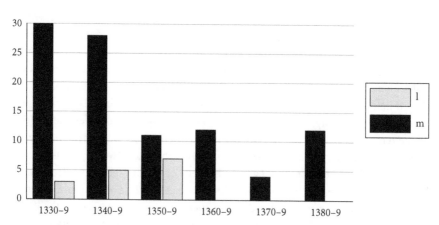

Figure 3.3 Size of payments (d.) for female merchet, and leyrwite at Norton (Herts.) 1330 to 1389
Source: Foden 2013

reveals rapid and significant changes to the rent package of villein service tenancies in the generation after the arrival of plague.

(iii) Conversion of villein land to monetarized tenures

The dilution of the rent package on non-commercial tenures after 1349 was one major strand of lordly concessions on the terms on which villein land was held. The other was the conversion of the dominant, non-commercial service tenancies to cash-based tenancies set at a commercial rate. While this development is well documented in existing studies, few historians have commented explicitly upon the speed and scale of its spread.[195] The trigger for these conversions was the abandonment of land in the hands of the lord following the death of the tenant and the failure of any heir to claim it. Under these circumstances, the lord could grant the land to a new, unrelated, tenant, but could also opt to change the terms of the tenancy. Vacant peasant—especially villein—land was increasingly granted for a straight cash rent set at a commercial level at the point of the initial grant, usually with an entry fine and suit of court (and often a heriot for villein land). The grant was heritable for a term of stipulated lives. The cash rent remained fixed and immutable thereafter, until the end of the life tenancy or unless the land happened to revert to the lord without an heir. Hence the fixed rent was closer to the market value of land than on the old non-commercial tenancy, although it was not yet a sensitive and changeable commercial rent because it was not varied in response to fluctuations in the actual market value. These heritable cash tenures were occasionally called 'fee-farms'. For example, in 1353 the lord of Bredfield (Suffolk) granted half an acre of villein land—previously held on a service tenancy but abandoned since 1349 without a known heir—to William le Smith of Bredfield as a 'feoda firma ... to hold to William and his heirs at the will of the lord paying 18d. annually'.[196] The phrase 'fee farm' had emerged during the thirteenth century to describe a heritable or perpetual free tenure paying a rent, where the fee to the land was effectively being farmed in perpetuity for 'a substantial, that is more than nominal, rent'.[197] The use of free fee farms had declined after the 1290s, so the adoption of the term to describe heritable customary land granted for a fixed cash rent was unequivocally an attempt to improve the dignity of the tenure.[198]

These cash-based heritable and life tenures spread rapidly after 1349 in many areas. Part of the difficulty in assessing the pace and extent is that the process was piecemeal and gradual, and hard to trace and pin down in the extant sources. Wholesale conversions of all villein land on a manor to a cash rent on a single date are rare, and the handful of documented examples date from the early fifteenth century.[199] A careful re-reading of the published studies, however, provides unequivocal evidence that in the 1350s the rate of conversions of villein land to money rents increased sharply. For example, villein holdings were extensively converted to cash rents on the Staffordshire and Derbyshire properties of the bishopric of Coventry and Lichfield.[200] Monastic landlords with estates in the east Midlands and East Anglia converted some holdings to cash in the 1350s in order to encourage new tenants to take on customary holdings.[201] Landlords who resisted pressure to convert empty servile holdings from service to cash tenancies risked vacancies well into the 1350s, and a requirement to perform labour services was often cited as the reason for a failure to find tenants for vacant holdings on the old terms on the Winchester estate.[202] A switch to a straight cash rent was invariably required to get such holdings back into occupation and tilth.[203]

The second outbreak of plague in 1361 resulted in another spate of relinquished holdings in many places and triggered another surge of conversions to cash tenancies.[204] In 1361–2 the lord converted five empty virgates to cash rents in Bishop's Tachbrook, Bishop's Itchington and Chadshunt (Warks.), four on hereditary grants at a set rate of 15s. per annum for a messuage and a virgate, while the fifth was a lease for six years at the reduced rate of 8s. for a messuage and virgate: clearly, a hereditary cash tenancy carried a rental premium above leasehold.[205] All five were grants of untenanted land direct from the lord on new terms, and two of the tenants were hereditary serfs of the manor, indicating that the lord was unable or unwilling to compel his own serfs to hold on the traditional tenure. At Englefield (Berks.) in the 1370s the old villein tenure was virtually 'obsolete' because customary land had been converted to monetary tenures of various sorts.[206] By the 1390s conversions of service tenancies to monetarized tenures are well documented throughout England (see pp. 300–3).[207]

The second form of conversion from the old non-commercial tenancies was leasehold, which involved the grant of freehold or customary land to a named tenant in a contractual relationship for a limited and specified term at a fixed annual rent, the latter reflecting the market not customary value of the land.[208] There has been a widespread assumption that conversions of customary land to leaseholds were unusual before the fifteenth century. This is understandable because leases were certainly uncommon on some estates before then and, even where they had already become established, historians have made little attempt to measure the scale of their spread.[209] For example, neither of the indexes to the two medieval volumes of *The Agrarian History of England and Wales* contains a separate entry for leases of customary land.[210] This reflects a wider inattentiveness to the evolution of leasehold among agrarian histories of north-west Europe, despite its importance.[211] While the short-term lease was relatively uncommon in England before the Black Death, its use expanded rapidly thereafter on demesne and customary land.[212] Examples of the expansion of leases on customary land in the 1350s and 1360s abound.[213] While the shift to leasing was most pronounced in east and south-east England, underlining the association of the lease with higher levels of urbanization and commercialization, it is also readily identifiable—albeit often on a smaller scale—in many other areas of the country. For example, in Gloucestershire 'the plague was swiftly followed by comprehensive leasing' of customary land on the Berkeley estate, and also occurred on manors held by major ecclesiastical lords in the west Midlands.[214] In the early 1350s conversions of untenanted customary land to short-term leases were common on Wakefield (Yorks.) manor.[215] It was also common enough in the Home Counties;[216] the east Midlands;[217] Lincolnshire;[218] the southern counties and south Midlands;[219] Somerset;[220] Cornwall;[221] and the North.[222]

An institutional dimension to the spread of leases is also discernible because certain landlords utilized them more than others.[223] For example, within the estate of Westminster abbey the abbatial manors deployed leases more than did the conventual manors: similarly, whilst Durham priory actively deployed leases after *c.*1390, the bishop did not.[224] But the main institutional contrast is between the greater and the lesser landlords because contractual tenures were more common on the estates of the latter.[225] Gentry lords were relatively impoverished and had to manage their estates in decidedly different ways: as Fryde observes, lesser lords occupied 'a very different world' to the magnates and prelates.[226] Historians have not been able to pay much attention to that world because few sources have survived from it, although most gentry manors were dominated by freeholdings yielding immutable low returns, which raised the pressure to squeeze cash from the demesne land and to maximize cash income from the small areas of customary land.[227] Villeinage featured less prominently on gentry estates than ecclesiastical and aristocratic estates, and gentry lords lived among their tenants, knowing most of them personally.

The extent to which lesser landlords, and those holding the smaller manors, switched to leasing quickly and extensively can be illustrated by the evidence from a small sample of eleven such manors in East Anglia, for which a reasonable number of court rolls and/or accounts survive.[228] Before the arrival of plague hereditary non-commercial tenures had dominated every one of these eleven manors, but within a generation leases had become the main tenurial form of customary land on seven of them and a sizeable minority on a further two.[229] In successive courts in late 1349 and early 1350 officials granted nineteen untenanted customary holdings on short-term leases at Merton (Norfolk).[230] In 1352–3 three-quarters of customary holdings at Loudham (Suffolk) were either held on leases or derelict, and over 90 per cent in the 1380s.[231] In 1374–5 leases dominated customary tenures, and labour services had disappeared, at Cretingham (Suffolk).[232] In the 1380s only *c.*10 per cent of all customary holdings at Akenham (Suffolk) remained on traditional villein tenure, and the majority were leased instead in fifty-one separate parcels usually for one year or for a short term of years.[233] The disappearance of labour services from Horham (Suffolk) by 1352–3, and evidence for a sharp increase in the amount of customary land at lease in the 1360s, is strongly indicative of a major swing away from service tenure.[234] In 1373–4 around half of the customary land at Walsham High Hall (Suffolk), and in 1376–7 around three quarters of that at Laxfield (Suffolk), were leased.[235] There were no leases of peasant land at Easton Bavents (Suffolk) in 1343–4, but in 1356–7 nearly half of rents of assize were decayed, over half of customary labour services were uncollectable because the land was in the lord's hands, and leases of land now comprised 52s. 6d.[236] By the mid-1370s over half of the customary land remained on short-term leases for years, and by the mid-1390s nearly all had been converted.[237] On the remaining four manors, heritable service tenancies were still the main form on villein land to varying degrees.[238]

Hence gentry estates were more likely than aristocratic to switch to leasing after 1349 because they tended to be run on tighter financial margins and were more likely to struggle with cash flow in the face of rising costs. Converting customary tenures to leases at market rates (and, indeed, freeholds that reverted into their hands following the failure of heirs) would have provided a more reliable and predictable source of income, and so was likely to have been an attractive option. As small gentry manors were numerically much more commonplace than large aristocratic manors, we might suppose that the swing to leasing of villein land was much more common than the extant sources indicate.

The third and final form of monetarized tenancy was tenure-at-will, which was less permanent and secure than a lease. It was used extensively at Birdbrook (Essex) in 1349–50 'to ride out the storm...a necessary evil while a new tenant was found', and in the same year it was used to find temporary tenants for 11 per cent of all customary land at Brandon (Suffolk) (see fig. 6.1).[239] It served as an emergency mechanism to deal with the immediate post-plague distress, which usually resulted in low rental values. Occasionally, it was renewed year after year for much longer periods, acquiring a *de facto* permanency in the process.[240] Some East Anglian manors of the earls of Norfolk were still using tenancies-at-will in the early 1390s to tenant a sizeable minority of customary holdings, which were routinely renewed year after year to the same tenant.[241] A similar trend is apparent on the estate of the bishop of Winchester, where some tenancies-at-will granted in the 1350s endured into the 1380s: most of this land was being used for rough pasture, although small areas would also have been sown with grain.[242] On some manors it comprised one element in a mix of tenures, reflecting the preparedness of landlords to respond flexibly to whatever expedient was needed to attract and retain tenants. In the 1370s customary virgates at Birdbrook (Essex) were held on a mixture of hereditable service tenancies, life cash tenancies, leases for years, and tenancies-at-will, and likewise customary land at Thaxted (Essex) was held on a mixture of leases for life and tenancies-at-will.[243]

Calculating the exact proportion of villein land held on different tenures on a given date and manor is often impossible because the calculation is dependent not only upon the survival of manorial accounts but also upon extant accounts containing sufficient detail. Where such accounts do survive, however, they can reveal high rates of conversion to contractual tenures soon after the Black Death. At Fornham All Saints (Suffolk) in 1347–8 93 per cent of customary land was held on a non-commercial tenancy, yet by 1360–1 only 28 per cent was on such tenure and 44 per cent was leased (the remainder was vacant, see fig. 3.4), and in 1376–7 47 per cent was still leased. At Chevington (Suffolk) 96 per cent of customary land was on service tenancy in 1347–8, but in 1365–6 31 per cent was leased, 8 per cent was vacant and the remainder were still on service tenancies (see fig. 3.5), yet in 1380 65 per cent was leased.[244] Leases spread quickly on three Gloucestershire manors held by the Berkeley family. At Ham the area of customary land held on hereditary villein tenure fell from 1,230 acres in 1348 to 255 acres in 1363, while the remaining 975 areas was mainly leased and the rest untenanted: at Hinton in 1356 23 per cent of all customary land had been converted to leases, rising to

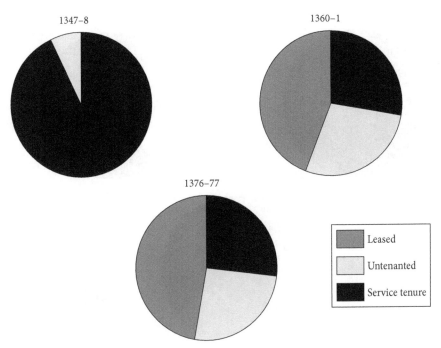

Figure 3.4 Tenurial status of the main customary holdings at Fornham All Saints (Suffolk), 1347 to 1377 (%)
Source: SROB E3/15.7/2.3; E3/15.6/2.28, 2.34b

41 per cent in the early 1370s.[245] At Alkington in 1345–6 all customary land was on service tenancy, but just 14 per cent in 1357–8 when the remainder were on leasehold (see fig. 3.6), and in 1366 91 per cent was leased.[246] Conversions of customary land to leasehold on other manors on the Berkeley estate did not occur to anything like the same extent, however, which underlines the fact that highly localized local market conditions drove tenurial change rather than a uniform estate policy.[247]

Estate-wide surveys can provide some rough and ready indication of the scale of conversions to monetary tenures across whole estates. These reinforce the argument that cash tenures had established a strong foothold within a generation of the plague across all parts of England. A valor of Lord Hastings' estate in 1391 included information about the structure of rental income from peasant holdings on forty-four manors distributed from Shropshire to Kent, whether rents of assize (service tenancies), or cash rents and/or leases. Non-commercial tenures continued to dominate on 47 per cent of the manors, commercial cash tenures characterized some peasant land on 42 per cent of the manors, and commercial cash tenures predominated on 11 per cent (see fig. 3.7).[248] Similarly, between 1360 and 1366 39 per cent of the villein land on four Oxfordshire manors of Eynsham

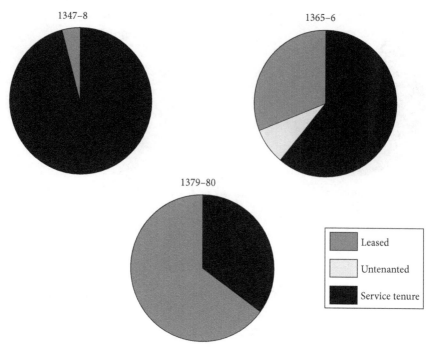

Figure 3.5 Tenurial status of the main customary holdings at Chevington (Suffolk), 1347 to 1380 (%)
Source: SROB E3/15.3/2.7, 2.10d, 2.11

abbey was held on service tenancies, 59 per cent on cash tenancies of various sorts, and 7 per cent leased (see fig. 3.8). The examples of Eynsham abbey and lord Hastings underline the point that even powerful, conservative landlords were incapable of enforcing a single tenurial policy across the whole of their estate, but were instead obliged to adapt to local conditions in order to keep it tenanted. These two examples underline that cash tenancies were common enough outside the commercialized heartlands of south-east England and East Anglia in the generation after the Black Death.

(iv) Explaining tenurial change
Soon after the Black Death conversions of villein land to cash and leasehold tenancies made major inroads into the redoubt of traditional service tenure. We might estimate that in the 1340s around 90 per cent of all customary land had been held on service tenancies, but by the 1370s that figure had reduced to just over one-half. It was to fall further by the end of the century (see p. 301). What, then, explains this dramatic tenurial change?

After the Black Death three major changes created an institutional environment greatly conducive to the spread of monetarized tenures. The first was the

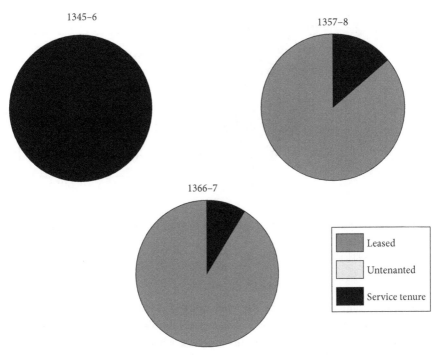

Figure 3.6 Tenurial status of customary land at Alkington (Gloucs.), 1345 to 1367 (%)

Source: Berkeley Castle Muniments A/1/3

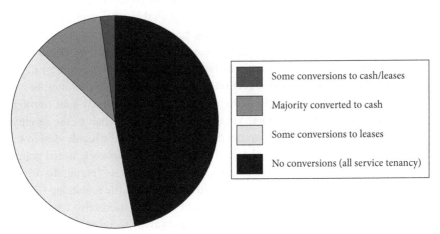

Figure 3.7 Percentage of manors with some conversions to leases or contractual rents on the Hastings estate, 1391–2

Source: TNA DL43/14/3

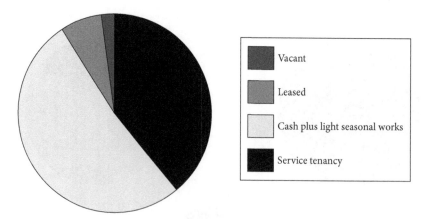

Figure 3.8 Tenurial status of customary land on four manors of Eynsham abbey (Oxon), 1360 to 1366 (%)
Source: Salter 1908, pp. 7–11, 61–4, 128–33

widespread failure of heirs in the epidemics of 1348–9 and 1361–2, and the tendency of land to remain for a while in the lord's hands, which provided a lord with the option to vary the terms of tenure when granting the land to a new tenant. A lord could not alter the terms unilaterally if an heir claimed a landed inheritance, so during periods when heirs were in ready supply—such as the conditions of acute land scarcity in the decades before the Black Death—lords had few opportunities to convert customary land to commercial tenures. After 1349 frequent episodes of high mortality and general shortages of heirs caused more land to revert to the lord, and a rising proportion of grants from the lord correlates strongly with an increase in monetarized tenures. For example, in 1330–9 thirty-four transfers of villein land are recorded in the court rolls of Bredfield (Suffolk), all of them direct transfers from one peasant to another and none directly from the lord: thirty-two (94 per cent) of these thirty-four transfers were on hereditary service tenure. Yet in 1350–9 nearly one-half of the seventy-four villein land transfers were grants directly from the lord's hands, due to the abandonment of land following the deaths of tenants. Of these seigniorial grants, seven (21 per cent) were granted on the old service tenancies (mainly to distant heirs who eventually came to claim their inheritance) while the remaining twenty-eight (79 per cent) were granted on a variety of cash and fixed-term tenures.[249]

The second major contextual change was the dramatic increase in the liquidity of the economy during the 1350s and 1360s, as the amount of coin in circulation in both real and per capita terms rose markedly (see below, pp. 157–8). Increased flows of coin facilitated a sudden swing to cash tenures. Finally, the widespread use of fixed-term leases was dependent upon the pre-existence of a system of secure property rights, including a clear and reliable system of registration ensuring clarity about its terms, because otherwise the lessor risked losing control of the land.[250] In this way, lords were assured that a temporary lease would not compromise their title to villein land, while lessees could be sure that their contractual rights within the terms of the lease would be respected.[251]

Contractual tenancies spread quickly after the Black Death because tenants preferred them. We know this for two reasons. First, the greater landlords' preference for traditional hereditary service tenancy is evident in a number of ways. They instructed their estate officials to seek out tenants willing to hold land on the old terms, and some offered special deals to entice such tenants.[252] Their prejudice against leases is sometimes revealed by the reasons given for conversions, such as refusals to hold on the old terms or shortages of tenants, and also by the description applied to them in the works' section of manorial *compoti*: abandoned 'in the lord's hands', even though in reality they were tenanted on new terms.[253] Second, servile holdings lying abandoned for a number of years invariably found a tenant once they were offered on a contractual tenancy, although even then the lord might flag an intention to return the land to traditional service tenure at the end of the lease.[254] Occasionally a tenant even relinquished land held on a service tenancy in order to re-enter the same holding immediately on a cash or contractual tenure.[255]

It is therefore indisputable that after 1349 tenants tended to prefer cash and contractual tenures.[256] The reasons for this are not difficult to surmise. The language used in grants of monetarized tenures was more dignified than in the old villein tenures, and the cash rent, and the absence of various servile incidents, more closely resembled the rent package of free tenure. They carried no (or hardly any) liability for the heaviest and most demeaning labour services.[257] The opportunity cost of labour services to peasant farmers had been much lower in the 1340s, when labour was abundant and wage labour brought modest rewards, but it rose sharply after the ravages of plague because it deflected family labour from their own holdings and from lucrative wage labouring. These changes removed a good deal of the stigma attached to servile land. A rental of 1378 described leases of customary land at Ham (Gloucs.) as 'villein land held freely by copy'.[258] Hence the aversion of many tenants to the traditional service tenure also reflects an aversion to the residual trappings of villeinage.[259]

The main difference between hereditary (fee farms) or life cash tenures and leasehold tenures was that the former possessed seisin of the land and therefore customary rights to inherit and alienate, whereas the leaseholder did not. The notion that tenants preferred customary land on insecure leasehold rather than on secure tenure seems counterintuitive, and, indeed, historians have habitually portrayed leases as inimical to peasant interests due to their vulnerability to punishing rent hikes and to eviction at the end of the term.[260] These assumptions are valid in periods of chronic land shortages, but are less applicable in a buyer's or an uncertain market. Peasants seeking cheap and flexible access to the land market, or facing uncertain circumstances (whether personal or commercial) and therefore seeking ease of egress, would find short-term leases well suited to their needs. Leases did not require an initial capital payment (such as a hefty entry fine or a purchase sum), and involved no loss of capital through the render of a heriot at the expiry of the term, and so offered an easier exit if the venture did not work out. Consequently, they were especially attractive to new entrants in the rural land market, and to inexperienced smallholders seeking to expand the size of their holdings cautiously during a period of volatile and uncertain agrarian conditions. Leases offered flexibility to expand and contract holdings as needed, for a temporary foray into the property market, to acquire an adjacent parcel of land to engross an existing holding, or for a newcomer to rent while deciding whether to settle permanently.[261]

Who were these new lessees and tenants? Land grants seldom contain their biographical details, although it is sometimes possible to ascertain their background from tangential information in manorial court rolls. Some were existing landholders seeking to augment their holdings, while others were incomers in search of new opportunities a niche within the village community.[262] After 1348–9 the proportion of outsiders holding customary land rose sharply. In the period 1320–49 41 per cent of those admitted to customary holdings on the estate of the bishop of Winchester were outsiders, yet this rose to 61 per cent in the period 1350–79 due to a combination of a failure of heirs with refusals to hold inherited land.[263] Newcomers were more likely to negotiate a cash or contractual rent, and this correlation is sometimes stated explicitly. In 1351 Richard le Clerk of Warwick was granted an abandoned tenement in Ashorne (Warks.) for a straight money rent of 10s. per annum, and outsiders ('adventiti') entered some vacant servile holdings on cash rents at Haywood and Brewood (Staffs.).[264] In May 1349 a family from Dorchester (Dorset) obtained a cottage and curtilage in nearby Fordington for the term of three lives, paying a set cash rent of 6d. per annum instead of the usual services and customs, and in 1353 an empty holding in Codicote (Herts.) was granted for a cash rent to a 'freeman and incomer'.[265] Clearly, cash and contractual tenancies were important in enticing outsiders to become tenants of customary land, as well as for retaining some existing tenants or persuading some existing residents to hold land locally rather than migrate elsewhere.[266] Even if the outsiders were hereditary serfs of other lords, they were simply tenants of customary land on their new manor because a flown serf whose status had not been proven was routinely treated as a freeman.[267] They may even have posed as freemen.

Before the Black Death some freemen held villein land, but in the immediate aftermath they flooded into the customary land market.[268] Their presence is not easy to detect, however, because land transfers seldom recorded the personal status of a tenant, and so this phenomenon is easy to overlook. Fortunately, fealty lists complied on the accession of a new lord of the manor are sometimes explicit about the personal status of tenants, and reveal the extent to which freemen had infiltrated the customary land market. In the early 1350s freemen had occupied eleven of the twenty-seven (41 per cent) customary bovates at Sawley (Derbys.), and four of the nine (44 per cent) customary virgates at Durrington (Wilts.) by 1359.[269] At Walsham (Suffolk) a detailed fealty list of 1361 lists twenty-seven 'freemen holding villein land', four 'free tenants of villein land', and twenty-seven 'native' tenants of villein land, which meant that a striking 53 per cent of customary tenants were freemen.[270] At Wimbotsham (Norfolk) in February 1353 11 per cent of all tenants performing fealty were freemen, 23 per cent were serfs 'making fealty to the lord with their bodies and chattels', and 58 per cent were 'freemen holding servile land'.[271] In February 1329 forty-five tenants of Bredfield were described simply as either 'nativi' or 'others', yet in 1354 45 per cent of the thirty-eight tenants performing fealty were 'freemen holding by the rod', and in 1361 41 per cent of the fifty-four tenants were 'freemen holding native land': others were described as serfs by blood.[272] At Iken (Suffolk) in 1363 a fealty list identified thirteen serfs by blood, ten free tenants and twelve tenants of native land, so the latter were either freemen or the flown serfs of other lords.[273]

These examples prove that on some manors freemen comprised a significant proportion of customary tenants in the 1350s and 1360s, and the changing format of the record of fealty implies that the proportion had risen markedly after the Black Death. Why were freemen so willing to occupy customary land when land in general and free tenure in particular was now readily available? The answer lies in the chronic impoverishment of the majority of freeholders on the eve of the Black Death, who occupied smallholdings due to the splintering effects of sustained population growth, partible inheritance, and an active land market.[274] Impoverished survivors of the plague were eager to obtain more land, but they lacked the working capital to purchase additional freeholds. Now, however, they were able to acquire abandoned customary land without any capital payment through a leasehold or through a hereditary cash tenure if the lord was willing to waive the entry fine. The quickest and cheapest way for poor freeholders to build up their meagre landholdings was to obtain customary land on cash or contractual tenancies. Freemen featured prominently among lessees of villein land on the Berkeley estate in Gloucestershire, and their influx among customary tenants at Bredfield corresponded with a major shift to contractual tenancies.[275]

Thus tenants from various backgrounds—existing landholders, landless residents, sub-tenants, hereditary serfs, incomers of unknown status, freemen—were all beneficiaries of the sudden expansion of cash and contractual tenancies on servile land. Yet it would be wrong to equate benefits for the peasantry with major losses for the seigneury. Replacing the sub-economic rent package of service tenancies with commercial cash tenures boosted headline rental income, and explains why rents recovered to pre-plague levels or even higher rents rose after 1348–9 on some manors: not because of coercion or surplus extraction but because of a change in rental structure.[276] For example, in 1347–8 99s. ½d. of rental income was received from peasant land at Chevington (Suffolk) compared with 194s. 3½d. in 1364–5: not because of seigniorial exploitation but because eight of the twenty-three main customary holdings had been converted to commercial leaseholds and they alone generated 108s. per annum.[277] The hikes in headline rental income accruing from conversions to leasehold and cash tenures disguise the costs to the lord incurred through losses of labour services, and of the incidental income from entry fines, merchet, and heriot, on the old service tenancy. Yet at least the leasehold income was predictable during a period of uncertainty, and it was also much better for cash flow. Furthermore, conversions to leases helped to fill manorial rent rolls at a time of collapsing land values, widespread vacancies, and unparalleled uncertainty. Thus the spread of leases and cash rents at the expense of service tenancies after 1348–9 brought finely weighed advantages and disadvantages for lords, and clear advantages for peasants. Leases promoted individualism among peasants and partnership with the lord on the manors of Durham priory, because the main lessees of customary and demesne land emerged as the leading figures within their communities, serving as manorial officials and receiving backing from the priory in disputes with other peasants.[278] Larson regards the spread of leases here as 'a fine example of compromise driven by mutual interests'.[279]

The spread of commercial cash tenures in general and of leaseholds in particular was an essential step towards the modernization of farming because they forced producers to respond directly to market forces and to maximize profits (see Chapter 6).[280] Similarly, the influx of freemen and incomers of indeterminate personal status into the villein land market in 1350s and 1360s severed finally and decisively the close association between tenure and status under villeinage, because many tenants of servile land were no longer the lord's hereditary serfs (*nativi domini de sanguine*, see below). Finally, the higher status of freemen and incomers, and their aversion to tenures characterized by villeinage, greatly reduced the likelihood of any future reversion to the old service tenancies: indeed, monetarized tenures increasingly attracted gentry, Londoners, and townsfolk into the customary land market.[281]

Personal servility

According to the narrative of the 'seigniorial reaction', manorial lords reinforced the action of the government's labour legislation by deploying all their legal powers under common law villeinage either to restrict or to profit from the movement of servile labour, and to attempt to enserf some of the free population. Thus, between 1350 and the Peasants' Revolt in 1381, it is held that some servile migrants were seized physically and forced to return to their home manor either to hold land or to work. Meanwhile, others were required to pay 'impossible fees' to license their absence from the manor (known as chevage payments), and both practices acted as a 'sharp brake' upon servile mobility.[282] Certainly, manorial documents suddenly displayed a new urgency in labelling and listing hereditary serfs, as seigniorial officials targeted them for servile dues and bound them into new forms of personal service contracts. Finally, the frequency of disputes over personal status increased greatly as lords attempted to enserf individuals whose status was uncertain.[283]

Soon after the Black Death two little-known government statutes enhanced the powers available to landlords to retrieve any serfs who had left the manor without permission. A landlord seeking to prove the status of a flown serf in a court of common law had to obtain a writ of neifty ('*de native habendo*'), but prior to the plague many defendants countered by obtaining a writ *de libertate probanda*, which enabled them to remain at liberty until the case was heard: in effect, a delaying tactic. In 1351, however, new legislation enabled lords to seize serfs following their acquisition of the writ of neifty, effectively nullifying the power of *de libertate probanda*.[284] Second, in 1361 a statute required borough authorities to return absconded serfs to any lord who requested their support. Any refusal to cooperate on the part of civic officials was reportable to the royal justices and subject to a £10 fine to the Crown and £5 damages to the lord.[285] Palmer regards such legislation as offering 'a powerful supplement to the lord's control'.[286] Yet there is little evidence that it was much enforced. Writs of neifty were seldom issued against serfs who had left the manor and had evaded its administration, who instead they behaved as if they were free. As Putnam observed, 'instead of bringing suit to recover his own fugitive villein, [lords] found it easier to employ the vagrant villein of some other lord'.[287]

Given that few lords bothered with even these enhanced legal processes, then taking direct action themselves represented 'the most complete form of social control available'.[288] Many lords instructed their officials to enquire about and to record absent serfs, and, as a result, lists of flown serfs now lengthened considerably or appeared for the first time in manorial court rolls.[289] Seigniorial officials placed pressure upon those attending the manorial court and/or relatives to supply information about, or to ensure the return of, fugitives, and the details of flown serfs (where they were, whether they had progeny) within many court rolls became richer.[290] Whether the rise in recorded departures represents a genuine increase or reflects greater administrative enforcement is impossible to know because we cannot reconstruct the real underlying rates of migration.[291] The key issue is that the sudden shortage of tenants and labourers greatly enhanced the *significance* of any migration: the compilation of extensive lists of departing serfs reflects heightened seigniorial sensitivity about the phenomenon.[292] Yet it would be misplaced to suppose that all or most lords recorded serfs with a new energy and assiduity after 1349, judging from the very different patterns of recorded departures from one manor to another. Some manors record few departures in the generation after the arrival of plague;[293] in some, lists of flown serfs first appear early in the 1350s and continue to be compiled for decades;[294] in others, numbers surged in the mid-1350s then declined dramatically during the 1360s.[295]

The most direct, but most confrontational, option available to lords when faced with absent serfs was to dispatch a party of officials to seize and return them forcibly, and in the 1350s manorial courts often contain sharply-worded directives for fugitives to be seized 'by body'.[296] It is less clear how far manorial officials took such orders literally, although some did result in the return of serfs. For example, between 1356 and 1359 eight out of thirteen absent serfs were returned to the manor of Chilton (Suffolk), and in the early 1350s the prior of Durham authorized expenses for those of his officials tasked with retrieving flown serfs from Seaham (Co. Durham).[297] The Durham example underlines that physical seizures carried a direct financial cost to the lord and some opportunity cost of diverting officials from other tasks, and could involve violent confrontation if the serf resisted. The obstacles, costs, and risks involved with physical seizures meant that, in general, they were rare in the 1350s and are seldom recorded thereafter.[298]

The experience of the cellarer of St Albans abbey on his manor of Winslow (Bucks.) illustrates the problems associated with forcible returns. In the early 1350s manorial officials successfully seized and restored three serfs to Winslow, but all three disappeared again soon afterwards, never to return. None were pursued again, and no further attempts to seize other serfs are recorded. The case of one of these Winslow serfs, William Adam, is especially instructive because following his forced return in 1353 one Richard le Barn immediately marched into Winslow and took him away again. Richard might have been William's employer, and therefore claiming him under the contract clause of the Statute of Labourers, or he might have been a gentry lord of a nearby manor who had granted land to William. Whatever the reason, the response of the cellarer to this re-seizure of his serf was to instruct his estate officials to procure a writ, presumably to seek William's return through the common law courts. He seems, however, to have been unsuccessful because William never again appears in Winslow. In a second case, also from 1353, one of the lord's officials, Henry Boveton (who was also a villein tenant on the manor), had seized the absent John Adam, held him in custody temporarily, but then released him rather than bringing back to Winslow.[299] Henry readily admitted his change of heart, although his motive was not stated: no punishment is documented. Physical seizures were unlikely to be a successful or sustainable policy when they relied upon the agency of manorial officials, who were often serfs themselves who knew the migrants personally and who had little incentive to pursue doggedly an elusive escapee.[300] Lords occasionally amerced those officials who had failed a direct order to retrieve a serf, but their general lack of vigour in dealing with such failures reflects an underlying pragmatism.[301]

The aggressive behaviour of Richard le Barn in retrieving a serf who was not his own is characteristic of the general unwillingness of other lords and employers to return flown serfs to their manor of origin.[302] After all, they were under no legal obligation to do so, in contrast to some other systems of European serfdom where lords were required to return migrant serfs.[303] To make matters worse, an English lord who retrieved a serf already bound in a contract of employment with a third party was vulnerable to legal challenge for breaching the contract clause of the Statute of Labourers. Another difficulty was how a lord was to retain a serf once the latter had been forcibly returned to the home manor. A couple of days in the stocks might have served as an example and a deterrent, but serfs could not be restrained indefinitely and, once released, there was little to prevent them departing again.[304] Lords could require relatives or pledges to stand surety for the serf, strengthened by the threat of steep financial penalties, or alternatively could seize the goods and chattels of flown serfs as a means of distraint, but neither tactic was common: indeed, few flown serfs left behind many goods worth seizing.[305] Lords who had leased their manors faced even greater challenges because they no longer possessed a framework of local officials to supervise and monitor returnees. In these circumstances, the manorial lessee was often made responsible for the custody of returning serfs, whose lack of incentive in such matters was unlikely to lead to a successful long-term policy.[306]

The existence of such obstacles explains why the incidence of physical recovery of flown serfs was exceptional rather than commonplace.[307] Instead, lords sought to record and to license departures (chevage), enabling them to track the whereabouts of serfs and to levy a fee as compensation for the absence.[308] In the 1350s and 1360s a few lords did introduce much higher fines for chevage payments, rising from the mainly nominal sums charged in the 1340s to sizeable levies such as 40d. per annum, or even 20s. or 40s. per serf.[309] For example, in 1355–6 three men paid an average of 14s. each to be absent from the manor of Woolston (Berks.).[310] In the pre-plague era Ramsey abbey had charged absentees small annual payments of cash or capons, but in the 1350s introduced individual charges of between 40d. and 6s.8d. per annum.[311] The largest fees were usually levied upon serfs from well-established families with considerable fixed assets within the manor, who could afford (however reluctantly) to pay them.[312] High fees were unquestionably onerous and novel, and added materially to the cost of servile migration, but any assessment of their broader significance in restraining the mobility of labour requires a proper understanding of their frequency, typicality, and context. In fact, a close reading of the published case studies reveals that high fees were atypical and usually confined to the 1350s and 1360s.[313] For example, high charges in the 1350s on the Ramsey abbey estate were short-lived and soon 'the nominal customary fee ... regained prominence'.[314] The standard fee at Ingoldmells (Lincs.) fell from a mere 4d. in the 1340s to 3d. after 1349, and that at Esher remained constant at 2d.[315] Some manors hardly charged chevage at all.[316]

The most common record of flown serfs in manorial court rolls is not the payment of chevage but the presentment of the serf for absence each year, often with a statement of their current place of residence.[317] Manorial officials still sought their return, and preferably a chevage payment, but their absence was essentially unlicensed. For example, between 1350 and 1374 three chevage payments and 215 presentments for absence are recorded at Winslow (Bucks.), and likewise ten chevage and forty-five absence presentments at Bredfield (Suffolk) over a similar period.[318] The relative infrequency of chevage payments reflects the difficulties of enforcing them, and suggests that, in reality, it was a system of self-registration. Absent serfs *opted* to pay chevage to license their departure, usually because they were seeking to retain an interest in an inheritance in their home manor. They may also have done so to remove the seigniorial pressure on resident relatives to secure their return, or to eliminate anxiety about having to evade detection as an unlicensed migrant.[319]

Although bodily seizures, annual chevage payments, and presentments for absence all increased in frequency in many places in the generation after the Black Death, and although they were undoubtedly irksome to serfs in various ways, did they act as a significant break upon peasant mobility? Did they enable lords to reassert control over their villein labour as part of a seigniorial reaction? Certainly, these measures must have persuaded some uncertain migrants to return to the home manor, and dissuaded others from leaving in the first place, while increasing the marginal costs of those who did migrate.[320] In general, though, they did not discourage migration, as evidenced by the very high proportion of flown serfs who were unlicensed and never returned.[321] Landlords had exercised little control over flown serfs in the pre-plague era, and, despite their energetic endeavours, this did not change much afterwards.[322] Raftis concluded that Ramsey abbey 'was able to exert no coercive pressure through the courts for the recovery of a villager'.[323] Even the bishop of Durham, who wielded extensive judicial powers in north-east England, was unsuccessful in persuading or forcing most serfs to return.[324] Muller captures the consensus among historians when observing 'even when the whereabouts of runaways became known there was usually little that could be done to bring them back'.[325] Lordly efforts succeeded mainly in inconveniencing serfs, because the repetitive record of absences in manorial court rolls must have generated considerable resentment among the migrants and their families, and repeated labelling as serfs was demeaning and stigmatizing.

A corollary of the increased tracking of flown serfs after 1349 was a greater administrative assiduity in identifying and documenting hereditary serfs. Before the plague manorial documents did not label an individual as *nativus/nativa domini de sanguine* routinely or persistently, because for all practical purposes tenurial and personal unfreedom were deemed to be the same.[326] Thereafter, labelling hereditary serfs explicitly became common.[327] Additionally, a few landlords began to compile lists of all serfs on their manors, or occasionally extracted snippets of proof of the servility of a targeted family from earlier court rolls (such as evidence of paying merchet or leyrwite) and consolidated the information in a single document.[328] Contemporary documents never reveal the motive behind this routine labelling and occasional listing, although one possibility is that it represented the administrative groundwork 'to impose a sort of second serfdom'.[329] Dyer argues that the explicit identification of serfs was a prelude to the imposition of special 'work agreements'—such as binding them to work on the demesne, or to return to the manor at harvest time, or to serve the lord if required—which were sealed through either oath-taking in the manor court or included in the terms for holding customary land.[330] As he states, 'if they could be kept on the manor they would have been useful workers on the lord's demesne'.[331] He is correct to emphasize the novelty of these special conditions after 1349, but their significance depends upon frequency, context, and effectiveness. Dyer himself admits that work agreements 'are rather scarce' in the documentary record, but he 'suspect[s] that many more grants of land were made on the basis of informal and unwritten agreements'.[332] Yet this is speculative. It is more plausible to suppose that special work agreements would have been recorded explicitly in manorial court rolls than not, given the simplicity and ease of recording them, the growing precision of tenurial forms, and the importance of written proofs. The rarity of written agreements most likely means that such impositions were themselves rare.[333]

If the purpose of labelling and listing of serfs routinely after 1349 was to extort more and higher monetary fines from the personal dues of servility, then we would expect to find a strong correlation between the two. In general, however, evidence for the subsequent adoption of an aggressive policy of imposing personal dues upon serfs is weak. Durham priory introduced annual lists of *nativi* in the 1360s, but did not follow up with a programme of coercion or higher dues against those named.[334] Indeed, the frequency and size of servile incidents tended to fall in most places. Some chevage rates rose after 1349 and were high on a few manors, but on most manors they were low and the vast majority of fugitives did not pay chevage. Again, while the size of fines levied for merchet and leyrwite increased on some manors, especially in the 1350s, this was not a common experience.[335] The size of fines most often fell after 1349, and the incidence of merchet and leyrwite usually declined faster than the fall in population, and even disappeared entirely on some.[336] For example, the frequency of merchet at Norton (Herts.) declined from thirty-one cases in the 1340s to just six in the 1350s, and the average fine for women fell by over half (figs. 3.2 and 3.3). Similarly, at Halesowen (Warks.) there were around forty-five recorded merchets per decade in each of the 1330s and 1340s, but then around seventeen per decade in the 1350s and 1360s, seven in the 1370s, and just one in the 1390s.[337] On some manors, the evidence is more ambiguous. For example, at Winslow (Bucks.) between 1330–49 and 1350–69 the number of merchets fell by 46 per cent, although the mean charge for merchet rose 16 per cent between 1330–49 and 1350–9, before falling in the 1360s.[338] Part of the explanation for differences in the evidence for merchet from one manor to another reflects local differences in the way it was customarily applied and managed.[339]

Thus, it is not at all obvious that lords who labelled their serfs more assiduously after 1349 intended to do anything specific or immediate with the information. Instead, it is likely that their motive was to establish reliable and cheap written proof of personal servility in order to support any future legal claim over their serfs, irrespective of any pressing intent. Before the Black Death there had been limited incentive to record such proofs routinely or precisely because a combination of acute land shortages and common-law doctrine had effectively fused tenurial and personal unfreedom: in other words, the vast majority of villein tenants were also hereditary serfs.[340] After 1349 the sudden influx of freemen and incomers to the customary land market shattered the close and implied association between customary tenure and servile status, forcing manorial authorities to identify hereditary serfs explicitly as a separate process.[341] The drive to register and to track serfs in manorial court rolls was primarily an administrative response to the legal imperative of obtaining secure proof of servility for every serf. As such, it reflects bureaucratic habits and a legal mentality among lords, and perhaps a cock-eyed optimism that the good old days would return once again. It also reflects the old belief that the relationship between lords and serfs was personal.[342] Of course, this system of record was not neutral because earmarking individuals in this manner was unquestionably socially demeaning. In addition, the identifications and lists would have greatly aided any lord who was determined to impose heavy dues on his servile population or to surprise a wealthy but long-flown serf with an extortionate demand for cash.[343] Yet it was primarily an exercise in legal observance and conservative bureaucratic reflex rather than a prelude to sustained coercion.

One inevitable by-product of the lordly determination to document hereditary serfs more assiduously after 1349 was an increase in disputes over personal status in manorial court rolls. Disputes over status were primarily a matter for the courts of common law, which from the late twelfth century had developed procedures for establishing whether a defendant was free or unfree.[344] This legal process was, however, notoriously lengthy and cumbersome, and the presumption towards liberty meant that the burden of proof rested upon the landlord.[345] Even when a case reached court, the lord still had to overcome the challenge of ensuring that the defendant and all witnesses arrived for the hearing at the right time and place.[346] The expense, effort, and uncertainty associated with this slow and formal process meant that prior to the Black Death landlords seldom used the king's courts for this purpose, but instead usually sued on tenure.[347]

No research has yet ascertained whether after 1349 the volume of cases disputing personal status rose sharply in the courts of common law. One or two eye-catching legal cases have attracted attention, however, which may exemplify a wider and heightened interest in such matters. For example, in 1356 the Cellarer family of Wawne (Yorkshire) had left the manor to work elsewhere and claimed to be hereditary freemen. Their lord—the abbot of Meaux—was alarmed at the example this might set to other serfs, so his officials seized the three most defiant males in the family and imprisoned them for a short while in the abbey. The dispute rumbled on until 1361, when finally a hearing in front of royal justices confirmed the family's servile status, but urged the abbot to treat its members with restraint. The abbot's notion of restraint was to require the serfs to stand in the choir in front of the monks on successive Sundays with bare heads and feet, offering wax candles as tokens of subjection.[348]

Whether this case was typical of many others in the generation after the Black Death in the courts of common law is not yet clear. What is clear is that in the 1350s the volume of disputes over status recorded in manorial courts increased.[349] The length of time and expense involved in suing in courts of common law may well have encouraged lords to deal with status in their own manorial courts, either through a personal confession of servile status under oath or by the verdict of an inquisition jury, because a confession in *any* court constituted proof of servility.[350] For example, before 1349 no disputes are recorded on the cellarer of St Albans abbey's manors of Norton (Herts.) and Winslow (Bucks.), but then two occurred in the early 1350s: in 1352 a jury confirmed that Robert Williams and his family of Winslow were serfs, while in 1353 a Norton jury declared John le Neweman to be free.[351] No further disputes are recorded subsequently on either manor.

The increase in disputes over personal status has been cited as another aspect of the seigniorial reaction, because they are interpreted as seigniorial attempts either to impose servitude on those previously considered free or to coerce others who had escaped supervision.[352] Indeed, at one level the dispute between Meaux abbey and the Cellarer family appears to be a tale of subjection, conflict over serfdom, and frustrated freedom and humiliation, and therefore, perhaps, indicative of the heightened struggle over serfdom after the Black Death. When viewed from another perspective, however, it exhibits enough peculiar features for us to question its wider typicality. The flaring of the dispute in 1356 coincided with the eruption of serious political divisions within the abbey, and for some reason the royal escheator in Holderness was inciting the family's behaviour, both of which suggest that this episode comprised one tactic to exert political pressure as part of a wider and complex intrigue within the abbey.[353]

In the two decades after 1350 disputes over personal status in manorial courts throughout England rose slightly, but they remained exceptional cases rather than commonplace in these courts.[354] Of course, there may be many such cases awaiting discovery in the extant courts of common law. But, in any event, evidence for an increase in such disputes does not prove that landlords were attempting to enserf the population as part of a seigniorial reaction. English freemen and women had considerable legal protection against false claims, and proving personal status was a relatively difficult, complex, and risky area of law. This encourages us to seek other reasons for the rise in challenges over personal status in the 1350s and 1360s in manorial courts. The most obvious explanations are the sudden divorcing of personal status from tenure, the influx of incomers and freefolk into the customary land market, and the sudden realization on many estates that lords did not possess explicit written proof of the identity of their hereditary serfs. The rapid and dramatic changes within the customary land market after 1348–9 led to genuine uncertainty and confusion about the personal status of some individuals, as well as some pushing at the bounds, and triggered a drive for administrative clarity and certainty. In some specific cases, challenges over personal status are undoubtedly explained by a very particular set of local circumstances that are scarcely visible to the historian, as implied in the Meaux abbey affair. For example, an on-going attempt to establish the servile status of one Peter Waryn between 1354 and 1356 in the manorial court of Drinkstone (Suffolk) acquires a different meaning through the chance discovery that Peter was simultaneously suing his lord for a debt of 60s. in the court of common pleas.[355]

Conclusion

We can only guess at the terror, bewilderment, and psychological trauma experienced by those who lived through the first and second epidemics of plague. Hopelessness and lassitude overwhelmed some people, while others made the best of the opportunities created by the sudden surfeit of land and the shortage of workers. The experience of hardship was greatest in the early 1350s because of the extreme weather conditions, the soaring prices of necessities, high levels of taxation, and the initial poverty of many survivors. Consequently, the general recovery from the 1348–9 outbreak was slow and delayed.

The immediate responses of the government did not aid the general populace's attempts to cope with the initial shock waves. It continued to raise taxes as if the catastrophe had not happened, it devised novel ways to tighten collection of those taxes, and it transformed itself from an emergency crisis manager of the commodity and labour markets to the standing authority. The latter represents a milestone in the expansion of state power in England. The government's rationale for intervention was to uphold contemporary notions of social order, which inevitably meant new legislation that was inequitable and prejudicial to the lowers orders of society. The labour legislation coerced and restricted workers, and it attempted to manipulate and enforce contracts in favour of employers. Such profound discrimination became a source of injustice, tension, and major divisions within communities, and a significant negative influence in the run-up to the Peasants' Revolt of 1381. Yet, while the government's social agenda was unjust and inequitable, it was also too ambitious to be sustainable and deliverable, and its effectiveness declined after the zealous enforcement wave of the 1350s and the second epidemic of 1361. Hence, while the legislation distorted labour and commodity markets, it was unable to control them.

Manorial lords reacted to the first epidemic in various ways. In the 1350s seigniorial sensitivity to the lack of tenants and workers, and the prospect of reduced income, resulted in the adoption of some aggressive polices, such as the seizure or careful tracking of flown serfs, increased fines for servile dues (such as chevage), and challenges to the personal status of targeted individuals on some—but by no means all—estates. Even on estates where coercive policies are evident, many were relaxed after the 1350s. In most places, lords conceded on the terms and conditions of villein land, such as diluting the rent package of service tenancies and converting service tenancies to contractual tenancies, and were powerless to prevent the out-migration of their serfs. Lords had to compete with one another for tenants and workers because they could not control the land and labour markets through coercion or other non-economic means. The rarity of physical seizures of flown serfs, and the commitment to strengthening written proofs of servility in manorial documents, confirm that lords, by and large, continued to abide by established legal principles and culture.

Thus the immediate response of the ruling elite to the demographic catastrophe was a predictable combination of repression and concession through both government legislation and seigniorial administration. During the 1350s the effect of these actions was to heighten social conflict. Whilst this decade yields the most compelling evidence for a 'seigniorial reaction' to the plague in England, there is little evidence that such a reaction prevailed beyond the 1350s or that it occurred on the majority of manors. Instead, there is compelling evidence that the 1350s and 1360s represented a watershed in the history of tenure in England, one characterized by a major swing from the old service tenancies to monetarized and commercial rents, the flooding of the villein land market with freemen and non-serfs, and the decisive separation of tenurial from personal unfreedom. These developments increased the mobility of land, reduced the obstacles to the poorer sections of society accessing land, and broke the main bond in the relationship between lord and servile peasant. The result was major and irreversible institutional change (see pp. 297–306).

So why did the ruling elite fail to bend tenants, serfs, and workers to their collective will? The customs and the laws of engagement in the land market were hostile to forcible or arbitrary intervention, and this vital institutional arrangement meant that commercial forces prevailed after 1349 within the most important factor market. The government made no attempt to intervene here, because law and custom dictated that landed property was the domain of the lord and the freeman. The government's far-reaching and novel intervention in the labour market confirms that this factor market was already well established, but hardly regulated, on the eve of the Black Death: indeed, little regulation was necessary in the 1340s, because underlining market conditions were favourable to the ruling elite. The sudden and immense reversal of fortune required coercive intervention to protect seigniorial interests and to control the movement of workers. Yet the government ultimately failed to control the labour market, and lords failed to control their serfs, because of two major weaknesses. First, they possessed neither the apparatus nor the capacity (nor perhaps the will) to enforce their formal legal powers. Second, employers and other lords were not legally required to return flown serfs to their home manors, and they displayed little inclination to do so voluntarily. As a result, the ruling elite had to adopt competitive, conciliatory, and contractual strategies over personal, coercive, and arbitrary ones. In this sense, the Black Death revealed quickly and graphically just how diluted manorial lordship and the common law of villeinage had already become, and the extent to which custom, the market, and a legal culture based on precedents and due process was already conditioning social relations and behaviours.[356] Historians have portrayed the Statute of Labourers primarily as an instrument of oppression, understandably so, but it is essentially about contract enforcement. The catastrophe resulted in the spread and tightening of contractual arrangements in both the labour and the land markets.[357]

Notes

1. Barbara Harvey, 'The abbot of Westminster's demesnes and the Black Death of 1349', in Marion Meek, ed., *The modern traveller to our past. Festschrift in honour of Ann Hamilton* (Dublin, 2006), pp. 292–8; John Hatcher, *The Black Death: a personal history* (London, 2008); Larson, *Conflict and compromise*, pp. 71–142; Stone, 'Black Death', pp. 213–44; James Davis, 'Selling food and drink in the aftermath of the Black Death', in Bailey and Rigby, eds., *Town and countryside*, pp. 351–406.
2. Razi, *Life, marriage*, pp. 104–5.
3. Ray Lock, 'The Black Death in Walsham-le-Willows', *Proceedings of the Suffolk Institute of Archaeology and History*, 37 (1992), pp. 327–8.
4. Bridbury, *English economy*, pp. 215–16; Campbell, *Great transition*, p. 14.
5. Stone, 'The Black Death', pp. 213–18; Campbell, *Great transition*, pp. 295–315; David J. Stone, *The accounts for the manor of Esher in the Winchester Pipe Rolls 1235–1376*, Surrey Record Society (2017), p. 283.
6. Bruce M.S. Campbell, 'Population pressure, inheritance and the land market in a fourteenth-century peasant community', in Richard M. Smith, *Land, kinship and life cycle* (Cambridge, 1984), pp. 94, 132.
7. John Mullan, 'The transfer of customary land on the estates of the bishopric of Winchester between the Black Death and the plague of 1361', in Richard H. Britnell, ed., *The Winchester pipe rolls and medieval English society* (Woodbridge, 2003), pp. 81–108, at p. 83, fns 4 and 5.
8. Robo, 'Black Death', pp. 562–4; Razi, *Life, marriage*, pp. 110–11; Campbell, 'Population pressure', p. 120.

9. Ada E. Levett, *Studies in manorial history* (Oxford, 1938), table 3. The manors are Barnet, Cashio, Codicote, Park, Norton, and Langley: 272 admissions were heirs, 66 strangers/unrelated or doubtful, and 'no evidence is provided for the remaining 30 admissions'.

10. Mullan, 'Transfer of customary land', pp. 87–91.

11. '*Usque mundus melioretur*', Paul H.W. Booth, *Accounts of the manor and hundred of Macclesfield, Cheshire, Michaelmas 1361 to Michaelmas 1362*, Record Society of Lancashire and Cheshire, 138 (2003), p. lxiv.

12. Larson, *Conflict and compromise*, pp. 119–20; David J. Stone and Richard Sandover, eds., *Moor medieval: exploring Dartmoor in the Middle Ages* (Exeter, 2019), pp. 99–100; Edmund King, 'Tenant farming: east Midlands', in Miller, *Agrarian History III*, pp. 630–1.

13. Norfolk Record Office, Walsingham III/3, court held June 1350 and WKC2/192, court held September 1351. See also Paul H.W. Booth, *The financial administration of the lordship and county of Chester 1272-1377*, Chetham Society, 3rd series, 28 (1981), p. 89.

14. Henry C. Darby, *The medieval fenland* (Cambridge, 1940), p. 152.

15. For example, Levett, *Black Death*, pp. 82–3; Stone, *Moor medieval*, p. 104.

16. Lock, 'The Black Death', pp. 329–36; Razi, *Life, marriage*, p. 110. See also, Levett, *Studies*, p. 255; John Hatcher, *Rural economy and society in the Duchy of Cornwall 1300-1500* (Cambridge, 1970), pp. 104–5.

17. Edmund B. Fryde, *Peasants and landlords in later medieval England* (Stroud, 1996), pp. 58–60; NRO WKC/2/54; Henry E. Salter, ed., *Cartulary of abbey of Eynsham, vol. II*, (Oxford, 1908), pp. 19–20.

18. Hatcher, *Duchy of Cornwall*, pp. 110–13.

19. Page, *Villeinage*, pp. 53, 73; Adolphus Ballard, *The Black Death on the estates of the see of Winchester* (Oxford, 1916), p. 198; Mark Bailey, 'The Prior and Convent of Ely and the manor of Lakenheath in the fourteenth century', in Christopher Harper-Bill and Michael Franklin, eds., *Ecclesiastical studies in honour of Dorothy M Owen* (Woodbridge, 1994), p. 8. For an example from Cheshire, see Horrox, *Black Death*, p. 281 and Booth, *Financial administration*, pp. 91, 128–9; from the north-east, Larson, *Conflict and compromise*, p. 74; from Shropshire, Kettle, '1300–1540', p. 76; from the west Midlands, Edmund B. Fryde, 'The tenants of the bishops of Coventry and Litchfield, and of Worcester, after the plague of 1348-9' in Roy F. Hunnisett and J.B. Post, eds., *Medieval legal records: essays in memory of C.A.F. Meekings* (London, 1978), pp. 229–30 and from Devon, Stone, *Moor medieval*, p. 104, fn. 38.

20. Compare Levett, *Black Death*, pp. 76, 82–85, with Jan Z. Titow, 'Lost rents, vacant holdings, and the contraction of peasant cultivation after the Black Death', *Agricultural History Review*, 42 (1994), pp. 97–114; and Mullan, 'Transfer of customary land', pp. 85–6.

21. Levett, *Black Death*, pp. 145–6, 152–3.

22. Mark Bailey, 'The transformation of customary tenures in southern England c.1300 to c.1550', *Agricultural History Review*, (2014), pp. 222–3.

23. Larson, *Conflict and compromise*, pp. 74–5, 84–6.

24. Broadberry et al., *Economic growth*, p. 125, table 3.21.

25. Robo, 'Black Death', p. 563; Ballard, *Black Death*, pp. 196–7. See also Wells-Furby, *Berkeley estate*, pp. 133, 271.

26. Page, *Crowland abbey*, p. 124; Larson, *Conflict and compromise*, p. 74; Stone, 'Black Death', pp. 222, 239.

27. See, for example, Robo, 'Black Death', pp. 566, 569–70; Horrox, *Black Death*, pp. 292–5, 304; Larson, *Conflict and compromise*, p. 86.

28. John Langdon, *Mills in the medieval economy: England 1300–1540* (Oxford, 2004), p. 28. See Stone, *Moor medieval*, p. 99.

29. Page, *Crowland abbey*, pp. 121–2; Stone, 'Black Death', p. 234. See also Wells-Furby, *Berkeley estate*, p. 134; Bailey, 'Prior and convent', p. 10; Kettle, '1300–1540', p. 75.

30. Wells-Furby, *Berkeley estate*, p. 169. See also Ballard, *Black Death*, p. 198.

31. Hatcher, *Duchy of Cornwall*, p. 182.

32. Robo, 'Black Death', pp. 566, 569–70; see also Hatcher, *Duchy of Cornwall*, p. 205, and Booth, *Financial administration*, p. 91.

33. Hatcher, *Duchy of Cornwall*, pp. 105–7; Levett, *Black Death*, p. 136.

34. Fryde, 'Tenants of the bishops', pp. 224–5. The household income of Elizabeth de Burgh fell by *c.*35% between the mid-1340s and 1349, Bailey, *Medieval Suffolk*, p. 180.

35. Fryde, 'Tenants of the bishops', pp. 225, 230, 235.

36. Stone, 'Black Death', p. 233. See also Wells-Furby, *Berkeley estate*, p. 63. Phillips, 'Collaboration and litigation', pp. 42, 46.

37. Davis, 'Selling food and drink', pp. 363–8.

38. Larson, *Conflict and compromise*, p. 86; Harvey, 'Abbot of Westminster's demesnes', p. 292.

39. Prices were generally lower throughout 1349, and began to rise from the end of the year, R. Braid, 'Economic behaviour, markets and crises: the English economy in the wake of plague and famine in the fourteenth century', in Silvia Cavaciocchi, ed., *Economic and biological interactions in pre-industrial Europe between the thirteenth and eighteenth centuries* (Florence, 2010), pp. 353–4.

40. Horrox, *Black Death*, p. 73; Stone, 'Black Death', p. 234. No wheat was sown on three manors on the Westminster estate in 1349–50, and problems were still recorded in 1350–1, because of lack of ploughmen to prepare the ground, Harvey, 'Abbot of Westminster's demesnes', pp. 294, 297. See also Wells-Furby, *Berkeley estate*, p. 161.

41. Harriss, *King, parliament*, pp. 379–81; Sharp, *Famine and scarcity*, pp. 91–7.

42. PROME Online, February 1351, accessed 18 October 2017.

43. Dodds, *Peasants and production*, p. 73.

44. CUL EDC 7/14/C/16 to 18. See also, Terrence H. Lloyd, 'Some documentary sidelights on the DMV of Brookend', *Oxoniensa*, 64 (1964–5), p. 121.

45. DeWindt, *Land and people*, pp. 91–2; Ray Lock, ed., *The court rolls of Walsham-le-Willows, vol. II, 1351–1399*, Suffolk Records Society, 45 (2002), pp. 39–42; Muller, 'Peasants, lords', p. 169; Bailey, *Decline of serfdom*, pp. 110, 209, 230.

46. Dodds, *Peasants and production*, p. 75.

47. Bruce M.S. Campbell, 'Grain yields on English demesnes after the Black Death', in Bailey and Rigby, eds., *Town and countryside*, pp. 121–74, at p. 144; Harvey, 'Abbot of Westminster's demesnes', pp. 293–4.

48. Bruce M.S. Campbell, 'Nature as a historical protagonist: environment and society and pre-industrial England', *Economic History Review*, 63 (2010), pp. 301–5; Campbell,

'Grain yields', pp. 140, 144; Stone, 'Black Death', p. 236; Wells-Furby, *Berkeley estate*, p. 152; Campbell, 'European mortality crisis', fig. 2.7.

49. Campbell, 'Grain yields', pp. 144–5.
50. Levett, *Black Death*, p. 123; Harvey, 'Abbot of Westminster's demesnes', p. 293; James A. Galloway, 'Storm flooding, coastal defence and land use around the Thames estuary and tidal river c.1250–1450', *Journal of Medieval History*, 35 (2009), fig. 2; Wells-Furby, *Berkeley estate*, pp. 83, 105, 128, 134, 151–2; L. Kathleen Pribyl, *Farming, famine and plague: the impact of climate in late medieval England* (Berlin, 2017), p. 133; Stone, *Esher*, p. 273.
51. Campbell, 'Grain yields', pp. 145, 159; Campbell, 'Physical shocks', p. 24.
52. Pribyl, *Farming, famine*, pp. 130–6.
53. Braid, 'Economic behaviour', pp. 354–6; Harvey, 'Abbot of Westminster's demesnes', pp. 294–5.
54. Stone, 'Black Death', pp. 223–4.
55. From a standard rate of 2½d. per 120 during the 1340s to 4d. in 1349–50, SROB E3/15.10/2.4 to 2.7.
56. Hatcher, *Duchy of Cornwall*, p. 103; John Hatcher, *English tin production and trade before 1550* (Oxford, 1973), p. 156; Langdon, *Mills*, pp. 174–5.
57. *Calendar of Fine Rolls*, November 1349, p. 188; Horrox, *Black Death*, p. 73.
58. Stone, *Decision-making*, pp. 103–5; Stone, 'Black Death', p. 237; Stone, *Esher*, pp. lxix, lxxiii, 273, 283.
59. Larson, *Conflict and compromise*, p. 101.
60. Stone, *Esher*, p. 293. See also Stone, *Moor medieval*, pp. 100–1. Enterprising peasants on the Winchester estate acquired more land and even stepped in to buy up supplies of grain from local landlords struggling to dispose of them, Levett, *Black Death*, pp. 137–8.
61. Larson, *Conflict and compromise*, p. 75.
62. Levett, *Studies*, pp. 275–9, 281–4 (the second court at Codicote was held in October).
63. Horrox, *Black Death*, p. 327; Larson, *Conflict and compromise*, pp. 75, 85, 112, 115, 122. For similar observations elsewhere in England, see also Stone, 'Black Death', p. 234; Edmund B. Fryde and Natalie Fryde, 'Peasant rebellion and peasant discontents', in Miller, ed., *Agrarian History III*, p. 747.
64. Hatcher, *Duchy of Cornwall*, p. 120.
65. Mullan, 'Transfer of customary land', pp. 85–6.
66. Bruce M.S. Campbell and Cormac O Grada, 'Harvest shortfalls, grain prices and farmers in pre-industrial England', *Journal of Economic History*, 71 (2011), pp. 869–70.
67. Farmer, 'Prices and wages', pp. 512–13.
68. Stone, 'Black Death', table 11, p. 232.
69. Woods, *Medieval Hadleigh*, p. 57.
70. This data is very hard to win from the sources, but in 1336–7 and 1338–9 a grand total of 2,780 faggots were sold for 462d. from Chevington manor, which is 17d. per hundred: SROB E3/15.3/2.2d and 2.3. In 1352–3, 1355–6, and 1356–7 1,345 faggots were sold at Chevington, South Elmham and Kelsale for 550d., which is 41d. per hundred, SROB E3/15.13/2.10a, SROL 741 HA12/C2/62b (the catalogue dates this to 1346–7, but the account is 29–30 Ed.III) and SROI HD1538/279/2. In 1371 4,200

faggots were sold at Hundon for 121s., or 35d. per hundred, TNA SC6/999/25. I am grateful to Rosemary Hoppitt for this information.

71. In the 1330s production costs were 3d. per hundred in the Chevington accounts cited above. Compare with 12d. per hundred at South Elmham in 1372, SROL 741/HA12/C2/65 and the same in 1399 at Staverton, SROI HD1538/356.

72. Clark, 'Long march', table 5.

73. Braid, 'Economic behaviour', pp. 355–6, 361.

74. Tony K. Moore, 'War and finance in late-medieval England', paper presented to the Anglo-American Seminar on the Medieval Economy and Society, Stirling 2016.

75. Braid, 'Economic behaviour', pp. 360–1.

76. Between October 1348 and January 1350 79 holdings were relinquished and 29 granted to either widows or children (and 7%, or 9%, remained untenanted), Page, *Crowland abbey*, p. 123; Alex Sapoznik, 'Resource allocation and peasant decision making: Oakington, Cambridgeshire, 1360–99', *Agricultural History Review*, 61 (2013), p. 204.

77. Fryde, 'Peasant rebellion', p. 747; Fryde, 'Tenants of the bishops', p. 230. See also Razi, *Life, marriage*, pp. 149–50.

78. Alexandra Sapoznik, 'Peasant agricultural productivity', paper presented to the Anglo-American Seminar on the Medieval Economy and Society, Worcester, 2019.

79. Two iron wheels (7d.), two iron feet (6d.), and an iron ploughshare (12d.) cost a total of 25d. in the mid-1340s, yet the same parts cost 41d. in the early 1350s (11d. wheels, 10d. feet, 20d. ploughshare), Stone, *Esher*, pp. 247, 256, 276, 283, 286. All prices exclude the labour costs of fitting them to the plough. See also Stone, 'Black Death', pp. 232–3; Seabourne, *Royal regulation*, pp. 85–6.

80. Farmer, 'Prices and wages', p. 465–6.

81. From 7d. in 1348 to 14d.–17d. in 1351–2, Stone, 'Black Death', table 11, p. 232.

82. Chris Briggs, *Credit and village society in fourteenth century England* (Oxford, 2009), pp. 198–200, 205–6, 211.

83. Levett, *Black Death*, p. 123; Braid, 'Economic behaviour', p. 354; Stone, 'Black Death', pp. 239–41. For some recovery in peasant litigation at Redgrave after 1354, see Phillips, 'Collaboration and litigation', pp. 42, 46, 153–4.

84. Simon Walker, 'Order and law', in Horrox and Ormrod, eds., *Social history*, p. 91; Wood, *Medieval economic thought*, pp. 143–4; Davis, *Medieval market morality*, p. 60; Braid, 'Behind the Ordinance', pp. 3–10; Sharp, 'Royal paternalism', pp. 628–47.

85. Kaye, *History of balance*, pp. 390–2.

86. Farmer, 'Prices and wages', p. 483.

87. Horrox, *Black Death*, pp. 287, 312–13.

88. The new contract clause 'bestowed far more important advantages on employers than they had possessed at common law, both as against their employees and as against competing employers', Bertha H. Putnam, *The enforcement of the Statutes of Labourers during the first fecade after the Black Death, 1349–1359* (New York, 1908), pp. 194–5; Clark, 'Medieval labour law', p. 334.

89. For useful summaries, see Farmer, 'Prices and wages', pp. 483–90; Larry R. Poos, 'Social context of the Statute of Labourers enforcement', *Law and History Review*, 1 (1983), pp. 28–33; Bennett, 'Compulsory service', pp. 10–28; Braid, 'Economic behaviour', pp. 358–61.

90. The statute is reproduced in Horrox, *Black Death*, pp. 312–16.

91. Palmer, *English law*, p. 294.

92. Samuel Cohn, 'After the Black Death: labour legislation and attitudes towards labour in late-medieval western Europe', *Economic History Review*, 60 (2007), pp. 457–87; Bennett, 'Compulsory service', p. 11–12; Fryde, 'Peasant rebellion', pp. 753–60.

93. Palmer, *English law*, pp. 14–17.

94. Horrox, *Black Death*, p. 288; '*Proviso quod domini preferantur aliis in nativis seu terram suam tenetibus*', Putnam, *Statutes of Labourers*, appendix p. 9*.

95. Chris Given-Wilson, 'Service, serfdom, and English labour legislation 1350–1500', in Curry and Matthews, eds., *Concepts and patterns*, pp. 23–4.

96. Kaye, *History of balance*, pp. 374–5; Mark Bailey, 'Peasants and the Great Revolt', in Stephen H. Rigby and Sian Echard, eds., *Historians on Gower* (Woodbridge, 2019), pp. 170–7, 183–4.

97. The same argument has been made about the 'common profit', see David Harry, *Constructing a civic community in late medieval London: the common profit, charity and commemoration* (Boydell, 2019), pp. 3–7.

98. Poos, 'Social context', pp. 29–50; Farmer, 'Prices and wages', pp. 484–5.

99. Paul H. Booth, 'The enforcement of the Ordinance and Statute of Labourers in Cheshire, 1349 to 1374', *Archives*, 127 (2013), pp. 1–16, at 8–10; Larson, *Conflict and compromise*, p. 172. For a cautionary note, see Stone, 'Black Death', p. 231.

100. Poos, 'Social context', p. 48; Fryde, *Peasants and landlords*, p. 35; Stephen H. Rigby, 'Justifying inequality: peasants in medieval ideology', in Kowaleski et al., eds., *Landlords and peasants*, p. 190.

101. Poos, 'Social context', pp. 37–44.

102. Farmer, 'Prices and wages', pp. 484–5.

103. The quote is from Given-Wilson, 'Problem of labour', p. 98, and broadly reflects the judgement of most historians. See also Putnam, *Statutes of Labourers*, p. 221; Levett, *Black Death*, pp. 101–6; Nora Kenyon, 'Labour conditions in Essex in the reign of Richard II', in Eleanor M. Carus-Wilson, ed., *Essays in economic history, volume II* (London, 1962), pp. 91–2; Bridbury, *English economy*, pp. 30–1; Poos, 'Social context', pp. 28–30; Anthony J. Musson and W. Mark Ormrod, *The evolution of English justice: law, politics and society in the fourteenth century* (Basingstoke, 1999), pp. 94–5; Given-Wilson, 'Service, serfdom', pp. 22–5; Fryde, *Peasants and landlords*, pp. 33–6, 64–5, 118; Farmer, 'Prices and wages', pp. 485, 489; Fryde, 'Peasant rebellion', pp. 756–8; Bennett, 'Impact of the Black Death', pp. 197–8; Mavis E. Mate, 'Labour and labour services on the estates of Canterbury Cathedral Priory in the fourteenth century', *Southern History*, 7 (1985), pp. 60, 65; Booth, 'Enforcement', pp. 6–7; Clark, 'Long march', pp. 116–17.

104. Anthony J. Musson, 'Reconstructing English labour laws', in Robertson and Uebel, eds., *The Middle Ages at work*, p. 121.

105. Braid, 'Economic behaviour', pp. 354–7.

106. Hatcher, 'England in the aftermath', pp. 21–4. See also Levett, *Black Death*, pp. 97–102; Farmer, 'Prices and wages', pp. 438, 469–70; Wells-Furby, *Berkeley estate*, p. 86; Stone, 'Black Death', pp. 231–2.

107. Britnell, *Colchester*, p. 137.

108. Fryde, 'Peasant rebellion', p. 756.
109. Bailey, 'Peasants and the Great Revolt', pp. 177–80.
110. Musson and Ormrod, *Evolution of English justice*, p. 85; Bridbury, *English economy*, p. 31.
111. Given-Wilson, 'Problem of labour', p. 98.
112. In addition, the county-based structure of administration meant that information and intelligence about offenders fell between the cracks of county boundaries; see Rees-Jones, 'Regulation of labour', pp. 143–5; Booth, 'Enforcement', p. 7.
113. Bailey, 'Peasants and the Great Revolt', pp. 177–82; Anne Middleton, 'Acts of vagrancy in the C-version autobiography and the Statute of 1388', in Steven Justice and Kathryn Kerby-Fulton, eds., *Written work: Langland, labour and authorship* (Philadelphia, 1997), pp. 224–8; Given-Wilson, 'Problem of labour', p. 86.
114. Palmer has suggested that the Crown's policy in the grain and processed foodstuffs markets after 1349 constituted a qualitative and novel intervention in economic affairs, although most historians emphasize its increased scale, and the enhanced powers of enforcement rather than its novelty. Compare Palmer, *English law*, pp. 1–16, with, for example, Seabourne, *Royal regulation*, pp. 160–2; Davis, 'Market regulation', pp. 103–4; Braid, 'Economic behaviour', pp. 345–51; Davis, 'Selling food and drink', pp. 354–6; and Sharp, *Famine and scarcity*, pp. 11–20.
115. Sharp, *Famine and scarcity*, pp. 91–7; Rigby, *Medieval Grimsby*, pp. 53, 55.
116. Sharp, *Famine and scarcity*, pp. 88, 102–10; John S. Lee, 'Grain shortages in medieval towns', in Dodds and Liddy, eds., *Commercial activity*, p. 74.
117. Pamela Nightingale, *A medieval merchant community: the Grocers' Company and the politics and trade of London 1000–1485* (New Haven, 1995), p. 205.
118. *Statutes of the Realm*, I, pp. 307–8.
119. *Statutes of the Realm*, I, pp. 315–16 and 378–9.
120. *Statutes of the Realm*, I, pp. 313; Braid, 'Behind the ordinance', pp. 24–5; Sharp, *Famine and scarcity*, pp. 97–113; Seabourne, *Royal regulation*, pp. 128–9.
121. Calculated from Seabourne, *Royal regulation*, pp. 141–2, fn. 117.
122. Seabourne, *Royal regulation*, pp. 131–8.
123. Madonna J. Hettinger, 'The role of the Statute of Labourers in the social and economic background of the Great Revolt in East Anglia' (PhD thesis, University of Indiana, 1986), table 3.3.
124. The London authorities were active in pillorying or imprisoning forestallers of poultry, passing ordinances to address profiteering among fishmongers, butchers, and poulterers, and capping prices in the plague year of 1361: *Statutes of the Realm*, I, p. 351; David L. Farmer, 'Marketing the produce', in Miller, ed., *Agrarian history III*, pp. 393, 427–8; Seabourne, *Royal regulation*, pp. 140–5, 149. For assiduous enforcement in provincial towns and local markets, see Larson, *Conflict and compromise*, pp. 98–9; Davis, *Medieval market morality*, pp. 226, 370; McGibbon Smith, 'Reflections', pp. 174–5; Davis, 'Selling food and drink', pp. 364–9, 391; Phillips, 'Collaboration and litigation', p. 137.
125. Judith M. Bennett, *Ale, beer and brewsters in England: women's work in a changing world 1300–1600* (Oxford, 1996), pp. 43–51, 113–14; James A. Galloway, 'London's grain supply: changes in production, distribution and consumption during the

fourteenth century', *Franco-British Studies*, 20 (1995), pp. 23–34; James A. Galloway, 'Driven by drink?: ale consumption and the agrarian economy of the London region, c.1300–1400', in Martha Carlin and Joel L. Rosenthal, eds., *Food and feasting in medieval Europe* (London, 1998), pp. 92–6; Stone, 'Field crops', pp. 23–4; Stone, 'Black Death', p. 235; Gregory Clark, *A farewell to alms: a brief economic history of the world* (Princeton, 2007), p. 54.

126. Bennett, *Ale, beer*, pp. 20–1, 45, 113–14; Mavis E. Mate, 'Work and labour', in Horrox and Ormrod, eds., *Social history*, pp. 285–6; Davis, 'Selling food and drink', pp. 381, 383, 385.

127. Stone, 'Consumption', p. 23.

128. An additional pressure was created by the structure of the assize of ale, which meant that profits were smaller when grain prices were higher, Bennett, *Ale, beer*, pp. 43–5; Stone, *Esher*, p. lxxii.

129. Hettinger, 'Role of the Statute of Labourers', table 3.3.

130. Davis, *Medieval market morality*, pp. 314–17, 328–30; Seaborne, *Economic regulation*, pp. 102–4, 160–1; Davis, 'Selling food and drink', pp. 369–70, 374, 395; Britnell, *Colchester*, pp. 134–7.

131. Seabourne, *Royal regulation*, pp. 160–2.

132. Horrox, *Black Death*, pp. 340–2.

133. Hatcher, 'England in the aftermath', pp. 3–35.

134. Dyer, 'Work ethics', pp. 27, 35–6.

135. Howell, *Commerce*, pp. 225–6, 233–5.

136. Nineteenth- and early twentieth-century historians developed the idea of a severe class reaction after 1348–9, stated evocatively in Charles H. Pearson, *English history in the fourteenth century* (London, 1876), pp. 229–30 and summarized in Hybel, *Crisis and change*, pp. 4–15. For later refinement of the argument, see, for example, George C. Homans, *English villagers of the thirteenth century* (Oxford, 1943), p. 275; Clive Holmes, *The estates of the higher nobility in fourteenth-century England* (Cambridge, 1957), p. 115; Rodney H. Hilton, *Bondmen made free: medieval peasant movements and the English rising of 1381* (London, 1977), pp. 154–7; Hilton, 'Crisis of feudalism', p. 132; Bolton, *Medieval English economy*, p. 213; Maurice Keen, *English society in the later Middle Ages* (Harmondsworth, 1990), pp. 38–41; Fryde, 'Peasant rebellion', pp. 765–6; Christopher Dyer, 'The social and economic origins of the Great Revolt of 1381', in Rodney H. Hilton and Trevor H. Aston, eds., *The English Rising of 1381* (Cambridge, 1984), pp. 23–36; Bolton, 'The world upside down', pp. 45–6; Paul V. Hargreaves, 'Seigniorial reaction and peasant responses', *Midland History*, 24 (1999), pp. 52–5; Fryde, *Peasants and landlords*, pp. 33–4; Christopher Dyer, 'Villeins, bondmen, neifs and serfs: new serfdom in England 1200–1600', in Freedman and Bourin, eds., *Forms of servitude*, pp. 428–34; Richard H. Britnell, 'Feudal reaction after the Black Death in the Palatine of Durham', *Past and Present*, 128 (1990), pp. 28–40: for summaries of the literature, see Rigby, *English society*, pp. 110–27; Bailey, *Decline of serfdom*, pp. 307–8; Mark Bailey, 'The myth of the seigniorial reaction in England', in Kowaleski et al., eds., *Peasants and landlords*, pp. 147–9; Schofield, *Peasants and historians*, pp. 102–4.

137. Keen, *English society*, pp. 39–40; Bolton, *Medieval English economy*, p. 213. See also, Dyer, 'Social and economic', p. 23.

138. Miriam Muller, 'Conflict and revolt: the Bishop of Ely and his peasants at the manor of Brandon in Suffolk c. 1300–81', *Rural History*, 23 (2012), p. 2. See also Hilton, *Bondmen made free*, pp. 156–7; Fryde, 'Peasant rebellion', pp. 765–6.

139. Holmes, *Higher nobility*, p. 115; Christopher Dyer, *Standards of living in the later Middle Ages: social change in England c.1200–20* (Cambridge, 1989), pp. 147–8; Richard H. Britnell, 'Tenant farming: eastern England', in Miller, ed., *Agrarian history III*, p. 618.

140. Mavis E. Mate, 'Agrarian economy after the Black Death: the manors of Canterbury Cathedral Priory', *Economic History Review*, 37 (1984), p. 342; Holmes, *Higher nobility*, p. 114; Bailey, *Decline of serfdom*, p. 121. See also Bridbury, *English economy*, pp. 203–4; Booth, *Financial administration*, pp. 97, 99.

141. Dyer, 'Social and economic', pp. 28–9.

142. Michel Mollat and Phillippe Wolff, *The popular revolutions of the late Middle Ages* (London, 1973), pp. 201, 203; Dyer, 'Villeins, bondmen', pp. 430–1.

143. The quotes are from Hargreaves, 'Seigniorial reaction', p. 52 and Bolton, *Medieval English economy*, p. 213.

144. Paul Freedman and Monique Bourin, 'Introduction', in Freedman and Bourin, eds., *Forms of servitude*, p. 16; Muller, 'Conflict', pp. 1–3.

145. Britnell, *Britain*, p. 432.

146. Bolton, *Medieval English economy*, p. 215. For a good example of resistance, see Britnell, 'Feudal reaction', pp. 40–7.

147. Fryde, *Peasants and landlords*, pp. 30–3; Bailey, *Decline of serfdom*, pp. 307–11; Bailey, 'Myth', pp. 147–72.

148. For example, Bolton, *English economy*, p. 213, claims without any supporting reference that villeins were forced to work holdings or to pay fines to avoid doing so. Zvi Razi, 'Serfdom and freedom: a reply to the revisionists', in Dyer et al., eds., *Rodney Hilton's Middle Ages*, p. 186 makes the same claims, citing just two pages from one article in support. Herbert Eiden, 'Joint action against "Bad" lordship: the Peasants' Revolt in Essex and Norfolk', *History*, 269 (1998), pp. 6–7 argues in favour of the seigniorial reaction, citing Bolton (above) and one article by Dyer.

149. Bailey, 'Myth', pp. 164–7; McGibbon, 'Reflections', pp. 180–4. Edmund Fryde supported the concept of a seigniorial reaction, while also observing of the 1350s that 'the great divergence in the nature and size of concessions wrung from unwilling landlords was itself a very disorganizing feature of the years after the first plague', Fryde, 'Peasant rebellion', p. 750.

150. Britnell, 'Feudal reaction', pp. 33–8; Larson, *Conflict and community*, pp. 86–9, 117–24; Horrox, *Black Death*, p. 327. See also Dyer, 'Social and economic', p. 23.

151. Britnell, 'Feudal reaction', pp. 33–8; Larson, *Conflict and community*, pp. 118–41.

152. Mullan, 'Transfer of customary land', pp. 85–6. See also Robo, 'Black Death', pp. 567, 569; Levett, *Black Death*, p. 85.

153. Mullan, 'Transfer of customary land', p. 87.

154. Mullan, 'Transfer of customary land', p. 85; John Mullan and Richard H. Britnell, *Land and family: trends and local variations in the peasant land market on the Winchester bishopric estates 1263–1415* (Hatfield, 2010), pp. 127–9.

155. Bailey, 'Myth', pp. 153–4.

156. A handful of examples of compulsion in the 1350s in Essex were part of a 'carrot-and-
     stick' approach from landlords, Poos, *Rural society*, p. 20. On the prior of Ely's estate
     six tenants between 1356 and 1361 were 'elected by the whole homage' to hold
     customary land in Sutton (Cambs.), though two successfully resisted the imposition,
     McGibbon Smith, 'Reflections', p. 173. Three examples have been identified on the
     St Albans abbey estate in the 1350s, where the practice was otherwise rare, Levett,
     Studies, p. 254; Noy, *Winslow, I*, pp. 248, 250. Ramsey abbey distrained heirs who
     failed to take up their customary landholdings, but did not compel, Raftis, *Tenure and
     mobility*, p. 143. In the 1390s serfs holding land on some Crowland abbey manors
     were required to occupy additional holdings, Page, *Crowland abbey*, pp. 152-3. See
     also Harold S.A. Fox, 'Occupation of the land: Devon and Cornwall', in Miller, ed.,
     Agrarian history III, p. 170.
157. Shakespeare Birthplace Trust, Stratford, DR10/2585 to 2598; see/2593 court held
     17 October 1360 for the assessment of vacant lands, and then/2594 court held
     March 1361 for the grants. The lord was the bishop of Lichfield.
158. Salter, ed., *Cartulary of the abbey of Eynsham, vol. II*, pp. 61-2.
159. Edward Miller, 'Occupation of the land: Yorkshire and Lancashire', in Miller,
     ed., *Agrarian history III*, pp. 46-7; Edmund King, 'Occupation of the land: East
     Midlands', in Miller, ed., *Agrarian history III*, pp. 71-2; Bailey, *Decline of serfdom*,
     pp. 120-1, 157, 187; Mullan, 'Transfer of customary land', p. 85.
160. See, for example, *Norton*, p. 102. Such proclamations were also common on the
     Winchester estates, Mullan, 'Transfer of customary land', p. 85. See also Phillips,
     'Collaboration and litigation', p. 74.
161. *Norton*, p. 149. See also, Constance M. Fraser, ed., *The court rolls of the manor of
     Wakefield from October 1350 to September 1352*, Wakefield Court Rolls Series of the
     Yorkshire Archaeological Society, volume 6 (1985), p. 56.
162. Bridbury, *English economy*, pp. 212, 215.
163. Mullan, 'Transfer of customary land', pp. 86-7. For the impotence of lords when faced
     with coordinated refusals to perform services and rents after 1349, see Bailey, *Decline
     of serfdom*, pp. 110-11, 139; and Booth, *Financial administration*, pp. 90-1.
164. Bailey, *Decline of serfdom*, pp. 16-61.
165. Calculations of entry fines per unit area are rare in published case studies, but where
     they exist and are analysed systematically all reveal marked falls in land values. See, for
     example, Mullan and Britnell, *Land and family*, pp. 76-9; Stone, *Esher*, pp. lxix, 283;
     Poos, *Rural society*, p. 50, fig. 2.4; Wells-Furby, *Berkeley estate*, p. 106; Graham Platts,
     Land and people in medieval Lincolnshire (Lincoln, 1985), p. 171; Phillips,
     'Collaboration and litigation', p. 63; Bailey, *Decline of serfdom*, pp. 109, 128, 166,
     172, 193, 208, 235; Ros Faith, 'Berkshire: fourteenth and fifteenth centuries', in
     Harvey, ed., *Peasant land market*, pp. 116, 132. For a contrary statement, see Dyer,
     'Social and economic', pp. 26-7.
166. Hargreaves, 'Seigniorial reaction', p. 58; Thornton, 'Rural society', pp. 135-9.
167. Fryde, 'Tenants of the bishops', pp. 232, 234-7; Bailey, *Decline of serfdom*, pp. 107,
     115-16, 123, 139, 150, 163, 201, 223; Bailey, 'Tallage-at-will', pp. 46-8. On the estate of
     the bishop of Winchester between 1346-47 and 1376-77 the annual tallage rendered
     by the bishop's villein tenants fell by 65%; the aggregate amount of annual recognition

payable on the Taunton group of manors (Holway, Poundsford, Bishop's Hull, Nailsbourne, Staplegrove, Rimpton and Downton) was 49s. 8d. in 1346-7 and 17s. 5d. in 1376-7, and it had disappeared from Poundsford and Staplegrove; see Levett, *Black Death*, pp. 127, 151-2, 171-7.

168. Fryde, 'Tenants of the bishops', pp. 232, 234, 236-8 and table E.

169. Richard Holt, *The mills of medieval England* (Oxford, 1988), pp. 160-2; Langdon, *Mills*, pp. 273-7; Bailey, *Medieval Suffolk*, pp. 57, 198.

170. Langdon, *Mills*, pp. 283-7; Bailey, *Decline of serfdom*, pp. 56, 108, 115, 123, 138-9, 151, 160, 173, 188, 201, 222, 234, 262. Contrast the rapid decay of milling monopolies in England under conditions of labour scarcity with seventeenth-century Bohemia, where under similar conditions such monopolies were re-imposed, Alexander Klein and Shelagh Ogilvie, 'Occupational structure in the Czech lands under the second serfdom', *Economic History Review*, 69 (2016), p. 514.

171. Mullan and Britnell, *Land and family*, pp. 26-7; Bailey, *Decline of serfdom*, pp. 111, 115, 124, 160-1, 174, 188, 203, 265-6; Fryde, 'Peasant rebellion', pp. 749-53; Woods, *Medieval Hadleigh*, p. 113. For a rare, and unequivocal, example of merchet remaining as a tenurial incident rather than as a personal incident, see William O. Massingberd, *Court rolls of the manor of Ingoldmells, Lincolnshire* (London, 1902), p. 185.

172. Between 1350 and 1360 nearly half of all entry fines due from seigniorial grants of customary land were excused at Halesowen (Warks.) in order to entice new tenants, Razi, *Life, marriage*, p. 112. In the 1350s labour services and tallage disappeared permanently from some servile holdings in Staffordshire and Derbyshire on the estate of the bishopric of Coventry and Lichfield, and in 1353 labour services were no longer liable on villein tenures at Fladbury and Ripple (Worcs.), 'because their tenure has been changed into a different service', Fryde, 'Tenants of the bishops', p. 231; Fryde, 'Peasant rebellion', p. 751; Fryde, *Peasants and landlords*, pp. 62-3. See also Wells-Furby, *Berkeley estate*, pp. 103-4.

173. Fryde, 'Tenants of the bishops', pp. 231-2, 234, 236-7; Fryde, *Peasants and landlords*, p. 61.

174. Campbell and Bartley, *Lay lordship*, pp. 253-4.

175. See, for example, Page, *Villeinage*, pp. 41-7; Edward P. Cheyney, 'The disappearance of English serfdom', *English Historical Review*, 15 (1900), pp. 32-7; Levett, *Black Death*, pp. 86-97, 147-56; Mate, 'Labour', pp. 55-67; Campbell, 'Agrarian problem', p. 37; Campbell, 'Factor markets', p. 84.

176. Levett, *Black Death*, pp. 88, 108, 151; Fryde, 'Tenants of the bishops', p. 234; Mullan and Britnell, *Land and family*, p. 59; Fryde, 'Peasant rebellion', p. 761; Page, *Villeinage*, pp. 47, 53, 66. Royal officials administering the Berkeley estate temporarily during its forfeiture to the Crown attempted to raise labour services and the charge for commutation, but this was never a feature of the estate under the Berkeley lords, Wells-Furby, *Berkeley estate*, pp. 116-18. Compare this English experience with of seventeenth-century Bohemia, where labour services were widely re-imposed in conditions of labour shortages, Klein and Ogilvie, 'Occupational structure', pp. 514-15.

177. Levett, *Black Death*, p. 146; Ballard, *Black Death*, pp. 199-200, 203; Fryde, 'Tenants of the bishops', pp. 231-3; Mary Saaler, 'The manor of Tillingdown: the changing

economy of the demesne 1325-71', *Surrey Archaeological Collections*, 81 (1991-92), p. 35; Bailey, *Decline of serfdom*, p. 139.

178. Cited in Horrox, ed., *Black Death*, p. 80.

179. Levett, *Black Death*, p. 97. For a similar examples, see Page, *Villeinage*, p. 65; Bailey, *Decline of serfdom*, pp. 125, 139, 162, 189-90, 203, 224, 255-6.

180. TNA SC6/1304/25 to 35.

181. Page, *Villeinage*, pp. 56-65; Ballard, *Black Death*, pp. 198-9; Levett, *Black Death*, pp. 108-9, 142, 147-8, 152; Mate, 'Labour', pp. 62-3; Britnell, 'Feudal reaction', p. 45; Kenneth C. Newton, *Thaxted in the fourteenth century: an account of the manor and borough* (Chelmsford, 1960), pp. 25-6; Edward Miller, 'Occupation of the land: southern counties', in Miller, ed., *Agrarian history* III, p. 142; Dyer, 'Tenant farming: west Midlands', p. 639; Harvey, 'Tenant farming: Home Counties', in Miller, ed., *Agrarian history* III, p. 667; Mullan and Britnell, *Land and family*, pp. 59-61; Bailey, *Decline of serfdom*, pp. 125, 139, 161-2, 176, 190, 224, 233, 256; Stone, *Esher*, p. 349.

182. Wells-Furby, *Berkeley estate*, pp. 103, 105, 135.

183. Bailey, *Marginal economy?*, pp. 309-10; Dyer, 'Social and economic', p. 29; Lock, 'Black Death', pp. 325-6; Hargreaves, 'Seigniorial reaction', pp. 62-71; Bailey, *Medieval Suffolk*, pp. 235-38; Matthew Tompkins, 'Peasant society in a Midlands manor: Great Horwood 1400 to 1600' (PhD dissertation, University of Leicester, 2006), pp. 65-6; Raftis, *Tenure and mobility*, pp. 191-2.

184. Jane Whittle and Margaret Yates, 'Pays real or pays legal: contrasting of patterns of land tenure and social structure in eastern Norfolk and western Berkshire, 1450-1600', *Agricultural History Review*, 48 (2000), pp. 9, 13; Thornton, 'Rural society', pp. 144-6.

185. Dyer, 'Social and economic', p. 33; Bailey, *Decline of serfdom*, pp. 205, 224-5; Stone, *Esher*, pp. lxxiii-iv.

186. Bailey, *Decline of serfdom*, pp. 290-2; Bailey, 'Transformation', pp. 216-20. These studies confirm Edmund Fryde's instincts that this subject 'is very significant and deserves much more systematic study than it has received hitherto', Fryde, 'Peasant rebellion', pp. 814-18, quote at p. 814.

187. Cecily Howell, 'Inheritance customs in the Midlands, 1280-1700', in Jack Goody, Joan Thirsk and Edward P. Thompson, eds., *Family and inheritance: rural society in western Europe, 1200-1800* (Cambridge, 1986), pp. 132-3; Thornton, 'Rural society', pp. 133-4.

188. Andrew Jones, 'Bedfordshire: the fifteenth century', in Paul D.A. Harvey, ed., *The peasant land market in England* (Oxford, 1984), p. 203.

189. Faith, 'Berkshire', pp. 130, 133, 138, 140; Bailey, 'Transformation', p. 220.

190. The following is based on a much more detailed study of Norton, using *Norton*, pp. 138-85.

191. Extensive data about the value of entry fines are not available from Norton because the exact acreage is not usually stated in land transfers.

192. Peter Foden, trans., *Records of the manor of Norton in the liberty of St Albans 1244-1539*, Hertfordshire Record Society 29 (2013), p. 171. For other examples of waived entry fines in the mid-1360s, see *Norton*, pp. 170, 172-73.

193. *Norton*, p. 147.

194. *Norton*, pp. 156, 176, 179.

195. Hilton, *Decline of serfdom*, pp. 44–51; Howell, 'Inheritance customs', pp. 133–4; Paul D.A. Harvey, 'Conclusion', in Harvey, ed., *Peasant land market*, pp. 328–38; Dyer, 'Social and economic', pp. 26–7; Robert C. Allen, *Enclosure and the yeoman: the agricultural development of the south Midlands 1450-1850* (Oxford, 1992) p. 67; Frances G. Davenport, *The economic development of a Norfolk manor* (Cambridge, 1906), pp. 70–5; Richard A. Lomas, 'Developments in land tenure on the Prior of Durham's estate in the later Middle Ages', *Northern History*, 13 (1977), pp. 37–40; Faith, 'Berkshire', pp. 124–5, 133–8; Hatcher, *Duchy of Cornwall*, pp. 122–47; Richard H. Britnell, 'Landlords and tenants: eastern England', in Miller, ed., *Agrarian History* III, pp. 615–16; J. Ambrose Raftis, 'Peasants and the collapse of the manorial economy on some Ramsey abbey estates', in Richard H. Britnell and John Hatcher, eds., *Progress and problems in medieval England* (Cambridge, 1996), pp. 193–4; G. Rosser, *Medieval Westminster 1200-1540* (Oxford, 1989), pp. 52–3; Schofield, 'Tenurial development', pp. 250–67; Wells-Furby, *Berkeley estate*, pp. 106–11; Bailey, 'Transformation', pp. 213–18; Bailey, *Decline of serfdom*, pp. 28–34.

196. SROI HA91/1, m. 62. For other, albeit later, examples, see Bailey, *Decline of serfdom*, pp. 173, 200, 222, 233, 248–9.

197. John M. Kaye, *Medieval English conveyances* (Cambridge, 2010), pp. 104–5. See also Paul R. Hyams, 'Notes on the transformation of the fief into the common law tenure in fee', in Susanne Jenks, Jonathan Rose, and Christopher Whittock, eds., *Laws, lawyers and texts: studies in medieval legal history in honour of Paul Brand* (Leiden, 2012), pp. 38–9.

198. A.W. Brian Simpson, *A history of the land law* (2nd edition, Oxford, 1986), pp. 78–9.

199. David Moss, 'The economic development of a Middlesex village', *Agricultural History Review*, 28 (1980), p. 109; DeWindt, *Land and people*, p. 135; and Howell, 'Inheritance customs', pp. 132–4.

200. Fryde, 'Tenants of the bishops', pp. 232, 234, 236; Fryde, 'Peasant rebellion', pp. 752–3; Fryde, *Peasants and landlords*, p. 62.

201. Raftis, *Ramsey abbey*, pp. 251–3; DeWindt, *Land and people*, p. 65; Matthew Tompkins, 'Park, one of the St Albans manors', in *The Peasants' Revolt in Hertfordshire* (Stevenage, 1981), p. 73; Mate, 'Labour', pp. 62–3.

202. As late as 1358 12¾ virgates of servile land across three Warwickshire manors were still unoccupied because no-one was willing 'to perform the services which the previous tenants had been accustomed to perform before the pestilence', Fryde, 'Tenants of the bishops', p. 233 and table F; Mullan and Britnell, *Land and family*, pp. 59, 62.

203. Faith, 'Berkshire', pp. 137–8; Bailey, 'Prior and convent', pp. 8–9; Bailey, *Decline of serfdom*, pp. 187, 250–2.

204. Fryde, 'Tenants of the bishops', pp. 224, 235, 237; Fryde, *Peasants and landlords*, pp. 56–7, 60, 64, 68; Rodney H. Hilton, 'A rare Evesham abbey estate document', in Rodney H. Hilton, *Class conflict and the crisis of feudalism* (1st edition, London, 1985), pp. 102–3, 105; Harvey, *Westminster abbey*, pp. 270–1; Page, *Villeinage*, p. 74;

DeWindt, *Land and people*, pp. 134–5; Schofield, 'Tenurial developments', pp. 255–6; Wells-Furby, *Berkeley estate*, p. 105.

205. Shakespeare's Birthplace Trust, Stratford, DR10/2594, court held March 1361 and/ 2596, court held March 1362.

206. Faith, 'Berkshire', p. 151.

207. Fryde, 'Tenants of the bishops', pp. 235–8; Fryde, *Peasants and landlords*, pp. 68–75; Finberg, *Tavistock abbey*, p. 252; Miller, 'Tenant farming: Yorkshire and Lancashire', p. 605; Harvey, 'Tenant farming: Home Counties', p. 669; Miller, 'Tenant farming: Southern Counties', pp. 708–9; Raftis, 'Peasants', p. 197; DeWindt, *Land and people*, p. 135; Raftis, *Peasant economic development*, pp. 72–5; Peter Coss and Joan C. Lancaster Lewis, eds., *Coventry priory register*, Dugdale Society 46 (2013), pp. 503–85, Sowe examples at pp. 550–6. In 1391 all the customary half-virgaters and cottars in Birdingbury (Warks.) were paying fixed money rents with no other services, as were six virgaters in Barford (Warks.) and 94 virgaters in Worfield (Shrops.): TNA DL43/14/3, folio numbers confused. The Birdingbury half-virgaters paid 8s. 11d. each year; the six virgaters in Barford paid a total of 68s., or 11s. 4d. each; and 94 virgaters at Worfield paid a total of £29 19s. 1d, or 6s. 4d. each.

208. van Basel, 'Land lease', p. 23; B. van Basel and P.R. Schofield, 'The emergence of lease and leasehold in a comparative perspective: definitions, causes and consequences', in van Bavel and Schofield, eds., *Development of leasehold*, pp. 12–13; Whittle, 'Leasehold tenure', pp. 139–40.

209. John P. Cooper, 'In search of agrarian capitalism', in Aston and Philpin, eds., *Brenner debate*, p. 161; Dyer, 'Social and economic', pp. 26–7; Poos and Bonfield, *Select cases*, p. clviii. Leases were rare on the bishopric of Winchester estates, Levett, *Black Death*, pp. 127–8, 151, and at Great Horwood, see Tompkins, 'Great Horwood', pp. 174–6; Bailey, 'Transformation', p. 218; John M.W. Bean, 'Landlords', in Miller, ed., *Agrarian history* III, pp. 569–70.

210. Hubert E. Hallam, ed., *The Agrarian History of England and Wales, vol. II* (Cambridge, 1988), pp. 1078–86; Miller, ed., *Agrarian History* III, p. 958. The latter does, however, contain an entry covering the leasing of demesnes.

211. This inattentiveness is noted in van Bavel and Schofield, 'Emergence', p. 11, although those two scholars have done more than any others to rectify the situation: see, for example, Schofield, 'Tenurial developments', pp. 250–67; van Bavel, *Manors and markets*, pp. 170–8; Whittle, 'Leasehold tenure', pp. 139–51.

212. For the leasing of demesne land, see Chapters 3 and 5. For the leasing of freeholds (usually land escheated into the lord's hands and without heirs to claim), see Wells-Furby, *Berkeley estate*, pp. 128–9. See also van Basel and Schofield, 'Emergence', p. 15; Christopher Dyer and Richard H. Hoyle, 'Britain 1000–1500', in Bas van Bavel and Richard H. Hoyle, eds., *Rural economy and society in north west Europe 500–2000: social relations, property and power* (Turnhout, 2010), pp. 57–8. For a comparison with the Low Countries, where the lease increased in importance in the fourteenth century in areas of stronger manorialism, see van Basel, 'Land lease', pp. 24, 28–9.

213. Kenneth G. Feiling, 'An Essex manor in the fourteenth century', *English Historical Review*, 102 (1911), pp. 334–5; Poos, *Rural society*, p. 243; Faith, 'Berkshire', pp. 122,

124–5; Phillips, 'Collaboration and litigation', pp. 130–1; Muller, 'Peasants, lords', pp. 162–5; Schofield, 'Tenurial development', pp. 253–5; Jack Ravensdale, 'Population changes and the transfer of customary land on a Cambridgeshire manor in the fourteenth century', in Smith, ed., *Land, kinship,* pp. 205, 216; Campbell, 'Population change', p. 121; TNA Dl4314/3, f. 21; Bailey, *Marginal economy?,* pp. 225–6; Newton, *Thaxted,* p. 24; Bailey, *Decline of serfdom,* pp. 232–3, 250–3; Margaret E. Briston and Timothy M. Halliday, eds., *The Pilsgate manor of the Sacrist of Peterborough abbey,* Northamptonshire Record Society, 43 (2009), pp. 377–403.

214. Wells-Furby, *Berkeley estate,* pp. 105–7; Dyer, *Lords and peasants,* p. 293; Fryde, 'Tenants of the bishops', pp. 234, 237–8; Dyer, 'Tenant farming: West Midlands', pp. 640–1; Razi, *Life, marriage,* p. 111; Fryde, *Peasants and landlords,* p. 140.

215. Fraser, ed., *Court rolls of Wakefield,* pp. xvi, 9, 23–4, 56, 60, 64, 73–4, 100.

216. Levett, *Black Death,* p. 127; Harvey, 'Tenant farming: Home Counties', pp. 670–1; Holmes, *Higher nobility,* p. 90.

217. Some customary holdings, and some small parcels of customary land, were converted to a new form of cash rent ('*arentata*') on the Ramsey abbey estate in the immediate aftermath of the Black Death. Although the exact details of this tenure are not revealed, it looks like a short-term lease, Raftis, *Ramsey abbey,* pp. 251–2, 285. See also DeWindt, *Land and people,* pp. 134–5; Page, *Crowland abbey,* pp. 128–9; Ravensdale, 'Population changes', p. 205; King, 'Tenant farming: East Midlands', p. 624.

218. Platts, *Land and people,* pp. 172–3.

219. Harvey, *Westminster abbey,* pp. 250–1; Simon Townley, 'Crawley', in *Victoria County History of Oxfordshire, volume 14* (Woodbridge, 2004), p. 180; Mullan and Britnell, *Land and family,* p. 80.

220. Holmes, *Higher nobility,* p. 108.

221. Hatcher, *Duchy of Cornwall,* p. 112.

222. Booth, *Financial administration,* pp. 128–9; Miller, 'Tenant farming: Yorkshire and Lancashire', p. 598; Dodds, *Peasants and production,* p. 80; Richard H. Britnell, Claire Etty, and Andy King, eds., *The Black Book of Hexham: a northern monastic estate in 1379* (Hexham, 2011), pp. 52–6, 64–5, 74–5.

223. In the Gelderland after 1400 the larger landlords and burghers were most likely to lease land, whereas charitable and parochial institutions were slower to turn to leases: peasants seldom leased to other peasants, van Basel, 'Land lease', pp. 26–8.

224. Harvey, *Westminster abbey,* pp. 257–8; Andrew T. Brown, *Rural society and economic change in County Durham: recession and recovery, c.1400–1640* (Woodbridge, 2015), pp. 104–6.

225. Sandra Raban, 'Landlord return on villein rents in north Huntingdonshire in the thirteenth century', *Historical Research,* 66 (1993), pp. 21–34.

226. Fryde, 'Peasant rebellion', p. 630; Campbell, 'The land', p. 236.

227. Campbell, 'Agrarian problem', pp. 27–8, 44; Campbell, 'The land', pp. 193–4.

228. The manors are Merton (Norfolk), and Akenham, Boulge, Cretingham, Easton Bavents, Kingston, Laxfield, Loudham, Tattingstone, Walsham, Walsham High Hall (Suffolk). Accounts are more useful than court rolls for quantifying in a single

snapshot the extent of conversions to leasehold, but accounts seldom survive from such manors.

229. The six are Akenham, Cretingham, Easton Bavents, Laxfield, Loudham, Merton, and Walsham High Hall.

230. Norfolk Record Office, Walsingham III/1, courts held December 1349 and March 1350.

231. In 1352-3 494 ex 656 winter works (75%) were not available because they were in the lord's hands, along with 28 ex 32 threshing works (88%), and 355 ex 609½ harvest works (58%), and leases yielded 41s. 8d., SROI HD1538/295/2. In the 1384-5 leases had jumped to £12 5s. 8d. and just 36 harvest works were now available: there were no sales of labour services, SROI HD1538/295/6.

232. Leases of customary tenements yielded £7 9s. 4d., compared with assize rents of 76s. 2½d. 29s. of assize rents (38%) were decayed. SROI HA10/50/18/4.4(8).

233. Of 800 winter works in the mid 1380s, 40 were used and 760 allowed because in the hands of the lord (95%); of 317½ winter works, 278½ were in the lord's hands (88%); and of 143 harvest works, 134 (94%) were in the lord's hands. Meanwhile leases of land fetched £11 10s. 6d. in 1392-3 in 51 parcels, 30 for a single year, 15 for a term of years, 3 for the term of an individual's life, and 3 unstated, SROI HD1469/7.

234. In 1328-9 62 acres of demesne had to be reaped, a further 22 boon works were due, and 310 muck-spreading works were owed. None are recorded, not even sold, in 1352-3. Leases of land fetched 3s. in 1363-4, and 76s. in 1371-2, SROI HA68/484/318. The increase in leases after the 1361 epidemic, including in 1363 a tenant relinquishing a holding on a service tenancy in order to be re-granted it on leasehold, is evident in contemporary court rolls, HA68/484/79 and 80.

235. There were no such leases in 1327-8 at Walsham High Hall, SROB HA504/3/1b. In 1373-4 leases generated rents valued at 66s. 1d., and decays (21s. 11d.) were 57% of notional assize rents: meanwhile, 23 ex 39 (59%) hen rents, 40 ex 80 (50%) half week works, and 55 ex 124 (44%) harvest works were 'in the lord's hands', an accounting device to cover the conversion to leases, HA504/3/1c. At Laxfield in 1376-7 one-third of the cash rents of assize were decayed, and leases of customary land generated nearly £11. 81% of customary winter works and 78% of harvest reaping works were uncollectable because the land was 'in the lord's hands due to the pestilence' (i.e. either abandoned or converted to leases), CUL Vanneck Mss, box 8.

236. SROI V5/19/1.1, 1.2 and 1.4. In 1343-4 11 'average' and 45 'turbary' works were due from customary tenants, and all were used by the demesne, but in 1356-7 eight of the average and 23 of the turbary works were decayed: the remainder were sold. In 1343-4 all the harvest works were used, but in 1356-7 20% (50 ex 245) were allowed. This lower figure must reflect the fact that free tenures also owed harvest works, most of which remained occupied on service tenures. Many of the leases related to grants of customary land until the heir reached the age of majority.

237. SROI V5/19/1.6 and 1.10. In 1376-7 revenues from leases of land fetched 59s. 4d., and 73% of customary 'average' works and 51% of turbary works were decayed, while in 1395-6 the proportions had risen to 91% (ten ex 11 decayed) and 64% (29 ex 43 decayed).

238. There was not a single lease of customary land at Tattingstone (Suffolk) in the late 1360s and 1370s, SROI HB8/1/817, 818 and 819. At Kingston in 1368-9 a mere nine parcels of customary land were leased for a mixture of years and for life, CUL EDC 7/14/C/27. At Boulge (Suffolk) in 1372-3 around 25% was leased, based on evidence that around 25% of harvest and winter works were 'in the lord's hands', and eleven separate leases yielded 32s. 1d., SROI HD1538/139/2.; and at Walsham in 1390 c.20% of customary holdings were leased, based on the proportion of egg rents (17%), half-day winter works (18%), and harvest works (15%) recorded as decayed, and income received from leases of customary land, SROB HA504/3/3.

239. Schofield, 'Tenurial developments', p. 255.

240. For an example from Cheshire, see Stuart Harrop, ed., *Extent of the Lordship of Longdendale 1360*, The Record Society of Lancashire and Cheshire, 140 (2005), pp. 49-59.

241. For the earls of Norfolk, see Bailey, *Decline of serfdom*, pp. 199-200, 220-1. For elsewhere in East Anglia, see Holmes, *Higher nobility*, pp. 92-3, and Newton, *Thaxted*, p. 68.

242. Ballard, *Black Death*, pp. 197, 214; Titow, 'Lost rents', pp. 101-6.

243. Schofield, 'Tenurial developments', pp. 257-8; Newton, *Thaxted*, p. 68.

244. This calculation supersedes the figures in Bailey, *Decline of serfdom*, p. 170, where I had originally misread some aspects of the 1350s and 1360s works' accounts, which were difficult to read on poor quality microfilm: these revised figures are based upon a thorough check of the original documents, SROB E3/15.3/2.7 and 2.10(d).

245. Wells-Furby, *Berkeley estate*, pp. 106-7. See also Finberg, *Tavistock abbey*, p. 251; and Bailey, 'Transformation', p. 218.

246. Berkeley Castle Muniments, A/1/3.

247. Wells-Furby, *Berkeley estate*, pp. 106-7, 217.

248. TNA DL43/14/3.

249. SROI, HA91/1.

250. van Bavel and Schofield, 'Emergence', pp. 17-18, 21.

251. van Bavel and Schofield, 'Emergence', pp. 14-23; van Bavel, *Manors and markets*, pp. 170-3.

252. Page, *Villeinage*, pp. 67-8, 84-5, 87; Levett, *Black Death*, p. 152; Page, *Crowland abbey*, pp. 128-9; Harvey, *Westminster abbey*, pp. 244-5, 247-8; Britnell, 'Feudal reaction', p. 44; Schofield, 'Tenurial developments', pp. 257-60; Bailey, 'Prior and convent', p. 8; Tompkins, 'Park', p. 73; Bailey, *Decline of serfdom*, pp. 120-1, 187, 251; Bailey, 'Myth', pp. 162-4.

253. Comments in contemporary manorial accounts also noted explicitly that rents at farm related to customary land 'leased for want of tenants'. For example, Booth, *Financial administration*, p. 129; Mullan and Britnell, *Land and family*, pp. 80, 99; Titow, 'Lost rents', pp. 97-106; Schofield, 'Tenurial developments', p. 255; Fryde, 'Tenants of the bishops', pp. 231, 234-8; TNA DL43/14/3.

254. For example, Hatcher, *Duchy of Cornwall*, p. 112; Bailey, *Marginal economy?*, pp. 225-6; Booth, *Financial administration*, p. 129; Fryde, *Peasants and landlords*, p. 68; Mullan and Britnell, *Land and family*, pp. 80, 99; Bailey, 'Prior and convent', pp. 8-9. In 1363 the grant of a messuage and acre of customary land at Iken (Suffolk) on a leasehold for

the life of John Holeway for 8d. per annum was explained by the fact that one Roger Melle had abandoned it in the lord's hands two years previously, SROI HD32/293/390, m. 39.

255. In 1373 John Polstead abandoned a coterell and three acres, formerly held by Alex le Coo, in Hargrave, but then he reoccupied them on leasehold at 2s. rent per annum, SROB E3/15.10/2.19. These smallholdings owed a rent package dominated by labour services, made up of a disproportionately heavy loading of week works and ploughing services.

256. Ravensdale, 'Population changes', pp. 224–5; Schofield, 'Tenurial developments', pp. 257–8; Dyer, *Making a living*, p. 295.

257. Levett, *Black Death*, pp. 86, 97; Mullan and Britnell, *Land and family*, pp. 58–63.

258. Wells-Furby, *Berkeley estate*, p. 106.

259. Bailey, 'Transformation', pp. 222–6.

260. Hilton, 'Evesham abbey', p. 105; Brenner, 'Agrarian', pp. 46–50; Fryde, *Peasants and landlords*, p. 270; Dyer, 'Social and economic', p. 26; Raban, 'Landlord return', p. 25; Poos and Bonfield, eds., *Select cases*, p. lxxxiv; Bavel and Schofield, 'Emergence', pp. 21–2; Muller, 'Conflict', p. 6; Bailey, 'Transformation', p. 222.

261. Edward Miller, 'Tenant farming and farmers: Yorkshire and Lancashire', in Miller, ed., *Agrarian history, III*, pp. 598–9; Mavis E. Mate, 'Tenant farming and farmers: Kent and Sussex', in Miller, ed., *Agrarian history, III*, p. 689; Harvey, *Westminster abbey*, pp. 250–1; Schofield, 'Tenurial development', pp. 258, 261–4; Larson, *Conflict and compromise*, p. 165; Bavel and Schofield, 'Emergence', p. 22.

262. Hatcher, *Duchy of Cornwall*, pp. 119–20; Schofield, 'Tenurial developments', pp. 251, 261–4; Britnell, 'Land and lordship', p. 161; Razi, *Life, marriage*, pp. 118–20; Mullan, 'Transfers of customary land', pp. 89–91; Wells-Furby, *Berkeley estate*, p. 105.

263. Mullan and Britnell, *Land and family*, pp. 87, 127–9.

264. Shakespeare Birthplace Trust, DR10/2588, court held 20 June 1351; Fryde, *Peasants and lords*, p. 63.

265. TNA SC2/169/28, m. 5.

266. Bailey, 'Prior and convent', pp. 8–9; Larson, *Conflict and compromise*, p. 167; Mullan and Britnell, *Land and family*, p. 62; Ravensdale, 'Population changes', pp. 224–5; Larson, *Conflict and compromise*, p. 167. Some landlords were alert to the pull exerted by competitive tenures, such as when the court of Bishop's Itchington (Warks.) decreed in 1354 that no customary tenants could hold land in two vills (there is no evidence the order was enforced), Shakespeare's Birthplace Trust, DR10/2594.

267. Vinogradoff, *Villeinage*, p. 85.

268. For evidence of freemen holding villein land before 1349, see Hatcher, 'English Serfdom', p. 26; Britnell, 'Tenant farming: eastern England', p. 619; Briggs, 'English serfdom', p. 27; Bailey, *Medieval Suffolk*, p. 46; Page, *Villeinage*, p. 52; Phillips, 'Collaboration and litigation', pp. 98, 165–6.

269. Fryde, *Peasants and landlords*, pp. 26, 63; John Hare, *A prospering society: Wiltshire in the later Middle Ages* (Hatfield, 2011), p. 124. See also Wells-Furby, *Berkeley estate*, p. 105.

270. After 1361 scribes returned to the practice of simply naming those performing fealty without distinction, Lock, *Walsham, vol. 2*, pp. 59, 105, 122.

271. Norfolk Record Office, Hare 4238. There were fifty-seven performing fealty: eleven freemen holding free land, eleven *nativi*, and thirty-five freemen holding '*terram nativam*'. Two of the names in the last category are crossed out, and *nativi* written as superscript. Thus the calculation of the percentages is based on thirteen serfs and thirty-three freemen holding customary land.

272. In March 1354 there were nine freemen, seventeen freemen holding by the rod, and twelve *nativi*; in March 1361 there were nineteen freemen, twenty-two freemen holding native land, and thirteen *nativi*. SROI HA91/1, court held February 1329 and mm. 68, 88.

273. SROI HD32/293/390, m. 37, court held April 1363. Seven serfs performed fealty, six more were attached by body to do so at the next court.

274. Kanzaka, 'Villein rents', p. 598 estimates that in 1279 60% of feeholdings were under six acres; Campbell, 'Agrarian problem', pp. 34, 50–1, 57–8, 61; Bekar and Reed, 'Land markets and inequality', pp. 306–9.

275. Wells-Furby, *Berkeley estate*, p. 105; Bailey, 'Bredfield', forthcoming.

276. Britnell, 'Tenant farming: eastern England', pp. 618–19; Bailey, *Decline of serfdom*, pp. 121, 188, 251; Bailey, 'Myth', pp. 149–54.

277. SROB E3/15.3/2.7 and E3/15.3/2.10(d); see Bailey, *Decline of serfdom*, p. 171.

278. Larson, *Conflict and compromise*, pp. 178–9, 191.

279. Larson, *Conflict and compromise*, p. 165; Bailey, 'Transformation', p. 222.

280. Whittle, 'Leasehold tenure', pp. 139–40.

281. Britnell, 'Tenant farming: eastern England', pp. 619–20; Bailey, 'Transformation', pp. 225–6.

282. Brenner, 'Agrarian class structure', pp. 27, 35; Dyer, 'Social and economic', p. 24. The general assumption about the immobility of serfs is surveyed by Briggs, 'English serfdom', p. 14.

283. See, for example, Hilton, *Decline of serfdom*, pp. 41–3; Hilton, *Bondmen made free*, pp. 153–6; Dyer, 'Social and economic', pp. 26, 31–2; Hargreaves, 'Seigniorial reaction', pp. 52–78; Juliet Barker, *England, arise: the people, the king and the Great Revolt of 1381* (London, 2014), pp. 64–71.

284. *Statutes of the Realm*, I, p. 323; Fryde, *Peasants and landlords*, pp. 19–21; Fryde, 'Peasant rebellion', p. 767; Ormrod et al., *Early petitions*, pp. 169–71.

285. *Statutes of the Realm*, 1, p. 367.

286. Palmer, *English law*, p. 27; Bennett, 'Compulsory service', pp. 25–6; Putnam, *Statutes of Labourers*, pp. 78, 174–84, 201–6; Clark, 'Medieval labour law', p. 338; Poos, 'Social context', pp. 30–1; Poos, *Rural society*, pp. 216–17.

287. Putnam, *Statutes of labourers*, p. 206; Paul Vinogradoff, *Villeinage in England* (Oxford, 1892), p. 85.

288. Dyer, 'Social and economic', p. 23.

289. For increased record of migration, see, for example, Page, *Villeinage*, pp. 55–7; Cheyney, 'End of serfdom', pp. 27–9; Page, *Crowland abbey*, pp. 137–8; William Page, ed., *Victoria County History of Gloucestershire, volume II* (London, 1907), p. 146; Raftis, *Tenure and mobility*, pp. 143, 151; Razi, *Life, marriage*, pp. 119–20; Dyer, 'Social and economic', p. 24; Harvey, 'Tenant farming: Home Counties', pp. 675–6; Fryde, 'Peasant rebellion', p. 767; Campbell, 'Population pressure', p. 100; Swanson, *Medieval British*

towns, p. 70; McGibbon Smith, 'Reflections', p. 148; Bailey, *Decline of serfdom*, pp. 123, 141, 161, 179; Britnell, 'Feudal reaction', p. 37; Muller, 'Conflict', p. 8.

290. For example, Muller, 'Conflict', p. 8; Sherri Olson, *A Chronicle of all that Happens: voices from the Village Court in Medieval England* (Toronto, 1996), pp. 84–8.

291. Britnell, 'Tenants and tenant farming: Eastern Counties', p. 621.

292. Olsen, *Chronicle*, p. 163.

293. There are no presentments for absence at Ingoldmells, for example, Massingberd, *Ingoldmells*, pp. 138ff. The frequency of departures from Ramsey abbey manors did not rise after 1348-9, Raftis, *Tenure and mobility*, pp. 145–50; Mavis E. Mate, *Daughters, wives and widows after the Black Death: women in Sussex 1350-1500* (Woodbridge, 1999) pp. 91–2; King, 'Tenant farming: East Midlands', p. 631; Harvey, 'Tenant farming: Home Counties', p. 677; Bailey, *Decline of serfdom*, pp. 123-4, 129, 226.

294. Poos, *Rural society*, p. 246; Briggs, 'English serfdom', pp. 28–30; Phillips, 'Collaboration and litigation', p. 62; Bailey, *Decline of serfdom*, pp. 140-1, 204-5, 226-8, 234.

295. Bailey, *Decline of serfdom*, pp. 110, 180, 190, 227-8.

296. Levett, *Studies*, p. 255; Raftis, *Tenure and mobility*, p. 143; Christopher Dyer, 'The Revolt of 1381 in Suffolk: its origins and participants', *Proceedings of the Suffolk Institute of Archaeology and History*, 36 (1988), pp. 274-87, at p. 278; Larson, *Conflict and compromise*, pp. 120-7.

297. Page, *Villeinage*, p. 56, fn. 2; Larson, *Conflict and compromise*, p. 158; Dyer, 'Villeins, bondsmen', p. 432. Flown villeins were imprisoned at Launton (Oxon) in 1372, Harvey, 'Tenant farming: Home Counties', p. 669.

298. Harvey, 'Tenant farming: Home Counties', p. 677; Poos, *Rural society*, p. 246; Fryde, 'Peasant rebellion', p. 767; Larson, *Conflict and compromise*, p. 158; Thornton, 'Rural society', pp. 249-50.

299. Noy, *Winslow*, I, pp. 280-1.

300. Davenport, *Norfolk manor*, p. 74; Larson, *Conflict and compromise*, p. 114.

301. Levett, *Studies*, p. 255; Britnell, 'Feudal reaction', p. 40.

302. Bailey, 'Myth', pp. 160-1.

303. Cerman, *Villagers and lords*, pp. 22-7.

304. Britnell, 'Feudal reaction', p. 33.

305. For example, Page, *Villeinage*, pp. 65-6; Dyer, 'Social and economic', p. 24; Bailey, *Decline of serfdom*, pp. 179-82.

306. For an example on the estate of Bury St Edmunds abbey, see SROB E3/15.6/1.18, court held July 1388.

307. See, for example, Harvey, 'Tenant farming: Home Counties', p. 677.

308. See, for example, Larson, *Conflict and compromise*, pp. 147-8; Briggs, 'English serfdom', pp. 28-30.

309. Raftis, *Tenure and mobility*, p.143; Dyer, 'Social and economic', p. 24; Bailey, *Decline of serfdom*, p. 204. Brenner, 'Agrarian class structure', p. 35.

310. Page, *Villeinage*, p. 56, fn. 2.

311. Raftis, *Tenure and mobility*, pp. 143-4.

312. Campbell, 'The land', pp. 204-5.

313. Bailey, *Decline of serfdom*, pp. 178, 189, 204, 216, 226.

314. Raftis, *Tenure and mobility*, p. 145.

315. Chevage was also infrequent in both places: Stone, *Esher*, pp. 329, 346, 352; Massingberd, *Ingoldmells*, pp. 47, 130, 138, 153, 164, 188.

316. The court rolls of Waldringfield (Suffolk) between 1356 and 1375 contain four payments 'to work elsewhere' between 1356 and 1359, i.e. no explicit reference was made to chevage, but thereafter contain no other references to servile departures, SROI HD2454/1/1. The account and court rolls of Kingston (Suffolk) between 1349 and 1380 record one chevage payment from one flown serf and the unlicensed absence of two, CUL EDC 7/14/C/18 to 32 and EDC 7/14/B/1. There are no chevage payments and no reported absences in the 54 extant courts of Westhall (Suffolk) between 1346 and 1355, SROI HA30/50/22/20.9 (1).

317. See, for example, Raftis, *Tenure and mobility*, p. 151; Phillips, 'Collaboration and litigation', p. 62; McGibbon Smith, 'Reflections', pp. 95–7, 148–9; Bailey, *Decline of serfdom*, pp. 110–12, 116, 124, 129–30, 140–1, 153, 162, 180, 190, 206–7, 227–8; Muller, 'Conflict', p. 8.

318. Noy, *Winslow*, I, pp. 250–49; SROI HA91/1.

319. Raftis, *Tenure and mobility*, p. 169; Olson, *Chronicle*, p. 189; Bailey, *Decline of serfdom*, pp. 271–2.

320. Ogilvie, 'Choices and constraints', pp. 280–1.

321. Raftis, *Tenure and mobility*, p. 169.

322. For the ineffectiveness of lordly efforts, Raftis, *Tenure and mobility*, p. 168; Thornton, 'Rural society', pp. 249–50.

323. Raftis, *Tenure and mobility*, p. 168.

324. Britnell, 'Feudal reaction', pp. 32–3, 40; Larson, *Conflict and compromise*, pp. 113–14, 147–8, 158.

325. Muller, 'Conflict', p. 8. See also Levett, *Studies*, p. 255; Fryde, 'Peasant rebellion', p. 767; Hare, *Prospering society*, p. 124.

326. Peter Coss, 'Neifs and villeins in later medieval England', *Reading Medieval Studies*, 40 (2014), pp. 197–8. For a lack of distinction in personal status pre-1349 see, for example, Edward Britton, *The Community of the Vill: a study in the history of the family and village life in fourteenth-century England* (Toronto, 1977), p. 167. Of the hundreds of individuals named in the Redgrave and Hinderclay courts, 9% at Redgrave were identified explicitly as unfree and 16% of those at Hinderclay, Phillips, 'Collaboration and litigation', pp. 164–5.

327. Mark Bailey, 'Blowing up bubbles: some new demographic evidence for the fifteenth century?', *Journal of Medieval History*, 15 (1989), pp. 350, 352; Mark Bailey, 'Rural society', in R. Horrox, ed., *Fifteenth-century attitudes* (Cambridge, 1995), pp. 158–9; Phillips, 'Collaboration and litigation', pp. 42, 46; Larson, *Conflict and compromise*, pp. 63–5, 104, 158, 180–1, 187; Dyer, 'Were late-medieval villages self-contained?', p. 13; Coss, 'Neifs and villeins', pp. 192–3. On the bishop of Durham's estate, however, after the 1350s serfs were no longer identified, Larson, 'Village Voice', p. 697.

328. Ernie D. Jones, 'Going round in circles: some new evidence for population in the later Middle Ages', *Journal of Medieval History*, 15 (1989), pp. 329–45; Bailey, 'Blowing up

bubbles', pp. 349–53; Larson, *Conflict and compromise*, pp. 157–9; Bailey, *Decline of serfdom*, p. 143; Coss, 'Neifs and villeins', pp. 201–2.

329. Dyer, 'Villeins, bondsmen', p. 429; Dyer, 'Work ethics', p. 40; Dyer, 'Social and economic', pp. 24–6.

330. Dyer, 'Social and economic background', pp. 24–6; Page, *Villeinage*, p. 56, fn. 2. See also a complex example in DuBoulay, *Lordship of Canterbury*, pp. 183–4.

331. Dyer, 'Villeins, bondmen', pp. 429–30. Dyer supports this argument by stating explicitly that the separate identification of thirteen *nativi domini de sanguine* within a 1361 fealty list of Bredfield (Suffolk) was a new development designed to earmark a servile workforce for future coercion, Dyer, 'Villeins, bondsmen', p. 430. The court roll reference for this entry is SROI HA91/1, m. 88. While the identification of personal status in fealty lists was indeed a new development at Bredfield, Dyer does not mention that the same list also identifies twenty-two 'freemen holding customary land' (the omission recurs in Dyer, 'Rising of 1381', p. 275). This additional information is contextually important because it makes the likely purpose of the list to distinguish *nativi* from other customary landholders of free status, not to earmark them for work service or future exploitation. Likewise, when a fealty list of Walsham High Hall in 1351 identified four customary tenants and one serf holding land in bondage, the purpose must have been to indicate that the four were not hereditary serfs of the manor, Lock, *Walsham, vol. 2*, p. 38.

332. Dyer, 'Villeins, bondmen', p. 429; Dyer, 'Work ethics', p. 40. For evidence of the rarity of work agreements, see Bailey, *Decline of serfdom*, pp. 113, 126, 142–3, 209, 229–30, 275–6.

333. Bailey, *Decline of serfdom*, pp. 164–5, 275, 308; Bailey, 'Myth', pp. 160–4. The possibility that some serfs entered agreements with special conditions willingly, because of benefits that are not apparent to the historian, merits consideration.

334. Tuck, 'Tenant farming: northern borders', p. 593; Larson, *Conflict and compromise*, pp. 157–8, 209.

335. Razi, *Life marriage*, p. 139 estimates that fines for merchet rose 300% after 1349. In contrast, see Dyer, 'Social and economic background', pp. 23–4; Miriam Muller, 'The function and evasion of marriage fines on a fourteenth-century English manor', *Continuity and Change*, 14 (1999), p. 183; Bailey, *Decline of serfdom*, p. 202.

336. Razi, *Life marriage*, pp. 138–9 documents the collapse of leyrwite; Larson, *Conflict and compromise*, p. 94; Mullan and Britnell, *Land and family*, pp. 26–7; McGibbon Smith, 'Reflections', pp. 144–6; Bailey, *Decline of serfdom*, pp. 108, 115–16, 124, 129, 139, 160, 174, 189, 202, 223, 264–6; McGibbon Smith, 'Court rolls', table 16, p. 270; Thornton, 'Rural society', p. 248; the number of merchets at Halesowen fell from 44 per decade in the 1330s and 1340s to 17 per decade in the 1350s and 1360s, seven in the 1370s, and one in the 1390s, Razi, *Life marriage*, pp. 48, 133. A 'very sharp decline in the number of marriage fines' is recorded on a sample of manors spread across southern England, Richard M. Smith, 'Moving to marry among the customary tenants of late thirteenth and early fourteenth century England', in Peregrine Horden, ed., *Freedom of movement in the Middle Ages* (Donington, 2007), p. 177.

337. Razi, *Life, marriage*, pp. 48, 133.

338. Between 1330–49 there had been an average of 59.5 merchets per decade, compared with 33 in 1360–69 and 21 in 1370–7, Muller, 'Function', p. 183.

339. Phillips, 'Collaboration and litigation', pp. 185–6.

340. Whittle, 'Individualism', p. 46; Coss, 'Neifs and villeins', pp. 197–8.

341. Raftis, 'Peasants', pp. 197–8; Dyer, 'Villeins, bondsmen', p. 424.

342. Coss, 'Neifs and villeins', pp. 201–2.

343. Eleanor M. Carus Wilson, 'Evidence for industrial growth on some fifteenth-century manors', in Carus-Wilson, ed., *Essays in economic history, volume II*, pp. 162–3; R.K. Field, 'Migration in the later Middle Ages: the case of the Hampton Lovell villeins', *Midland History*, 9 (1983), pp. 33–5; Bailey, *Decline of serfdom*, pp. 58–9.

344. Hyams, *King, lords and peasants*, pp. 29, 162; Henry S. Bennett, *Life on the English manor* (Cambridge, 1937), pp. 309–12; Fryde, *Peasants and landlords*, pp. 18–21; Postles, 'Migration', pp. 294–5; Briggs, 'English serfdom', pp. 294–5.

345. Pollock and Maitland, *The history of English law*, I, p. 426; Hyams, *King, lords, and peasants*, p. 29.

346. Hyams, *King, lords, and peasants*, pp. 29, 118, 171–4, 182; Fryde, *Peasants and landlords*, pp. 19–21.

347. Pollock and Maitland, *History of English Law*, I, pp. 426; Page, *Crowland abbey*, p. 152; Raftis, *Tenure and mobility*, p. 141; Salter, *Cartulary of Eynsham abbey, volume II*, p. xxvii; Bennett, *English manor*, pp. 307, 310–14; Hyams, *King, lords and peasants*, p. 118.

348. M.J.O. Kennedy, 'Resourceful villeins: the Cellarer family of Wawne in Holderness', *Yorkshire Archaeological Journal*, 48 (1976), pp. 107–18.

349. For the increase in disputes, and especially the 1350s, see Dyer, 'Social and economic background', pp. 31–2; Larson, *Conflict and compromise*, p. 120; Bailey, *Decline of serfdom*, pp. 274–5. The rarity of disputes in general in manorial court rolls is confirmed in Raftis, *Tenure and mobility*, p. 151n., and in Bailey, *Decline of serfdom*, pp. 113, 126, 142–3, 209, 229–30.

350. Vinogradoff, *Villeinage*, p. 63; Baker 1977, 187.

351. Noy, *Winslow*, I, p. 270; *Norton*, pp. 152, 155.

352. Paul Freedman, *Images of the medieval peasant* (Stanford, 1999), p. 262.

353. Kennedy, 'Resourceful villeins', pp. 110–13; Horrox, *Black Death*, pp. 331–8.

354. Bailey, *Decline of serfdom*, pp. 274–5, 300.

355. The case is documented in Bailey, *Decline of serfdom*, p. 274, but Nick Amor subsequently discovered the debt plea in the court of common pleas, TNA CP 40/402.

356. Hatcher, 'English serfdom', p. 33.

357. For the labour market, Dyer, 'Work ethics', p. 39.

4

A Mystery within an Enigma.
The Economy 1355 to 1375

Introduction

The sudden collapse of the English population from perhaps 5.5 million people in June 1348 to 2.8 million in December 1349, and the thwarting of any demographic recovery following the recurrence of plague in 1361–2, resulted in a sudden and severe contraction in the economy. GDP fell by an estimated 30 per cent between 1347 and 1353, and did not recover thereafter.[1] A demand-side collapse of this magnitude should also have caused the prices of grain and other essential food-stuffs to fall dramatically and to remain low, while the halving of the labour force should have caused wages to rise sharply. A scissor movement of falling prices and rising wages would have cut deep into the profits available from agriculture, especially for landlords running large-scale demesne operations, causing them to curtail direct husbandry or to abandon it entirely. Peasant producers, too, should have responded to the smaller population and falling profits by cutting back production, causing the permanent abandonment of many holdings and marginal land. Thus landlords should have faced shortages of tenants and dwin-dling rental and demesne income, while surviving peasants considered the pros-pect of improved real wages and, if they chose, expanded landholdings.

The general view is that hardly any of these seemingly predictable consequences of demographic collapse are actually observable until the late 1370s, and, instead, historians have marvelled at how little economic life changed in the wake of the Black Death.[2] Platt expresses wonderment at 'the strikingly rapid social and economic recovery' and Bridbury states that 'however hard the community may have been hit, the economy was scarcely affected'.[3] The third quarter of the fourteenth century is widely portrayed as an 'Indian Summer' for landlords, i.e. as an extension to the pre-plague season rather than the start of post-plague winter.[4] The delay in the economic impact of plague is therefore mysterious and enigmatic, and is usually attributed to the unanticipated buoyancy of prices for basic commodities and the social agency of the ruling elite, who coerced peasants to hold land and to work on terms favourable to the landlords: the so-called 'seigniorial reaction'.[5] But this explanation begs as many questions as it answers, and does not adequately address the many confusing and contradictory

After the Black Death: Economy, Society, and the Law in Fourteenth-Century England. Mark Bailey, Oxford University Press (2021). © Mark Bailey. DOI: 10.1093/oso/9780198857884.003.0004

characteristics of the period.[6] As Hatcher observes, 'there is a library of economic, social and demographic theory that tells us what should have happened... but most of it fails to explain what actually happened'.[7]

The reality is that we have tended to generalize too broadly about the third quarter of the fourteenth century and paid too little attention to exactly what did happen.[8] Local studies often focus upon the immediate pre-plague era in search of signs of crisis, then skate over the nuances in the responses to plague.[9] The neglect contrasts markedly with the lavish attention paid to the two landmark events at either end of the period: the demographic implosion in 1348–9 and the social explosion of the Peasants' Revolt in 1381. The main consequence of this neglect has been a serious underestimation of the extreme and highly disruptive succession of environmental and epidemiological events that occurred in the intervening three decades. Rescuing those events from obscurity and reconstructing a full and accurate picture of exactly what happened is essential to explaining the contradictions and paradoxes of the period. Casting it as a balmy 'Indian Summer' is misleading, because, as we shall discover, there was no neat or consistent pattern of recovery, and instead the economy was turbulent, volatile, and uncertain. In addition, major economic and social changes were occurring in many communities.[10] The extreme exogenous events amplified the enormous challenges of adjustment to the Black Death in the labour and commodity markets, and added greatly to the complexity of the period. The first part of this chapter seeks to document the main economic events and trends, then the second section attempts to explain them. It does not claim to offer a definitive narrative or explanation, but it does seek to improve our knowledge of what happened and, in the light of that, to re-consider the influence of a range of hitherto underexplored supply-side factors.

The enormity of the epidemic in 1348–9 largely explains why the second national plague epidemic in 1361–2 (*pestis secundis*) has only received fleeting attention, even though it stands unrivalled as the second greatest public health crisis of the second millennium.[11] It raged in London from March 1361, reached many areas of south-east England by late summer and early autumn, and the far north and Scotland in early 1362.[12] Estimates of mortality during this outbreak are less easy to recover than for 1348–9, although it struck widely throughout England and killed a higher proportion of the population than had the Great Famine of 1315–17.[13] Recorded deaths of tenants on a handful of manors scattered across England suggest a 10 per cent to 15 per cent mortality, while the rates among extant samples of the clergy and nobility were higher at around 19 per cent to 24 per cent.[14] The death rate in London and elsewhere might have reached 24 per cent.[15] The outbreak triggered more short-term economic instability and proved a watershed in tenurial conditions on some manors.[16] Peasant grain production was once again disrupted sharply.[17]

The second plague outbreak was a decisive event in long-term demographic history, too, because it savagely halted any recovery from the first epidemic. The Malthusian conditions for demographic recovery were ripe in the 1350s, and a surge of recorded marriages must have resulted in a baby boom.[18] Yet the second epidemic prevented that generation from blooming through high mortality, probably because death rates were higher among the young and those in the prime of life, which skewed the age distribution within the surviving population and depressed its reproductive capacity.[19] It is also possible that the changing behaviour of young women exacerbated the consequent fall in birth rates, because their pursuit of employment opportunities—especially in servanthood—might have resulted in a rise in the average age at first marriage and in the proportion of women never marrying (see pp. 286–9).[20] The next outbreak in 1369 was manifestly less widespread, but killed at least 10 per cent of the population in those places where it did strike.[21] The outbreak of 1375 and subsequent epidemics were progressively less extensive in their geographical coverage, but could still be severe locally.[22] From an estimated population of 5.5 million in 1348, the poll tax returns of 1377 provide a reliable basis for calculating a population of 2.5 million people.

In the 1360s humans were not the only victims of epidemic disease. In 1365–7 some chroniclers record the visitation of an animal disease dubbed the 'pokkes', and further epidemics among demesne livestock are recorded between 1367 and 1369 on various manors.[23] Shortages were reflected in the mean price for livestock, which in 1368 was 47 per cent higher than it had been in 1361, and in escalating prices for meat and leather (see table 4.1).[24] The scale of sheep deaths nationwide

Table 4.1 Some price and wage indices in England, 1341 to 85 (1451–75 = 100)

Years	CPI	Grains PI	Meat PI	Dairy PI	Threshing Wages	RWI (A)	RWI (C)
1341–45	85	81	90	89	52	61	63
1346–50	100	101	95	97	56	56	59
1351–55	126	131	114	103	60	46	50
1356–60	118	116	108	113	55	47	61
1361–65	138	130	131	105	60	44	55
1366–70	136	150	132	107	64	47	58
1371–75	127	134	144	107	72	55	60
1376–80	110	96	119	105	74	67	69
1381–85	113	104	111	106	78	68	69

Source: Munro, 'Late medieval decline', tables 18, 20A, 21A.

CPI = Composite Price Index; RWI = Real Wage Index, calculated by Nominal Wage Index/CPI; RWI (A) = agricultural real wage (based on threshing and winnowing wages); RWI(C) = craft worker real wage rate (based on carpenters' wages).

was sufficient to cause wool prices to rise dramatically during the late 1360s—28 per cent higher in 1366–70 than in 1356–60—and only when sheep flocks had eventually recovered in the early 1380s did wool prices begin to fall.[25] The scale and impact of these animal murrains in the second half of the 1360s have passed virtually unnoticed in historical accounts, but the subject will reward more detailed research if the wretched experience of the manor of Brandon (Suffolk) is typical. In the winter of 1365–6 one-third of the herd of demesne cows died of 'murrain', prompting the sale of the remaining stock, and a similar proportion of lambs were killed.[26] Then in 1367–8 one-quarter of all demesne lambs died of disease, one-fifth in 1368–9, and almost one-half of the remaining stock in 1369–70: ewes were also afflicted by the 1368–9 and 1369–70 epidemics, and in the summer of 1370 all the ewes that had survived successive waves of disease were transferred to another manor on the estate.[27] All these deaths were attributed to the generic noun 'murrain', so we cannot know if it was the same recurring disease or a succession of different diseases. Whatever the causes, the outcome is clear enough: in just five years the combined demesne lamb and ewe flock at Brandon had been devastated, collapsing from 540 in the autumn of 1365 to 15 in autumn 1370, and not until the late 1370s was the flock restored to its former size.[28]

Recurrent human and livestock epidemics struck against a background of extreme and changeable weather conditions, whereby phases of cool and wet weather alternated with dry and warm.[29] Intense global cooling during the 1340s and 1350s was followed by a rise in solar irradiance between the 1360s and 1380s, peaking at a level not matched again until the seventeenth century.[30] This major climatic shift provides a backdrop to the extraordinary volatility of the weather between the 1350s and 1370s, characterized by harvests that were highly variable from year to year and from manor to manor.[31] Extremely cold and wet weather caused harvest failure in 1349–52; the summer of 1361 was one of the hottest of the late-medieval centuries; then the winter of 1363–4 was one of the coldest of the millennium.[32] Poor weather caused repeated attacks of mildew in the mid-1360s in Kent.[33] Concerns about, and royal commissions into, the effects of marine surges and flooding in coastal areas increased between the 1350s and 1370s.[34] In 1367 manorial officials at Hutton (Essex) were neither exaggerating nor making excuses when they complained of an exceptional combination of wind, rain, drought, and animal murrain, and their accounts show that arrears of rent and the number of abandoned holdings rose.[35] The widespread failure of the harvest in 1367 was followed by a modest harvest in 1368, and that of 1369 was disrupted by plague.[36] The succession of poor harvests conceivably made the population more vulnerable to plague, but the compound effect of three consecutive poor harvests certainly explains the exceptionally high prices of grain in the summer of 1370.[37] According to one long-term index of grain prices, the level in 1370 was 227 per cent above the long-term average, the highest recorded adverse variation in the whole of the last millennium.[38] Complaints about grain shortages resurfaced in towns until the harvest of 1370 brought some relief.[39] The severity of conditions in 1370 has passed virtually unobserved because it created local hardship rather than a national crisis of subsistence. The extraordinary combination of adverse events between 1367 and 1370 is worth underlining: these years witnessed extreme and highly changeable weather, three poor harvests in succession, the third plague epidemic in 1369, and persistent if localized outbreaks of animal murrain.

The dramatic climatological and epidemiological events of the 1360s exemplify the exceptional, volatile, unpredictable, and disruptive characteristics of the third quarter of the fourteenth century. The historical literature does not emphasize enough the frequency and scale of these events, as exemplified by the cursory treatment of the second epidemic of 1361–2, despite its standing as a health catastrophe only surpassed by the 1348–9 epidemic. Consequently, we have not fully grasped how these events compounded the survivors' sense of fear, uncertainty, and turbulence as they attempted to respond to the challenges presented by the catastrophe of 1348–9. Yet this was the critical phase of adjustment, because demographic collapse filtering through the extant institutional structures produced social and economic changes in England that were very different from those in other European countries such as Spain.[40] Indeed, this short period could even be regarded as the defining moment of the last millennium, when 'profound and irreversible changes occurred in both environmental and human conditions'.[41] It is to these responses and changes that we now turn.

Reconstructing Economic Change

GDP per head

The collapse of population meant that the total output of the economy contracted sharply, with one recent set of estimates proposing that between the early 1340s and the late 1370s GDP fell by around 30 per cent.[42] However, population fell even further, by 46 per cent according to the same set of estimates. In some areas of Europe both GDP and GDP per head contracted, whereas English GDP per head rose by an estimated 25 per cent.[43] The rise in GDP per head was both immediate and sustained, estimated at £6.07 in the 1300s, £7.85 in the 1350s, and £8.86 in the 1400s (based on prices in 1700, see fig. 4.1).[44]

These are currently the best estimates available: even if they are not definitively provable, they offer a good representation of the direction and approximate scale of change. GDP per head rose for a number of reasons. The proportion of people who were landless fell because in the wake of plague they were able to obtain a foothold on the property ladder. Surviving smallholders could increase the size of their holdings. The availability of paid work increased sharply. Rural labour could be diverted from grain production towards pastoral pursuits and poultry rearing.

Figure 4.1 Estimated GDP per head in England, 1335 to 1404
Source: Broadberry et al. 2015, pp. 229–31. 100 = 1700–50

The lower orders of English society enjoyed a swift decisive improvement in their material welfare in the immediate aftermath of the plague.[45] At a stroke, the Black Death reduced inequalities of wealth, which in turn stimulated changes to patterns of mass consumption.[46] Consumption of foodstuffs per head increased, from an estimated 2,056 kilocalories per person per day in the 1310s to 2,467 kilocalories in the 1380s, and preferences shifted from cheaper to more expensive foods.[47] Ordinary people bought more and better household and personal goods. Hence they began to consume more wheat, ale, meat, and dairy produce, and less fish and vegetables, and to buy textiles for clothing and bedding.[48] The government's sumptuary legislation in 1363 was directed at the 'inappropriate', 'outrageous', and 'excessive' clothing and eating of the lower orders, confirming the speed and scale of the post-plague changes in their consumption habits.[49] Kowaleski identifies the stirrings of a consumer revolution in the wake of the Black Death, based on the penetration of consumer demand down the social scale, the expansion of mass consumer goods, changing attitudes towards spending, and the increasing quantity and diversity of personal possessions.[50] Certainly, the most likely initial outcome of any rise in disposable income among the lower orders in the 1350s and 1360s was an increased consumption per head of better quality food and clothing.

Prices and wages

At some stage during the 1350s, prices, wages, and rents should have lowered to a new post-plague equilibrium. Instead, grain, livestock, wool, and salt prices were higher in the 1350s than they had been in the 1340s, and continued to rise during the 1360s and early 1370s before falling markedly and persistently from the mid-1370s.[51] Rises in prices were higher than those in wages, so that despite the continued shortage of labour nominal real wage rates for ordinary labourers in the 1360s were actually lower than they had been before the plague. Furthermore, Clark has argued that agricultural rents remained flat between the 1330s and the 1390s.[52] Many historians and economists have expressed astonishment and puzzlement at the perverse behaviour of prices and rents, and especially the fall in real wage rates, between 1350 and 1375.[53] Consequently, the consensus view is that there was no 'change in the relative scarcity of land and labour until very near the end of the century'.[54]

The information contained in table 4.1 reveals that the prices of individual commodities did not all rise at the same rate. Grain prices registered the highest and most sustained increases, peaking in 1366–70 at a level 85 per cent higher than in 1341–5, and these drove the contemporary rise in prices for bread and ale.[55] Successive harvest failures in 1349–52 eroded stocks of grain, especially the reserves of seed corn. Prices for meat produce rose modestly in the 1350s, but soared in the 1360s and early 1370s due to shortages caused by successive murrains. Prices for diary produce rose by 20 per cent between the early 1340s and late 1360s, because demand for dairy produce was more elastic than for grain, and the rise in dairy stocks per head of population meant that its supply was more stable.[56] The chronic shortages of labour after 1349 generated upward pressure on wages, which rose after every successive plague epidemic.[57] By 1366–70 threshing wages were 25 per cent higher than they had been in 1341–5, and did not reduce thereafter, although they still lagged well behind the rise of the Composite Price Index until the mid-1370s.

Thus nominal real wages in the 1350s and 1360s were consistently lower than they had been in the 1340s, and Munro estimates at their lowest point they were down 20 per cent.[58] This evidence formed the cornerstone of the belief that the living standards of the many labourers and smallholders who depended wholly or partly upon waged employment fell in the immediate aftermath of plague.[59] Yet John Hatcher has warned against a heavy reliance upon nominal real wage data when assessing standards of living and the warning is especially apposite in this period.[60] The information about daily wages contained within historical datasets understates the wages actually paid because they exclude the bonuses and payments in kind demonstrably paid to labourers as part of the attempts to circumvent the restrictions of the labour legislation. Furthermore, attempts to project the living standards of labourers from nominal real wages are problematic because we cannot know how many days they worked each year, at what rates of daily pay, and what alternative sources of income (such as from a smallholding) were available. After 1349 the ready availability of both land and employment must have improved the living standards of ordinary people.[61] Likewise, the proportion of landless people declined, and the proportion on or below the poverty line may have halved.[62] The acquisition of a smallholding must have been the priority because land provided status and offered a more controllable and predictable form of livelihood than complete dependence upon hired labour. It is inconceivable that the average person was worse off in the 1360s than in the 1340s, despite the sustained fall in the nominal real wage data. A much higher proportion of the population now had at least some alternative sources of subsistence—a garden, a couple of acres, a little livestock, and some poultry—which reduced the absolute dependence upon income from day labouring while increasing levels of disposable income. This conclusion is consistent with the contemporary disapproving statements about the improved living standards of the lower orders of society.[63]

The issue is the extent of the gains. According to one optimistic estimate, real agricultural output per head rose by nearly one half between the 1340s and the 1360s, and real annual incomes by well over one-half, based on a working year of 250 days for a landless labourer.[64] There are grounds, however, for caution about the extent of those initial gains. Many labourers may have chosen not to accept all the work available to them, preferring instead to increase their leisure time.[65] Casual and unskilled work remained discontinuous and seasonal, and the government's labour legislation increased the costs and risks of participating in it. Payment for workers on annual contracts rose after 1350, but not as generously as the rise in day rates.[66] Another estimate posits a fall in the number of days worked each year, from c.200 days before the Black Death to c.140 days in the 1350s and 1360s, and by extension a more modest improvement in the real annual income of the average worker of around 15 to 20 per cent between the 1340s and the 1360s, with even fewer gains for those on annual contracts.[67] Caution about the extent of gains in living standards also applies to landholders with more than 15 acres of land. While their incomes would have swelled from expanding pastoral operations and the profits from grain surpluses, their expenditure undoubtedly rose due to the sharply rising costs of equipment, the replacements costs of livestock following bouts of murrain, and the costs and risks of having to hire labour themselves.[68] This section of peasant society was certainly better off in the 1360s than the 1340s, but it is difficult to know by how much.

Agricultural output

It is widely argued that the uptake of arable land in the immediate aftermath of plague was rapid and relatively complete.[69] Levett stated that most peasant landholdings were reoccupied by the early 1350s on the large estates of the bishopric of Winchester and St Albans abbey, and Page was struck by the comparatively few holdings remaining vacant on the estate of Crowland abbey.[70] Demand for land remained buoyant, so that in the 1360s the volume of land transactions had recovered to something approaching pre-plague levels and mean holding size remained stubbornly small in many places.[71] At Hinderclay (Suffolk), for example, in 1301 92 per cent of the unfree tenantry held less than 15 acres of land and 96 per cent in 1362: expressed another way, in 1301 fifty-two unfree tenants held an average of 7.4 acres of land and in 1362 forty-nine tenants held an average of 7.3 acres.[72] No obvious change in mean holding size between the 1340s and 1360s does not, however, mean that little had changed, because it disguises the fall in the proportion of the landless, many of whom had joined the property market, and the likely fall in yields and the area cropped each year on most holdings (see below, pp. 158-68). On the surface, however, the semblance of normality and continuity is powerful. Bridbury captures the general view when admiring 'the astonishing rate at which things got back to normal on most of the estates'.[73]

Nevertheless, whilst the evidence for recovery is impressive and indeed surprising given the scale of the mortality, the examples cited above must be balanced against the many other examples of places where large areas of peasant arable land remained uncultivated throughout the 1350s and 1360s.[74] Levett's claim that customary arable land was soon reoccupied on the Winchester estate is correct for the most populous manors, but subsequent research has shown that on many others large areas of land remained uncultivated well into the 1360s.[75] Considerable disruption and extended vacancies are recorded on the Duchy of Cornwall's central and north-eastern Cornish manors, and similar examples can be found from northern England, through the west Midlands to East Anglia.[76] For example, in 1362 half the peasant arable at Rollright (Oxon) was still uncultivated, and in 1365 up to one-quarter of arable was still unoccupied on various Derbyshire manors.[77] On manors across England during the 1350s large standardized holdings—those comprising perhaps 15 to 40 acres of arable land—often proved the most difficult land to fill.[78] In the late 1350s tenants could not be found for many customary virgates in parts of Warwickshire for as long as labour services remained part of the rent package.[79] This seems incongruous after decades of land hunger, especially when such holdings offered the tenant a large area of land suited to commercial production in a period of buoyant grain prices. Localities experiencing the most severe contraction had not usually suffered significantly higher levels of mortality, but their problems were a function of chronic difficulties finding replacement tenants (see above, pp. 91–3).[80]

Evidence from descriptions of the land use of freeholds transacted after the Black Death recorded in feet of fines also reinforces the sense that grain production did not collapse in line with population. These fines record mainly sales, including a lawyer's description of the land and sometimes a statement of the area transacted.[81] They distinguish arable from pasture, separating land nominally under the plough from that designated as permanent pasture land (the area of arable left fallow each year is not recorded). The fines further distinguished between good permanent pasture (including meadows) and rougher forms of grazing land, such as marsh, moor, and heathland (designated 'pasture plus', see fig. 4.2). Thus this information can be aggregated to provide an approximation of changes in the main forms of land use over time. The information contained within all the feet of fines for Essex, Norfolk, Suffolk, and Kent recorded during 1327–33 and 1366–72 is shown in fig. 4.2.[82] The most notable and distinctive trend is the failure of the proportion of nominal arable land to decline significantly between 1327–33 and 1366–72, which reinforces the view that no major or permanent conversions to pastoral land had yet occurred.

Overall, wide regional variations are evident in the extent to which arable was either abandoned or reoccupied after 1348–9. Hence, it is difficult to weigh the local examples of severe contraction against those of recovery in order to produce a national balance sheet of change in any meaningful way.[83] Yet it is indisputable that between the 1340s and 1350s the area under cultivation did not fall as far as the population. Reasoned, but tentative, estimates suggest that the total area under cultivation in England was one-third lower in the aftermath of plague than it had been in the 1300s, compared with a loss of population of one-half.[84]

Another oft-cited symptom of the unexpected buoyancy of arable farming in the aftermath of plague is the failure of grain production on seigniorial demesnes to collapse. According to Bolton 'there was little interruption in the pattern of demesne farming in the 1350s and 1360s, profits were being made and seigniorial incomes were buoyant'.[85] Some estates leased all their arable demesnes in the 1350s, while others began leasing some parcels of demesne, but for the most part the great landlords did not move decisively away from direct cultivation until the end of the fourteenth century.[86] The area sown on demesnes still in direct

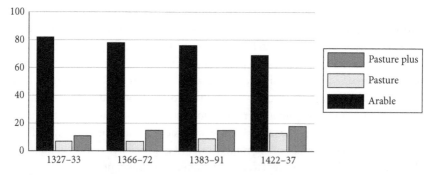

Figure 4.2 Percentage of land described as arable and pasture in the feet of fines for Essex, Kent, Norfolk, and Suffolk, 1327 to 1437
Source: see endnote 82

cultivation invariably fell severely in the 1350s, but then recovered in the 1360s and early 1370s, and on some manors it recovered to within 10 per cent of pre-plague levels.[87] The production of rye and oats bore the brunt of the decline, whereas the proportion devoted to brewing grains generally increased.[88] Buoyant grain prices enabled landlords to generate some profits from grain production, despite the vast mortality and upward shift in wages.[89]

Establishing precisely what happened to peasant grain production is impossible due the absence of any direct records, but indirect evidence from tithe records points to a general recovery of production between the mid-1350s and the late 1360s.[90] According to one estimate, grain output per head was 13 per cent higher in 1375 than it had been on the eve of plague.[91] For example, tithe receipts at Feering (Essex) in 1348–55 had fallen by around one-third compared with 1331–47, but by 1367–72 had recovered to within 11 per cent of the earlier figure, while those in County Durham had returned to pre-plague levels by 1358, suffered serious disruption in the 1360s, but then recovered and reached a post-plague peak by the early 1370s.[92] The subtle changes in crop selection apparent on demesnes are also evident on peasant holdings. A swing to brewing grains was especially apparent in regions geared to commercial output, such as the light soils of East Anglia, and elsewhere a shift to fodder crops occurred in areas where peasant production was focused more upon livestock husbandry.[93] In general, grain production per head of population was higher in the 1360s than it had been in the 1340s, although this was mainly the consequence of the reduction in the tail of landless, the agriculturally unproductive section of the population. Output per acre on peasant holdings almost certainly fell due to inclement weather (see below, pp. 159–60) and the diversion of labour to employment and pastoral tasks. Furthermore, as we shall see, it is also likely that the uncertainty created by poor weather, the threat of epidemic disease, increased government intervention, and disrupted networks caused some reduction in the supply of grain to market (see below, pp. 165-8).

While the arable sector performed better than might be expected, the pastoral sector expanded strongly (table 4.2). Although some livestock died through neglect and lack of supervision during 1348–9, the vast majority survived the plague year unscathed and so numbers of cows, beef cattle, and sheep in the 1350s were only slightly lower than they had been earlier in the century (table 4.3). Consequently, total agricultural output did not fall as much as the loss of population and had swung strongly from grain towards livestock rearing. Hence, within the context of contracting overall agricultural production between the 1300s and 1350s, the estimated contribution of livestock to total agricultural output had increased 39 per cent.[94] The lower costs of livestock rearing in an age of rising labour costs reinforced the swing because livestock required around one fifth of the labour per unit of land necessary to produce grain.[95] In general, peasant producers concentrated on lower capital-intensive and higher labour-intensive

Table 4.2 Estimated total agricultural output in England, 1300 to 1409

Decade	Population	Arable share of output	Livestock share of output	Total agricultural output
1300s	100	100	100	100
1350s	56	80	139	76
1400s	44	87	126	67

Source: Broadberry et al., *British economic growth*, table 3.21.

Table 4.3 Estimated numbers of livestock in England, 1300 to 1409

Decade	Dairy cows	Beef stock	Sheep
1300s	600,000	540,000	15,700,000
1350s	510,000	460,000	15,300,000
1400s	400,000	360,000	11,300,000

Source: Broadberry et al., *British economic growth*, table 3.11.

pastoral activities (pigs, diary, poultry), because the daily tasks of animal super-vision, feeding, milking, and butter and cheese making were most readily under-taken by family labour.[96] Lords concentrated more on higher capital-intensive, lower labour-intensive, activities such as sheep and rabbit rearing, and those who retained dairy herds invariably leased them to peasants rather than exploit them directly.[97]

The relative importance of livestock production was further enhanced by a shift to a higher consumption of meat and dairy products among the surviving population. Contemporary moralists complained about the new-found fussiness of the eating habits of the lower orders, and landlords had to substitute lesser foods such as potage with meat and better quality bread grains to attract workers.[98] While some pastoral produce was consumed within the household, rising demand from urban dwellers and non-agricultural workers—reflected in the buoyant prices of much pastoral produce—encouraged peasants to increase their commercial output. This orientation towards the market also helps to explain the revival of commercial leasehold rents for pastures and meadows in some places during the 1360s and early 1370s.[99] Prices for dairy products rose in the 1350s and held their level until the mid-1380s (table 4.1), the size of some demesne dairy herds expanded during the 1350s and early 1360s, and the rates paid for leasing a cow ('lactage') held or even rose.[100] The speed of the rise in the immediate aftermath of plague could be dramatic: for example, in the ten years after 1351 the number of cattle agisted on Dartmoor yearly rose from c.3,000 to 13,500.[101] The number of sheep on the bishop of Winchester's estate was a third higher in the 1350s than in 1348, and in 1354 the Black Prince established a large cattle herd at Macclesfield (Cheshire) to breed oxen and cows for sale as mature beasts, and to generate revenue from dairy produce.[102] In both cases, the expansion reflects the willingness of wealthy lords to invest large capital sums in livestock immediately after the plague.[103] Buoyant prices acted as an incentive. Poultry prices rose steeply in the 1350s, resulting in a rise in sales to market on some manors, although production shifted from demesnes to the peasant sector.[104] Indeed, in the 1350s the Wisbech (Cambs.) demesne diverted most of its pig production from household consumption to commercial sales.[105]

The growing demand for textiles for basic clothing and bedding in the 1350s fuelled demand for wool, whose price rose sharply and encouraged the expansion of sheep flocks.[106] Expansion could be rapid on manors where sheep rearing had been previously unimportant.[107] Production of leather goods grew, generating increased demand for hides.[108] During the 1350s and 1360s rabbit rearing in demesne warrens on the sandy soils of East Anglia transformed from a low-output, domestic-orientated activity to a major commercial enterprise in response to rapidly increasing urban demand for its meat and fur.[109] Output from Lakenheath (Suffolk) warren tripled between the 1340s and 1350s (see fig. 6.2), while the proportion of rabbits sold rose from 17 per cent to 71 per cent, and thereafter output continued to rise as the lord invested in watchtowers to protect the stock from predators and poachers.[110] London was the principal market for the produce of most commercial rabbit warrens.[111] The remarkable speed of the response to some new commercial opportunities in pastoral production in the immediate aftermath of the Black Death is manifest, yet its speed and significance is often understated in the existing scholarship.

For all the buoyant demand for the produce of livestock rearing, the sector also suffered a series of setbacks. The plague epidemics of 1361–2 and 1369 caused some short-term disruption to livestock production due to neglect and economic dislocation.[112] Then animal murrain caused even greater disruption to both the domestic and commercial supply of pastoral produce. The impact of the succession of livestock epidemics in the second half of the 1360s is reflected in the fall in both numbers of sheep and the quality of fleeces: demand, too, began to falter as both the penetration of English woollen textiles into overseas markets slowed and the level of domestic demand stabilized.[113] Disease also decimated supplies of beef stock and dairy cows in some localities. For example, during the course of the 1360s the manor of Tillingdown (Surrey) lost its entire cattle and dairy herds through a combination of murrain and sales.[114] The variable weather repeatedly curtailed the size of rabbit stocks in carefully supervised warrens because the medieval rabbit was especially vulnerable to cold winters, which severely restricted the ability of landlords to raise levels of bunny production consistently to meet the buoyant demand.[115] These challenges warn against excessive optimism about the scope for expanding livestock operations after the Black Death. The Black Prince's impressive new cattle herd at Macclesfield (Cheshire) could only turn a modest profit, and in 1372 no-one could be found to lease the dairy, and by the mid-1370s its size shrank rapidly through sales.[116]

The land market

The loss of half of the population should have severely reduced both activity in the peasant land market and the rental income from landholdings. Demand had certainly dampened. Land occupancy fell, each plague epidemic caused significant short-term disruption to the land market, and the volume of transactions did not return to pre-plague levels. The market for freehold land had lost its hair-trigger sensitivity to high grain prices, indicating the reduced vulnerability of rural society to the effects of famine. Similarly, the small, lower-value transactions that had dominated the pre-plague freehold market declined in importance in favour of larger, higher-value, and more complex transactions.[117] Yet the freehold market recovered in the 1360s, so that the fall in levels of activity were not commensurate with the fall in population. Rental income recovered in many places, and by the early 1370s the number of annual transactions recorded in the feet of fines in some counties had returned to the levels recorded in some pre-plague years.[118] This rebound in the face of successive plague epidemics reflects the pitiful size of many landholdings and the long tail of impoverished and unmarried landless people on the eve of the Black Death, who now stepped forward to remove the slack in the land market. It also reflects easier access to land, more attractive tenures, and the ability of survivors to combine a smallholding with more plentiful opportunities for paid employment.[119]

The customary land market had also lost a good deal of its pre-plague buoyancy and its sensitivity to peaks in grain prices.[120] In the late 1350s there were less than 400 transactions of customary land each year on the Winchester estate, compared with an annual average of 570 in the 1340s.[121] Evidence for untenanted holdings and concerns about shortages of tenants had been unusual before 1348–9, but now became more common.[122] The proportion of inter-peasant transactions fell and the proportion of grants directly from the lord rose, because more land parcels were being abandoned in the lord's hands and were tending to stick there for longer before tenants for them could be found. Subletting between peasants had been an important feature of the pre-plague land market as a way of redistributing land during a period of land scarcity, but thereafter the practice quickly disappeared as tenants could now acquire land directly.[123] Then, in the 1360s and early 1370s, demand for land began to pick up again, rental values increased on the 1350s, and in places the volume of transactions reached levels not far below those recorded in the immediate pre-plague period.[124]

Thus the customary and free land markets shared many traits. They were less volatile, less harvest sensitive, and less active than they had been in the second quarter of the century, but showed consistent signs of recovery in the 1360s. Despite this, the average size of landholding does not appear to have increased demonstrably until the last quarter of the fourteenth century.[125] Two other differences between the pre- and post-plague periods are less immediately apparent, but they carried great significance for long-term economic development. First, as we have emphasized, the proportion of landless adults had fallen, because not to hold land was now more a matter of personal choice and less a matter of availability. Second, commercial forces were beginning to exert a greater influence on the transfer of land through changes in tenurial structure and in patterns of disposal. Contractual tenures increased in importance (pp. 90–6, 300–6), and so the proportion of tenancies owing commercial head rents for cash rose sharply, albeit from a low base. A higher proportion of land was now transferred outside the family entirely.[126] In 1320–49 59 per cent of customary land had been transferred within the family on the bishop of Winchester's estate, and the rest to outsiders, whereas in 1350–79 only 39 per cent had been retained within the family.[127] Likewise, outsiders and non-heirs were able to acquire untenanted land directly from the lord. For example, nearly every transfer of customary land in the 1330s and 1340s at Bredfield (Suffolk) had been between peasants—and therefore were either sales or inherited—whereas in the 1350s and 1360s nearly one-third of transfers were grants of vacant land direct from the lord.[128] So market forces were more influential in the disposal of land after 1348–9. We must not overstate this point, however, because family and custom were still the main influence, and newcomers to the land market were principally seeking a holding for subsistence purposes.[129]

The continued buoyancy of rents in the generation after the Black Death has attracted a good deal of comment from historians. Of course, during the 1350s manorial rental income from rural landholdings fell on those manors where many holdings remained empty.[130] For the most part, however, historians have marvelled at the recovery of rents in most places, which seldom fell as far as the population, and often returned to pre-plague levels or even, in a few places, exceeded them: it was not until the 1370s that they began to fall.[131] By the late 1350s rental income on the estate of Canterbury Cathedral Priory had returned to within 4 per cent of the pre-plague level; to within 10 per cent by 1370s on the western manors of the estate of the earls of Clare; while on Merton College's manor of Cuxham (Oxon) money rent from peasant holdings soared from 45s. per annum in the mid-1340s to over £7 in 1359.[132] These generalizations disguise the considerable variety that could exist locally, even on the same estate.[133] For example, between the 1340s and 1360s total income from freeholds on the Berkeley estate rose c.10 per cent on its manors around Ham (Gloucs.), but fell 15 per cent on its manors around Coaley (Gloucs.).[134]

The general failure of rental income from peasant land to decline after the Black Death is traditionally attributed to a combination of buoyant grain prices and the 'strength and determination of the ruling class' to apply 'a degree of non-economic compulsion' to prevent customary rents falling in line with market forces.[135] Landlords are said to have forced villeins 'to work vacant holdings or pay fines for the privilege of not doing so', and restricted the mobility of serfs so that they had no option but to remain as tenants on their home manor.[136] Yet the reality was very different, as we argued in Chapter 2, because landlords could not alter customary rents at will and tenants were rarely coerced to hold land on terms unacceptable to them.

The discussion of rents in the aftermath of plague in the scholarly literature is, in fact, confused and lacking in rigour. Too often it fails to distinguish with sufficient care between rental income and rental values per unit area. The recovery of rental income after 1349 was occasionally due to exceptional local economic conditions, but more often than not was due to the conversion of holdings from non-commercial service tenancies to commercial cash rents.[137] Thus buoyant levels of aggregate rental income received from peasant land are not evidence of the oppressive imposition of high rents, or indeed of rises in rent values, but instead they reflect changes in tenurial arrangements and they disguise a loss of supplementary income from customary dues such as labour services and tallage. The swing to commercial tenures meant that aggregate levels of rental income could hold or even rise even if rental values per unit area were falling. Unfortunately, we know little about changes in the market value of agricultural land during the fourteenth century because there is no data for rent values to compare with the reliable information about prices and wages. Annual freehold rents and relief payments (upon entry to the land) were fixed, and so do not reflect changes in market value. The capital sums paid for freeholds by commercial buyers recorded in feet of fines provide a crude indication of broad shifts in land values and transaction size, but little reliable information about the value of land per fixed unit of area.[138] New tenants of customary land did, however, pay entry fines that were more sensitive to market conditions than were reliefs on free tenure, and so offer a more secure basis for reconstructing annual values. Nevertheless, few studies have attempted to convert fines into land values, because of various difficulties in extracting meaningful rental data from customary entry fines.[139]

Gregory Clark has postulated that if market forces had been the primary influence upon English agricultural rent values, then the latter should have fallen by c.30 per cent between the 1340s and 1350s, and by a further 10 per cent in the 1390s.[140] Yet his own rent series confounds these predictions by showing that average decennial values of arable land were marginally higher between the 1350s and 1380s than they had been in the immediate pre-plague period.[141] He does not discuss the reason for this anomaly in any detail, other than to comment on the simultaneous rise in grain prices.[142] Clark's attempt to construct an agricultural rent series is commendable and innovative, although the material draws mainly from the evidence of demesne leases (not peasant land), the number of observations per decade is relatively small, and the methodology is obscure. Clark does not engage at all with any of the more reliable rent data from published studies of customary arable land and which reveal a widespread fall in unit rent values after 1348–9.[143] For example, rents per unit area on a handful of Essex manors fell 25 per cent between the 1340s and 1350s, stabilized in the 1360s and early 1370s, then sagged again in the 1380s, while the level at Ham (Gloucs.) fell by 20 per cent between the 1340s and 1380s.[144] At the very least, the discrepancies between these localized but reliable and unequivocal examples of decline, and the evidence for growth in the Clark series, demand an explanation.

Figs. 4.3 and 4.4 offer a new rent series derived from the unit values of customary arable land, based on both capital values (entry fines per unit, fig. 4.3) and annual commercial rentals (leasehold per acre, fig. 4.4) from seven manors across southern and eastern England. The trends in decennial rent levels are fairly consistent from manor to manor, and overall the mean value across all seven manors fell by around one-third between the 1340s and 1360s, then stabilized in the 1370s before a further fall in the 1380s. As both graphs reveal, in the 1350s and 1360s grain prices soared while customary rents fell sharply. In the 1370s prices tumbled and rents values declined gently. Only in the 1380s and 1390s do the movements of grain prices and customary rents display a close correlation.

The fall in customary land values revealed by this rent series is consistent with a land market that had lost a good deal of its vitality after 1348–9, and where tenants exercised a greater degree of choice and bargaining power. The trend conforms closely to what Clark predicted should have happened to rents in the aftermath of the Black Death.[145] As such, it confirms that market forces did mainly determine capital values and leasehold rents of customary land. While the consistency of these findings cast serious doubt upon the reliability and validity of the Clark

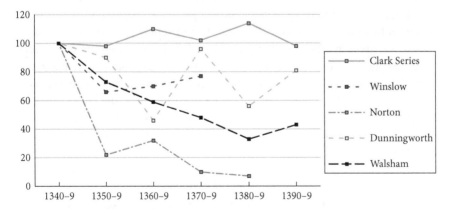

Figure 4.3 Index of capital values of customary land, 1340 to 1399 (100 = 1340–9)
Source: Noy 2011, Foden 2013, Bailey 2014, Clark 2016

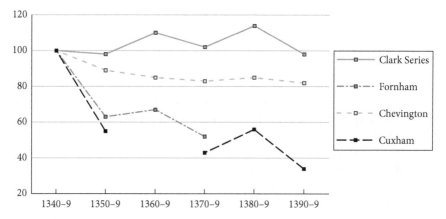

Figure 4.4 Index of rental values of customary land, 1340 to 1399 (100 = 1340–9)
Source: Bailey 2014, Clark 2016

series, there remains the difficulty of reconciling the decline in customary rent values with the buoyancy in the freehold land market and, especially, the buoyancy of agricultural prices. The conundrum of rising grain prices and falling customary land values in the 1350s and 1360s epitomizes the contradictions within this period and the turbulence within the rural economy. There are two likely explanations. The first is that the customary land market bore the brunt of the decline in the demand for arable land because it was the most stigmatized and unattractive form of tenure. Freeholdings were now widely available and represented the tenure of choice, and consequently in the short term the market for freeholds suffered less from the consequences of plague. Customary land values represent the rump end of the land market. The second possibility is that buoyant grain prices reflected a deficiency in the supply of foodstuffs to the commercial market, but not a deficiency of foodstuffs per se. The modern mind automatically assumes that grain prices will reflect the state of supply and demand across the whole of grain production, but in the mid-fourteenth century they simply reflected the intersection of supply and demand in the commercial market. In the 1340s at least two-thirds of all English grain never reached the market at all (see p. 41), and it is possible that in the 1350s and 1360s the fall in aggregate output coincided with an increase in the proportion consumed within the household, and an associated fall in the proportion available commercially (see below pp. 164–8).

In summary, then, the demand for land in the third quarter of the century was characterized by swirling cross-currents. On the one hand, the area under cultivation fell by around one-quarter, unit rental values for customary land and the volume of land transactions also fell, and distress sales largely disappeared. On the other hand, the reoccupation of arable land after 1348–9 was quicker and more complete than we might have expected, aggregate rental income recovered to a remarkable degree, and in the 1360s the volume of transactions almost returned to pre-plague levels. The fall in the rent value of customary arable land provides the clearest indication that the land market had indeed lost its buoyancy in the aftermath of plague. Customary land values fell c.30 per cent between the 1340s and 1360s, a function of its relative unpopularity, the falling productivity of arable land, and the pervading sense of uncertainty. We have underestimated the economic disequilibrium and turbulence of the 1350s and 1360s, stirred by plagues, murrains, and extreme weather and characterized by demographic collapse yet buoyant grain prices. From the mid-1370s many of these swirling and contradictory cross-currents disappeared, and the behaviour of the land market, of rental income and rent values became more consistent, and correlated more closely with the declining profitability of agriculture (see pp. 237–48).

Non-agricultural output

The industrial sector also emitted some contradictory signals. On the one hand, output from the extractive industries declined significantly and its recovery was delayed by disruption to markets and labour shortages.[146] Tin production was volatile and risky. In 1371 a shortage of workers was blamed for the abandonment of iron forges and coal mines in the forest of Macclesfield (Cheshire).[147] Similarly, construction work on major building projects ceased abruptly with the arrival of plague, and in the atmosphere of uncertainty in the 1350s few new projects were started.[148] Consequently, during the 1350s the wage rates of skilled building workers lagged behind those of other workers.[149] The expertise of such skilled workers was difficult to replace—and even harder for the historian to measure— but the loss of human capital in the first two plague epidemics must have been considerable. Yet the speed and the scale of the increase in GDP per head—which rose by perhaps one-quarter between 1335–44 and 1355–64 (fig. 4.1)—stimulated an immediate demand for basic manufactured goods. The evidence of rapid growth in some industrial (such as low-grade textiles) and retail (such as ale) trades in the 1350s confirms that labour and capital was being transferred quickly into those activities requiring limited amounts of capital, skill, and knowledge. Overall, estimated aggregate industrial output fell, but not as far as the fall in population over the same period (table 4.4).

The rapid rise in the consumption per head of clothing and basic domestic goods was directed mainly towards artisan-produced, cheaper goods from specialist towns and regions, and away from coarse wares manufactured locally by generalists.[150] Such specialists were responding to dramatic changes in fashion and dress among the lower orders, including a culture of emulating novelties of attire and keeping up with new modes of dress.[151] The main area of growth in the

Table 4.4 Estimated GDP per head and total output of the industrial sector in England, 1335 to 1404 (1700–50 = 100)

Period	GDP per head	Industrial sectoroutput
1335–44	49.1	29.1
1345–54	54.6	24.8
1355–64	62.7	19.7
1365–74	59.2	17.7
1375–84	60.5	16.9
1385–94	68.6	20.0
1395–1404	70.9	21.0

Source: Broadberry et al., *British economic growth*, pp. 229–31.

1350s and 1360s occurred in textile manufacture, partly in response to this rising domestic demand but largely to expanding overseas markets.[152] These were mass-produced cloths of good quality for general use as clothing and bedding, made by specialists using English wools rather than coarse textiles or indeed intricate, high-quality fabrics. In the 1350s localized expansion in towns and industrialized villages specializing in the production of such textiles is recorded in parts of Essex, Wiltshire, Somerset, Suffolk, and Yorkshire.[153] The speed of growth in a handful places displaying brash enterprise—such as Colchester (Essex) and Hadleigh (Suffolk)—is startling.[154] A timber-framed building in Bocking (Essex) constructed in the mid-1350s from trees felled in 1353–4 was custom-built to provide a spacious, but crudely finished, ground floor, most likely used for sorting and selling wool to local clothmakers.[155] Not only was the market for wool buoyant but it was also restructuring rapidly into the hands of domestic merchants operating from urban centres.[156] Similarly, the number of fulling mills in England rose by around 50 per cent between the 1340s and late 1360s, often by converting idle grain mills.[157] Production of leather goods expanded, especially gloves, purses, hats, belts, and doublets, alongside that of domestic utensils and furniture, such as pots, pans, cutlery, and beds.[158] Thicker and warmer clothing and bedding was not just fashionable but practical given the colder and wetter weather.

The buoyancy within some sectors of industry is impressive, but the scale and geographical distribution should not be overstated. Most areas of England had little specialist industry. The construction of a new fulling mill at Yeardsley (Cheshire) in 1367 was intended to exploit the growing demand for cloth, but it proved a folly and shut soon afterwards.[159] Nevertheless, there was sufficient buoyancy in localized pockets of specialized industrial activity to cause a distinct 'occupational migration of labour from agriculture to manufacturing'.[160] The poll tax returns of 1381 provide the most secure basis for estimating the composition of the English labour force in the immediate post-plague era, of which an estimated 19 per cent worked in industry, 24 per cent in services, and 57 per cent in agriculture.[161] These returns confirm that manufacturing activity was both a rural and urban phenomenon.[162] They also confirm that specialized manufactures were now expanding in regions—such as Derbyshire, Devon, Wiltshire, and Yorkshire— far outside the established economic heartlands of south-east England and East Anglia, a development confirmed by other local sources.[163] In the longer term, this had the important effect of distributing wealth more equitably across the country by increasing the availability of specialist craft-based employment outside urban areas and by greatly extending its geographical distribution.

Attempts to generalize about the fortunes of towns in the immediate aftermath of plague have usually begun by commenting upon the difficulty of the task because the available sources do not permit detailed reconstructions over short periods. Consequently, most case studies offer generalized observations about urban performance across the second half of the fourteenth century rather than focusing specifically upon the 1350s and 1360s. The urban land market is very difficult to reconstruct due to the lack of detailed records comparable to those from the countryside. As most urban populations were smaller after 1348–9, and as most civic property was residential rather than agricultural, we would anticipate the land market became much less active. In the 1350s attractive properties in desirable locations were usually re-tenanted quickly, but other properties struggled to find tenants: as a consequence many towns (including London) experienced reduced rental income, vacant tenements, the amalgamation of some holdings, and the demolition of empty houses.[164] By the 1360s demand for properties had recovered in those towns where industrial manufacture was expanding, including new housing, but remained sluggish in those that did not.[165] Westminster (Middlesex) experienced rapid immigration from the mid-1350s, prompting the main landlord to invest in a building spree of new housing and retail outlets within the town.[166]

Some general observations hold, however. The conditions conducive to the growth of the urban sector in the pre-plague period—a growing population and high volumes of trade—no longer prevailed, undermining the function of many markets and towns and narrowing their economic base.[167] New foundations of towns and markets virtually ceased.[168] Most towns had smaller populations as a consequence of the Black Death, the volume of trade in basic commodities and services contracted, and the regulation of urban economic activity and the costs of civic life rose. These adverse trends could only be countered if a town was able to capitalize upon the growing demand for mass consumption goods and the deeper penetration into overseas markets of English manufactures, and if it could minimize the institutional inflexibility and high fixed costs that were often a feature of urban administration.[169]

The manner in which these cross-currents affected individual towns depended upon the extent to which they relied upon a manufacturing base, their ability to access distant markets, the dynamics of local trade routes, and their structures of government. Between 1348 and 1353 all towns suffered severe economic disruption.[170] Rental income declined sharply, properties remained unoccupied, and the volume of market activity fell.[171] Recovery thereafter was quickest in a handful of towns able to respond to the growing demand for English textiles, notably Colchester (Essex), Coventry (Warks.), Lincoln (Lincs.), Hadleigh (Suffolk), Lavenham (Suffolk), and Leeds (Yorks.).[172] London experienced a surge of immigration during the 1350s, and its economy boomed over the next three decades: thereafter its relative importance and wealth continued to grow, suffocating the trade of some towns while stimulating those of others.[173] Competition for all types of trade was undoubtedly keener after 1350, and many towns suffered declining economic fortunes as a result.[174]

The proportion of people living in towns held constant across the Black Death: 15 per cent to 20 per cent of the English population lived in towns on its eve, and the poll tax evidence from 1377 suggests that around 18 per cent of the population were townsfolk.[175] Other methods of calculating the urbanization rate draw a similar conclusion.[176] Sustained immigration from rural areas was essential to maintaining the urbanization rate.[177] Before the Black Death much urban migration had been driven by rural poverty and desperation, but thereafter most was driven by choice and opportunity: towns experiencing economic growth attracted more immigration than those experiencing difficulties.[178] The granular details of immigration into towns are difficult to document precisely from urban sources, which provide few details about the origins or the status of immigrants.[179] Yet it is likely that labour shortages encouraged more rural women to move to towns in search of employment in servanthood, especially in the retailing trades, and contemporaries were especially sensitive to the flight of hereditary serfs into towns.[180]

The fortunes of towns could change rapidly. This was especially true of textile manufacturing centres, as we have seen, but it could also apply to localized markets. For example, the old borough of Standon (Herts.) and the small market settlement of Chipping (Herts.) declined rapidly in the 1350s and 1360s due to the meteoric rise of nearby Buntingford (Herts.), reflecting the radical and sudden restructuring of local marketing patterns in the new conditions.[181] Grimsby (Lincs.) flourished while its competitor across the river Humber, Ravensrodd (Yorks.), suffered coastal erosion.[182] Finally, the loss of human capital was significant in certain sectors. The sudden and unexpected deaths of so many highly skilled craftsmen, knowledgeable merchants, and experienced administrators represented a profound loss of expertise and know-how.[183] The composition of urban elites altered radically between the 1340s and 1360s as long-established families with vast accumulated experience in trade and town government died out.[184] Around two-thirds of the leading gildsmen of Henley (Oxon) died in the first epidemic, and nearly one-third in the second.[185]

During the 1350s and 1360s the reoccupation of land in some places, the eye-catching growth in some industrial sectors of the economy, and the speed with which a few towns expanded, are impressive. They reflect rapid changes in the consumption preferences of the lower orders of society from low-quality foodstuffs to meat and dairy products, and from coarse wares to cheap manufactures produced by specialists. They also reflect a relatively fast and nimble supply-side response, and an expanding engagement with the market, which could not have happened unless commodity and labour markets were already well established before the Black Death. The modest levels of skill and the relatively low levels of capital required to manufacture these types of textiles and leather goods, and to rear animals such as rabbits, also help to explain the speed of the response. Yet it is important to emphasize that the majority of towns did not develop such specialisms, and other industries were severely disrupted. The milling, extractive, and construction industries were badly hit. Changes to the most important factor market—land—were slower and more complex because of the institutional rigidities that already existed there, notably the high the degree of fragmentation and the knotty tangle of subtenancies. Likewise, adjustments within the commercial grain market were slow. The historian's dispassionate and retrospective analysis of price, wage, and rent data can obscure just how the sequence of extreme epidemiological and climatic events hampered and distorted the realignment of factor and commodity markets, and increased general sense of uncertainty and turbulence. In the 1350s and the 1360s the decision facing any one individual about their options must have been evenly balanced and difficult to resolve: whether to produce for subsistence or consumption; how far to switch to livestock rearing, and which aspect of pastoral farming to pursue; whether to acquire more agricultural land or to seek wage labour instead; whether to work in agriculture or industry; and whether to remain in the countryside or migrate to a town? Uncertain opportunities had now replaced the economic certainties of the 1340s.

Explaining Economic Change

Demand-side buoyancy

As we have seen, historians have placed most emphasis upon the evidence for economic buoyancy in the third quarter of the fourteenth century, despite the tremendous mortality, and have puzzled over the paradoxical rise of prices and the profitability of grain production in its wake.[186] The standard explanation for these astonishing trends is the failure of aggregate demand to fall anything like as far as the population and an expansion in the supply of money per head. The former was a function of the pent-up demand in the pre-plague economy, characterized by the extreme subdivision of holdings, widespread landlessness, and chronic underemployment, which meant that after the appalling mortality a 'submerged and pullulating throng' of replacements surged forward to take up the slack capacity.[187] The release from the choking congestion triggered an increase in average earnings and output per capita.[188] There were, however, limits to the immediate gains, because the scale of landlessness and the extreme fragmentation of holdings had been so great before the plague that the average size of customary landholdings appear not to have risen before the last quarter of the century.[189]

The second explanation for the buoyancy of the post-plague economy is the increase in both the aggregate and per capita supply of money, which contributed to the inflationary pressures.[190] The loss of bullion overseas in the 1330s and 1340s had reduced mint output to an unusually low level, from an estimated c.£1.5m–c.£2m in 1332 to c.£700k in 1351, and had contributed to a period of deflation. An influx of bullion in the 1350s and 1360s resulted in a rapid rise in the amount of money in circulation from c.£700k in 1351 to c.£1.4m–c.£2.4m in 1377.[191] As a result, the supply of coin per head rose approximately fourfold. The composition of the currency also changed, with gold coins quickly dominating mint output and the introduction of larger denominations of silver coins with a lower silver content.[192] Debasement of the currency and an increased velocity of circulation added to the inflationary effect. Other possible inflationary pressures were a reduction in hoarding in the 1350s due to the high levels of taxation, thus further increasing the amount of coin in circulation, and a greater income velocity of circulation due to a 'spending spree' mentality among survivors.[193]

Supply-side shocks

According to the traditional narrative and explanation, the buoyant demand-side responses meant that the immediate impact of the Black Death was 'purgative not toxic'.[194] There is no question that these demand-side influences were very important. However, this explanation does not sufficiently accommodate the many contradictory and turbulent elements within the economy, and it does not consider properly the range of supply-side problems facing certain sectors and some producers. The rapid changes in patterns of demand created manifold opportunities in the wake of the first epidemic, but, for the next two decades, the combination of market uncertainty, extreme weather, labour shortages, and repeated outbreaks of human and animal disease continued to hamper the responses to those opportunities. The severity of these problems extended the time lag of supply-side adjustments to the new patterns of demand, contributing to the inflationary pressures within the economy. Nowhere is this more evident than in the severe disruption to the supply of grain, which was exacerbated by consistently poor yields. In the 1360s grain yields on English demesnes were 15 per cent lower than they had been in the 1340s, and the fall was especially severe—around 30 per cent—in East Anglia and south-east England, where production was most commercialized.[195] Campbell concludes that 'in large parts of the country [grain yields] remained depressed and it took twenty-five years for yields of all three principal grains to regain their pre-plague level'.[196] If these depressed demesne yields were also a feature of peasant holdings, then the output of the arable sector fell much further than the estimated 27 per cent fall in the sown area in the 1350s, perhaps by over 40 per cent.[197]

The sharp and sustained fall in demesne grain yields between 1349 and the mid-1370s is paradoxical given that, other things being equal, they should have risen following the sudden release of severe population pressure upon landed resources. There are various reasons why land productivity should have jumped under the new demographic conditions: the abandonment of the most marginal, exhausted, and intractable soils; the sudden rise in the supply of manure from the improved ratio of livestock to the area under cultivation; and the adoption of less punishing crop rotations.[198] Yet the unequivocal and significant drop in demesne yields means that powerful countervailing forces must have overcome these potentially beneficial developments. The main cause of the lower yields was persistently poor weather, just as persistently fine weather in the last quarter of the fourteenth century was to bring good harvests and plummeting grain prices.[199] In Campbell's words, from 1349 'cooler, wetter and stormier conditions persisted for the next twenty to twenty-five years and inhibited yields from recovering to their pre-Black Death average. Conditions changed suddenly and dramatically in 1376 with the onset of a twenty-year growth bonanza', due to the onset of a phase of warmer weather dubbed the 'Chaucerian Anomaly'.[200] Campbell has also suggested that yields in the 1350s and 1360s were further depressed by 'a progressive depletion of the botanical quality of seed stocks, in terms of their resistance to disease, resilience to the weather, and capacity to reproduce', because economic conditions after the plague were not conducive to systematic seed selection, exchange, and importation.[201]

While poor demesne grain yields owed much to environmental factors, reductions in labour inputs must also have contributed because important tasks—such as weeding, marling, manuring, and even harvest reaping—were skimped.[202] In part, this was rational economic decision-making, given the rising wages and the difficulties finding seasonal labourers.[203] Yet the most severe decline in grain yields occurred in those areas—such as East Anglia and south-east England—where before the Black Death highly intensive farming techniques had prevailed. This may have been due to regionally adverse weather conditions, but was more likely due to a dramatic reduction in labour inputs.[204] There is certainly evidence of a fall in the quality of work on some demesnes between the 1340s and 1350s, where the efficiency and effectiveness of workers fell by around one-third.[205] The post-plague workforce was probably more inexperienced, reluctant, and truculent.[206]

The mass dereliction of holdings and the disruption to the agricultural labour force between 1348 and 1350, and the on-going difficulties with labour thereafter, must have resulted in a severe infestation of the arable with weeds, and this must also have contributed to the fall in grain yields. Farmers of every generation have understood the adverse impact of weeds upon grain yields, yet historians have scarcely considered its relevance to post-plague agriculture. Our difficulty is that contemporary sources cast little direct light onto the matter: we can establish from manorial accounts when grain yields fell, but the reasons are rarely given. There are, however, powerful grounds for arguing that the growth of weeds over abandoned holdings and the lack of sufficient labour to remove them from land still under cultivation contributed to the depressed yields in 1349–52 and, indeed, for the next two decades. It may not be coincidental that John Gower was fond of using weeds as a metaphor in his contemporary poetry: for example, he opines that 'the teasel harmfully thins out the standing crops if it is not thinned out itself'.[207]

A weed is defined simply as a plant growing where it is not wanted by humans, and the main unwanted plants on the medieval arable were thistle, mayweed, charlock, poppy, nettle, teasel, dog fennel, corncockle, corn marigold, dock, and darnel.[208] Arable land is difficult to keep clear of weeds because of their prolificacy, their tolerance of adverse conditions, and the profusion of their seeds in the soil.[209] The extent to which weed infestation became an acute and chronic problem in the wake of the Black Death can be estimated by drawing upon modern studies of the extent and speed to which weeds become established on untreated set-aside land, which indicate that 70 per cent of the arable becomes weed-infested within ten months, and 95 per cent after 24 months.[210] Flowering annuals dominate in the first year, but these quickly decline over the next two years as broadleaf biennials and perennials take over. The latter are dominated by grasses, such as couch and darnel, and increasingly feature tenacious woody species such as oak, maple, ash, and willow. The seedbank of weeds in the soil rises rapidly, and after two years the coverage of grass over the arable is almost complete.[211] The initial growth of broadleaf weed cover also causes the plant-parasitic nematode population in the soil to increase rapidly, further restricting the growth of grain shoots, and some nematodes also contribute to infection in livestock.[212]

The rate of weed spread on the medieval arable was likely to be faster and more complete than on the modern arable because the latter is intrinsically cleaner through the use of both herbicides and deep ploughing, both of which reduce the presence of weeds and, crucially, the bank of weed seeds in the soil. Such practices have extirpated many once-common weeds, such as corncockle and cornflower, from modern fields.[213] In contrast, the medieval arable was chronically weed-infested, because not enough resources were devoted to the task of removing them and because the sickle used at harvest left standing a thicker batch of weeds, including grasses, than do modern machines.[214] The only way to treat weeds was to remove them from growing grain either by hand or by using a spud (a sort of hoe) or a long weeding hook and fork, and to remove them from the fallow by ploughing, preferably cross-ploughing: in other words, through the application of hard labour.[215] One of the major weeds, thistle, was best targeted through intensive weeding between June and the harvest. The rate of weed spread on modern set-aside can be adapted to estimate the *minimum* rate of spread on abandoned holdings in the wake of plague. A holding abandoned in March 1349 and remaining unoccupied until, say, the following November would have suffered weed growth across at least one-half of its surface area.[216] Arable unoccupied for this length of time was a common enough experience in the first year of plague: on many manors between a quarter and two-thirds of all customary arable lands were still unoccupied in the autumn of 1349.[217] Arable remaining untenanted from March 1349 into 1351 would have reverted entirely to grass and begun to sprout tree shoots, and by 1353 the latter would be well established. The demesne at Chastleton (Oxon) remained wholly uncultivated as late as 1352.[218] Weed seeds from abandoned arable would disperse seasonally and infest nearby cultivated holdings, as any modern allotment holder would attest.

Thus the temporary abandonment of arable land and the reduction of weeding on cultivated land must have resulted in a step-like increase in weeds, weed seeds, and plant parasites, which in turn would have contributed to the reduced productivity of cultivated land.[219] The only insights we have into the scale and nature of this problem are derived from demesne accounts, although even these seldom provide a clear picture. Occasionally, they attribute low yields explicitly to weeds, as when darnel was blamed for blighting the 1351 and 1367 harvests in two Fenland communities, and poppies caused problems at Ickham (Kent) in 1356.[220] In general, though, weeds are not recorded explicitly, although one suspects that the frequent references in the 1350s to the 'debility' and 'impoverishment' of land may have been referring obliquely to the same problem.[221] The chronic shortages of labour during the initial plague crisis were likely to cause lords to hurry or neglect weeding. Throughout 1349 to 1351 a handful of manors on the Westminster abbey estate were unable to secure enough labourers to plough the demesne arable to sow the wheat crop, let alone to cross plough the fallow to kill weeds.[222] The amount of weeding fell on many demesnes in the years of initial crisis.[223] On those occasions in the early 1350s when increases in the level of weeding are identifiable on manorial demesnes, the additional effort did not improve yields, so its purpose appears to have been simply to try and impose some kind of control over weed growth.[224] Cross-ploughing the fallow offered a less labour-intensive solution to weeds on fallows, although its success depends upon the thoroughness of the work, and upon the sun drying out and killing the exposed roots of weeds: the wetter and cooler weather of the 1350s and 1360s was not conducive in this regard. The only other method of suppressing weeds was to smother them with heavy sowing of grain seed, but all the demesne evidence shows that after 1350 grain was actually sown more thinly.[225] If demesnes devoted less resource to weeding, then it is likely that peasant holdings did the same. The shortages of family labour and the availability of increasingly well-paid work off the farm would all have reduced the incentive and capacity of peasants to weed as assiduously as they had before the plague.[226] Cultivated land must have been much dirtier and weedier in the 1350s and 1360s than it had been in the 1340s.

Arable holdings that lay abandoned for years also posed severe difficulties for any tenant prepared to occupy them for the first time since the plague outbreak, because they would now have been entirely covered with stubborn perennial grasses and woody species whose impact on crop yields (especially on heavy soils) could be 'calamitous'.[227] Consequently, new tenants tackling holdings that had remained unoccupied for a decade after plague first struck would have needed many months or even years to restore them to a decent state of cultivation.[228] The example of Brandon (Suffolk) can illustrate this scenario because for the whole of the 1350s over four-fifths of its customary arable land lay abandoned.[229] This began to be reoccupied in the 1360s on leasehold, although the rents per acre were low initially (4d. per acre in the 1350s) and then rose to a mean of 6.7d. in the 1370s as the leases were systematically renegotiated.[230] Muller attributes these rent rises to seigniorial exploitation, but a simpler explanation is that when these holdings were first re-tenanted after years of neglect they were completely overrun with weeds, gorse, heather, and bracken, and were virtually indistinguishable from the surrounding heathland.[231] The initial low rentals acknowledged the back-breaking work and constant weeding over successive seasons required to restore the land to proper tilth, and the rental was then raised when the lands were finally restored to a reasonable level of cleanliness, and yields began to recover.

Wandering livestock posed another serious challenge to grain producers in regions of regular and irregular open fields, where small strips of cultivated arable lay intermingled with fallow and abandoned strips with few physical barriers to separate them.[232] These systems of husbandry required constant supervision of livestock to prevent the flattening and grazing of standing crops—whether through herding or tethering or the regular movement of wooden hurdles to pen animals in particular areas of the open fields—and therefore operated most effectively when labour was abundant and cheap. The shortages of labour after 1348–9 resulted in less attentive supervision, as evidenced by sharp rises in recorded crop damage by livestock.[233] This increased tensions between grain producers and stock rearers in the short term, while in the long term the best solution was permanent separation of arable strips from livestock through hedged, ditched, or stone enclosures.[234]

One other post-plague development must have also contributed to the reduction in the aggregate grain output of both demesne and peasant holdings: the rise in the proportion of arable left fallow, and therefore not cultivated, each year within a given holding. Annual grain yield data provide a reliable measure of the output of the arable land under cultivation. This is subtly different, however, from the total output of a given arable holding, which was a function of both the yield of the cultivated arable and the proportion of arable sown. The latter fell sharply after 1348–9 on most demesnes, reflecting the extension in the area fallowed.[235] For example, on four Suffolk demesnes in the 1350s and 1360s the proportion of the arable sown fell by 15 per cent from the average level of the 1340s.[236] We cannot know whether a fall of this magnitude was also a feature of peasant holdings, but *any* rise in the area left fallow would have compounded the effects of lower grain yields in reducing total output of the holding. If we assume that the yields and the proportion of arable sown recorded on demesnes were replicated on peasant holdings, then the grain output of a ten-acre peasant holding would have fallen by nearly one-half between the 1340s and the 1360s.[237] Of course, the additional fallow offered more grazing for animals, and the swing to livestock rearing meant that the pastoral output of the same holding probably rose, but the impact on grain production is clearly apparent.

We have tended to assume that the recorded *c.*15 per cent fall in grain yields on seigniorial demesne was also a feature of peasant holdings, although it is probable that the latter fell a great deal further. This point is impossible to prove definitively due to the absence of any reliable yield data from the latter. If we accept, however, that on the eve of the Black Death land productivity on peasant holdings was higher than on demesnes, because of the heavy application of otherwise under-employed family labour (see pp. 7–8), then it follows that the rapid and precipitous withdrawal of the latter would have caused peasant grain yields to fall even further.[238] Smaller families, and the diversion of labour from arable farming into livestock rearing and into the rapidly expanding industrial and service sectors, meant less labour for peasant arable holdings.[239] Survivors may also have opted to work less frequently and hard on their holdings, reckoning that lower yields were preferable to the most arduous, unpleasant, seasonal work in arable farming—weeding, muck spreading, ploughing—and, perhaps, an acceptable price to pay for increased leisure time.[240] Hence, there are strong grounds for arguing that the output of grain per acre on peasant holdings fell further than the documented fall in demesne grain yields in the 1350s and 1360s.

Campbell's research on demesne grain yields is the first to grasp and document the scale and persistence of supply-side difficulties in the post-plague world. Poor weather, a step-like increase in weeds, and wandering livestock all contributed to the dramatic fall in grain yields in the 1350s and 1360s. The effects of low yields on levels of aggregate grain output were exacerbated by the rise in the area left fallow each year, which reduced output per holding. All these factors affected demesne and peasant holdings. But they do not adequately explain why customary land values fell by around one-third, when grain prices rose by a similar order of magnitude. Nor do they explain why the largest customary holdings were prominent among those lands remaining tenantless until the late 1350s or even the 1360s, when such holdings offered any willing peasant a straightforward opportunity to produce grain surpluses for the buoyant market. The answer must lie in changes in the behaviour of peasant grain producers in the aftermath of the Black Death. Human decision-making must also have contributed to the severe and sustained supply-side shock. One obvious line of inquiry is whether the high grain prices reflected relative shortages of commercially available grain— which in the 1340s had absorbed around one-third of all grain—rather than shortages of grain per se. As the peasant sector was the main source of commercial supplies, then changing attitudes to market production and perhaps a shift to self-sufficiency among the peasantry might explain the lack of interest in cultivating large customary holdings while grain prices remained high. Another line of inquiry is the operational difficulties facing the new generation of peasant grain producers, who had to cope with impoverishment, inexperience in larger scale enterprises, the diversion of labour from grain production into other tasks, the spread of weeds across the arable, and the perceived and actual risks associated with commercial production. It is to these human factors that we now turn.

After the seismic shock of 1348–9, a succession of catastrophes continued to pose major challenges to agriculturalists. The plague outbreaks of 1361–2 and 1369, the animal murrains of the later 1360s, and the highly volatile weather added to a pervasive sense of uncertainty and risk. Unexpected losses of seed corn through poor harvests, and of livestock through murrain, could only be replaced quickly through expensive purchases, but many producers would have struggled to raise the necessary capital.[241] Peasant grain output, as indicated by tithe receipts, fell sharply in the year following each harvest failure because of the reduction of available seed corn.[242] The losses of skilled artisans and the disruption to marketing networks also contributed to the high costs of key agricultural equipment and repairs, which prevailed far beyond the initial crisis of 1348–53. In the 1360s the price of lath nails was still more than double that of the immediate pre-plague era.[243] Likewise, the high price of iron meant that the cost of acquiring a heavy plough, and its on-going maintenance, had more than doubled.[244] These persistent and challenging conditions meant that some peasant landholders continued to suffer hardship. The difficulties were real enough for smallholders, but they were much worse for anyone with slender resources attempting to work a large holding in excess of 20 acres, because of the scale of the problems posed by weeds, and the costs of stock and equipment. Indeed, the unwillingness of tenants on the estate of the bishopric of Worcester to occupy large holdings in the 1350s was attributed partly to the cost of equipment, coupled with their lack of cash reserves and expertise.[245] The rapid deterioration of agricultural buildings, and the build-up of weeds, during the weeks, months, or years of vacancies meant that considerable reserves of capital and labour were needed to restore them, which some landlords acknowledged through additional remission of rent and/or entry fines.[246] Even in the 1360s some tenants were still abandoning large customary holdings on the Winchester estate for reasons of incapacity and poverty.[247]

The persistently heavy burden of direct and indirect taxation further hampered the attempts of landholders to build up stocks, equipment, and reserves. Moore has calculated that the total tax burden rose from an estimated c.4d. per head per annum in the mid-1340s to nearer 10d. in the 1350s, peaking at 11d. in the mid-1370s. At its fourteenth-century peak in 1378, taxation absorbed an estimated 4.5 per cent of GDP.[248] The drastic increase in the weight of the individual tax burden in the early 1350s, and its shift down the social order, came at a time when the sums demanded were less affordable to unskilled labourers than at any other point between the 1270s and 1450s.[249] Peasant grain producers in south-east England and the east Midlands were also troubled by the Crown's continued requisitioning of grain and livestock for royal armies though purveyance, which during the 1350s and 1360s generated a volley of complaints and caused real local difficulties in places such as Kent.[250] A combination of exceptional outgoings and escalating costs of farm equipment would have depleted the wealth of newcomers to the land market, and hindered their attempts to invest in the resources necessary to build a successful agrarian enterprise.

Thus there are various grounds for supposing that the productivity of peasant grain output fell sharply during the 1350s and 1360s, and probably more than on demesnes. There are also grounds for supposing that, at the same time, peasant production became more self-sufficient, so that a smaller proportion of its output found its way to market. As the peasant sector was the main source of commercial supplies of grain, then this change would have exacerbated the effects of poor harvests upon the high grain prices of the 1350s and 1360s.[251] We can be certain that demesne production did not become more market orientated in this period. The proportion of demesne grain sold commercially fell slightly between c.1300 and c.1400, and, if anything, in the 1350s and 1360s the fall was more severe.[252] We cannot know what happened on peasant holdings because no accounts documenting their activities have survived. Tithe receipts offer insights into cropping strategies and are suggestive of greater caution. For example, Sapoznik has shown how in the 1360s peasant households in Oakington (Cambs.) prized stability of yields, and prioritized the calorific value of grain for their domestic needs, above commercial opportunities.[253] Given all the risks and uncertainties in the 1350s and 1360s, it is distinctly possible that peasants were retaining more grain within their household, either for consumption, or to be fed to animals, or reserved as seed corn for the following year. If so, then high grain prices after 1349 also reflected a sharp contraction in the proportion of grain supplied to market, while disguising a general sufficiency of grain in rural households for domestic purposes. The sufficiency of supply of grain within rural households, and the insufficiency of supply from the peasant sector to the commercial market, explains why the rural land market had lost its hair-trigger sensitivity to poor harvests yet, paradoxically, why the government remained concerned about grain shortages in major cities, especially London and Bristol, until the early 1370s.[254]

It might seem perverse to the modern mind that peasant producers in the 1350s and 1360s remained stubbornly unresponsive to the shortfall in the commercial supply of grain signalled by persistently high prices. Yet this perspective is based upon a presumption that peasant producers were primarily focused upon market opportunities, whereas their decision-making was also strongly influenced by other factors, such as consumption needs, attitudes to risk, transaction costs, and, indeed, the prospect of switching production to goods other than grain.[255] Furthermore, in the pre-plague era selling grain had not been a voluntary strategy for many smallholders, who had to sell in order to obtain cash to pay rent, fines, and taxes, even though the strategy could be deleterious to their welfare.[256] After 1349 more plentiful and better-paid employment provided an alternative source of cash, so they could now pursue the more rational strategy of consuming their own produce when grain prices were steep.[257] The modern mind would also take it for granted that peasants possessed the requisite commercial acumen to respond successfully to market stimuli. In reality, the relative inexperience of many newcomers to the land market and their inability to access a ready supply of family labour created obstacles to adapting to larger-scale grain production, irrespective of the deterioration in the weather or the build-up of weeds. Running a large holding orientated to the market required specific expertise in managing a seasonal hired labour force, and then in disposing of surpluses through commercial networks, but the landless and smallholding survivors of the Black Death who filled the shoes of dead tenants after 1348–9 did not initially possess such expertise. Even canny and experienced commercial producers would have found planning and production for the market unpredictable and precarious in the challenging circumstances of the 1350s and 1360s. This provides a good example of the ways in which the relative absence of relevant human capital and knowledge in some sectors of the economy could have contributed to a decline in productive efficiency and to a sluggishness in reacting to dramatic changes in market conditions.[258]

The expectation that peasants would respond enthusiastically to the stimuli of high prices also assumes that grain production was their primary objective, whereas many peasants might have been focusing their resources and production upon the expanding commercial opportunities in the livestock and poultry sectors. If so, their interest in crop production might not have extended beyond the subsistence needs of the household, or indeed the requirement to provide fodder for their animals, and so they might have ignored cash crops entirely.[259] Peasants were suddenly presented with a wide range of opportunities and choices for participating in chronically undersupplied commodity and labour markets, and therefore many of them might have opted for those activities that yielded more immediate returns to their labour. Activities such as paid employment for others, poultry rearing, dairy produce, and so on produced a fairly quick and tangible return, whereas grain production involved considerable work and no little financial outlay throughout the year, but no cash from sales until after the harvest.

Another possible reason for disengaging from the market is changing attitudes to risk. The knowledge about, and the ability to read, market conditions among grain producers probably deteriorated after the major epidemics of 1348–9 and 1361–2 due to the destruction of established, personal, commercial contacts. The 'particularized trust' that characterized trade between people with personal affiliations, and even the 'generalized trust' necessary for high volume transactions between strangers, must have broken down to varying degrees, diminishing confidence in the market and increasing the risk and cost of transactions.[260] If personal trading contracts had been extensively broken, and confidence in trading with strangers badly shaken, then both would have caused producers to shy from the market: rebuilding networks between survivors and restoring confidence in the market may well have taken years. Credit was harder to obtain, anxiety about the ability of debtors to repay rose.[261] Finally, psychological states of uncertainty tend to trigger greater reliance upon affective decision-making among consumers and producers—rather than cognitive, reason-based and evaluative judgements—where the preference is focused towards immediate and small rewards rather than large, distant, and delayed rewards.[262] This argument has been used to explain consumption patterns immediately after the Black Death, but it can also be applied to production strategies.[263] Decision-making in grain production shifted more towards satisfying the immediate subsistence needs of the household in the immediate aftermath of plague. Peasants could see regular income and rewards from poultry and dairy production, but delayed and uncertain returns from the arduous seasonal work in commercial grain production.

Peasants trying to make decisions in the 1350s and 1360s about how to respond to the widespread changes in consumption patterns and the associated opportunities did not necessarily prioritize grain production, despite the incentive of sustained high prices. Instead, they saw opportunities in casual employment and in livestock production. They would have weighed the quick returns and the benefits to their cash flow generated through paid work and regular sales of livestock produce against the slower and delayed returns from commercial grain production. They might have prioritized the consumption of their grain ahead of its sale. They would have struggled to see beyond the immediate challenges, conflicting signals, and uncertainties all around them: poor weather, depleted seed stocks, labour shortages, volatile yields, empty holdings, weeds, and risky commercial contacts. The government's zealous regulation of the commercial sale of grain and basic foodstuffs after 1349 added to such obstacles and uncertainty. The risks and complexities facing peasants in the aftermath of plague help to explain why those at Oakington 'did not respond with flexibility to market indicators'.[264] They also explain why large, standardized, villein holdings—15 to

40 acres of arable—proved among the most difficult holdings to fill in the 1350s and early 1360s, despite their obvious benefits to anyone with an eye for the market.[265] They explain why customary land values were tumbling. Rural households were consuming a higher proportion of their grain output. The sufficiency of grain in rural households, but the undersupply of grain to commercial outlets, also explains the continued sensitivity to grain shortages in towns during years of poor harvest, and the absence of similar distress signals in rural areas.

Conclusion

The traditional argument that the English economy was able to absorb the immediate shock of the Black Death with relative ease, so that it 'was scarcely affected' by plague before the mid-1370s, is no longer tenable.[266] We now know that between 1348 and 1375 English people endured the worst succession of extreme epidemiological and environmental events in recorded history. The two plague outbreaks of 1348–9 and 1361–2 killed over half the population; successive winters between 1349 and 1352, and in 1363–4, were among the coldest of the millennium, and the summer of 1361 was one of the hottest; and the visitations of epidemic disease among livestock in the 1360s were among the most severe in the medieval centuries. It is inconceivable that these extreme events left the economy unaffected. They created new patterns of demand, and triggered rapid readjustments to supply chains in some sectors of the economy. They also created complexity, turbulence, uncertainty, and volatility within an economy already struggling to adjust to the greatest demand-side shock ever known. The challenges were most evident in grain production. In the immediate aftermath of any one of these events, depleted stocks of seed corn and beasts of burden were expensive to replace. The general costs of buying and maintaining basic farming equipment had doubled. The result was swirling cross-currents, contradictory and paradoxical signals, and very mixed fortunes for different groups of people.

More detailed reconstructions of what actually happened during the third quarter of the fourteenth century, and more careful contextualization and weighing of the contradictory trends, are essential to understanding its complexities. This chapter has provided the first systematic attempt to catalogue the succession of exogenous shocks and to explore the human responses during this period. In doing so, it has reinforced the view that GDP fell while GDP per head rose, partly due to the reduction in the proportion of the landless population, but also due to gains in annual earnings and disposable income among ordinary people. A sudden increase in the supply of money in the 1350s lubricated the rise in wealth per head and stoked demand further. Patterns of consumption shifted quickly, and aggregate demand fell less than the drop in population. The survivors of plague were soon consuming more ale, higher-quality bread, more dairy produce, and meat.

They burnt more fuel, acquired warmer clothing and bedding, constructed robust housing, and accumulated a wider range of possessions. The speed of the response in various sectors of the economy in the 1350s—such as the professionalization of baking and brewing, the expansion of textile manufacture, and the surge of immigrants into certain towns—provides further confirmation that petty commodity markets were already well established in pre-plague England, and that labour was already relatively mobile and unregulated.[267] The labour market subtly changed its complexion, shifting from arable towards pastoral, industrial, and service pursuits in both rural and urban settings. Responses were most rapid in sectors requiring limited human skills and financial capital, such as poultry and dairy farming, and low-grade manufactures. These examples of rapid responses have to be balanced against the severe contraction in sectors relying on highly skilled workers—such as the high-end construction industry—whose lost expertise could not be quickly replaced.

Some sectoral adjustments occurred with impressive speed, and historians have explained them mainly in terms of the demand-side stimuli of monetary inflation, higher disposable incomes, and the slack capacity within the pre-plague economy. While these were powerful influences, they cannot explain all of the economic signals and contradictions of the 1350s and 1360s. The most paradoxical aspect is the behaviour of grain prices, which jumped in 1349 and remained high until 1376, and were primarily responsible for driving upwards the Composite Price Index in general and the prices of other basic foodstuffs (ale and bread) in particular. Demesne grain yields per acre fell around 15 per cent on pre-plague levels, peasant yields much further, mainly due to persistently poor weather and a reduction of labour inputs in arable production. In other words, serious supply-side problems existed in this sector of the economy. Following the crisis of 1348–53, the impoverishment and inexperience of new landholders, the proliferation of weeds, the diversion of labour into other tasks, and a reduction in the proportion of grain sent to market from the peasant sector, all contributed to the disruption in grain supplies. Personalized marketing contacts and networks fractured, knowledge of the market fell, credit dried up, and fear of reneging on debts increased. It was not until the early 1370s that corrective forces began to gain traction, setting the scene for the sudden swing to oversupply from the mid-1370s.

Our understandable fascination with the Black Death of 1348–9, and with the Peasants' Revolt of 1381, has for too long diverted our attention from the extraordinary succession of calamitous events in between. In this chapter, we have attempted to explore in more detail what happened, then to consider the wider implications for the economy. Some of the ideas discussed here are raised in the spirit of exploration. Certainly, the enormous change in the demographic paradigm created immense challenges of economic and psychological adjustment for the survivors, and we should consider more carefully how the sequence of extreme climatic and epidemiological events extending into the early

1370s greatly complicated the process of economic adjustment. Wealth per head was rising, but consumers initially prioritized the acquisition and disposal of food, drink, clothing, and fuel. Meanwhile, the costs of farm equipment jumped skyward, and losses of livestock through heriots, mortuaries, or disease proved expensive to replace. Heightened taxation, borne by a smaller number of taxpayers, added materially to outgoings. As a result, newcomers to the land market would have struggled to invest in the resources necessary to build a successful agrarian enterprise, which would explain the continued references in manorial documents to the poverty and incapacity of tenants.

These events also created uncertainty, risks, and turbulence, which commercial grain producers felt most keenly. Contemporaries must have regarded the succession of plagues, poxes, and wild weather as foreboding and portentous. The losses of human capital, experience, and networks were grievous. We should understand better how the lived experience of these afflictions shaped the economic decision-making of ordinary people, and avoid assessing this period with the benefit of hindsight and the presumption that peasants will respond directly and rationally to the stimulus of price. Survivors of the plague often thought differently and reacted in ways that were rational and reasonable to them. They were likely to opt for activities that provided quick returns and mitigated risks rather than ones that might make most profit. Historians see clearly the incentive of buoyant grain prices and profits that persisted well into the mid-1370s, but ordinary people living through the period stared at turbulence, uncertainty, hazards, risks, increased government regulation, and, of course, weeds. Our past was their 'present', and their present was even more uncertain than our future.

Notes

1. Broadberry et al., *British economic growth*, p. 229.
2. Levett, *Black Death*, pp. 75, 97, 140, 142, 145–6; Page, *Crowland abbey*, p. 125; Levett, *Manorial studies*, pp. 253–5, 294; Bolton, *Medieval English economy*, pp. 61–2, 201–11.
3. Platt, *King Death*, p. 10; Bridbury, *English economy*, p. 301. For similar sentiments, see Bolton, *Medieval English economy*, p. 214; Levett, *Black Death*, p. 140; Page, *Crowland abbey*, p. 125; Holmes, *Higher nobility*, p. 115; Hatcher, 'England in the aftermath', p. 6.
4. Bridbury, *English economy*, pp. 212–13.
5. For useful summaries, see Rigby, *English society*, pp. 83–5, and John H. Munro, 'The late-medieval decline of English demesne agriculture: demographic, monetary and political-fiscal factors', in Bailey and Rigby, eds., *Town and countryside*, pp. 300–15; Dyer, *Standards of living*, p. 219; Hatcher, 'England in the aftermath', pp. 6–9.
6. The quotes are from Harriss, *Shaping the nation*, p. 227 and Britnell, *Colchester*, p. 113. See also Hatcher, 'England in the aftermath', pp. 31–2.
7. John Hatcher, 'Unreal wages: long-run living standards and the "golden age" of the fifteenth century', in Dodds and Liddy, eds. *Commercial activity*, p. 2.

8. For a notable exception, see Stone, *Decision-making*, pp. 81–220.

9. Bridbury, *English economy*, p. 203.

10. Larson, *Conflict and compromise*, pp. 237–8.

11. Campbell, *Great transition*, p. 319; Dewitte and Kowaleski, 'Black Death bodies', pp. 12–14.

12. Philip Slavin, 'The second wave: contours of the *Pestis secunda* in England and Wales 1361-2', paper to the Anglo-American Seminar on the Medieval Economy and Society, Worcester 2019.

13. Shrewsbury, *Bubonic plague*, pp. 126–32; Hatcher, *Plague, population*, p. 35; Larson, *Conflict and compromise*, p. 143; Campbell, *Great transition*, pp. 315–16; Pribyl, *Farming, famine*, p. 201.

14. Josiah C. Russell, *British medieval population* (Albuquerque, 1948), p. 222; Razi, *Life, marriage*, p. 127; Bailey, *Medieval Suffolk*, p. 183; Campbell, *Great transition*, pp. 315–16.

15. Barron, *London*, p. 239; Slavin, 'Second wave'.

16. Fryde, 'Tenants of the bishops', p. 235; Campbell, 'Population change', p. 121; Fryde, *Peasants and landlords*, pp. 63–4.

17. See, for example, Ben Dodds, *Peasants and production in the medieval north-east: the evidence from tithes, 1275-1536* (Woodbridge, 2007), p. 73, 80; Titow, 'Lost rents', p. 100.

18. Bridbury, *English economy*, p. 214; Razi, *Life, marriage*, pp. 117, 125–9; Chavas and Bromley, 'Modelling population', pp. 230–1, 233; Campbell, *Great transition*, pp. 315–16, 352.

19. Razi, *Life, marriage*, pp. 128–30, 150–2; Dewitte and Kowaleski, 'Black Death bodies', pp. 13–15.

20. See, for example, Smith, 'Human resources', pp. 208–12; P. Jeremy and P. Goldberg, *Women, work and life cycle in a medieval economy: women in York and Yorkshire c.1300-1520* (Oxford, 1992), pp. 345–61.

21. Shrewsbury, *Bubonic plague*, pp. 134–5; Razi, *Life, marriage*, pp. 125–8; Bailey, *Medieval Suffolk*, p. 183; Campbell, *Great transition*, pp. 316–17.

22. See, for example, the outbreak in north-east England in 1379–80, Dodds, *Peasants and production*, p. 97. For a comprehensive assessment of the continued presence of epidemic disease and high mortality in the fifteenth century, see Richard M. Smith, 'Measuring adult mortality in an age of plague', in Bailey and Rigby, eds., *Town and countryside*, pp. 43–85.

23. Shrewsbury, *Bubonic plague*, pp. 133–4; Britnell, 'Farming practice: eastern England', p. 208; Pribyl, *Farming, famine*, pp. 29, 176–7; Raftis, *Ramsey abbey*, p. 140, 258; Mate, 'Agrarian economy', pp. 344, 352; Bailey, *Marginal economy?*, pp. 245, 250, 257; Saaler, 'Tillingdown', pp. 31–2; Titow, 'Lost rents', p. 101; Bailey, 'Prior and convent', pp. 12, 14; CUL EDC 7/15/I/22; Stone, *Decision-making*, pp. 115–16; Bailey, *Medieval Suffolk*, p. 215; Booth, *Macclesfield*, pp. xliii, xlix–l; Broadberry et al., *British economic growth*, pp. 145–7.

24. Farmer, 'Prices and wages', pp. 508–9.

25. Mate, 'Agrarian economy', p. 352; Munro, 'Late medieval decline', pp. 302, 307.

26. UC, Bacon Ms 649.

27. TNA SC6/1304/31 to 33.
28. University of Chicago, Bacon Mss. 649, 650; TNA SC6/1304/34. Animal murrain in the 1360s most likely explains the 24% fall in the number of peasant sheep in nearby Lakenheath between the 1340s and 1360s, Bailey, *Marginal economy?*, p. 250.
29. Pribyl, *Farming, famine*, pp. 83–4, 95, 102–4, 112–16, 135, 167, 227–8.
30. Campbell, *Great transition*, pp. 337–40.
31. Pribyl, *Farming, famine*, p. 167; Farmer, 'Prices and wages', p. 449; Dodds, *Peasants and production*, p. 73.
32. Pribyl, *Farming, famine*, pp. 83–4, 95, 102–4, 112–16, 135, 167, 201, 208–9, 231; Campbell, *Great transition*, p. 340; Wells-Furby, *Berkeley estate*, p. 169; Booth, *Macclesfield*, pp. xl.
33. Campbell and O Grada, 'Harvest shortfalls', p. 867.
34. Galloway, 'Storm flooding', pp. 180–1.
35. Feiling, 'Essex manor', pp. 335–6. The harvests of 1366 and 1367 were exceptionally poor in north-east England, Dodds, *Peasants and production*, p. 73.
36. Campbell, 'Grain yields', pp. 143, 165; Pribyl, *Farming, famine*, pp. 113–15, 208.
37. Mate, 'Agrarian economy', p. 349; Farmer, 'Prices and wages', pp. 445, 447, 449. A consignment of rye sold early in the accounting year 1369–70 at Brandon fetched 5s. per quarter, yet one sold later in the year when supplies were lowest fetched 10s., TNA SC6/1304/33.
38. Mark Casson and Catherine Casson, 'Economic crises in England 1270–1520: a statistical approach', Alex T. Brown, Andy Burn, and Rob Doherty, eds., *Crises in Economic History: a comparative approach* (Woodbridge, 2015), p. 100; Bruce M. S. Campbell, 'Global climates, the 1257 mega-eruption of Samalas volcano, Indonesia, and the English food crisis of 1258', *Transactions of the Royal Historical Society*, 6th series, 27 (2017), p. 90.
39. Sharp, *Famine and scarcity*, p. 88; The B text of Langland's Pier Plowman refers to famine in London in 1369–70, Helen Jewell, 'Piers Plowman a poem of crisis: an analysis of political instability in Langland's England', in John Taylor and Wendy R. Childs, eds., *Politics and crisis in fourteenth-century England* (Stroud, 1990), p. 65. Derek Keene, 'Crisis management in London's food supply 1250–1500', in Piet van Cruyningen and Eric Thoen, eds., *Food supply, demand and trade: aspects of the economic relationship between town and countryside (Middle Ages to nineteenth century)* (Turnhout, 2012), pp. 19–20.
40. Broadberry, 'Accounting', pp. 4, 7.
41. Campbell, *Great transition*, p. 2; also p. 328.
42. Broadberry et al., *British economic growth*, table 5.03.
43. Broadberry et al., *British economic growth*, p. 207, table 5.03.
44. Broadberry et al., *British economic growth*, table 5.06.
45. Hatcher, 'England in the aftermath', pp. 3–35.
46. Dyer, *Age of transition*, pp. 131–2.
47. Broadberry et al., *British economic growth*, table 7.06.
48. Dyer, *Everyday life*, pp. 85–8, 96–7.
49. Horrox, *Black Death*, pp. 340–2; Dyer, 'Work ethics', pp. 35–6.
50. Kowaleski, 'Consumer economy', pp. 238–43; Dyer, 'Work ethics', pp. 36–7.

51. Farmer, 'Prices and wages', pp. 456–8, 465.

52. Clark, 'Microbes and markets', pp. 150–1.

53. Farmer, 'Prices and wages', p. 450; Bridbury, *English economy*, p. 204; Chavas and Bromley, 'Modelling population', p. 232; Sharp, *Famine and scarcity*, p. 89; Campbell, 'Physical shocks', p. 29; Munro, 'Late medieval decline', pp. 307–9; Braid, 'Economic behaviour', p. 357.

54. Bridbury, *English economy*, pp. 30–1, 200–9, quote at 201; Bean, 'Landlords', pp. 579–80.

55. Campbell, 'Grain yields', pp. 160–1.

56. Mate, 'Agrarian economy', pp. 342, 344–6; Britnell, *Britain*, p. 421; Bailey, *Medieval Suffolk*, p. 220; Philip Slavin, 'Death and survival: Norfolk cattle, c.1280–1370', *Fons Lumini*, 1 (2009), pp. 54–6.

57. Clark, 'Long march', p. 117.

58. Munro, 'Late medieval decline', p. 311.

59. Aberth, *From the brink*, pp. 132–3, 135–6.

60. Hatcher, 'England in the aftermath', pp. 9–25; Hatcher, 'Seven centuries', pp. 15–18, 33–5; Hatcher, 'Unreal wages', pp. 232–6.

61. Farmer, 'Prices and wages', p. 452; Scott L. Waugh, *England in the reign of Edward III* (Cambridge, 1991), pp. 91–2; Hatcher, 'England in the aftermath', pp. 9–25, 29–30; Britnell, *Britain*, pp. 388–9; Braid, 'Economic behaviour', pp. 351–7; Broadberry et al., *British economic growth*, pp. 248–50.

62. Broadberry et al., *British economic growth*, p. 320 and table 5.03.

63. Hatcher, 'England in the aftermath', pp. 13–19; Bailey, 'Peasants', pp. 175–7; Dyer, 'Work ethics', pp. 21–41; Kowaleski, 'Consumer economy', p. 241.

64. Gregory Clark, 'Farming in England', *Economic History Review*, 71 (2018), p. 73, from an index of 45.8 in 1340–9 to 67.2 in 1350–9 (1860–9 = 100); Humphries and Weisdorf, 'Unreal wages', fig. 2.

65. Karl G. Persson, 'Consumption, labour and leisure in the later Middle Ages', in D. Merijot, ed., *Manger et boire au Moyen Age*, vol. I (Nice, 1984), pp. 211–23. Braid, 'Economic behaviour', pp. 362–3.

66. Jane Humphries and Jacob L. Weisdorf, 'The wages of women in England, 1260–1850', *Journal of Economic History*, 75 (2015), pp. 417–18, 425.

67. Humphries and Weisdorf, 'Unreal wages', pp. 11–14, figs. 2, 4, and 5.

68. Dodds, *Peasant production*, pp. 9, 160; Sapoznik, 'Resource allocation', pp. 189, 196–205.

69. For example, Hatcher, *Duchy of Cornwall*, p. 104; Mate, 'Occupation of the land: Kent and Sussex', p. 119; Miller, 'Occupation of the land: southern counties', pp. 140–1; Mate, 'Agrarian economy', p. 343; Fryde, *Peasants and landlords*, pp. 57–8, 61, 64–5; Bolton, *Medieval English economy*, pp. 210–11; DeWindt, *Land and people*, p. 65; Booth, *Financial administration*, p. 90; Hatcher, 'England in the aftermath', p. 6; Sapoznik, 'Resource allocation', pp. 191, 204.

70. Levett, *Black Death*, pp. 82–6; Levett, *Studies*, p. 253; Page, *Crowland abbey*, p. 151.

71. Page, *Crowland abbey*, pp. 152–3; Campbell, 'Population pressure', pp. 103, 130; Dyer, *Standards of living*, pp. 141–3; Richard H. Britnell, 'Land and lordship: common themes and regional variations', in Ben Dodds and Richard H. Britnell, eds.,

Agriculture and Rural Society after the Black Death (Hatfield, 2008), pp. 149-67; Alexandra Sapoznik, 'The productivity of peasant agriculture: Oakington, Cambridgeshire, 1360-1399:', *Economic History Review*, 66 (2013), pp. 522-3; Alexandra Sapoznik, 'Resource allocation and peasant decision-making: Oakington, Cambridgeshire, 1360-99', *Agricultural History Review*, 61 (2013), p. 191.

72. Phillips, 'Collaboration and litigation', pp. 97-8.

73. Bridbury, *English economy*, pp. 30-1, 204.

74. Lodge, 'Social and economic history', p. 187; Platts, *Land and people*, p. 170; Kettle, '1300-1540', p. 76; Stone, *Decision-making*, pp. 95-6; Bailey, *Decline of serfdom*, pp. 120-1, 156-8, 187, 251; Stone, *Moor medieval*, p. 104.

75. Compare Levett, *Black Death*, p. 146, with Ballard, *Black Death*, pp. 198-200, 206-11, 213-14, and also with Titow, 'Lost rents', pp. 99-100 (who notes that in 1364-5 8,156 acres of customary arable across the Winchester estate were still vacant); Mullan, 'Transfer of customary land', pp. 85-6; and Mullan and Britnell, *Land and family*, pp. 59-61, 65, 78-80.

76. Lodge, 'Social and economic history', p. 187; Hatcher, *Duchy of Cornwall*, pp. 104-7; Tuck, 'Occupation of the land: northern borders', pp. 37, 40; Miller, 'Occupation of the land: Yorkshire and Lancashire', pp. 43, 46; King, 'Occupation of the land: east Midlands', p. 73; Dyer, 'Occupation of the land: west Midlands', pp. 82-3; Harvey, 'Occupation of the land: Home Counties', p. 116; Miller, 'Occupation of the land: southern counties', pp. 140-1; Fox, 'Occupation of the land: Devon and Cornwall', pp. 161-3, 168-9; Fryde, 'Tenants of the bishops', pp. 229, 223-4; Wells-Furby, *Berkeley estate*, pp. 141-5; Fryde, *Peasants and landllords*, pp. 57-8, 63-5; Bailey, *Decline of serfdom*, pp. 120-1, 156-8, 187, 251.

77. Lloyd, 'Brookend', p. 122; Titow, 'Lost rents', p. 100; Ian Blanchard, 'Industrial employment and the rural land market, 1380-1520', in Smith, ed., *Land kinship*, p. 274.

78. Page, *Villeinage*, p. 53, fn. 1; Ballard, *Black Death*, pp. 198-9; Lodge, 'Social and economic history', p. 185; Bailey, *Marginal economy?*, pp. 226-7; Bailey, 'Prior and convent', p. 8; Mullan, 'Transfer of customary land', p. 85; Bailey, *Decline of serfdom*, pp. 120-1, 146, 186-8, 252-3, 313-14.

79. Fryde, *Peasants and landlords*, p. 63; Fryde, 'Peasant rebellions', p. 752.

80. Titow, 'Lost rents', p. 100.

81. The recording of the exact area of land is not always given, and in many parts of England the details are provided in customary measures such as virgates, which limit the uses to which the fines can be put. But the quantity of fines, their consistent format and uniform layout make them well suited to aggregate analysis, and they have provided the material for a growing number of interesting studies. For the form and possible historical uses of feet of fines, see Mike Davies and Jonathan Kissock, 'The feet of fines, the land market and the English agricultural crisis of 1315 to 1322', *Journal of Historical Geography*, 30 (2004), pp. 215-18; M. Yates, 'The market in freehold land, 1300-1509: the evidence of feet of fines', *Economic History Review*, 66 (2013), pp. 580-5; Hannah Ingram, 'Crisis and conscious property management: reconstructing the Warwickshire land market', *Midland History*, 40 (2015), pp. 182-4; Adrian R. Bell, Chris Brooks, and Helen Killick, 'A reappraisal of the freehold property market in later medieval England' (Working Paper, ICMA Centre, University of Reading, 2018), accessed 22 July 2019, pp. 5-11.

82. These four counties were chosen for four reasons: their feet of fines usually provide descriptions of the different types of land use land in acres; large numbers of fines survive, which improves reliability when sampling short periods; a high proportion of these fines comprise measured land rather than manors or messuages of unquantified extent; and they were among the most commericalized agricultural counties in England, and so are likely to be highly sensitive to changes in market conditions. The four time-intervals chosen for the samples were 1327–33 to provide a pre-plague benchmark; 1366–72 to capture the highpoint of the post-plague recovery; 1383–91 to capture the major downturn in the economy; and 1422 to the mid-1430s to capture the post-plague 'equilibrium'. The four periods from the four counties yielded a total of 3,207 fines providing details of the land use of 171,953 acres of transacted freehold. The exact timeframes for capturing the data were 1383–90 for Norfolk and Kent, 1384–91 for Essex and Suffolk; 1422–34 (Essex), 1422–37 (Suffolk), 1422–35 (Norfolk), 1422–33 (Kent). TNA CP25/1/63/163–7, CP25/1/67/220–7, CP25/1/68/228, CP25/1/71/270–4 (Essex). TNA CP25/1/102/118–26, CP25/1/106/178–90, CP25/1/109/221–34, CP25/1/114/295/30 (Kent). TNA CP25/1/164/146–8, CP25/1/167/168–72, CP25/1/168/178–9, CP25/1/169/186–7 (Norfolk). TNA CP25/1/218/68–72, CP25/1/221/95, CP25/1/222/96–7, CP25/1/223/104–6, CP25/1/224/114–16 (Suffolk).

83. Britnell, *Britain*, pp. 391–3.

84. Britnell, *Britain*, p. 389; Broadberry et al., *British economic growth*, table 2.10.

85. Bolton, *Medieval English economy*, p. 211.

86. For examples of leasing in the 1350s, 1360s and 1370s, see Booth, *Financial adminis-tration*, p. 97; Wells-Furby, *Berkeley estate*, pp. 215–16; Fryde, *Peasants and landlords*, pp. 65, 76–9. For general surveys, see Bridbury, *English economy*, pp. 207–8; Bolton, *Medieval English economy*, pp. 211–12, 214, 220; Mate, 'Agrarian economy', pp. 341, 345, 348; Britnell, *Britain*, pp. 430–1.

87. Bruce M.S. Campbell, *English seigniorial agriculture 1250–1450* (Cambridge, 2000), pp. 233–8. Between the 1340s and the 1370s the demesne area under cultivation fell around 15% to 20% across the estates of the bishopric of Winchester, Levett, *Black Death*, pp. 132–3, 151–2; Bolton, *Medieval English economy*, pp. 211–12; Bailey, *Medieval Suffolk*, pp. 205, 212.

88. Bailey, *Marginal economy?*, pp. 237–45; Britnell, *Britain*, pp. 396–7; Bailey, 'Prior and convent', pp. 11–12; Campbell, *English seigniorial agriculture*, pp. 238–48; James A. Galloway, 'Driven by drink?', pp. 96–8; Stone, *Decision-making*, pp. 81–95; Broadberry et al., *British economic growth*, table 3.07.

89. Mate, 'Agrarian economy', p. 347; Stone, *Decision-making*, pp. 84–6.

90. For tithes as a source of information about peasant production, see Dodds, *Peasants and production*, pp. 23–32.

91. Kitsikopoulos, 'England', p. 39.

92. Britnell, *Britain and Ireland*, p. 391; Dodds, *Peasants and production*, pp. 26, 28, 73–7, 80.

93. Dyer, 'Occupation of the land: west Midlands', p. 229; Bailey, *Medieval Suffolk*, p. 212; Dodds, *Peasants and production*, pp. 72, 76, 81–3.

94. Broadberry et al., *British economic growth*, pp. 106–7, 118, table 3.17; Munro, 'Late-medieval decline', pp. 323–30.

95. Campbell, *Seigniorial agriculture*, p. 10.

96. Philip Slavin, 'Chicken husbandry in late-medieval eastern England, 1250–1400', *Anthropozoologica*, 44 (2009), pp. 36–7, 47–8; Jeremy Edwards and Shelagh Ogilvie, 'Did the Black Death cause economic development by "inventing" fertility restriction?', CESifo Working Paper No. 7016, p. 11; Stone, *Esher*, p. lxxi.

97. See, for example, Bailey, *Medieval Suffolk*, pp. 214–16, 227–30; Miller, 'Yorkshire and Lancashire', pp. 602–3.

98. Hatcher, 'England in the aftermath', pp. 13–19; Dyer, *Everyday life*, pp. 85–8, 96–7.

99. Britnell, *Colchester*, pp. 150–1; Britnell, *Britain*, pp. 409–28.

100. Harvey, 'Occupation of the land: Home Counties', p. 115; Mate, 'Occupation of the land: Kent and Sussex', p. 120; King, 'Occupation of the land: east Midlands', pp. 219–20; Bailey, 'Prior and convent', p. 14; Saaler, 'Tillingdown', pp. 30–1; Bailey, *Medieval Suffolk*, pp. 219–20; Slavin, 'Death and survival', pp. 55–6.

101. Stone, *Moor medieval*, fig. 4.5.

102. David J. Stone, 'The productivity and management of sheep in late medieval England', *Agricultural History Review*, 51 (2003), p. 1; Booth, *Macclesfield*, pp. xxiv–lxiv. See also Miller, 'Occupation of the land: Yorkshire and Lancashire', p. 48.

103. Martin Stephenson, 'Risk and capital formation: seigniorial investment in an age of diversity', in Bailey and Rigby, eds., *Town and countryside*, pp. 205–6.

104. Slavin, 'Chicken husbandry', fig. 3, pp. 43–4, 47–8; Philip Slavin, 'Late-medieval goose farming: evidence from eastern England, c.1280–1400', *Agricultural History Review*, 58 (2010), pp. 8, 20, 22–3.

105. Stone, *Decision-making*, p. 85.

106. Bailey, *Marginal economy?*, pp. 245–51; Dyer, 'Farming practice: west Midlands', p. 236; Britnell, *Britain*, p. 413; Hare, *A prospering society*, pp. 63–4; John Oldland, 'Wool and cloth production in late medieval and early Tudor England', *Economic History Review*, 67 (2014), p. 26.

107. Bailey, *Marginal economy*, pp. 246–60; Campbell, *Seignorial agriculture*, pp. 159–60; Stone, 'Productivity', p. 1; Bailey, *Medieval Suffolk*, p. 214.

108. Broadberry et al., *British economic growth*, p. tables 4.02, 4.03, 4.10, 7.06. For the growth of textile and leather industries in towns in the 1350s, see Richard H. Britnell, 'The Black Death in English towns', *Urban History*, 21 (1994), 195–210, pp. 209–10.

109. Mark Bailey, 'The rabbit and the medieval East Anglian economy', *Agricultural History Review*, 36 (1988), pp. 6, 10–12; Bailey, *Marginal economy?*, pp. 251–3.

110. Bailey, 'Prior and convent', p. 13; CUL EDC 7/15/I/10–16.

111. Bailey, 'Rabbit', pp. 13, 15; David Gould, 'The distribution of rabbit warrens in medieval England: an east-west divide', *Landscape History*, 38 (2017), pp. 35–6, 39.

112. Booth, *Macclesfield*, pp. xxxii, liii; Stone, *Moor medieval*, p. 115.

113. Broadberry et al., *British economic growth*, pp. 145–7; Bailey, *Marginal economy?*, pp. 245–8.

114. Saaler, 'Tillingdown', p. 31.

115. Bailey, *Medieval Suffolk*, pp. 229–30.

116. Booth, *Financial administration*, pp. 96–7; Booth, *Macclesfield*, pp. xxxv, lvii–viii, lx–lxi.

117. Yates, 'Market in freehold land', pp. 583, 586–7, 593–6; Bell, Brooks, and Killick, 'Reappraisal', pp. 12–20; Adrian R. Bell, Chris Brooks, and Helen Killick, 'The first real estate bubble? Land prices and rents in medieval England c.1300–1500' (Working Paper, ICMA Centre, University of Reading, 2018), accessed 22 July 2019, p. 11.

118. Yates, 'Market in freehold land', pp. 584, 588–9, 597–8; Bell, Brooks, and Killick, 'Reappraisal', pp. 16–17 and figure 1.

119. The extent and plight of the pre-plague poor are summarized in Bennett, 'Wretched girls', pp. 321–35.

120. See, for example, Razi, *Life, marriage*, p. 111; Mullan, 'Transfer of customary land', pp. 82–3; Campbell, 'Population pressure', pp. 108–10, 122; Ravensdale, 'Population changes', pp. 210, 216; Phillips, 'Collaboration and litigation', figs. 3.2 and 3.3; Campbell and O Grada, 'Harvest shortfalls', pp. 869, 872; Sapoznik, 'Resource allocation', pp. 201–3.

121. Mullan, 'Transfer of customary land', pp. 82–3.

122. Ballard, *Black Death*, p. 200; Campbell, 'Population pressure', pp. 120–4; Fryde, 'Peasant rebellion', pp. 746–8; Larson, *Conflict and compromise*, pp. 162, 200–1; Kettle, 1300–1540', p. 76; Fryde, *Peasants and landlords*, p. 63; Bailey, 'Prior and convent', p. 8; Titow, 'Lost rents', pp. 100, 106.

123. Campbell, 'Agrarian problem', pp. 55–9; McGibbon Smith, 'Reflections', pp. 169–73; Phillips, 'Collaboration and litigation', p. 130.

124. Raftis, *Ramsey abbey*, p. 265; Campbell, 'Population pressure', p. 121; Bailey, *Marginal Economy*, p. 228; Phillips, 'Collaboration and litigation', figure 2.9; Wells-Furby, *Berkeley estate*, pp. 105–6, 128–9, 212–13, 217; Bailey, *Decline of serfdom*, pp. 166, 172, 208.

125. DeWindt, *Land and people*, pp. 110–15; Harvey, *Westminster abbey*, pp. 288–90; Miller, 'Tenant farmers and farming: Northern Borders', pp. 704–6, 714–16; Campbell, 'Population change', p. 103; Poos, *Rural society*, pp. 18–19; Dyer, 'Tenant farmers and farming: West Midlands', p. 636; Hatcher, *Duchy of Cornwall*, p. 139; Mullan and Britnell, *Land and family*, pp. 136–40, 145–8; Olsen, *Chronicle*, pp. 162–3; Britnell, *Britain*, p. 379; Mullan and Britnell, *Land and family*, pp. 136–40.

126. Dyer, *Lords and peasants*, p. 302; Faith, 'Berkshire', pp. 116, 121; De Windt, *Land and people*, p. 134; Campbell, 'Population change', p. 121; Tuck, 'Northern Borders', p. 592; Hatcher, 'Devon and Cornwall', pp. 726–7; Mullan, 'Transfer of customary land', pp. 87–95; Mullan and Britnell, *Land and family*, pp. 87–90, 101–2.

127. Mullan and Britnell, *Land and family*, p. 89.

128. SROI HA91/1.

129. Mullan and Britnell, *Land and family*, pp. 118–31.

130. Michael Prestwich, *The three Edwards: war and state in England 1272–1377* (London, 2003), p. 263; Platts, *Land and people*, p. 170–1; Bailey, 'Prior and convent', pp. 8–9; Booth, *Financial administration*, pp. 128–9; Bailey, *Marginal economy?*, pp. 223–5; Mullan and Britnell, *Land and family*, pp. 59–61, 65, 80; Stone, *Moor medieval*, p. 104, fn. 38.

131. Bridbury, *English economy*, pp. 203, 211, 215.

132. Mate, 'Agrarian economy', p. 342; Holmes, *Higher nobility*, p. 114; Bailey, *Decline of serfdom*, p. 121. See also Bridbury, *English economy*, pp. 203–4; Booth, *Financial administration*, pp. 97, 99.

133. Bell, Brooks, and Killick, 'Reappraisal', p. 17; Davies and Kassock, 'Feet of fines', p. 222.

134. Wells-Furby, *Berkeley estate*, pp. 128–9.

135. Rodney H. Hilton, 'A crisis of feudalism', in Aston and Philpin, eds., *Brenner Debate*, p. 132; Dyer, *Standards of living*, pp. 147–8; Waugh, *Reign of Edward III*, pp. 106, 112–13.

136. Bolton, *Medieval English economy*, p. 213; Brenner, 'Property and progress', p. 96; Dyer, 'Villeins, bondmen', pp. 430–1.

137. Britnell, *Britain*, p. 431; Bailey, *Decline of serfdom*, pp. 121, 171, 188; Bailey, 'Myth', pp. 151–2; Hatcher, *Duchy of Cornwall*, pp. 104–5, 111–12. For an example of exceptional local conditions, see the expanding textile town of Hadleigh, Mate, 'Agrarian economy', p. 351; Wood, *Medieval Hadleigh*, pp. 93, 97, 161–94.

138. Yates, 'Market in freehold land', pp. 580–2, 585–8.

139. See, for example, Ravensdale, 'Population changes', pp. 209–10. The area of land being transacted is not always stated explicitly in the court roll and, when it is, the transaction usually included an enclosure of indeterminate size—such as a messuage, cottage, croft, garden, or orchard—containing housing and outbuildings of unknown number and quality, all of which could significantly alter the value of the property and hence the level of the entry fine.

140. Gregory Clark, 'Microbes and markets: was the Black Death an economic revolution?' (Working paper, University of California Davis, 2013), accessed 19 January 2019, pp. 8–9.

141. Clark, 'Microbes and markets', p. 149, states there was 'no decline in nominal farmland rents'.

142. Clark, 'Microbes and markets', p. 150.

143. Raftis, *Ramsey abbey*, pp. 260–1, 264–5; Platts, *Land and people*, p. 171; Ravensdale, 'Population changes', p. 210; Poos, *Rural society*, p. 50; Wells-Furby, *Berkeley estate*, p. 106; Bailey, *Decline of serfdom*, pp. 109, 128, 172, 193, 208, 235. Comparing 1263–1348 with 1350–1415 entry fines fell from 4% at Harwell to 78% at Witney on the Winchester estate, Mullan and Britnell, *Land and family*, pp. 76–9. At Esher, on the same estate, entry fines fell from an average of 40d. per acre in the 1340s to 6d. per acre in the 1350s, Stone, *Esher*, pp. lxix, 283.

144. Poos, *Rural society*, p. 50, fig. 2.4; Wells-Furby, *Berkeley estate*, p. 106.

145. Clark, 'Microbes' (working paper)', pp. 8–9.

146. Hatcher, *Duchy of Cornwall*, pp. 119, 146–7; Hatcher, *English tin production*, pp. 156–7; Britnell, 'Urban demand', pp. 13–14; Broadberry et al., *British economic growth*, pp. 138–9.

147. Booth, *Financial administration*, pp. 97–8.

148. Broadberry et al., *British economic growth*, pp. 138–9, 151; Campbell, *Great transition*, pp. 310–13. For an exception, see Mark Bailey, 'John de Wingfield and the foundation of Wingfield College', in Peter Bloore and Edward Martin, eds., *Wingfield College and its patrons: piety and patronage in medieval Suffolk* (Woodbridge, 2015), pp. 44–6.

149. Munro, 'Late medieval decline', p. 317.

150. Britnell, 'Urban demand', pp. 12–14.

151. Kowaleski, 'Consumer economy', pp. 247–8.

152. Wendy Childs, 'The English export trade in cloth in the fourteenth century', in Britnell and Hatcher, eds., *Progress and problems*, pp. 126, 137; Munro, 'Late medieval decline', pp. 330–4; B. Lambert and M. Pajic, 'Immigration and the common profit: native cloth workers, Flemish exiles, and royal policy in fourteenth-century London', *Journal of British Studies*, 55 (2016), pp. 645–9; J. Oldland, *The English woollen industry c.1200–c.1560* (Abingdon, 2019), chapter 6.

153. Miller, 'Yorkshire and Lancashire', pp. 599–600; Britnell, 'Black Death', p. 209; Hare, *Prospering society*, pp. 179, 181–8; Bailey, *Medieval Suffolk*, pp. 270, 285–6; Britnell, *Britain*, p. 352; Nicholas Amor, *From wool to cloth: the triumph of the Suffolk clothier* (Bungay, 2016), pp. 33–4, 40, 47–8, 52; Bart Lambert and Milan Pajic, 'Drapery in exile: Edward III, Colchester and the Flemings 1351–1367', *History*, 338 (2014), pp. 749–53.

154. Britnell, *Colchester*, pp. 80–3, 85, 87; Wood, *Medieval Hadleigh*, pp. 93, 97.

155. John Walker and David Andrews, '65–69 Bradford St, Bocking, Essex: an unusual timber framed building of the mid-14th century', *Essex Historic Buildings Group Newsletter* (No 7, October 2018), pp. 5–8. In 1353 warehousing facilities for the collection of wool were created in Winchester, Patrick Ottaway, *Winchester: an archaeological assessment* (Oxford, 2017), p. 356.

156. Britnell, 'Urban demand', pp. 15–16.

157. John Langdon, *Mills in the medieval economy: England 1300–1500* (Oxford, 2004), pp. 28–9, and figs. 2.8 and 2.9. The fulling mill in the expanding industrial town of Haldeigh was rebuilt in 1363, Woods, *Medieval Hadleigh*, p. 162.

158. Newton, *Thaxted*, p. 27; Kowaleski, 'Consumer demand', pp. 250–1, 253–4. Broadberry et al., *British economic growth*, tables 4.02, 4.03, 4.10, 7.06; Britnell, 'Black Death', pp. 209–10.

159. Booth, *Financial administration*, p. 98.

160. Campbell, *Great transition*, pp. 360–1.

161. Gregory Clark, '1381 and the Malthus delusion', *Explorations in Economic History*, 50 (2013), table 2 and p. 13; Stephen Broadberry, Bruce M.S. Campbell and Bas van Leeuwen, 'When did Britain industrialise?: the sectoral distribution of the labour force and labour productivity in Britain, 1381–1851', *Explorations in Economic History*, 50 (2013), pp. 17–18.

162. Goldberg, *Women, work and life-cycle*, pp. 40–8; Hare, *Prospering society*, p. 121; Bailey, *Medieval Suffolk*, pp. 269–86; Bailey, *Marginal economy*, pp. 158–86, 259–64; Amor, *Wool to cloth*, pp. 21–57.

163. Blanchard, 'Industrial', pp. 229–31, 270–1; Kowaleski, *Local markets*, pp. 18–19, 21, 23, 27, 30–1; Britnell, *Britain*, p. 352; Hare, *Prospering society*, pp. 177–82; Goldberg, *Women, work*, pp. 39–48, 75; Amor, *From wool to cloth*, pp. 30, 33–4, 36; Stone, *Moor medieval*, pp. 107–10.

164. Barron, *London*, p. 241; Britnell, 'Black Death', pp. 206–7; Kowaleski, *Local markets*, pp. 87–9; Ottaway, *Winchester*, pp. 358, 379–81.

165. See, for example, the contrasting fortunes of Salisbury and Wilton, Hare, *Prospering society*, pp. 150–2, 159–62. Also Kowaleski, *Local markets*, pp. 88–9.

166. Gervase Rosser, *Medieval Westminster 1200–1540* (Oxford, 1989), pp. 55–7, 65–6, 171.

167. Britnell, 'Urban demand', pp. 9–19; Campbell, *Great transition*, pp. 356, 364–5.

168. Although for some exceptions see Keith D. Lilley, 'Urban planning after the Black Death: townscape transformation in later medieval England (1350–1530)', *Urban History*, 42 (2015), pp. 26, 32–4.

169. Swanson, *Medieval British towns*, pp. 15–21; Britnell, *Britain and Ireland*, pp. 347–61.

170. Britnell, 'Black Death', pp. 206–10; Richard Goddard, *Lordship and medieval urbanisation: Coventry, 1043–1355* (London, 2004), pp. 252–3.

171. Britnell, 'Black Death', pp. 206–7.

172. Britnell, 'Black Death', p. 209; Britnell, *Colchester*, pp. 64, 68, 82–5, 98–103, 109–11; Britnell, *Britain*, pp. 351–2; A. Kissane, *Civic community in late medieval Lincoln: urban society and economy in the age of the Black Death, 1289–1409* (Woodbridge, 2017), pp. 4, 86–7; Britnell, 'Urban demand', pp. 10, 14; Kowaleski, *Local markets*, pp. 88–90; Bailey, *Medieval Suffolk*, pp. 285–6; David Palliser, *Medieval York 600–1540* (Oxford, 2014), pp. 189–90; Lambert and Pajic, 'Drapery in exile', pp. 749–53; Goddard, *Lordship*, pp. 253–4; Woods, *Medieval Hadleigh*, pp. 93, 177–9, 188.

173. Pamela Nightingale, 'The growth of London in the medieval English economy', in R.H. Britnell and J. Hatcher, eds., *Progress and problems in medieval England* (Cambridge, 1996), pp. 95, 98–100, 105–6; Caroline Barron, *London in the later Middle Ages: government and people 1200–1500* (Oxford, 2004), pp. 395–40; Pamela Nightingale, *A medieval mercantile community: the Grocers' Company and the politics and trade of London, 1000–1485* (1995), pp. 201, 206–10; Goldberg, *Medieval England*, p. 168.

174. Newton, *Thaxted*, pp. 20–4; Rigby, *Medieval Grimsby*, pp. 114–15; Mark Bailey, 'A tale of two towns: Buntingford and Standon in the later Middle Ages', *Journal of Medieval History*, 19 (1993), pp. 361–2, 367–8; Anthony Tuck, 'A medieval tax haven: Berwick-upon-Tweed and the English crown, 1333–1461', in Britnell and Hatcher, eds., *Property and progress*, p. 166; Hare, *Prospering society*, pp. 150–2, 159–62; Christine M. Newman, 'Marketing and trade networks in medieval Durham', in Dodds and Liddy, eds., *Commercial activity*, pp. 137–8.

175. Britnell, *Commercialisation*, pp. 115, 170; Holt, 'Society', pp. 103–4; Dyer, *Making a living*, p. 312; Galloway, 'Metropolitan' p. 7; Britnell, *Britain*, pp. 74, 306–7; Stephen H. Rigby, 'Urban population in late medieval England: the evidence of the lay subsidies', *Economic History Review*, 63 (2010), pp. 393–417. In contrast, the urbanization rate in Holland rose during this period; see van Bavel, *Manors and markets*, p. 281.

176. Broadberry et al., *British economic growth*, p. 153.

177. Britnell, 'Black Death', pp. 205–6; Newton, *Thaxted*, p. 31; Reynolds, *English medieval towns*, p. 69; Britnell, *Colchester*, pp. 96, 204; Goldberg, *Women, work and life-cycle*, pp. 77, 281–304; Shaw, *Creation of a community*, pp. 58–9; Swanson, *Medieval British towns*, p. 113; Dyer and Slater, 'Midlands', p. 635; Rosser, *Westminster*, pp. 171–2, 177–9, 182–3; Goldberg, *Medieval England*, pp. 168–72; Campbell, *Great Transition*, p. 365.

178. Dyer, 'Importance of small towns', p. 18; Holt, 'Society and population', pp. 97, 100–3; Britnell 2004, 152; Routledge, 'Immigration', pp. 25–7; Britnell, *Colchester*, p. 205; Rosser, *Medieval Westminster*, p. 189.

179. Given-Wilson, 'Service, serfdom', p. 23; Britnell, 'Black Death', pp. 205–6. Surprisingly little has been written on the nature, extent, and significance of immigration into English towns after 1350, as indicated by the diminutive section on immigration contained within the index of the medieval volume of *The Cambridge Urban History of Britain*, (Palliser, ed., *Cambridge Urban History*, p. 810), though this observation does not detract from the volume's significance and quality. Similarly, Swanson's

excellent introductory survey of medieval towns contains just two short sections on migration, Swanson, *Medieval British towns*, pp. 70, 113.

180. P. Jeremy and P. Goldberg, 'Female labour, service and marriage in the late medieval urban north', *Northern History*, 22 (1986), pp. 18–38; Goldberg, *Women, work and life-cycle*, pp. 82–157; Shaw, *Creation of a community*, p. 100; Kowaleski, *Local markets*, p. 88; Mavis E. Mate, *Daughters, wives, and widows after the Black Death: women in Sussex, 1350–1535* (Woodbridge, 1998), p. 92.

181. Bailey, 'Tale of two towns', pp. 361–3.

182. Rigby, *Medieval Grimsby*, pp. 114–15.

183. Britnell, 'Black Death', pp. 205, 208; Robert B. Peberdy, 'The economy, society and government of a small town in late medieval England: a study of Henley-on-Thames c.1300 to c. 1540', (PhD thesis, University of Leicester, 1994), pp. 114–16; Campbell, *Great Transition*, pp. 310–13.

184. Anthony Saul, 'English towns in the late middle ages: the case of Great Yarmouth', *Journal of Medieval History*, 8 (1982), p. 82; Nightingale, *Medieval mercantile community*, pp. 198–200.

185. Perberdy, 'Henley', pp. 114–16.

186. See, for example, Bridbury, *English economy*, pp. 212–13; Chavas and Bromely, 'Modelling population', p. 232; Braid, 'Economic behaviour', p. 357.

187. Bridbury, *English economy*, p. 215.

188. Bridbury, *English economy*, p. 216. See also Mate, 'Agrarian economy', p. 354; Farmer, 'Prices and wages', pp. 441, 451; Munro, 'Late medieval decline', pp. 299–305. Campbell, *Seigniorial agriculture*, p. 430; Campbell, 'The land', p. 232; Broadberry et al., *British economic growth*, pp. 207–9, 316–22.

189. Page, *Crowland abbey*, pp. 152–3; Campbell, 'Population change', pp. 103, 130; Dyer, *Standards of living*, pp. 141–3; Britnell, 'Land and lordship', pp. 149–67; Sapoznik, 'Productivity', pp. 522–3; Sapoznik, 'Resource allocation', p. 191; Hatcher, 'England in the aftermath', pp. 25–7.

190. Mate, 'Agrarian economy', p. 345; Farmer, 'Prices and wages', p. 441; Rigby, *English society*, pp. 99–100; John H. Munro, 'Wage-stickiness, monetary changes and real incomes in late-medieval England and the Low Countries, 1300–1500: did money matter?', *Research in Economic History*, 21 (2003), pp. 207–17; Pamela Nightingale, 'Gold, credit, and mortality: distinguishing deflationary pressures on the late medieval English economy', *Economic History Review*, 63 (2010), pp. 1081–5; Braid, 'Economic behaviour', pp. 356–7; Martin Allen, *Mints and money in medieval England* (Cambridge, 2012), pp. 263–6; Nicholas Mayhew, 'Prices in England 1170–1750', *Past and Present*, 219 (2013), pp. 23, 31; Allen, 'Transformation of the English coinage' (2016).

191. Summarized in Mayhew, 'Prices in England', table 3; Allen, *Mints and money*, p. 344.

192. Mavis E. Mate, 'The role of gold coinage in the English economy, 1338–1400', *Numismatic Chronicle*, 18 (1978), pp. 126–41, at pp. 131–41. The shortage of smaller silver coins, which were the lubricant of trade in petty commodities, was due to a shortage of silver reaching the mints and an unwillingness to mint sufficient quantities of smaller coin. See also Jim L. Bolton, *Money in the medieval English economy 973–1489* (Manchester, 2012), pp. 244–8; Allen, *Mints and money*, pp. 264–6, 285,

291, 313, 411–15; N. Palma, 'Reconstruction of money supply over the long run: the case of England, 1270–1870', *Economic History Review*, 71 (2018), pp. 377, 384, 387.

193. John H. Munro, '"Money matters": a critique of the Postan thesis on medieval population, prices and wages', in John Drendel, ed., *Crisis in the later Middle Ages: beyond the Postan-Duby paradigm* (Turnhout, 2015), pp. 127–94, at 167–8.

194. Bridbury, *English economy*, p. 216. See also Mate, 'Agrarian economy', p. 354; Farmer, 'Prices and wages', pp. 441, 451; Munro, 'Late medieval decline', pp. 299–305.

195. David L. Farmer, 'Grain yields on Westminster abbey manors, 1271–1410', *Canadian Journal of History*, 18 (1983), pp. 331–48; Campbell, 'Grain yields', pp. 125–8, 137–8, 156; Mate, 'Agrarian economy', pp. 346–8; Britnell, *Britain*, p. 400; Wells-Furby, *Berkeley estate*, pp. 151–3.

196. Campbell and O Grada, 'Harvest shortfalls', p. 869; Campbell, 'English yields', pp. 144, 148.

197. Broadberry et al., *British economic growth*, tables 3.07 and 3.21.

198. Farmer, 'Grain yields on the Winchester manors in the late Middle Ages', *Economic History Review*, 30 (1977), pp. 555–61; Britnell, *Britain*, pp. 396 (table 19.4), 398; Stone, *Decision-making*, p. 101; Broadberry et al., *British economic growth*, table 3.10.

199. Campbell, 'Grain yields', p. 129; Sharp, *Famine and scarcity*, pp. 89–91; Wells-Furby, *Berkeley estate*, pp. 169–71.

200. Campbell, 'Grain yields', p. 159; Campbell and O Grada, 'Harvest shortfalls', p. 869; Pribyl, *Farming, famine*, pp. 83–4, 102–4, 113, 167, 201, 208–9, 231.

201. Campbell, 'Grain yields', pp. 158–9.

202. Farmer, 'Grain yields on the Winchester manors', 561; Campbell, 'Grain yields', p. 124; Munro, 'Late medieval decline', p. 322.

203. Stone, *Decision-making*, pp. 244–6.

204. Mate, 'Agrarian economy', p. 347; Britnell, *Britain*, p. 400; Campbell, 'Grain yields', pp. 157–8.

205. Stone, *Decision-making*, pp. 102–5.

206. Campbell, 'Grain yields', p. 124.

207. Eric Stockton, *The voice of one crying: the major works of John Gower*(Seattle, 1962), p. 209,.and *Vox Clamantis*, 'a tiller who tills the soil badly brings forth thistles, if well bears grain' (VI.1,001–2); and in *Mirour de l'Omme* 'when the grain loses its roots in the fields, the land becomes a wasteland and thereafter bears nettles and thorny brambles', W.B. Wilson, ed., *Mirour de l'Omme* (East Lancing, 1992), p. 261.

208. Edward Salisbury, *Weeds and aliens* (London, 1961), pp. 35–7, 146–7; J. Grieg, 'Plant resources', in Astill and Grant, eds., *Medieval countryside*, pp. 113–14; John B. Letts, *Smoke-blackened thatch* (Reading, 1999), pp. 39–41; Myrdal and Sapoznik, 'Technology, labour', pp. 202–6.

209. Salisbury, *Weeds and aliens*, p. 17.

210. P.J. Wilson, 'The natural regeneration of vegetation under set-aside in southern England', in James Clarke, ed., *Set-Aside*, British Crop Protection Council 50 (1992), p. 74; J. Wade, 'Set-aside land study' http://www.setasidestudy.cu.uk/2-3-vegetation-studies-on-set-aside, accessed 14 September 2016. I am grateful to John Belcher and Jeremy Macklin for these references.

211. Wilson, 'Natural regeneration', pp. 75–7; D.H.K. Davies and N.M. Fisher, 'Weed control implications of the return of set-aside land to arable production', in Clarke, ed., *Set-Aside*, pp. 130–1 (129–34); I.D.S. Brodie, C. Gallagher, S. Hitchin, and T. Noel, 'Spatial and temporal variation in the vegetation in set-aside fields at Conington, Cambs.', in Clarke, ed., *Set-Aside*, pp. 136 (135–42).

212. B. Bony, 'Effect of set-aside on soil nematode fauna and vertebrates in eastern Scotland', in Clarke, ed., *Set-Aside*, pp. 153 (153–8).

213. Letts, *Smoke-blackened thatch*, p. 41.

214. Salisbury, *Weeds and aliens*, p. 32; W. Harwood Long, 'The low corn yields of medieval England', *Economic History Review*, 32 (1979), pp. 469 (459–69); Harold S.A. Fox, 'Some ecological dimensions of medieval field systems', in Kathleen Biddick, ed., *Archaeological approaches to medieval Europe* (Kalamazoo, 1984), pp. 127–8 (119–58); John Langdon, 'Agricultural equipment', in Astill and Grant, eds., *Medieval countryside*, p. 99.

215. Dave Postles, 'Cleaning the medieval arable', *Agricultural History Review*, 37 (1989), pp. 138–42; Langdon, 'Agricultural equipment', p. 99; Myrdal and Sapoznik, 'Technology, labour, and productivity', pp. 203–5.

216. Based on the observation that 70% of modern set-aside has such weed growth within ten months.

217. Bailey, *Marginal Economy?*, p. 223; Fryde, *Peasants and landlords*, pp. 58–9; Kettle, '1300–1540', p. 76. The statement that one half of the arable was covered with weeds is based on the evidence that one-third of modern arable becomes weed-infested during the same length of time.

218. Lloyd, 'Brookend', p. 121.

219. For the deleterious impact of weeds on grain yields, see Harwood Long, 'Low yields', pp. 468–9; Stone, *Decision-making*, p. 111.

220. Stone, 'Black Death', p. 237; Mate, 'Agrarian economy', p. 349; Bruce M.S. Campbell, 'Agriculture in Kent in the high Middle Ages', in Sheila Sweetinburgh, ed., *Later medieval Kent 1220–1540* (Woodbridge, 2010), p. 47 n. 80; Stone, *Decision-making*, p. 109.

221. See, for example, Richard H. Britnell, 'Agrarian technology and the margin of cultivation', *Economic History Review*, 30 (1977), pp. 61–2 (53–66); Mate, 'Agrarian economy', p. 347; Larson, *Conflict and compromise*, p. 114; Levett, *Studies*, p. 293; Booth, *Financial administration*, p. 91.

222. Harvey, 'Agriculture of Westminster demesnes', pp. 294, 297. See also Dyer, *Lords and peasants*, p. 127.

223. Campbell, 'Agriculture in Kent', pp. 46–7; Stone, *Decision-making*, pp. 109–11; Stone, 'Black Death', p. 228.

224. Stone, *Decision-making*, pp. 101, 109.

225. Campbell, 'Grain yields', pp. 124, 126, 137.

226. Myrdal and Sapoznik, 'Technology, labour, and productivity', pp. 205–6, 212.

227. Harwood Long, 'Low yields', p. 469.

228. See, for example, Fryde, *Peasants and landlords*, 61–4; Bailey, 'Prior and convent', p. 8; Bailey, *Decline of serfdom*, pp. 120, 136, 157, 187, 251.

229. The abandonment of most of the customary land in 1349 is documented in TNA SC6/ 1304/27, when nine full-lands (of 40 acres) and four half-lands (of 20 acres), totalling 440 acres, lay in the lord's hands: around 90% of all week works were unavailable in this year because of these and other abandonments. By 1362–3 around 40 acres of customary arable had been leased in small parcels, leaving around 400 acres still uncultivated, University of Chicago, Bacon Ms 647.

230. Bailey, *Marginal Economy?*, pp. 226–30. Standardized full-lands only began to be leased from the mid-1360s, and the rents were raised when many of these were renegotiated in 1374, Muller, 'Peasants, lords', p. 172.

231. Muller, 'Peasants, lords', p. 172; Muller, 'Conflict', p. 6.

232. Bruce M.S. Campbell, 'The regional uniqueness of English field systems?: some evidence from eastern Norfolk', *Agricultural History Review*, 29 (1981), pp. 20–6; Mark Bailey, 'The form, function and evolution of irregular field systems in Suffolk, c.1300 to c.1500', *Agricultural History Review*, 57 (2009), pp. 17–19, 24–5.

233. Dyer, *Standards of living*, p. 144; Jack Ravensdale, *Liable to floods: village landscape on the edge of the Fens AD 450 1850* (Cambridge, 1974), pp. 77–8; McGibbon Smith, 'Reflections', pp. 138–41, 212–13; Thornton, 'Rural society', p. 84; Muller, 'Conflict', pp. 9–10.

234. Britnell, *Britain*, pp. 412–13; Dodds, *Peasants and production*, pp. 81–83; Bailey, 'Irregular fields', pp. 21–3, 25–9.

235. Campbell, *English seigniorial agriculture*, pp. 275–302.

236. The proportion of fallow arable jumped from 42% to 64% at Brandon, from 37% to 51% at Lakenheath, from 14% to 25% at Risby, and from 18% to 30% at Fornham All Saints, Bailey, *Marginal economy?*, pp. 214–15.

237. A ten-acre holding with 30% of the arable lying fallow and yielding ten bushels for each cultivated acre in the 1340s would have produced 70 bushels of grain: the same holding in the 1360s with 45% of the arable lying fallow and yielding seven bushels per cultivated acre produced 38.5 bushels, a fall of 45%.

238. See also Britnell, *Britain*, pp. 399–400.

239. Broadberry et al., *British economic growth*, tables 4.02, 4.03, 4.10.

240. Braid, 'Economic behaviour', pp. 363–4.

241. Munro, 'Late medieval decline', p. 336.

242. Britnell, *Britain*, p. 392.

243. Around 8d per thousand in the late 1330s and early 1340s, yet 19d. in the early 1360s, Stone, *Esher*, pp. 231, 257, 318–19.

244. For the sustained high prices of iron pieces for ploughs into the 1360s, see Stone, *Esher*, pp. 247, 256, 276, 330, 338.

245. Fryde, 'Tenants of the bishops', p. 230.

246. Hatcher, *Duchy of Cornwall*, pp. 109, 120; Horrox, *Black Death*, pp. 280–3.

247. Titow, 'Lost rents', p. 100.

248. Tony K. Moore, 'War and finance in late-medieval England', paper to the Anglo-American Seminar on the Medieval Economy and Society, Stirling 2016.

249. Moore, 'War and finance'; Gerald L. Harriss, *King, parliament, and public finance in medieval England to 1369* (Oxford, 1975), pp. 333–4.

250. Harriss, *King, parliament*, pp. 376–83; Maddicott, 'English peasantry', pp. 23–4; Mate, 'Agrarian economy', p. 350; McIntosh, *Autonomy and community*, p. 80; Given-Wilson, 'Purveyance', p. 154; Sharp, *Famine and scarcity*, pp. 116–17.

251. James A. Galloway, 'One market or many?: London and the grain trade of England', in Galloway, ed. *Trade, urban hinterlands*, pp. 33–4, 39, 42.

252. Campbell, *Seigniorial agriculture*, pp. 205–7, 275–6, 431–4, estimates that *c*.40% of demesne grain was sold commercially in *c*.1300 and *c*.36% in *c*.1400. For examples of a sharp decline in commercial sales on some demesnes in the generation after the Black Death, see Richard H. Britnell, 'Production for the market on a small fourteenth-century estate', *Economic History Review*, 19 (1966), pp. 381, 386; Bailey, *Marginal economy?*, pp. 241–4.

253. Sapoznik, 'Resource allocation', pp. 194, 202–4.

254. Campbell, 'Population change', pp. 108–10, 122; Sharp, *Famine and scarcity*, pp. 88, 102–10; John S. Lee, 'Grain shortages in medieval towns', in Dodds and Liddy, eds., *Commercial activity*, p. 74; James A. Galloway, 'Metropolitan food and fuel supply in medieval England: regional and international contexts', in van Cruyningen and Thoen, eds., *Food supply*, p. 12.

255. Campbell, *Seigniorial agriculture*, p. 303; Sapoznik, 'Resource allocation', p. 197.

256. Bailey, 'Peasant welfare', pp. 233–8.

257. Hatcher, 'England in the aftermath', p. 26; Hatcher, 'Unreal wages', p. 15.

258. Chavas and Bromley, 'Modelling population', pp. 233–4.

259. Munro, 'Late medieval decline', pp. 302, 307.

260. Chavas and Bromley, 'Modelling population', pp. 233–4; Philip Slavin, 'Market failure during the Great Famine in England and Wales (1315–1317)', *Past and Present*, 222 (2014), pp. 35–42; Briggs, 'Introduction', pp. 7–8.

261. Pamela Nightingale, 'The impact of crisis on credit in the late medieval economy', in Brown et al., eds., *Crises in economic and social history*, pp. 26–71.

262. Michel T. Pham, 'Emotion and rationality: a critical review and interpretation of empirical evidence', *Review of General Psychology*, 11 (2007), pp. 155–78; Hannah Chang and Michel T. Pham, 'Affect as a decision-making system of the present', *Journal of Consumer Research*, 40 (2013), pp. 42–63; Ali Faraji-Rad and Michel T. Pham, 'Uncertainty increase the reliance on affect in decisions', *Journal of Consumer Research*, 44 (2017), pp. 1–21.

263. Braid, 'Economic behaviour', pp. 363–4.

264. Sapoznik, 'Resource allocation', p. 189.

265. Page, *Villeinage*, p. 53, fn. 1; Ballard, *Black Death*, pp. 198–9; Lodge, 'Social and economic history', p. 185; Bailey, *Marginal economy?*, p. 224; Bailey, 'Prior and convent', p. 8; Bailey, *Decline of serfdom*, pp. 120–1, 146, 186–8, 252–3, 313–14.

266. Bridbury, *English economy*, p. 30.

267. Britnell, *Commercialisation* (second edition), p. 232.

5

Injustice and Revolt

Introduction: the Causes of the Peasants' Revolt

The events of the Peasants' Revolt in the summer of 1381 are well known. The uprising began in parts of Essex and Kent in May, quickly spread to London where the rebels effectively controlled the capital for several days in mid-June, then spilled over into the Home Counties and East Anglia. The holders of four major offices in central government were murdered in separate incidents (Robert Hales, the treasurer, Simon Sudbury, the chancellor and archbishop of Canterbury, and John de Cavendish, the Lord Chief Justice). Order began to be restored from 16 June, although sporadic outbreaks of unrest continued for several weeks. Trials of the rebels began in July. The uprising represents one of the most serious outbreaks of civil and political unrest in English history.

Historical interest in the revolt shows little sign of abating. Indeed, there is still a good deal to discover about the origins of the revolt, and about the nature and complexion of the local disturbances. In this chapter, we explore the background to the revolt and, in particular, examine in what ways and to what extent the revolt was linked to the social and economic changes of the three decades after the Black Death (Chapters 3 and 4). As early as 1906, Oman laid out the basic framework for modern studies of the causes of the Peasants' Revolt. He argued that after the Black Death oppressive manorial lordship and the restrictive new labour legislation escalated social tensions between lord and peasant, and these social and economic grievances combined with political discontent over taxation and an unsuccessful war to create the 'real determining cause' of the rebellion.[1] Many recent accounts continue in Oman's footsteps in drawing together a wide range of both socio-economic issues—notably the supposed 'seigniorial reaction' and the labour legislation—and political, fiscal, and legal grievances to explain the rising.[2] As Whittle has pointed out, 'popular movements are always multi-causal', and it is impossible to disagree with Thomson's observation that the actions and the demands of the rebels 'reflect both political and social aims'.[3] Yet, in general, historians of the revolt have been reluctant to settle for such generalizations, but instead have sought to identify the ultimate or primary cause of the revolt. Consequently, they tend to fall into one of two camps: those who promote the primacy of political causes, and those who promote the primacy of social and economic causes.

After the Black Death: Economy, Society, and the Law in Fourteenth-Century England. Mark Bailey, Oxford University Press (2021). © Mark Bailey. DOI: 10.1093/oso/9780198857884.003.0005

In the first camp, Postan argued explicitly that it would be wrong to place 'an undue emphasis on economic causes of the revolt', so instead he focused on the deteriorating political situation of the late 1370s: the senility of Edward III, the minority of Richard II, the unpopularity of John of Gaunt, and the expensive and unsuccessful war in France.[4] Similarly, for Goldberg, the rebels targeted people whose profile 'more obviously represented royal government than the seigneurial order per se'.[5] These explanations sit comfortably within a wider framework for interpreting pre-industrial European revolts and rural unrest in terms of the role of the state and increasing fiscal and military demands.[6] In such perspectives, 'it remains very doubtful whether a general revolt would have resulted' in 1381 without the heavy taxation and the political instability of the late 1370s.[7] Even Whittle, for whom popular revolts are multi-causal, argues that the uprising was based upon a 'political division rather than an economic one: a division between those who held power in government, in lordship, in urban oligarchies, in the legal system, and those who did not'.[8]

In contrast, other scholars have emphasized the primacy of social and economic causes of the revolt, arguing that after 1349 social tensions rose as landlords exploited their villeins in novel and humiliating ways.[9] This so-called 'seigniorial reaction' was designed to re-impose villeinage by forcing tenants to hold land on the old terms, restricting the migration of serfs, increasing rents, and imposing the arbitrary incidents of serfdom vigorously. The 'ruthless exploitation' and 'overt seigniorial oppression' triggered a rising tide of peasant resistance, which by the 1370s had become 'widespread ... and all classes of the peasantry were involved', culminating in the revolt of 1381.[10] Ormrod observes that 'this feudal reaction of the 1370s explains many of the grievances and fears aired during the Peasants' Revolt of 1381'.[11] As Holmes put it, the revolt was 'essentially a protest against the manorial landowner by his tenants', and for Bridbury the root cause of mounting social tensions in the 1370s 'is to be found ... in the persistent attempts made by manorial lords and employers of all degrees to halt changes which no power on earth could check or halt, still less reverse'.[12] Mollat and Wolff argue that—for all the political and fiscal triggers in 1381—the rebels 'most keenly resented' the grievances associated with rural and social life, and especially with villeinage.[13] For Keen the great 'dividing line' in society was social and economic, between those who worked for themselves and for others and those 'who depended on the work of others to maintain them'.[14] Aers described English bondage as involving the 'extremely heavy exploitation of villeins' resources', which, if correct, would explain why the 'masses ... fought covertly and openly against villeinage and persuaded King Richard, on that memorable day in June 1381, to abolish serfdom'.[15]

The primacy of social and economic causes, and in particular the desire to be free from the shackles of serfdom, is strongly associated with the work of Hilton and those influenced by his historical materialist account of the 1381 rising. Hilton was well aware of the wide range of political and fiscal causes contributing to the revolt: indeed, he argued that the rising social tensions generated by the seigniorial reaction were 'not enough to provoke a general rebellion' on their own. Nevertheless, 'judging by [the rebels'] actions and demands', he concluded that it was 'serfdom and those things which flowed from the rights of lords over tenants which bulked largest' in their grievances, and these were 'the most important of the elements of social tension in the years after the Black Death'.[16] Thus it was the manipulation of rents and 'the renewed emphasis on servile villeinage' after the Black Death which were 'at the forefront' of the causes of the revolt because 'the basic motive force of discontent and action is to be found in the landlord-tenant relationship, which was... the defining relationship of feudal society'.[17] In the same tradition, Dyer stresses that the majority of the rebels in Essex, Suffolk, and Norfolk were customary tenants, whose aim was to pressurize the state to 'set aside the property rights of lords and free the serfs'. The rebels 'did not mention the poll taxes but instead demanded their freedom' in their meetings with the king in London. Dyer regards the issue of serfdom as being of 'central importance' to the rebels, while acknowledging the contribution of taxation and misgovernment to the rising.[18] Historians in this camp would accept Rollison's view that 'the abolition of serfdom was a primary aim' of the insurgents in 1381.[19]

Many who emphasize the primacy of socio-economic factors also link them to political factors by portraying the state as 'increasingly identified' with the interests of the landlords in the years leading up to the rising.[20] The extension of state power through the labour legislation after 1349 is depicted as creating a new form of serfdom and forging a new and powerful alliance between the government and landlords, because of the close 'social identity between the justices enforcing the statute [of labourers] and the lords of the manors who were the principal interested employers'.[21] This intertwining of manorial lordship with the administration of royal justice increased conflict along class lines 'between lords of manors on the one hand and the plebian mass on the other'.[22] Dyer concludes that lords 'showed class solidarity in the adverse circumstances after the Black Death' and Brenner states that lords used parliament 'to tighten controls over peasant mobility'.[23] The alliance 'helped the lords to plan the imposition of a second serfdom', which in turn led to 'exploitation of the peasants in excess of even the bad old days of the thirteenth century'.[24] Other historians have endorsed the view that the appointment of the gentry to justices of the peace closed the ranks of the political establishment and blurred the distinction between royal and feudal authority, strengthening the coercive powers of the ruling elite over the labour of the lower orders of society and threatening the latter's economic and social well-being.[25] For instance, Palmer states that 'king, magnates, and gentry coalesced into a governing elite under the umbrella of state authority'.[26] According to Michael Bennett 'the coercive power of the magnates and gentry, previously given expression through the manor courts, increasingly began to operate through the agencies of the centralized state and the common law of the land... it is even possible to talk in terms of a deal consciously struck in the aftermath of the plague between the Crown and the classes represented in Parliament'.[27] The knotty entanglement of state power and manorial lordship explains why the insurgents in 1381 targeted the 'unjust and bad exercise of lordship on the manorial, communal, and governmental level'.[28]

The discussion so far has attempted to do justice to the extensive literature on, and the debate surrounding the causes of, the revolt of 1381. It confirms that underlying tensions generated by rising class conflict over serfdom and the labour laws are a recurrent theme in all explanations, irrespective of whether they are regarded as a primary cause or one of a number. Yet this theme is difficult to reconcile with the arguments developed earlier in this book that villeinage in England was weak on the eve of the Black Death (pp. 25–52), that it withered rapidly soon afterwards, and that the so-called seigniorial reaction was limited and short-lived in its extent (pp. 83–110). Furthermore, the theme of rising class conflict sits uncomfortably with the hard evidence that most of the rebels were not serfs but comprised a diverse group of people from urban and rural areas, and that most of their targets were political and judicial figures (see pp. 196–200). Consequently, this chapter will explore an alternative explanatory framework. It agrees that serfdom was a key issue for some of the rebels, and socio-economic tensions certainly contributed to the revolt, but the former has been overstated and the latter has been misunderstood. Conflict over serfdom was just one element within a wider crisis of authority, and the new labour legislation did not create conflict along crude class lines. It focuses upon the one experience that unified the wide variety of rebels from very different backgrounds: the growing pains of the state in the wake of the Black Death, expressed through the heavy burden of taxation and the rapid expansion of royal justice.

The heavy burden of taxation is well established in the scholarship. More people became caught in the government's fiscal net after 1348–9, and the burden of tax per head rose threefold between the 1340s and the 1370s (see p. 165). The experiments with taxation in the 1370s, and the perceived flittering of the revenues, created a tinderbox of resentment that was ignited by attempts in May 1381 to enforce collection of the third poll tax in four years. The argument about royal justice is not that the new gentry justices generated tensions along class lines. Instead, the line of inquiry explored here is that much of the rebels' frustration with royal justice emanated from both the drafting of the social legislation and the mechanics of its enforcement, which had created wide inconsistencies in the treatment of similar wrongs and greatly increased the scope for arbitrary action among local officials of the Crown. The resulting tensions were sustained and widespread, and they created fracture lines *within* local communities and *among* the lower orders. In other words, the labour legislation and gentry justices did not generate a simple dichotomous conflict between the lordly class and the plebeian mass, because the whole raft of government reforms after 1349 generated new tensions across communities. The labour legislation did not necessarily increase solidarity among the lower orders, even though at first glance their interests might appear to be closely aligned. By recreating the lived experience among the lower orders of society of the novel and rapid expansion of royal justice after 1349, we can obtain a clearer sense of how a mounting sense of injustice came to bind disparate groups of people, and contributed to the revolt of 1381. It also exposes the oversimplicity of any attempt to establish the primacy of 'socio-economic' causes of the revolt—narrowly defined as class conflict over serfdom and the labour laws—over 'political and legal' causes—narrowly defined as taxation, corruption, war, and the creation of gentry JPs—or indeed vice versa. Instead, the interplay between law, justice, economic change, and social conflict was more complex and fluid.

Serfdom and the Law in the Peasants' Revolt

Serfdom and the revolt

The argument that a rising tide of resistance against deep-rooted social inequalities and serfdom was the critical element behind the revolt continues to attract support, as exemplified in two recent reconstructions of localized actions within the revolt.[29] Muller identifies the 'exploitation' and 'subjugation' of the peasantry as an 'integral feature' of the manorial system after the Black Death in Brandon (Suffolk) and links it directly to the participation of some of its residents in the revolt.[30] Whilst Eiden adopts a more pluralist approach to the revolt in Essex and Norfolk, recognizing the many different targets and motivations behind the rebellion, he also points to the 'lack of fit' between the heightened aspirations of the peasantry and the adherence of 'many lords' to outmoded policies of 'subordination'. In particular, he attributes the June attack upon the abbey of St Benet Holme (Norfolk) to its recent imposition of 'highly oppressive and unjust seigniorial restrictions' on its servile peasantry, and points to the extensive burning of manorial documents as a protest against the onerous burdens of villeinage.[31] He notes that 'a significant minority [of rebels] held land on disadvantageous terms', implying that this motivated their participation.[32]

These two case studies typify the conventional approach to the social and economic causes of the revolt, but they also exemplify some of its untested assumptions and its slender evidentiary base. Even if we accept at face value Muller's evidence for rising tensions between the villeins of Brandon and their lord in the 1360s and 1370s, it is distinctly odd that in 1381 the Brandon rebels did not target their own manorial lord or attack any of his properties. Instead, they left the manor to join attacks on political and judicial targets many miles away in

Norfolk and another part of Suffolk, a discrepancy which Muller does not seek to explain.[33] Likewise, Eiden's attribution of some of the rebel action in Essex and Norfolk to the oppressive imposition of serfdom is unsupported by any direct evidence or footnote: for example, there is no evidence at all for oppressive policies on the estate of the abbey of St Benet Holme after 1349.[34] Instead, the attacks on the abbey have more plausible, alternative explanations. One of its manors was sacked due to the presence there of an unpopular JP, while the motives for attacking the abbey itself were various. The rebels seem to have thought that the abbey building might offer a good defensive stronghold and they also believed (mistakenly) that the bishop of Norwich was hiding there: furthermore, the abbey was linked through patronage to the unpopular John of Gaunt, duke of Lancaster and a central figure in the political scandals of the late 1370s.[35]

These case studies exemplify both the enthusiasm for placing serfdom at the heart of the revolt and some of the difficulties in sustaining this approach. These difficulties are exacerbated by the growing doubts about whether a 'seigniorial reaction' occurred at all after the Black Death. The idea of the reaction is founded upon a deduction of what should have happened within a conflict-based model of social change, rather than upon any convincing evidence that it *did* happen. The evidence advanced in support of the 'reaction' is anecdotal and unquantified, and some categories of evidence—such as increases in manorial rental income and court revenues—are capable of other, more credible explanations (pp. 101–2, 149–50). Furthermore, there is no evidence for any seigniorial reaction on many manors.[36] As we argued in Chapter 3, in the 1350s and 1360s evidence for coercion in the villein land market is thin, whereas indications that landlords were making significant concessions on tenure are plentiful. The rent package attached to villein service tenures was diluted to make it more attractive to tenants from a variety of backgrounds, and a sizeable minority of villein land was converted to contractual tenures for money rents. Retaining and recruiting tenants of customary land in the immediate aftermath of the Black Death involved far more concession than coercion.

Those who see conflict over serfdom as the pre-eminent cause of the revolt can appeal for support to the burning of manorial court rolls during the rebellion, to the royal grants of manumission (freedom from serfdom) made at the height of the revolt in London, and to the calls for the abolition of serfdom included among the rebel demands in London.[37] Certainly, according to the *Anonimalle* chronicler, one of the rebel demands put forward at Mile End on 14 June was freedom 'from all manner of serfdom'.[38] Next day at Smithfield the abolition of serfdom was again included among the rebels' demands.[39] However, whilst the chroniclers convey the impression of an orderly presentation of demands, legal records indicate that in reality the meetings featured 'a chaotic series of demands for justice by many petitioners from many parts of the country'.[40] The concise and precise accounts of the chroniclers have therefore benefited from a good degree of sifting, editing, and prioritization of the rebels' demands. While serfdom was an important and very personal issue for those rebels who were either serfs or held servile tenure, it had no direct relevance for the many others who were townsfolk and freemen. It is more convincing to regard the call for abolishing serfdom as one specific element within a much broader, unifying ideology at the heart of the revolt, one based on a desire to reform the legal system and to abolish intermediary layers of courts and lordship (see below, pp. 200–2).

At first glance, the burning of manorial documents in general, and of court rolls in particular, does seem to offer powerful evidence for placing serfdom at the centre of the revolt. After all, these documents were the principal repository of information about the local management of villeinage, including proofs of personal servility (mainly merchet and chevage) and the status of customary land, and, as such, they have been portrayed as instruments of oppression.[41] Literary scholars have argued that illiterate peasants targeted written documents as the symbols and instruments of oppression of the literate culture of the landlords who opposed them.[42] Some historians have warmed to the same theme. For example, Muller portrays the destruction of manorial records as symbolizing 'the complete rejection of manorial rule' and Eiden argues that it reflects 'the tenants' aspiration to get rid of constraints imposed upon them by seigneurial authority'.[43]

Whatever the extent of the burning of manorial documents, its significance is not straightforward to interpret.[44] Certainly, the targeting of manorial court rolls was not always the result of a grievance about lordship on a particular manor, and very few such explicit linkages have been established so far.[45] In fact, the burning of manorial documents could have nothing to do with oppressive seigniorial policies towards serfs. Thus rebels from all over East Anglia descended on manors held by John of Gaunt, such as Methwold (Norfolk), and revelled in the destruction of his property and muniments for political reasons rather than out of hostility to Gaunt as a manorial lord.[46] Similarly, the insurgents at Bridgwater (Somerset) burned the court rolls of a rural manor held by an unpopular burgess of the town as an act of spite rather than as a complaint against his management of his villeins.[47] Furthermore, the frequency and extent of document destruction requires careful reconstruction because it was not as widespread as sometimes portrayed: for example, such incidents were rare in Cambridgeshire and unusual in Suffolk.[48] The pattern of destruction is suggestive of copycat behaviour among bands of rebels operating locally, some of whom burnt documents and others of whom did not. Furthermore, the rebels targeted all manner of written documents, including judicial and urban records (for example, in Canterbury (Kent)) and university muniments (in Cambridge), not just manorial material.[49] Any such documents also provided a handy, effective, and satisfying form of kindling to light the traditional bonfires that marked the ritual year around midsummer and the feast of Corpus Christi.[50] Furthermore, the seizure of manorial and borough court rolls, of university muniments, and of records of sessions of justices of the peace for destruction are all consistent with a rebel aspiration to remove all lordship other than the king, thereby abolishing the clutter of intermediate jurisdictions between the central courts and the local leets (see below, pp. 200–2). The destruction of manorial records cannot be interpreted straightforwardly as proof of either a seigniorial reaction or a revolt against an oppressive lord, and the local context needs to be established and explained precisely in order to understand the rebels' motives.

Indeed, there were good reasons why the burning of manorial rolls was *not* in the rebels' own interests. After all, the argument that illiterate peasants burnt manorial documents to rid themselves of the instruments of their oppression does not fit with the abundant recent research revealing that many peasants were actively engaged in literate modes of thinking and working.[51] For instance, Olson has argued that peasants in general and villeins in particular were major participants in manorial court activity, both as leaders of their communities and as officials acting on behalf of their lord, who consequently shaped the contents of the courts' records and used them regularly to defend or improve their position both individually and collectively.[52] Peasants participated actively in court roll creation, and the rolls provided a record of a variety of peasant and community functions.[53] While court rolls did indeed provide proof of servility, they also documented precedents, proof of titles to land, and customs which were beneficial to peasants in general, and to villeins in particular, which meant that their destruction also carried risks.[54]

The ambiguities and uncertainties behind the motives for burning manorial documents urge caution in interpreting such actions either as evidence of the centrality of serfdom to the revolt or as the iconoclastic acts of an illiterate peasantry against a literate culture. The destruction of the written proofs of the residual burdens of servility is consistent with the aspiration to abolish all lordship except the king and all local courts other than the leets (see below, p. 201), because manorial court rolls would have no place in such a world. In 1382 the scribe of Wivenhoe manor (Essex) explained the destruction of its court rolls in the revolt as an expression of the rebels' desire 'to hold the said tenements at their own will, freely, and not at the will of the lord'.[55] Rather than interpreting this narrowly as a rejection of the oppressions of servile tenure, we should regard this more broadly as being consistent with the greater desire to remove all intermediary curial layers between local leets and the central royal courts. The lack of access to the royal courts for matters relating to the title of customary land would have been especially frustrating to the many freeholders who had poured into the customary land market in the period after the plague. Rebels who were serfs shared this frustration at their exclusion from the royal courts and, furthermore, their exclusion from either litigating or serving on juries there, because these exclusions perpetuated the dishonour and stigma of their bond status.[56] As Musson and Ormrod state, 'access to the royal courts was clearly regarded as an important advantage to be preserved or acquired by whatever means available'.[57] Where the rebels did ascribe a symbolism to their destruction of manorial documents—indeed, of any legal document—then it was arguably their desire to replace old with new documents within a reformed legal system.[58]

The third strand of evidence used to support the view that serfdom lay at the heart of the revolt is Richard II's instructions to a team of royal scribes to produce the royal charters of manumission and pardon for the rebels which were issued on 14 and 15 June.[59] The manumissions bestowed grants of royal freedom on all hereditary serfs in each of the counties represented among the London rebels and were issued as letters patent under the Great Seal, a grand gesture that implies villeinage was a key issue in the revolt.[60] Holmes believed that such charters of liberties 'expressed [the rebels'] social dreams'.[61] Barker has recently developed this approach in arguing that Richard II was sincere in issuing these grants and, by extension, was sympathetic to the abolition of villeinage. Her argument rests on three points. First, she claims that at Mile End Richard committed himself to carry out wide-ranging and radical reforms by promising to abolish not just personal serfdom but also tenurial villeinage and all seigniorial trading monopolies. Second, she interprets the extended time lapse between the suppression of the London revolt on 15 and 16 June and the revocation of the grants of freedom on 2 July 1381 as evidence for Richard's reluctance to revoke the manumissions, reflecting his personal sympathy for the rebel cause, and she also argues that the delay encouraged the provincial rebels to believe that they were acting with royal authority. Finally, in November 1381, the king appealed directly to parliament over the heads of his advisors for the abolition of villeinage.[62]

The grants made to the rebels on 14 and 15 June were not just of manumissions, however, but also included royal pardons to all participating rebels. The inclusion of pardons is vital to understanding the significance of these grants, although historians often overlook it.[63] The most straightforward interpretation is that the manumissions and pardons served an immediate and tactical purpose for both parties.[64] From the perspective of the authorities, the grants placated the rebels, bought precious respite at a critical juncture, and presented a pretext for some of the rebels to leave London. The authorities knew full well that the pardons could be revoked retrospectively by arguing that they had been issued under duress and that the manumissions were invalid because the king did not have the legal right to manumit the serfs of other lords. From the perspective of the rebels, the grants represented a tangible gain to show for their actions and offered immunity from prosecution. Thus the king's grants of manumissions and pardons helped to avert the immediate crisis and to thin the rebel ranks in London, albeit at the cost of spilling disorder out into Hertfordshire and the eastern counties in the king's name. Rebels present in London in the early stages of the revolt left the capital and became active in Hertfordshire and Cambridgeshire.[65]

The tactic of using manumissions and pardons to placate the London rebels on 13 and 14 June is also consistent with the evidence that the king's counsellors were already considering how to deal with the rebels once the immediate and present danger to public order had passed.[66] Yet, as we have seen, Barker claims that Richard II was sincere in his sympathy with the rebels' cause in the summer of 1381 and that as late as November 1381 in a speech made to parliament he 'was still prepared to plead with parliament to allow the abolition of villeinage'. In fact, Richard did not plead this case explicitly but stated that he would be supportive if the lords and commons were inclined to manumit their serfs.[67] As evidence for this view, Barker cites a passage in Walsingham's chronicle—but not mentioned in any other source—indicating that Richard was committed to the abolition of both tenurial villeinage and seigniorial trading monopolies.[68] Yet, whilst Barker accepts Walsingham's account of this matter without question, she routinely dismisses his testimony as tendentious and unreliable on a host of other points.[69] For example, when Walsingham states that on 22 June Richard informed the Essex rebels that he would *not* stand by his grants of manumission—a statement which undermines the view that the king was sympathetic towards the rebels and reluctant to move against them—Barker dismisses his claim as being the chronicler's own fabrication.[70] Therefore she appears to rely upon Walsingham as a source when it suits the argument, but selectively dismisses him when it does not.

There are two other objections to Barker's argument. The first—and most powerful—is that if Richard really was sincere in a desire to abolish villeinage, why did he not issue charters of manumission to the villeins on the manors on the royal estate? After all, as the lord of these villeins he was fully empowered to grant them legal freedom at any time without interference. Yet he did not do so. On the contrary, on 22 July 1381 Richard explicitly revoked a charter of manumission known to be circulating among the villeins on his manor of King's Langley (Herts.), almost certainly a copy of the general manumission and amnesty issued on 15 June to the people of Hertfordshire.[71] The second is that the king had no legal right to bestow freedom upon the serfs of other lords or to interfere in any way with their villein tenure. We cannot know whether the 14-year-old king was aware of this legal principle when facing the rebels at Mile End. Nevertheless, the evidence does suggest that he was acting on advice to agree to the rebels' demands simply as a short-term expedient to avert the immediate crisis.[72]

Thus, rather than providing evidence for royal sympathy for the rebels, the issuing of royal pardons to them on 14 and 15 June was primarily a pragmatic gesture designed to buy time for the authorities. The coupling of the pardons with manumissions is harder to explain, because the majority of rebels were already personally free and the grants were easily revoked as they had no standing under the common law. Their inclusion probably signalled the rebels' faith in the power and intent of the king to abolish intermediary forms of lordship and legal jurisdiction because only in such a world would royal manumissions carry any legal credibility.[73] It symbolized the rebels' fundamental belief in the proper exercise of the king's law and justice, and their reverence for charters.[74] As Freedman states, 'English peasants demonstrated a peculiarly persistent faith in the possibility of achieving exemption from servitude by means of formal legal procedures'.[75]

It would thus seem that, contrary to a strong historiographical tradition, there are a number of grounds for arguing that oppressive policies by manorial lords were not a significant cause of the Peasants' Revolt, and that the abolition of serfdom was not the revolt's central element. This is not to argue, however, that serfdom was irrelevant, either in the revolt or as an issue more widely. After all, villeinage continued to influence the lives of a sizeable minority of the population: in 1381 perhaps one-fifth of England's population was still hereditary serfs (see p. 265), and around one-third of the country's arable land was unfree. The main source of frustration for all tenants of villein land was the inability to defend the title to villein tenure in the courts of common law, and, for some tenants, another source was the continued requirement to perform labour services (see pp. 255–8). Both of these issues created a sense of relative deprivation when compared with other tenants, especially among those freemen and outsiders who had entered the customary land market since the plague. Two residual elements of personal serfdom continued to generate complaint and resistance: its dishonour and social stigma, and the scope for an unscrupulous lord to abuse custom and extort serfs for money.[76] For the minority of unfree tenants and hereditary serfs, there was still plenty to dislike about serfdom and a good deal to gain from its abolition.[77]

The law and the revolt

As we have seen, one of the main reasons for doubting the centrality of serfdom to the 1381 rising is the fact that the main targets were political and judicial figures rather than manorial landlords, and that many of the rebels were free or urban dwellers.[78] Certainly, the single-mindedness with which the rebels pursued the person or the property of leading political figures, lawyers, justices, and jurors is remarkable.[79] This was especially true of events at the epicentre of the uprising in London and Kent, where there was no serfdom.[80] Another feature of the London disturbances was the murderous attacks on Flemings, which drew upon long-standing frustrations with royal immigration policy.[81] The properties of the same political targets, and even some Flemings, featured prominently in the rural unrest in the Home Counties and East Anglia. Above all, it was those individuals deemed to have served improperly as royal justices, sheriffs, and tax collectors, who faced 'popular odium and personal violence'.[82] For example, the main targets in Essex were 'a county *Who's Who* or staff list of the judicial establishment'.[83] Likewise, the Essex rebels were 'a mixed bag', although their ranks were dominated by craftsmen, labourers, and servants, and included many men who had served as tax assessors, constables, and manorial officials.[84]

Recent local case studies reinforce these conclusions strongly. Chick shows that the two primary targets in Suffolk were political and judicial figures: Sir John de Cavendish (Lord Chief Justice) and Richard Lyons (the prominent Londoner who was a political target because of his role in national politics in the late 1370s). Most of the other attacks in Suffolk were on government officials—such as the escheator of Norfolk and Suffolk, justices, and poll tax commissioners—while some rebel bands left the county to attack property belonging to John of Gaunt in Norfolk.[85] The main exception to this pattern was the violent attack on the abbey of St Edmund led by burgesses of Bury St Edmunds, who used the wider breakdown of order to resurrect an old dispute over urban privileges with the abbey.[86] In Suffolk there is little evidence of coordinated activity, central leadership, or a common ideology amongst the rebels, whose disparate bands resorted to localized looting and extortion: furthermore, the burning of manorial documents was rare.[87] Likewise, Xu demonstrates that the disorder in Cambridgeshire, which was orchestrated by five main rebel bands over four days (15 to 18 June) of violent activity, focused upon 'primarily political rather than feudal and manorial' targets.[88] Nearly 90 per cent of rural acts of violence recorded in legal documents were against political figures and royal officials, especially poll tax commissioners and JPs known to have been hardline implementers of unpopular government initiatives, such as the price-setting and labour legislation.[89] Urban uprisings in Cambridge and Ely were partly a revival of existing disputes between the townsfolk and resident institutional landlords (such as the university and the prior of Ely) over the latter's restriction of urban privileges. Finally, Liddy has shown that the disturbances in York emanated directly from political factionalism and pressures within the city, intensified in the three decades after the Black Death by the financial demands of the Crown.[90]

These detailed analyses of disturbances in three localities reinforce the argument that grievances about the exercise of royal justice and the extension of state power since 1349 were important and consistent elements within the revolt.[91] This subject has already attracted a good deal of attention from scholars. The Crown's ambitious intervention into the labour and commodity markets (see pp. 77–83) increased the influence of the key personnel tasked with its implementation, notably the justices of the King's Bench and the magnates serving on royal commissions, which inflamed concerns about corruption, bribery, and special favours.[92] Various checks and balances needed to operate if the system was to work effectively, but by the 1370s it seemed that such checks had broken down.[93] The cosy relationship between the central justices and members of the nobility, and the suspicion that together they were manipulating the work of the King's Bench and specific royal commissions for their own benefit, had become major political issues.[94]

Historians have argued that similar concerns were swirling around those people serving in the new role of justices of the peace, who were drawn mainly from the ranks of the county gentry.[95] The reforms of the 1350s and 1360s had invested them with novel powers and considerable personal discretion to influence local affairs, but these new arrangements could cut both ways. On the one hand, people of local standing and knowledge were now empowered to deal directly with the myriad social and economic challenges of the era. On the other hand, the gentry were more susceptible to influence and pressure from local interest groups than were the central justices, and the office of county justice offered unscrupulous individuals an opportunity to pursue their own personal agendas.[96] The scope for abuse in this extended and reformed judicial system is often illustrated by an example from Essex, where in the late 1350s Lionel de Bradenham terrorized the countryside around Colchester by extorting money from merchants and fishermen while serving as a justice of labourers.[97] Certainly, in the 1360s and 1370s there seems to have been a mounting concern that members of the gentry had switched 'roles with apparent effortless ease...first as poachers then as gamekeepers, first as lawbreakers then as lawmakers'.[98] A small number of 'gentlemen justices' are perceived to have dominated royal judicial appointments in the localities, thus effectively taking over the administration of the shires for their own benefit. The appointment of some of these men on judicial commissions to inquire into the local administration of the poll tax in south-east England in March 1381 raised fears that they were now also taking over the collection of royal finances, stirring the anger of those local people who had been forced to collaborate with them previously as jurors, officials, and constables.[99]

There is no doubt that much of the popular concern about the ruling elite's manipulation of royal justice for its own purposes stemmed from the implementation of new labour legislation, which provided a unifying target for villeins, freemen, and townsfolk alike.[100] The compulsory service clause was the most humiliating, enduring, and controversial aspect of this new legislation, and was the target of the Smithfield rebels in 1381 when they demanded that 'no-one should serve anyone except by his/her own will and by means of a drawn covenant'.[101] For Palmer, the government's legislation in the 1350s amounted to the introduction of a new social policy which was 'directed to the problem of retaining traditional society in the wake of the demographic collapse' and which involved 'the coercion of the people to stand to their duties'.[102] Many historians have depicted the creation and implementation of the labour laws as having the effect of uniting the various subgroups within the ruling elite into a formidable and consolidated alliance against ordinary workers, as the former sought to 'redefine their feudal powers' through the extension of royal justice to introduce 'a new form of bondage'.[103] The result was a sharpening of social conflict along class lines between the unified ruling elite and an increasingly united 'plebian mass'.[104] Hilton captures this view by stressing that the legislation did not cause 'social conflicts between peasant employers and their employees', because he assumed that rich peasants were not the main employers of wage labour and, when they did use hired workers, they were 'prepared to offer higher wages' in order to avoid conflict with their comrades.[105] Yet, although this view is still widely held, it is founded upon an assumption about the nature of the labour market which, as we shall argue, is open to challenge.

The disquiet about royal justice also extended to the behaviour of lesser royal officials working under the justices and county sheriffs. In *Mirour de l'omme*, written around 1376–9, John Gower criticized royal officials alongside judges for accepting bribes and dispensing favours within the law.[106] Other contemporary sources express similar complaints about official corruption, extortion, and belligerence.[107] In the 1360s royal officials administered the estate of Hornchurch priory (Essex) harshly when it was temporarily in the king's hands, imprisoning two tenants, and during the 1370s tensions rose between officials and the inhabitants of Havering (Essex).[108] The common people of Denbighshire complained that local officials extorted fines and tolls, and imprisoned people without the opportunity for a proper defence.[109] The practice of purveyance—whereby royal officials were able to insist upon the compulsory purchase of food, fodder, and fuel for either military purposes or the consumption of the royal household—was also a common cause of complaint, but especially so in the 1350s.[110] This led to attempts at reform in 1362, but these were only partially successful.[111] For example, in 1376 residents of Norfolk complained that they still had not been paid for large quantities of grain requisitioned over the previous two years, whilst in the southern counties it was claimed that soldiers had seized crops and livestock in the king's name but that the royal purveyors refused to honour these debts.[112] There were also intermittent protests and local riots against the heavy imposition of direct taxation, which after 1349 was borne by a much higher proportion of the population.[113]

Thus the general view among historians is that the hostility towards the legal profession in the summer of 1381 was in direct response to heightened tensions over the bribery of justices, their maintenance by the nobility, the pursuit of personal agendas by justices of labourer/peace, corruption among local royal officials, and the labour legislation.[114] Of course, complaints about the abuses of justices and royal officials were not new in the generation after the Black Death.[115] Nevertheless, the intrusion of government into the affairs of the localities after 1349 had broadened the scope for such behaviour, and petitions to parliament confirm the popular perception that extortion, corruption, and injustice had worsened. Such popular views were likely to be well informed because ordinary people possessed a good knowledge and understanding of the royal judicial process, either through their involvement in legal tribunals of various kinds or from serving on juries or as local officials. They had a robust sense of how it was faring, how it should operate, and how it might be reformed.[116] By the 1370s the concerns were widespread and had 'united a diverse group of people—burgesses, gentry, artisans, and peasants—in outrage at an oppressive law administered from London'.[117] Ormrod captures this general view when concluding that the revolt was 'a protest against twenty years of mismanagement, during which a small number of prominent local landholders sitting on the commissions of the peace had effectively taken over the administration shires and run it largely for their own benefit'.[118] The rebels were demanding the proper exercise of royal justice.[119]

Rethinking Injustice, 1349 to 1381

The1381 revolt is an episode so well researched, and so multi-faceted, complex, and varied, that the prospect of any fresh approach generating new conclusions seems unlikely.[120] Here, however, we offer a new perspective on injustice in the years between the Black Death and the uprising. It considers the experience of royal justice from the bottom up (how it worked on the ground) rather than from the top down (the legislative framework, and the behaviour and profile of the justices). This approach draws encouragement from the work of Andrew Prescott, who has argued that we have failed to appreciate fully the geography and complexity of events in 1381, and have not properly explored the common threads of conflict and frustration that forged temporary coalitions between otherwise disparate groups of urban and rural rebels. As Firnhaber-Baker and Watts have suggested, modern conceptions of statehood and ideological preoccupations with class and revolution have been far too influential in historical approaches to pre-industrial revolts. Insufficient attention has been paid to the ways in which the diffuse and polycentric power structures of late fourteenth-century England shaped the actions of the rebels.[121]

Royal authority was not exercised through the single, narrow agency of a standing bureaucracy but through multi-layered and dispersed jurisdictional structures. It relied upon extensive work by local officials of the Crown at the level of the hundred and the vill, some of whom were salaried, but most of whom were unpaid and elected from within their own communities. Furthermore, a system of borough, manorial, and other local courts existed that both fragmented and overlapped this system of royal courts, creating scope for both duplication and competition.[122] Understanding how these structures and jurisdictional configurations interacted, overlapped, and conflicted, and how these officials behaved when utilizing them, is essential to understanding how justice actually worked on the ground and how it shaped the lived experience of ordinary people.[123] This approach is especially relevant during periods of upheaval and change, such as the post-plague decades, when the government was introducing novel and ambitious social objectives, and inserting new jurisdictional layers, into the legal system.

Two hints from the events of the Peasants' Revolt itself suggest that the extension of the state's legislative power to gentry justices was not the only source of tension and conflict, but also the additional problems emanating from the *mechanics* of implementing the new legislation. The first hint is the view expressed soon after the revolt by senior figures in the government that the behaviour of lesser officials of the Crown had been a major factor in causing the uprising.[124] In November 1381, Sir Richard Waldegrave, the speaker of the House of Commons, addressed parliament on the causes of the revolt, followed in 1383 by the chancellor, Michael de la Pole, and both accused petty royal officials of 'grievous oppressions' and acting 'like kings in the country, so that justice and law are scarcely administered to anyone'.[125] Both men were, of course, deflecting attention from the actions of those at the centre of government to a convenient scapegoat, but they were touching a popular gripe about the administration of law and government at the coalface.[126] The second hint lies within the demand of the London rebels at Smithfield that there must be 'no law but the law of Winchester'.[127] Although this demand has often been seen as cryptic and enigmatic, its meaning becomes clearer when coupled with the demand that 'no lord should have lordship in future ... except for the king's own lordship' and with the stated aim of Essex rebels to abolish all local courts other than the leet court.[128] In effect, the rebels were proposing the removal of all intermediary courts—seigniorial, ecclesiastical, and royal—leaving just the king's central courts and a civil leet court in every vill.[129] Representatives of every community would run its leet on behalf of the community, and each leet would maintain a dialogue with the centre through petitioning.[130] These proposals would streamline and simplify the responsibility for implementing government policy, and by extension remove a good deal of the tension surrounding the labour legislation and the extension of royal justice since 1349.[131] The direct appeal to the king for such reforms also offers support for Dyer's view that the rebels believed that 'only the authority of the state could overcome the lord's power of private jurisdiction'.[132]

The streamlining of lordship, and the curbing of royal authority as exercised by lesser officials in the provinces, was a unifying theme across the rebels' demands. This involved the stripping out of the intermediary layers from the legal system, and providing all subjects with access to the central courts of common law. In this way, all could petition the king directly, and local people could run their own leet courts according to statute and criminal law and free of corrupting external influences. This aim was also consistent with attitudes expressed in the burning of all forms of court records, in the call for the end of serfdom, and in grievances about the behaviour of petty royal officials. It reflected the frustration of many disparate groups of people with the way in which local officials had exercised royal justice in the generation after 1349 and indeed with the structural flaws within the new system. These frustrations can be readily illustrated. First, changes to the administration of some hundreds within each county resulted in the manipulation of royal justice by local officers for personal profit. Second, a dissection of the labour and profit-capping legislation reveals how both its construction and the mechanics of its implementation greatly enhanced the personal discretion of local officials to direct the affairs of their communities, in ways that could often be prejudicial, self-serving, and highly divisive. We will consider each in turn.

The leasing of hundreds

Royal justice generated considerable revenue for the Crown through the payment of fees of various sorts, and increasing judicial activity to generate funds was a legitimate, though occasional, practice. For example, in the 1350s and 1360s the Black Prince used a combination of established and exceptional royal judicial powers to generate cash for his various military campaigns from the county of Cheshire.[133] One cash-generating option available to the Crown was to 'outsource' lower-tier judicial franchises to third parties for an agreed annual rental for a fixed period.[134] This provided a predictable source of revenue for the Crown for little administrative effort, but it carried some risk because it transferred the responsibility for the running the franchise from the direct control of royal officials—accountable to the Crown—to the lessee (accountable for the rental). The judicial tier most easily farmed out in this manner was the administrative unit of the hundred, which was ordinarily run directly by royal officials under the supervision of the county sheriff. Indeed, for centuries successive kings had granted a single hundred, or groups of hundreds, as an act of patronage to a third party (usually a major monastic house), either on a permanent basis or for a fixed period.

Any such grant to a third party resulted in the Crown handing over the machinery of the hundred, including the running of the hundred court and the execution of royal writs along with all the associated revenues. If the grant was permanent as an act of royal charity, then all the profits accrued to the recipient: if the grant was a lease for a stipulated period, then the lessee paid the stipulated annual rent and kept the net revenue. In both cases, the hundred was effectively privatized. The recipients of the grant appointed their own officials to manage the hundred and its monthly court, and to handle its revenues. Ormrod has suggested that the practice of leasing out individual hundreds for cash increased during the late 1360s and 1370s, as a small group of nobles around the ageing Edward III manipulated the machinery of royal patronage for their own advantage.[135] If Ormrod is indeed correct about the growth of leasing, then there may have been other possible motives. It might have been an expedient forced upon the king and other major landlords after the Black Death due to a shortage of the experienced officials capable of administering the hundreds effectively, or it might have been a method of securing a fixed and reliable stream of income during a period of financial uncertainty.

There is clear evidence to confirm that the Crown, and some monastic land-lords who had been granted permanent private control of hundreds, did indeed increase the extent of 'outsourcing' of hundreds for cash leases in the generation after the Black Death in south-east England. A key source here is the number of leases of royal hundreds recorded in the royal fine rolls (fig. 5.1), and the number of references to leases of hundreds in the patent and close rolls (fig. 5.2), both of

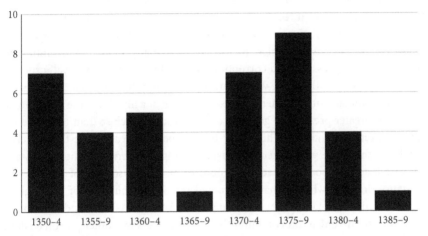

Figure 5.1 Number of leases of hundreds recorded in the Calendar of Fine Rolls, 1350 to 1389
Source: CFR

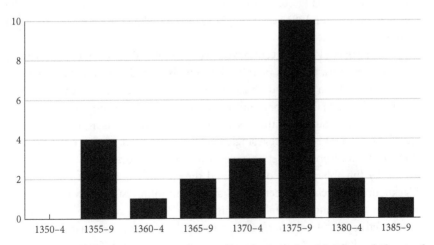

Figure 5.2 Number of references to leases of hundreds in the Calendars of Close and Patent Rolls, 1350 to 1389
Source: CCR, CPR

which reveal two surges, one in the 1350s and the other in the 1370s. The number of recorded grants peaked in the period 1375–9 in both sources, then fell suddenly in the 1380s and remained low thereafter. Furthermore, the contents of two contemporary parliamentary petitions reinforce the evidence for outsourcing during the 1370s, and that it was associated with a perceived decline in the quality of royal justice. One commons petition from the 1370s complained that the sums payable for these leases were excessive, whilst another in 1376 stated that landlords holding hundreds as private liberties were now leasing them to third parties for large annual rents and causing 'great extortions to the people'.[136]

The significance of these developments is that royal powers over the affairs of local communities had now been transferred to third parties without adequate controls or supervision, which in turn created many more opportunities for interference, oppression, and corruption in the administration of royal justice.[137] The first priority of the lessee was to turn enough profit from the hundred court to cover the annual rental payment. If the rent was set at a high level, the lessee would be under greater pressure to generate cash from the franchise than to ensure the proper exercise of justice. This seems to have been the case since there is clear evidence that lease values were increasing during this period as the Crown and private landlords sought to squeeze more from flexible sources of income. For instance, in 1379 when Richard II granted the Suffolk hundred of Lothingland (with the manor of Lowestoft) for seven years to William Ashman and Edmund de Lakenheath, he did so on condition that 'if in future some other person shall be willing to pay more for the manor and hundred, then the lessees could only retain the lease if they paid more'.[138] It may not be coincidental that de Lakenheath was a key target of the East Anglian rebels in the revolt of 1381.[139] The milking of these privatized yet essentially 'communal' jurisdictions for cash represented exactly the type of abuse that the 1381 rebels sought to prevent when calling for the abolition of lordship.

The rare survival of two centralized accounts detailing the abbey of Bury St Edmund's revenues from its privatized hundreds provides unequivocal evidence that the switch from direct administration to leasing resulted in sizeable hikes in revenues (table 5.1). The abbey enjoyed the ancient right to administer the seven hundreds of west Suffolk within its Liberty of St Edmund as a private jurisdiction.[140] An account relating to a single year from sometime in the period between 1350 and 1353 records the net revenues from six of the seven main hundreds run directly by the abbey's own officials, and the receipt of £31 from one hundred (Blackbourne) which had been leased at farm to John Aston, who was a gentry lord from neighbouring Cambridgeshire.[141] By 1360 six of the seven hundreds were leased separately, although unfortunately the lessees are not named. The five new leases (Babergh, Cosford, Lackford, Thedwastre, and Thingoe) yielded a combined rent of £89, compared with only £56 10s. when they had been exploited directly, a rise of 58 per cent (see table 5.1). In contrast, the revenue from the

Table 5.1 Annual income from seven hundreds within the Liberty of St Edmund, *c*.1353 and 1360

Hundred	*c*.1349–53	1359–60
Babergh and Cosford	£23 5s 8d	**£36**
Blackbourn	£31	**£36**
Lackford	£3 7s 3d	**£8**
Risbridge	£6 10s 8d	£7 16s 8d
Thedwastre	£26 19s	**£35**
Thingoe	£2 19s	**£10**

Sources: SROB A6/1/18; E3/15.51/1.1. Bold font signifies hundred at lease.

single 'control' hundred that was directly exploited throughout (Risbridge) had grown by only 19 per cent.

The Bury St Edmunds example shows clearly that the lessees must have been under financial pressure to cover the basic cost of their annual farm. In these circumstances, an obvious response would have been to manipulate the business of the hundred in a variety of ways, such as diverting business from local leets, preventing hundredal business from reaching the JPs' sessions, encouraging more private suits, and even by making malicious presentments.[142] Having increased the volume of business in the court, the lessee could further increase revenues through raising the level of fines themselves. Hundred courts usually appointed affeerors from among those attending to assess fines impartially, but a forceful lessee could appoint cronies as affeerors or even dispense with them altogether and determine fines personally. No evidence has survived to establish whether the Bury abbey lessees engaged in such ruses, but they are documented in other courts.[143] For example, in 1368 a royal inquiry revealed that one William Rous of Dennington (Suffolk) had compiled for himself a portfolio of local administrative roles for both the Crown and prominent landlords, including acting as the steward of various hundredal and manor courts. It alleged that William had devised the practice of setting and collecting the amercements from these courts at his own house a week or so after the court session, rather than at the court itself, which gave him to scope to manipulate the level of fines 'to the manifest oppression of the people'.[144] Another possible ruse was for the lessee of a hundred to change the location of the court from its traditional meeting place to a less convenient one as a pretext for fining suitors for their non-attendance. While this might sound improbable, fines for non-attendance were a routine item in many hundred courts and the shifty practice of switching curial location was the subject of a petition to the king in the 1370s.[145] Finally, lessees who were also local residents might use their control over the hundred's processing of royal orders and its court to manipulate events in their favour.[146]

Hence after 1349, and especially in the 1370s, the Crown and some major landlords increasingly privatized hundreds for cash, removing the levers of royal justice from their direct control and placing them into the hands of private individuals. While this transfer of administrative responsibility did not have to result in a diminution in the quality of justice within the hundredal court, this was a much more likely outcome in those cases where the lord raised the value of the lease above the level of income received when under direct management. Under these circumstances, the private lessees were likely to generate more cash by diverting cases to the hundred court and finding ways to increase fines. In other words, the balance shifted towards cash-generating justice and away from fair justice or justice according to the norms of the established legal culture.

Implementing the labour and price-setting legislation

The two main manifestations of the growth of state power after the Black Death and of its intrusion into local communities were increased taxation and the raft of new economic and social legislation. The scale and novelty of taxation after the Black Death, its increased burden upon a drastically shrunken population, and its role in generating social tensions in the run-up to the revolt of 1381 are all well documented.[147] The experimentation with new and regressive forms of direct taxation—such as the parish tax and the poll taxes of the 1370s—meant that a higher proportion of the population was now caught in the fiscal net. The annual burden of direct and indirect taxation per head more than doubled between the mid 1340s and early 1350s, peaking in the late 1370s when it absorbed an estimated 4.5 per cent of GDP.[148] There were widespread concerns that this money was being used to support the personal agendas of leading figures in the government.[149] In contrast, less consideration has been given to the drafting of the new legislation and the mechanics of its implementation as major sources of grievance and injustice. This section explores the inherent flaws in the detail of the legislation and in the manner in which it was actually implemented on the ground, and argues that the government's new social policy was impossible to implement in a manner which was equitable or consistent.

The role of the government in price-setting and profit-capping was already well established long before the Black Death (pp. 42–4). Royal justices sometimes enforced this legislation, but for the most part civic and manorial authorities appointed their own officials to implement it locally. These local officials largely decided what commodities were to be regulated, what constituted a reasonable price or profit, and what punishments to impose, which inevitably meant that its interpretation on the ground varied by time and place.[150] The theory and the primary purpose of the system was worthy—to defend the common good by preventing traders from exploiting consumers through excessive profiteering and by ensuring that prices of essential foodstuffs were affordable—but in practice the system was inexact, arcane, and inherently flawed. While flagrant breaches of the legislation were obvious and straightforward, especially in the wholesale trade, the vast majority of cases, especially in the petty retail trade, were not. Setting a fair price required officials to disentangle the effects of fraudulent and dishonest practices on rising prices from other legitimate inflationary pressures, such as genuine shortages and monetary debasement, just as determining whether a profit was reasonable in every case required detailed knowledge of the price of raw materials and the cost of labour. Hence establishing whether lowly retailers and artisans were forestalling or excessively profiteering was, at best, a haphazard and inequitable process, and, at worst, vexatious and arbitrary.[151] Recognition of these systemic flaws and of the vulnerability to abuse led to a pragmatic approach to its implementation in most places, whereby it was applied as a low-level licensing system for foodstuff traders, supplemented occasionally with direct and specific action against the worst offenders (pp. 42-4).

From 1349, however, the government's intervention increased the scope and powers of the extant legislation. The Ordinance of Labourers in 1349 decreed that all retailers of foodstuffs must sell their wares at a 'reasonable' price, one which would allow the vendor a 'modest but not excessive profit'.[152] Sustained high prices over the next two years probably convinced the King's council of the necessity for stricter enforcement and so the Statute of Labourers of 1351 transferred oversight of these powers to the newly-created justices of labourers, who were empowered to prosecute all 'those that sell by victual or retail, and other things here not specified'.[153] The Statute of Forestallers in 1351 underlined the point that price and profit regulations were henceforth to be applied to all victuals and wares, as directed by the royal justices, and it also laid down new statutory punishments, from forfeiture of the offending goods to two years' imprisonment for recidivists.[154] Thus, from 1351, price- and profit-setting was now formally to be applied to all commodities and its implementation locally was to be supervised by the royal justices. In theory, the justices had overall powers to determine what constituted a reasonable price and profit in every locality, and how far to apply these criteria to goods beyond basic foodstuffs. They could direct, override, or ignore local officials, and they could also impose more severe punishments than lesser courts if they chose. However, very few justices had much, if any, relevant experience of such issues because they were drawn mainly from the ranks of the gentry and the legal profession whereas people reared in the commercial world—borough and market officials of the middling sort—were unlikely ever to serve as royal justices.[155] As a consequence, if the justices were to exercise their powers with any semblance of fairness, then they had to depend heavily upon the borough and hundredal jurors who did have this knowledge.

Thus the government took an already inexact system of economic regulation, one which was already liable to abuse, then extended and enhanced it, and, finally, placed it under the supervision of justices inexperienced in such matters. There is no evidence that the government provided guidance to its justices on the implementation of this new legislation, nor that the county justices provided any guidance to the local officials, such as jurors and constables, who were responsible for bringing such cases to court. Given the considerable discretion enjoyed by county justices and local jurors in what and who to prosecute, it is unsurprising that the quantity and types of cases coming before different sessions of justices were highly inconsistent.[156] For example, in the 1360s and 1370s most sessions in Lincolnshire paid hardly any attention to the price and profit legislation, but, among the few that did, the principal targets were cases involving the sale of ale and hides.[157] Occasional and selective forays into the sale of other goods also targeted fish,[158] turves,[159] oil,[160] lead,[161] cloth,[162] poultry,[163] salt,[164] and shoes.[165] The wide inconsistencies from one session of the royal justices to another, and the apparent arbitrariness of the commodities targeted, seem to have reflected the personal priorities and agendas of the justices or, or likely, of the hundredal jurors who were responsible for making the presentments.

The inherent flaws in the price-setting and profit-capping legislation are also apparent in the labour legislation. Its loose drafting is readily illustrated by the vagueness of key passages relating to labour in the Ordinance of Labourers in 1349.[166] The able-bodied were to be put to work, but without any direction on what constituted 'able-bodied'. Workers were to be hired 'openly not privately', without any guidance on the boundary between these two states. Servants were to receive 'appropriate, not excessive, food and drink', without any advice on how to interpret these value-laden terms.[167] The ordinance exempted from its provisions artisans, commercial traders, and peasants fully occupied on their own holdings, but how was peasant self-sufficiency or commercial engagement to be reliably determined in a society where workers were very flexible in their sources of employment? Finally, wages were to be pegged at the going rate in 1346–7, but there was no objective or definitive local estimation of the rates from that year, and so this was bound to generate local disputes over exactly what the rates had been for different tasks.

The revisions to the ordinance of 1349 in the statute of 1351 partly addressed some of these issues, but much vagueness still remained. For example, the statute stipulated the maximum rates (based on 1346–7 levels) to be paid for an explicit but narrow range of tasks, and yet remained silent on the rates to be paid for countless others. The continuing problems created by these omissions are implied by the attempts to address them in subsequent revisions of the statutes, which added wage rates for a wider range of roles, such as building trades (1361), chaplains (1362), and a range of agricultural tasks (1388).[168] The statute also clarified that artisans were to work as they had before plague, and that artisans who had taken up a new trade since the plague were no longer exempt from prosecution.[169] But this still left plenty of room for confusion surrounding the exemptions (how, for example, did officials know for sure the pre-plague occupational status of all survivors?), which led to some private litigation in the central courts of common law.[170] So the revisions of 1351 left clouds of uncertainty swirling around the legislation, and the definitions of fundamental concepts—able-bodied, private—remained as vague as before. The point here is not that these definitions fell short of modern standards of exactitude in contractual terms and conditions, because the vagueness was deliberate: medieval legislators *intended* that judicial officers should exercise their discretion.[171] The point is that the vagueness increased the personal discretion and power of the local officials empowered to implement the legislation and, in doing so, amplified greatly the inconsistency of decision-making within an ostensibly standardized system.

Another example of the inherent flaws within the legislation is the practical difficulties in enforcing the contract clause of the Statute of Labourers. The statute sought to take firm action on workers who breached the terms of their employment contract, yet this could only be enforced fairly and equitably if there was clarity and precision about those terms and conditions in the first place. Most such contracts, however, were informal or *de facto* arrangements based loosely on headline terms or on a mutual or implied understanding, with little detail about terms and conditions.[172] The overwhelming majority of them were verbal 'bargains' and 'covenants', not written, which presented greater difficulties in proving a breach.[173] Prudent employers and servants could mitigate some risk by ensuring that third parties witnessed the covenant who, if necessary, could later provide testimony on oath to the original agreement. The legislation encouraged both parties to arrange witnesses to verbal agreements, which was another reason why the 1351 statute explicitly required workers to be hired publicly not privately. It is likely, therefore, that the legislation resulted in greater precision in stating contractual terms and conditions in advance, but this was still new territory, and informal and loose practices must have left plenty of scope for subsequent dispute and uncertainty.[174]

The net effect was inequitable to workers because the legislation favoured employers even when the contractual terms were imprecise. Furthermore, the 1351 statute tilted the scales even further away from workers by reducing the standards of proof through its provision that the oaths of two trustworthy men were now sufficient to pronounce guilt in cases where an able-bodied person had refused to work.[175] The only remedies available to a worker wrongly accused of a breach were to request an inquest jury to pronounce on the matter, to wage law, or to bring private suit. The vast majority of defendants pleaded guilty and accepted a modest fine as the most pragmatic response to an indictment or presentment.[176] In other words, the legislation required constables and local presentment jurors to make clear-cut legal judgements in manifold cases where the original contract itself was likely to have been unclear, where standards of proof for breaches had been lowered, and the presumption was to guilt. Very few defendants bothered to have their case considered by an inquest jury, which meant that the vast majority simply accepted the monetary fine, perhaps because they came to regard it as part of their operating expenses in the labour market.

The loose drafting of the legislation greatly increased the scope for petty royal officials to exercise their own judgement and discretion after 1349, which in turn rendered the experience of royal justice much more uneven. Furthermore, the creation of county justices to implement this legislation inserted another jurisdic-tional layer into the system of royal justice, which added complexity and perhaps even confusion, as well as creating even greater scope for manipulation. The jurisdictional structure for handling cases was now so diffuse that the same petty offence could be handled in any one of a variety of jurisdictions. For example, a routine case of a humble brewer breaching the price- or profit-capping legislation might be heard in seven different jurisdictions, from the lowly manorial court leet all the way to the King's Bench.[177]

Despite adding another jurisdictional layer to deal with economic offences, the government did not provide guidance to its county and local officials on how it fitted within the existing layers. So what determined, and who decided, where a given case would be heard? Was it decided by local officials (royal bailiffs, hundred and leet jurors, and constables) acting alone or guided by JPs, or did central royal officials dictate from the top down?[178] No evidence exists to indicate that the government provided the county justices with any answer to these questions, or that the justices then provided any guidance to their subordinate officials. The earliest-known articles of presentment for jurors attending JP sessions (dating from 1403) direct jurors to present infractions of the assizes of bread and ale and cases involving the regrating and forestalling of 'all manner of victuals', but offered no threshold of severity to guide which cases to refer to the justices and which to one of the local courts.[179] One might expect the more severe cases to be reserved for higher courts, but this was not so, because extant sessions of the justices meted out petty fines for humdrum price- and profit-setting offences similar to those in lesser courts.[180] Consequently, the decision about whether to take such offences to the royal justices and, if so, how many and which cases, must have been a matter left almost entirely to local initiative. This explains the wide variations in the types of cases recorded from one session to another. Thus the Norfolk justices operating between 1375 and 1378 paid little attention to price-setting offences, dealing with a mere nineteen cases which amounted to less than 4 per cent of all their business, whereas their counterparts in Suffolk between 1361 and 1364 handled 106 cases which made up 13 per cent of their total business.[181] Furthermore, there was little consistency in the commodities targeted from session to session: the main target was usually ale, but presentments for the sale of other goods were so inconsistent and occasional that they appear arbitrary. Hettinger suggests that the main driver for hearing offences under the price and labour legislation in the peace sessions was financial, because the fines went directly to the Exchequer rather than via the stickier hands of county officials.[182] County justices and jurors decided for themselves how much business relating to economic and labour offences to present, and the counties most active in these spheres were also those where rebel activity in the revolt was subsequently high.[183]

The heightened interest of the courts of King's Bench and county justices, and of specific royal commissions of oyer and terminer, in enforcing the price- and profit-capping legislation did not deter local authorities from enforcing the same legislation in their borough and manorial courts. It is apparent, however, that after the 1350s these local authorities largely followed their own agendas on the frequency of prosecutions and the punishments imposed.[184] Local officials usually adopted a pragmatic approach, allowing most individual traders some flexibility while punishing the worst offences.[185] However, the insertion of a new jurisdictional layer generated complaints that royal justices were dealing with cases that were properly the domain of local courts.[186] In extreme circumstances, both justices and local courts ended up fining individuals for the same offence.[187] Hence, at the very least, the multi-layered jurisdictions resulted in greater inconsistencies in the treatment of similar wrongs under the legal system. As such, it must have fuelled the rebel demand in 1381 for the simplification of the curial structure.

Given that no central or set guidelines existed to guide choices about which cases to prosecute under the price-setting and labour legislation, where to prosecute them, or even how to punish them, such decision-making was left to local discretion.[188] The implied assumption among historians is that the justices of the peace were actively directing cases in pursuit of their own interests and agendas in ways that heightened social tensions.[189] For example, Aberth states that they 'had a vested interest in the statute [and]...played off one element of community against the other, undoubtedly creating tensions in society that contributed to the revolt'.[190] But this is scarcely credible because it would have required the handful of unpaid justices to sift through hundreds if not thousands of individual cases from the scores of leets under their jurisdiction to determine what to prosecute and where. They simply cannot have had the time, or the resource, or the inclination to do so. Instead, they were more likely to issue periodically generic and verbal guidance to lesser officials of the various hundreds under their control, but not to direct personally the vast majority of individual cases.[191] If this assumption is correct, then the key decision-makers were the jurors and constables from every vill and hundred.[192] They swore on oath to enforce the legislation, they were responsible for identifying all breaches within their jurisdiction, and so they had to determine how to deal with each breach. They chose whether to ignore a breach, or issue an informal warning, or impose a summary punishment (stocks or compelled to work within the vill), or present to the next session of the leet court, or report it upwards to the hundred court, or to the justices.[193] It follows that after 1349 these local office holders wielded enhanced powers, and exercised considerable discretion. Hence their behaviour, in particular whether they discharged their office for the common good or according to their own personal agenda, became the primary influence upon the quality and the local experience of royal justice.

Who were these local constables and jurors, and how well equipped were they to exercise their enhanced discretionary powers? We know little about the profile of jurors at the sessions of King's Bench and justices of the peace because lists naming them are unusual and, even when such lists survive, it can be very difficult to reconstruct biographical details.[194] Plucknett argued long ago that the jurors were minor gentry, i.e. from the same social background as the justices themselves, and therefore their presentments and judgements were likely to reinforce the entrenched interests of the ruling elite.[195] Yet subsequent analyses of named presentment jurors serving the sessions of royal justices in the eastern counties indicate that they were actually from further down the social scale.[196] Jurors at judicial sessions were representatives of their hundred or borough, the former being drawn from the leading peasant landholders within rural communities while the latter were usually burgesses, many of whom were active traders and employers.[197] Yet even these representatives were sifting and synthesizing information provided to them by leet jurors and constables from every vill within a hundred or every ward within a borough, and these, too, were drawn from the resident and wealthier members of their communities.[198] A study of the social backgrounds of the 652 jurors named in peace sessions held in Suffolk between 1361 and 1364 confirms that the leading rural jurors were the larger peasant landholders, while the urban jurors belonged to some of the wealthiest burgess families.[199]

The unpaid constables and subconstables of each vill were drawn from the same social groups as the jurors. Indeed, some of them served as jurors when not acting as constable.[200] They stood on the front line, and played a pivotal role in the enforcement of the labour legislation.[201] After 1349 they shouldered immense responsibility and wielded considerable power over the work habits and routines of every adult in their community. They largely determined whether and how to interpret the legislation locally, and so had constantly to assess who was able-bodied and who was not, whether hiring had taken place openly or privately, and whether contracts had been breached. The constables determined how to resolve breaches of the legislation (including the power to force servants to work for particular employers) and which punishments to apply. Within their communities they were busy hearing oaths under the statute, putting people to work, addressing disputes over contracts, placing transgressors in the stocks and deciding what to report to the hundred jurors.[202] Yet they did so without any training, or any guidance about how to deal with the complex cases they encountered or the vague and confusing aspects of the legislation. Some of them may have been reluctant office holders, or unsuited to the demands and dilemmas of the post. Constables had considerable powers to dispense summary justice, but only their personal skill, diligence, and disposition determined whether that justice was to be fair or rough.[203] If their justice was rough, then the tithing groups who had elected them now had diminished powers to censure or hold them to account formally, because in the matter of the labour laws and price legislation constables and jurors were accountable directly to the justices of the peace.[204]

It is possible to illustrate the discretion vested in constables and the dilemmas such men faced from an actual incident of the time. In 1373 the unnamed constable of Northolme (Lincs.) put Alicia de Ingoldmels to work as a servant of Thomas Walsh of Wainfleet, but Alicia left before the end of the contract without good reason or Thomas's permission.[205] The royal justices in Lincolnshire then heard the case and fined Alicia. This concise official narrative of events hides the various options available and the decisions taken at each step in the case. Let us speculate that Alicia had suffered maltreatment and had not been provided with board as originally covenanted, and so *did* have a lawful reason for leaving, but could not find two witnesses able to swear definitively either to the maltreatment or to the detail of the original agreement. Without any defence in law, she had no other options for redress and the constable could not investigate her version of events further, even if he suspected that Alicia was a vulnerable and innocent woman wronged by an employer with a reputation for abuse. The constable now had to decide what sanction to apply. If the constable believed that she had been wronged, and considered minimizing the punishment, he risked criticism from Thomas Walsh and the justices of the peace who favoured a tougher line against offenders. The lowest level of sanction, and the most pragmatic and kindly, was to try and persuade Alicia to return to Thomas's employment and to persuade Thomas to remove any possible grounds for future complaint. However, the constable manifestly decided to take a harder line, so his three options were either to put her to work elsewhere (again); to place her in the stocks for the recommended three days; or to report the case to the justices, either for fining or imprisonment.[206] He chose the last option, probably because Alicia was a recidivist, or possibly because she had irked the constable previously, or because she had failed to offer a discreet bribe or had refused an explicit demand for money to lighten the punishment.[207] The choices and the dilemmas are starkly apparent. Honest and sensitive constables had limited scope to manage injustice: dishonest and insensitive ones enjoyed considerable scope for exercising—or manipulating or abusing—the king's justice.

While the challenges facing constables enforcing the labour laws have been acknowledged, their implications for the quality of justice after 1349 have not been fully explored. The advantage of bestowing so much discretion upon local constables and jurors was that they were well informed about local issues, problems, and troublemakers. The disadvantage was that they could be personally involved or had conflicts of interest in some cases and might use the authority of office to pursue their own agendas or those of local cliques. After all, as resident and established landholders within their communities, they had a vested interested in upholding the established social hierarchy, which increased the scope for prejudice against outsiders, newcomers, and the poorer and more mobile elements of society. They also faced various conflicts of interest. Some constables forced individuals, whom they had deemed to be the idle able-bodied, to work in their own households.[208] Urban jurors who were themselves established retailers could easily use their office to target outsiders and occasional traders within the price- and profit-setting legislation. In 1356 a royal commission was sent to Scarborough (Yorks.) to investigate claims that royal officials had abused their positions under the Statute of Labourers and pocketed the fines for themselves.[209] In the 1370s public concern about corruption in the retail trades and other abuses by royal officials formed an important backdrop to the 1381 revolt in London.[210] It cannot be coincidental that immediately after the revolt parliament addressed such issues when stipulating that in future no practising victualler could serve in a judicial office within a royal borough, and that profit- and price-setting was to be implemented without favour.[211]

The most obvious and cogent manifestation of the presence of bias and weighted agendas in enforcing the legislation is the rarity of prosecutions against employers in general and landlords in particular.[212] For every labourer who had received an excessive wage, an employer had paid one, so employers should have featured in the court records as frequently as employees. Indeed, the Ordinance of Labourers even contained a clause empowering justices to punish employers more severely than workers.[213] There is no doubt that even the major landlords were openly flouting the labour legislation: they paid bonuses in cash and kind, and slipped in other hidden perks such as food and drink; and their auditors reduced the day rates paid to workers recorded in manorial accounts, when they knew full well that higher wages had been paid.[214] Yet, despite all this, constables, jurors, and justices routinely turned a blind eye. Out of 467 cases relating to the labour legislation handled by the justices in Norfolk and Suffolk in the 1360s and 1370s, just one involved an individual paying excess wages; likewise, there were few prosecutions against employers in Cheshire.[215] Only when an employer had flagrantly procured or incited a servant to walk out of an existing contract did a prosecution follow.[216] Yet the possibility of prosecuting employers provided the labour legislation with real bite and offered its best chance of success. The failure to do so implies either that justices directed jurors not to present employers, or that jurors and constables chose not to. Whatever the reasons, it exposes starkly the deep social prejudice at the heart of the labour legislation, and the hypocrisy and blatant unfairness in its implementation. Its objective was to restore balance within the ordained social order by enforcing social inequality, not to promote economic equality in the radically-changed circumstances of the post-plague world. The wage and compulsory service clauses of the labour legislation were probably the source of greatest resentment towards the government's social and economic policies.[217]

Although the experience of royal justice after 1349 unquestionably increased the divisions within society, it is no longer credible to argue that these divisions were mainly along class lines, i.e. between the justices and landlords on the one hand and the plebian mass on the other.[218] The central role of local jurors and constables in implementing the legislation on the ground undermines any notion of class solidarity among the 'plebian mass'. One reason why some among the ranks of the lower orders may have supported the legislation in the 1350s was the incentive to use fines collected under the statute to offset their contribution to royal lay subsidies (see above, p. 79). But the main reason is that enough people within every English community had sufficient interest in making aspects of the legislation work because they themselves—not the landlords—were the main employers of day workers and servants.[219] One recent estimate suggests that fourteenth-century England contained around 19,000 seigniorial employers and 450,000 peasants, artisans, and townsfolk with enterprises large enough to require hired labour.[220] The latter were usually those serving as jurors and constables, who were making most decisions about whom to prosecute and where, and who would have shared the seigniorial aversion to prosecuting employers.[221] Cases recorded in sessions of the justices are explicit that many labour offences were not against lords but against ordinary employers. Offenders 'would not serve within the vill', 'would not work in the harvest', 'would not labour for their neighbours', or had refused to work when requested to do so by the 'good people of the vill'.[222] Such behaviour was 'damaging' to their neighbours or to their community, or 'to the great annihilation and impoverishment of the vill'.[223] Likewise, borough courts and jurors had no interest in or business implementing the legislation in support of rural lordship: they were implementing it strictly on behalf of urban employers, sometimes rigorously.[224] The implementation of the legislation must have significantly increased social tensions *within* the lower orders of society in both town and countryside, splitting local communities in complex, shifting, and fluid ways between those who supported it, those who supported it in principle but objected to its abuses, and those opposed to it.[225]

Thus lords and the government were not the only groups in English society who believed that underemployed workers should be available to work for a reasonable wage, and that wandering and indigent labourers represented a threat to social order.[226] Central royal and county gentry justices were incapable of making this legislation work on their own initiative: it was effective only because local constables identified dissidents within their own communities and took action against them, and because local jurors brought thousands of cases to the justices. All of these officials were under oath, and some were also under duress, but many of them performed their duties as resident members of their community who themselves depended upon hired labour, who had an interest in upholding the local social hierarchy, and who may well have had a strong sense of their social responsibilities in this regard.[227] A number of the jurors serving on peace sessions in Ipswich (Suffolk) in the 1360s were employers who themselves litigated in private pleas against some of their former employees for breach of contract.[228] Studies of pre-plague rural communities have shown that the strongest and closest social ties existed among the middling sort, whereas the wealthier peasants and the poor had more distant and socially differentiated networks.[229] The labour laws provided village elites with new powers to control the lives and behaviour of the poorer and most unruly elements of their communities.[230]

Nevertheless, if the labour legislation received some support among sections of the lower orders, certain aspects of its implementation could still be a source of concern even to its supporters.[231] The first was the scope it provided for the unscrupulous or dishonest to abuse their position of authority flagrantly.[232] The second was the impossible dilemmas it could sometimes create for the honest office holders, as explored above in the case of Alicia de Ingoldmels. The third was the blunt, undifferentiated, nature of the legislation, which could be used to punish both the enterprising and industrious employed, *and* the idle, resentful, and underemployed. Thus, although migrant and seasonal workers were among the worst offenders against the labour legislation, they often escaped punishment because they were the most difficult to oblige to attend judicial sessions, whereas resident members of communities were easier to pressurize to attend and to punish.[233] Objections and concerns such as these might well explain why some members of the clergy openly questioned the legitimacy of the laws.[234] In 1374 two local chaplains and an acolyte assaulted the constables of Wyberton (Lincs.) for placing one Richard Rote in the stocks after he had refused to be put to work.[235] Two Hertfordshire men prosecuted in the 1350s under the legislation were punished further for openly expressing a desire to strike William Shareshull, the Lord Chief Justice responsible for the laws.[236]

The role of the constable became much more prominent and onerous under the new legislation, but many of the people tasked with the office were trapped between two concepts of order.[237] One, exerted from above and by certain sections of their own community, obliged them to enforce the legislation zealously; the other, exerted from others within their own community, required them to resist its implementation and oppose its abuses.[238] Some jurors and constables must have 'dreaded the difficulties and dangers of enforcing the labour laws'.[239] Tangential evidence of such dilemmas, tensions, and divisions are apparent in the sources. In 1370s some constables informed the Lincolnshire justices that *no-one* in the district had transgressed the statute on their watch, while others informed the justices that *everyone* had done so: both reports are implausible.[240] Some constables refused to make presentments to the justices.[241] For example, in 1375 William Bateson, the constable of Cold Hanworth (Lincs.), refused either to respond to a summons to attend the sessions of the peace or to convey a summons to other representatives of the vill in his place.[242] Explicit refusals of jurors to take their oaths or to attend the session are occasionally recorded.[243] For example, in 1373 the vills of Grainsby, Swinhope, and North Thoresby (all Lincs.) were described as 'rebellious and would not come to present in front of the justices of the lord king'.[244] Passive collective resistance was less confrontational, but was nonetheless effective. Failures—as opposed to refusals—of jurors from specified townships to attend a particular peace session are regularly recorded.[245] The dilemmas facing constables must also explain their mixed roles and fortunes during the 1381 uprising. Rebels targeted them in some places, along with active jurors and unpopular justices, while in other places rebel bands included men who had served as jurors and constables.[246] Indeed, some constables and jurors may have sprung quickly to support the revolt as a pre-emptive move against becoming a target themselves.[247] Rebel bands in 1381 must also have included people who had been responsible for enforcing aspects of the government's social policies within their own communities at various times in the 1360s and 1370s, but who objected to the role they were required to perform or were outraged at some of the abuses they witnessed around them.

Enhancing both the powers and the discretion of local officials, whose experience in judicial matters was variable, to implement the raft of new government legislation after 1349 was bound to result in wide inconsistencies in the nature and quality of their decision-making. The loss of experienced local officials in successive plague outbreaks certainly thrust more inexperienced people into public office, although whether the overall impact was detrimental to the quality of officialdom or beneficial (because of the opening up of office holding to new talent) is impossible to gauge.[248] There are, however, three reasons to suspect that, in general, the consequences were detrimental. First, the significant extension of powers was not supported by any close direction or training about how to exercise them. Individual officers had to make their own judgements with little guidance on what to ignore, what to pursue, whether to mitigate, and so on, but few were able to learn by observing or obtaining advice from others with a deep well of experience. They had to rely instead mainly upon their personal experience in this field, which was decidedly limited. Second, moralists captured popular concerns about the quality of petty officialdom and advocated better civic governance, and in the early 1380s their concerns were partly addressed through legislation restricting the influence of royal officials in the retail trades.[249] Third, the prominence of long-established families as office holders within local communities declined after the Black Death and their places taken by recent immigrants with few local contacts or loyalties, and with less understanding of the local context.[250] Olson regards the generation after the Black Death as a period of severe discontinuity in village communities and of a breakdown in the old forms of internal social cohesion because of the high turnover of established families, the decline of pledging as a system of social self-regulation, a reluctance to hold local office, and the influx of newcomers. As a result, social control was increasingly imposed upon the village from outside, which meant the role of constable 'became far more visible in the more troubled village society after 1350'.[251]

Conclusion

After 1349 the expanding activity of the state—through novel forms of taxation and a new social policy—was a common experience forging common grievances across the lower orders of English society. The transformation of England from a 'demesne' state, where the Crown was largely dependent upon its own financial resources, to a 'fiscal' state, in which the resources of the realm were mobilized through regular indirect and direct taxation to support the Crown's dynastic ambitions, dramatically increased the tax burden upon a greatly reduced population.[252] The burden was greatest in the 1370s, when the government also experimented with new forms of direct taxation and when its management of the war with France was inept. The price- and profit-capping legislation was not new after 1349, but its zealous enforcement increased the exposure of ordinary people to its arbitrary and vexatious characteristics. The labour laws represented a novel, major, and socially inequitable intrusion into a labour market that had previously operated with little regulation. In addition, the Crown created a new category of county justices to enforce the legislation and loaded the commissions with members of the local gentry, who could use the position to pursue their own political agendas. The Statute of Labourers effectively imposed an indirect tax upon hired labour and upon those working in the retail and wholesale trades. These intrusive innovations frustrated many among the lower orders at a time when their expectations and living standards were rising. A sizeable minority of the population were hereditary serfs and tenants of villein land, who were frustrated further by the residual stigma associated with serfdom.

All of these developments have been well researched and documented, and all contributed to the Peasants' Revolt of 1381 to varying degrees. This chapter has focused upon one under-researched aspect of the revolt, namely how the behaviour of some lesser royal officials after 1349 fuelled concerns and anger about the deteriorating quality of royal justice. The practice of leasing the judicial unit of the hundred to a third party increased in the 1350s, and again in the 1370s, which increased the likelihood that the business of the hundred court would be manipulated for profit at the cost of the quality of royal justice. The drafting and the structure of the economic and social legislation after 1349, and the system of its implementation, enhanced the systemic opportunities for manipulation, misuse, abuse, extortion, and corruption, whilst, at the same, failing to install adequate checks and balances that would have discouraged such behaviour. The statutory provisions for the economic legislation were always cursory, sometimes vague, and lacking detail and precision for those tasked with implementing them.[253] The same offences could be handled within a tier of courts, so the scope for jurisdictional confusion, duplication, and manipulation was enhanced. The legislation handed those individuals elected to serve as constables and jurors significant discretionary powers to exercise their version of social control within their communities, greatly increasing the scope for prejudice and conflicts of interest.[254] It also shifted the accountability of those officials from the communities that had elected them to the justices of the peace, creating another source of contention.

These issues affected men and women from a wide range of different backgrounds and communities: townsfolk, the free, the unfree, migrants, and residents. They affected people especially in the south-east, the Home Counties, and East Anglia, where the labour market and retail trades were most widely established. It is therefore reasonable to deduce that the experience on the ground of this very prominent and intrusive manifestation of royal justice wove common threads of frustration among disparate groups of society in regions where the Peasants' Revolt was fiercest. It helps to explain the heightened anxieties within English society in the wake of plague about the abuses committed by those engaged in commercial practices and the legal profession.[255]

The resultant social conflict cannot, however, be categorized simplistically or crudely along class lines, i.e. between landlords and the plebian mass, because the experience of royal justice affected elements of the lower orders in different ways. The new legislation appears to have set the landlord class against the peasantry, but, on closer inspection, the interests of the latter were not closely aligned. Enough ordinary people within every English community had a vested interest in enforcing many aspects of the legislation because they were regular employers of hired labour and consumers of basic foodstuffs. They served as the jurors and constables who were pivotal to making the system work. They recognized the benefits it might bring to the common good as well as some of the difficult dilemmas it posed: and even those who supported the legislation in principle would have baulked at the opportunities it presented for some of their peers to manipulate and abuse their positions of responsibility. They were as likely to regard vagrants and the able-bodied poor as a threat to social order, and to regard them as scapegoats, as the ruling elite. As a result, the very nature of the legislation and the detailed mechanics of its enforcement caused deep divisions within local communities, although the lines of rupture were neither horizontal nor clean nor fixed. These complex economic and social grievances were inextricably intertwined with the political ambitions and legal reforms of the post-plague era, so it is difficult to categorize them cleanly as either a 'socio-economic' cause of the revolt or a 'political' cause. In this sense, it underlines the challenges of attempting to weigh and prioritize the causes of the revolt according to some clear and definitive hierarchy.

The exploration of how the legislation worked on the ground casts new light upon the ways in which the extension of royal justice after 1349 also fuelled grievances about its deteriorating quality. The sense of grievance was amplified by the heightened demands for taxation and its perceived waste. These experiences helped to develop further the political consciousness of the lower orders because it raised urgent and persistent questions about how the Crown should govern, and with what authority and accountability. Ordinary people possessed a good knowledge and understanding of the royal judicial process, and so they had an informed sense of how it was faring, how it should operate, and how it could be reformed.[256] This experience explains the rebels' demand in 1381 for one lord and the removal of the intermediary layers of overlapping jurisdictions between the local community leet court and the royal central courts.[257] The Peasants' Revolt of 1381 was not a movement seeking to reject the law per se, but it was a movement which, in Musson's words, reflected 'an exasperation with the judicial system. Their revolution was intended to be a cleansing of the Augean stables rather than an overthrow of the whole system'.[258] The rebels sought reform of certain institutions of government (taxation, aspects of the legal system) and the correction of the leading individuals, which reflects an underlying faith in the principle of royal authority, despite its manifest failings in this period.[259] Indeed, Faith argues that the English peasantry displayed a distinct lack of revolutionary fervour, exhibiting instead a social traditionalism harking back to an idealized past rather than looking forward to an idealized future.[260] From a European perspective, English peasants demonstrated a peculiarly persistent faith in legal records and the possibility of achieving reform by means of formal legal procedures.[261]

The English peasantry in 1381 sought reform of the various layers of royal legal jurisdictions and of manorial lordship, but their fundamental belief in royal justice held steadfast. This belief reflects the immersion of all levels of society in a legal culture during the course of the thirteenth century through the spread of standardized legal procedures within a multiplicity of local legal tribunals. By the time of the Black Death this culture was deeply established: it conditioned behaviour, shaped expectations, and had created a belief in a rudimentary legal due process and in the broadly consistent treatment of similar wrongs. The innovations in royal justice under the unprecedented conditions created by the Black Death fell short of those expectations. The aspirational reach of the state after 1349 had far overextended its systemic grasp, and the revolt served as a dire warning of the consequences.

Notes

1. Charles Oman, *The Great Revolt of 1381* (Oxford, 1906), pp. 5–12, 152–4, quote at p. 5; see also Edgar Powell, *The rising in East Anglia in 1381* (Cambridge, 1896), pp. 62–4.
2. See the summary in Rigby, *English Society*, pp. 110–24.

3. Jane Whittle and Stephen H. Rigby, 'England: popular politics and social conflict', in S. H. Rigby, ed., *A companion to Britain in the late Middle Ages* (Oxford, 2003), p. 73; Thomson, *Transformation*, p. 28; see also Harriss, *Shaping the nation*, pp. 232–4.

4. Michael M. Postan, *The medieval economy and society: an economic history of Britain in the later Middle Ages* (London, 1972), p. 154; also the summary in Rigby, *English society*, pp. 121–2.

5. Goldberg, *Medieval England*, p. 180.

6. Summarized in Rigby, *English society*, pp. 122–4; and J. Firnhaber-Baker, 'Introduction', in Justine Firnhaber-Baker and Dirk Schoenaers, eds., *The Routledge handbook of medieval revolt* (Abingdon, 2017), pp. 3–4.

7. May McKisack, *The fourteenth century 1307–1399* (Oxford, 1964), p. 422.

8. Whittle and Rigby, 'Popular politics', p. 72.

9. This tradition can be traced back to Powell, *Rising in East Anglia*, pp. 1–2. Summarized in Aberth, *From the brink*, pp. 140–2; Schofield, *Peasants and historians*, pp. 99–102.

10. Quotes from Bolton, *Medieval English economy*, pp. 215–17. See also Barbara Hanawalt, 'Peasant resistance to royal and seigniorial impositions', in Francis X. Newman, ed., *Social unrest in the late Middle Ages* (New York, 1986), pp. 23–7; Bolton, 'World turned upside down', pp. 45–9; Hargreaves, 'Seigniorial reaction', pp. 52–5; Kitsikopolous, 'Impact of the Black Death', pp. 82–3. This line of argument is summarized clearly in Rigby, *English society*, pp. 113–18; for an example of resistance, see Britnell, 'Feudal reaction', pp. 40–7.

11. W. Mark Ormrod, *The reign of Edward III: Crown and political society in England* (New Haven, 1990), p. 31. See also Campbell, 'The land', pp. 222–5.

12. Holmes, *Higher nobility*, pp. 116–17; Bridbury, *English economy*, p. 37. See also, for example, Keen, *English society*, pp. 39–43; J. Lander, *Conflict and stability in fifteenth-century England*, p. 72.

13. Mollat and Wolff, *Popular revolutions*, pp. 201–3, quote at p. 201.

14. Keen, *English Society*, p. 40.

15. David Aers, 'Justice and wage-labor after the Black Death: some perplexities for William Langland', in Allen J. Frantzen and Douglas Moffat, eds., *The work of work: servitude, slavery, and labour in medieval England* (Glasgow, 1994), p. 172.

16. Rodney H. Hilton, *Bondmen made free: medieval peasant movements and the English rising of 1381* (London, 1973), pp. 156–7. Also, the demands of the rebels emerged 'specifically from the conflict between landlords and tenants', Hilton, 'English Rising', p. 19.

17. Rodney H. Hilton, 'Introduction', in Rodney H. Hilton and Trevor H. Aston, eds., *The English Rising of 1381* (Cambridge, 1984), p. 8; and Hilton, 'English Rising', p. 18. In this tradition, see also Ros Faith, 'The class struggle in fourteenth-century England', in Raphael Samuel, ed., *Peoples' history and socialist theory* (London, 1981), pp. 50–60; Christopher Dyer, 'The social and economic background to the rural revolt of 1381', in Hilton and Aston, eds., *The English Rising*, pp. 9–42; Dyer, *Everyday life*, pp. 221–40; idem, 'The causes of the revolt in rural Essex', in W.H. Liddell and R.G. Wood (ed.), *Essex and the Great Revolt of 1381* (Chelmsford, 1982), pp. 21–36; Kitsikopoulos, 'Impact of the Black Death', pp. 82–3.

18. Dyer, *Standards of living*, p. 147; Dyer, *Making a living*, pp. 286–90.

19. David Rollison, *A Commonwealth of the people: popular politics and England's long social revolution, 1066-1649* (Cambridge, 2010), p. 96.

20. Rigby, *English society*, p. 123.

21. Hilton, *Bondmen made free*, p. 155. For the labour legislation as new serfdom, see Alan Harding, 'The revolt against the justices', in Hilton and Aston, eds., *The English Rising*, p. 187; Beier, 'A new serfdom', pp. 40-5.

22. Hilton, *Bondmen made free*, p. 154.

23. Christopher Dyer, 'The ineffectiveness of lordship in England', in Dyer et al. eds., *Rodney Hilton's Middle Ages*, p. 84; Brenner, 'Property and progress', p. 96.

24. The quotes are from Dyer, 'Villeins, bondsmen', p. 434 and Bolton, *Medieval English economy*, p. 213.

25. Keen, *English society*, pp. 39-41; Bennett, 'Impact of the Black Death', pp. 200-1; Palmer, *English law*, pp. 23-4; Dyer, 'Villeins, bondmen', p. 434; Fryde, 'Peasant rebellion', p. 755; Nigel Saul, 'Conflict and consensus in English local society', in Taylor and Childs, eds., *Politics and crisis*, p. 40.

26. Palmer, *English law*, pp. 11-12.

27. Bennett, 'Impact of the Black Death', p. 200.

28. Herbert Eiden, 'Joint action against "bad" lordship: the peasants' revolt in Essex and Norfolk', *History*, 83 (1998), p. 29. Dyer, 'Social and economic', pp. 40, 42.

29. Eiden, 'Joint action', pp. 5-30; Müller, 'Conflict', pp. 1-19; Herbert Eiden, 'The social ideology of the rebels in Suffolk and Norfolk in 1381', in M.-L. Heckmann and Jens Rohrkasten, eds., *Von Novgorod bis London* (Gottingen, 2008), pp. 425-40 at p. 436.

30. Muller, 'Conflict', pp. 1-3, 13-15.

31. Eiden, 'Joint action', pp. 22-3, 28.

32. Eiden, 'Joint action', p. 28. This statement is not quantified, and his analysis of 110 Norfolk rebels reveals that nine were servile tenants or tenants at will, p. 23.

33. Dyer, 'Social and economic', p. 38 explains such discrepancies by the ability of the rebels to generalize their actions and demands rather than pursuing personal vendettas. Since we cannot recover the motives of the rebels definitively, we can never know, but it is evident that the Brandon rebels were motivated by wider political, not just narrowly local, issues.

34. Eiden's two citations in support of this argument relate to the seigniorial reaction in general not the abbey of Benet Holme specifically: two pages of an article by Dyer and one page from Bolton's survey of the post-plague economy, Eiden, 'Joint action', pp. 7, 10, 23, 28.

35. William Page, ed., *Victoria County History of Norfolk, volume 2* (London, 1906), pp. 330-6; Powell, *Rising*, pp. 30, 34; John F. Maddicott, 'Law and lordship: royal justices as retainers in thirteenth- and fourteenth-century England', Past and Present Supplements, 4 (1978), p. 74; Juliet Barker, *England arise: the people, the king and the Great Revolt of 1381* (London, 2014), p. 347.

36. Bailey, 'Myth', pp. 164-5.

37. Hilton, *Bondmen made free*, pp. 137-40; Rigby, *English Society*, p. 117; Eiden, 'Bad lordship', p. 29; Muller, 'Conflict', p. 5.

38. R. Barrie Dobson, ed., *The Peasants' Revolt of 1381* (second edition, Basingstoke, 1983), pp. 159, 161. Henry Knighton also notes the demand at Mile End to be free of

'intolerable servitude and heavy oppressions', and Froissart records the rebels' call for freedom for themselves, their heirs and lands, Dobson, *Peasants' Revolt*, pp. 183, 192.

39. Dobson, *Peasants' Revolt*, pp. 164–5.

40. Alan Prescott, '"Great and horrible rumour": shaping the English revolt of 1381', in Firnhaber-Baker and Schoenaers, eds., *Routledge handbook*, p. 85.

41. Robin DuBoulay, *The lordship of Canterbury: an essay in medieval society* (London, 1967), pp. 188–9; Susan Crane, 'The writing lesson of 1381', in Barbara A. Hanawalt, ed., *Chaucer's England: literature in historical context* (Minneapolis, 1992), p. 204; Dyer, *Everyday life*, p. 224; Eiden, 'Joint action', pp. 22, 29; Musson, *Medieval law in context*, p. 245; Muller, 'Conflict', p. 5; Hilton, *Bondmen made free*, p. 156; Andy Wood, *Memory of the people: custom and popular senses of the past in early modern England* (Cambridge, 2013) p. 52.

42. Nick Ronan, '1381. Writing in revolt: signs of confederacy in the chronicle accounts of the English rising', *Forum for Modern Language Studies*, 25 (1989), pp. 304–14; Crane, 'Writing lesson', pp. 203–6. They would presumably omit charters of manumission from this targeting of written records.

43. Muller, 'Conflict', p. 5; Eiden, 'Bad lordship', p. 29.

44. Green, *Crisis of truth*, pp. 199–203.

45. For one example, see the destruction of some estate documents belonging to Waltham abbey (Essex) following the abbey's drawing up in the late 1370s of written proofs of servility, Poos, *Rural society*, p. 250.

46. Muller, 'Conflict', pp. 13–14; Barker, *England arise*, p. 344. See also Holmes, *Higher nobility*, pp. 127–8; Fryde, 'Peasant rebellion', p. 775.

47. Prescott, 'Great and horrible rumour', pp. 83–4.

48. Eiden, 'Joint action', p. 22; Eiden, 'Social ideology', p. 435; Mingjie Xu, 'Disorder and rebellion in Cambridgeshire in 1381' (PhD dissertation, University of Cambridge, 2015), pp. 31, 56, 62.

49. Putnam, *Proceedings*, pp. cxxii–iii; Richard W. Kaeuper, *War, justice and public order: England and France in the later Middle Ages* (Oxford, 1988), p. 371; Barker, *England arise*, pp. 180, 184, 189, 192, 198–200, 276–7, 282, 293–4, 314, 383; Xu, 'Disorder and rebellion', pp. 47, 55.

50. Musson, *Medieval law in context*, pp. 245–46; Eiden, 'Social ideology', p. 436; Freedman, *Images*, p. 260; Barker, *England arise*, p. 339; Xu, 'Disorder and rebellion', p. 39.

51. Steven Justice, *Writing and rebellion: England in 1381* (Oakland, 1996) p. 41; Richard F. Green, *A crisis of truth. Literature and law in Ricardian England* (Philadelphia, 2002), pp. 165–8, 199–202; Sherri Olson, *A mute gospel: the people and culture of the medieval English common fields* (Toronto, 2009), pp. 124–5; Wood, *Memory of the people*, p. 50.

52. J. Ambrose Raftis, 'Social change versus revolution: new interpretations of the Peasants' Revolt of 1381', in Newman, ed., *Social unrest*, pp. 6–13; Olson, *A mute gospel*, pp. 124–30.

53. Olson, *Chronicle*, pp. 3–9; Olson, *Mute gospel*, pp. 124–30.

54. Beckerman, 'Procedural innovation', p. 226, n.133; Musson, *Medieval law in context*, p. 120; Birrell, 'Manorial customs', pp. 10–37.

55. Eiden, 'Joint action', p. 29.
56. Freedman, *Images*, p. 264; Musson, *Medieval law in context*, pp. 170, 248.
57. Musson and Ormrod, *Evolution of English justice*, p. 133.
58. Barker, *England arise*, p. 383.
59. Helen Lacey, 'Grace for the rebels', *Journal of Medieval History*, 34 (2008), pp. 40–1, 45.
60. Hilton, *Bondmen made free*, pp. 224–5; Andrew Dunn, *The Peasants' Revolt: England's failed revolution* (Stroud, 1994), pp. 120–3; Lacey, 'Grace for the rebels', p. 45; Barker, *England arise*, pp. 250–1, 256.
61. Holmes, *Higher nobility*, p. 116.
62. Barker, *England arise*, pp. 250–6, 375, 385–6, 393–4. See also Mollat and Wolff, *Popular revolutions*, p. 200.
63. Lacey, 'Grace for the rebels', pp. 40–1.
64. Dunn, *Peasants' Revolt*, pp. 120–2; Lacey, 'Grace for the rebels', pp. 45–6.
65. Barker, *England arise*, p. 281; Xu, 'Disorder and rebellion', pp. 31–2, 40–3.
66. Lacey, 'Grace for the rebels', pp. 46–7.
67. Barker, *England arise*, pp. 255, 375.
68. Barker, *England arise*, pp. 252–3, fns 50 and 52, and pp. 393–4; Fryde, 'Peasant rebellion', pp. 767–8.
69. See, for example, Barker, *England arise*, pp. x, 5, 217, 261–2, 350, 375, 401, 425.
70. Barker, *England arise*, pp. 374–5.
71. Barker, *England arise*, p. 383; the Hertfordshire charter is printed in full in Dunn, *Peasants' Revolt*, p. 121. King's Langley was probably singled out because Richard stayed there in July 1381 in the clean-up operation after the revolt, Lacey, 'Grace for the rebels', p. 52.
72. Lacey, 'Grace for the rebels', p. 45.
73. As stated explicitly by the Essex rebels on 22 June, Barker, *England arise*, p. 167.
74. Green, *Crisis of truth*, pp. 165–8; Ros Faith, 'The Great Rumour of 1377 and peasant ideology', in Hilton and Aston, eds., *English Rising of 1381*, pp. 61–2, 69; Freedman, *Images*, pp. 130, 265.
75. Freedman, *Images*, p. 129.
76. Levett, *Black Death*, pp. 134–5; Page, *Villeinage*, pp. 66–71; Fryde, 'Tenants of the bishops', pp. 231–9; Bailey, 'Blowing up bubbles', pp. 349–50; Mark Bailey, 'Rural society', in R. Horrox, ed., *Fifteenth-century attitudes: perceptions of society in late medieval England* (Cambridge, 1994), 158–9; Bailey, *Decline of serfdom*, pp. 56–65; McGibbon Smith, 'Reflections', p. 184; Coss, 'Neifs and villeins', pp. 198–9; Bailey, 'Tallage-at-will', pp. 50–7.
77. See, for example, the survey in Wood, *Memory of the people*, pp. 43–5.
78. Maddicott, 'Law and lordship', pp. 62–4; Rigby, *English society*, p. 123; Goldberg, *Medieval England*, pp. 174–85; Jane Whittle, 'Peasant politics and class consciousness: the Norfolk rebellions of 1381 and 1549 compared', in Dyer et al., eds., *Rodney Hilton's Middle Ages*, p. 245; Xu, 'Disorder and rebellion', pp. 124, 171–4.
79. Harding, 'Revolt against the justices', p. 180.
80. Dobson, *Peasants' Revolt*, p. 375; Thomas E. Tout, *Chapters in the administrative history of medieval England*, volume III (Manchester, 1928), pp. 365–70; Lambert and Pajic, 'Immigration and the Common Profit', pp. 633–57; Barker, *England arise*, pp. 174–93.

81. Lambert and Pajic, 'Immigration and the Common Profit', pp. 633–57; Samuel K. Cohn, *Popular protest in late medieval English towns* (Cambridge, 2012), pp. 287–8.

82. Quote from Poos, 'Social context', p. 28. For attacks on Gaunt's provincial estates, see Powell, *Rising*, p. 28; Harding, 'Revolt against the justices', pp. 187–8, esp. fn. 90; Bailey, *Marginal economy*, pp. 235–6; Dobson, *Peasants' Revolt*, pp. 278–9; Platts, *Land and people*, p. 177; Barker, *England arise*, pp. xiv, 192, 202, 316, 324, 328–9, 344, 365–6; Xu, 'Disorder and rebellion', pp. 99–100; Prescott, 'Great and horrible rumour', p. 92. For attacks on properties associated with Treasurer Robert Hales as Grand Prior of the Knights Hospitallers, see Xu, 'Disorder and rebellion', pp. 99–100, 113–17; Vanessa McLoughlin, *Medieval Rothley, Leicestershire: manor, soke and parish* (PhD dissertation, University of Leicester, 2006), pp. 109–13; Barker, *England arise*, pp. 196–7, 311, 319, 328. For Flemings, see Powell, *Rising*, pp. 31–2, 36; Barker, *England arise*, p. 345. For judicial targets, see Maddicott, 'Law and lordship', pp. 61–2; Harding, 'Revolt against the justices', p. 180; Jewell, 'Piers Plowman', pp. 67–71. For local examples, see Tout, *Administrative history*, pp. 365–6; Nicholas Brooks, 'The organization and achievements of the peasants of Kent and Essex in 1381', in Henry Mayr-Harting and Robert I. Moore, eds., *Studies in medieval history presented to R.H.C. Davies* (London, 1985), pp. 250–2, 262; J. Anthony Tuck, 'Nobles, commons and the Great Revolt of 1381', in Hilton and Aston, eds., *English Rising*, p. 205; Fryde, 'Peasant rebellion', pp. 759–60; Powell, *Rising*, pp. 28–36; Eiden, 'Joint action', pp. 18–21; Xu, 'Disorder and rebellion', pp. 44–5, 52, 96–9, 102, 110–11; Barker, *England arise*, pp. 146–7, 175–6, 179–82, 185, 188–9, 191–2, 197–202, 293–4, 308, 310, 319–20, 328–31, 336, 338–9, 342–4, 369–70.

83. Quote from Eiden, 'Joint action', p. 14. See also McIntosh, *Autonomy and community*, pp. 80–5; Poos, *Rural society*, pp. 239–51; Eiden, 'Joint action', pp. 14–15; Eiden, 'Social ideology', p. 435.

84. Eiden, 'Joint action', pp. 10, 23–8; Xu, 'Disorder and rebellion', pp. 67–81.

85. Eiden, 'Social ideology', pp. 435–6; Joe Chick, 'Leaders and rebels: John Wrawe's role in the Suffolk rising of 1381', *Proceedings of the Suffolk Institute of Archaeology and History*, 44 (2018), pp. 214–34; Muller, 'Conflict', pp. 13–14; Barker, *England arise*, pp. 202–3.

86. Joe Chick, 'The 1381 rising in Bury St Edmunds: the role of leaders and the community in shaping the rebellion', *Pons Aelius*, 13 (2016), pp. 35–47.

87. Eiden, 'Social ideology', p. 435; Chick, 'Leaders and rebels', pp. 217–19, 224–6.

88. Xu, 'Disorder and rebellion', pp. 20–4, 128–9, 169, quote from p. 169.

89. Fryde, 'Peasant rebellion', p. 760; Xu, 'Disorder and rebellion', pp. 44–5, 52, 96–9, 102, 110–11.

90. Christian Liddy, 'Urban conflict in late fourteenth-century England: the case of York in 1380–1', *English Historical Review*, 475 (2003), pp. 1–32.

91. For general summaries of what follows, see Maddicott, 'Law and lordship', pp. 59–71; Kaeuper, *War, justice*, pp. 367–70; Jewell, 'Piers Plowman', pp. 59–71; Goldberg, *Medieval England*, pp. 180–3; Seabourne, *Royal regulation*, pp. 1–4, 160–5; Lacey, 'Grace for the rebels', pp. 36–9.

92. Maddicott, *Law and justice*, pp. 1–13.

93. Maddicott, *Law and lordship*, pp. 13–25; Durant W. Robertson, 'Chaucer and the economic and social consequences of the plague', in Newman, ed., *Social unrest*, pp. 51–6.

94. Harding, 'Revolt against the justices', p. 171; Lacey, 'Grace for the rebels', p. 53; Maddicott, 'Law and lordship', pp. 59–61.

95. Harding, 'Revolt against the justices', p. 168; W. Mark Ormrod, 'The politics of pestilence: government in England after the Black Death', in Ormrod and Lindley, eds., *Black Death*, pp. 155–9.

96. Ormrod, *Edward III*, pp. 155–60; Harding, 'Revolt against the justices', pp. 183–6; Dobson, *Peasants Revolt 1983*, p. 68; Tuck, 'Nobles, commons', p. 206.

97. Britnell, 'Production for the market', p. 385; Poos, 'Social context', p. 43; Britnell, *Colchester*, p. 137; Fryde, 'Peasant rebellion', p. 755.

98. Saul, 'Conflict and consensus', p. 40. See Poos, 'Social context', pp. 40–1 for an example of the ways in which local people appointed to royal commissions were accused of extortion and abuse of their authority.

99. Musson and Ormrod, *Evolution of English justice*, p. 97. W. Mark Ormrod, 'The Peasants' Revolt and the government of England', *Journal of British Studies*, 29 (1990), pp. 13–14.

100. Putnam, *Proceedings*, pp. cxxiii, cxxv; Fryde, 'Peasant rebellion', pp. 759–60; Campbell, 'Factor markets', p. 98.

101. Bennett, 'Compulsory service', pp. 14–19, 23–7, 47; Bennett, 'Impact of the Black Death', pp. 200, 202; Poos, 'Social context', pp. 30–1.

102. Palmer, *English law*, pp. 12, 294. See also Kaeuper, *War, justice*, pp. 386–7; Harriss, *King, parliament*, pp. 35–45.

103. Quote from Bennett, 'Impact of the Black Death', pp. 200–1. See also Palmer, *English law*, pp. 11, 15–18, 23–4; Given-Wilson, 'Service, serfdom', p. 22; Bennett, 'Compulsory service', pp. 14–16. Hilton, *Bondmen made free*, p. 152; Alan Harding, *The law courts of medieval England* (London, 1973), p. 118; Hettinger, 'Role of the Statute', pp. 5–7; Dyer, 'Ineffectiveness of lordship', p. 84; Dyer, 'Social and economic', p. 38; Aberth, *From the brink*, pp. 135–9, 144–7; Cohn, *Popular protest*, pp. 125–8.

104. Hilton, *Bondmen made free*, p. 154.

105. Hilton, *Bondmen made free*, pp. 154, 184.

106. For the latest dating of the poem, see Stephen H. Rigby, 'Gower's works', in Rigby and Echard, eds., *Historians on John Gower*, pp. 124–5. For Gower's observations on officialdom, see William B. Wilson, ed., *Mirour de l'omme* (East Lansing, 1992), pp. 323, 330; Musson, *Medieval law in context*, pp. 69–72; Robertson, 'Chaucer', pp. 51–6.

107. Fryde, 'Peasant discontent', pp. 747–9; Booth, *Financial administration*, p. 90; Cohn, *Popular protest*, pp. 118–22.

108. McIntosh, *Autonomy and community*, pp. 78–81; see also Fryde, 'Peasant rebellion', pp. 748–9.

109. Holmes, *Higher nobility*, p. 100.

110. Seabourne, *Royal regulation*, pp. 121–2; Sharp, *Famine and scarcity*, pp. 113–19; Cohn, *Popular protest*, p. 117; Jennifer Hole, *Economic ethics in late-medieval England* (Palgrave, 2016), pp. 169–77.

111. *Statutes of the Realm*, I, pp. 371–3; Hole, 'Justification for wealth', pp. 39–43.

112. Ormrod, *Edward III*, p. 158.

113. Cohn, *Popular protest*, pp. 118, 124.

114. Musson, *Medieval law in context*, pp. 69, 72, 75; Green, *Crisis of truth*, pp. 128–43; Walker, 'Order and law', pp. 106–7; Bailey, 'Peasants and the Great revolt', p. 187.

115. Lacey, 'Grace for the rebels', pp. 42–3.

116. Brooks, 'Organization and achievements', pp. 250–2, 265–6; Musson, *Medieval law in context*, pp. 84–5, 243; Freedman, *Images*, p. 266.

117. Harding, 'Revolt against the justices', p. 180; Jewell, 'Piers Plowman', pp. 67–71; Robertson, 'Chaucer', pp. 53–6; Peter Coss, 'An age of deference', in Horrox and Ormrod, eds., *Social history*, pp. 160–2.

118. Ormrod, 'The Peasants' Revolt', p. 14.

119. Cohn, *Popular protest*, pp. 125–6.

120. Rigby, *English society*, pp. 123–4; Goldberg, *Medieval England*, pp. 176–8.

121. Justine Firnhaber-Baker, 'Introduction', in Firnhaber-Baker and Schoenaers, eds., *Routledge handbook*, pp. 3–6; Prescott, 'Great and horrible rumour', pp. 94–6; John Watts, 'Conclusion', in Firnhaber-Baker and Schoenaers, eds., *Routledge handbook*, pp. 370–7; John Watts, *The making of polities: Europe 1300–1500* (Cambridge, 2009), pp. 205–8, 216–19, 238–44, 253–4, 363–7, 275–82.

122. Briggs, 'Introduction', pp. 9–11.

123. Hettinger, 'Role of the Statute', pp. 197–8; Prescott, 'Great and horrible rumour', pp. 88–96.

124. Maddicott, *Law and lordship*, pp. 63–5; Fryde, 'Peasant rebellion', pp. 782–3; Anthony J. Musson, 'Sub-keepers and constables: the role of local officials in keeping the peace in fourteenth-century England', *English Historical Review*, 470 (2002), pp. 21–3.

125. Tuck, 'Nobles, commons', p. 205; Jewell, 'Piers Plowman', p. 74; Barker, *England arise*, pp. 386, 411–12.

126. For example, Green, *Crisis of truth*, pp. 127–86.

127. The other Smithfield demands were: no serfdom, no type of service to any lord, and all to be free and of one condition; rents fixed at 4d. per acre; no requirement for anyone to be forced to serve (i.e. work as a hired labourer or servant), except by their own will and a regular covenant; no outlawry; no lordship other than the king; and one bishop, and the wealth of the church to be shared, Dobson, *Peasants' Revolt*, pp. 164–5.

128. The demands are recorded in Dobson, *Peasants' Revolt*, p. 164, who notes the cryptic nature of the Winchester reference. For other references to the latter, see Goldberg, *Medieval England*, p. 175 and Barker, *England, Arise*, pp. 268–9, but also Green, *Crisis of truth*, pp. 198–9. The specific aims of the Essex rebels are described in Barker, *England, Arise*, pp. 167, 269–70. For a basic introduction to leet courts, see Bailey, *English manor*, pp. 178–88; for the Statute of Winchester in its local context, see Musson, 'Sub-keepers and constables', pp. 3–5.

129. Harriss, *Shaping the nation*, pp. 233–4; Eiden, 'Social ideology', pp. 437–8; Musson, *Law in context*, pp. 250–2; Barker, *England, Arise*, pp. 268–70.

130. Anthony J. Musson, 'Patterns of supplication and litigation strategies: petitioning the Crown in the fourteenth century', in Thomas W. Smith and Helen Killick, eds., *Petitions and strategies of persuasion in the Middle Ages: the English Crown and the church, c.1200–c.1550* (York, 2018), pp. 96–104.

131. Harding, 'Revolt against the justices', p. 187.

132. Dyer, 'Memories', p. 295.

133. Paul H. Booth, 'Taxation and public order: Cheshire in 1353', *Northern History*, 12 (1976), pp. 16–31; Paul H. Booth, 'The enforcement of the Ordinance and Statute of Labourers in Cheshire, 1349 to 1374', *Archives*, 127 (2013), pp. 8–10. See the farming of royal offices in Wales at this time, Matthew F. Stevens, *The economy of medieval Wales 1067–1536* (Cardiff, 2019), pp. 88–9.

134. Waugh, *England*, p. 115.

135. Bean, 'Landlords', p. 572; Ormrod, *Edward III*, pp. 117–19; Ormrod, 'Politics of pestilence', p. 169 and fn. 65.

136. W. Mark Ormrod, Helen Killick, and Phil Bradford, eds., *Early commons petitions in the English parliament c.1290–c.1470*, Camden 5th Series, 52 (2017), pp. 40–1. Moralizers recognized the potential this created for extortion; see Michael Haren, *Sin and society in fourteenth-century England: a study of the Memoriale Presbiterorum* (Oxford, 2000), p. 130; *PROME, volume V, Edward III 1351–77*, p. 322.

137. Musson and Ormrod, *Evolution of English justice*, pp. 50–3, 89–100.

138. *CFR, 1377–1383*, p. 131 (dated 24 March 1379).

139. Powell, *Rising in East Anglia*, pp. 21–2.

140. For a general background to this private franchise, see Helen Cam, *Liberties and communities in medieval England* (Cambridge, 1944), pp. 183–204; Bailey, *Medieval Suffolk*, pp. 3–4.

141. The account is not dated, but the catalogue and internal evidence suggests it is from the early 1350s, SROB A6/1/18. I have not identified any lord named John Astoun in Suffolk, but in 1346 a man of that name held a manor in Woodditton just across the county border in Cambridgeshire, William Farrer, *Feudal Cambridgeshire* (Cambridge, 1920), pp. 158–9.

142. Hundred courts could handle public and private cases under the labour legislation; see Booth, 'Enforcement', pp. 3–4.

143. Rosamund Sillem, ed., *Some sessions of the peace in Lincolnshire 1360–1375*, Lincoln Record Society, 30 (1937), p. 30. For affeerors, see Bailey, *English manor*, p. 171.

144. *CPR 1367–70*, p. 137; *CIM, vol. 3*, pp. 263–5.

145. Ormrod et al., eds., *Early petitions*, pp. 38–9.

146. For example, two local men were granted two Norfolk hundreds in separate grants in 1369 and 1370, *CFR, 1368–77*, pp. 31, 64.

147. Rigby, *English society*, pp. 119–21; Ormrod, 'Politics of pestilence', pp. 159–67; Harriss, *Shaping the nation*, pp. 58–61; Given-Wilson, 'Problem', pp. 94–7; Moore, 'War and finance', figs. 2–3.

148. Moore, 'War and finance'.

149. Kaeuper, *War, justice*, pp. 353–60.

150. Davis, *Medieval market morality*, pp. 226, 231.

151. De Roover, 'Just price', pp. 425, 430; Seabourne, *Royal regulation*, p. 136; Kaye, *History of balance*, pp. 71–87, 95–125. Hence local officials could easily bring poorly founded charges against vulnerable targeted individuals or groups, such as outsiders and occasional dealers, and so institutionalize prejudice against certain types of retailer, Britnell, *Commercialisation*, p. 174.

152. '*Modestum lucrum non excessivum*', Horrox, *Black Death*, p. 289.

153. Quote from *Statutes of the Realm*, I, p. 313; Seabourne, *Royal regulation*, pp. 77, 85, 98; Davis, *Medieval market morality*, pp. 225-6.

154. *Statutes of the Realm*, I, pp. 315-16.

155. Hettinger, 'Role of the Statute', pp. 163-6; Seabourne, *Royal regulation*, p. 95; Davis, *Medieval market morality*, pp. 226-30, 233-5, 243-4; Braid, 'Behind the ordinance', pp. 13-15.

156. Putnam, *Proceedings*, pp. cxiii, cxxii.

157. Sillem, ed., *Some sessions of the peace*, pp. 17, 84, 157, 168-9, 177-8, 201, 211 (ale); 26, 49-50, 58-9, 62-3, 72, 84, 197-8, 220 (hides).

158. Sillem, ed., *Some sessions of the peace*, pp. 52, 85, 100, 157, 227-8.

159. Sillem, ed., *Some sessions of the peace*, pp. 94, 237-8.

160. Sillem, ed., *Some sessions of the peace*, pp. 89, 157.

161. Sillem, ed., *Some sessions of the peace*, pp. 43-4.

162. Sillem, ed., *Some sessions of the peace*, pp. 157-8, 222.

163. Sillem, ed., *Some sessions of the peace*, p. 85.

164. Sillem, ed., *Some sessions of the peace*, p. 89.

165. Sillem, ed., *Some sessions of the peace*, pp. 26, 198-9. Interestingly, given the government's concerns about grain shortages in the 1350s and 1360s, there is no record of the Lincolnshire justices addressing sales of grain before the mid-1370s, Sillem, ed., *Some sessions of the peace*, pp. 95-9, 101, 168, 172, 182. This is consistent with the evidence from London, Braid, 'Behind the ordinance', p. 5.

166. Musson, 'Reconstructing', pp. 114-15; Braid, 'Behind the Ordinance', pp. 23-8.

167. Horrox, *Black Death*, p. 342.

168. Given-Wilson, 'Service, serfdom', pp. 24-6.

169. Bennett, 'Compulsory service', p. 18; Palmer, *English law*, pp. 21-2. The 1351 statute stated that artisans 'shall be sworn before the justices to perform and carry out their crafts and jobs in the same manner as in the said 20th year and before, without any refusal on the grounds of this ordinance', Horrox, *Black Death*, p. 314; *Statutes of the Realm*, 1, p. 313.

170. A.W. Brian Simpson, *A history of the common law of contract: the rise of the action of assumpsit* (Oxford, 1975), *Contract*, pp. 49-51; Musson, 'Reconstructing', pp. 15-16.

171. Sandy Bardsley, 'Women's work reconsidered: gender and wages differentiation in late medieval England', *Past and Present*, 165 (1999), p. 18 cites a case of a constable and bailiff determining the able-bodied within their vill.

172. Simpson, *Common law of contract*, pp. 49-52, 149.

173. These phrases feature in *Statutes of the Realm*, I, p. 366.

174. Dyer, 'Work ethics', p. 39.

175. Bennett, Compulsory service', p. 15; Palmer, *English law*, p. 18.

176. Hettinger, 'Role of the Statute', pp. 97, 104, 108; Booth, 'Enforcement', p. 7.

177. The other five tribunals were the market court; borough court; hundred court; royal commission of oyer and terminer; and JP session.

178. Hettinger, 'Role of the Statute', pp. 21-4; Booth, 'Enforcement', pp. 2-5.

179. The earliest surviving copy of articles of presentment for jurors attending JP sessions (from 1403) is a miscellaneous compilation bearing all the hallmarks of having been

drawn up locally and borrowed from similar articles created for use within another county: locally-generated copies indicate the absence of centrally-issued templates, Putnam, *Proceedings*, pp. xxxii–xxxv, 15.

180. Hettinger, 'Role of the Statute', pp. 97, 104, 108; Sillem, ed., *Some sessions of the peace*, pp. 179–81.
181. Hettinger, 'Role of the Statute', table 3.3.
182. Hettinger, 'Role of the Statute', pp. 28–89, 92, 108.
183. Putnam, *Proceedings*, p. cxiii; E.C. Furber, ed., *Essex sessions of the peace 1351, 1377–79*, Essex Archaeological Society, Occasional Papers, 3 (1953), pp. 38, 42, 47; Alfred L. Brown, *The governance of late medieval England* (London, 1989), p. 126.
184. *Statutes of the Realm*, I, p. 351; Davis, *Medieval market morality*, pp. 226, 314–17, 328–30, 380–1, 395; Britnell, *Colchester*, pp. 133–5; Seaborne, *Economic regulation*, pp. 102–4; Braid, 'Behind the ordinance', pp. 6–15.
185. Davis, *Medieval market morality*, pp. 314–17, 380–1; Seabourne, *Royal regulation*, pp. 102–4.
186. *PROME, volume V, Edward III 1351–1377*, p. 405.
187. Putnam, *Statutes of Labourers*, p. 164.
188. Seabourne, *Royal regulation*, pp. 96–117.
189. Musson, 'Reconstructing', pp. 117–18.
190. Aberth, *From the brink*, p. 145.
191. Hettinger, 'Role of the Statute', pp. 114–15.
192. Musson, 'Sub-keepers and constables', pp. 1–22.
193. The constable and usually a couple of other representatives from each vill were required to elect representatives from their hundred to attend each peace session within their county and, if they were not on the jury personally, to brief the presentment jury concerning any cases from their vill: R. Sillem, ed., *Some sessions of the peace in Lincolnshire, 1360–1375*, Lincoln Record Society, 30 (1937), pp. xxxv–xxxvii.
194. Elizabeth G. Kimball, ed., *Rolls of the Warwickshire and Coventry sessions of the peace 1377–1397*, Dugdale Society, 16 (1939), pp. l–liii; Furber, ed., *Essex sessions of the peace*, pp. 32–5.
195. Writing a commentary on the indictments in Putnam, *Proceedings*, pp. cxxxviii–cxxxix. See also J.B. Post, 'Some limitations of the medieval peace rolls', *Journal of the Society of Archivists*, 4 (1973), pp. 633–5; Poos, 'Social context', p. 34.
196. Furber, ed., *Essex sessions of the peace*, p. 37; Hettinger, 'Role of the Statute', pp. 185–92; Post, 'Some limitations', p. 635.
197. Kimball, *Rolls*, pp. lii–liii; Furber, ed., *Essex sessions of the peace*, pp. 32–7; Hettinger, 'Role of the Statute', pp. 185–92.
198. Hettinger, 'Role of the Statute', pp. 108, 161–2, 200–16; Poos, 'Social context', p. 35; Larson, 'Village voice', pp. 698–706.
199. Nicholas Amor, 'Justices and jurors in fourteenth-century Suffolk' (forthcoming).
200. Kimball, *Rolls*, p. liv.
201. Putnam, *Proceedings*, p. cxxvi; Poos, 'Social context', pp. 31–3, 35; Musson, 'Reconstructing', p. 124; Bennett, 'Compulsory service', pp. 21–2; Musson, 'Sub-keepers and constables', pp. 5–19.

202. Sillem, ed., *Some sessions of the peace*, pp. 31, 70, 81 (hearing oaths); pp. 5–6, 22, 24–8, 32–4, 36, 42, 47–8, 67, 74, 91 (putting able-bodied to work); 1 (contract disputes); 8, 18, 241 (stocks and imprisonment). Poos, 'Social context', pp. 30–3.

203. Bennett, 'Compulsory service', pp. 14–16, 28.

204. Poos, 'Social context', pp. 34–5; Horrox, *Black Death*, p. 315; Palmer, *English law*, pp. 18–20.

205. '*Alicia de Ingoldmeles de Northolm iuxta Waynflete nuper assignata Thome Walsshe per constabularium de Northolm ad seruiendum eiden Thome in autumpno anno xlvij capiendo mercedes et salarium iuxta ordinacionem inde editam videlicet apud Waynflete dicta Alicia a seruicio ipsius Thome ante finem termini predicti since causa racionabili et licencia ipsius Thome recessit contra formam ordinacionis predicte*', Sillem, ed., *Sessions of the peace*, p. 48.

206. Putnam, *Statutes of Labourers*, pp. 73, 82–3; Bennett, 'Compulsory service', pp. 17, 21–2, 28.

207. The likelihood of bribes was so obvious to the drafters of the Statute of Labourers that they included specific clauses to deal with the issue, Horrox, *Black Death*, p. 315.

208. Poos, 'Social context', p. 35.

209. Cohn, *Popular protest*, p. 127.

210. Helen Carrel, 'Food, drink and public order in the London *Liber Albus*', *Urban History*, 33 (2006), pp. 180–1, 184–7; James Davis, 'Towns and trade', in Rigby and Echard, eds., *Historians on Gower*, pp. 195–211.

211. *Statutes of the Realm*, II, pp. 28–9; Davis, *Medieval market mortality*, pp. 65, 67.

212. Putnam, *Enforcement*, pp. 82, 179; Fryde, 'Peasant rebellion', p. 758; Given-Wilson, 'Service, serfdom', p. 27; Dyer, *Making a living*, p. 283; Booth, 'Enforcement', p. 8.

213. Horrox, *Black Death*, p. 288; Palmer, *English law*, p. 18.

214. Farmer, 'Prices and wages', pp. 483–5; Hatcher, 'England in the aftermath', pp. 21–4; Stone, 'Black Death', pp. 231–2.

215. Hettinger, 'The role of the Statute', table 3.3 and pp. 118–19; Booth, 'Enforcement', p. 8.

216. John Gale of Edlington was presented to the justices for enticing John Donney from his service contract with the offer of an excessive salary, Sillem, ed., *Sessions of the peace*, p. 63: for other examples, see pp. 34, 45.

217. Fryde, *Peasants and lords*, p. 35; Given-Wilson, 'Service, serfdom', p. 27; Goldberg, *Medieval England*, pp. 182–3.

218. Hilton, *Bondmen made free*, pp. 154–5.

219. Kosminsky, *Studies in the agrarian history*, pp. 315–17; Hettinger, 'Role of the Statute', pp. 7–8, 24, 127–9, 161–2, 197–202; Poos, 'Social context', pp. 35–6, 51–2; Rees Jones, 'Regulation of labour', p. 139; Dyer, 'Work ethics', pp. 33–4; Bennett, 'Compulsory service', pp. 12–13; Booth, 'Enforcement', p. 10.

220. Broadberry et al., *British economic growth*, p. 321 and table 8.03.

221. Poos, 'Social context', pp. 35–6; Given-Wilson, 'Service, serfdom', p. 27; Hettinger, 'Role of the Statute', pp. 7–8, 124–60, 196–223. For examples where judicial sessions identify explicitly the social status of employers, see Sillem, ed., *Sessions of the peace*, pp. 2, 20, 22–8, 33–4, 36–8, 42, 45–8, 52, 54, 57–8, 62.

222. '*Ad laborandum [cum] vicinis ville*'; '*ad seruiendum...ad operandum...refutavit seruire...in eadem villa*'; '*ad seruiendum communitati eiusdem ville tempore autumpni*'; '*et alios probos homines eiusdem ville ad seruiendum de artificio suo in*

eadem villa', Sillem, ed., *Sessions of the peace*, pp. 6, 24, 32–4, 36, 41, 46–7, 92; Faith, 'Berkshire', pp. 163–4; Booth, 'Enforcement', p. 10.

223. Sillem, ed., *Sessions of the peace*, p. 92; Hettinger, 'Role of the Statute', pp. 102, 149.

224. Rees Jones, 'Regulation of labour', pp. 139; Britnell, *Colchester*, p. 136.

225. Poos, 'Social context', pp. 28, 31–7, 50–2.

226. Hettinger, 'Role of the Statute', pp. 7–8, 24, 127–9, 161–2, 197–20; Booth, 'Enforcement', p. 10.

227. Hettinger, 'The role of the Statute', pp. 161–2, 200–16; Given-Wilson, 'Problem of labour', pp. 98, 100; Musson, 'Reconstructing', p. 119.

228. Nicholas R. Amor, *Keeping the peace in medieval Suffolk* (forthcoming) .

229. Stephen Mileson, 'Openness and closure in the later medieval village', *Past and Present*, 234 (2017), pp. 14–18.

230. Poos, 'Social context', pp. 34–51; Clark, 'Medieval labour laws', p. 334.

231. Bennett, 'Compulsory service', pp. 22–3.

232. Musson, 'Sub-keepers and constables', pp. 20–3.

233. Booth, 'Enforcement', p. 7.

234. Putnam, *Proceedings before the Justices*, p. cxxv; Bennett, 'Impact of the Black Death', pp. 201–2; Poos, 'Social context', pp. 28, 31, 33; Beier, 'A new serfdom', p. 43; Bennett, 'Compulsory service', pp. 23–5, 42–4.

235. Sillem, ed., *Some sessions of the peace*, p. 241.

236. Putnam, *Proceedings*, p. cxxv. See also, Cohn, *Popular protest*, pp. 125–8.

237. Olson, *Chronicle*, pp. 44–55, 128–31.

238. Poos, 'Social context', p. 35; Marjorie K. McIntosh, *Controlling misbehaviour in England 1370–1600* (Cambridge, 1998), pp. 206–8; Musson, 'Reconstructing', p. 121.

239. Putnam, *Proceedings before the Justices*, p. cxxvi; Poos, 'Social context', pp. 34–5; Bennett, 'Compulsory service', p. 22.

240. Putnam, *Statutes of Labourers*, p. 76.

241. Poos, *Rural society*, pp. 241–2.

242. Sillem, ed., *Sessions of the peace*, p. 55.

243. Sillem, ed., *Sessions of the peace*, pp. 3–4, 32, 34, 55, 70–1; Booth, 'Enforcement', pp. 7–8.

244. Sillem, ed., *Sessions of the peace*, p. 16.

245. Sillem, ed., *Sessions of the peace*, pp. 10, 14, 21, 23, 33, 35, 39, 54–5, 75, 84.

246. Putnam, *Proceedings*, p. cxxvi; Poos, 'Social context', pp. 33–4; Hettinger, 'The role of the Statute', pp. 191–2, 208–11; Eiden, 'Social ideology', p. 435; Eiden, 'Joint action', pp. 10, 23, 26, 28; Musson, 'Reconstructing', pp. 121; Barker, *England arise*, pp. 184–5, 189–90, 204; Xu, 'Disorder and rebellion', pp. 103, 119, 123, 125. The William Rous of Dennington, whose extortionate practices when collecting court fines is documented above (p. 205), was chief constable of Hoxne hundred (Suffolk) and targeted in the revolt, Powell, *Rising in East Anglia*, pp. 21, 130–1.

247. Hettinger, 'The role of the Statute', pp. 210–11. For a possible case of a juror behaving this way, see Furber, ed., *Essex sessions of the peace*, p. 36.

248. Britnell, 'Black Death in towns', pp. 203, 208. See Larson, *Conflict and community*, pp. 136–7.

249. G.R. Owst, *Literature and pulpit in medieval England* (Oxford, 1933), pp. 162, 169–70, 328–9; James Davis, 'Towns and trade', in Rigby and Echard, eds., *Historians on Chaucer*, pp. 208–11; *Statutes of the Realm*, II, pp. 28–9.

250. Raftis, 'Social change', pp. 15–17; Razi, *Life, marriage*, pp. 123–4; Britnell, 'Black Death in towns', p. 208; Sherri Olson, 'Jurors of the village court: local leadership before and after the plague in Ellington, Hunts.', *Journal of British Studies*, 30 (1991), pp. 237–56, at 240–3; Olson, *Chronicle*, p. 141.

251. Olson, *Chronicle*, pp. 84–8, 147–9, 106, 128, 141, 229–30, quote at p. 128; Larson, *Conflict and compromise*, pp. 136–7.

252. Waugh, *England*, pp. 178–89; Cohn, *Popular protest*, pp. 160–2.

253. Britnell, *Commercialisation*, p. 174; Seabourne, *Royal regulation*, p. 15; Davis, *Medieval market morality*, p. 226.

254. Hettinger, 'Role of the Statute', p. 108.

255. Davis, 'Towns and trade', pp. 206-211; Anthony J. Musson, 'Men of law', in Rigby and Echard, eds., *Historians on Gower*, pp. 226–38.

256. Brooks, 'Organization and achievements', pp. 250–2, 265–6; Musson, *Medieval law in context*, pp. 84–5, 243; Freedman, *Images*, p. 266.

257. Harding, 'Revolt against the justices', p. 166; Musson, *Medieval law in context*, pp. 250–2; Eiden, 'Social ideology', p. 437; Barker, *England arise*, pp. 268–70, 374.

258. Musson, *Medieval law in context*, p. 242.

259. Green, *Crisis of truth*, pp. 167–8.

260. Faith, 'Class struggle', p. 50; Faith, 'Great Rumour', p. 70; Freedman, *Images*, p. 129; Musson, *Medieval law in context*, p. 252.

261. Freedman, *Images*, p. 129.

6

A New Equilibrium? Economy and Society, 1375 to 1400

Introduction: a New Equilibrium?

Following the volatility and unpredictability of the third quarter of the century, the orthodox view is that from the mid-1370s the English economy and society finally settled at their post-plague equilibrium. According to Bolton 'only in the mid-1370s did plague really begin to bite hard into the traditional manorial economy...it was not until the years 1370–90 that the tide turned full'.[1] Similarly, Bridbury states that 'the effects of cumulative attacks of the Black Death first manifested themselves' in the 1370s, reiterating that 'it is in the seventies, rather than in the mid-century decades' that its 'dynamic' impact was felt.[2] The harvest of 1376 was bountiful, causing grain prices to fall dramatically. During the previous quarter-century prices had always bounced back quickly after good harvests—such as in 1354–5, and 1366—but after 1376 grain prices and the Composite Price Index lost their bounce, and thereafter remained persistently lower (table 6.1).[3] Wages, meanwhile, continued to rise after successive plague outbreaks.[4] As a result, nominal real wages rose appreciably in the years 1376 to 1380 (table 6.1) and remained high thereafter.[5] From the mid-1370s agricultural land values, rents, and levels of occupation all fell, and agrarian production swung decisively towards pastoral pursuits.[6]

Thus, according to this widely-accepted narrative, the economy at last reached its new equilibrium, in which the relative abundance of land to labour was now fully reflected in factor and commodity prices. The population settled at around 2.5 million, benign weather greatly improved grain supplies, and monetary deflation exacerbated the decline in commodity prices. More arable was converted to pasture because stock rearing and pastoral produce required fewer labour inputs and offered greater opportunities to reduce unit costs of production. The sustained fall in agrarian profits caused economic distress to many landlords, forcing even the most conservative of them to abandon the direct cultivation of their demesnes. This reduced the seigniorial need for labour services at the same time as the chronic shortage of tenants forced them to make concessions to the old terms of tenure.

This orthodox narrative also identifies a neat contrast between the third and fourth quarters of the century in the social relations between lords and peasants.

After the Black Death: Economy, Society, and the Law in Fourteenth-Century England. Mark Bailey, Oxford University Press (2021). © Mark Bailey. DOI: 10.1093/oso/9780198857884.003.0006

Table 6.1 Some price and wage indices in England, 1361 to 1400 (1451–75 = 100)

Years	CPI	Grains PI	Meat PI	Dairy PI	Threshing Wages	RWI (A)	RWI (C)
1361–65	138	130	131	105	60	44	55
1366–70	136	150	132	107	64	47	58
1371–75	127	134	144	107	72	55	60
1376–80	110	96	119	105	74	67	69
1381–85	113	104	111	106	78	68	69
1386–90	101	83	108	97	72	71	75
1391–95	104	97	106	73	72	69	74
1396–1400	111	105	111	101	77	69	70

Source: Munro, 'Late medieval decline', tables 18, 20A, 21A.
CPI = Composite Price Index; RWI = Real Wage Index, calculated by Nominal Wage Index/CPI; RWI (A) = agricultural real wage (based on threshing and winnowing wages); RWI(C) = craft worker real wage rate (based on carpenters' wages).

In the 1360s and 1370s relations are supposed to have deteriorated sharply, as peasants were coerced into accepting terms in the land and labour markets that were favourable to the lords and contrary to market forces. Resistance became widespread during the course of the 1370s, when 'all classes of the peasantry were involved'.[7] As we saw in Chapter 5, the heightening of lord–peasant tensions in this decade is seen as leading directly to the Peasants' Revolt of 1381, which was 'essentially a protest...against the seigniorial reaction by which landowners were trying to hold their own against the economic tide'.[8] In this perspective, the revolt of 1381 is depicted as a key watershed in social relations, after which lords abandoned their harsh and exploitative policies and sought to accommodate peasants with more attractive tenures and concessions on serfdom.[9] The rapid descent into anarchy during the summer of 1381 and the shocking violence sent a chilling warning to landlords to beware the consequences of prolonging the 'seigniorial reaction'.[10] Managerial policies after 1381 thus became studiously moderate, servile tenancies and incidents gradually dissolved, and the government's labour legislation was incapable of preventing a sustained rise in wages.[11] Serfs now enjoyed greater freedom in determining their own lives and left their home manors in droves in search of better terms elsewhere, and their lords lacked the power or will to prevent them.[12]

Thus from the early 1380s powerful and self-reinforcing social and economic forces caused serfdom to dissolve, gradually releasing the land and labour markets from non-commercial influences and propelling them towards full market development.[13] The shifting balance of economic power heralded the advent of a golden age for the lower orders of English society.[14] The flood of demesne land onto the land market, tumbling land values, and the desperation of lords to retain tenants all worked to the advantage of peasants, enabling most to benefit and a small minority to increase substantially the size of their landholdings. This peasant elite now began to construct large commercial farms, and to lease demesne flocks, herds, arable, and woodland, so that by the early fifteenth century they were self-identifying as the economically prosperous and socially influential 'yeomen' and 'husbandmen'. Meanwhile, smallholders, labourers, and servants reaped the rewards of both higher earnings and nominal real wages. Opportunities for women's work increased, whether in urban servanthood or rural day labour, enhancing their economic standing and offering them wider choices about when, where, and whether to marry.[15]

While there is a good deal to commend in this orthodoxy, a reassessment of some of its central elements is overdue. First, a closer analysis of the key economic indicators reveals that the final quarter of the fourteenth century did not constitute a single homogeneous or stable period but rather was comprised of three distinct but subtly different sub-periods. Historians often imply that economic and social conditions remained stable and consistent between c.1375 and c.1430, but in reality those between 1375 and 1395 were rather different from those that followed.[16] Second, historians usually attribute the sudden swing in the mid-1370s from buoyant to depressed conditions for grain producers to bumper yields from improved weather and the sapping of demand through recurrent plague epidemics. While this explanation makes good sense, it overlooks the contribution of grain producers to the conditions of oversupply. It is likely that high grain prices and the experience of harvest failures during the late 1360s had stimulated an expansion in commercial grain production in the peasant sector: the notion that they waited until the profitability of agriculture had collapsed before constructing large agricultural holdings is counter-intuitive. Their re-engagement with the market would have exacerbated the problems of oversupply in the mid-1370s, and their economic pain when profits slumped fuelled the social unrest in the run-up to the revolt. Third, the argument that this period heralded a golden age for the peasantry is attractive, but the evidentiary base is less compelling upon close scrutiny.[17] Fourth, the narrative that serfdom mainly disappeared after 1381 does not fit with the evidence from Chapter 3 that it was already dissolving in the 1350s, nor with the arguments in Chapter 5 that the Peasants' Revolt was primarily an angry response to the expansion in state power, rather than a protest against bad manorial lordship.[18] Here, then, we seek to offer a more nuanced, complex, and multi-factored assessment of the last quarter of the fourteenth century.

Economic Change

GDP per head

Real GDP per head grew at an estimated 0.76 per cent per annum throughout the second half of the fourteenth century, an exceptional rate not bettered until the late seventeenth century, before levelling off in the early fifteenth century.[19] The most recent and reliable calculations of annual GDP per head reveal that it remained flat between 1365 and 1384, then rose more than ten per cent from (an index of) 60.5 per annum in 1375–84 to 68.6 in 1385–94 (fig. 4.1 and table 4.4).[20] It rose marginally to 70.9 in 1395–1404 and levelled off thereafter. Likewise, the index for industrial output rose from 16.9 in 1375–84 to 20.0 in 1385–94, and marginally thereafter (table 4.4). These figures are, of course, estimates, but they are broadly consistent with the evidence from various sectors of the economy, and so identify confidently the main direction of economic change. They also point to the period 1385–94 as another phase of structural change within the economy, away from agriculture towards industrial pursuits. As we shall see, the fortunes of individual sectors of the economy after c.1400 support the argument that GDP per head was now levelling.

Prices and wages

On closer analysis, it becomes apparent that the economy did not settle into its post-plague equilibrium in the mid-1370s. In fact, three distinct and subtly different sub-periods are identifiable in the last twenty-five years of the century. The first began in the mid-1370s and lasted until the mid-1380s. The Composite Price Index fell 14 per cent in the second half of the 1370s and remained there until the mid-1380s. It was driven principally by a sustained fall in grain prices, and the associated fall in the price of bread, ale, and, to a lesser extent, meat, while the prices of other agricultural produce—such as dairy produce—remained relatively stable (table 6.1). Wages continued to rise, and consequently the level of the Real Wage Index moved decisively upwards between 1375 and 1380. The cumulative effect was to improve the purchasing power of labour: the estimated living costs of a farm labourer fell by around one-fifth.[21]

The second sub-period extended from the mid-1380s until the mid-1390s. If the period 1375 to 1385 represented a cold snap for commercial producers, then 1385 to 1395 was a harsh winter. The Composite Price Index declined by a further 11 per cent, mainly as a result of another slump in grain prices, but this time due to falls in the prices of poultry, meat, dairy produce, and clothing.[22] According to one price series, the fall from a high point in the early 1370s to the low point of the late 1380s represents the greatest single decennial price drop in more than five centuries of English history.[23] Wages held steady or declined only marginally after 1385, which meant a further squeeze on agrarian profitability and a slight rise in the Real Wage Index (table 6.1). Indeed, agricultural conditions in the late 1380s were worse than commercial producers had faced at any time in the previous two centuries (they became even worse in the mid-fifteenth century).[24] The third sub-period began in the mid-1390s, when these severe conditions eased slightly. The Composite Price Index rose 7 per cent, wages held or drifted up marginally and so the Real Wage Index held more or less steady. Thereafter, price indices for agricultural, industrial and service goods remained broadly constant into the early fifteenth century.[25] Hence the mid-1390s, rather than the mid-1370s, was the period when the economy settled at its post-plague equilibrium.

The opening up of the price-wage scissors in the mid-1370s and the associated fall in the profitability of grain production is usually attributed to the combined effects of three powerful forces. First, the successive outbreaks of plague gradually sapped the economy's buoyancy by preventing any demographic recovery and levelling aggregate demand. Second, demesne grain yields in the period 1375–90 were c.20 per cent higher than they had been in 1355–70, which greatly boosted the supply of grain.[26] Campbell attributes the recovery of yields to the sudden onset of drier, warmer, and more stable weather, reinforced by higher stocking densities and the abandonment of marginal lands.[27] Finally, during the 1380s and 1390s a general monetary deflation reinforced the downward pressure on prices.[28] Mint output fell from the late 1360s, reaching its lowest point in the late 1370s and early 1380s, due to reduced exports and mounting bullion shortages.[29] The severe conditions between 1385 and 1395 were principally a function of exceptional monetary deflation.

While these three forces provide a convincing explanation for the fall in prices, one other hitherto unexplored factor deserves closer consideration: the possibility that a recovery of peasant grain production by the early 1370s also contributed to the subsequent conditions of oversupply and low grain prices. The evidence of tithe payments indicates a widespread and sustained recovery of peasant grain output during the course of the 1360s, which rose to a peak in the early 1370s.[30] For example, tithe receipts at Feering (Essex) in 1348–55 had fallen by around one-third from their level in 1331–47, but by 1367–72 had recovered to within 11 per cent of that pre-plague level.[31] Similarly, the value of grain tithes at Kingston (Suffolk) had returned to its pre-plague level by 1374–5, while tithe receipts in County Durham reached a post-plague peak in the early 1370s.[32]

How was this growth in peasant grain output achieved during a period when the evidence from seigniorial demesnes indicates that yields were dire (see pp. 158-9)? One possibility is that peasants began to increase the inputs of labour to their own holdings, resulting in improved yields, although this is impossible to prove one way or the other. However, the most obvious and likely explanation is that it was achieved through a rise in the area under cultivation. This possibility has not really been considered before, because of a general sense that no significant rise in the mean size of peasant holdings is detectable before the late fourteenth century. Certainly, the accumulation of substantial landholdings was rare in the 1350s.[33] There are two grounds, however, for challenging the assumption that peasants did not construct larger holdings before the 1380s. First, there are clear signs from manors across the country that levels of occupancy of peasant arable land, and the construction of larger holdings, rose during the course of the

1360s.[34] The experience of back-to-back harvest failures between 1367 and 1369 might have been a trigger to take on more arable land. For example, in 1365 between 16 per cent and 25 per cent of all customary land was still abandoned on four Derbyshire manors, but by 1375 three of them recorded full occupancy while just 11 per cent of customary land remained unoccupied on the fourth.[35] The number of tenants holding more than one virgate of land increased markedly on pre-plague levels in parts of the east Midlands and on the estate of the bishop of Winchester.[36] In the early 1370s the mean holding size was at least 27 per cent higher, and on one manor 83 per cent higher, than it had been in the 1340s across four Cornish manors.[37] Elsewhere, standardized holdings for which it had proved impossible to find tenants during the 1350s were gradually re-let during the course of the 1360s, often by converting the land from the old service tenure to a cash tenancy.[38] Most of the standardized customary holdings in Brandon (Suffolk) had been abandoned during the first epidemic, and they remained vacant until the early 1360s, so that in 1361–2 79 per cent of all customary arable land was still untenanted, 9 per cent was held on the old service tenancy, and 12 per cent had been converted to cash leases. Yet by 1371–2 all of this land was now tenanted, with 94 per cent on cash leases and only 6 per cent on the old service tenancy (fig. 6.1). Clearly, conversions to leases had played an important role in encouraging new tenants to take on the larger holdings and existing tenants to expand theirs.[39] The extent of accumulation of land holding on some manors could be

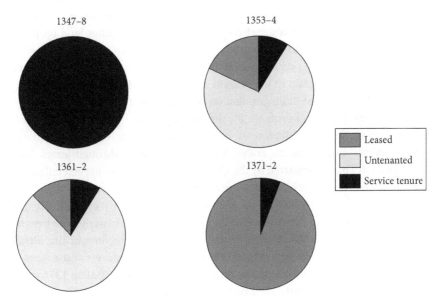

Figure 6.1 Tenurial status of the main customary holdings at Brandon (Suffolk), 1347 to 1372 (%)

Sources: TNA SC6/1304/26, 28, 29, 35

impressive: for example, by 1380 the accumulation of 60-acre plus holdings was greater than or equal to the post-1380 level on eleven out of a sample of twenty-six manors in southern England.[40]

The second challenge to the assumption that mean holding size did not rise until the end of the fourteenth century is that conventional calculations of the size of peasant landholdings can be misleading. The calculations are usually based upon the mean holding size for villein tenants, and sometimes for free tenants, on a given manor. They do not include additional land held on other forms of tenure and/or from other manors.[41] Few peasants would have held multiple tenancies in the land hungry conditions of the pre-plague era, but the practice became much more common after 1348–9, when land of varied status (free, customary, and demesne) was now readily available on more varied forms of tenure (non-commercial/service, contractual, lease) from different manors. In other words, it is highly likely that peasants were constructing larger holdings during the 1360s and early 1370s on different tenancies, but that these are difficult for the historian to identify and quantify because the sources do not routinely identify leaseholders and freeholders.[42] For example, in 1371–2 Walter Alcock was the tenant of a 40-acre full-land on a service tenancy in Brandon (Suffolk). The unusual detail of the Brandon manorial sources reveals that he also held another full-land at leasehold, and an additional 7 acres 3 roods of demesne arable on another lease.[43] Walter might also have held free land, and land from another local manor, but these are not recorded in the extant documentation. Thus, on the basis of the conventional calculation of landholdings, Walter was a customary tenant holding 40 acres of land, whereas his acquisitions of other land on leases meant that he actually held a minimum of 87 acres 3 roods.

Thus there is a strong possibility that the adverse forces which had contributed to the undersupply of grain in the peasant sector since 1349 had begun to ease by the early 1370s. Peasant grain production reached a post-plague peak, which is consistent with piecemeal evidence for the reoccupation of abandoned standardized holdings, the accumulation of holdings on different tenancies, and the transfer of yet more demesne arable into peasant control through leases. This could well have been stimulated by the chastening experience of harvest failures in the late 1360s. The government's zealous regulation of grain markets and foodstuffs had eased, and producers had the time and opportunity to construct new marketing contacts and networks. Finally, the diminution in extreme weather and epidemiological events from the 1370s reduced the levels of economic turbulence and uncertainty, which in turn reduced the risks to grain producers and generated greater confidence in market production. It is significant that after 1376 grain prices were not only persistently lower but they were also less volatile from one year to another, which is suggestive of a better integrated grain market.[44] All of these developments would have improved the prospect of more grain reaching the market each year from the peasant sector.[45] There is clear evidence of London's grain supply stabilizing along restructured lines in the last quarter of the century, after considerable disruption and shortages in the 1350s and 1360s.[46] From the early 1370s, then, a number of factors converged to shift the commercial grain market from conditions of under- to oversupply, reinforcing the effects of more benign weather and higher yields.

Agricultural output

The double-dip in grain prices in 1385–95 was compounded by the resilience of wages, causing profits in arable production to be squeezed. The extent of the fall is evident in calculations of the marginal product of farm labour, which convey the changing cost to the farmer of hiring labour compared with the value of goods being produced on the farm.[47] As such, it illustrates how the relative shifts in labour costs and product prices altered agrarian profitability over time: these costs rose by c.15 per cent between 1360–9 (90) and 1370–9 (104), and again by a similar magnitude in the 1380s (128). The indexed figure for the 1380s is comfortably the highest for any decade in the whole of the thirteenth and fourteenth centuries, and twice the level of the 1340s.[48] On this measure, economic conditions in the late 1380s were worse than anything commercial agricultural producers had faced in the previous two centuries.

The significant deterioration in agrarian conditions between 1385 and 1395 provides the context for the final and decisive withdrawal of the greater landlords from direct demesne cultivation on their manors. By the early 1390s many such aristocratic and institutional landlords had finally abandoned their efforts to maintain direct management and had leased out their demesnes, reflecting the difficulties of securing a seasonal workforce and of turning a worthwhile profit in such harsh conditions.[49] On the estate of Canterbury Cathedral Priory, for instance, attempts to revive demesne agriculture in the early 1380s were quickly abandoned with the collapse in grain and wool prices.[50] Even where direct management of demesnes was retained, the area sown with grain fell. For example, in 1377–80 an average of 159 acres were sown per annum on the Stanton Lacy (Salop) demesne compared with 84 acres in 1385–90, and at Lakenheath (Suffolk) 48 per cent of the total demesne area was sown between 1350 and 1379, but only 37 per cent in 1380–99.[51] Where demesnes were retained in hand, they tended to concentrate upon wheat and barley for bread and ale, or fodder crops for animals.[52] The sustained fall in the populations of the largest towns resulted in a marked fall in concentrated urban demand, which is reflected in less intensive and less specialized arable cropping regimes on many demesnes in south-east England.[53] These general trends explain why the financial returns from arable farming at Wisbech (Cambs.) in 1376–1409 were 41 per cent lower than they had been in 1349–75, and why in the 1380s the return on demesne arable land at Ham

(Gloucs.) collapsed and recorded a loss.[54] Likewise, in 1385 the manor of Ladbroke (Warks.) made no profit at all from its arable operations.[55] A survey of the Duchy of Lancaster estates in 1388 regarded grain production as a 'graunde mischief': the report from two Northamptonshire manors stated 'husbandry is no value beyond the costs there, which are so great each year that the said husbandry is a great loss to my lord'.[56]

Peasant producers also felt the consequences of the sharp downturn in agrarian fortunes. Tithe receipts of grain fell by around one-third between the 1370s and 1380s in north-east England, and did not recover thereafter.[57] Tithe output at Feering (Essex) in 1393–8 was down 17 per cent compared with the peak years of 1367–72.[58] It is possible to illustrate notionally how the compound effects of the price and wage scissors in the 1380s could severely diminish the profitability of commercial grain production for the larger peasant producers. Table 6.3 models the fall in notional profits between the 1360s and the 1380s to reveal the impact of the relative changes in grain yields, prices, and waged labour. It is *not* an attempt to model the total output or budget of a typical peasant household or holding, but to demonstrate how the interaction of rising yields and costs, but falling prices, presented enormous challenges to the largest grain producers. The results are striking. The notional cash profit from 30- and 40-acre holdings in the 1380s was *c.*45 per cent down on the level of the 1360s, but over 70 per cent from a 60-acre holding. The reason is that the cultivation of the smaller holdings could be mainly covered using mainly family labour at no direct monetary cost, topped up with some hired labour, whereas the 60-acre holding relied to a much greater degree upon paid day labour, the direct costs of which had to be weighed against falling sale prices for grain. The larger the commercial holding, the greater reliance upon hired labour, and the more difficult it was to squeeze profits from grain production in the bleak conditions of the 1380s. Indeed, it indicates that the challenges faced by such farms in the mid-fifteenth century—as demonstrated by Hatcher— were already apparent at the end of the fourteenth century.[59] A tenant with 60-plus acres could only make a living from commercial grain production by restricting the use of hired *day* labour to a minimum—perhaps by employing

Table 6.2 Estimated output per head of key industrial and service sectors in England, selected decades 1300 to 1409

Decade	Metals/ Mining	Textiles/ Leather	Other Industries	Total Industrial Sector	Total Service Sector
1300s	100	100	100	100	100
1350s	98	220	89	133	115
1400s	413	221	83	164	115

Source: Broadberry et al., *British economic growth*, table 4.11.

Table 6.3 Notional changes in profits from commercial grain production for 30-acre, 40-acre, and 60-acre holdings, 1360–9 and 1380–9 (pence)

	30-acre	30-acre	30-acre	40-acre	40-acre	40-acre	60-acre	60-acre	60-acre
Decade	Gross income from grain sales	Gross labour costs	Notional profit	Gross income from grain sales	Gross labour costs	Notional profit	Gross income from grain sales	Gross labour costs	Notional profit
1360–9	831d.	260d.	**571d.**	1,125d.	520d.	**605d.**	1,663d.	1,040d.	**623d.**
1380–9	651d.	293d.	**358d.**	908d.	585d.	**323d.**	1,346d.	1,170d.	**176d.**

Calculations: See Appendix 1.

servants on yearly contracts whose rate per diem was considerably lower, or by putting labourers into tied cottages and cutting a deal on day rates—and/or by complementing arable with pastoral interests.[60]

The downturn in the profitability of grain production after the mid-1370s did not immediately result in the conversion of large areas of arable to permanent pasture in many parts of the country. Indeed, this development only becomes prominent in the documentary record around the end of the century.[61] This is especially the case in those areas of the country where commercial grain production was most strongly developed. For example, the proportion of pasture recorded in the feet of fines for Norfolk, Essex, Suffolk, and Kent changed little between 1366–72 and 1383–91, but a discernible shift did occur between 1383–91 and 1422–37 (fig. 4.2). The proportion of arable fell from 76 per cent to 70 per cent, pasture rose from 9 per cent to 12 per cent, and 'pasture plus' from 15 per cent to 18 per cent.[62] The latter would have included the regeneration of woodland stocks over abandoned arable land and less intensively managed pasture.[63] In the most commercialized counties of England agriculture did not settle at its post-plague 'equilibrium' of extended pastoral and severely contracted arable production until after the double-dip of the late 1380s.

The impact of the price falls on pastoral production is less straightforward to assess than for arable because the prospects were more mixed. On the one hand, since pastoral production was less labour intensive than arable, it offered more opportunities to control unit costs and so offered better prospects in a period of falling prices. On the other hand, the economic conditions between c.1385 and c.1395 were so severe that the prices of pastoral products fell sharply—for example, prices of dairy produce fell around 20 per cent—and squeezed profits. Peasants needed capital to buy livestock, or time to build up their herd through natural replacement, and so could not switch sectors easily or quickly, especially when the availability of local credit in many rural communities shrank in the tougher economic conditions.[64] Opportunities for profit were delicately balanced, which is reflected in signs of both growth and retrenchment in pastoral pursuits, and the abandonment of direct livestock rearing on some demesnes yet the development of more commercial enterprise on others, depending on the locality and the estate. In general, the pastoral sector was not expanding as rapidly as in the third quarter of the century, so that the pastoral share of agricultural output was now stabilizing.[65] Even those who continued to pursue commercial opportunities in pastoral production perforce resorted to some cost-cutting in stock management by lowering standards of supervision and care in order to maintain profitability.[66]

The experiences of the various subsectors of the pastoral economy exemplify these mixed fortunes. Demesne dairy herds expanded in a few places, usually due to the consolidation of operations into a single manor, or a smaller number of manors, within an estate in an attempt to reduce unit costs.[67] In other places, they were sold off or reduced in size: meanwhile, lactage rates (the demesne's charge for leasing a milking cow) either held or drifted down slightly.[68] After c.1400 the scale of, and profits from, dairy farming declined gently.[69] Similarly, in the 1390s cattle rearing began to level off in many parts of the country, but continued to expand until the early fifteenth century in certain areas of northern and southern England.[70] Chicken prices fell from the volatile highs of the 1350s and 1360s and remained stable throughout the 1380s and 1390s, albeit at a higher level than in the pre-plague period.[71] In the 1380s demesne poultry rearing contracted and became less commercialized, perhaps due to a transfer of production to the peasant sector.[72] The fall in wool prices prompted a fall in demesne flock size in some places.[73] In others, landlords leased their flocks or consolidated them into a smaller number of larger production units.[74] The weight of fleeces fell due to less careful management of flocks following cost-cutting measures, and landlords relied more on natural replacement rather than purchases.[75] The profits of sheep rearing might have fallen in the 1380s, but it still offered one of the best opportunities to turn a profit from agriculture in a tough period. Consequently, expansion of and investment in sheep flocks continued in the 1380s and 1390s among some demesne and peasant producers in specialist sheep-rearing regions, such as the East Anglian Breckland and the west country.[76] It is estimated that in the 1390s there were 11.3m sheep in England, compared with 13.7m in the 1310s.[77] After c.1400, however, sheep rearing at best held level then began to decline.[78] Overall, then, at the very end of the fourteenth century the levelling off of animal numbers, and a lurch towards overproduction, is evident across the pastoral sector.[79]

Commercial rabbit rearing provides an interesting illustration of the opportunities and the challenges facing the pastoral sector in this period. Production in the largest warrens in East Anglia expanded significantly in the 1380s, as lords vastly increased cullings and sales to satisfy market demand and to compensate for declining revenues in other sectors of agriculture.[80] Output from Lakenheath (Suffolk) warren rose from c.850 per annum in the 1370s to c.3,600 in the 1380s (fig. 6.2), that from Brandon (Suffolk) warren increased fourfold, while output from Methwold (Norfolk) soared from c.350 in the 1350s to 9,500 in the 1390s.[81] Sales from these great commercial warrens were mainly to urban markets, with some onward exports of fur to the Low Countries.[82] The sudden expansion in supply was due to a combination of environmental change and intensive stock management. Medieval rabbits were especially vulnerable to cold and wet conditions, so the warmer, more benign, weather after c.1375 would have resulted in lower winter mortalities among the warren population. Greater capital investment in watchtowers and stone lodges, and seasonal hiring of additional labour, reduced losses to predators and poachers.[83] As a result, the rabbit population increased dramatically. These eye-catching gains were not widely spread, however, and they proved unsustainable. Most commercial warrens were located in eastern England,

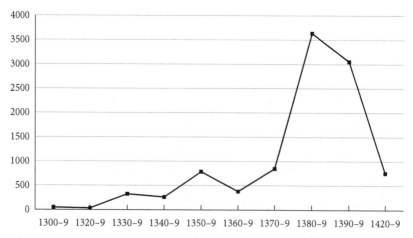

Figure 6.2 Number of rabbits culled in Lakenheath warren (Suffolk), decennial means 1300 to 1429
Source: Bailey 1988

and those elsewhere remained small and focused upon production for seigniorial consumption.[84] The astounding revenues generated in the 1380s and 1390s from the greatest warrens were not sustained after *c*.1400, when warren output fell precipitously in many places to around one-third of the late fourteenth-century peak (fig. 6.2).[85] Similarly, the values of warren leases remained flat or declined during the fifteenth century, and the sale price of a rabbit fell steadily, both of which are indicative of an oversupplied market after the 1390s.[86]

The experiences of the reproductive rabbit exemplify the continuing opportunities for growth after 1375 within some sectors of pastoral production, but underline that they were restricted spatially and that after *c*.1400 they narrowed considerably. Our most reliable and direct sources of evidence about pastoral operations derive from the demesne sector, and to some extent the signs of contraction there may disguise a transfer of activity to the peasant sector. This would be most likely in those activities requiring daily or frequent inputs of labour, such as poultry and swine rearing, and dairy production, which were therefore well suited to family farms.[87] But the fall in the prices of all pastoral produce from the 1370s, and the levelling out of those prices after the 1390s, is indicative of flattening levels of consumption per head and oversupplied markets.[88]

The land market

From the mid-1370s the peasant land market contracted markedly almost everywhere. Evidence points unequivocally to a significant downturn in customary land values, contracting levels of rental income from peasant holdings, and an upturn in the area of untenanted land.[89] Local responses were varied, but, overall, these traits are most strongly apparent from the mid-1380s and in the 1390s. Leasehold values for customary land in the 1390s reached their lowest point in the whole of the fourteenth century, and capital values were lowest in the 1380s (figs. 4.3 and 4.4). Land values on a handful of Essex manors fell by at least a quarter between the 1370s and 1380s, and halved on others in the west Midlands.[90] In the 1390s vacant arable land had become commonplace in north-east England, and both entry fines for customary land and income from servile dues were persistently and significantly lower than they had been in the 1350s.[91] Sea banks and defences were maintained less carefully due to the cost and shortages of labour, and consequently flooding and marine encroachments became more common in places as far apart as the Humber, Severn, and Thames estuaries, and the Wash.[92]

The volume of market activity also declined markedly. The evidence from the freehold market is mainly confined to the feet of fines, where the number of transactions nationally fell by around one-half between the late 1360s and late 1390s, and the area of land transacted also fell sharply across the same period: the main period of decline was the 1380s.[93] The volume of customary land transactions at Coltishall (Norfolk) collapsed in 1386, and in the 1390s the market was heavily depressed.[94] In the 1380s and 1390s in places as far apart as Hargrave (Suffolk), Norton (Herts.), and Totton (Hants) the number and proportion of inter-peasant customary land transfers fell to a fourteenth-century low.[95] At the same time, the number of holdings abandoned into, or remaining in, the lord's hands rose sharply; grants made directly from the lord increased, together with the proportion of contractual tenures; and entry fines were either greatly reduced or waived.[96] These trends are captured in the grant in 1392 of an abandoned cottage and enclosure of two acres in Westhall (Suffolk) to John le Reve for a contractual hereditary tenancy of 3s. 8d. per annum and a nominal 6d. entry fine: the grant was also explicit that the size of the entry fine would be capped in perpetuity at a maximum of 12d. whenever the land was transferred or sold.[97] The dampening of the market is also reflected in the slowing down of the numbers of outsiders taking up land on manors held by the bishop of Winchester.[98] These are all symptoms of a depressed land market, in which landlords had to offer widespread concessions in order to retain and attract tenants. The accelerating trend towards demesne leasing increased the amount of land available to local peasants and so inadvertently exacerbated the conditions of oversupply in local land markets. All the indicators reveal that any buoyancy in the land market in the generation after plague had now been sapped, underlining the sense that the period of transition had passed and the land market had settled at its post-plague equilibrium.[99]

The tendency for the renders attached to villein service tenancies—such as tallage, labour services, millsuit, and entry fines—to diminish in frequency and value, or even to disappear, accelerated everywhere.[100] The swing from non-commercial service tenures (characterized by labour services and other dues, and sub-economic cash rents) to contractual tenures (such as renewable cash leases, and fee-farms and life tenancies fixed at a commercial cash head rent at the time of the initial grant) continued during the last quarter of the fourteenth century. We have already noted the 1391 survey of Lord Hastings' estate, where peasant holdings were now partially or predominantly held on contractual tenures on over half of the forty-four manors, and the adoption of leases on many gentry manors (pp. 92–7). The wholesale conversion of customary land to leases at Brandon (Suffolk) was largely completed by the mid-1370s (see figs. 3.7 and 6.1). Conversions of customary land to leases accelerated in the 1380s and 1390s on the Westminster abbey estates, and on one manor (Birdbrook, Essex) both the number of leases of customary land doubled between the 1370s and the 1390s.[101] This general trend is observable across the country, from East Anglia to the west Midlands.[102] Similarly, conversions of customary land from non-commercial tenancies to cash head rents on heritable and life tenancies increased. By c.1400 the preference for cash tenancies for lives in areas of southern and western England, and of heritable tenancies in the east, was already becoming clear.[103]

The cumulative effect of this swing to contractual tenures by c.1400 was considerable. In the 1340s peasant land comprised two-thirds of all arable land, of which an estimated 90 per cent was held on non-commercial tenures.[104] Demesne land comprised the remaining one-third, of which just over one-quarter was exploited directly and the rest leased.[105] Consequently, we estimate that in the 1340s c.20 per cent of all arable land in England was held on contractual tenures (see fig. 7.7). By the 1390s the head rents on the majority of free tenures remained fixed and non-commercial, mainly because heirs and buyers sought out free tenures in preference to any other type of land, and so it tended not to stick in the lord's hands.[106] Perhaps c.12 per cent of free land had been converted to contractual tenures, through re-grants of the small proportion of free tenures that had reverted to the lord through the failure of heirs and of free tenures purchased by lords from their free tenants.[107] In contrast, perhaps over one half of villein land had been converted to contractual tenures by the 1390s.[108] Similarly, by this date around three quarters of all demesne land was leased.[109] Thus in the 1390s an estimated 45 per cent of the total arable land of England was held on contractual tenancies, and 45 per cent in the 1390s (fig. 7.7), 33 per cent on leases (mainly demesne, and some villein land) and 12 per cent on quasi-commercial head rents.[110] As a consequence, by the late fifteenth century direct demesne exploitation contributed little to agricultural output, and demesne land had been effectively reallocated to the leasehold and peasant sector.[111]

Although the volume and value of peasant land transactions had fallen sharply, the mean size of both free and unfree land transactions, and of peasant landholdings in general, rose almost everywhere.[112] For instance, at Coltishall (Norfolk), the average size of individual customary land transactions in the period

1376–1405 was double that of the early 1370s, albeit from a low base.[113] Three other developments of significance are also apparent. First, poor harvests no longer triggered distress sales, underlining the eradication of the chronic rural poverty of the pre-plague period. Second, transfers of property to other family members through inheritance and marriage were still important, but a rising proportion of transfers was made to outsiders and non-kin. The bond between an individual family and a particular landholding weakened.[114] Land was increasingly a marketable asset, sometimes purchased by higher status, non-resident, individuals for the purposes of status or investment. The growing variety of tenurial forms, and the removal of many of the stigmatizing aspects of villein tenure, increased the portability of land and the options available for its acquisition and disposal.[115] Third, the increasing size of peasant landholdings and the leasing of demesnes to peasants meant that the supply of grain and other agricultural produce to market became even more the preserve of the peasantry.[116] The long-term significance of these developments are considered further in Chapter 7.

Non-agricultural output

The 1381 poll tax returns contain occupational details about individual taxpayers and so provide a more secure basis than any other extant medieval source for estimating the distribution of the workforce across the main sectors of the economy. Two separate analyses of the 1381 poll tax returns suggest that around 57 per cent of the workforce was employed in agriculture, 19 per cent in industry, and 24 per cent in services (fig. 7.5).[117] These estimates are likely to be over-generous to non-agricultural occupations, however, because a single occupational designation obscured the ways in which individuals turned their hands to a variety of paid activities (work was diversified not just specialized). Furthermore, the attempts through the labour legislation to prevent the migration of workers from agriculture to manufactures would have encouraged people to self-identify as an industrial rather than agricultural designation. Hence we should regard the estimates as maxima. These figures also provide a basis for estimating the maximum contribution of each sector to the overall size of the economy (sector share in GDP): agriculture comprised around 45 per cent of GDP, industry 29 per cent, and the service sector 26 per cent (fig. 7.1).[118] Even if these estimates are also overly-generous to the non-agricultural sector, they do capture the swing to rural and urban industrial and service employment that had taken place since 1348–9.

We have no source comparable to the 1381 poll tax to estimate how far the shift away from agricultural employment continued during the 1380s and 1390s. A range of indirect indicators, however, all suggest that industrial output continued to expand after 1381. The first indicator is the sudden growth in the estimated levels of GDP per head between the mid-1380s and late 1390s, which are usually associated with rising consumption of services and manufactured goods. Over the same period the estimated indexed output of the industrial sector rose around 20 per cent from 16.9 in 1375–84 to 20 in 1385–94 (table 4.4). Both GDP and industrial output indices indicate that the growth then slowed and flattened thereafter (fig. 4.1).

The second indicator of the continued expansion of industry in the final quarter of the fourteenth century is evidence from local sources for the buoyant performance of key industries within the sector. Textile and leather production formed the bedrock of English industrial output, although Broadberry et al.'s calculations assume that their output plateaued after the rapid expansion of the 1350s (table 7.2).[119] This was probably true of leather manufacture, but it does not adequately reflect the local evidence for expanding output at the end of the century in many of the major textile-producing centres.[120] Exports of lower-quality broadcloths, cheap straits, and kerseys continued to grow into the 1390s, and one estimate suggests that at this date the total volume of English cloth exports was three times greater than it had been in the 1350s.[121] The number of recorded fulling mills rose in the 1380s to a peak in the 1390s, after which numbers began to fall then remained at the lower level throughout the fifteenth century.[122] All this evidence supports Amor's argument that English textile manufacturing continued to grow until c.1400.[123]

Other industries were also expanding in the 1380s and 1390s, especially metals and mining, which recovered strongly after the collapse of the 1350s (table 6.2).[124] Metal working in general, and the production of cutlery in particular, flourished in the 1380s and 1390s.[125] The output of tin in areas of Cornwall and Devon, and of lead in the Mendips and Derbyshire, increased sharply from the 1380s.[126] Coal production was undeveloped and haphazard, but there are signs of a surge in output at the end of the century in various coalfields.[127] Marine and estuarine fishing exhibits clear signs of expansion in a number of ports in the last two decades of the century despite the well-documented decline of the great herring fair of Great Yarmouth (Norfolk).[128] Output in many of these activities then levelled or declined during the first half of the fifteenth century.[129]

The third indicator of the continued expansion of industrial output at the end of the fourteenth century is the evidence for economic and even demographic growth in those towns specializing in industrial production. Harriss dates the main period of expansion of such towns to the two generations after 1370, when the demand for manufactures 'was working through the economy'.[130] The population of Westminster continued to grow, and in response Westminster abbey invested further in the construction of small-scale housing and retail outlets within the town.[131] Major textile manufacturing centres such as Norwich and York, and lesser ones such as Mildenhall, Kersey, and Hadleigh (all Suffolk), all reached their peak in the last two decades of the fourteenth century.[132] Rural dwellers struggling to cope with the downturn in agriculture streamed into

Colchester (Essex) seeking work in its booming textile manufacturing.[133] Thaxted (Essex) expanded rapidly in the 1380s and 1390s through its manufacture of cutlery.[134] Not all industrial towns expanded in this period, however, and Lincoln declined after growing in the immediate aftermath of plague.[135] Moreover, few textile towns continued their expansion in the early fifteenth century. Even buoyant Westminster experienced a sharp economic and perhaps demographic downturn after c.1400.[136]

Finally, aspects of the government's legislative activity suggest that the swing from agricultural to industrial employment continued apace. After 1376 the contraction in commercial grain production, the levelling of output in the pastoral sector, and the expansion of certain industrial activities all created the conditions for rural dwellers to increase their occupational flexibility, to seek more by-employment in rural crafts or to migrate to dynamic urban centres. A royal commission in Essex in 1377 noted a movement of workers from agriculture to fishing, and a parliamentary petition in 1393 argued that East Anglian textile workers were fully employed in their craft, implying insistent demand for workers.[137] An analysis of the cases presented to the royal justices under the labour legislation in the later fourteenth century reveals the wide variety of occupations and the occupational flexibility of individual workers who turned their hand to a variety of different tasks, although levels of skill were unlikely to have been especially high.[138] Kenyon's analysis of labour cases presented to one session of the King's Bench in Essex in 1389 suggests that the justices were particularly targeting individuals leaving agricultural employment for work in trades and industry.[139] Indeed, the ruling elite was now so concerned about the shortage of cheap labour in agricultural areas that it introduced drastic new legislation in 1388, the so-called Statute of Cambridge, to attempt to prevent rural dwellers from taking up employment in industry (see pp. 266–7).[140]

A golden age for the peasantry?

After the 1370s the peasantry stood to benefit from the sizeable gains in nominal real wages and the slackening of demand in the land market, which has encouraged a belief in a golden age for the peasantry—and especially labourers—that peaked around the 1460s.[141] This belief is encouraged by the buoyancy of real wages between c.1380 and c.1470 for those choosing to earn a living through paid employment, and the ready availability of land on increasingly favourable terms for those seeking a livelihood through agrarian production. Opportunities to lease more demesne arable, along with demesne herds and flocks, increased further in the 1380s and 1390s as the greatest landlords withdrew from direct exploitation, enabling some peasants to construct sizeable agricultural enterprises from different types of land on various types of tenure.

Despite the manifold opportunities to acquire land at the end of the fourteenth century, only a small minority in each community managed to construct sizeable landholdings.[142] The risks of large-scale farming, the difficulties acquiring capital and credit, and the failure of heirs presented significant obstacles. The small elite who succeeded in accumulating land came to be known as the yeomanry, and they become easier to identify under this label after the Statute of Additions in 1413, which required that henceforth the personal status of defendants in certain legal cases should be recorded. The rise of the yeoman is traditionally dated to the fifteenth century, yet the rural yeomanry were unquestionably on the rise in the last two decades of the fourteenth century.[143] The term 'yeoman' was originally applied to either a high-ranking servant in a noble household or a soldier—usually an archer—but its application to the upper ranks of the peasantry was occasioned by the leasing of the demesnes of the greater landlords.[144] As this process accelerated in the 1380s and 1390s, so many such landlords provided their lessees with livery (outer clothing carrying the insignia of the lord) equivalent to that provided to their household yeomen as part of the terms of the lease.[145] The leasing of demesnes also diminished the visibility and influence of the officials of the great landlords within local communities, creating a social space into which the yeomanry now stepped.[146] Indeed, the forging of a tangible social affiliation between rentier landlords and their new agents in the localities served the interests of both parties and, perhaps, underlined their shared concerns about the problem of labour (see below, pp. 266-8).[147] By c.1410 rural yeomen are already clearly identifiable as a social group in East Anglia.[148] By the 1430s the label is usually applied to landholders with more than c.40 acres of land and incomes of between £5 and £19 per annum: in the 1430s they probably comprised 2 per cent of the national population.[149]

Middling landholders—people with c.10 to 40 acres of land—benefited from the downturn in the land market, which made arable land easier and cheaper to acquire. As a result, they exercised a good deal of choice about the size and the nature of their enterprises. They enjoyed a sturdy self-sufficiency, relying mainly upon commercial pastoral activities for cash revenues, supplemented by sales of grain surpluses as the opportunity arose. Their children may have supplemented the household income with some paid employment, but this was not a major component of their livelihood. This stratum of rural society was increasingly self-identifying as 'husbandmen'. The emergence and growing usage of labels such as husbandmen and yeomen at the end of the fourteenth century in part reflects the breakdown of the old link between tenure and status. The many freemen who had acquired customary land, and the flown serfs who had settled away from their home manor and constructed sizeable landholdings, did not fit the traditional nomenclature based on land tenure, such as freemen, mollmen, or villein, and so they self-identified with contemporary descriptors that better reflected the new social order and their aspirations.

Most people within rural communities were either smallholders (with less than ten acres of land), day labourers (either smallholders, or simply with a cottage and garden), or resident servants on annual contracts.[150] The jump in nominal real wages from the mid-1370s unquestionably increased their standards of living. Between the 1370s and 1390s the estimated living costs of a farm labourer fell by 20 per cent and the estimated number of days per year a rural labourer had to work to purchase a fixed basket of essential commodities fell by a similar order of magnitude.[151] The contribution of a smallholding to the living standards of the lower ranks of society is often overlooked, especially in this period when land was easier to acquire, but it enhanced their capacity to supply themselves with food and to engage in petty pastoral production for the market: married women and children reared poultry, collected eggs, made cheese and butter, some of which was sold. We simply cannot know what proportion of their labour smallholders devoted to their own holding, what was spent in paid employment, and how far women and children contributed to household income.

There is no doubt that from the 1370s the lower orders benefited from the further fall in rent values and from the rise in real wages. But without knowing how much time smallholders spent on their holding or in paid employment, we cannot estimate reliably the extent to which their living standards improved. A similar challenge exists for landless labourers because the number of days worked depended upon how much work was available and whether workers chose to maximize income or to settle for a comfortable standard of living and maximize their leisure time.[152] Consequently, historians make various assumptions in order to calculate average annual incomes, but, of course, different assumptions generate very different results. For example, the most generous estimate assumes that the average labourer worked for 250 days a year at prevailing day rates for wages, in which case purchasing power rose relentlessly between the 1350s and the 1390s, and by 1400 was almost double the level of the 1340s.[153] Alternatively, if one uses day rates calculated from annual contracts, then the average income of the labourer increased marginally in the 1350s and 1360s, then rose by around one-third between the 1370s and 1390s. Certainly, annual contracts for servants, and day rates for women, were the least generous forms of pay. Humphries and Weisdorf show that day rates for women rose from 1.2d. per day in the 1340s to 2.2d. in the 1360s and 2.72d. in the 1390s, whereas annual contracts for women were a good deal less generous at 0.97d. per day in the 1340s, 1.23d. in the 1360s, then 0.97d. in the 1390s.[154]

Generalizations are difficult, given all these indeterminate variables, although some basic observations still hold. First, during the 1360s and early 1370s the purchasing power of wages was relatively low (table 6.1) while work was widely available in most sectors of the economy. Smallholders and landless labourers who opted to accept most, or all, of the available work would have enjoyed demonstrable gains in their annual incomes: for those who did not, their gains would have been modest given the limited purchasing power of wages. Second, from the mid-1370s the rise in the purchasing power of wages meant that smallholders and landless labourers could enjoy higher standards of living, while working fewer days each year than in the 1360s. Indeed, paid work in arable districts might have become harder to find now that the profits of commercial grain production had collapsed and the area under cultivation had contracted sharply. As a result, the length of the working year probably fell in the 1380s and 1390s for many ordinary people.[155] It is very doubtful whether at the end of the fourteenth century the average labourer would opt to (or indeed could find) work for 250 days per annum. Third, servants on annual contracts did not receive wage packages as generous as workers hired by the day, although their remuneration still improved by around one-third between the 1370s and 1390s. These observations caution against highly optimistic claims for the living standards of workers in c.1400, and dissipate some of the aura surrounding the supposed golden age of the peasantry in the fifteenth century. It seems reasonable to suppose that the average annual income within the lower orders of society rose by c.40 per cent between c.1370 and c.1400, and stabilized thereafter.[156]

Social Conflict and Change

The received version of social change during the last quarter of the fourteenth century offers a powerful narrative and a clear chronology. During the 1370s tensions between lords and tenants rose sharply in the build-up to the Peasants' Revolt of 1381, followed by their sudden release in its aftermath as chastened landlords changed tack and pursued policies conciliatory to peasants in general, and to serfs in particular. Studies of the revolt comment on the general respect for the due process of law in its aftermath, and the leniency of many of the punishments meted out to the rebels: in Cambridgeshire, for example, the government crackdown was sharp, carefully targeted, and short-lived, and a good deal of clemency and restraint was shown.[157] In this interpretation, political society had 'peered into the abyss' and thereafter 'took heed' by recognizing economic reality and abandoning coercive policies towards the peasantry.[158]

Yet a good deal of evidence does not support this seemingly clear sequence of mounting tension, revolt, and, finally, long-term appeasement. First, we have already argued that the empirical evidence for a seigniorial reaction in the 1360s and 1370s is weak, and specific evidence for increased social conflict in the 1370s is anecdotal rather than quantified. The principal example of mounting unrest in the lead-up to the revolt—the 'Great Rumour' of 1377—actually occurred in places that were subsequently unaffected by the events of 1381 and, as we will argue, should be considered on its own terms within the specific context of the changed economic conditions of the late 1370s rather than interpreted through the lens of the revolt.[159] Second, instead of a seigniorial policy of appeasement after 1381, there is a good deal of evidence for a handful of landlords adopting tougher policies against labourers and serfs in the 1380s and 1390s.[160] This crack-down resembled the limited, short, but ultimately unsuccessful 'reaction' of the early 1350s, and it coincided with draconian revisions to the labour legislation in the 1388 Statute of Cambridge. Given-Wilson has described the contents of the latter 'breathtaking', and its language as 'uncompromising', while Judith Bennett argues that it 'created substantive new law'.[161] Hence there are powerful grounds for reassessing the received interpretation, and for disputing the view that the revolt constituted a decisive watershed in lord–peasant relations. The combination of hardening attitudes to the problem of labour and the further deterioration in the agrarian economy in the 1380s resulted in tougher government legislation and the adoption of harsher policies on some estates: a mini seigniorial reaction.

Rural conflict in the late 1370s

Those who see the years before the 1381 uprising as a period of mounting social friction often cite the 'Great Rumour' during the summer of 1377 to prove their point.[162] The 'Rumour' involved villeins on at least forty manors between Surrey and Devon, whose common objective was to obtain personal freedom and to evade labour services by claiming that they were tenants of manors once held as part of the royal estate (known as Ancient Demesne).[163] Although the rebellion was largely contained within a tract of countryside from Berkshire and Wiltshire to Dorset, it created considerable consternation among the ruling elite and formed a major topic of discussion at the October parliament of 1377.[164] Parliamentary representatives accused peasants of binding together in confederations, withholding labour services, collecting money to obtain legal advice, and seeking exemplifications from Domesday Book to prove that their manor had once been Ancient Demesne. The appeals to Domesday reveal the capacity among the peasantry for a powerful collective memory, while the recourse to law reflects a touching belief that the king's justice would uphold their objection to performing labour services.[165] The king's council was sufficiently alarmed about the wider threat to public order that it agreed to send specific royal commissions into the affected areas to support landlords in upholding their rights to insist upon the performance of labour services.[166]

The two distinctive features of the 'Rumour' were requests for exemplifications from Domesday Book and refusals to perform labour services.[167] The requests came primarily from villein tenants on manors held by prominent ecclesiastical landlords in one particular area of England. Thus the aims, participants, and geography of the rebellion of 1377 were manifestly different from those of the Peasants' Revolt of 1381, and the only common thread between them was the implied quest for freedom and for money-based rents. These differences encourage us to decouple the two events, to consider the 'Rumour' on its own terms, and to place it within the context of the unfolding agrarian difficulties from the mid-1370s, rather than regarding it as a prelude to the revolt.

Requests from peasants for exemplifications from the king were very unusual. Between 1340 and 1404 there were only thirty-one such requests enrolled in the Calendar of Patent Rolls for the whole of England (fig. 6.3).[168] Yet they were a very prominent feature of the 'Rumour' in the summer of 1377 because nearly half (fourteen) of these thirty-one requests date from July and August 1377. Of the fourteen connected with the 'Rumour', thirteen were from tenants of ecclesiastical landlords and twelve from Wiltshire.[169] Tenants from Wiltshire had also featured in the earlier attempts to gain exemplifications.[170] Indeed, there is independent evidence around this time of at least one man—John Godfray—providing legal advice to villeins in Wiltshire on exactly this issue.[171] Other requests for exemplifications during the 'Rumour' from manors outside Wiltshire were all from villein tenants of ecclesiastical landlords.[172] Once the 'Rumour' had passed, the interest in exemplifications quickly evaporated, with just four enrolled requests in the 1380s, and four more from the 1390s (fig. 6.3).

The second main feature of the 'Rumour'—challenging the requirement to perform labour services—was tightly intertwined with the request for exemplifications. If the exemplifications proved that their manor had once been part of the royal estate (Ancient Demesne), then the protestors could access the royal courts to make representations in matters of tenure and thereby challenge the

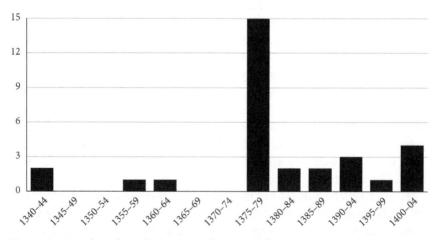

Figure 6.3 Number of enrolled requests for exemplifications in England, 1340 to 1404
Source: CPR

requirement to perform labour services.[173] Labour services were an especially irksome element of villeinage for those required to render them, and were a rumbling source of conflict between peasants and lords throughout the Middle Ages.[174] This conflict over labour services suddenly flared up again in the late 1370s in various places throughout England.[175] For instance, in 1379 villeins on the estate of Worcester Cathedral Priory refused to perform labour services, and the priory responded with an aggressive order to seize all their goods and chattels.[176]

The targeting of labour services requires some explanation, given their relative unimportance. As we saw in Chapter 1, they were not especially common on the eve of the Black Death—absorbing just 10 per cent of all expended labour—and they had declined further after 1349 through a combination of commutations and conversions of service tenure to leases and contractual rents (see pp. 90-6). By the 1370s they absorbed little more than perhaps 5 per cent of total labour, and the most onerous form—week works—were now rare and survived mainly on the estates of ecclesiastical landlords. Seasonal services—such as mowing hay or reaping grain—proved more enduring, but were still relatively light. So what explains the sudden surge of resentment and anger towards labour services in the late 1370s? The most likely explanation is that it was a consequence of the dramatic and sustained fall in the profitability of grain production after 1375, as a result of which tenants sought better rental terms and conditions. Those peasants who in the favourable conditions of the late 1360s and early 1370s had accumulated standardized customary holdings on a service tenancy with liability for labour services were suddenly faced with reduced revenue from the sale of agricultural produce after 1376 when the price-wage scissors cut against them. Yet they were stuck with the requirement to fulfil labour services for the lord, a burden which was more endurable in the favourable economic conditions of the early 1370s, but which weighed more heavily after the fall in prices and surge in wages, because they could obtain better rewards for their labour on the open market.[177] In the late 1370s, just as in the early 1350s, customary landholders sought real concessions on their rent packages. Conversely, the same scissor movement encouraged those ecclesiastical landlords who were still owed labour services to insist on their performance, rather than allowing them to be commuted for cash, because this guaranteed a free seasonal workforce for their demesnes at a time when market rates were soaring. For example, in 1374 the abbot of St Edmund used 38 per cent of all due week works on his manor of Hargrave (Suffolk) but then claimed 63 per cent in 1377, which must explain the sudden increase in 1378 of the number of recorded refusals to perform them.[178] The use of royal commissions during the 'Rumour' to support those landlords seeking to enforce their customary right to labour services signifies the sudden escalation and seriousness of the conflict over them. It also testifies to the weakening of seigniorial power and the stiffening of peasant resistance because, strictly speaking, tenure was a private matter between lord and tenant and not a matter for royal intervention.

Hence the combination of the fall in grain prices in the mid-1370s and rising peasant expectations of improved conditions were likely to have triggered unrest over rent packages in general, and conflict over labour services in particular. Tenants of customary land after 1349 exhibited an aversion to labour services out of all proportion to their economic significance, as evidenced by their will-ingness to pay much higher head rents per acre on leaseholds instead of perform-ing services (see pp. 98-102).[179] The explanation for this aversion must lie in the background of the tenants, many of whom were freemen and flown serfs of other manors who had acquired customary land on service tenancies after the Black Death. After 1375 the increased opportunity costs of performing labour services, and/or the renewed insistence of landlords that they were performed, heightened the aversion and therefore the sense of grievance. Yet they could not pursue the freeholder's usual option for dispute resolution through the courts of common law because they were tenants of villein land. Likewise, flown serfs were no longer serfs on their new manors, but neither were they legally free. Frustration over the inability to challenge lords over villein tenure is surely behind the rush to seek exemplifications in the late 1370s. The frustration was felt most keenly by those freemen and flown serfs who had acquired customary land on service tenure from stubborn ecclesiastical landlords. It may have been further heightened by some calculated lordly attempts to intimidate peasants into not raising challenges in the royal courts.[180]

Peasant landholders with sizeable holdings on contractual rents and demesne lessees also caught the economic chill after 1375, because in many cases their cash rents had been fixed in the buoyant conditions of the early 1370s and so their outgoings remained high as prices and profits tumbled.[181] This surely explains why at Smithfield in 1381 the rebels called for all rents to be monetary *and* fixed at a very modest 4d. per acre, when at this date many leasehold rents were charged at between 9d. and 12d. per acre.[182] Hence the sudden onset of falling prices of agricultural goods caused economic distress to the larger peasant landholders, not just to landlords, which in turn generated resentment at rent packages that now seemed unacceptably high or unattractive. The wider variety of contractual terms on which villein land was held also created a sense of relative deprivation, which Barbara Harvey suggests might have added to the general discontent.[183] Whatever the explanation, the rural discontent of the late 1370s defies any simple categor-ization along class lines because heightened conflict is also evident between peasants, not just between peasants and lords. For example, Larson has identified a peak in violent disputes between villagers from the 1360s to the mid-1380s in north-east England.[184] Dodds argues that the increase in violence was especially prominent from the mid-1370s in arable villages because of the heightened tension between large arable producers and smallholding livestock rearers as the former struggled to maintain profitability.[185]

Rural conflict after 1381

The conventional narrative is that conflict over serfdom and tough seigniorial policies diminished markedly after the shock of the Peasants' Revolt, and thereafter landlords adopted a softer line to appease the peasantry. This interpretation forges a clear and causal link between rising peasant resistance and the subsequent decline of serfdom as a very distinctive element of the English experience. Yet this argument is difficult to sustain in the light of a large body of evidence for continued unrest and conflict in the 1380s and 1390s—a mini seigniorial reaction—which can be categorized in three main areas: on-going disputes over labour services, including wider use of royal commissions to deal with the problem; a hard crackdown on the mobility and activities of hereditary serfs on some estates; and, finally, the introduction of tough new labour laws. Most of this unrest was concentrated in the late 1380s and early 1390s, coinciding with the second dip in grain prices and the onset of harsh winter for large-scale grain producers, and was characteristic of the estates of the greatest ecclesiastical landlords.

Disputes over labour services continued to rumble well into the 1380s and 1390s. The most powerful way of illustrating this point is the continued use of royal commissions to help landlords deal with refusals to perform labour services among their villein tenants. Historians associate this tactic primarily with the government's response to the 'Rumour', following the petitioning for such support at parliament in October 1377.[186] Less well known, however, is that the Crown had been deploying royal commissions for this very purpose since the 1350s.[187] Between 1350 and 1374 eleven such commissions had been dispatched to various parts of the country (see fig. 6.4). Between 1375 and 1379 another eighteen were created, most of them to deal with the 'Rumour'. Interestingly, the king's council had sent five such commissions during September 1377, i.e. pre-dating the opening of parliament on 13 October: it had not waited until parliament had assembled to take action against the unrest.[188]

Nor did the creation of royal commissions to investigate disputes over labour services cease with the passing of the 'Rumour'. Tillotson found that between 1385 and 1399 twenty such commissions were sent to twenty-three places in eleven counties located in southern England, most of them in response to pleas from religious landlords in the face of peasant recalcitrance.[189] In fact, a re-working of the evidence for such royal commissions in the both the calendars of patent rolls *and* inquisitions miscellaneous reveals an even more striking pattern than

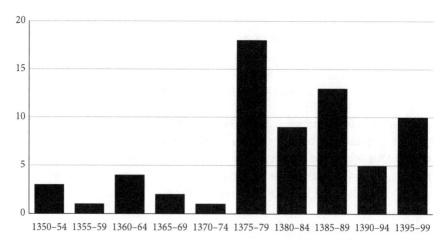

Figure 6.4 Number of royal commissions into peasants withholding labour services recorded in the Calendars of Patent Rolls and Inquisitions Miscellaneous, 1350 to 1399

Tillotson realized. Between 1380 and 1399 a total of thirty-seven commissions were dispatched, peaking in 1385–9 (fig. 6.4). These covered a much wider geographical area than in 1377–8, stretching from the southern counties to manors across East Anglia and the east Midlands. Of the grand total of fifty-five commissions dispatched in the whole of the last quarter of the century, the majority (twenty-eight or 51 per cent) were to manors held by major ecclesiastical landlords in southern and eastern England. These were the exactly the type of landlords most likely to be still persevering with direct demesne arable cultivation, most likely to have unfree tenants still liable for labour services, and most likely to be wrangling over their performance.[190]

The evidence of royal commissions shows that disputes over labour services continued throughout the 1380s and 1390s, at a level well above anything recorded in the 1350s and 1360s. Indeed, if anything the issue worsened after the revolt rather than ameliorated. If we exclude the commissions associated with the 'Rumour' of 1377–8, then the period of greatest unrest was the mid-1380s to the mid-1390s (fig. 6.4). Indeed, evidence from other local sources confirms that in the 1380s and 1390s petty disputes over labour services continued across East Anglia and the Home Counties.[191] Collective refusals to perform labour services on the Ramsey abbey manor of Holywell (Hunts.) peaked between 1386 and 1396.[192] In 1390 the archbishop of Canterbury took the exceptional step of disciplining six of his customary tenants for their half-hearted performance of labour services by requiring them to parade around Wingham (Kent) church as penitents carrying sacks of hay and straw.[193] The disputes were mainly on the manors of great ecclesiastical landlords located in arable districts. These lords felt the shortages of labour most keenly because they were among the rapidly declining number who were still endeavouring to maintain direct cultivation on their arable demesnes.[194] Their large arable demesnes had substantial and fixed seasonal requirements for agricultural labour, while they were also the type of lords most likely to be owed heavy labour services and most likely to insist upon their tenants standing to their obligations.[195] Indeed, for as long as their demesnes were being cultivated directly, these lords still maintained an administrative framework of officials who could try to mobilize the remnants of the servile labour force. The archbishop of Canterbury's humiliation of his Wingham tenants is oft-cited to illustrate the demeaning character of serfdom (which it unquestionably is), but without any proper consideration as to why the archbishop chose this particular moment to impose such an unusual and symbolic sanction. Yet the context is clear: he was frustrated with attempting to exploit his demesne directly at a time when agrarian conditions were dire and difficulties securing a cheap seasonal labour force were acute. Many bishoprics and monastic houses finally accepted economic reality during the course of the 1390s by moving finally to wholesale leasing of their demesnes, a policy which continued throughout the fifteenth century.[196]

The lesser gentry were the other main subset of the landlord class still attempting to cultivate their demesnes directly at the end of the fourteenth century. They were a sizeable group, but we know little about them because their estate records have rarely survived. However, villeinage did not tend to feature prominently on their estates and labour services tended to be lighter than on those of the greater lords.[197] The lesser gentry often ran their small estates directly and personally, so were likely to be employers of a sizeable casual workforce at key moments in the agrarian year.[198] They were also among those willing to lease the demesnes of the greater landlords, and these leases usually granted to the lessee the use of any remaining labour services. For all these reasons, the gentry formed the other category of landlords seeking royal commissions to force tenants to perform labour services. Indeed, they were also active in litigating against employees in the royal courts. A sample of all cases relating to breaches of contract under the Statute of Labourers in the Court of Common Pleas during the Trinity, Easter, and Michaelmas terms 1377 reveals that gentry and heads of minor religious houses were the most active category of lordly litigants.[199] The rewards of further research into the records of royal courts are likely to be considerable.

One example of a case brought by a gentry lord before the royal justices in September 1385 offers an illuminating insight. The gentry lord of the manor of Littlehawe in Thurston (Suffolk) alleged that fifteen serfs and customary tenants had conspired together to withhold all the labour services owed to the lord, 'claiming to be free from all excepting 4d. rent per acre'.[200] The justices heard a plea from the tenants that they held their customary land by hereditary villein tenure, owing no week works, a cash rent equivalent to 5d. per acre, and a range of light seasonal works, the most onerous of which was six days reaping in the harvest on a 24-acre holding. The jury found that the tenants had withheld their services for the past three years, had threatened the lord's officials and had refused to allow them to distrain goods, were bound together in an allegiance, and had raised £6 per annum as a legal war chest. They were being advised by the parish vicar and chaplain, and various others. The appearance of such a case before the King's Bench probably reflects continued official nervousness in the wake of 1381 about coordinated challenges to lordly authority, especially when the call for rents at 4d. per acre echoed a specific demand of the London rebels.[201] It is instructive, however, that *seasonal* labour services were the focus of the dispute, as they were in a similar case nearby in November 1385.[202] The shortages of rural labour were most keenly felt in the key seasons of the grain-producing year, and so seasonal services were worth fighting for in such bleak conditions.

The second category of evidence for the continuation of social conflict in rural areas after 1381 is the sudden and energetic attempts in the late 1380s and early 1390s of a handful of major landlords to restrict the mobility of hereditary serfs.[203] For example, officials on the East Anglian manors of the earls of Norfolk paid much closer attention to the identity and whereabouts of migrant serfs, and introduced special licences for those wishing to pursue a trade.[204] Likewise, in 1390–1 an extensive survey of the newly-inherited estate of John Hastings, Lord Abergavenny, was undertaken to establish a centralized and up-to-date record of the annual revenues liable from over forty manors scattered from Shropshire to Kent, and to identify assets which might be liquidated for ready cash, such as stocks of mature timber. The survey included lists of all the hereditary serfs on each manor as written proof of their servility, presumably to track their mobility and potentially to target them for servile dues.[205]

Tougher policies against serfs between the mid-1380s and mid-1390s are especially evident on the estate of the abbot of Bury St Edmunds. There had been no seigniorial reaction here between the Black Death and the Peasants' Revolt, when the abbot paid little interest in the mobility of serfs (figs. 6.5 and 6.6), and most of the old hereditary villein tenancies were converted to cash leaseholds.[206] As a result, most of the original labour services had disappeared. For example, at Chevington (Suffolk) in 1379–80 three-quarters of all week works and four-fifths of harvest works were no longer available due to conversions to leases.[207] Yet the abbot was still managing many of his arable demesnes directly, so the sudden fall in grain prices and profitability in the mid-1380s must have posed serious challenges. The shortages of agricultural labour in such circumstances and its associated cost hardened attitudes towards the estate's servile labour force. From the mid-1380s estate officials took a sudden and sustained interest in the identity and whereabouts of hereditary serfs (see figs. 6.5 and 6.6).[208] The court rolls of many abbatial manors now recorded absences extensively, updated the movement of serfs annually, and threatened stiff financial penalties on migrants who failed either to return or to pay a licence for their absence (fig. 6.5). The

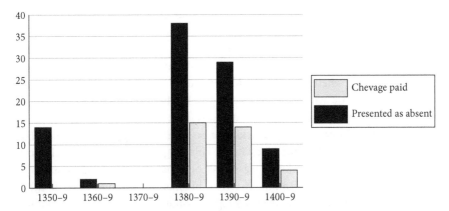

Figure 6.5 Recorded departures of serfs from Chevington (Suffolk), by decade 1350 to 1409

Source: Bailey 2014

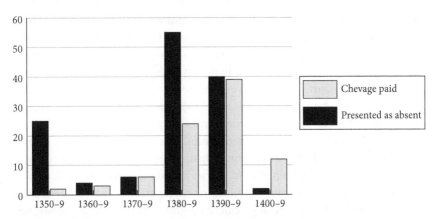

Figure 6.6 Recorded departures of serfs from Hargrave (Suffolk), by decade 1350 to 1409

Source: SROB E3/15.10/1.1 to 1.20; E3/15.10/2.8 to 2.20

timing cannot have been a coincidence: from the perspective of this conservative landlord, a combination of economic necessity and a wider hardening of attitudes towards labour justified the sudden use of action targeted against the only section of manorial population whose movements the lord could legally control.

The crackdown on migrant serfs on the abbot of Bury St Edmunds' manors was an enforcement wave rather than a response to a sudden flood of departing serfs. The Hargrave (Suffolk) court rolls, for example, record not a single absent serf during the 1370s, although it is inconceivable that none had left the manor. Then in 1384 the rolls record six migrants, followed by eleven in 1385 (fig. 6.6). Furthermore, the rolls also record a great deal more information about servile progeny after 1384, and the number of fines for childwite and the number of merchet fines also rose. Threats of large financial penalties against the relatives of flown serfs are recorded. This tactic was novel but not indiscriminate because it was carefully targeted at four serfs whose close relatives held sizeable landholdings from the manor, where pressure could be brought locally to bear to secure their return.[209] The tactic achieved little success.[210] The attention to serfs then ceased in the mid-1390s, almost as abruptly as it had started.

The abbot of Bury's ten-year crackdown on serfs at Hargrave was repeated on other manors across the abbatial estate.[211] This tough policy provides an important context for the extraordinary clash over personal status in 1393 between the abbot's officials and one prominent serf of his manor of Redgrave (Suffolk).[212] *Roge* Furthermore, in 1388 John le Reve of Redgrave—the sole surviving son of ~~William~~ (see p. 50)—decided to purchase the freedom of his son, Henry, for an undisclosed sum, and the timing must have been influenced by John's concerns about the abbot's new policy and its longer-term implications for his family.[213] In stark contrast, there was no comparable crackdown on the manors of the sister estate of the cellarer of the abbey of Bury St Edmunds because personal servility had almost disappeared there by the 1380s.[214] The hard line on the abbatial manors may have been a personal response from a controversial abbot—John de Timworth—whose disputed election in 1379 was a factor in the extreme violence shown by the rebels against the abbey during the revolt of June 1381.[215] Timworth did not become abbot until the resolution of the dispute in 1384, which coincided closely with the start of the new policy, although it continued even after his death in 1389. In the mid-1390s, however, the policy ceased abruptly on most of the abbot's manors: enforcement of servile incidents diminished, threats of financial penalties on relatives ceased, and the frequency of entries and information about flown serfs became less detailed. This mini seigniorial reaction fizzled out as quickly as it had started, without the abbot having achieved a great deal: hardly any flown serfs returned. Neither the financial returns from the small number of merchet and chevage fines, nor the conflict it must have generated with tenants at a time when the land market was deteriorating, justified the administrative effort involved.

The sudden determination to identify and control the movement of serfs between the mid-1380s and mid-1390s on the estate of the abbot of Bury St Edmunds illustrates admirably the character of English serfdom. On the one hand, it reveals how a powerful lord could suddenly choose to be more aggressive in the management of villeinage in ways that were troubling, stigmatic, and irksome to those subjected to it. The abbot's change of policy towards serfs certainly alarmed John le Reve sufficiently that he arranged the purchase of a charter of freedom for his son and took the precaution of recording the fact in the manor court. On the other hand, it reveals how such aggressive policies required a good deal of administrative effort, without yielding much revenue or securing more labour. It was neither cost-effective nor successful. The actions of the abbot of Bury between c.1385 and c.1395 exemplified what some landlords occasionally attempted under English serfdom rather than what most landlords routinely did. The deteriorating economic conditions provided the trigger for an aggressive policy against serfs on the estate, but the determination to pursue it was influenced by a particular social attitude and mindset as much as economics. Further research is required to establish how widespread were coercive policies against serfs in the 1380s and 1390s. In all likelihood, they were restricted to those conservative landlords with a high proportion of serfs on their estates and the administrative infrastructure to monitor them. Such estates comprised a small minority of the whole.

What proportion of the total population did hereditary serfs comprise at the end of the fourteenth century? On the eve of the Black Death villeins had comprised around 40 per cent of the population, most of whom were also hereditary serfs. The scale and rate of attrition after 1348–9 is not definitively knowable, although there is no doubt that the proportion declined. English lords could not enserf new populations because of the protection offered to people of free status under the common law, so the proportion could not increase. The main source of attrition was the unlicensed flight of serfs from the home manor, never to return, who thereby acquired de facto freedom in their new place of residence. In addition, on many (and especially gentry) manors lords simply ceased record-ing and tracking personal serfdom after the 1350s as tenurial villeinage declined.[216] Finally, some serfs bought their freedom formally through the pur-chase of charters of manumissions. Consequently, both Dyer and Campbell have estimated independently that the proportion of serfs fell to c.25 per cent of the population in the 1380s, and continued to decline thereafter.[217]

A fall from 40 per cent in the 1340s to 25 per cent in the 1380s represents a reasonable estimate for the proportion of serfs among the English population, although there are grounds for arguing that it is generous. Twenty-five per cent is a fair guess if the reference point is the prominence of references to serfs in the extant estate records of the greater landlords during the 1380s. However, it is impressionistic and liable to overstate the proportion of serfs for two reasons. First, our impression of the extent and survival of serfdom on the estates of greater landlords is exaggerated, if the exceptional evidence from a survey in 1391 of the whole estate of John de Hastings—a member of the lesser nobility—is typical. This document provides summary extents for numerous manors located between Shropshire and Kent, many of which also include lists of the number of adult serfs and, in some cases, their progeny. Although it is impossible to calculate the proportion of serfs as a percentage of the manorial population from the informa-tion provided, the survey does provide a rare opportunity to establish quantita-tively the presence or absence of serfs on each manor across a large aristocratic estate. Of the forty-three manors for which a sufficiently detailed extent is given, 63 per cent had no recorded serfs, 16 per cent had fewer than five recorded adult serfs, and 21 per cent had more than five.[218] In other words, where a surviving document enables some quantification of the presence of serfs on an aristocratic estate, it proves that they were much less common that we have assumed. The proportion of manors with no serfs is remarkably high and, even allowing for some scribal omissions, it likely that by 1391 at least half the manors on this estate had none.[219] Second, serfs were much less common on the manors of the lesser gentry, which constituted a large majority of manorial forms, although few records have survived from such estates. One case study has shown that by the late fourteenth century there is no record of personal servility on nine out of a sample of fifteen gentry manors (60 per cent), and the remaining manors in the sample contained just a handful of serfs.[220] Hence if Hastings is typical of aristocratic estates, and if greater weighting is given to gentry estates, then the estimate of 25 per cent in the 1380s is too high: it is more likely that less than 20 per cent of the population were serfs and, due to continued attrition, the figure in 1400 might have been as low as 10 per cent.

The third, and final, category of evidence for the continuation of social conflict in rural areas after 1381 is the revision of the government's labour legislation in the 1380s.[221] The Statute of Cambridge of 1388 introduced major revisions to the 1351 labour legislation, and Fryde captured the view of many historians when he described these as 'startlingly oppressive provisions'.[222] These included a prohibition on children who had worked in agriculture to the age of 12 years from taking up a trade; a requirement for craft workers to participate in the harvest if not otherwise employed; leisure time to be directed productively to hone military skills and not dissipated unproductively in frivolous games; able-bodied vagrants to be returned to their home village and put to work; itinerant workers to carry testimonials cleared by justices of the peace explaining their need to travel; and the introduction of penalties for employers who breached the legislation, including imprisonment for the worst cases. English wage rates fell temporarily in 1389, a phenomenon which Gregory Clark describes as 'mysterious', but must have been the consequence of a sharp, short crackdown following the 1388 statute.[223] Indeed, the chance survival of the sessions of the court of the King's Bench in Brentwood (Essex) in 1389 reveals a preoccupation with cases relating to the agricultural labour force and a much greater willingness to mete out heavier fines in such cases than previously.[224]

Yet, in general, the bark of the new legislation was far worse than its bite because many of its provisions were unrealistic and difficult to enforce.[225] The penalties on employers, for example, were little used before they were formally retracted in 1402, few punishments are recorded for playing the wrong games in the 1390s, and the frequency of cases under the labour laws reduced to a trickle in extant sessions of justices of the peace.[226] The significance of the Statute of Cambridge lies in its intent and in what it reveals about changing attitudes to labour, not in its effectiveness. The initial, towering ambition in 1351 to use the legislation to restore the labour market to pre-plague conditions was formally abandoned, and replaced instead with a pragmatic determination to target the most pressing problems: labour mobility, able-bodied beggars, and the shortage of agricultural labourers. In this sense, 1388 represents a resolution of years of debate among the ruling elite over the problem of labour and what areas to prioritize.[227]

Perhaps the only surprise is that it had taken so long for this narrower and more targeted approach to be enshrined in legislation. After all, the failure of the Statute of Labourers to restrict wage rises and to enforce annual contracts had become starkly obvious as early as the 1360s, when for the first time a parliamentary petition raised concerns about the statute's shortcomings.[228] In 1372 another petition argued that tougher punishments were needed to deter contract breakers, then another in 1376 bemoaned the widespread evasion of the legislation, ana-lysed the likely reasons for this, and proposed some radical solutions.[229] The petitioners identified the mobility of labourers and servants as the main problem, because the latter could breach contracts and obtain better-paid work elsewhere with relative impunity, and so they now directed their anger primarily against the idle beggars and drifting vagrants who supposedly chose not to work.[230] In 1383 the first reiteration of the labour legislation in the wake of the revolt included the usual directives about wages and contracts, but also empowered royal officials and constables to stop and question 'vagabonds', the first time this word had been used in an official context.[231] A narrower preoccupation with the mobility of rural labour is reflected in a succession of five parliamentary petitions between 1377 and 1402, each complaining about the flight of rural villeins to towns or the failure of villeins to perform labour services.[232] For example, in 1385 a petition complained about the migration of villeins to 'cities, towns, and places enfranchised ... to the intent to make them free', in response to which parliament passed legislation reiterating that lords should not be 'forebarred of their villeins'.[233] The 1391 petition was from the 'knights of the shires'—rural landlords—who complained that townsfolk were obstructing their attempts to retrieve flown villeins, suggest-ing a conflict of interest between rural landlords and urban burgesses on this issue.[234] Another petition in 1391 requested royal action against villeins who bought freehold land and sought to educate their offspring, even though in law these were matters exclusively for lords and not for the Crown.[235]

Just as parliamentary petitions after 1368 reveal the narrowing of emphasis upon the perceived or most pressing issues of rural mobility and able-bodied beggars, so contemporary sermons and literature reassessed the nature and value of labour, and portrayed the idle vagrant as a bogeyman associated with crime and sedition.[236] The revolt of 1381 had also signalled the dangers of bestowing upon local officials considerable discretion to enforce wide-ranging but loosely-drafted legislation, an experience which must have convinced many among the ruling elite to reduce its scope and to sharpen its focus. Hence the Statute of Cambridge represented a major watershed, when the scope of labour legislation narrowed to provide pragmatic remedies aimed at addressing the shortages of rural agricultural labour.[237] This also provides another context for understanding the crackdown on serf migration and labour services from the mid-1380s on some estates, discussed above. In many ways, a seigniorial reaction to enforce serfdom in the last quarter of the fourteenth century makes much more sense than one in the third quarter now that the economic situation of landlords had deteriorated so badly. Tenants for customary land were harder to attract, profits in agriculture were tumbling, the government's original labour legislation had palpably failed, seigniorial revenues were declining sharply, labour costs were rising, and seasonal workers in agriculture were more difficult to find.[238] Those landlords who were still cultivating their arable demesnes directly at this time, who could still call upon labour services, and who still had a corpus of hereditary serfs on their estates, had little to lose by clamping down on them hard, especially with the onset of economic winter in the mid-1380s. Yet historians have hardly considered the possibility of a mini seigniorial reaction *after* the revolt of 1381 because it does not fit the conventional narrative of post-revolt appeasement.

Conclusion

The received wisdom is that from the mid-1370s the economic and social equilibrium of the post-plague era was finally established. The economic buoyancy of the 1350s and 1360s finally ceased, the price-wage scissors opened decisively and persistently to the benefit of labourers and smallholders, and seigniorial polices of appeasement towards peasants after 1381 diminished social conflict. Yet this chapter has proposed a different interpretation, arguing instead that economic conditions were neither unchanging nor stable in the final quarter of the fourteenth century, and that three distinct economic sub-periods are identifiable. First, there was a sharp deterioration in agrarian profitability between 1375 and 1385. Second, a further worsening of conditions for agricultural production between 1385 and 1395, caused by a sharp monetary deflation, but a growth in industrial output. Finally, a general stabilizing and levelling of most sectors of the economy after 1395, as the acute monetary factors eased. These broad phases provide a context for reassessing the nature of social relations, and the revision of the labour legislation, in the 1380s. They also warn against any tendency to represent the late fourteenth and fifteenth centuries as an undifferentiated and homogenous economic period.

Between the early 1370s and early 1380s a steep decline in grain prices was the driving force behind the 14 per cent fall in the Composite Price Index, while wages remained high. Larger peasant grain producers now felt the economic chill and the peasant land market slowed, whereas labourers enjoyed a marked gain in earning power and annual incomes. Lower grain prices after 1376 were due mainly to the confluence of benign weather and monetary deflation, although the conditions of oversupply also owed something to the increased productive capacity of the peasant sector and its re-engagement with the commercial grain market. Short-term leases of demesne and peasant land were especially important in aiding this process of market re-engagement, especially in the most commercialized areas of the country, because they increased the mobility of land while reducing the risks and capital costs of its acquisition. These peasant producers suddenly had to adapt to a much less favourable commercial environment, which fuelled some of the rural discontent in the late 1370s: their labour services or fixed cash rents now appeared onerous and irksome at a time when they—no less than landlords—had to find ways of reducing their costs.

After 1385 the Composite Price Index fell a further 10 per cent and remained low until the mid-1390s, although now the prices of all basic commodities sagged as the effects of a wider and severe monetary deflation began to grip. This double-dip further reduced the profitability of commercial grain production and so caused real economic difficulties for the greater landlords, who consequently moved decisively and extensively towards the leasing of their demesnes. The result was a significant and ultimately a permanent transfer of land from the seigniorial to the peasant sector, and an increase in the proportion of land held on contractual tenures. This development, together with the slackening land market and the practice of providing lessees with the lord's livery, accelerated the emergence of a new social order within rural society. It reinforced the breakdown of the old link between tenure and status, and further reinforced the irrelevance of traditional social labels based on tenure, such as freeman and villein. No wonder the many freemen and flown serfs who had constructed agrarian enterprises from a mixture of demesne, free, and customary land on various forms of tenure began to self-identify as husbandmen and yeomen.

In the harsher agrarian conditions of the late 1380s livestock rearing offered better opportunities for profit than grain production, because markets for pastoral products remained more resilient and labour costs were lower and easier to control, but the opportunities for expansion were fewer and the commercial risks were greater than they had been in the third quarter of the century. Despite the difficulties in agriculture, estimated GDP per head rose 10 per cent in the mid-1380s. Industrial output continued to expand, especially in mining, marine fishing, and the manufacture of certain textiles. Urban fortunes were very mixed, but those towns specializing in the most dynamic industries and the ports servicing them enjoyed economic buoyancy and even some demographic growth. Employment opportunities in industry exacerbated the chronic shortages of labour in agriculture.

The failure of the Statute of Labourers to restore the conditions of the pre-plague labour market, coupled with the agrarian downturn of the mid-1370s, created the backdrop for a national debate among the ruling elite about the problem of labour. Either radical new remedies were needed to increase the supply of agricultural labour, or a more pragmatic, and targeted, approach was required. The sudden deterioration in the agrarian economy in the mid-1380s proved the tipping point. The labour legislation was substantially revised in 1388 with a narrower focus on controlling the mobility of rural labour, regulating able-bodied vagrants, stemming the flow of workers into trades, and restricting the leisure activities of the lower orders. Landlords in the last throes of direct management of their demesnes had little to lose by insisting upon the performance of residual labour services and by clamping down on the movement of their hereditary serfs. Now was the moment for a last stand on targeted elements of serfdom. Consequently, social relations between lords and tenants did not obviously ameliorate after the Peasants' Revolt of 1381. Ecclesiastical landlords, in particular, continued to request royal commissions to support their attempts to force the tenants of their customary land to perform labour services. Their desire to impose labour services would have met most resistance from tenants of customary land who were legally free or who were the flown serfs of other lords. The combination of new government legislation and a clampdown on the movement of servile labour on some estates between the mid-1380s and mid-1390s has parallels with the mini seigniorial reaction of the 1350s: both occurred on some estates in response to rapidly changing and deteriorating economic conditions, and both proved unsustainable.

From the mid-1390s the severe conditions in agriculture eased slightly as the monetary squeeze was released. There are clear signs of activity flattening out across all sectors of the economy. Markets for agricultural products show signs of stability or even oversupply, and after 1400 few sectors of the economy exhibit substantial or sustained signs of growth. This supports arguments that after c.1400 annual incomes and spending power reached a plateau and that estimated GDP per head flattened (fig. 4.1). A deteriorating climate and repeated outbreaks of disease reinforced the levelling of demand.[239] Peasants still faced the risks associated with trade cycles, the levelling of demand, and depressed profits, and their response was probably to manage such risks by minimizing their engagement with the market. Whatever the reasons, the economy had lost the turbulence and uncertainty of the third quarter of the century and as such had finally settled at its new post-plague equilibrium.

Notes

1. Bolton, *Medieval English economy*, pp. 214–15, 217–20, quote at p. 214.
2. Bridbury, *English economy*, pp. 31–2, 208–10, 217, quotes at 31, 217. See also Kitsikopoulos, 'England', pp. 34–5.
3. Farmer, 'Prices and wages', pp. 502–3.

4. Farmer, 'Prices and wages', pp. 471–2, 485, 489; Munro, 'Late medieval decline', table 20a; Clark, Long march', p. 117.
5. Monro, 'Late medieval decline', pp. 299–305.
6. Edward Miller, 'Introduction: people and land', in Miller, ed., Agrarian history, III, pp. 12–13, 22.
7. Bolton, Medieval English economy, p. 215; Britnell, 'Feudal reaction', pp. 40–7.
8. Holmes, Higher nobility, pp. 116–17; Hilton, Bondmen made free, pp. 156–7; Keen, English society, pp. 39–43; Bridbury, English economy, pp. 34–7; Eiden, 'Bad lordship', pp. 29–30; Muller, 'Conflict', pp. 2–3; van Bavel, Manors and markets, p. 273.
9. See, for example: Razi, 'Myth', pp. 38–43; Dyer, Making a living, pp. 271–97; Harriss, Shaping the nation, pp. 222–3, 234–42, 651–3; Munro, 'Late medieval decline', pp. 299–305; Larson, Conflict and compromise, pp. 143–69; Rigby, English society, pp. 80–7, 110–27; Fryde, Peasants and landlords, pp. 113–34; Thomson, Transformation of medieval England, pp. 18–20; Goldberg, Medieval England, pp. 192–4; Dyer, Age of transition, p. 96.
10. Harriss, Shaping the nation, pp. 234–5; Dyer, Lords and peasants, p. 275; Fryde, Peasants and landlords, pp. 69, 116–17; Britnell, Britain, p. 430.
11. Hilton, 'Crisis of feudalism', pp. 132–3; Tuck, 'Nobles, Commons', pp. 201–3; Bolton, Medieval English economy, pp. 217–18; Eiden, 'Bad lordship', pp. 29–30; Kitsikopoulos, 'England', pp. 34–5.
12. Brenner, 'Agrarian class structure', p. 35; Fryde, Peasants and landlords, pp. 69, 116–17, 123–7; Brenner, 'Property and progress', pp. 96–7.
13. Miller, 'Introduction', p. 16; Ghosh, 'Rural economies', pp. 280–4; van Bavel, Invisible hand, pp. 211–18.
14. Summarized in Hatcher, 'Unreal wages', pp. 1–5.
15. Recent summaries of this debate can be found in Dyer, Making a living, pp. 276–81; Humphries and Weisdorf, 'Women's wages', pp. 419–26; and Bennett, 'Wretched girls', pp. 315–20.
16. See, for example, Fryde, Peasants and landlords, chapter 8; Goldberg, Medieval England, pp. 186–99; Harriss, Shaping the nation, pp. 234–42.
17. See Chapter Six, and the summaries in Humphries and Weisdorf, 'Women's wages', pp. 419–26; and Bennett, 'Wretched girls', pp. 315–20.
18. Bailey, Decline of serfdom, pp. 285–337; Wells-Furby, Berkeley estate, pp. 106–7, 212, 217.
19. Broadberry et al., British economic growth, pp. 207–9.
20. Broadberry et al., British economic growth, table 5.06.
21. Clark, 'Long march', table 5.
22. The falls in the prices of rabbits and poultry are documented in Bailey, 'Rabbit', p. 11, and Slavin, 'Goose management', pp. 8, 23.
23. Mayhew, 'Prices in England', table 1.
24. As revealed through calculations of the marginal product of labour, Clark, 'Long march', table 1, pp. 99–100.
25. Broadberry et al., British economic growth, pp. 189, 256. Agricultural prices rose in the 1430s due to exceptional weather and famine conditions.
26. Campbell, 'Grain yields', fig. 16B, p. 131; Britnell, Britain, p. 400.

27. Campbell, *Seigniorial agriculture*, pp. 372–3; Campbell, 'Grain yields', p. 159; Pribyl, *Farming, famine*, pp. 83–4, 102–4, 113, 167, 201, 208–9, 231; Campbell, *Great transition*, pp. 338–40.
28. Munro, 'Money matters', pp. 168–72; Munro, 'Late medieval decline', pp. 303–4; Nuno Palma, 'Reconstruction of money supply over the long run: the case of England, 1270–1870', *Economic History Review*, 71 (2018), pp. 377, 384.
29. Britnell, *Britain*, pp. 457–8; Palma, 'Reconstruction', fig. 1, p. 377.
30. For tithes as a source of information about peasant production, see Dodds, *Peasants and production*, pp. 23–32.
31. Britnell, *Britain*, p. 391.
32. Dodds, *Peasants and production*, pp. 26, 28, 73–7, 80.
33. Larson, *Conflict and compromise*, pp. 195, 217; Mullan, 'Transfer of customary land', pp. 103–6.
34. For example, see Tuck, 'Occupation: Northern Borders', p. 39; Tuck, 'Tenant farming: Northern Borders', pp. 590–1; John Mullan, 'Accumulation and polarisation in two bailiwicks of the Winchester bishopric estates, 1350–1410', in Ben Dodds and Richard H. Britnell, eds., *Agriculture and rural society after the Black Death* (Hatfield, 2008), pp. 179–98; Mullan and Britnell, *Land and family*, pp. 145–8.
35. Blanchard, 'Industrial employment', pp. 249–50, 258–9, 274.
36. King, 'Tenant farming: East Midlands', p. 625; Harriss, *Shaping the nation*, p. 238; Mullan and Britnell, *Land and family*, pp. 142–3.
37. Fox, 'Tenant farming and farmers: Devon and Cornwall', p. 724.
38. Fryde, *Peasants and landlords*, pp. 61, 63–4.
39. Leases were an important element in retention in the north-east, where there was a chronic shortage of tenants, Larson, *Conflict and compromise*, pp. 162–7.
40. Mullan and Britnell, *Land and family*, table 9.4.
41. A point made by Whittle, *Agrarian capitalism*, pp. 183–90, 224, for the fifteenth century, but it applies equally to the second half of the fourteenth century.
42. See, for example, Miller, 'Tenant farming: Yorkshire and Lancashire', p. 597.
43. TNA SC6/1304/35 records that just one (40-acre) full-land was still held on the old service tenancy, and as Walter was elected reeve that year then I have assumed he was the tenant. It also records that Walter was leasing another full-land, formerly of Bartholomew Clement, for 4s. per annum. From another account (Bacon Ms 648), we know that he had first acquired the latter on a six-year lease at Michaelmas 1363, and had subsequently renegotiated. He was not one of the named Brandon rebels during the uprising of 1381, Muller, 'Conflict', p. 11.
44. Galloway, 'One market or many', pp. 36–7; Campbell and O. Grada, 'Harvest shortfalls', pp. 879–81; Bateman, 'Evolution', p. 464.
45. A possibility raised by Farmer, 'Prices and wages', p. 451.
46. Galloway, 'One market or many?', pp. 32–8; Galloway, 'Driven by drink', pp. 96–9; Galloway, 'Metropolitan food', pp. 12–13.
47. Clark, 'Long march', table 1, pp. 99–100.
48. Clark, 'Long march', tables 1 and 5. The index is based on 1860–9 = 100, and on 1360–9 = 90, on 1370–9 = 104, and 1380–9 = 128.

49. Marjorie Morgan, *The English lands of the abbey of Bec* (Oxford, 1946), pp. 113–15, 118; Reginald A.L. Smith, *Canterbury Cathedral Priory: a study in monastic administration* (Cambridge, 1943), pp. 190–1; Bean, 'Landlords', pp. 573–5, 580–2; Raftis, 'Peasants', pp. 195–6; Farmer, '*Famuli*', pp. 219–20; Harvey, *Westminster abbey*, p. 268; Dyer, *Lords and peasants*, p. 147; Moss, 'Economic development', p. 112; Bolton, *Medieval English economy*, pp. 212, 214, 220; Tuck, 'Tenant farming: Northern Borders', pp. 588–9; Miller, 'Occupation: Southern Counties', p. 143; Fryde, *Peasants and landlords*, pp. 71–5, 80–2; Britnell, *Britain*, pp. 399, 401, 430–1; Stone, *Decision-making*, pp. 121–2; Munro, 'Late medieval decline', pp. 299–00; Wells-Furby, *Berkeley estates*, pp. 201, 216–17; Mullan and Britnell, *Land and family*, p. 66.

50. Mate, 'Agrarian economy', pp. 352–4.

51. Kettle, '1300–1540', table III, p. 88, and Bailey, *Marginal economy?*, p. 214. See also Dyer, *Lords and peasants*, pp. 122–3; Britnell, 'Occupation: Eastern England', p. 58; Mate, 'Occupation: Kent and Sussex', p. 121.

52. Britnell, 'Occupation: Eastern England', pp. 64–5; Campbell, *Seigniorial agriculture*, pp. 275–6.

53. Stone, *Decision-making*, pp. 126–40; Campbell, *Seigniorial agriculture*, p. 433.

54. Stone, *Decision-making*, p. 133; Wells-Furby, *Berkeley estate*, pp. 170–1.

55. Jean Birrell, ed., 'The *Status Maneriorum* of John Catesby 1385 and 1386', *Dugdale Society*, 31 (1977), pp. 15–28 at 21, 27.

56. Holmes, *Higher nobility*, pp. 118–19, 126–7; Dyer, *Age of transition*, p. 100.

57. Dodds, *Peasants and production*, pp. 74–83, fig. 5.

58. Britnell, *Britain*, p. 391.

59. Hatcher, 'Unreal wages', pp. 14–19; Harry Kitsikopoulos, 'The impact of the Black Death on the peasant economy in England, 1350–1500', *Journal of Peasant Studies*, 29 (2002), p. 82.

60. See, for example, Deborah Youngs, 'Servants and labourers on a late medieval demesne: the case of Newton, Cheshire, 1498–1520', *Agricultural History Review*, 47 (1999), pp. 148–9, 159–60; Mate, 'Occupation: Kent and Sussex', p. 134; Dyer, 'Work ethics', pp. 40–1.

61. King, 'Occupation: East Midlands', p. 72; Dyer, 'Occupation: West Midlands', p. 80; Andrew Watkins, 'Cattle grazing in the Forest of Arden in the late Middle Ages', *Agricultural History Review*, 37 (1989), p. 21. See also Poos, *Rural society*, pp. 46–9; Amor, 'Late medieval enclosure', pp. 186–7; Peberdy, 'Henley', p. 112; Dyer, *Age of transition?*, pp. 32, 129. The exception is parts of the north and west where stock rearing had long been important, where the shift from arable to pasture occurred on a larger scale soon after the first plague outbreak, Tuck, 'Occupation: Northern Borders', pp. 40–1.

62. See Ogilvie and Edwards, 'Did the Black Death', p. 10.

63. Campbell, *Great transition*, pp. 312–13; Harvey, 'Occupation: Home Counties', p. 117.

64. Briggs, *Credit and village society*, pp. 55–6, 209–10.

65. Broadberry et al., *British economic growth*, tables 3.17 and 3.18. See M. Stephenson, 'Risk and capital formation: seigniorial investment in an age of adversity', in Bailey and Rigby, eds., *Town and countryside*, pp. 205–7, and Kettle, '1300–1540', pp. 92–3.

66. Stone, *Decision-making*, pp. 126–7, 149–54; Wells-Furby, *Berkeley estate*, p. 205; Stone, 'Productivity', pp. 1–22.
67. Bailey, *Marginal economy?*, p. 257; Bailey, 'Prior and convent', p. 14.
68. Dyer, *Lords and peasants*, pp. 134–6; Munro, 'Late medieval decline', p. 307; Bailey, *Marginal economy?*, pp. 256–8; Kettle, '1300–1540', p. 92; Bailey, *Medieval Suffolk*, pp. 215–16, 219–22; Wells-Furby, *Berkeley estate*, p. 183.
69. Bailey, *Marginal economy?*, pp. 294–5.
70. Britnell, *Britain*, pp. 421–2.
71. Slavin, 'Chicken husbandry', fig. 3.
72. Slavin, 'Goose management', pp. 9–10, 14–15, 23; Slavin, 'Chicken husbandry', pp. 47–54.
73. Britnell, 'Production for the market', p. 387; Bailey, 'Prior and convent', pp. 12–13; Britnell, 'Occupation: Eastern England', p. 58; Miller, 'Occupation: Southern Counties', p. 144.
74. Dyer, *Lords and peasants*, pp. 138–40; Bailey, *Marginal economy?*, pp. 249–51; Britnell, *Britain*, pp. 413–14; Oldland, 'Wool and cloth production', p. 26.
75. Miller, 'Farming practice: Southern Counties', pp. 296–7; Stone, 'Productivity', pp. 3–20; Britnell, *Britain*, pp. 414–15; Oldland, 'Wool and cloth production', p. 42.
76. Bailey, *Marginal economy?*, pp. 249–50; Kettle, '1300–1540', pp. 95–6; Wells-Furby, *Berkeley estate*, pp. 201, 217; Harvey, 'Occupation: Home Counties', p. 115; Stephenson, 'Risk', pp. 208–9.
77. Oldland, 'Wool and cloth production', p. 29.
78. Bailey, *Marginal economy?*, pp. 246–7, 289–95; Britnell, *Britain*, pp. 414–19; Oldland, 'Wool and cloth production', pp. 27, 29, 39.
79. Campbell, *Seigniorial agriculture*, pp. 433–5.
80. Bailey, 'Rabbit', pp. 10–12; Bailey, *Marginal economy?*, pp. 251–6.
81. Bailey, 'Rabbit', p. 6; Bailey, 'Prior and convent', p. 13.
82. Bailey, 'Rabbit', pp. 13, 15; Gould, 'Distribution', p. 38.
83. Bailey, *Marginal economy?*, pp. 254–55.
84. Gould, 'Distribution', pp. 39–40.
85. Bailey, *Marginal economy?*, pp. 252, 296–8.
86. Bailey, 'Rabbit', pp. 10–11, 13–14.
87. Dyer, 'Farming practice: west Midlands', pp. 236–7; Slavin, 'Goose management', pp. 9–10, 14–15.
88. Campbell, *Seigniorial agriculture*, pp. 433–5.
89. Raftis, 'Peasants', p. 196; Britnell, 'Production for the market', p. 386; Dyer, 'Occupation: West Midlands', p. 83; Harvey, 'Occupation: Home Counties', p. 110; Miller, 'Occupation: Southern Counties', p. 145; Fox, 'Occupation: Devon and Cornwall', pp. 157–8; Britnell, 'Tenant farming: Eastern England', p. 610; Mullan and Britnell, *Land and family*, p. 122; Bailey, 'Prior and convent', pp. 14–16; Wells-Furby, *Berkeley estate*, p. 268.
90. Poos, *Rural society*, p. 50, fig. 2.4; Dyer, *Lords and peasants*, p. 290, fig. 5. See also Mullan and Britnell, *Land and family*, figs. 5.5 and 5.8, pp. 80–2.
91. Larson, *Conflict and compromise*, pp. 200–2.

92. Miller, 'Occupation: Yorkshire and Lancashire', p. 44; Mate, 'Occupation: Kent and Sussex', p. 124; Miller, 'Occupation: Southern Counties', p. 139; Galloway, 'Storm flooding', pp. 180–1, 184; Stone, *Decision-making*, pp. 123, 149; Wells-Furby, *Berkeley estate*, pp. 203–4.

93. Yates, 'Market in freehold land', fig. 1, pp. 583, 585; Bell et al., 'Reappraisal', figs. 1 and 7.

94. Campbell, 'Population pressure', pp. 123–4.

95. Mark Bailey, *Studies in villeinage*, forthcoming.

96. See also Faith, 'Berkshire', pp. 117, 128; Schofield, 'Tenurial developments', pp. 258–9; Whittle, 'Individualism', pp. 46–9; Mullan and Britnell, *Land and family*, pp. 81–2, 153–5.

97. SROI HA/30/50/22/20.9 (2), court held November 1392.

98. Between 1350 and 1379 60% of admissions to customary land on the Winchester estate were outsiders, and 61% between 1380 and 1415, Mullan and Britnell, *Land and family*, pp. 87, 127–9.

99. Larson, *Conflict and compromise*, pp. 199–20, 212, 22, 237–8.

100. Tuck, 'Tenant farming: Northern Borders' pp. 587, 591; Britnell, 'Tenant farming: Eastern England', pp. 620–1; Dyer, 'Tenant farming: West Midlands', pp. 639–41; Harvey, 'Tenant farming: Home Counties', p. 667; Miller, 'Tenant farming: Southern Counties', p. 710; Bailey, 'Tallage-at-will', pp. 46–52.

101. Harvey, *Westminster abbey*, pp. 256, 261–4, 270; Schofield, 'Tenurial developments', fig. 1 and table 2, pp. 256, 249.

102. Britnell, 'Tenant farming: Eastern England', p. 635; Dyer, *Lords and peasants*, pp. 120, 292–3; Fryde, *Peasants and landlords*, pp. 139–41; Dyer, 'Tenant farming: West Midlands', pp. 639–41; Miller, 'Tenant farming: Yorkshire and Lancashire', pp. 598–9; Harvey, 'Tenant farming: Home Counties', p. 671.

103. Bailey, *Decline of serfdom*, pp. 322–6.

104. It is not possible to establish precise and definitive figures, but this does not mean that we cannot confidently guess the approximate magnitudes. We estimate that in the 1340s 0.9 of all free land was held on non-commercial/service tenancies, 0.07 was leased, and 0.03 on quasi-commercial head rents; likewise 0.9 of all villein land on non-commercial/service tenure, 0.05 leased, and 0.05 on quasi-commercial tenures.

105. We estimate that in the 1340s 0.6 of all demesne land was directly exploited, 0.4 leased; in the 1390s 0.25 directly exploited, 0.75 leased.

106. For example, Britnell, 'Tenant farming: eastern England', p. 618. In the 1390s we estimate 0.88 of all free land on non-commercial/service, 0.07 leased, and 0.05 quasi-commercial.

107. Harvey, 'Tenant farming: Home Counties', p. 672; Sandra Raban, *A second Domesday?: the Hundred Rolls of 1279–80* (Oxford, 2004), p. 136; Wells-Furby, *Berkeley estate*, pp. 125–9.

108. The estimated proportions are 0.45 non-commercial/service, 0.25 leased, and 0.3 quasi-commercial.

109. In the 1390s 0.25 of all demesne land was directly exploited, 0.75 leased. The leasing of demesnes after 1350 is documented above, pp. 92–5 and pp. 251–2, and the sharp fall

276   AFTER THE BLACK DEATH

in demesne share of agriculture as a consequence of leasing is estimated in Broadberry et al., *British economic growth*, p. 82.

110. This calculation applied the proportions estimated above to the following distribution: 30% of all land held as demesne in *c*.1300, 35% as free land, and 35% as unfree. Hence in the 1340s the 20% of contractual rents is comprised of 12% = leased demesne, plus 4% = peasant leased, plus 4% = peasant quasi-commercial. In the 1390s 45% contractual rents is comprised of 22% demesne leased, plus 2.5% = free leased, plus 1.5% = free quasi-commercial, plus 8% = villein leased, plus 11% = villein quasi-commercial.

111. Broadberry et al., *British economic growth*, p. 82.

112. Razi, *Life, marriage*, pp. 147–50; Campbell, 'Population pressure', pp. 123-5; King, 'Tenant farming: East Midlands', pp. 624–5; Fox, 'Tenant farming: Devon and Cornwall', pp. 723–5; Britnell, *Britain*, pp. 238–40, 378–9; Goldberg, *Medieval England*, pp. 193–4; Mullan and Britnell, *Land and family*, pp. 139–51; Yates, 'Market in freehold land', fig. 2, pp. 586–7; Bell et al., 'Reappraisal', pp. 20–1.

113. Campbell, 'Population pressure', pp. 123, 125, fig. 2.6.

114. Zvi Razi, 'The erosion of the family-land bond in the late fourteenth and fifteenth centuries: a methodological note', in Smith, ed., *Land, kinship*, pp. 295–304; Faith, 'Berkshire', pp. 129–30, 132; Whittle, *Agrarian capitalism*, pp. 86–177.

115. Razi, 'Myth', pp. 25–37; Whittle, 'Individualism', pp. 44–9, 62; Bailey, 'Transformation', pp. 210–30; Mullan and Britnell, *Land and family*, pp. 84–102, 118–31; Sheila Sweetinburgh, 'Farming the Kentish marshlands', in Sweetinburgh, ed., *Medieval Kent*, pp. 88–90.

116. Britnell, *Britain*, pp. 402–3.

117. Figures from Broadberry and Campbell, 'Why did Britain industrialise?', pp. 17–18 are very similar to those from Clark, '1381 and the Malthus delusion', pp. 6–11, despite the deployment of different methods of calculating the percentages.

118. Broadberry et al., *British economic growth*, table 5.01.

119. Broadberry et al., *British economic growth*, pp. 81–3, 138, 146–7.

120. Wendy Childs, 'English export trade in cloth', in Britnell and Hatcher, eds., *Problems and progress*, p. 137; Poos, *Rural society*, pp. 70–1; Goldberg, *Women, work and life-cycle*, p. 73; Hare, *Prospering society*, pp. 152, 165–6, 179–80, 191–2; Bailey, *Medieval Suffolk*, pp. 270, 272; Amor, *Wool to cloth*, pp. 31, 33–4, 42–3, 52, 55–7; Britnell, *Britain*, p. 351; Goddard, *Lordship*, p. 231; John Oldland, *The English woollen industry c.1200 to c.1560* (London, 2019) pp. 193–7, 211–12.

121. Oldland, *English woollen industry*, p. 221.

122. Langdon, *Mills*, pp. 29–30, 47, figs. 2.8 and 2.9.

123. Amor, *Wool to cloth*, pp. 55–7.

124. Broadberry et al., *British economic growth*, pp. 138–9; Hatcher, *Tin production*, pp. 156–8; Dodds, *Peasant and production*, pp. 85–8.

125. Newton, *Thaxted*, pp. 26–7; Hatcher, *Coal production*, p. 151.

126. Hatcher, *Duchy of Cornwall*, p. 143, 147; Fox, 'Occupation of the land: Devon and Cornwall', p. 162, fn. 358; Stone, *Moor medieval*, pp. 107–10; Blanchard, 'Industrial employment', pp. 232, 237.

127. Hatcher, *Coal production*, pp. 26–9, 76–7, 124, 137, 151; Dodds, *Peasants and production*, pp. 85–9.

128. Rigby, *Medieval Grimsby*, pp. 122, 137; Mark Bailey, 'Coastal fishing off south east Suffolk in the century after the Black Death', *Proceedings of the Suffolk Institute of Archaeology and History*, 37 (1990), pp. 109–10; Kowaleski, *Local markets*, pp. 311–12; Bailey, *Medieval Suffolk*, pp. 276–7; Dodds, *Peasants and production*, pp. 89–92. For Great Yarmouth see Anthony Saul, 'English towns in the late middle ages: the case of Great Yarmouth', *Journal of Medieval History*, 8 (1982), pp. 83–4.

129. For example, in north-east coal and fishing Dodds, *Peasants and production*, pp. 89, 90–1; fulling mills nationally, Langdon, *Mills*, p. 47, fig. 2.11; cloth manufacture in Essex and Derbyshire, Poos, *Rural society*, pp. 70–1, and Blanchard, 'Industrial employment', p. 234; and Mendip and Derbyshire lead mining, Blanchard, 'Industrial employment', pp. 233, 237.

130. Harriss, *Shaping the nation*, p. 247. See also Britnell, *Colchester*, p. 159; Kowaleski, *Local markets*, pp. 89–92; Rigby, *Medieval Grimsby*, pp. 114–15.

131. Rosser, *Medieval Westminster*, pp. 73–4, 171.

132. Amor, *Wool to cloth*, pp. 31, 33–4, 42–3, 52, 55–7; Palliser, *Medieval York*, pp. 195–200, 299; Britnell, *Colchester*, pp. 65, 69–73, 90, 95, 122–4, 151–2, 160; Bailey, *Medieval Suffolk*, pp. 281–2, 285–6.

133. Britnell, *Colchester*, pp. 157–8. Similarly, the highest rate of recorded migration from Coltishall and Martham (Norfolk) occurred in the 1370s and 1380s, with a particular focus upon urban destinations in an area experiencing growth in textile manufacture, Campbell, 'Population pressure', p. 100.

134. Newton, *Thaxted*, pp. 26–7.

135. Kissane, *Lincoln*, pp. 25–9, 33, 48.

136. Rosser, *Medieval Westminster*, pp. 74–5, 171.

137. CIM, 1348–1377, pp. 406–7; Poos, *Rural society*, p. 59. See also Blanchard, 'Industrial employment', p. 250.

138. Kenyon, 'Labour conditions', pp. 92–5; Penn and Dyer, 'Wages and earnings', pp. 171–8; Poos, *Rural society*, pp. 220–1.

139. Kenyon, 'Labour conditions', pp. 94–5; Penn and Dyer, 'Wages and earnings', p. 175.

140. Given-Wilson, 'Problem of labour', pp. 88–9.

141. For a recent summary of the literature on the so-called golden age, see Hatcher, 'Unreal wages', pp. 1–24.

142. Razi, *Life, marriage*, pp. 147–51; Mullan and Britnell, *Land and family*, pp. 136–50.

143. Louisa Foroughi, 'What makes a yeoman?: status, religion, and material culture in later medieval England' (PhD thesis, Fordham University, 2020), chapter 1.

144. Anthony J. Pollard, 'The yeoman', in Rigby and Minnis, eds., *Historians on Chaucer*, pp. 77–81. It may also reflect their military service.

145. Pollard, 'Yeoman', pp. 79–80; Christopher Dyer, 'A fifteenth-century Suffolk farmer', *Agricultural History Review*, 55 (2007), p. 9.

146. Larson, *Conflict and compromise*, pp. 197–8.

147. Given-Wilson, 'Problem of labour', pp. 88–9, 98–100; Bailey, 'Ploughman', pp. 365–7.

148. Foroughi, 'What makes a yeoman?', fig. 1.1.

149. Bolton, 'World turned upside down', p. 57.

150. In some places, smallholders still comprised well over half of the landholding tenantry: for example, Britnell, 'Tenant farming: Eastern England', pp. 616–17; Dyer,

'Tenant farming: West Midlands', p. 636. Mere cottagers probably declined as a percentage of the population, as most labourers obtained a basic smallholding; see Mullan and Britnell, *Land and family*, pp. 149–50.

151. Clark, 'Long march', table 5; Allen and Weisdorf, 'Industrious revolution', fig. 1.

152. See, for example, Dyer, 'Work ethics', pp. 30–1; Hatcher, 'Seven centuries', pp. 41–3; Broadberry et al., *British economic growth*, pp. 248–50.

153. This optimistic scenario, and the more pessimistic one that follows, is illustrated clearly in Humphries and Weisdorf, 'Unreal wages', fig. 2, p. 11.

154. Jane Humphries and Jacob L. Weisdorf, 'The wages of women in England 1260–1850', *The Journal of Economic History*, 75 (2015), pp. 423–6, 431; Humphries and Weisdorf, 'Unreal wages', fig. 5.

155. Mate, 'Work and leisure', p. 285.

156. For the highly optimistic estimates based on 250 days and day wages, and more cautious estimates, see Humphries and Weisdorf, 'Unreal wages', figs. 2 and 5.

157. Bolton, *Medieval English economy*, pp. 217–18; Xu, 'Discontent and rebellion', pp. 135–6, 167–8.

158. Harriss, *Shaping the nation*, p. 234; Fryde, *Peasants and landlords*, p. 128.

159. J.H. Tillotson, 'Peasant unrest in the England of Richard II: some evidence from royal records', *Historical Studies*, 16 (1974), p. 9.

160. Powell, *Rising in East Anglia*, pp. 64–6; Eiden, 'Bad lordship', pp. 29–30; Tuck, 'Nobles, Commons', p. 210; Bailey, *Decline of serfdom*, pp. 182–4, 191–2, 203, 209–10, 226–8, 268–9, 276.

161. Given-Wilson, 'Problem of labour', p. 89; Given-Wilson, 'Service, serfdom', pp. 21, 24, 28, 30, 34; Bennett, 'Compulsory service', p. 11.

162. Tillotson, 'Peasant unrest', pp. 1–2, 7–9; Rigby, *English society*, pp. 116–17.

163. Background Tillotson, 'Peasant unrest', pp. 1–3; Faith, 'Great Rumour', pp. 43–7; Lodge, 'Economic and social history', pp. 189–90.

164. Faith, 'Great Rumour', pp. 44–5.

165. Faith, 'Great Rumour', pp. 51–63; Dyer, 'Memories of unfreedom', p. 291.

166. Faith, 'Great Rumour', pp. 43–51; *Statutes of the Realm*, II, pp. 2–3.

167. Another objective was resistance to distraints of goods, Hanawalt, 'Peasant resistance', p. 39.

168. The Patent Rolls do not provide a definitive list of exemplifications because not all requests were enrolled there: Faith suggests that around half of all exemplification requests were enrolled, Faith, 'Peasant Rumour', pp. 71–3.

169. CPR, 1377–1381, pp. 9–10, 12, 15–16, 18, 23; Tillotson, 'Peasant unrest', p. 3.

170. Tillotson, 'Peasant unrest', pp. 2–3.

171. Putnam, *Proceedings*, p. cxxvi; Faith, 'Great Rumour', pp. 60–2.

172. These further exemplification requests were from a handful of manors in Surrey, Berkshire, and Hampshire, but were not enrolled in the Patent Rolls and therefore not included in fig. 5.3, Faith, 'Great Rumour', pp. 45–6, 71–3.

173. Faith, 'Great Rumour', pp. 48–9; Marjorie K. McIntosh, 'The privileged villeins of the English Ancient Demesne', *Viator*, 7 (1976), pp. 296–7, 325; Kettle, '1300–1540', pp. 112–13.

174. Whittle and Rigby, 'Popular politics', pp. 76–7; Tillotson, 'Peasant unrest', p. 9; Muller, 'Conflict', p. 3; Mullan and Britnell, *Land and family*, p. 57.

175. Lodge, 'Economic and social history', pp. 189–90; Platt, *King Death*, pp. 125–6; Bailey, *Decline of serfdom*, p. 177.

176. Hilton, *English peasantry*, pp. 161–2; Bolton, *Medieval English economy*, p. 215 states that the order was carried out, but there is no evidence that it was, Fryde, *Peasants and landlords*, pp. 68–9. Also see Poos, *Rural society*, p. 247.

177. Kenyon, 'Labour conditions', p. 98.

178. SROB E3/15.10/2.19, 2.20; E3/15.10/1.16, 1.17.

179. See also, Mate, 'Tenant farming: Kent and Sussex', pp. 682–3.

180. Musson, 'Patterns', pp. 99–100.

181. Britnell, *Colchester*, pp. 151–2, notes the tendency in the late 1360s and early 1370s to re-negotiate contractual rents upwards due to the prevailing high grain prices.

182. The demand for 4d. per acre is documented in Oman, *Great Revolt*, pp. 9–10; Dobson, *Peasants' Revolt*, pp. 164–5. For leasehold valuations around 9d. to 12d. per acre, see Miller, 'Tenant farming: Southern Counties', p. 709; Dyer, *Making a Living*, p. 289; Bailey, *Decline of serfdom*, pp. 172, 193, 235.

183. Harvey, *Westminster abbey*, pp. 245–6.

184. Larson, *Conflict and compromise*, pp. 178–88, 196–7, 199, 213.

185. Dodds, *Peasants and production*, pp. 94–5. See also, King, 'Occupation: East Midlands', p. 70.

186. Tillotson, 'Peasant unrest', pp. 1–3; Faith, 'Great Rumour', pp. 43–51; *Statutes of the Realm*, II, pp. 2–3.

187. Tillotson, 'Peasant unrest', p. 6.

188. CPR, 1377–81, pp. 20, 24, 50.

189. Tillotson, 'Peasant unrest', pp. 9–16. Upon investigation, the royal justices usually discovered that beneath the protests lay a specific point of conflict between lord and tenant, such as an irksome obit payment or a refusal to undertake carrying services.

190. King, 'Tenant farming: East Midlands', pp. 629–30; Mate, 'Tenant farming: Kent and Sussex', p. 683.

191. Poos, *Rural society*, pp. 250–2; Harvey, 'Tenant farming: Home Counties', p. 668; Bailey, *Decline of serfdom*, pp. 110, 177, 258.

192. DeWindt, *Land and people*, pp. 91–2.

193. DuBoulay, *Lordship of Canterbury*, p. 189.

194. Britnell, *Britain*, p. 599; Mate, 'Agrarian economy', pp. 352–3.

195. Stone, *Decision-making*, p. 227; Hatcher, 'Unreal wages', p. 8; King, 'Tenants: East Midlands', pp. 629–30; Bailey, 'Prior and convent', p. 18.

196. For the 1390s as a major watershed in demesne leasing on the estates of ecclesiastical landlords, see Dyer, *Lords and peasants*, p. 147; Harvey, *Westminster abbey*, p. 268; Mate, 'Agrarian economy', p. 354; Smith, *Canterbury Cathedral Priory*, pp. 190–1; Bolton, *Medieval English economy*, pp. 214, 220; Britnell, *Britain*, pp. 401, 430–1.

197. Kosminsky, *Studies in the agrarian history*, pp. 156–96.

198. Bean, 'Landlords', pp. 575–6; Bailey, *Medieval Suffolk*, pp. 208–10.

199. TNA CP40/466, 483, 541, 555.

200. Reproduced in Powell, *Rising in East Anglia*, pp. 64–6.

201. A list of demands made by London rebels was found in the possession of a Suffolk man in the aftermath of the revolt, Andrew Prescott, 'Writing about rebellion: using the records of the Peasants' Revolt of 1381', *History Workshop Journal*, 45 (1998), pp. 13–14.

202. Labour services were also the source of dispute in November 1385 on a nearby manor, CPR, 1385–8, p. 88.

203. For example, Massingberd, *Ingoldmells*, pp. 180–1, 185–6; Holmes, *Higher nobility*, pp. 128–9; Fryde, 'Peasant rebellion', p. 764. The highest recorded rate of servile out migration from Coltishall and Martham date from the 1370s and 1380s, Campbell, 'Population pressure', p. 100.

204. Bailey, *Decline of serfdom*, pp. 141, 182–4, 191–2, 203, 209–12, 226–30, 268–9, 273–4, 279, 281. See also, King, 'Tenant farming and farmers: East Midlands', p. 631.

205. TNA DL43/14/3.

206. Bailey, *Decline of serfdom*, figs. 10.5, 10.13, pp. 176, 190.

207. In 1379–80 68% of week works were unavailable because of conversions to leasehold, 15% were used, and 79% of harvest works were unavailable for the same reason and the rest were used, SROB E3/15.3/2.11.

208. Bailey, *Decline of serfdom*, pp. 182–3, 191.

209. Campbell, 'The land', pp. 224–5.

210. With one limited exception. In 1389 John atte Hill was threatened with a 100s. fine if he failed to track down the flown John Page, and the latter did indeed render chevage the following year, SROB E3/15.10/1.19, courts held November 1389 and October 1390.

211. Bailey, *Decline of serfdom*, pp. 179–83, 188–92, 194–5.

212. Phillipp R. Schofield, 'Lordship and the peasant economy, c.1250–c.1400: Robert Kyng and the Abbot of Bury St Edmunds', in Dyer et al., eds., *Rodney Hilton's Middle Ages*, pp. 53–68. Schofield uses the case to make a general point about the political nature of feudal rent, although, given the knowledge of the local context, it might be re-interpreted as an exceptional case.

213. UC, Bacon Ms 28. An entry in the manorial court roll records the existence of the charter of manumission, not the charter itself or the size of the fine paid to acquire it. Henry does not otherwise feature in the Redgrave court rolls, so he was not living on the manor. In these circumstances, John must have been moving to protect his son's future, and his insistence on having the existence of the charter noted formally in the court roll offered a layer of protection against its future loss or targeting of Henry.

214. The policy was not pursued on the cellarer's manors of Great Barton and Fornham St Martin; see Bailey, *Decline of serfdom*, p. 271, and also SROB E18/151/1 and 2, and SROB E3/15.9/1.5. Nine full courts have survived for the cellarer's manor of Little Barton between 1377 and 1384, where not a single case of millsuit, merchet, heriot, chevage, leywite, or even presentment for absence is recorded: there is a single amercement for marrying without licence, SROB E7/24/1.3.

215. Robert S. Gottfried, *Bury St Edmunds and the urban crisis 1290–1539* (Princeton, 1982), pp. 231–5; Chick, '1381 Rising', pp. 39–40.

216. See, for example, the manors of Debach, Drinkstone, High Hall, Holywell, Radclive, Runton Hayes, Walsham, High Hall, Bailey, *Decline of serfdom*, pp. 111–16, 129–30, 259.

217. Dyer estimates 200,000 serfs, which, given the estimate of 2.5m population from the poll taxes, is 25% of the total population, Dyer, 'Villeins, bondsmen', p. 433; Campbell, 'Factor markets', p. 82. See also, Razi, 'Myth', p. 39.

218. TNA DL43/14/3.

219. It is possible that the document omitted to record serfs on some of the manors where extents are provided due to scribal carelessness. For example, no serfs are recorded on the manor of Lidgate (Suffolk), though court rolls dating from the late 1390s reveal a handful of serfs on the manor, Bailey, *Decline of serfdom*, p. 269. But this is unlikely to have been a major omission, given the care with which serfs were recorded in many places and the importance of this information to the construction of the manorial extents. A further *c.*20 manors are recorded in the document beyond the sample used here, but no detailed extent is provided and therefore they were omitted from these calculations.

220. Bailey, *Decline of serfdom*, pp. 279–80.

221. Tuck, 'Nobles, commons', pp. 209–19.

222. Fryde, 'Peasant rebellion', p. 784; Edward M. Thompson, ed., *Chronicon Angliae* (London: Rolls Series, 1874), p. 316; Tuck, 'Nobles, commons', pp. 209–10.

223. Clark, 'Long march', p. 117. See Fryde, 'Peasant rebellion', p. 792, and Farmer, 'Prices and wages', pp. 489–90.

224. Kenyon, 'Labour conditions', pp. 92–4, 98–9.

225. Fryde, 'Peasant rebellion', p. 784.

226. Given-Wilson, 'Problem of labour', p. 87; McIntosh, *Controlling misbehaviour*, pp. 97–106; Musson, 'Reconstructing', p. 112.

227. Musson, 'Reconstructing', p. 115; Bailey, 'Peasants and the Great Revolt', pp. 177–82.

228. *PROME, volume V, Edward III 1351–1377*, p. 211; Bridbury, *English economy*, p. 33.

229. *PROME, volume V, Edward III 1351–1377*, pp. 264, 337–40.

230. *PROME, volume V, Edward III 1351–1377*, pp. 337–40. 211. Given-Wilson, 'Problem of Labour', pp. 88–9. In 1374 the bishop of Ely had required his serfs of Brandon to swear fealty and not to leave the vill without permission, Muller, 'Conflict', p. 8.

231. *PROME, volume VI, Richard II 1377–1384*, p. 342; *Statutes of the Realm, II*, pp. 32–3; Farmer, 'Prices and wages', p. 486; McIntosh, *Controlling misbehaviour*, pp. 89–90, 130. The word *vacabunus* is used only once—in the mid-1370s—in the extant JP and King's bench rolls for Lincolnshire, Sillem, *Some sessions*, p. 241.

232. Given-Wilson, 'Service, serfdom', pp. 23–4. *PROME, volume VI, Richard II 1377–1385*, p. 47; *PROME, volume VII, Richard II 1385–1397*, pp. 23, 218–19; *PROME, volume VIII, Henry IV 1399–1413*, p. 189. The 1399 petition does not appear in the recent versions of PROME but is documented in J. Strachey, ed., *Rotuli Parliamentorum*, volume III, (London, 1783), p. 448.

233. Given-Wilson, 'Service, serfdom', p. 23; *Statutes of the Realm*, vol. II, p. 38; *PROME, volume VII, Richard II 1385–1397*, p. 23.

234. *PROME, volume VII, Richard II 1385–1397*, p. 218–19; Given-Wilson, 'Service, serfdom', p. 24.

235. *PROME volume VII, Richard II 1385–1397*, p. 213.

236. Hatcher, 'England in the Aftermath', pp. 13–19, 32; Ann Middleton, 'Acts of vagrancy in the C version autobiography and the Statute of 1388', in Steven Justice and Kathryn Kerby-Fulton, eds., *Written work: Langland, labour and authorship* (Philadelphia, 1997), pp. 208–17; Anne P. Baldwin, *The theme of government in Piers Plowman*

(Cambridge, 1981), pp. 356–63; Derek Pearsall, '*Piers Plowman* and the Problem of Labour', in Rothwell et al., eds., *Problem of Labour*, 127–32; Bennett, 'Compulsory Service', pp. 26–8; Bailey, 'Ploughman', pp. 360–7; Bailey, 'Peasants and the Great Revolt', pp. 180–2.

237. Musson, 'Reconstructing', p. 115.
238. Bridbury, *English economy*, p. 209.
239. Campbell, *Great transition*, pp. 344–5, 378, 388.

7

The Decline of Serfdom and the Origins of the 'Little Divergence'

Introduction: the Black Death and the 'Little Divergence'

As we saw in Chapter 1, many historians and economists now argue that the age of the Black Death—defined expansively as the era of the second pandemic between the mid-fourteenth and the early eighteenth centuries—was a period of momentous change in the economic, social, and institutional history of Europe, when parts of north-west Europe took a clear lead on the road to modernity ahead of the rest of the continent.[1] The epidemics of the mid-fourteenth century led to different economic outcomes across the continent, but many of its peoples enjoyed an increase in real wages and GDP per capita to varying degrees in the late fourteenth and fifteenth centuries. However, these gains largely disappeared across most of the continent in the sixteenth and seventeenth centuries when population eventually recovered. In contrast, in a few regions of north-west Europe, such as the Netherlands and England, real wages declined less and so opened up a gap in average incomes within Europe: the so-called 'Little Divergence'.[2] Real wages have long been deployed as the principal measure of economic performance, but recently econometricians have developed a range of other salient measures, such as GDP per capita, household incomes from annual contracts, urbanization rates, and agricultural productivity. These, too, confirm that the seventeenth century was the key period when a yawning gap in economic performance opened between these areas of north-west Europe and the rest of the continent.[3]

The Little Divergence occurred because of a complex combination of changes and forces that evolved over a long period of time. The main variables—not in any particular order—were agricultural changes leading to higher levels of productivity, such as the land/labour ratio, the balance between livestock and grain production, and farm structure and size; the size and dominance of intercontinental trade; high investment in labour-saving and expensive capital goods; the replacement of manorial lordship with market institutions more favourable to labour and more conducive to productivity gains; the rise of representative government; the development of a culture in which material self-interest was regarded positively;

After the Black Death: Economy, Society, and the Law in Fourteenth-Century England. Mark Bailey, Oxford University Press (2021). © Mark Bailey. DOI: 10.1093/oso/9780198857884.003.0007

and the accumulation of human capital.[4] The relative importance of these explanatory variables is a matter of on-going debate.

The debate over the Little Divergence has transformed the discipline of economic history in the past two decades, although it raises almost as many challenges and questions as it answers. It relies a great deal upon the construction of aggregate data for key indices of economic performance over large areas and over long periods but, inevitably, such estimates vary markedly according to the quality of the data, the size of the sample, and the underlying assumptions about key imponderables. For example, estimates of annual English household incomes fluctuate significantly depending upon whether they derive from daily real wages, annual contracts, or output-based estimates of GDP per capita.[5] Likewise, Pamuk and Allen estimate independently that the urbanization ratio of England nearly doubled between 1300 and 1400, in contrast to Malanima who estimates that it fell by almost one-half: meanwhile, the consensus among English medievalists is that it remained constant or rose marginally.[6] The manifold difficulties of quantifying the main indicators of economic performance are equally (if not more) apparent in attempts to quantify the extent and chronology of changes in the various explanatory factors. How, for example, to measure the accumulation of human knowledge? The methodological problems of rising to these challenges explain some of the very different conclusions that emerge when deploying different measures for the same phenomenon. For example, Allen concluded on one set of statistical measures that intercontinental trade was the most significant influence on economic progress, while literacy (human knowledge) and representative government were unimportant, whereas de Pleijt and van Zanden concluded from a different set of measures that trade was less important, but literacy and government were more so.[7]

Even if we were to reach agreement about the level, direction, and differences in economic trends between countries, and even if we were able to construct reliable data series for the main explanatory variables (such as human capital formation), establishing a clear causal relationship between them would still remain a formidable challenge. First, establishing a positive correlation between a given trend and particular variable does not mean that a causal relationship exists. Second, isolating individual variables is difficult because many of them are interlinked and interdependent.[8] For example, agricultural productivity interconnects closely with the urbanization rate and extent of non-agricultural employment because the proportion of people earning a living in towns, industry, or services is dependent upon the capacity of the agricultural sector to feed them. Finally, the forces driving gains within any given variable are numerous and complex, and therefore difficult to untangle and isolate. Hence, increases in agricultural productivity were caused by, inter alia, changes in product and factor prices, enclosures, farm size and structure, tenures, market integration, and capital investment, although the relative importance of these and other forces varied over time and place. Indeed, it may be that the relative importance of each differed from country to country, and that no one broad explanatory model fits all.[9] In the ambitious and laudatory quest to explain the Little Divergence, and the understandable desire to cut through detail and the atypical, it is deceptively easy to slip into overgeneralizations and oversimplifications of the nature of key institutional arrangements, and also of complexity of the relationships between and within trends and variables.[10]

To some extent, a gap is growing between econometricians who input macro-level data into mathematical models in search of the big picture and historians who conduct micro-level, empirical case studies. If we are not careful, scepticism about the quality of the data being fed into statistical models, and about the lack of precision and understanding of the nature of institutional changes in different countries, will expand the gap between historians and econometricians. A closer dialogue between the two approaches, and more comparative studies, will greatly aid the reconstruction and understanding of the key institutional changes in the wake of plague.[11] The priorities of econometricians should be more influential in directing historical research, including collaborative ventures to generate more reliable data and to quantify key trends as far as the sources will allow. Historians have been slow to respond to these needs, not least historians of medieval England, who until recently had not seriously attempted to quantify key developments such as the proportion of non-agricultural employment or the rate of decline of serfdom.[12] Equally, the knowledge of historians should better direct the theorizing and judgements of econometricians because only careful empirical investigation can reconstruct the key institutional differences between countries and the linkages between economic progress and specific institutional changes.[13] Describing institutional arrangements accurately and fully is essential to undertaking effective and reliable comparisons across time and pace, and is only possible through detailed—and properly directed and informed—historical research.[14]

The various indicators of long-term economic progress across Europe point to three consistent characteristics of England's performance. First, on the eve of the Black Death estimates for GDP per capita, real wages, urbanization, and agricultural productivity indicate that, in European terms, England was not a leader economically or socially.[15] Second, by every indicator it emerged as a leading performer within Europe in the seventeenth and eighteenth centuries.[16] Finally, even though it emerged late in the race, England was the only European country to exhibit consistent growth across all the main indicators of development between c.1300 and c.1800.[17] To what extent, then, did developments in the wake of the epidemic of 1348–9 contribute to England's march to modernity? After all, urban real wage data from England first show signs of moving ahead of those from southern Europe during the course of the fifteenth century, which indicate that some institutional changes of significance were already in motion.[18] Indeed, Britnell—the leading historian of commerce in medieval England—argued that most of the key institutional features underpinning Britain's precocious economic development in the sixteenth and seventeenth centuries were already in place by c.1500.[19] What were they, and what was the role of the Black Death?

In attempting to answer these questions, we have consciously restricted the time span of our inquiry to the second half of the fourteenth century in order to identify the most distinctive short- and medium-term responses to the initial, sudden, and dramatic demographic decline. Clearly, in 1400 England's economy was neither prominent in European terms nor in any sense modern, so any changes that had occurred were not in themselves sufficient to alter radically its economic and social paradigm. By narrowing the chronology, by reconstructing more precisely and accurately the institutional arrangements governing factor and commodity markets, and by charting subsequent changes, we can identify more accurately the key developments in some of the main variables driving economic performance. In particular, how quickly and how far were the pre-plague obstacles to growth within factor and commodity markets reduced?[20] This exercise in quantitative empiricism can then provide a benchmark for comparative studies with both early modern England and other areas of late-medieval Europe. It will also provide a more secure chronology for identifying when specific institutional changes occurred, and for better evaluating how the pre-conditions to England's later divergent surge were shaped. Hence we have sought to reconstruct the key institutional features in the organization of England's land, labour, capital, and basic commodity markets on the eve of the Black Death, thereby creating a benchmark from which to reconstruct and chart the main contours of change by the 1390s. Chapters 2 to 6 have comprehensively reassessed the short and medium impact of the Black Death in England through a thorough re-examination of the established historiography and new archival research. In this chapter, we pull together the main themes and assess their significance for the wider debates about the decline of serfdom and the origins of the Little Divergence.

Institutional Change after the Black Death

Both Campbell and Pamuk have speculated that after the Black Death some institutional changes occurred quickly in England, which in turn must have had their roots in the pre-plague period, without elucidating the point.[21] Their instincts are surely correct. In the 1340s the land, labour, petty commodity, and capital markets had grown large enough, and their operation had become sufficiently protected by a relatively standardized and independent legal system, not just to survive the onslaught of plague but also to enable the forces of supply and demand thereafter to become increasingly influential in determining their allocation. The pre-existing weaknesses of manorial lordship also help to explain why post-plague institutional change occurred rapidly. The nature of that change was momentous, in the sense that it accelerated the end of villeinage and laid the foundations for future efficiency gains that ultimately enabled English society to avoid falling into another dire Malthusian trap when population rose again in the sixteenth century.

Five key institutional changes are identifiable between the 1340s and c.1400: a marked and sustained rise in GDP her head; sectoral shifts in the economy; relatively high levels of non-agricultural employment; the decline of villeinage; and the expansion of contractual tenures. We deal with each of these changes below. To begin, however, we should explain the most prominent *omission* from this list: the European Marriage Pattern (EMP).

The EMP has attracted a great deal of attention from econometricians seeking to identify the key features of the Little Divergence. It describes a dominant demographic system in which the average age of women at first marriage was relatively late and a relatively high proportion of women did not marry, causing fertility rates and family size to be low by the standards of pre-industrial societies. Consequently, productivity gains were translated into higher annual incomes instead of a larger population. The system was certainly in place at the end of the sixteenth century, when the available evidence shows clearly that women in England and Germany were marrying in their mid-20s on average and between 15 per cent to 20 per cent never married. Some historians have argued that it emerged in the aftermath of the first epidemic in the North Sea region, but not elsewhere.[22] Voigtlander and Voth even claim this to be a consensus view among medieval historians, because environmental conditions here were well suited to the types of pastoral produce suddenly in demand among the survivors of plague, and English landlords in particular responded by expanding their commercial sheep and cattle rearing activities. They argue that seigniorial pastoral enterprises depended heavily on single female servants on annual contracts, and were large enough to draw a sizeable proportion of young women into the labour market, driving a rise in the average age of women at first marriage (by perhaps four years) and in the proportion of those opting not to marry.[23] In a similar vein, De Moor and van Zanden have argued that the general increase in women's wages and employment opportunities after the Black Death incentivized women to defer marriage.[24] The result was a fall in fertility rates. The economic significance of this became fully apparent when population rose again in the early modern period, because the lower fertility regime translated to higher incomes and consumption per capita under a high demographic pressure in north-west Europe, whereas other parts of Europe were still caught in a Malthusian trap. This particular response to the Black Death—the rise of 'Girl Power'—is deemed a watershed event in world history because it formed new patterns of behaviour that fundamentally changed household formation, marriage patterns, and by extension demographic structure.[25]

This powerful, influential, and popular thesis is, however, the subject of intense debate. Voigtlander and Voth's claim that a scholarly consensus exists on the emergence of the EMP after the Black Death in north-west Europe is neither an accurate nor fair reflection of the views of English historians on the subject.[26] The latter agree broadly that the aristocracy and gentry tended to marry earlier than the peasantry, that migratory service and employment could delay female marriage, and that considerable variety (regional, personal, positional) existed in marriage patterns.[27] Otherwise, there is little agreement on the nature of the dominant demographic structure of late-medieval England. For example, Judith Bennett has shown that all the main characteristics of the EMP were observable as early as the thirteenth century among the rural poor in the densely populated Lincolnshire silt fens, so not only does it pre-date plague but it was a consequence of dire poverty, not of expanding employment opportunities.[28] Goldberg and Poos showed that after 1348–9 delayed marriage and non-marrying females became a discernible feature of rural Essex and the urban north, but others have disputed the scale and typicality of these developments.[29] So delayed age at marriage, and a rising proportion of never marrying females, were certainly features of some places and social groups both before and after the Black Death, but this does not mean that the EMP had yet emerged as a widespread and enduring demographic *system* in England.

There is simply no consensus on when the characteristics of the EMP became sufficiently widespread to be regarded as the dominant system in England.[30] Historians such as Benedictow, Foreman-Peck, and Zhou agree that the EMP emerged when the late-medieval regime of persistently high mortality rates finally eased, but they propose very different dates for when this happened. Benedictow and others suggest the second quarter of the sixteenth century, citing the evidence of changing mortality and fertility rates from parish registers, whereas Foreman-Peck and Zhou's theoretical models of simulated and observed demographic data point to the second quarter of the fifteenth century.[31] The reason for the lack of consensus is simple: there is no reliable evidence for the age of marriage prior to the survival of parish registers in the sixteenth century, so we cannot know the extent to which the EMP did or did not exist. Medievalists have tried to wring reliable data out of fragmentary medieval sources and failed. As there is no evidence that can ever answer this question reliably, it will remain a source of controversy.[32]

While the debate may be irresolvable, it is possible to assess the quality of the evidence used to promote some of the lines of argument within it. Voigtlander and Voth argue that a major driver behind the emergence of the EMP after 1350 was the increased reliance of English landlords upon live-in—and therefore single—female servants to operate their expanded and large-scale pastoral enterprises, but their assertions are not supported by credible evidence on the ground.[33] Many landlords were not directly involved in livestock rearing, but instead leased their pastures, herds, and flocks to yeomen or gentry farmers. Where landlords did retain a direct interest, then they tended to concentrate upon sheep and cattle rearing, and perhaps some rabbit and pig keeping, none of which required live-in female servants. The types of commercial pastoral production that did require daily inputs of labour—dairying and poultry rearing—were largely the preserve of the peasantry, who could deploy family including child labour for such tasks as required and so minimized the need for live-in servants. So whilst commercial pastoral operations were a strong feature of post-plague England, they were not wholly or even substantially dependent upon single female servanthood.[34]

The argument that women entered the labour market in droves as single servants in preference to operating as married (or indeed single) day labourers also implies that servanthood was remunerated attractively, but recent research on day rates and annual contracts for women has revealed that neither rose dramatically and that the latter was less generously remunerated.[35] Humphries and Weisdorf show that mean day rates for women rose from 1.2d. in the 1340s to 2.2d. in the 1360s, and 2.72d. in the 1390s, whereas the equivalent rates for women earning board and lodging on annual contracts were 0.97d. per diem in the 1340s, 1.23d. in the 1360s, then 0.97d. in the 1390s.[36] Since women's work in servanthood was poorly remunerated compared with day rates, it was less likely to have exerted such a strong incentive for young women to enter the labour market. This may explain why the proportion of recorded servants in some pastoral districts—such as the far north of England—was very low.[37] Indeed, we estimate that in the 1390s around 15 per cent of all labour was absorbed in servanthood, of which perhaps just under half of all servants were women.[38] This argument also underplays the ease and attractions to young people of acquiring land, marrying early, and seeking paid employment within marriage. Thus it is arguable that neither the availability of work in servanthood nor its levels of remuneration was sufficiently high in the late fourteenth century to attract a significant proportion of young single women.

The argument that the EMP became quickly established as the dominant demographic system in post-plague England is therefore reliant upon debatable *a priori* economic arguments, not on any hard demographic evidence that it existed. The turbulence of the post-plague period created demographic cross-currents whose relative strengths are impossible for the historian to measure accurately. Mortality rates rose, and remained higher than pre-plague, but how long did they persist and to what extent did fertility rates creep up over time? If chronic shortages of land and work in the pre-plague era had created poverty so dire that it delayed or prevented household formation in some communities, then the improved availability of land and work in the post-plague period should have encouraged household formation, earlier marriage of women, a higher proportion of married women, and a consequent boost to fertility rates.[39] Indeed, there is evidence for a marriage boom, and perhaps a baby boom, in the 1350s.[40] The

290 AFTER THE BLACK DEATH

second plague epidemic of 1361–2 certainly thwarted any immediate demographic recovery, but what then happened? Did England settle into a demographic regime of high mortality and high fertility—and no population growth—until the sixteenth century?[41] Or were there two late-medieval demographic regimes, the first between the 1370s and 1450s, and the second between the 1460s and 1540s?[42] In the first phase, mortality rates rose and fertility rates fell, the latter due to the changing patterns of women's work and/or the age-specific mortality in the second epidemic which had skewed the age distribution of the population towards the elderly.[43] In the second phase, mortality rates rose even further and fertility rates drifted upwards. The evidentiary base simply will not permit definitive answers to these possibilities and questions.

The debate over the EMP exemplifies the wider challenges within the divergence debate presented by the variable quality of data and the difficulties of isolating causation. The available evidence confirms that the EMP existed in England by the mid-sixteenth century, but there is no evidence to determine reliably or definitively when it emerged before that date as the dominant demographic form. Without certain knowledge of when it emerged, we cannot be certain why it emerged. This has led to contradictory lines of argument: land and labour shortages in the pre-plague era discouraged early marriage, whereas their abundance in the post-plague era had the same—not the opposite—effect. Furthermore, even if we are able to establish the existence of the EMP in late-medieval England, scholarly opinion differs sharply on its significance. Edwards, Ogilvie, and Dennison doubt whether the EMP was a significant element in divergent, long-term economic growth—pointing to its presence in slow-growing and less progressive European economies—and argue that the reasons for the Little Divergence are to be found instead in regional differences in non-familial institutions.[44] Foreman-Peck and Zhou agree that the EMP was not of itself a sufficient condition for divergence, although they suggest that it did contribute to the superior development of human capital in north-west Europe.[45] The debate shows little sign of abating.

We can now turn to the five major institutional changes identifiable by c.1400.

Output per head

Output per head rose immediately after the Black Death, by perhaps 25 per cent, and by the 1390s estimated GDP per head was around 40 per cent higher than it had been in the 1340s (fig. 4.1).[46] Annual incomes estimated from day rates (based on 250 days' work per annum) also soared in the 1350s, and by the 1390s were around double the level of the 1340s.[47] The initial gains in the 1350s were mainly due to the greater availability of work and land, and received a further boost from the 1370s by gains in the purchasing power of wages.[48] The proportion of landless and those living on or below the poverty line fell, although it is impossible to be exact about the extent: one plausible estimate suggests it fell from c.40 per cent in the 1340s to c.15 per cent in the 1390s.[49] Proponents of the golden age of the peasantry contend that the gains in annual incomes and output per head continued to rise until the mid-fifteenth century before declining with renewed population growth in the sixteenth. However, there is powerful evidence—from, for example, sectoral output and wage rates calculated from annual contracts—that they had reached a plateau around 1400, then in the sixteenth century they did not fall as steeply as other parts of Europe.[50] The rise in GDP per head in England after 1349 contrasts with the experience of Spain, where in the wake of demographic collapse a fragile commercial infrastructure fragmented and income per head fell.[51] During the third quarter of the century England's GDP per head rose above that of Italy for the first time.[52] The uplift did not match the levels of GDP per head attained in parts of the Low Countries at the same time, however, so while England was now moving up the league table of European economic performance, it was not yet a major force.[53]

Sectoral shifts within the economy

The increase in incomes per head and the reduction in wealth inequality increased the consumption of better-quality foodstuffs and household goods among the lower orders of society, which in turn triggered three significant and permanent changes in the structure of the English economy. The first was a shift within agriculture from an emphasis upon cereal production towards pastoral pursuits. According to one estimate, the livestock share of agriculture rose from c.40 per cent in the 1270s to c.51 per cent in the 1350s, to c.54 per cent in the 1400s: this contrasts with modern India, where the figure is closer to 20 per cent.[54] The second major shift was from agriculture to industrial production, mainly in textiles and household utensils, and in services, such as ale production and retailing. Industrial output per head was an estimated 64 per cent higher at the start of the fifteenth century than it had been a century earlier.[55] In 1381 agriculture comprised an estimated 45 per cent of English GDP, industry 29 per cent, and services 26 per cent (fig. 7.1).

These figures are, of course, estimates, and they mark the maximum extent of such developments by 1381 (pp. 249–51), but there is no doubting that the swing away from agriculture was a feature of the English experience. This development was also associated with the greater dependency of ordinary people upon the market for some subsistence commodities (bread and ale) and for cheap non-subsistence goods. Before the Black Death these had usually been produced either in the home or by local generalists, but afterwards they were increasingly supplied by specialists, many of them working some distance from the place of purchase

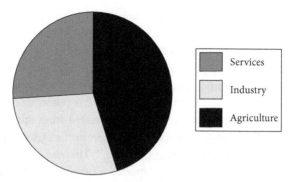

Figure 7.1 Estimated sectoral composition of the English economy in 1381 as a percentage of GDP
Source: Broadberry et al. 2015, table 5.01

and consumption. It is striking how quickly these changes occurred, as exemplified by the contents of the 1363 sumptuary legislation, and the rapid expansion and commercialization of textile manufacture and rabbit rearing during the course of the 1350s and 1360s. Demand rose sharply in such sectors, and elicited prompt supply-side responses, which proves that both labour and capital could be transferred swiftly into those industrial and pastoral activities where both inputs of capital and levels of technical skill were relatively modest. It also serves as a reminder of the relative freedom and flexibility of the labour market when plague first struck. The growth of commercial activity in such sectors also came to be associated with changes to the systems of industrial production, such as the emergence of clothiers deploying an outwork system to control the quality of cloths destined for the export market.[56]

In the second half of the fourteenth century London was also growing in relative importance, as evidenced by the buoyancy of its economy, its growing control of England's overseas trade, and its surges of immigration.[57] The extent of that growth between *c.*1340 and *c.*1400 is impossible to measure quantitatively, although between the tax assessments of 1334 and 1515 London's share had increased from 2 per cent to 9 per cent of the country's assessable wealth.[58] London had certainly come to dominate England's overseas trade by 1400.[59] In the pre-plague era the demand generated by London for food and fuel had already begun to shape agricultural production strategies throughout the Home Counties and East Anglia, although after 1349 the reduction in population and rising transport costs caused the size of the regular provisioning zone for grain and fuel to shrink.[60] Yet the supply lines to the city restructured as well as contracted, due to Londoners' increased per capita and changing consumption patterns of foodstuffs and essential goods. By the end of the century the dramatic rise in the consumption of ale, for example, had increased the percentage of malting grains sown and the proportion sold on demesnes in London's broad hinterland, and supplies came increasingly from the counties located to the north and west of the city, as far as Huntingdonshire and Oxfordshire.[61] Similarly, the capital's demand for pastoral produce strengthened a long supply chain of livestock, stretching to Wales and to south-west and north-west England. The towns and fairs heavily involved in this trade—such as Birmingham, Coventry (both Warks.) and Bishop's Stortford (Herts.)—show signs of prosperity.[62] By c.1400 Londoners were trading with these areas more frequently.[63] They were also investing in land in rural areas at greater distances from the capital.[64] In other words, the growing relative importance of London deepened economic linkages between the capital and far-flung regions, many of them marginal for grain production.[65] These important changes were to become even more pronounced over the next three centuries.[66]

These sectoral shifts carried real significance for the long-term development of the English economy. First, the dynamism of the pastoral sector and the strengthening of inter-regional trade in its produce increased the degree of market dependence and integration across the country.[67] Second, in the pre-plague era the density of taxpayers and assessable wealth was concentrated mainly to the south and east of a line between the rivers Severn and Humber.[68] The swing towards pastoral and industrial specialisms occurred predominantly in areas outside this zone, especially the south-west, the west Midlands, and Yorkshire.[69] It therefore stimulated a redistribution of regional wealth and population density. The speed of change is apparent from the shifting geographical distribution of taxpayers towards the north and the south-west of England, and to the textile areas of south Suffolk and north Essex, between the 1332 lay subsidy and the 1377 poll tax (fig. 7.2).[70] The relative shift of population towards north-west and south-west England continued further between 1377 and the sixteenth century (fig. 7.3).[71] Similarly, significant changes in the regional distribution of assessable wealth are evident between the Lay Subsidy of 1334 and that of 1524, with marked relative gains in the industrialized and pastoral areas of the south-west, south, and north (fig. 7.4).[72] In other words, wealth and people became more equitably distributed across England in the wake of plague, which meant that, when population began to rise again in the sixteenth century, the spatial distribution of demand and consumption was more even than it had been in the early fourteenth century. Consequently, in 1400 the economy was less two-paced and imbalanced than it had been in 1300. The combination of higher wealth per head, greater economic diversification, and greater regional diversity and specialization combined to reduce the dependence upon the staple product of grain, thus reducing susceptibility to future growth reversals and harvest failures.[73]

Non-agricultural employment

The third major change after the Black Death was an increase in non-agricultural employment.[74] Two different methods of calculating the share of non-agricultural employment from the poll tax returns of 1381 have both concluded that around

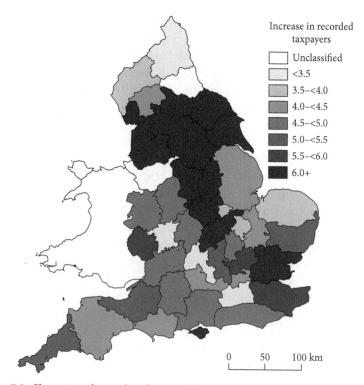

Increase in recorded
taxpayers

☐ Unclassified
☐ <3.5
☐ 3.5–<4.0
☐ 4.0–<4.5
☐ 4.5–<5.0
☐ 5.0–<5.5
☐ 5.5–<6.0
☐ 6.0+

0   50   100 km

Figure 7.2 Changing relative distribution of English taxpayers, 1332 to 1377
Source: Campbell and Bartley 2006, map 18.11

57 per cent of the labour force was employed in agriculture, 19 per cent industry, and 24 per cent services (fig. 7.5).[75] We have no comparable source to enable measurement of how far these proportions had changed since the 1340s, but the widespread evidence for industrial growth in various localities and expanding employment opportunities from the 1350s confirms that the Black Death must have accelerated the swing away from agriculture and increased the frequency and reliability of non-agricultural work. Indeed, the government's revision of its labour legislation in 1388 attempted to restrict any further movement by prohibiting children who had worked in agriculture from then transferring into a trade. The estimate of 43 per cent of the labour force in non-agricultural employment is a highly distinctive feature of the English economy by the standards of pre-industrial Europe because as late as 1700 the comparable figure was merely c.20 per cent–30 per cent in Finland, Poland, Bohemia, and many parts of eastern Europe.[76] This calculation for England should be regarded as the maximum extent of non-agricultural employment in the 1380s, and may be overgenerous, but the important point is that a substantial swing to non-agricultural employment had already become a distinctive feature of its economy. It explains the precocity of

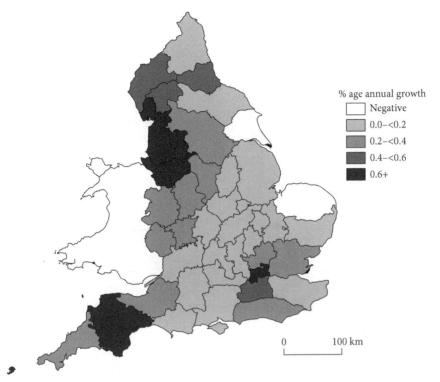

Figure 7.3 Changing relative distribution of the population in England, 1377 and 1600
Source: Broadberry et al. 2015, fig. 1.03

English commercialization, even though levels of urbanization remained relatively low until the seventeenth century.[77]

These comparisons reinforce the point that the labour market in England was already relatively large on the eve of the Black Death and it had grown even further by the end of the century. Labour services continued to decline after 1348–9 (fig. 7.6), so that by *c*.1400 less than 5 per cent of all expended labour was coerced, an estimated 55 per cent was self-employed on the holding or in the household (including leisure), and *c*.40 per cent was hired (of which, perhaps 25 per cent in waged labour and 15 per cent in annual servanthood).[78] Most labourers were also smallholders who sought paid work as a supplement to their own activities and who could turn their hands to a variety of tasks: there was not yet a rural proletariat of landless wage labourers seeking work on large commercial farms.[79] These proportions disguise the fact that the lower orders now exercised much greater choice over how and where to expend their labour, and that hired work was more readily available, compared with the 1340s (see fig. 2.1). It also ignores the intervention of the government in attempting to regulate the hired market after 1349.

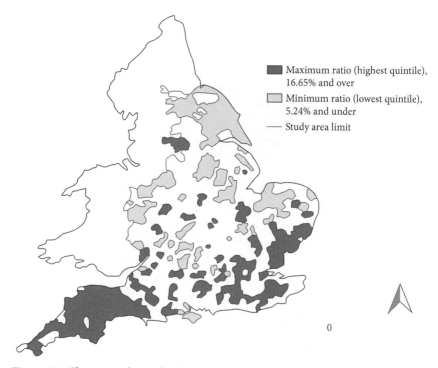

Figure 7.4 Changing relative distribution of taxable wealth in England, 1334 and 1524
Source: Campbell 1990, fig. 4.1

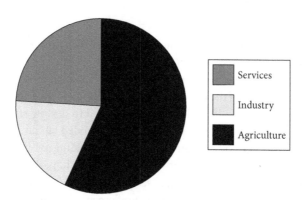

Figure 7.5 Sectoral share of employment in England in 1381 (%)
Source: Broadberry et al. 2015, fig. 5.02

Thus between the 1340s and the 1390s gains are demonstrable in output per head, annual incomes, the pastoral share of agriculture, the proportion of people in non-agricultural employment, and a more even spatial distribution of wealth and people. These changes strengthened England's comparative advantage in

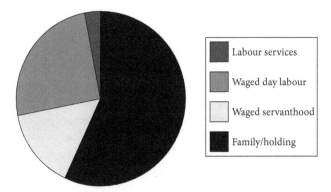

Figure 7.6 Estimated expenditure of productive labour in England, *c.*1390 (%)

pastoral pursuits and manufacturing, and increased the dependency of ordinary people on the market for basic consumption goods, both of which help to explain why England's urbanization rate did not fall after the Black Death.[80] Although that urbanization rate remained low by European standards until the seventeenth century, the precociousness of England's economic development owed much to the high proportion of the population in non-agricultural employment.[81] These represent permanent changes to the structure of the English economy and society. For example, the estimated livestock share of agriculture achieved in 1400 changed little for the next four centuries, and, similarly, the estimated size of the industrial sector, and of industrial output per head in 1400 did not change substantially until the late sixteenth century.[82] Likewise, analysis of the muster returns of the 1520s indicates that 58 per cent of the labour force was employed in agriculture, 23 per cent in industry, and 19 per cent in services, which hardly differs from the distributions calculated from the 1381 poll tax.[83] In other words, many of the major economic changes of long-term significance triggered by the Black Death had largely worked through the economy by 1400.

Decline of serfdom

The fourth major change was the rapid decline of villeinage. In the early 1350s a handful of powerful landlords adopted coercive policies to force villein tenants and hereditary serfs to hold land and remain on the manor, but such policies were exceptional, unsustainable, and soon abandoned. The forces of supply and demand quickly increased their influence in the dramatically changed land market, and the government did not attempt to intervene, because land was strictly a matter for lord and tenant under the common law. The state did intervene in the labour market through the Ordnance and Statute of Labourers, which applied equally to the free and the unfree, but the nature of its intervention confirms that seigniorial powers over labour were already weak and that hitherto regulation of the labour market had been minimal. While this ambitious legislation was highly inequitable and divisive, and transformed the role of the state from emergency regulator to standing authority in matters of social policy, its economic effectiveness was limited after the 1350s. The initial attempts of the state and manorial lords to seize control of the land and labour markets—control that they had not exerted in the 1340s—had failed within a few years of the first epidemic (pp. 79–112).

The personal and tenurial elements of villeinage declined precipitously in the second half of the fourteenth century. The proportion of the English population who were hereditary serfs declined from a maximum of c.40 per cent in the 1340s to between 25 per cent and 20 per cent in 1381, and perhaps as low as 10 per cent in 1400. Certainly, by the latter date the servile incidents levied upon the rapidly shrinking serf population had become markedly less burdensome. Leyrwite—a charge for illegitimacy—had virtually disappeared everywhere, special licences (to be educated, or to pursue a craft) were very rare, and merchet was much reduced in frequency.[84] Chevage survived as the most prominent and onerous incident, mainly because it served as a written proof of status and as an effective tracking device.[85] It perpetuated the dishonour and social stigma of personal servility, and enabled a handful of unscrupulous lords to make sudden and unwelcome demands for money from those flown serfs who had made their fortunes elsewhere.[86] However, even chevage had disappeared from a sizeable minority of manors by c.1400, and on many more the frequency was very low, with just a couple of cases a year.[87] The annual charge was a few pennies, too low to exert a brake on the mobility of the servile population, although sufficient to add to the costs of evading serfdom. In any case, many of the serfs who continued to pay chevage to their home manor chose to do so for a variety of personal reasons, including to retain an interest in a landed inheritance on their home manor.[88]

Villein tenure had undergone a dramatic transformation between the 1340s and 1390s. The received wisdom that it changed little until the 1380s then declined is no longer tenable. Conventional unfree service tenure—with a rent package comprised of labour services, tallage, heriot, millsuit, entry fine, payments in kind, and a fixed cash head rent—'was in headlong retreat from the 1350s, and had largely decayed by the 1380s, on all types of manors'.[89] Tallage, millsuit, labour services, entry fines, and merchet had either become much reduced or had disappeared entirely on this form of tenure.[90] Other measures further enhanced the attractiveness of unfree land to freemen and flown serfs, notably the removal of overtly servile language from conveyances and the issuing of copies of the court roll transfer to emulate the charter of free tenure.[91] A growing proportion of unfree land was converted from service tenures to either leaseholds for a commercial money rent, or hereditary or life tenures for a cash rent fixed at a commercial or quasi-commercial level at the time of the grant, plus an entry fine and often a heriot: a prototype copyhold.[92] The decline of tenurial and personal villeinage after 1348–9 occurred more quickly and extensively than traditionally portrayed. This is consistent with the arguments that villeinage was already weak on the eve of the Black Death; that the role of social conflict in liberating the land and labour markets has been overstated; and that serfdom was but one element in the Peasants' Revolt.

The decline of serfdom is usually linked to the rise of the state because a centralized authority has to displace the dwindling role of manorial lordship to provide the public goods of protection and justice.[93] As we have seen, after the Black Death the English Crown increased its regulatory profile and activity in the commodity and labour markets (pp. 77–83). Its initial attempts to control the labour market proved too ambitious, and subsequently had to be narrowed to a more pragmatic agenda, but the initial intervention established a precedent that was to shape governmental social policy for centuries.[94] The sharp expansion in governmental activity bestowed enhanced powers upon some members of the gentry (as justices) and of the upper ranks of the peasantry and urban society (as jurors and constables) as officials of the state. The government also dramatically increased the scale of direct and indirect taxation on the surviving population, effectively tripling the tax burden per head between the 1340s and 1370s. England had completed its transformation from a demesne state to fiscal state, deploying a mixture of sophisticated fiscal instruments to finance its activities.[95] The English state was strong enough to tax regularly, and to tax the nobility alongside the peasantry (including serfs), but only in return for political representation at parliament for the upper elements of the taxable population. Even then, taxation sparked revolt when running as high as $c.5$ per cent of GDP during the 1370s and when the competence and honesty of the government was suspect. These checks set limits to the state's fiscal powers, and it was not sufficiently strong to appropriate significant proportions of wealth through taxation.[96]

The increased scale of the English state's activity, its energy, and its greater reliance on lesser and (mainly) unpaid lay officials in the aftermath of the Black Death are remarkable. Palmer argues that the government's immediate responses to the Black Death were both ground-breaking and deliberate, because they conformed to a 'consistent policy line' and featured a range of innovations from new legal devices to the origins of chancery as an equity court. The cumulative effect was far-reaching, transforming English government from its feudal origins into 'one truly of inherent authority; legitimately competent and accustomed to handle generally the needs of a whole society'. As such, the Black Death 'generated agreement on the plenary extent of state authority and, in the law, set the structures and forms that would dominate Anglo-American law into the nineteenth century'.[97] Similarly, Michael Bennett states that 'under the long shadow of the Black Death some of the most distinctive features of the English constitutional and legal systems came to be firmly set in place'.[98] Other legal historians are more cautious, however, arguing that Palmer overstates both the novelty of the economic reforms and the importance of other post-plague legal developments.[99] Nevertheless, in the 1350s the centralization of justice and the increased scale of the government's interventions in the labour and commodity markets were major features of change. Nor should we underestimate the importance or novelty of the labour legislation. The government had not previously regulated the labour market, but thereafter it sought to determine social policy through regulating wage levels, contracts, labour mobility, and compulsory service.[100] While these policies did not significantly distort the operation of the labour market, they increased the costs and reduced the choices of some participants, increased the inequalities of treatment, and conditioned the behaviour of all participants. State interference in the labour market also contrasted with its absence from the land market.

Ironically, the most significant contribution of the English state to the profound social and economic changes of the fourteenth century pre-dated the arrival of plague, and it was not a deliberate or coherent act of policy. The most striking aspect of the 1350s and 1360s is the extent to which the radically changed forces of supply and demand influenced the allocation of resources in the land, labour, and commodity markets, and, in contrast, how limited were the coercive powers of manorial lordship when faced with the dramatic change in the land/labour ratio. This simply would not have been possible without the prior existence of the rudimentary framework of public and private 'contracting institutions' that provided some protection to key assets, such as land and goods, and also cheap and accessible means of dispute resolution, based on a common system of proofs, precedents, and fixed procedures.[101] This provision was an inadvertent by-product of the growth of royal justice and the common law from the late twelfth century because the success of the royal courts in generating business and revenues encouraged local and seigniorial courts to import many of their procedures and some of their business. This unanticipated process of emulation and assimilation had created a system of local tribunals deploying relatively standardized and consistent legal practices throughout England on the eve of plague, with the common law and the system of royal justice at its heart. Most ordinary peasants and townsfolk could therefore access a range of local legal tribunals for relatively cheap and effective petty dispute resolution and contract enforcement, reducing transaction costs and the risks of their participation in the land, labour, and commodity markets.[102] This system of contract enforcement was still uneven and inequitable, but it was more robust and standardized than in other European systems of serfdom, such as Russia.[103] As a result, by the standards of pre-modern systems, it provided 'reasonably good property rights and contract enforcement to rural people'.[104]

This legal framework was essential in determining the re-allocation of key resources in the wake of plague because it discouraged attempts at forced and arbitrary seizures of land, chattels, and body. Indeed, the use of more formal contracts in everyday life rose after 1349, and their precision improved. This was most evident in the land market (see above, pp. 90–6, and below, pp. 300–7), but the government's determination after 1351 to regulate breaches of contracts and modes of hiring of labour must have promoted greater contractual and procedural precision in the labour market. The main consequence of greater contractual rigour was to reduce the risks of participation in markets.

Contractual tenures

The structure of the tenancies that displaced traditional non-commercial tenures, and the extent to which they displaced them, during the second half of the fourteenth century carried significance for England's long-term economic development, although this important subject has received little detailed attention.[105] By the 1390s a larger proportion of agricultural land was held on either commercial or quasi-commercial head rents due to the conversion of some peasant land to contractual rents and the leasing of demesnes. In the 1340s over one half of all demesne land was in direct exploitation and the rest leased, but by 1400 the proportion leased had risen to at least three quarters.[106] Similarly, in the 1340s around 90 per cent of all peasant land was held on non-commercial tenancies (see p. 301), but by 1400 only a small majority of villein land remained on such tenures (albeit diluted) and a sizeable minority had been converted to either quasi-commercial head rents on hereditary/life tenancies or to commercial cash leaseholds (see pp. 300–7).[107] Consequently, we estimate that 20 per cent of all arable land in England was held on some form of contractual tenancy in the 1340s, which had risen to 45 per cent by the 1390s (fig. 7.7).[108] The 45 per cent of land on contractual rents comprised 33 per cent leases (mainly demesne, and some villein land) plus 12 per cent quasi-commercial head rents. The leasing of demesnes and the associated withdrawal of landlords from direct cultivation was never subsequently reversed, so that by the late fifteenth century the seigniorial class contributed little to English agricultural output and almost all demesne land had been permanently added to the peasant sector through leasehold.[109] As a consequence, the latter had become even more important as the source of commercial agricultural produce.

The erosion of non-commercial tenures after 1340 also had the effect of undoing much of the tenurial tangle that had been responsible for fragmenting holdings in the pre-plague era. The swing to commercial head rents discouraged subletting and fragmentation. Conveyances of villein land—whether contractual or the old non-commercial tenures—began to drop the vocabulary of servility, even though the land itself was still carefully identified as unfree or bond. As a wider range of tenures came to be used, so conveyances became more precise about the terms of the grant, detailing the number of years of the lease or whether

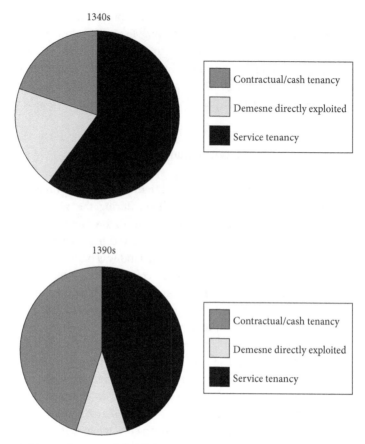

Figure 7.7 Tenurial status of arable land in England, 1340s and 1390s (%)

the grant was for lives or heritable. Some grants of small parcels of land contain more detail about their location and abuttals. The issue of a copy of the grant of a piece of unfree land recorded in the manorial court also became fashionable, so that references to 'copies' were more frequent in the second half of the century (although 'copyhold' was not yet in use).[110] Of course, fixed cash head rents on heritable and life tenures were not pure commercial tenancies, and there was still a long way to go before copyholds and leaseholds fully displaced villein tenure: leases would not dominate land tenures generally until the early seventeenth century.[111] Yet the changes in the second half of the fourteenth century represented a major and irreversible step forward, and a large minority of land was now held on commercial or quasi-commercial terms.[112]

The greater use of contractual tenures in the half century after 1350 also reduced some of the stigma and uncertainty associated with traditional villein tenure. Similarly, short-term leases increased the turnover, mobility, and flexibility of land transfer and acquisition, without the need for its sale or permanent alienation. These developments promoted a number of important changes to the character of the English land market. First, in the 1350s leases helped the poorer survivors of the plague to take their first step on the property ladder—a cottage and garden, a smallholding—without any sizeable pre-capital payment, and so greatly facilitated the fall in landlessness and the rapid rise in disposable incomes and purchasing power. Second, the variety of tenurial forms enhanced the scope for, and strategies available to, peasants to accumulate landholdings and to use land to store wealth and to provide for their families.[113] Third, leases offered peasants a way of acquiring land while mitigating the risk of such acquisition in a period of unprecedented turbulence and uncertainty. Fourth, they initially encouraged freemen, and later gentry, clerics and townsfolk, to acquire villein land, either to cultivate directly or increasingly as an investment.[114] Finally, they weakened the old link that had existed between a particular family and its landed holding, and contributed to the increased proportion of land transferred outside the family.[115] In short, the spread of more contractual tenures accelerated the commoditization of land as a marketable asset.

A further motive for acquiring land on leasehold was the opportunity it provided for individuals to consolidate and concentrate their landholdings in a particular area of the village fields. Large standardized customary holdings such as virgates and yardlands did not usually lie in a single block but comprised numerous small parcels scattered throughout the open fields. Consolidating some of those parcels would reduce the time spent shifting workers and equipment to cultivate detached and dispersed parcels of arable land, which carried clear benefits in an era of rising labour costs and uncertain or declining profits.[116] The process of consolidation and engrossment was slow and opportunity-led, because the chance to acquire the key land parcel may not have arisen for many years, and it is exceptionally difficult to illustrate because manorial documents do not often record the distribution of standardized villein holdings and the exact location of land parcels. But the process was more likely to accelerate in eras of slack demand for land, and on manors where lords were willing to break up standardized customary holdings to offer small individual parcels of land on contractual tenancies, or indeed to offer contiguous parcels of demesne land. The opportunities were greater in regions of irregular open field systems and enclosures, where land holdings tended to be comprised of larger parcels that were concentrated in a particular area of the village field system.[117] Consolidation of land parcels was also an important preliminary step to the enclosure of land in such regions.[118]

This process must have been the driver behind some of the acquisitions of small parcels of land on different tenancies in the late fourteenth century, but at this date the descriptions of land in manorial documents are not sufficiently precise to enable its reconstruction. By the fifteenth century, however, some manorial documents do provide fuller descriptions of abuttals of land held by the same tenant but on different tenures, which can reveal its scale and nature. For example, a rental of Fornham All Saints and Fornham St Martin (Suffolk) in 1459 (held by the abbey of Bury St Edmunds) details the location of all the land held by each tenant, whatever its status and its tenurial form, thus permitting a rare glimpse into the ways in which some had consolidated blocks of land on a variety of tenures. Fornham was situated in a region of irregular open fields, with an active land market including widespread leasing of single parcels of demesne and customary land.[119] The rental reveals how one tenant, Walter Spalding, held a customary messuage with a croft of five roods in the Weststreet of Fornham All Saints, together with a further 3½ acres of customary land in five parcels, 4½ acres of free land in two parcels, and 7½ acres of leased land (a mixture of demesne and customary land) in a croft and seven parcels. Therefore his holding totalled 16 acres 3 roods plus a croft, of which leases comprised 45 per cent of the arable, and the customary and leased lands were heavily concentrated in the irregular open fields around areas known as 'Daleway' and 'Galtonway' in the south-west of the parish. Of the six different parcels of customary land, five abutted either each other or land leased by Walter.[120] In other words, Walter was restructuring and reconfiguring his farming unit in one area of the village, and the numerous abuttals reveal that the holding was partially consolidated and engrossed. Similar traits are discernible in the construction of the holding of John Lunden, who held 5 acres 3 roods of free land (in eight parcels), an eight-acreware customary tenement containing 13 acres 3 roods in twelve parcels; 10 acres 2 roods of customary land at lease in five parcels, and a meadow at lease. The lands were located in the open fields to the south of Fornham All Saints, and the largest parcel of leased land abutted directly onto a parcel of John's own customary land in *le Hyde* to create a consolidated single block of 5½ acres of arable. John had also recently exchanged two parcels of free land with Walter Spalding to concentrate his own holdings further.[121] Much of this important reconfiguration of the layout of individual farming unit is impossible to recover from the record in the century after the Black Death.

Another development was the permanent alienation of some parcels of demesne land to the peasant sector as a hereditary grant held for cash, as opposed to a lease for a fixed term. While this was much less common than leasing, it offers an important counter to Brenner's supposition that English landlords sought to retain and accumulate as much peasant land as possible—especially vacant customary land—into the demesne sector in order to repackage it in competitive leases.[122] For example, John Sampson held a plot of land from the manorial demesne in Fornham St Martin that enlarged the curtilage of his customary tenement (and house) on Nethyr Street in the centre of the village. It was granted as a 'new rent' of 4d. per annum on a hereditary cash tenancy.[123] John also held the leases of two parcels of the abbot's demesne to the north and east of this plot, so he was clearly extending the garden around his property. Granting parts of the demesne to peasants on hereditary tenures for a quasi-commercial cash head rent is not well documented, although this may be because historians have not been alert to the development.[124] The cellarer of St Albans abbey, for example, made thirteen separate grants of demesne land between 1446 and 1459 totalling at least 42 acres on hereditary cash rents at Winslow (Bucks.), and, in addition, some expiring leases of demesne were also converted to hereditary tenures.[125] Some English landlords were permanently reducing their stock of demesne land, not seeking to add to it.

The Black Death played the central role in the acceleration of all these tenurial changes. The scale and frequency of epidemics (1348–9, 1361–2, 1369, 1375, 1390–3) dramatically increased the rate of turnover of peasant land, which correspondingly increased the opportunities for lords to change the terms of its tenure. Similarly, the epidemics increased the incidence of the failure of heirs, and the length of time land remained in the lord's hands without a tenant, creating even more opportunities and incentives for landlords to change the terms of tenure. These coincided with a fall in the value of land and a sharpened competition for tenants, especially for unfree land, which resulted in the dilution of the burdens of villein tenure and more conversions to contractual tenures and short-term leases.[126] These changes significantly reduced the barriers to entry to unfree land, which in turn resulted in a higher proportion of transfers to non-kin and the infiltration of incomers into local land markets. In the 1350s freemen poured into the customary land market and migrant serfs settled on land holdings as the customary tenants of other lords. By the end of the century, even townsfolk and gentry were acquiring customary land on contractual tenures. As a result of these changes, the strong links that had once existed between tenure and status were decisively and irreversibly broken. Meanwhile, reduced profits forced lords to lease their demesnes (mainly to peasants) and to make leases more attractive to peasants. The reduced demand for land, the abandonment of some house plots, and the availability of a wider variety of tenures made it easier for tenants to reconfigure and to engross, and even to enclose, their landholdings.[127] The traditional labelling of individuals on the basis of tenure or legal status lost its relevance, and the emerging elite within rural communities began to self-identify as husbandmen and yeomen. These developments reduced the influence of the family on the operation of the land market, and helped to improve the efficiency and reduce the unit costs of farms, and in turn these tentative structural reforms created the preconditions for the further expansion and commercialization of the land market and to the increased commercialization and productivity of agriculture during the sixteenth and seventeenth centuries.[128] They also promoted the growing privatizing of space and the social distancing of the village elite in post-plague communities.[129]

The growth of leases in a period of demographic decline is unusual from a European perspective and constitutes a peculiar feature of the English experience. In parts of the Low Countries, for example, leases had developed under the pre-plague conditions of high population pressure.[130] Leases proved popular among English tenants after 1348–9 because they stripped unfree land of its demeaning incidents, and offered flexible and relatively risk-averse access to the land market without the need for any frontloaded capital.[131] At this date, unlike in the late sixteenth century, leases were not negatively associated with a permanent loss of property ownership for large sections of the peasantry, nor with their displacement from family holdings or a decline in their social capital and credit-worthiness.[132] While converting villein land to leases was not the preferred option among lords, it did at least secure tenants without risk of permanent alienation of the land and generated ready cash in a challenging market. Likewise, they allowed lords to offload demesne land for a predictable cash rent without the fear of alienation. Leases only developed as a widespread tenure in places where a particular combination of institutional features had become established. Foremost among these were secure property rights, a reliable system of registration to record the terms and conditions of the lease, a legal system capable of providing remedies for a breach in the terms cheaply and equitably, commercial opportunities for the farmer to dispose of sufficient surpluses to cover the rent, and a sufficiently monetarized economy to lubricate exchange.[133] Leases are characteristic of regions with weak or declining manorial systems, and of growing levels of commerce and of involvement of urban investors in rural lands.[134] All these features became permanently established in post-plague England, although still some way behind the scale achieved in the Low Countries.

As we saw in Chapter 2, in the 1340s the vast majority of peasant-held land was held on service tenures with non-commercial head rents, and under high demographic pressure peasants either sublet some of their holding for rack rents or fragmented them through sales for high prices (with the profits accruing to them, not their lord). The collapse of demographic pressure immediately removed the rationale for, and the benefits of, such practices, and the swing to contractual tenures also removed many of the sub-economic head rents that had promoted such behaviour: consequently, the incentive to behave in the same manner when population eventually rose again was reduced. Leases ensured that the market value of the land accrued to the lord because the head rent was now a commercial rent and the tenant could not sell the land. Likewise, a quasi-commercial cash head rent on a copyhold for lives guaranteed the reversion of the land to the lord, and the opportunity to reset the head rent. A quasi-commercial head rent on a hereditary tenure offered some disincentive to subletting provided that the fixed head rent did not fall much below the market value of land. In these ways, contractual and institutional change in the second half of the fourteenth century laid the basis for the eventual construction of large farms over the next three centuries, and their preservation under future population upswings, by removing a good deal of the tenurial tangles and inefficiencies that had once promoted subdivision and fragmentation.[135]

The importance of the lease, and to a lesser extent of hereditary or life tenures on quasi-commercial rents, is worthy of emphasis in the long-term development of agrarian capitalism. Van Bavel has described the spread of the lease as 'perhaps the most important link' in the emergence of large commercial farms, because the increased mobility of land and labour promoted a growing social stratification and polarization within village communities between larger landholders and small-holding craft workers and labourers.[136] These changes occurred gradually between c.1300 and c.1800, and the spread of competitive tenures on commercial rents forced landlords to compete harder for tenants, required lessees to reduce their costs and increase profits, and so increased the orientation of production for the market and accentuated regional specialization in agriculture.[137] The increased orientation towards the market also promoted larger farms, and the displacement of the smallholder and the emergence of a rural waged proletariat.[138] The latter required a properly functioning labour market where lessees could acquire and compete for day-wage labour or live-in servants to undertake key agricultural tasks as required.[139]

While the spread of contractual rents was a significant feature of the second half of the fourteenth century, and while this development shifted the institutional framework in ways that encouraged the creation of larger and commercial farms, these changes did not mean that England was on the cusp of agrarian capitalism in 1400. Sluggish product prices relative to wages and deficient demand created risks for commercial producers, and acted as a disincentive to raising levels of market integration and efficiency, and of agricultural productivity.[140] The proportion of rural landholders actively accumulating land as a commercial asset was low.[141] The majority of farms were still smallholdings and a genuine rural waged prole-tariat did not yet exist.[142] Business calamities and the failure of heirs in an era of high mortality caused some large farms to be broken up.[143] During the fifteenth century some leases were converted to hereditary cash tenures with fixed head rents.[144] Custom and family remained important influences on the disposal of land in many places long after the Middle Ages, and a good deal of peasant land continued to be held on sub-economic head rents, which were still prone to promote subletting under renewed population pressure in the sixteenth century.[145] Many holdings still comprised small parcels of arable scattered around the village fields and intermingled with the land of others, a layout and structure that remained suboptimal. Residual seigniorial and customary rights continued to apply to varying degrees over villein land, including a theoretical vulnerability to arbitrary seizure and little protection in the common law. Hence in c.1400 there remained disincentives, obstacles, rigidities, constraints, and inefficiencies to productivity gains in commercial farming, which would take at least two centuries to erode. At this date, the contractual changes were more important for the tenurial tangle they had started to unpick, and their irreversibility, rather than for some brave new tenurial world they had created.

Explaining the Decline of Serfdom

What general conclusions can be drawn about the causes of the decline of European serfdom from the English experience? Put another way, why did sudden and severe demographic decline cause serfdom to decay in England, but either had no discernible effect on serfdom or caused it to be re-imposed or tightened elsewhere in Europe?[146] The standard explanation for the particular nature of the English experience—post-plague seigniorial reaction, followed by resistance, revolt then the bargaining away of serfdom from the 1380s—does not adequately fit the evidence. Resistance and conflict certainly formed part of the explanation, but in the 1340s manorial lordship was already too weak, and the state lacked the bureaucratic apparatus, to counteract the forces of supply and demand in the post-plague land and labour markets. In order to understand these processes better, it is helpful to step back and consider the general conditions underpinning serfdom in the first place.

Domar argued that when labour shortages coincided with sustained periods of warfare, lawlessness, and/or severe political instability, peasants would submit to serfdom because warrior lords could offer protection and justice to peasant families as a public good in exchange for the produce of their labour and land.[147] Peasants who submitted willingly to serfdom in return for protection would be cheaper to supervise and easier to hold to the terms of their social contract than those who did not. In the absence of any powerful military imperative or external threat, peasants were unlikely to submit to serfdom voluntarily, and therefore forcing peasants into servitude and keeping them there involved much greater supervision and enforcement costs.[148] If those costs could be controlled relative to revenues, then serfdom would still be cost-effective.[149] If not, then 'economic forces would reassert themselves and help the peasants'.[150] How inefficient and how costly also depended upon the mechanics of enforcement, which varied according to time and place. These mechanisms ranged from national legislation to restrict the movement of labour to the supervision of labour services, or the hiring of officials to restrain and recover migrants. Enforcement costs would rise in eras of labour shortages because rising wage rates would increase administration and supervisory costs, and any peasant resistance would increase the effort and expense of enforcing the system.

Domar's model of serfdom is based principally upon the twin variables of the peasant need for protection and the lord's willingness to supply this in exchange for coerced labour and land, although it also assumes a form of serfdom where lords prefer servile to other forms of labour, and where lords are the primary source of justice and protection. More recently, Acemoglu and Wolitzky have developed a theoretical framework to model how changes in two key variables (agricultural prices and the availability to serfs of alternative employment) determined the cost effectiveness of coercion during periods of labour scarcity.[151] They demonstrate how the mechanics of enforcement under serfdom (comprising anything from local armed guards and security fencing to national legislation strengthening the powers available to employers) are most cost-effective when agricultural prices are high (and can therefore cover the costs of enforcement) and when peasants possess few 'outside options' (thus limiting the costs of enforcement). Conversely, low agricultural prices and the widespread availability of outside options render coercion less cost-effective to lords and migration more viable for peasants.[152] Acemoglu and Wolitzky assume that the availability of rural outside options was highly restricted in pre-industrial Europe because of the seigniorial dominance and control of the land and labour markets in the countryside (they label lords as 'coercive producers'): consequently, the scale of outside options available to peasants was almost entirely determined by the number and size of towns.[153] This is a logical and common assumption. Millward, for example, regarded towns as the only viable destination for servile migrants, and Dennison has shown how most Russian serfs headed for the cities rather than to other rural estates.[154]

Acemoglu and Wolitzky illustrate the central elements of their model against the example of European serfdom during the later medieval and early modern periods. They suggest that a combination of high agricultural prices and low levels of urbanization made the supervision costs of coercion viable in many parts of eastern Europe, which explains the survival (or even tightening) of serfdom there under conditions of labour shortages. In contrast, the ready access to towns in many areas of western Europe increased the outside options of rural serfs sufficiently to reduce the cost-effectiveness of servile labour, and as a result serfdom dissolved.[155] Klein and Ogilvie have tested these principles in a case study of early-modern Bohemia and concluded that the relative absence of towns, supplemented by the existence of urban privileges that suppressed non-agricultural employment in the rural areas surrounding the towns that did exist, combined to limit the outside options for serfs and rendered labour coercion more cost-effective.[156]

In a similar vein, historians of late-medieval England have tended to assume that servile migrants were mainly attracted to towns. After all, a serf who resided in a royal borough for a year and a day could claim borough privilege and obtain legal freedom, and some historians have stressed how young women in particular sought employment as resident servants in urban households.[157] Contemporaries themselves complained that rural villeins were fleeing to towns with the intention of obtaining their freedom.[158] There have been few attempts, however, to test these complaints and assumptions systematically through quantitative research into servile patterns of migration, despite the abundant records of presentments for absence and chevage in manorial court rolls. Two notable exceptions are the work of DeWindt and Raftis. DeWindt showed that between 1400 and 1429 48 per cent of servile female migrants from the village of Warboys (Hunts.) moved to towns, and Raftis supplied details of the movements of 285 serfs from four rural manors in the post-plague era, 40 per cent of whom moved to towns.[159] Surprisingly, these studies reveal that towns were *not* the primary destination of those rural serfs for whom a destination is recorded. A much larger, and more recent, case study has reached the same conclusion.[160] Drawing upon the records of twenty manors from four counties and hundreds of reference points, it reveals that *c.*30 per cent of servile migrants (for whom the destination is recorded) resided in towns, and only one-third of these (i.e. 10 per cent overall) were in royal boroughs where their personal freedom would be assured under borough privilege.[161] In other words, the majority of servile migrants moved around the countryside, whether as landholders, craft workers, rural servants, or marriage partners. The preference of serfs for rural not urban destinations is, in fact, entirely consistent with the evidence for the ready availability of both land and employment in rural areas in the post-plague period. It might also reflect a reluctance to migrate to towns where plague was increasingly concentrated. This finding also underlines that serfs could obtain *de facto* freedom as tenants of other lords, and that the evasion costs of serfdom were irksome but not prohibitive. As a result, many serfs did not seek formal freedom through either borough privilege or the purchase of a charter of manumission.

The options available to, and the choices made by, English serfs can be illustrated by the example of Austin Crembell of Aldham (Suffolk). The significance of his case lies in our ability to track his movements and activities from the court rolls of both his departing and his destination manor, a dual perspective which is exceptionally rare. Austin lived mainly in the first half of the fifteenth century, i.e. after the period covered by the main body of this study, but the quality of the source material and the likely typicality of his case justifies a brief reconstruction of his migratory history. He was probably born in the mid-1380s and in 1399 left his rural home manor of Aldham to live in the neighbouring parish, the textile town of Hadleigh. This appears to be a classic case of a young hereditary serf leaving the home manor at an early opportunity to flee servile status for the attractions of a town. He lived in Hadleigh until 1416, but then returned home to Aldham (aged *c.*30) and became active in the community's affairs, serving as a manorial office holder. Then, between 1422 and 1426, Austin split his time between Aldham and the rural village of Bredfield (Suffolk), some 18 miles away. He married a Bredfield widow, Agnes, and became an active baker and brewer there, while simultaneously continuing to hold land and even to serve as a capital pledge in Aldham. In 1427 he left Aldham for good (aged *c.*40), settled permanently in Bredfield, and died in the 1450s.[162] He continued to be tracked as a hereditary serf in the Aldham court rolls, but in the Bredfield rolls he was described simply a tenant of customary land, never as a serf. Austin's activities reveal a wide, varied and dynamic range of motives behind his movements. He earned a living in a town for a while, then migrated to marry a widow miles away from his home, and for many years retained landed and commercial interests in two rural communities: there is no question that between 1422 and 1427 he was regularly commuting the 18 miles between Aldham and Bredfield, remaining active in both places. Towards the end of his adult life, he was most likely an alehouse keeper in Bredfield. Austin's case proves the existence and attractions of a good variety of *rural* 'outside options' available to English serfs after the Black Death.

At one level, these general conclusions from the English experience contradict the Acemoglu and Wolitzky model, because towns were relatively unimportant as an outside option for serfs when labour was scarce, yet serfdom still dissolved. Their model assumes a stereotypically restricted form of serfdom, where factor markets were poorly developed and where lords were the principal source of employment in rural areas. Under these conditions, only towns could offer any viable outside options for peasants.[163] Their model, no less than Domar's, is simplified in order to illustrate how changes in a limited range of key variables alter the cost-effectiveness of serfdom. Both models are effective in this task, albeit at the cost of oversimplifying historical reality, because European serfdom assumed a wide variety of complex forms, and operated within a variety of institutional frameworks. Serfdom was a genus with many species, where the precise form (tenurial or personal) and degree of subjugation, and the extent and type of forced labour, were highly heterogeneous; where there was little uniformity in the size and commercial orientation of demesne lordships; and where factor markets and contractual relationships existed at differing levels of maturity.[164] The nature of manorial lordship, the organization of local communities, the power of the state, and the formulation of legal systems all differed from place to place, and their complex interactions at a given time and place determined how far lords were able to impose their will or, conversely, how far peasants were able to exercise their own choices. This observation applies even to eastern Europe, where historians had once supposed that a highly restrictive and standardized system prevailed.[165]

Where manorial lordship was fragmented, where community controls over peasant activity were weak, where legal structures offered some form of redress to peasants—such as medieval England—then serfdom assumed a mild form. In contrast, societies characterized by communities with strong communal controls, consolidated lordship, and the absence of extra-manorial legal tribunals—such as eighteenth-century Russia—experienced more severe forms of serfdom.[166] The residual effects of manorial lordship in England were to increase the costs to the villein of disposing of or acquiring land (for example, through heriot or entry fines), and of migrating in search of paid work (for example, through chevage), and also to increase the risks of evading such charges (such as through the seizure of land or goods).[167] The costs and risks varied from place to place because on the eve of the Black Death villeinage comprised a complex set of customs and rules, varying in both the cogency and the rigour of enforcement from manor to manor, and so did not operate as a standardized system with equal force everywhere in England.[168] The reasons for this weakness are varied, but the important point is that it severely diluted the lords' capacity to coerce villeins to hold land or to work on demesnes on terms favourable to them. It had also contributed to the emergence of an infrastructure more conducive to the spread of market forces. The profound significance of these developments became clear in the dramatically changed circumstances of the post-plague era.

The example of fourteenth-century England reveals that, in weaker systems of serfdom, towns were just one of a number of outside options for serfs. The existence of a relatively large hired labour market and an active peasant land market, with few barriers to entry and few effective seigniorial controls, meant that English serfs enjoyed a good range of alternative external options within short distances in the countryside. Their options increased after 1348–9 through greater competition between landlords for both tenants and workers, and through the growing demand for commercial manufactured goods and quality foodstuffs. At the same time, rising wage rates increased the administrative costs of monitoring serfdom, reducing the options available to lords. The net effect was to increase the costs of enforcing an already diluted system of serfdom. In some ways, therefore, the English evidence provides support to Acemoglu and Wolitzky's contention that the availability of outside options was central to determining the cost-effectiveness of serfdom. Yet the point needs qualifying. Lords did not calculate the costs of restraining serfs in shillings and pennies—if they did, examples would have survived—nor did serfs construct careful cost–benefit analyses of unlicensed versus licensed migration. Both lords and serfs operated within a framework of opportunities: financial, economic, social, personal, ideological, emotional, and cultural. Some serfs found good reasons to stay on their home manor or, like Austin Crembell, to retain close links. Others left, and were eager to leave few traces of their destinations. A handful of conservative landlords in the 1380s took a tough stance on serfdom, based on hardening attitudes to labour within a particular social ideology as much as, if not more than, cost. The English experience encourages us to think more broadly in terms of the opportunity structure available to serfs—wide or narrow—and about social attitudes to serfdom, as well as cost-effectiveness.

A greater awareness of the variety and complexity of systems of European serfdom explains the shift in recent historical scholarship away from powerful but monocausal 'class-conflict'-based models in explaining the decline of such systems.[169] As there was no uniform system of serfdom, and as there was no uniform chronology of decline, then no general model of repression, exploitation, or enserfment can explain its survival or decline. Consequently, historians such as Cerman, Dennison, and Ogilvie emphasize the need to reconstruct and understand the wider institutional context in which local and regional systems of serfdom operated, and to analyse how custom, cooperation, negotiation, contestation, and conflict interacted to shape local power relations.[170] We manifestly need more comparative analyses, more focused assessments of the capacity of lords to intervene arbitrarily in local factor and commodity markets, and closer attention to the extent to which seigniorial prerogatives—whether exercised or not—restricted the choices of peasants.[171]

Conclusion

Between 1300 and 1800 parts of north-west Europe experienced economic progress, a sustained reduction in wealth inequality, and moved decisively towards liberal modernity. In contrast, much of eastern Europe experienced the reimposition or continuation of feudal relations and authoritarianism, remained economically backward, and any reduction in wealth inequality in the immediate post-plague era disappeared when sustained population growth returned.[172] Within this general picture, the headline indicators of economic progress reveal that in 1300 England was a laggard by European standards; its performance improved consistently thereafter; and only during the seventeenth century did it emerge decisively as a leader.

The key institutional changes behind this trajectory of development are complex, hard to unravel, and intensely disputed. Furthermore, they evolved over a long period. Yet many influential economists and historians are focusing upon the structural changes that occurred in north-west Europe during the late fourteenth and fifteenth centuries, when the visitations of the Black Death were most frequent and virulent, which created some of the preconditions for sustained economic growth (see above, pp. 5-6). The development of the law and a legal culture, the liberalization of seigniorial institutions, and a growing participation in commercial activity at all levels of society are all observable by degrees in late-medieval England. The purpose of this chapter has been to identify what, if any, major institutional changes had occurred in the immediate aftermath of the Black Death, and to assess their significance in creating the preconditions for England's future economic development.

On the eve of the Black Death the combination of high demographic pressure and the particular institutional arrangements had caused economic growth to falter. Mean output per head, household incomes, and real wages were low, landholdings for many were small and fragmented, and nearly half the population possessed no land. Society languished in the grip of what has been variously described as a Malthusian crisis, a crisis of feudalism, institutional sclerosis, and a tenurial tangle, and, as such, it had become acutely vulnerable to external shocks and calamities. The Black Death of 1348–9 removed the demographic pressure at a stroke and, under this very different demographic regime, the same institutional structure facilitated some redistribution of wealth down the social scale. For all the challenges in the 1350s—from the immediate crisis and inflation to a mini seigniorial reaction and the state's clampdown in the labour market—there is clear evidence for a reduction in wealth inequality: the tail of landless shrank, tenants obtained land on more favourable terms, industrious labourers earned higher annual incomes, and the lower orders were eating more and clothing themselves better. The institutional structure enabled the forces of supply and demand to prevail—by and large—in the immediate post-plague world.

Between the 1350s and 1390s further changes occurred that accelerated the redistribution of wealth down the social scale, reduced society's vulnerability to calamity, and removed some of the institutional inefficiencies that had choked the pre-plague economy, while also laying the foundations of future productivity gains. Estimated GDP per head rose by around 40 per cent and annual household income by at least the same magnitude. While neither measure matched the standards of contemporary European leaders, both had driven changes in the consumption of foodstuffs and household goods, and created a growing dependence upon the market for those products, which in turn caused important structural shifts within the economy. The first of these shifts was the rising proportion of the population in non-agricultural employment, which was high by European standards and by c.1400 might even have exceeded 40 per cent. Much of this employment was available in the countryside. The second was the growth in the livestock share of agriculture, which now probably exceeded 50 per cent. The effects of both of these were to spread wealth and employment more equitably throughout England, diminishing (but not yet eradicating) the spatial differentials between the south-east and the rest of the country, and reducing dependence upon the staple of grain. These in turn reduced society's vulnerability to future harvest sensitivity and famine, and helped to protect incomes and GDP per head when population rose again in the sixteenth century.

Villeinage declined rapidly between the 1340s and the 1390s. The proportion of hereditary serfs fell from c.40 per cent of the total population to little more than 10 per cent, and the personal dues associated with this status declined in size and frequency. Likewise, the proportion of unfree land held on the traditional villein service tenure probably halved, and the main servile dues of labour services, tallage, and millsuit were vastly reduced. The dilution of villeinage had the general effect of further reducing the influence of manorial lordship, thus diminishing the scope for arbitrary and coercive seigniorial behaviour in the allocation of land and labour, and in the provision of justice, even if the residual elements of villeinage proved socially demeaning and irksome to those still exposed to them. The decline of villeinage provided more space for the land, labour, and commodity markets to expand. The way in which it declined resulted in more contractual tenures, and greater precision within those contractual tenures, in the land market.

Given the way in which villeinage declined, in c.1400 the land market was qualitatively different from that of c.1300. The spread of contractual tenures over some free and a great deal of unfree land, the transfer of most demesne land into the peasant sector through leasing, the greater precision in contractual terms, the erosion of the family-land bond, the entry of freemen and outsiders into the customary land market, and the drift to engrossment were all important changes, whose net effect was to reduce the institutional inefficiencies in its operation.[173] Many of these developments accelerated over the next two centuries, so that the land market of c.1600 was qualitatively different again to that of c.1400.[174] These changes also increased the importance of the peasant sector in the supply of agricultural produce to market. Most importantly, when population rose again in the sixteenth century, the prior spread of contractual tenures and the increase in the percentage of land owing commercial and quasi-commercial head rents reduced the likelihood that holdings would fragment, as they had in the thirteenth century under similar demographic conditions. This reinforces the point that factor markets exist in various forms throughout English history, and they operated differently over time according to the institutional arrangements governing them.[175]

Although contractual tenures were still a minority form in c.1400, their rate of growth since 1349, their role in breaking the link between tenure and status, and in drawing freemen, townsfolk, and gentry into the unfree land market, all meant that the change was irreversible. They also accelerated the process of removing the sub-economic head rents that in the pre-plague period had caused many land-holdings to fragment under the pressure of population. This process was reinforced by the permanent transfer of most of the land in the demesne sector into the peasant sector on commercial leases. Both of these developments altered the tenurial structure of rural England. They accelerated the breakdown of the traditional bond between a particular family and its holding, and destruction of the long association between land tenure and personal status. They increased the mobility and portability of land, and enabled the layout of individual holdings to be reconfigured and rationalized. They encouraged the entry of outsiders of higher social status into the customary land market. The effects were to destroy the old link between tenure and personal status, to increase the use of land as a marketable asset, and to reduce the tenurial obstacles to the construction of large commercial farms.

In 1400 the significance of contractual tenures was more about the inefficient tenurial and rent structure they had begun to dismantle than for the new tenurial order that would eventually emerge in the future. England was not yet an economic pace- and trend-setter. Compared to the leading economies in Europe, its urbanization rates remained low, agricultural productivity was modest, and GDP per head still lagged. But the Black Death had proved a major watershed in English history. We have identified five major structural and institutional changes that occurred between the 1340s and 1390s, reflecting the shift in factor ratios and the progressive commoditization of those factors. We have emphasized the rapid decline of villeinage and the manner of its decline. The contrast between the dissolution of English serfdom under the shock of demographic collapse, and its survival or re-imposition elsewhere in Europe under the same demographic conditions, is partly due to the strength of the local system of serfdom when plague first hit (weak or strong), the framework of opportunities available to peasants, and the continued cost-effectiveness of enforcing a particular system under the conditions of labour scarcity. Different forms of serfdom experienced different trajectories of decline, and reconstructing and comparing the institutional structures in each case, and mapping in detail the specifics of decline, provide the clearest insights to explaining whether labour scarcity resulted in the liberation of the labour and land markets or the imposition of coercion.[176] Thus the reconstruction of the institutional framework within which factor and commodity markets operated enables historians to assess processes of intentional and unintentional change, and to analyse causation in non-deterministic ways. Causation in historical development is not constant over time but varies according to institutional context.[177] The implications of this point for attempts to identify the main explanatory variables behind the Little Divergence are obvious: different variables could carry different weight and power over both time and place.[178] Pandemics shift the paradigm, but they do not dictate the social, economic, and cultural outcomes.

Notes

1. See, for example, Allen, 'Great Divergence', pp. 411–47; Pamuk, 'Black Death', pp. 289–317; Robert C. Allen, *The British industrial revolution in global perspective* (Cambridge, 2009); de Pleijt and van Zanden, 'Accounting', pp. 387–409.
2. See, for example, de Pleijt and J.L. van Zanden, 'Accounting', figs. 1 and 2.
3. Robert C. Allen, 'Progress and poverty in early modern Europe', *Economic History Review*, 56 (2003), pp. 403–43; de Pleijit and van Zanden, 'Accounting', pp. 387–409; van Bavel, *Invisible hand*, pp. 15–16; Fochesato, 'Origins', pp. 91–4.
4. The literature is voluminous, but see Allen, 'Progress and poverty', pp. 403–43; Pamuk, 'Black Death', pp. 304–11; van Bavel, *Manors and markets*, pp. 353–71; de Pleijt and J. L. van Zanden, 'Accounting', pp. 387–96, 406–7; Fochesato, 'Origins', pp. 91–4, 104–11; and Foreman-Peck and Zhou, 'Late marriage', pp. 1073–99.
5. The range of estimates are illustrated in Humphries and Weisdorf, 'Unreal wages', fig. 2.
6. Allen, 'Progress and poverty', figs. 6 and 9, pp. 425, 429; Pamuk, 'Black Death', p. 305; Malanima, 'Italy in the Renaissance', p. 8. For medievalists' views, see Galloway, 'Metropolitan' p. 7; Dyer, *Making a living*, p. 312; Britnell, *Britain*, pp. 348–50, 403; Palliser, 'Introduction', p. 4; Christopher Dyer, 'How urbanised was medieval England' in Jean-Marie Duvosquel and Erik Thoen, eds., *Peasants and townsmen in medieval Europe* (Ghent, 1995), pp. 169–85; Broadberry et al., *British economic growth*, table 4.04.

7. Allen, 'Progress and poverty', pp. 431–4; de Pleijt and van Zanden, 'Accounting', pp. 396–407.

8. These challenges are acknowledged; see, for example, Allen, 'Progress and poverty', pp. 405–12.

9. de Pleijt and van Zanden, 'Accounting', pp. 391–6, although Allen, 'Progress and poverty', pp. 405–6 argues that one model might well fit all.

10. See, for example, Clark, *Farewell to alms*, pp. 147–8 for a simple and high-level scoring of the efficiency of English factor and commodity markets in *c.*1300; and the critique of its simplicity in Dennison, 'Institutional context', pp. 249–50. See also Pamuk, 'Black Death', p. 309, and Fochesato, 'Origins', pp. 109–10.

11. van Bavel, *Invisible hand*, pp. 27–8.

12. The work of Bruce Campbell is a notable exception to this observation.

13. Tracy K. Dennison and Shelagh Ogilvie, 'Institutions, demography and economic growth', *Journal of Economic History*, 76 (2016), pp. 205–16.

14. Briggs, 'Introduction', pp. 4–5.

15. Campbell, 'Factor markets', pp. 80, 96; de Pleijt and van Zanden, 'Accounting', figs. 1 and 2. Kitsikopoulos, 'Epilogue', pp. 331–7 places England at the back end of a progressive group of regional economies at this date.

16. Allen, 'Great divergence', figs. 6 to 8, pp. 425–6; Pamuk, 'Black Death', pp. 304–5; Broadberry, 'Accounting', tables 1 to 4; Campbell, *Great transition*, pp. 121–5; Broadberry et al., *British economic growth*, pp. 377–81; de Pleijt and van Zanden, 'Accounting', figs. 1 to 5, tables 1 and 2.

17. de Pleijt and van Zanden, 'Accounting', p. 390.

18. Allen, 'Great divergence', p. 413; Allen, 'Progress and poverty', fig. 1, p. 407; van Zanden, 'Revolt', pp. 622, 635–8; Pamuk, 'Black Death', pp. 289–93, 306–11; Fochesato, 'Origins', fig. 1, pp. 92–4, 111; Voigtlander and Voth, 'How the West', pp. 2227–64; de Pleijt and van Zanden, 'Accounting', fig. 4.

19. Britnell, *Britain*, pp. 515–17. Or, medieval commerce was the midwife of the age of capital, Howell, *Commerce before capitalism*, p. 8.

20. Campbell, 'Factor markets', p. 99.

21. Campbell, 'The land', p. 237; Campbell, *Great transition*, p. 328; Pamuk, 'Black Death', p. 313.

22. Tina de Moor and Jan Luiten van Zanden, 'Girl power: the European marriage pattern and labour markets in the North Sea region in the late medieval and early modern period', *Economic History Review*, 63 (2010), pp. 1–33; Voigtlander and Voth, 'How the West', pp. 2232–3, 2252–6, 2259–60; Foreman-Peck and Zhou, 'Late marriage', pp. 1076–8. For a general summary, see Stephen H. Rigby, 'Gendering the Black Death: women in later medieval England', *Gender and History*, 12 (2000), pp. 745–54; Bennett, 'Wretched girls', pp. 315–20.

23. Voigtlander and Voth, 'How the West', pp. 2228–33, 2252–6, 2259–60.

24. de Moor and van Zanden, 'Girl power', pp. 1–33; Tina de Moor and Jan Luiten van Zanden, 'Every woman counts': a gender-analysis of numeracy in the Low Countries during the early modern period', *Journal of Interdisciplinary History*, 41 (2010), pp. 179–208.

25. Pamuk, 'Black Death', p. 308; Voigtlander and Voth, 'How the West', pp. 2227–30.

26. Voigtlander and Voth, 'How the West', pp. 2228, 2232. For a recent summary of the extent of disagreement, see Edwards and Ogilvie, 'Did the Black Death?', pp. 2–5.

27. Bennett, 'Wretched girls', pp. 318–19.

28. Judith Bennett, 'Married and not: Weston's grown children in 1268–9', *Continuity and Change*, 34 (2019), pp. 151–82; Bennett, 'Wretched girls', pp. 336–9.

29. Poos, *Rural society*, pp. 81–228; Goldberg, *Women, work and lifecycle*; Razi, 'Myth', pp. 7–22; Mark Bailey, 'Demographic decline in late medieval England: some thoughts on recent research', *Economic History Review*, 49 (1996), pp. 1–19; Rigby, 'Gendering', pp. 745–54; Hatcher, 'Understanding the population history', pp. 91–9.

30. Richard M. Smith, 'Some emerging issues in the demography of medieval England and prospects for their future investigation', *Local Population Studies*, XX (2018), pp. 13–24.

31. Bailey, 'Demographic decline', pp. 15–17; Hatcher, 'Understanding the population history', pp. 99–104; Ole Benedictow, 'New perspectives in medieval demography: the medieval demographic system', in Bailey and Rigby, eds., *Town and countryside*, pp. 3–42; Yates, *Town and countryside*, p. 235; Foreman Peck and Zhou, 'Late marriage', pp. 1076–7, 1095.

32. Smith, 'Some emerging issues', p. 24.

33. Voigtlander and Voth, 'How the west', pp. 2252–6.

34. Edwards and Ogilvie, 'Did the Black Death', pp. 6–15.

35. Bennett, 'Compulsory service', pp. 44–7 for scepticism about the golden age of women.

36. Humphries and Weisdorf, 'Wages of women', pp. 423–6, 431; Humphries and Weisdorf, 'Unreal wages', fig. 5.

37. Tuck, 'Tenant farming: northern borders', p. 595.

38. The assumption that under half of all recorded servants were female is based upon the evidence from the early sixteenth century, when in *c*.1500 *c*.40% servants are women in north-east Norfolk, Whittle, *Agrarian capitalism*, pp. 259–60, 302.

39. Bennett, 'Wretched girls', pp. 320–5; Chavas and Bromley, 'Modelling population', pp. 230–1; Smith, 'Some emerging issues', p. 21.

40. Razi, *Life, marriage*, pp. 132–4; Campbell, *Great transition*, pp. 318–19; Aberth, *From the brink*, pp. 134–5.

41. Bailey, 'Demographic decline', pp. 15–17; Hatcher, 'Understanding the population history', pp. 99–104.

42. Smith, 'Measuring adult mortality', pp. 72–82.

43. Razi, *Life, marriage*, pp. 129, 150–1; Bolton, 'Looking for *Yersinia pestis*, p. 36; Dewitte, 'Anthropology', p. 116.

44. Tracy K. Dennison and Shelagh Ogilvie, 'Does the European Marriage Pattern explain economic growth?', *Journal of Economic History*, 74 (2014), pp. 651–93; Dennison and Ogilvie, 'Institutions, demography', pp. 205–17; Edwards and Ogilvie, 'Did the Black Death', pp. 21–34.

45. Foreman-Peck and Zhou, 'Late marriage', pp. 1073–4, but see also Jeremy Edwards and Shelagh Ogilvie, 'What can we learn from a race with one runner?: a comment on Forman Peck and Zhou', *Economic History Review*, 72 (2019), pp. 1439–46, and James Foreman-Peck and Peng Zhou, 'A response to Edwards and Ogilvie', *Economic History Review*, 72 (2019), pp. 1447–50.

46. Broadberry et al., *British economic growth*, pp. 229–30.

47. Humphries and Weisdorf, 'Unreal wages', fig. 2.

48. Monro, 'Late medieval decline', table 20A.

49. Broadberry et al., *British economic growth*, pp. 320–1.

50. Clark, 'Markets and microbes', pp. 139–44, 161; Broadberry et al., *British economic growth*, pp. 209, 273–4, fig. 7.06; Humphries and Weisdorf, 'Wages of women', p. 431; Humphries and Weisdorf, 'Unreal wages', figs. 2, 4, and 5.

51. Broadberry et al., *British economic growth*, pp. 273–4. Jutta Bolt and J.L. van Zanden, 'The Maddison Project: collaborative research on historical national accounts', *Economic History Review*, 67 (2014), table 2, p. 637; Malanima, 'Italy in the Renaissance', fig. 6, p. 19.

52. Campbell, 'European mortality crises', fig. 2.8.

53. Campbell, *Great transition*, table 5.1; de Pleijt and van Zanden, 'Accounting', fig. 2.

54. Broadberry, 'Accounting', table 5; Broadberry et al., *British economic growth*, table 3.18, p. 118.

55. Broadberry et al., *British economic growth*, table 4.11, p. 181.

56. Britnell, *Britain*, p. 519; Bailey, *Medieval Suffolk*, pp. 274–6; Amor, *Wool to cloth*, pp. 190–215; John S. Lee, *The medieval clothier* (Woodbridge, 2018), pp. 17–30, 65–114, 273–81.

57. Barron, *London*, pp. 45–83, 99–101; Alan Dyer, *Decline and growth in English towns 1400–1640* (Basingstoke, 1991), p. 26; Britnell, 'Urban demand', pp. 16, 18; Dyer, *Making a living*, pp. 304–7.

58. Nightingale, 'London', p. 89; Barron, *London*, p. 45.

59. Barron, *London*, p. 101.

60. Galloway et al., 'Fuelling the city', pp. 447–72.

61. Galloway, 'Driven by drink?', pp. 97–9. He estimates the total grain consumption (bread and ale) per head of Londoners to have increased by around one-third over the course of the century, Galloway, 'Metropolitan food', pp. 12–13.

62. Britnell, 'Urban demand', pp. 16–17; Galloway, 'Metropolitan food', pp. 13–14; Christopher Dyer and Terry Slater, 'The Midlands', in Palliser, ed., *Urban history*, pp. 635–7.

63. Derek Keene, 'Changes in London's economic hinterland as indicated by debt cases in the Court of Common Pleas', in Galloway, ed., *Trade, urban hinterlands*, figs. 4.1 and 4.4, pp. 60, 63.

64. Bailey, 'Transformation', pp. 202–3; Yates, *Town and countryside*, pp. 237–8; Adrian R. Bell, Chris Brooks, and Helen Killick, 'Medieval property investors 1300–1500', (Working Paper, ICMA Centre, University of Reading, 2018), accessed 22 July 2019, pp. 17–21.

65. Bailey, *Marginal economy?*, pp. 150, 263, 316; Kowaleski, *Local markets*, p. 273.

66. Dyer, *Decline and growth*, pp. 25–7; Britnell, *Britain*, p. 518; Keene, 'Changes', figs. 4.4 and 4.5, pp. 63–4; E. Tony Wrigley, 'A simple model of London's importance in changing English society and economy 1650–1750', *Past and Present*, 37 (1967), pp. 44–70.

67. Britnell, *Commercialisation* (second edition), p. 228.

68. Campbell and Bartley, *England*, maps 18.10 and 18.16.

69. Campbell, 'People and land', p. 72; Miller and Hatcher, *Medieval England Towns*, pp. 415–16; Broadberry et al., *British economic growth*, table 1.03D; Goldberg, *Women, work and life-cycle*, pp. 75; Miller, 'Occupation of the land: Yorkshire and Lancashire', p. 52; Miller, 'Tenant farming: Yorkshire and Lancashire', p. 600; Kowaleski, *Local markets*, pp. 17–38; Oldland, *English woollen industry*, pp. 200–12.
70. Dyer, *Decline and growth*, pp. 40–2; Campbell and Bartley, *England*, map 18.11.
71. Smith, 'Human resources', p. 202; Broadberry et al., *British economic growth*, fig. 1.03.
72. Dyer, *Decline and growth*, pp. 21–2.
73. Broadberry, 'Accounting', pp. 12–13; Campbell and O Grada, 'Harvest shortfalls', pp. 859–86.
74. Klein and Ogilvie, 'Occupational structure', pp. 493–8.
75. Clark, '1381 and the Malthus delusion', p. 9; Klein and Ogilvie, 'Occupational structure', p. 498; Broadberry et al., 'When did Britain industrialise?', p. 18; Broadberry et al., *British economic growth*, p. 195.
76. Clark, '1381 and the Malthus delusion', p. 9; Klein and Ogilvie, 'Occupational structure', pp. 496–9.
77. Britnell, *Britain*, pp. 517–18.
78. Clark, '1381 and the Malthus delusion', p. 9; Broadberry et al., 'When did Britain industrialise?', p. 18; van Bavel, *Invisible hand*, p. 211. See also Dyer 'Occupation: West Midlands', p. 646; Poos, *Rural society*, pp. 18, 24, 30–1, 186–8; Whittle, *Agrarian Capitalism*, pp. 228, 233.
79. Whittle, *Agrarian Capitalism*, pp. 302–4.
80. Ghosh, 'Rural economies', pp. 261–7.
81. Clark, '1381 and the Malthus delusion', p. 5; Klein and Ogilvie, 'Occupational structure', pp. 496–9.
82. Broadberry et al., *British economic growth*, pp. 118, 139, 181, tables 3.08, 4.03, 4.11.
83. Broadberry et al., *British economic growth*, pp. 195, 347; figs. 5.02 and 9.02.
84. Bailey, *Decline of serfdom*, pp. 38–41, 46, 111, 115–16, 142–3, 264–6, 273–4, 280.
85. Bailey, *Decline of serfdom*, pp. 42–6, 266–73.
86. Bailey, *Decline of serfdom*, pp. 58–9.
87. Bailey, *Decline of serfdom*, pp. 110–12, 124, 129, 140, 153, 162, 178, 189, 227–8, 268–9, 297.
88. Bailey, *Decline of serfdom*, pp. 271–3.
89. Bailey, 'Transformation', pp. 189–203; Bailey, *Decline of serfdom*, pp. 241–55, 287–93, quote at p. 287.
90. Langdon, *Mills in medieval economy*, pp. 286–7; Bailey, *Decline of serfdom*, pp. 47–56, 255–64, 287–93, 316–19; Bailey, 'Tallage-at-will' pp. 46–52.
91. Bailey, 'Transformation', pp. 190–1, 196–7.
92. Bailey, 'Transformation', pp. 193–203; Bailey, *Decline of serfdom*, pp. 316–22.
93. Douglas C. North and R. Paul Thomas, 'The rise and fall of the manorial system: a theoretical model', *Journal of Economic History*, 31 (1971), pp. 777–803; Douglas C. North and R. Paul Thomas, *The rise of the western world: a new economic history* (Cambridge, 1973), pp. 6–8, 79–86, 94–101.
94. Bennett, 'Compulsory service', pp. 7–8, 47.

95. W. Mark Ormrod, 'England in the Middle Ages', in Richard J. Bonney, ed., *The rise of the fiscal state in Europe* (Oxford, 1999), pp. 36–41; Harriss, 'Shaping the nation', pp. 58–66.

96. Broadberry, 'Accounting', pp. 13–15; Broad, 'English agrarian structures', p. 54.

97. Palmer, *English law*, pp. 294–306, quotes at pp. 295, 305.

98. Bennett, 'Impact of the Black Death', p. 203.

99. Musson, 'New labour laws', pp. 73–88; Seabourne, *Royal regulation*, pp. 160–2.

100. This does not mean, however, that government was constantly active in these spheres, because it alternated phases of intense activity (such as the 1350s to 1390s, the mid-sixteenth century, and the later eighteenth century), alternated with long periods of relative inactivity (such as the 1390s to the mid-sixteenth century). See Beier, 'A new serfdom', pp. 35–8; Bennett, 'Compulsory service', pp. 7–8, 11–12; Whittle, *Agrarian capitalism*, pp. 287–96; Marc W. Steinberg, *England's great transformation: law, labour and the Industrial Revolution* (Chicago, 2016), pp. 26–46.

101. Briggs, 'Introduction', pp. 3–18.

102. Ghosh, 'Rural economies', pp. 260–1, 278.

103. Tracy K. Dennison, *The institutional framework of Russian serfdom* (Cambridge, 2011), pp. 262–8; Tracy K. Dennison, 'Contract enforcement in Russian serf society, 1750–60', *Economic History Review*, 66 (2013), pp. 715–32.

104. Ogilvie, 'Choices and constraints', p. 296.

105. The importance of the subject is flagged in Brenner, 'Agrarian roots', pp. 295–9. For a summary of the broad changes, see Bailey, 'Transformation', pp. 210–30.

106. It is not possible to establish precise and definitive figures, but this does not mean that we cannot confidently guess the approximate magnitudes. We estimate that in the 1340s 0.6 of all demesne land was directly exploited, 0.4 leased; in the 1390s 0.25 directly exploited, 0.75 leased. See fig. 7.7. The leasing of demesnes after 1350 is documented above, pp. 92–3 and pp. 241–2, and the sharp fall in demesne share of agriculture as a consequence of leasing is estimated in Broadberry et al., *British economic growth*, p. 82.

107. We estimate that in the 1340s 0.9 of all free land was held on non-commercial/service tenancies, 0.07 was leased, and 0.03 on quasi-commercial head rents; likewise 0.9 of all villein land on non-commercial/service tenure, 0.05 leased, and 0.05 on quasi-commercial tenures. In the 1390s 0.88 of all free land on non-commercial/service, 0.07 leased, and 0.05 quasi-commercial; for villein land the proportions are 0.45 non-commercial/service, 0.25 leased, and 0.3 quasi-commercial. See fig. 7.7.

108. This calculation applied the proportions estimated above to the following distribution: 30% of all land held as demesne in c.1300, 35% as free land and 35% as unfree. Hence in the 1340s the 20% of contractual rents is comprised of 12% = leased demesne, plus 4% = peasant leased, plus 4% = peasant quasi-commercial. In the 1390s 45% contractual rents is comprised of 22% demesne leased, plus 2.5% = free leased, plus 1.5% = free quasi-commercial, plus 8% = villein leased, plus 11% = villein quasi-commercial.

109. For the prominence of peasants as lessees of demesne land, see Britnell, *Britain*, pp. 403–4; for the shift of demesne land to the peasant sector, Broadberry et al., *British economic growth*, p. 82.

110. Bailey, 'Transformation', pp. 210–16, 228–30; Bailey, *Decline of serfdom*, pp. 287–93, 316–26.

111. French and Hoyle, *English rural society*, pp. 31–3; Jane Whittle, 'Tenure and land-holding in England 1400–1580: a crucial period of the development of agrarian capitalism?', in Bas van Bavel and Peter Hoppenbrouwers, eds., *Landholding and land transfer in the North Sea areas (late Middle Ages – 19th century)* (Turnout, 2004), pp. 240–2; Broad, 'English agrarian structures', pp. 52–62.

112. Cf. Ghosh, 'Rural economies', p. 264, who states 'forms of tenure...whether custom-ary or leasehold were not in reality determined primarily by the market'.

113. Whittle, 'Individualism', pp. 47–8.

114. Whittle, 'Individualism', pp. 48–9, 62; Bailey, 'Transformation', pp. 225–6; Sheila Sweetinburgh, 'Farming the Kentish marshlands', in Sweetinburgh, ed., *Later medi-eval Kent,* pp. 88–90.

115. Razi, 'Myth', pp. 25–37; Mullan and Britnell, *Land and family*, pp. 84–102, 118–31.

116. Raftis, *Ramsey abbey*, pp. 285–6.

117. Dyer, 'Tenant farming: West Midlands', pp. 642–3.

118. Bailey, 'Form, function', pp. 24–32; Bailey, *Medieval Suffolk*, pp. 102–14, 225–6.

119. Bailey, 'Form, function', p. 20; Bailey, *Decline of serfdom*, pp. 188, 252–3.

120. SROB HA528, Hengrave Hall Deposit 114, ff. 6, 20, 40–1.

121. SROB HA528 Hengrave Hall Deposit 114, ff. 52–3.

122. Brenner, 'Agrarian class structure', p. 47; Brenner, 'Agrarian roots', p. 294.

123. SROB HA528 Hengrave Hall Deposit 114, f. 16.

124. A notable exception is Jane Whittle: Whittle, 'Individualism', p. 29.

125. They were all liable to an entry fine, and were all granted on cash rents, Noy, ed., *Winslow, II*, pp. 608, 628, 640, 646, 650, 663–6, 671, 673, 679, 684, 686, 698, and 702.

126. Whittle, *Agrarian capitalism*, p. 305; Pamuk, 'Black Death', pp. 309–11.

127. Bailey, 'Form, function', pp. 25–9.

128. Robert C. Allen, 'Tracking the agricultural revolution in England', *Economic History Review*, 52 (1999), pp. 209–35; Allen, 'Progress and poverty', fig. 7, p. 425; van Bavel, *Manors and markets*, pp. 179–81, 245–6; Campbell and O Grada, 'Harvest shortfalls', pp. 859–86; Richard M. Smith, 'Dearth and local political responses: 1280–1325 and 1580–1596/7 compared', in Kowaleski et al., eds., *Peasants and lords*, pp. 377–406; Broad, 'English agrarian structures', pp. 51–3, 55–61.

129. Mileson, 'Openness and closure', pp. 27–32.

130. van Bavel, *Manors and markets*, pp. 172–3; van Bavel, 'Land lease', p. 24.

131. van Bavel and Schofield, 'Introduction', pp. 15, 22.

132. van Bavel and Schofield, 'Introduction', pp. 21–5; Whittle, 'Leasehold tenure', pp. 139–49; cf. Cerman, *Villagers and lords*, pp. 29–31.

133. van Bavel and Schofield, 'Emergence', pp. 15–18; van Bavel, *Manors and markets*, pp. 174–5.

134. van Bavel and Schofield, 'Introduction', pp. 14–23; Van Bavel, 'Land lease', pp. 24–5.

135. French and Hoyle, *English rural society*, pp. 28–9.

136. van Bavel, 'Emergence and growth of short term leasing', p. 181.

137. van Bavel, *Manors and markets*, pp. 171, 179–80.

138. Whittle, 'Tenure and landholding', pp. 244–5; van Bavel, 'Land lease', pp. 35–7; Whittle, 'Leasehold tenure', pp. 139–40.

139. van Bavel, *Manors and markets*, p. 245.

140. Pamuk, 'Black Death', p. 309. This contrasts with the beneficial impact of rising product prices in these areas in the early modern period, French and Hoyle, *English rural society*, pp. 26–8.
141. Mullan and Britnell, *Land and family*, p. 131.
142. Whittle, 'Tenure and landholding', pp. 242–3; Mullan and Britnell, *Land and family*, pp. 148–9.
143. French and Hoyle, *English rural society*, p. 25.
144. Bailey, 'Transformation', p. 25.
145. In the early fourteenth century fragmentation was widespread: in the early seventeenth century it still occurred in some places, but now engrossment was much more common in others. Whittle, 'Individualism', pp. 28–46; Henry R. French and Richard W. Hoyle, 'The land market of a Pennine manor: Slaidburn, 1650–1780', *Continuity and Change*, 14 (1999), pp. 349–83; Henry R. French and Richard W. Hoyle, 'English individualism refuted and reasserted: the land market of Earls Colne (Essex), 1550–1750', *Economic History Review*, 56 (2003), pp. 595–622; Whittle, 'Tenure and landholding', pp. 238–40; French and Hoyle, *English rural society*, pp. 25–6, 30–1; Broad, 'English agrarian structures', pp. 59–61; Sweetinburgh, 'Farming on the Kent marshlands', pp. 86–93.
146. See, for example, seventeenth-century Russia, Evsey D. Domar, 'The causes of slavery or serfdom: a hypothesis', *Journal of Economic History*, 30 (1970), pp. 18–25; fifteenth-century Poland, Grzegorz Mysliwski, 'Central Europe', in Kitsikopoulos, ed. *Agrarian change*, pp. 269–70; and seventeenth-century Bohemia, Arnost Klima, 'Agrarian class structure and economic development in pre-industrial Bohemia', in Aston and Philpin, eds., *The Brenner Debate*, pp. 192–212; Klein and Ogilvie, 'Occupational structure', pp. 494–5, 509–18.
147. Domar, 'Causes', pp. 18–32; Douglas C. North and R. Paul Thomas, 'The rise and fall of the manorial system: a theoretical model', *Journal of Economic History*, 31 (1971), p. 778.
148. Domar, 'Causes', pp. 23–5; North and Thomas, 'Rise and fall', pp. 779; Daron Acemoglu and Alexander Wolitzky, 'The economics of labour coercion', *Econometrica*, 79 (2011), pp. 557–8.
149. Domar, 'Causes', pp. 23–5, 28–9; North and Thomas, 'Rise and fall', pp. 779, 798.
150. Domar, 'Causes', p. 29.
151. Acemoglu and Wolitzky, 'Labour coercion', pp. 555–600.
152. Acemoglu and Wolitzky, 'Labour coercion', pp. 555–8, 569–73, 587–8. 'Whether the labour demand effect or the outside option effect dominates simply depends upon whether the population change has a larger direct effect on the market price or on the workers' outside options' (p. 588).
153. Acemoglu and Wolitzky, 'Labour coercion', pp. 563–9.
154. Robert Millward, 'An economic analysis of the organisation of serfdom in eastern Europe', *Journal of Economic History*, 42 (1982), p. 515; Dennison, *Institutional framework*, pp. 153, 172–3. See also Brenner, 'Agrarian class structure', pp. 38–40.
155. Acemoglu and Wolitzky, 'Labour coercion', pp. 558, 577–8.
156. Klein and Ogilvie, 'Occupational structure', pp. 500–3.
157. Millward, 'Economic analysis', p. 515; Raftis, *Peasant economic development*, p. 99; Goldberg, *Medieval England*, pp. 169–70; Anne R. DeWindt, 'Leaving Warboys: emigration from a fifteenth-century English village', in Charlotte N. Goldy and

Amy Livingstone, eds., *Writing medieval women's lives* (New York, 2012), pp. 85–111; Mate, *Wives, daughters*, p. 92; D. Gary Shaw, *The creation of a community: the city of Wells in the Middle Ages* (Oxford, 1993), p. 100; Dennison, *Institutional framework*, pp. 153, 156–7, 166, 172–3.

158. *Statutes of the Realm*, II, p. 38; Given-Wilson, 'Service, serfdom', p. 23; Kowaleski, *Local markets*, p. 88.

159. DeWindt, 'Leaving Warboys', pp. 101–3. The four Ramsey manors used by Raftis are Alconbury, Ashton, King's Walden, and Wrestlingworth; he does not calculate the percentage heading to towns himself, so the figure of 40% is my calculation from Raftis, *Peasant economic development*, pp. 100–2.

160. Mark Bailey, 'Patterns of rural migration in south-east England 1300–1500', paper to the British Agricultural History Society winter conference, 2014, and forthcoming.

161. A serf migrating to either a manorial town—i.e. one defined as a town in economic but not institutional terms—or a mesne borough would be unlikely to claim borough privilege successfully.

162. The detailed reconstruction of his life from two court series is complex, but will be fully explicated in a forthcoming study on servile migration. The Aldham court rolls are CUL Vanneck Ms Box 1 and the Bredfield rolls are SROI HA91/2.

163. Acemoglu and Wolitzky, 'Labour coercion', pp. 563–9.

164. North and Thomas, 'Rise and fall', pp. 786–95; Cerman, 'Demesne lordship', pp. 242–48.

165. Stephen H. Rigby, 'Serfdom', in *The Oxford Encyclopedia of Economic History*, volume 4 (2003), p. 463; Markus Cerman, 'Demesne lordship and rural society in early modern east central and eastern Europe: comparative perspectives', *Agricultural History Review*, 59 (2011), pp. 239–40, 254; Erich Landsteiner, 'Demesne lordship and the early modern state in central Europe: the struggle for labour rent in lower Austria in the second half of the sixteenth century', *Agricultural History Review*, 59 (2011), pp. 266–92; Myrdal, 'Scandinavia', pp. 208–14; Mysliwski, 'Central Europe', pp. 268–77; Janet Martin, 'Russia', in Kitsikopoulos, ed. *Agrarian change*, pp. 299–309, 316–19; Markus Cerman, *Villagers and lords in eastern Europe 1300–1800* (Basingstoke, 2012), p. 132; Dennison, 'Institutional context', pp. 251–2; Ogilvie, 'Choices and constraints', pp. 276–8; Klein and Ogilvie, 'Occupational structure', p. 494.

166. Cerman, *Villagers and lords*, pp. 1–22; Dennison, *Institutional framework*, pp. 214–17; Dennison, 'Institutional context of serfdom', pp. 249–68; Ogilvie, 'Choices and constraints', pp. 269–305.

167. Ogilvie, 'Choices and constraints', pp. 274–80.

168. Bailey, 'Villeinage in England', pp. 433–55.

169. As discussed in Whittle, *Agrarian capitalism*, pp. 305–15; Cerman, 'Demesne lordship', pp. 243, 258.

170. Dennison, *Institutional framework*, pp. 213–22; Cerman, 'Demesne lordship', pp. 243–54; Dennison, 'Institutional context of serfdom', pp. 249–68; Ogilvie, 'Choices and constraints', pp. 269–305. See the initial exploration of some of these ideas in Whittle, 'Individualism', pp. 58–63, and Briggs, 'English serfdom', pp. 3–32.

171. Cerman, 'Demesne lordship', p. 254; Ogilvie, 'Choices and constraints', pp. 274–305.

172. Cerman, *Villagers and lords*, p. 1.
173. Campbell, 'Factor markets', p. 99.
174. French and Hoyle, *English rural society*, pp. 20, 25, 28–9.
175. This serves as an important counterbalance to the statements in Clark, *Farewell to alms*, pp. 160–3.
176. van Bavel, 'Factor markets', pp. 18–19.
177. Stephen H. Rigby, 'Historical causation: is one thing more important than another?', *History*, 259 (1995), pp. 227–42; Greif, *Institutions*, pp. 17–39, 155–6, 350–6, 379–80.
178. Campbell, *Great transition*, p. 395.

8

Conclusion

Early fourteenth-century England was in the grip of a severe socio-economic crisis. Furthermore, its economic performance lagged well behind the European leaders such as the Low Countries and northern Italy. In 1348–9 the Black Death struck, killing nearly half the population of Europe. By 1500 real wages and GDP per head had risen in England, so that the gap with the continental leaders had begun to close. The English form of serfdom—villeinage—had withered away, and factor and commodity markets were well established. England had reached the dawn of the modern age with many of the foundations for its extraordinary development in the seventeenth and eighteenth centuries already in place. Yet this same demographic shock—the loss of nearly half the population in the first epidemic, and repeated subsequent exposure to outbreaks of disease—had resulted in very different outcomes across Europe: serfdom was preserved in some places (much of eastern Europe), and GDP per head had remained constant or had even fallen in others (Spain and Ireland).

These broad trends are not disputed. The explanation for the different responses is, however, the subject of intense debate. The conventional narrative has emphasized the pervasive and ultimately stifling influence of manorial lordship ('feudalism') in explaining the distress and the backwardness of early fourteenth-century England. The distinctive strength of manorial lordship in England derived partly from the development of the common law, which during the thirteenth century had enhanced the legal powers of lords over servile land and labour. This stifled the development of land, labour, and commodity markets, and enabled lords to control those that did exist. Towns were relatively unimportant, and seigniorial demand for non-essential and luxury goods was the main driver behind commerce. This narrative provides a clear explanation as to why the English economy could not absorb the relentless growth in population before the Black Death, and why its performance was modest when compared to, say, the Low Countries, where manorialism had largely dissolved and factor markets had already developed apace.

This conventional narrative also explains why the attention of most historians writing in the twentieth century was focused so intently upon the crisis of the pre-plague period, why they relentlessly downplayed the impact of the Black Death, which was relegated to the role of an accelerator of a crisis already in motion. It also explains England's peculiar social and economic trajectory after the Black Death. Manorial lordship this powerful was capable of mounting a vigorous

After the Black Death: Economy, Society, and the Law in Fourteenth-Century England. Mark Bailey, Oxford University Press (2021). © Mark Bailey. DOI: 10.1093/oso/9780198857884.003.0008

seigniorial reaction in its immediate aftermath to compel peasants to work and to occupy land on terms favourable to lords, contrary to the forces of supply and demand now that workers were suddenly scarce and land abundant. This explains why little supposedly changed in the third quarter of the century and why historians have not looked very closely at this period. It also establishes a context for the state's decisive intervention in 1349 and 1351 in the labour and commodity markets: it supported the position of landlords, thereby forging a cogent new alliance between all forms of lordship against the plebian mass. The alliance was so successful that the effects of plague on society and the economy hardly showed until the late 1370s. Yet the rising tide of coercion and exploitation in the 1350s and 1360s generated a strengthening counter-current of peasant resistance, culminating in the Peasants' Revolt of 1381. Chastened government and manorial lords quickly abandoned their harsh policies in its wake. In the 1380s and 1390s prices, wages, and land rents at last behaved as economic theory predicted they should following a demographic cull of this magnitude. Hence in this interpretation, after the watershed of 1381 economic and social trends combined to dissolve serfdom, and as the edifice of manorial lordship crumbled over the next fifty years so markets became firmly established.

This book has drawn upon a large corpus of recent scholarship, a re-reading of older studies, and original research into legal and manorial documents to construct a subtly different version of events, and to explore an amended explanatory framework. It argues that the strength and influence of manorial lordship on the eve of plague has been overstated; in the 1350s and 1360s the effects of a succession of extreme events, and the resultant uncertainty and turbulence, have been overlooked; initial and patchy attempts at a seigniorial reaction had fizzled out before the end of the 1350s, and villeinage was in headlong retreat long before the Peasants' Revolt of 1381; the late 1380s saw renewed social conflict over labour and acute difficulties in agriculture; the post-plague equilibrium was not reached until the mid-1390s; and by 1400 the major structural adjustments triggered by plague had largely worked through. The forces of supply and demand were—for the most part—triumphing immediately after 1350, although the speed of responses varied by sector and the survivors faced sustained adversity and uncertainty that influenced their decision-making.

At the heart of this revised framework is a different view of the strength and influence of manorial lordship. Its powers were much weaker than portrayed in the conventional narrative, while factor and commodity markets in non-elite goods were larger, and, crucially, lords exercised little control over them. Consequently, peasants—including villeins—were able to access and to operate in them with limited seigniorial interference. In the 1340s two villeins—John Docke and Roger le Reve—were even running the small town of Botesdale (Suffolk) as lessees of its market from their own lord (see pp. 48–50). Yet this revisionist argument faces a major challenge because it begs two difficult questions. First, what then caused pre-plague stagnation and crisis? Second, if manorial lordship was too weak to mount a seigniorial reaction after 1350, how then do we explain the government's labour laws, the rapid decline of villeinage, and, for that matter, the Peasants' Revolt?

Research in the last two decades has confirmed that earlier narratives have underestimated the development of factor and commodity markets by the early fourteenth century, and overestimated the ability of lords to control what markets did exist. Likewise, as we saw in Chapter 2, the English peasantry did not conform to the stereotype of immobile, subsistence-orientated family units usually associated with traditional peasant societies. Relatively secure property rights had developed during the course of the thirteenth century, underpinning the emergence of a sizeable peasant land market, but by c.1300 landlords had lost control of the freehold market everywhere and much of the unfree market in south-east England and East Anglia. Peasants routinely bought and sold land among themselves for money, and paid the majority of agricultural head rents in cash. This did not mean, however, that the growth of a land market and the diminution of lordly control over its operation was beneficial to peasant welfare. Around 90 per cent of peasant land was held on service tenancies whose cash head rents had been fixed for decades, and so on the eve of plague their level had become ossified far below the prevailing commercial value of land. Yet, paradoxically and perversely, while rents on peasant land were largely non-commercial, land sales were determined by the forces of supply and demand, and the capital gains accrued to the peasant vendor not the lords. This peculiar mix of head rents fixed well below sub-economic levels, the ability of peasants to sell land on commercial terms, and high land values resulted in the extreme fragmentation of peasant landholdings in many places. The hired labour market was larger than usually depicted— absorbing about one-third of productive labour—and hardly controlled by either manorial authorities or the state: it was chronically oversupplied. Commodity markets for non-elite goods were well established (for example, about one-third of all grain was traded), but fragmented and inefficient. Credit was widely available, but it was expensive and tended to reinforce existing inequalities. Thus the institutional framework of markets served to increase inequality and risk under the pressure of high population.

In pre-plague England manorial lordship was one factor influencing the allocation of resources within a complex mix that included custom, family, tenurial arrangements, the market, and the law (Chapter 2). Its character had also changed, in the sense that rule- and procedure-governed behaviour had displaced a great deal of lords' personal and discretionary powers over its peasantry. The combined effect was to restrain and diminish the arbitrary aspects of manorial lordship. The particular combination of manorial lordship with these other factors had created an institutional mosaic which, when subject to the sustained pressure of high population in the late thirteenth and early fourteenth centuries, caused landholdings to splinter and real wages to plummet. The effect was to create chronic rural congestion and poverty, which not only depressed demand per head and mean disposable household income but also inhibited savings, investment, and the adaptation of agrarian techniques to commercial opportunities. The immiserated condition of the mass of the populace heightened the economic and social sensitivity to external shocks, such as extreme weather, a deteriorating climate, heavy taxation, intermittent warfare, recurrent harvest failures, and diseases of livestock. As the global climate system changed from the 1280s, such exogenous events increased in frequency and severity. The Black Death, however, dramatically changed the paradigm.

The first epidemic in 1348–9 reduced the population from around 5.5 million to 2.8 million, and coincided with a period of exceptionally cold weather, creating a crisis that did not abate until 1353. Harvest failures, labour shortages, and the disruption to trade caused a dramatic inflation of the prices of foodstuffs, fuel, and basic farm equipment. The soaring costs of salt and fuel indicate a period of extreme cold and reduced solar output. Taxation and purveyance added to the challenges faced by survivors. Landlords reacted initially with a predictable combination of concession and repression. Consequently, recovery from the demographic hammer blow during the 1350s for many people was less straightforward than traditionally supposed, and took longer in arable farming in particular, which explains the continued dereliction of large areas of arable and references to the poverty of tenants well into the 1360s in some parts of the country. Some survivors of the first epidemic, such as John Derling of Esher (Surrey), experienced bouts of impoverishment as he struggled to respond to the enormity of what had happened and its aftermath (p. 75).

Such challenges and disruption endured well into the 1360s, as plague returned (1361, 1369, 1375), the weather was highly variable, harvests continued to fail, and livestock suffered repeated attacks of disease. The population fell from c.2.8 million in the early 1350s to c.2.5 million in the late 1370s. The old notion that there were no fundamental social or economic changes in the third quarter of the fourteenth century is no longer credible. The succession of dramatic climatic and epidemiological events generated turbulence that has been gravely underestimated, but it goes a long way to explaining the many conflicting and paradoxical economic signals of this period: high prices for foodstuffs and basic commodities, falling purchasing power of wages, strong revenues from rents, and the tumbling value of customary land. The degree of buoyancy in the economy is striking and largely explained by the action of various demand-side factors, whose effects meant that the fall in output was not as great as the fall in population: monetary inflation, the falling proportion of landless people, rising household and disposable incomes, and increased consumption of basic foodstuffs and clothing among the lower orders.

The combination of increased incomes per head, turbulence, and uncertainty encourages much closer analysis of the nature of supply-side responses in the third quarter of the century (Chapter 4). The evidence points to rapid adjustments as early as the mid-1350s in some sectors of the economy: growth is manifest in brewing, basic manufactures (especially textiles), dairy produce, rabbit, and poultry rearing. Conversely, it also reveals very sluggish responses in other sectors, especially high-end construction, luxury goods, and the extractive industries (especially tin mining). In the middle of this spectrum, the supply of grain was sufficient for the subsistence purposes of most rural households, but persistently below the level of demand within the commercial market. The proportion of grain marketed from the key peasant sector had fallen for a variety of reasons, creating serious concerns about food shortages in the late 1360s in cities such as London and Bristol. The range of sectoral responses indicates that those relying upon low-skilled workers and limited capital inputs, and/or where the work was regular and the rewards were immediate and predictable, responded quickly and nimbly to the post-plague opportunities. In contrast, sectors requiring highly-skilled workers and/or large capital inputs, and/or where the work was arduous, monotonous, irregular, or dangerous, and rewards were more distant, delayed, or uncertain, struggled. In the wake of two catastrophic demographic events, and surrounded by volatility and uncertainty about the future, workers may well have become more affective in their decision-making, prioritizing short term rewards and minimizing risk in preference to responding directly to price stimuli and certain opportunities for profit.

One the eve of the Black Death round 20 per cent of the population lived in (mainly small) towns, many of which struggled to recover from the demographic blow. The vast majority were smaller after 1348-9, with substantially reduced levels of trade. A few maintained their populations or even grew (such as Westminster), especially those specializing in those manufactures in demand from the 1350s, such as the textile towns of Colchester (Essex) and Coventry (Warks.). Towns may have been fewer and smaller, but the proportion of the population living there held constant at around 20 per cent. Inflation and short-ages of foodstuffs in the 1360s were most keenly felt in urban centres. The experience of shortages of commercial supplies of grain in the late 1360s acceler-ated the take-up of arable holdings and an increase in commercial grain produc-tion during the early 1370s, although ironically this swing contributed to the sudden onset of conditions of oversupply after 1376. Monetary deflation, sus-tained demographic decline, and benign weather were other important factors in the sharp downturn in the Composite Price Index, driven by the fall in grain prices and its associated products. But the economy had not yet reached its post-plague equilibrium (Chapter 6). Between 1385 and 1395 severe monetary deflation exacerbated the tendency towards oversupply in agriculture, and resulted in the withdrawal of most of the great landlords from direct demesne exploitation. This recession highlighted the high cost and scarcity of hired seasonal labour in agriculture, sharpening the contemporary debate on labour, and triggering a mini seigniorial reaction on the estates of a handful of high-status landlords. The abbot of Bury St Edmunds (Suffolk) cracked down hard on the mobility of serfs on his estate between the mid-1380s and mid-1390s because attempting to exploit his arable demesnes directly in such dire conditions meant he had little to lose by such tough tactics. The land market slowed markedly, and arable was increasingly abandoned and allowed to revert to permanent pasture. The swing to manufacturing and to livestock rearing continued. The severe monetary conditions eased in the mid-1390s. By the end of the 1390s output in the vast majority of sectors had now stabilized at their post-plague level.

The forces of supply and demand—not the compulsion and power of manorial lordship—dominate this description of the key trends of the second half of the fourteenth century. Markets were inefficient, of course, a point underlined by the extended time-lags of adjustment in some sectors, but they were well established in the 1340s and growing in relative importance from the early 1350s. Shortages of tenants prompted isolated attempts in the 1350s to compel serfs to hold villein land on the old terms, but mostly forced landlords to make concessions on the terms of tenure to retain and attract tenants (Chapter 3). Many of the servile incidents on the traditional villein service tenure—tallage, millsuit, merchet, labour services—were eased or dropped, and a growing proportion of peasant land was converted to contractual tenures, mainly short-term leases for cash, but also quasi-commercial and fixed cash head rents on hereditary and life-tenancies. Land values per unit area fell by up to a third between the 1340s and 1360s. As a result of all of these changes, villein land became more accessible and more attractive to non-serfs and non-heirs, and freemen and incoming migrants of servile origin poured into the customary land market. By the end of the 1350s freemen already comprised nearly half the tenants of customary land in places as far apart as Sawley (Derbys.) and Durrington (Wilts.).

The Black Death increased the mobility of peasant land, and broke irreversibly the traditional link between tenure and status. The acceleration in the leasing of demesnes, especially from the 1380s, further increased the opportunities for an emerging peasant elite to obtain land and construct large commercial holdings. By the end of the fourteenth century this elite was self-identifying as yeomen and husbandmen, and the use of this novel nomenclature served the dual purpose of distinguishing them from the rest of peasant society—the smallholders, artisans, servants, and labourers—and of distancing many of them from their servile roots. The majority of rural dwellers were smallholders, combining a holding of a few acres with occasional paid employment for others, while a sizeable minority were cottagers earning a living mainly from paid labour or live-in servants on annual contracts. The mixed economy of smallholders, and uncertainty about the number of days labourers worked each year, makes it impossible to measure accurately the extent of their gains. Their incomes probably increased by nearly one-half between the 1340s and 1390s, although they were unlikely to have increased much thereafter. Likewise, the yeomanry would have struggled to make much profit from commercial grain farming after the 1380s. This was a comfortable—not an unbridled golden—age for the peasantry, and the rewards were not evenly distributed between them.

What, then, was the main contribution of the arrival of the Black Death to England's lurch towards modernity? We must, of course, be wary of viewing changes in the second half of the fourteenth century through the lens of the future: even as late as 1600, the cultural, social, and economic structure of England did not yet resemble modern capitalism.[1] The changes laying the road to industrialization were multi-faceted, complex, and occurred slowly over a long period of time. Hence in many ways the most informative approach is to look backwards, not forwards, to identify what had changed decisively or irreversibly since the pre-plague era.

Between the 1340s and 1400 GDP per head increased by at least one-third, reflecting the reduction in the tail of landless and poverty-stricken people, and some redistribution of wealth down the social scale. Production shifted from grain to livestock farming, and from agriculture to manufactures, and also involved greater dependence on the market among the lower orders. By 1400 perhaps 40 per cent of the population was employed outside agriculture, a good deal of it in rural settings. The livestock share of agriculture now exceeded 50 per cent, and its commercial orientation had increased. The effects of both of these structural changes were to spread wealth and employment more equitably throughout England, and to extend London's influence, diminishing (but not yet eradicating) the spatial differentials between the south-east and the rest of the country, and reducing dependence upon the staple of grain. These in turn reduced society's vulnerability to future harvest sensitivity and famine, and helped to protect incomes and GDP per head when population rose again in the sixteenth century.

The Black Death also precipitated the decline of villeinage. In the 1340s one-third of all arable land was unfree, c.90 per cent of which was held on non-commercial servile tenures, and around 40 per cent of the population were villeins. After 1348–9 the incidents associated with tenurial villeinage declined faster and further than those of personal servility. The dilution of servile incidents, the practice of issuing of copies of the terms of the tenancy to the tenant (the origin of copyhold), and conversions to cash tenancies were prominent features of the 1350s and 1360s, and by 1400 over one-half of villein land was now held on commercial or quasi-commercial cash tenancies. The breaking of the link between tenure and status encouraged some lords to record the status of hereditary serfs in manorial courts more assiduously in order to create written proof of their subordination and to track their subsequent movements. Plague, migration, grants of freedom, and even seigniorial indifference reduced the number and relative importance of serfs in the population at large, from 40 per cent in the 1340s, to perhaps 20 per cent in 1381, and by c.1400 perhaps as little as one tenth. Many of these remaining serfs must have sorely resented their labelling and status.

The reasons for the decline of villeinage in England are more complex than allowed in the traditional narrative, which proposes a seigniorial reaction, followed by resistance and revolt, and finally decay between the 1380s and 1430s. As manorial lordship and villeinage were too weak on the eve of the Black Death to enable lords to dictate the allocation of land, labour, and capital, or to alter arbitrarily the terms on which they were held, it follows that in its wake their powers were simply not strong enough to use force to impose unfavourable terms upon the peasantry. Some lords certainly attempted to do so in limited ways during the 1350s, and again to a lesser extent in the late 1380s, but there is no credible evidence to support the argument that a systemic, country-wide, seigniorial reaction occurred in the third quarter of the fourteenth century. Villeinage declined because it was already weak when plague struck, and because thereafter lords competed with each other for tenants and workers, irrespective of whose serf it was, as exemplified by the tug-of-war in 1353 over the Winslow (Bucks.) serf, William Adam, between the cellarer of St Albans abbey and a local lord. English serfs enjoyed flexible access to a variety of opportunities in town and countryside, in agriculture and in manufacturing, in self-employment and hired work, and the scale and immediacy of all these outside options rendered seigniorial coercion impractical and cost-ineffective. Austin Crembill, a serf of the earl of Oxford, maintained active business interests simultaneously in two villages 18 miles apart, before settling as an alehouse keeper on the manor of another lord (pp. 309–10). Although these were the principal reasons for the crumbling of the edifice of English villeinage, there is no doubt that resistance and conflict also hastened serfdom's decline. The inability to defend the title to this land in the courts of common law remained a source of resentment, especially for the freemen and non-serfs now holding most villein land, as did the last vestiges of the old servile incidents, such as residual labour services on the estates of conservative landlords. The very process of labelling 'serfs by blood' in court rolls was demeaning, and in the 1350s and again in the 1380s a handful of landlords sought to restrict their mobility and to raise revenues through more rigorous enforcement of the personal incidents of serfdom. Social stigma and these belittling traits made serfdom worth evading, and worth resisting as one of the elements in the Great Rumour of 1377 and the Peasants' Revolt in 1381.

The spread of contractual tenures on peasant land and the leasing of demesnes shifted the institutional paradigm of agriculture decisively and irreversibly (Chapter 7). In the 1340s perhaps 20 per cent of all arable land in England was held on some form of contractual tenure, and 45 per cent in 1400. These developments reduced the barriers to entering the land market, increased the mobility of land, and accelerated the commoditization of land as a marketable asset. They provided opportunities for scattered holdings to be consolidated and concentrated in a particular area of the village fields, reducing unit costs of production and increasing efficiency. They began the process of removing many of the sub-economic head rents that had caused holdings to splinter under population pressure before 1348, and of replacing them with more commercial tenures, both of which stimulated engrossment and discouraged fragmentation when population eventually rose again. The leasing of demesnes was never reversed, and so the process transferred more land to the peasant sector permanently and increased the commercial sector's reliance on the output of peasant farms. This bundle of institutional changes was irreversible, and laid the basis for the eventual construction of large commercial farms over the next three centuries. Plague was central to shifting the paradigm. Repeated outbreaks of epidemic disease increased significantly the turnover of land, the failure of heirs, and the proportion of untenanted land, all of which were crucial to providing more opportunities and incentives for lords to change the terms of tenure. Likewise, the reduced demand for land made it easier for tenants to reconfigure and to engross, and even to enclose, their landholdings. Landlords still recorded the status of land (whether free, unfree or demesne), although the tenure on which it was held was now more varied. Walter Spalding built a holding of 16 acres tightly concentrated in one area of his village from a combination of free, villein, and demesne land on a variety of different tenures (see pp. 303–4). Of course, in 1400 agriculture was still not capitalist, and many disincentives, obstacles, and rigidities remained to productivity gains and greater commercial orientation. But its institutional structure was now materially different to the 1340s, and it had begun to unravel the original tenurial tangle.

The emergence of the centralized state in matters of social and economic policy, and in the provision of justice, is another major theme in the rise of modern institutions. The Black Death provides a prominent and early example of a government taking decisive action at a moment of national crisis to protect what it regarded as the welfare of its peoples and to promote its notion of a good society (Chapter 3). The state intervened in both commodity and labour markets even as the first plague epidemic was still raging. Its objective was not to prevent them from existing or expanding but to strengthen existing legislation against profiteering in commodity markets, and to impose new controls over the operation of the labour market. The latter attempted to re-impose the labour conditions of the 1340s and to provide an appropriate supply of labour in agriculture, as if plague had never happened, with the objective of ensuring 'balance' within the social order in accordance with contemporary estates theory. In doing so, the labour legislation sought to enforce social inequality, and to ignore economic reality and equality. In the 1350s the government's policies enjoyed some success, but thereafter their principal success lay in constraining not compelling workers, thereby generating unrest and discontent. The drafting of the legislation and the mechanics of its enforcement resulted in wide discrepancies in its implementation and in the treatment of similar wrongs, because it bestowed upon local officials of the Crown considerable personal discretion in interpretation and action while subjecting them to too few supervisory checks. Employees were targeted for accepting excess wages, whereas employers were scarcely punished for paying them (Chapter 5).

In both conception and implementation, the price-fixing and the labour laws were highly inequitable. They reflected the innate social conservatism of the prevailing estates ideology and the ruling elite in their attempt to restore the pre-plague economic status quo and to protect vested interests in a radically altered world. They inevitably heightened conflict and contestation, but not along class lines of lords against peasants. The legislation served the interests of employers, which included many peasants. Peasant leaders of local communities were employers of hired labour, especially during the harvest, and they regarded the itinerant, the leisured, and the lazy worker with suspicion. Peasant and urban employers, not lords, implemented the legislation on the ground, which conse- quently generated swirling tensions within communities. The Peasants' Revolt served as a warning to the state about the ambitious expansion of its powers in matters of social policy, as well as a reminder of the need for competent govern- ment and for the consent of subjects when raising levels of taxation to uncom- monly high levels (Chapter 5). So, after 1349 the state had become more active and assertive in social affairs, although its objectives were backward-looking, moralis- tic, conservative, and unenforceable. The government's ambitions, idealism, and shortcomings in this arena are exemplified by its brief and unsuccessful attempt in 1363 to implement a sumptuary law.

The state's intervention in the labour market was designed to compel the idle to participate in it, and to tighten the contractual terms in private covenants—the level of pay, the length of contract, the mode of hiring—in favour of all types of employers. This encouraged a culture more generally of tighter contractual terms and conditions, including the witnessing of oral contracts. A parallel development is evident in land tenures after 1348–9, with the rapid expansion and tightening of contractual forms such as leases. The extended use of contracts was an important element in ensuring that the forces of supply and demand prevailed in commodity and factor markets in the aftermath of plague—rather than seigniorial coercion— although, of course, it depended on the pre-existence of a legal system capable of resolving breaches and an associated culture of using legal means for redress. In this respect, the provision and extension of royal justice during the twelfth and thirteenth centuries was a development of considerable importance within the institutional framework of England. As such, the English experience highlights the beneficial stimulus of the law in long-term economic development, although ironically this was not the intention of the common-law legislators. Nor was the provision of a broadly standardized system of justice primarily or exclusively a function of a powerful, centralized state: while the state initially promoted it, its subsequent spread and wide uptake by 1300 occurred principally because thou- sands of local and privatized legal jurisdictions emulated and utilized it.

The English experience provides a counter-balance to some of the established scholarship on pre-modern legal systems, which sometimes portrays the law as irrelevant to peasants, but more often as deleterious to their welfare and social standing.[2] The view that pre-modern laws and legal systems were detrimental to ordinary people draws upon the presumption that legal codes created the forms and practices through which ruling elites commodified and expropriated peasant land and labour. As elites controlled both the creation of new laws and their implementation, it seems logical to suppose that they would tend to construct laws and manipulate justice in ways that primarily served and furthered their own interests, and strengthened their powers of extra economic coercion over a dependent peasantry.[3] This presumption is implicit or explicit in most assessments of medieval England.[4] Kosminsky argued that the common law provided lords with a regulated and ordered means of increasing feudal rent and exploiting the peasantry or, as Brenner put it, 'an indispensable lever to raise dues arbitrarily on customary lands and tenants'.[5] Kitsikopoulos judges the overall impact of the common law on the peasantry to be negative: 'the judicial system acted as one of the instruments used to provide an appearance of legitimacy to exploitative extractive mechanisms'.[6] Likewise, van Bavel attributes the stifling of market growth and efficiency in thirteenth-century England to 'the interference of the ever more dominant social groups which have benefited from the market exchange...[who tend] to freeze and preserve the market institutions which had exerted their beneficial effect on them and helped them come to the fore'.[7] Hence the widespread assumption that the development of the common law increased seigniorial powers to restrict the economic freedom of villeins and to restrict the growth of markets, while also increasing the powers of merchants to operate markets in their own interests.[8]

There is no doubt that laws and legal codes promoted the interests of social elites and as such institutionalized inequalities, and the Statute of Labourers and the creation of gentry justices are prime examples. But this does not mean that the impact of the law on the freedom and welfare of peasants, or indeed on the size and operation of factor and commodity markets, was wholly or unremittingly negative. The legal developments were essential to contract enforcement—an essential building block to reducing risk in systems of exchange—and they help to explain the diverging historical pathways of different regions.[9] The Statute of Labourers was not a pure instrument of class power, and in some ways it encouraged more rigour in the drawing up of contractual terms among all levels of society. As Ogilvie states, in reality 'legal systems facilitated some peasant choices and constrained others'.[10] The balance sheet of the effects of the common law on the peasantry must weigh practice against theory, benefits against drawbacks. Certainly, the common law offered a good degree of protection to free tenure, and it protected people of free status against enserfment. Its presumption to liberty and upholding of borough privilege provided some protection to flown serfs, and the adoption of some of the practices relating to free tenure in the transfer of unfree land helped to strengthen property rights over the latter. The adoption of many of its practices and its culture in local privatized courts provided all peasants and townsfolk with a relatively cheap, accessible, and impersonal system of dispute resolution and contract enforcement. The latter point also underlines that a standardized legal code can develop even when a state is still relatively immature as an institution, because of the willingness of local lordship and people to emulate and adopt the processes.

The English experience also demonstrates how the operation of a state-instigated legal code can limit the exploitative and arbitrary powers of lords, and create a legal culture that promotes restraint, and a commitment to due process, written precedents, and proofs. The legal culture in medieval England came to alter social perceptions of justice, and conditioned the behaviour and expectations of lords, peasants, and townsfolk.[11] It provided a variety of tribunals for cheap, accessible, and relatively efficient contract enforcement, an essential element in reducing risk in impersonal exchange.[12] In short, it rendered the provision of local justice more impersonal, more standardized, more hostile to discretion, and friendlier to rigid rules and, by extension, fostered a respect for contracts and for due process.[13] The proliferation of this culture of law, and a concept of equity, had the consequence of weakening and limiting the potential for arbitrary seigniorial behaviour.[14] This was not the original intention of common-law legislators, which underlines that the evolution of legal institutions can carry unintended and inadvertent consequences. Nor was England now fixed on some linear and progressive pathway to its modern legal system. There was nothing certain about the pathway forward, and, for example, the use of local courts in contract enforcement and dispute resolution declined in the fifteenth and sixteenth centuries.[15] Nevertheless, the English system in the fourteenth century was distinctive, and contributed importantly to the growth of factor markets and their further development after 1350. In contrasting it with the legal framework of nineteenth-century Russia, Dennison concludes that the former fitted within a 'framework of interlocking legal institutions extending from the Crown to the manor', which helped to stimulate greater economic development in England and 'overtime appears to have evolved in a way that undermined the system of serfdom itself'.[16]

The Black Death killed between one-third and one-half of the population of Europe, but the same, sudden, universal, demographic shock stimulated very different social, economic, and cultural outcomes. It triggered the intervention of the state in social policy in England, whose effects are still felt today, but resulted in no state intervention in many other countries and even the fragmentation of state authority in some, such as Ireland. It resulted in very different patterns in wealth per head, and in long-term trajectories of growth, across the continent. Within England, demographic collapse shifted the balance of social and economic power away from lords to the peasantry, and the increased commoditization of factor markets, but their effects were not evenly spread. Male day-labourers enjoyed greater gains than women on annual contracts. Many peasants remained smallholders, whereas a small elite from varied social backgrounds began to construct sizeable, commercial, holdings. These examples—and there are many more throughout the book—reinforce the point that pandemics are watersheds in human history, but they do not dictate the direction, nature, and pace of change. The dislocation caused by pandemics opens up possibilities for change, for increasing the pace of change, or, indeed, for embedding vested interests even deeper. The interaction of natural and human agency is interlinked and interdependent in complex, fascinating, and, sometimes, impenetrable ways.

Notes

1. Howell, *Commerce*, p. 300.
2. Ogilvie, 'Choices and constraints', pp. 294–302.
3. Steinberg, *England's great transformation*, pp. 3–25, 32.
4. See, for example, Rodney H. Hilton, *A medieval society: the west midlands at the end of the thirteenth century* (London, 1948), 218–19, pp. 240–1; Hilton, *Bond men made free*, p. 151; Brenner, 'Rises and declines', pp. 260–1; Stephen H. Rigby, 'Historical Materialism: social structure and social change in the Middle Ages', *Journal of Medieval and Early Modern Studies*, 34 (2004), pp. 488–90.
5. Kosminsky, *Studies in the agrarian history*, pp. 328–54; Brenner, 'Agrarian roots', pp. 257–8.
6. Kitsikopoulos, 'England', p. 47.
7. van Bavel, *Invisible hand*, p. 20.
8. Hilton, *Medieval society*, pp. 140, 159, 166; Brenner, 'Agrarian roots', pp. 257–8; Ros Faith, *The English peasantry and the growth of lordship* (Leicester, 1997), pp. 248, 263–6; Brenner, 'Rises and declines', pp. 262–3; Kitsikopoulos, 'England', p. 46; Dyer, 'Memories', p. 277; Brenner, 'Property and progress', pp. 95–6; Adam Lucas, *Ecclesiastical lordship: seigneurial power and the commercialization of milling in medieval England* (Farnham, 2014), p. 308; van Bavel, *Invisible hand*, pp. 20–1. For summaries, see Razi and Smith, 'Origins', pp. 40–3; Rigby, *English society*, pp. 25–30; and Hatcher and Bailey, *Modelling the middle ages*, pp. 77–8.
9. Briggs, 'Introduction', pp. 3–5.
10. Ogilvie, 'Choices and constraints', p. 302.
11. Palmer, 'Economic and cultural origins', p. 376.
12. Briggs, 'Introduction', pp. 9–14.
13. Palmer, 'Economic and cultural origins', pp. 394–6; Hyams, *King, lords, and peasants*, p. 257.
14. Hyams, 'Edwardian villagers', pp. 92–9; Bonfield, 'Nature of customary law', p. 520.
15. Bailey, *English manor*, pp. 184–9; Briggs, 'Seigniorial control', p. 421.
16. Dennison, 'Institutional context', p. 268.

APPENDIX

Calculations in Table 6.3

The method for the calculations in table 7.3 is as follows.

Yields per acre, net of tithe and seed, were 5.1 bushels in 1360–9 and 6.3 in 1380–9. These figures were reached by calculating the mean yield per acre on pre-Black Death demesnes in Norfolk (6.3 bushels), FTC counties (5.3 bushels), and Winchester estates (5.1 bushels) = average of 5.6 bushels per acre, as documented in Campbell, *Seigniorial agriculture*, p. 335. Yields per seed for wheat, barley, and oats were then taken for every harvest between 1361 and 1369, and 1381 and 1389 to produce an average for the decade and expressed as an index of 1300–49 = 100, using Campbell, 'Grain yields', p. 165. The indices are 1360–9 = 91 and 1380–9 = 112. Using 5.6 bushels per acre as the mean for 1300–49, the mean yield per acre in 1360–9 = 5.1 bushels and in 1380–9 = 6.3 bushels per acre.

The price of grain was calculated by taking the mean price for wheat, rye, barley, oats, and beans for each year between 1360–1 and 1369–70, and 1380–1 and 1389–90, as provided in Farmer, 'Prices and wages', pp. 502–3. The mean was 1360–9 = 8.15d. per bushel of 'grain' and 1380–9 = 5.34d. per bushel.

We assume that family labour is capable of working the first 20 acres of an arable holding, i.e. without recourse to hired labour. By extension, hired labour will work every additional acre above the 20. We assume that 13 days of hired work are required for each additional acre, following Hatcher, 'Unreal wages', pp. 16–17.

The average cost of a day's agricultural labour is 2.74d. in 1360–9, and 3.09d. in 1380–9, taken from Clark, 'Long march', pp. 99–100. However, these neat averages disguise the reality of significant seasonal variation in rates of pay and the availability of work, which meant that around 20 per cent of all daily pay was higher than the average (say, 3d. per diem in 1360–9 and 3.25d. in 1380–9) and 80 per cent were lower (say, 1.7d. in 1360–9 and 2d. in 1380–9): see Hatcher, 'Unreal wages', pp. 18–19, esp. fn. 42. From this, we adjust the 1360–9 figure to 2d. per diem and the 1380–9 figure to 2.25d. per diem.

We assume that 66 per cent of the arable holding will be left fallow each year, and therefore the fallow third does not contribute either to the yield of the holding or the costs of the holding.

References

Aberth, John. 2001. *From the brink of the apocalypse: confronting famine, war, plague and death in the later Middle Ages*. London.

Acemoglu, Daron, and Wolitzky, Alexander. 2011. 'The economics of labour coercion', *Econometrica*, 79.

Aers, David. 1994. 'Justice and wage-labor after the Black Death: some perplexities for William Langland', in Allen J. Frantzen and Douglas Moffat, eds., *The work of work: servitude, slavery, and labour in medieval England*. Glasgow.

Allen, Martin. 2012. *Mints and money in medieval England*. Cambridge.

Allen, Robert C. 1992. *Enclosure and the yeoman: the agricultural development of the south Midlands 1450–1850*. Oxford.

Allen, Robert C. 1999. 'Tracking the agricultural revolution in England', *Economic History Review*, 52.

Allen, Robert C. 2001.'The Great Divergence in European wages and prices from the Middle Ages to the First World War', *Explorations in Economic History*, 38.

Allen, Robert C. 2003. 'Progress and poverty in early modern Europe', *Economic History Review*, 56.

Allen, Robert C. 2009. *The British industrial revolution in global perspective*. Cambridge.

Allen, Robert C., and Weisdorf, Jacob L. 2011. 'Was there an "industrious revolution" before the industrial revolution?: an empirical exercise for England, c. 1300–1830', *Economic History Review*, 64.

Amor, Nicholas. 2016. *From wool to cloth: the triumph of the Suffolk clothier*. Bungay.

Amor, Nicholas, *Keeping the peace in medieval Suffolk* (forthcoming).

Ault, Warren O. 1930. 'Some early village by-laws', *English Historical Review*, 178.

Ault, Warren O. 1972. *Open-field farming in medieval England: a study of village by-laws*. London.

Bailey, Mark. 1988. 'The rabbit and the medieval East Anglian economy', *Agricultural History Review*, 36.

Bailey, Mark. 1989. 'Blowing up bubbles: some new demographic evidence for the fifteenth century?', *Journal of Medieval History*, 15.

Bailey, Mark. 1989. *A marginal economy?: East Anglian Breckland in the later Middle Ages*. Cambridge.

Bailey, Mark. 1991. '*Per impetum maris*: natural disaster and economic decline in eastern England, 1275–1350', in Bruce M.S. Campbell, ed., *Before the Black Death: essays in the crisis of the early fourteenth century*. Manchester.

Bailey, Mark, ed. 1992. *The bailiff's minute book of Dunwich, 1404–1430*, Suffolk Records Society, 34.

Bailey, Mark. 1993. 'A tale of two towns: Buntingford and Standon in the later Middle Ages', *Journal of Medieval History*, 19.

Bailey, Mark. 1994. 'The Prior and Convent of Ely and the manor of Lakenheath in the fourteenth century', in Christopher Harper-Bill and Michael Franklin, eds., *Ecclesiastical studies in honour of Dorothy M. Owen*. Woodbridge.

Bailey, Mark. 1994. 'Rural society', in Rosemary Horrox, ed., *Fifteenth-century attitudes: perceptions of society in late medieval England*. Cambridge.

Bailey, Mark. 1996. 'Demographic decline in late medieval England: some thoughts on recent Research', *Economic History Review*, 49.

Bailey, Mark. 1998. 'Historiographical essay: the commercialisation of the English economy 1086–1500', *Journal of Medieval History*, 24.

Bailey, Mark. 1998. 'Peasant welfare in England, 1290–1348', *Economic History Review*, 51.

Bailey, Mark. 2002. ed., *The English manor c.1200–c.1500*. Manchester.

Bailey, Mark. 2007. *Medieval Suffolk: an economic and social history 1200 to 1500*. Woodbridge.

Bailey, Mark. 2009. 'The form, function and evolution of irregular field systems in Suffolk, c.1300–c.1550', *Agricultural History Review*, 57.

Bailey, Mark. 2009. 'Villeinage in England: a regional case study c.1250–1349', *Economic History Review*, 62.

Bailey, Mark. 2010. 'Beyond the Midland field system: the determinants of common rights over the arable in medieval England', *Agricultural History Review*, 58.

Bailey, Mark. 2011. 'Self-government in the small towns of late-medieval England', in Ben Dodds and Christian Liddy, eds., *Commercial activity, markets, and entrepreneurs in the Middle Ages: essays in honour of Richard H. Britnell*. Woodbridge.

Bailey, Mark. 2014. *The decline of serfdom in late-medieval England: from bondage to freedom*. Woodbridge.

Bailey, Mark. 2014. 'Patterns of rural migration in south-east England 1300–1500', paper to the British Agricultural History Society winter conference.

Bailey, Mark. 2014. 'The transformation of customary tenure in southern England c.1350 to 1500', *Agricultural History Review*, 62.

Bailey, Mark. 2015. 'John de Wingfield and the foundation of Wingfield College', in Peter Bloore and Edward Martin, eds., *Wingfield College and its patrons: piety and patronage in medieval Suffolk*. Woodbridge.

Bailey, Mark. 2015. 'The myth of the seigniorial reaction in England after the Black Death', in Maryanne Kowaleski, John Langdon, and Phillipp Schofield, eds., *Peasants and lords in the medieval English economy: essays in honour of Bruce Campbell*. Turnhout.

Bailey, Mark. 2019. 'Tallage-at-will in medieval England', *English Historical Review*, vol. 134 no. 566.

Baldwin, John W. 1959. 'Medieval theories of the just price: Romanists, canonists, and theologians in the twelfth and thirteenth centuries', *Transactions of the American Philosophical Society*, 92.

Ballard, Adolphus. 1916. *The Black Death on the estates of the see of Winchester*. Oxford.

Bardsley, Sandy. 1999. 'Women's work reconsidered: gender and wages differentiation in late medieval England', *Past and Present*, 165.

Barg, M.A. 1989. 'The social structure of manorial freeholders: an analysis of the Hundred Rolls of 1279', *Agricultural History Review*, 39.

Barker, Juliet. 2014. *England, arise: the people, the king, and the Great Revolt of 1381*. London.

Barron, Caroline. 2004. *London in the later Middle Ages: government and people 1200–1500*. Oxford.

Bateman, Victoria. 2011. 'The evolution of markets in early modern Europe, 1350–1800: a study of wheat prices', *Economic History Review*, 64.

Bavel, Bas van. 2001. 'Land lease and agriculture: the transition of the economy in the Dutch river area from the fourteenth to the sixteenth century', *Past and Present*, 172.

Bavel, Bas van. 2010. *Manors and markets: economy and society in the Low Countries, 500-1600*. Oxford.

Bavel, Bas van. 2016. *The invisible hand?: how market economies have emerged and declined since AD500*. Oxford.

Bavel, Bas van, de Moor, Tina, and Zuiten, Jan Luiten van. 2009. 'Introduction: factor markets in global economic history', *Continuity and Change*, 24.

Bavel, Bas van, and Schofield, Phillipp. 2008. 'The emergence of lease and leasehold in a comparative perspective: definitions, causes and consequences', in Bas van Bavel and Phillipp R. Schofield, eds., *The development of leasehold in northwestern Europe, 1200-1600*. Turnhout.

Bean, John M.W. 1991. 'Landlords', in Edward Miller, ed., *The agrarian history of England and Wales, volume III: 1348-1500*. Cambridge.

Beckerman, John S. 1992. 'Procedural innovation and institutional change in medieval English manorial courts', *Law and History Review*, 10.

Beckerman, John S. 1995. 'Toward a theory of medieval manorial adjudication: the nature of communal judgements in a system of customary law', *Law and History Review*, 13.

Beier, A. Lee. 2008. 'A new serfdom: labour laws, vagrancy statutes and labour discipline in England 1350-1800', in A. Lee Beier and Paul Ocobock, eds., *Cast out: vagrancy and homelessness in global and historical perspectives*. Athens, Ohio.

Bekar, Cliff T., and Reed, Clyde G. 2013. 'Land markets and inequality: evidence from medieval England', *European Review of Economic History*, 17.

Bell, Adrian R., Brooks, Chris, and Moore, Tony K. 2009. 'Interest in medieval accounts: examples from England 1272-1340', *History*, 92.

Bell, Adrian R., Brooks, Chris, and Moore, Tony K. 2017. '*Cambium non est mutuum*: exchange and interest rates in medieval Europe', *Economic History Review*, 70.

Bell, Adrian R., Brooks, Chris, and Killick, Helen. 2018. 'A reappraisal of the freehold property market in later medieval England', Working Paper, ICMA Centre, University of Reading.

Bell, Adrian R., Brooks, Chris, and Killick, Helen. 2018. 'Medieval property investors 1300-1500', Working Paper, ICMA Centre, University of Reading.

Bell, Adrian R., Brooks, Chris, and Killick, Helen. 2018. 'The first real estate bubble?: land prices and rents in medieval England c.1300-1500', Working Paper, ICMA Centre, University of Reading.

Benedictow, Ole J. 2004. *The Black Death 1346-1353: the complete history*. Woodbridge.

Benedictow, Ole J. 2012. 'New perspectives in medieval demography: the medieval demographic system', in Mark Bailey and Stephen H. Rigby, eds., *Town and countryside in the age of the Black Death: essays in honour of John Hatcher*. Turnhout.

Bennett, Henry S. 1937. *Life on the English manor: a study of peasant conditions 1150-1400*. Cambridge.

Bennett, Judith M. 1987. *Women in the medieval English countryside. Gender and household in Brigstock before the plague*. Oxford.

Bennett, Judith M. 1996. *Ale, beer and brewsters in England: women's work in a changing world 1300-1600*. Oxford.

Bennett, Judith M. 2010. 'Compulsory service in late medieval England', *Past and Present*, 209.

Bennett, Judith M. 2015. 'Women and poverty: girls on their own in England before 1348', in Maryanne Kowaleski, John Langdon, and Phillipp R. Schofield, eds., *Peasants and lords in the medieval English economy: essays in honour of Bruce M.S. Campbell*. Turnhout.

Bennett, Judith M. 2019. 'Married and not: Weston's grown children in 1268-9', *Continuity and Change*, 34.

Bennett, Judith M. 2019. 'Wretched girls, wretched boys, and the European marriage pattern in England (c. 1250-1350)', *Continuity and Change*, 34.

Bennett, Michael. 1995. 'The impact of the Black Death on English legal history', *Australian Journal of Law and Society*, 11.

Biddick, Kathleen. 1990. 'People and things: power in early English development', *Comparative Studies in Society and History*, 32.

Birkelbach, Karl. 2009. 'Plague debate: methodology and meaning in the retrospective diagnosis of the Black Death'. PhD dissertation, University of Western Australia.

Birrell, Jean. 2014. 'Manorial custumals reconsidered', *Past and Present*, 224.

Blanchard, Ian. 1984. 'Industrial employment and the rural land market, 1380-1520', in Richard M. Smith, ed., *Land, kinship, and life cycle*. Cambridge.

Bolt, Jutta, and Zanden, Jan Luiten van. 2014. 'The Maddison Project: collaborative research on historical national accounts', *Economic History Review*, 67.

Bolton, Jim L. 1980. *The medieval English economy 1150-1500*. London.

Bolton, Jim L. 1996. 'World turned upside down', in W. Mark Ormrod and Philip Lindley, eds., *The Black Death in England*. Stamford.

Bolton, Jim L. 2012. *Money in the medieval English economy 973-1489*. Manchester.

Bolton, Jim L. 2013. 'Looking for *Yersinia pestis*: scientists, historians and the Black Death', in Linda Clark and Carole Rawcliffe, eds., *The fifteenth century XII: society in an age of plague*. Woodbridge.

Bonfield, Lloyd. 1989. 'The nature of customary law in the manor courts of medieval England', *Comparative Study of Society and History*, 31.

Bonfield, Lloyd. 2000. 'The role of seigniorial jurisdiction after the Norman Conquest, and the nature of customary law, in England', in Lloyd Bonfield, ed., *Seigniorial jurisdiction*. Berlin.

Bony, B. 1992. 'Effect of set-aside on soil nematode fauna and vertebrates in eastern Scotland', in James Clarke, ed., *Set-Aside*, British Crop Protection Council, 50.

Booth, Paul H. 1976. 'Taxation and public order: Cheshire in 1353', *Northern History*, 12.

Booth, Paul H. 2013. 'The enforcement of the Ordinance and Statute of Labourers in Cheshire, 1349 to 1374', *Archives*, 127.

Booth, Paul H.W. 1981. *The financial administration of the lordship and county of Chester 1272-1377*, Chetham Society, 3rd series, 28.

Booth, Paul H.W. 2003. *Accounts of the manor and hundred of Macclesfield, Cheshire, Michaelmas 1361 to Michaelmas 1362*, Record Society of Lancashire and Cheshire, 138.

Boucoyannis, Deborah. 2021. *From roving to stationary judges: power, land and the origins of representative institutions*. Cambridge.

Braid, Robert. 2010. 'Economic behaviour, markets, and crises: the English economy in the wake of plague and famine in the fourteenth century', in Silvia Cavaciocchi, ed., *Economic and biological interactions in pre-industrial Europe between the thirteenth and eighteenth centuries*. Florence.

Braid, Robert. 2013. 'Behind the Ordinance of Labourers: economic regulation and market control in London before the Black Death', *Journal of Legal History*, 34.

Brand, Paul. 1992. *The making of the common law*. London.

Brand, Paul. 2002. 'Aspects of the law of debt, 1189-1307', in Nicholas J. Mayhew and Phillip R. Schofield, eds., *Credit and debt in medieval society, c.1180 to 1350*. Oxford.

Brand, Paul. 2003. *Kings, barons, and justices: the making and enforcement of legislation in thirteenth-century England*. Cambridge.

Brenner, Robert. 1985. 'Agrarian class structure and economic development in pre-industrial Europe', in Trevor H. Aston and Charles H.E. Philpin, eds., *The Brenner Debate: agrarian class structure and economic development in pre-industrial Europe.* Cambridge.

Brenner, Robert. 1985. 'The agrarian roots of European capitalism', in Trevor H. Aston and Charles H.E. Philpin, eds., *The Brenner Debate: agrarian class structure and economic development in pre-industrial Europe.* Cambridge.

Brenner, Robert. 1996. 'The rises and falls of serfdom in medieval and early modern Europe', in Michael L. Bush, ed., *Serfdom and slavery: studies in legal bondage.* London.

Brenner, Robert. 2007. 'Property and progress: where Adam Smith went wrong', in Chris Wickham, ed., *Marxist history-writing for the twenty-first century.* Oxford.

Bridbury, Anthony R. 1992. *The English economy from Bede to the Reformation.* Woodbridge.

Briggs, Chris. 2006. 'Manor court procedures, debt litigation levels, and rural credit provision in England, c.1290–c.1380', *Law and History Review,* 24.

Briggs, Chris. 2008. 'Seigniorial control of villagers' litigation beyond the manor in later medieval England', *Historical Research,* 213.

Briggs, Chris. 2009. *Credit and village society in fourteenth-century England.* Oxford.

Briggs, Chris. 2014. 'English serfdom, c.1200–c.1350: towards an institutionalist analysis', in Silvia Cavaciocchi, ed., *Serfdom and slavery in the European economy 11th–18th centuries.* Florence.

Briggs, Chris. 2014. 'Introduction: law courts, contracts, and rural society in Europe, 1200–1600', *Continuity and Change,* 29.

Briston, Margaret E., and Halliday, Timothy M., eds. 2009. *The Pilsgate manor of the Sacrist of Peterborough abbey,* Northamptonshire Record Society, 43.

Britnell, Richard H. 1966. 'Production for the market on a small fourteenth-century estate', *Economic History Review,* 19.

Britnell, Richard H. 1977. 'Agrarian technology and the margin of cultivation', *Economic History Review,* 30.

Britnell, Richard H. 1980. 'Minor landlords in England and medieval agrarian capitalism', *Past and Present,* 89.

Britnell, Richard H. 1986. *Growth and decline in Colchester 1300–1525.* Cambridge.

Britnell, Richard H. 1987. 'Forestall, forestalling and the Statute of Forestallers', *English Historical Review,* 102.

Britnell, Richard H. 1991. 'Occupation of the land: eastern England', in Edward Miller, ed., *The agrarian history of England and Wales, volume III: 1348–1500.* Cambridge.

Britnell, Richard H. 1991. 'Tenant farming and farmers: eastern England', in Edward Miller, ed., *The agrarian history of England and Wales, volume III: 1348–1500.* Cambridge.

Britnell, Richard H. 1993. 'Commerce and capitalism in late medieval England: problems of description and theory', *Journal of Historical Sociology,* 6.

Britnell, Richard H. 1993. *The commercialisation of English society 1000–1500.* 1st edition, Cambridge.

Britnell, Richard H. 1994. 'The Black Death in English towns', *Urban History,* 21.

Britnell, Richard H. 1995. 'Commercialisation and economic development in England 1000–1300', in Richard H. Britnell and Bruce M.S. Campbell, eds., *A commercialising economy: England 1086 to 1300.* Manchester.

Britnell, Richard H. 1996. 'Price setting in English borough markets, 1349–1500', *Canadian Journal of History,* 31.

Britnell, Richard H. 2000. 'Urban demand in the English economy 1300–1600', in James A. Galloway, ed., *Trade, urban hinterlands and market integration c.1300–1600*. Centre for Metropolitan History, Institute of Historical Research.

Britnell, Richard H. 2001. 'Specialization of work in England, 1100–1300', *Economic History Review*, 54.

Britnell, Richard H. 2004. *Britain and Ireland, 1050–1530: economy and society*. Oxford.

Britnell, Richard H. 2006. 'Town life', Rosemary Horrox and W. Mark Ormrod, eds., *A social history of England 1200–1500*. Cambridge.

Britnell, Richard H. 2008. 'Land and lordship: common themes and regional variations' in Ben Dodds and Richard H. Britnell, eds., *Agriculture and rural society after the Black Death*. Hatfield.

Britnell, Richard H. 2015. 'Making or buying?: maintaining farm equipment and buildings, 1250–1350', in Maryanne Kowaleski, John Langdon, and Phillipp Schofield, eds., *Peasants and lords in the medieval English economy: essays on honour of Bruce Campbell*. Turnhout.

Britnell, Richard H., Etty, Claire, and King, Andy, eds. 2011. *The Black Book of Hexham: a northern monastic estate in 1379*. Hexham.

Britton, Edward. 1977 *The community of the vill: a study in the history of the family and village life in fourteenth-century England*. Toronto.

Broadberry, Stephen. 2015. 'Accounting for the Great Divergence'. Unpublished Working Paper.

Broadberry, Stephen, Campbell, Bruce M.S., and Leeuwen, Bas van. 2013. 'When did Britain industrialise?: the sectoral distribution of the labour force and labour productivity in Britain, 1381–1851', *Explorations in Economic History*, 50.

Broadberry, Stephen, Campbell, Bruce M.S., Klein, Alexander, Overton, Mark, and van Leeuwen, Bas. 2015. *British economic growth 1270–1870*. Cambridge.

Brodie, I.D.S., Gallagher, C., Hitchin, S. and Noel, T. 1992. 'Spatial and temporal variation in the vegetation in set-aside fields at Conington, Cambs.', in James Clarke, ed., *Set-Aside*, British Crop Protection Council, 50.

Brooks, Nicholas. 1985. 'The organization and achievements of the peasants of Kent and Essex in 1381', in Henry Mayr-Harting and Robert I. Moore, eds., *Studies in medieval history presented to R.H.C. Davies*. London.

Brown, Alfred L. 1989. *The governance of late medieval England*. London.

Brown, Andrew T. 2015. *Rural society and economic change in County Durham: recession and recovery, c.1400–1640*. Woodbridge.

Cam, Helen. 1944. *Liberties and communities in medieval England*. Cambridge.

Campbell, Bruce M.S. 1981. 'The regional uniqueness of English field systems?: some evidence from eastern Norfolk', *Agricultural History Review*, 29.

Campbell, Bruce M.S. 1984. 'Population change, inheritance and the land market in a fourteenth century peasant community', in Richard M. Smith, ed., *Land, kinship, and life-cycle*. Cambridge.

Campbell, Bruce M.S. 1990. 'People and land in the Middle Ages, 1066–1500', in Robert A. Dodgshon and Robin A. Butlin, eds., *An historical geography of England and Wales*. 2nd edition, London.

Campbell, Bruce M.S. 1995. 'Measuring the commercialisation of seigniorial agriculture in c.1300', in Richard H. Britnell and Bruce M.S. Campbell, eds., *A commercialising economy: England 1086 to 1300*. Manchester.

Campbell, Bruce M.S. 2000. *English seigniorial agriculture 1250–1450*. Cambridge.

Campbell, Bruce M.S. 2005. 'The agrarian problem in the early fourteenth century', *Past and Present*, 188.

Campbell, Bruce M.S. 2006. 'The land', in Rosemary Horrox and W. Mark Ormrod, eds., *A social history of England 1200–1500*. Cambridge.

Campbell, Bruce M.S. 2009. 'Factor markets in England before the Black Death', *Continuity and Change*, 24.

Campbell, Bruce M.S. 2010. 'Agriculture in Kent in the high Middle Ages', in Sheila Sweetinburgh, ed., *Later medieval Kent 1220–1540*. Woodbridge.

Campbell, Bruce M.S. 2010. 'Nature as a historical protagonist: environment and society and pre-industrial England', *Economic History Review*, 63.

Campbell, Bruce M.S. 2012. 'Grain yields on English demesnes after the Black Death', in Mark Bailey and Stephen H. Rigby, eds., *Town and countryside in the age of the Black Death: essays in honour of John Hatcher*. Turnhout.

Campbell, Bruce M.S. 2016. *The great transition: climate, disease and society in the late-medieval world*. Cambridge.

Campbell, Bruce M.S. 2017. 'Global climates, the 1257 mega-eruption of Samalas volcano, Indonesia, and the English food crisis of 1258', *Transactions of the Royal Historical Society*, 6th series, 27.

Campbell, Bruce M.S. 2018. 'The European mortality crisis of 1346–52 and the advent of the Little Ice Age', in Dominik Collet and Maximilian Schuh, eds., *Famines during the Little Ice Age, 1300–1800: socionatural entanglements in premodern societies*. Cern.

Campbell, Bruce M.S., and Bartley, Ken. 2006. *England on the eve of the Black Death: an atlas of lay lordship, land and wealth, 1300–49*. Manchester.

Campbell, Bruce M.S., Galloway, James A., Keene, Derek, and Murphy, Margaret. 1993. *A medieval capital and its grain supply: agrarian production and distribution in the London region c.1300*, Historical Geography Research Series, 30.

Campbell, Bruce M.S., and O Grada. 2011. 'Harvest shortfalls, grain prices and farmers in pre-industrial England', *Journal of Economic History*, 71.

Carrel, Helen. 2006. 'Food, drink and public order in the London *Liber Albus*', *Urban History*, 33.

Carus Wilson, Eleanor M. 1962. 'Evidence for industrial growth on some fifteenth-century manors', in Eleanor Carus-Wilson, ed., *Essays in economic history, volume II*. London.

Casson, Mark, and Casson, Catherine. 2015. 'Economic crises in England 1270–1520: a statistical approach', in Alex T. Brown, Andy Burn, and Rob Doherty, eds., *Crises in economic history: a comparative approach*. Woodbridge.

Cerman, Markus. 2011. 'Demesne lordship and rural society in early modern east central and eastern Europe: comparative perspectives', *Agricultural History Review*, 59.

Cerman, Markus. 2012. *Villagers and lords in eastern Europe 1300–1800*. Basingstoke.

Chang, Hannah, and Pham, Michel T. 2013. 'Affect as a decision-making system of the present', *Journal of Consumer Research*, 40.

Chavas, John-Paul, and Bromley, Daniel W. 2005. 'Modelling population and resource scarcity in fourteenth century England', *Journal of Agricultural Economics*, 56.

Cheyney, Edward P. 1900. 'The disappearance of serfdom in England', *English Historical Review*, 15.

Chick, Joe. 2016. 'The 1381 rising in Bury St Edmunds: the role of leaders and the community in shaping the rebellion', *Pons Aelius*, 13.

Chick, Joe. 2018. 'Leaders and rebels: John Wrawe's role in the Suffolk rising of 1381', *Proceedings of the Suffolk Institute of Archaeology and History*, 44.

Childs, Wendy. 1996. 'The English export trade in cloth in the fourteenth century', in Richard H. Britnell and John Hatcher, eds., *Progress and problems in medieval England*. Cambridge.

Claridge, Jordan. 2017. 'The role of demesnes in the trade of agricultural horses in late medieval England', *Agricultural History Review*, 65.

Claridge, Jordan, and Langdon, John. 2015. 'The composition of *famuli* labour on English demesnes', *Agricultural History Review*, 63.

Clark, Elaine. 1981. 'Debt litigation in a late medieval English vill', in J. Ambrose Raftis, ed., *Pathways to medieval peasants*. Toronto.

Clark, Elaine. 1983. 'Medieval labour law and English local courts', *American Journal of Legal History*, 27.

Clark, Gregory. 1988. 'The cost of capital and medieval agricultural technique', *Explorations in Economic History*, 25.

Clark, Gregory. 2007. 'The long march of history: farm wages, population, and economic growth, England 1209–1869', *Economic History Review*, 60.

Clark, Gregory. 2007. *A farewell to alms: a brief economic history of the world*. Princeton.

Clark, Gregory. 2013. '1381 and the Malthus delusion', *Explorations in Economic History*, 50.

Clark, Gregory. 2013. 'Microbes and markets: was the Black Death an economic revolution?' Working Paper, University of California Davis.

Clark, Gregory. 2016. 'Microbes and markets: was the Black Death an economic revolution?', *Journal of Demographic Economics*, 82.

Clark, Gregory. 2018. 'Farming in England', *Economic History Review*, 71.

Cohn, Samuel K. 2007. 'After the Black Death: labour legislation and attitudes towards labour in late-medieval western Europe', *Economic History Review*, 60.

Cohn, Samuel K. 2012. *Popular protest in late medieval English towns*. Cambridge.

Cohn, Samuel K. 2013. 'The historian and the laboratory: the Black Death disease', in Linda Clark and Carole Rawcliffe, eds., *The fifteenth century XII: society in an age of plague*. Woodbridge.

Cooper, John P. 1985. 'In search of agrarian capitalism', in Trevor H. Aston and Charles H. E. Philpin, eds., *The Brenner Debate: agrarian class structure and economic development in pre-industrial Europe*. Cambridge.

Coss, Peter. 2006. 'An age of deference', in Rosemary Horrox and W. Mark Ormrod, eds., *A social history of England 1200–1500*. Cambridge.

Coss, Peter. 2014. 'Neifs and villeins in later medieval England', *Reading Medieval Studies*, 40.

Coss, Peter, and Lancaster-Lewis, Joan C., eds. 2013. *Coventry priory register*, Dugdale Society, 46.

Crane, Susan. 1992. 'The writing lesson of 1381', in Barbara A. Hanawalt, ed., *Chaucer's England: literature in historical context*. Minneapolis.

Darby, Henry C. 1940. *The medieval fenland*. Cambridge.

Davenport, Frances G. 1906. *The economic development of a Norfolk manor*. Cambridge.

Davies, D.H.K., and Fisher, N.M. 1992. 'Weed control implications of the return of set-aside land to arable production', James Clarke, ed., *Set-Aside*, British Crop Protection Council, 50.

Davies, Mike, and Kissock, Jonathan. 2004. 'The feet of fines, the land market and the English agricultural crisis of 1315 to 1322', *Journal of Historical Geography*, 30.

Davis, James. 2004. 'Baking for the common good: a reassessment of the Assize of Bread in medieval England', *Economic History Review*, 57.

Davis, James. 2011. 'Market regulation in fifteenth-century England', in Ben Dodds and Christian Liddy, eds., *Commercial activity, markets, and entrepreneurs in the Middle Ages: essays in honour of Richard H. Britnell*. Woodbridge.

Davis, James. 2012. 'Selling food and drink in the aftermath of the Black Death', in Mark Bailey and Stephen H. Rigby, eds., *Town and countryside in the age of the Black Death: essays in honour of John Hatcher*. Turnhout.

Davis, James. 2012. *Medieval market morality: life, law and ethics in the English marketplace, 1200–1500*. Cambridge.

Davis, James. 2015. 'A reassessment of village markets in late medieval England', in Maryanne Kowaleski, John Langdon, and Phillipp R. Schofield, eds., *Peasants and lords in the medieval English economy: essays in honour of Bruce M.S. Campbell*. Turnhout.

Davis, James. 2018. 'Towns and trade', in Stephen H. Rigby and Sian Echard, eds., *Historians on Gower*. Wodbridge.

De Moor, Tina, and Zanden, Jan Luiten van. 2010. 'Every woman counts': a gender-analysis of numeracy in the Low Countries during the early modern period', *Journal of Interdisciplinary History*, 41.

De Moor, Tina, and Zanden, Jan Luiten van. 2010. 'Girl power: the European marriage pattern and labour markets in the North Sea region in the late medieval and early modern period', *Economic History Review*, 63.

Dennison, Tracy K. 2011. *The institutional framework of Russian serfdom*. Cambridge.

Dennison, Tracy K. 2013. 'Contract enforcement in Russian serf society, 1750–1860', *Economic History Review*, 66.

Dennison, Tracy K. 2014. 'The institutional context of serfdom in England and Russia', in Chris Briggs, Peter T. Kitson, and Stephen J. Thompson, eds., *Population, welfare and economic change in Britain, 1290–1834*. Woodbridge.

Dennison, Tracy K., and Ogilvie, Shelagh. 2014. 'Does the European Marriage Pattern explain economic growth?', *Journal of Economic History*, 74.

Dennison, Tracy K., and Ogilvie, Shelagh. 2016. 'Institutions, demography and economic growth', *Journal of Economic History*, 76.

De Pleijt, Alexandra, and Zanden, Jan Luiten van. 2016. 'Accounting for the "Little Divergence": what drove economic growth in pre-industrial Europe, 1300–1800?', *European Review of Economic History*, 20.

De Roover, Raymond. 1958. 'The concept of the just price and economic policy', *Journal of Economic History*, 18.

De Vries, Jan. 1994. 'How did pre-industrial labour markets function?', in George Grantham and Mary McKinnon, eds., *Labour market evolution: the economic history of market integration, wage flexibility and the employment relation*. London.

DeWindt, Anne R. 1987. 'Redefining the peasant community in medieval England: the regional perspective', *Journal of British Studies*, 26.

DeWindt, Anne R. 2012. 'Leaving Warboys: emigration from a fifteenth-century English village, in Charlotte N. Goldy and Amy Livingstone, eds., *Writing medieval women's lives*. New York.

DeWindt, Edwin B. 1971. *Land and people in Holywell-cum-Needingworth: structures of tenure and patterns of social organization in an east Midlands village 1252-1457*. Toronto.

Dewitte, Sharon N. 2015. 'The anthropology of plague: insights from bioarchaeological analyses of epidemic cemeteries', in Monica H. Green, ed., *Pandemic disease in the medieval world: rethinking the Black Death*. Kalamazoo.

Dewitte, Sharon N., and Kowaleski, Maryanne. 2017. 'Black Death bodies', *Fragments*, 6.

Dobson, R. Barrie, ed. 2003. *The Peasants' Revolt of 1381*. 2nd edition, Basingstoke.

Dobson, R. Barrie. 2000. 'General survey 1300–1500', in David Palliser, ed., *The Cambridge Urban History of Britain: volume I, 600–1540*. Cambridge.

Dodds, Ben. 2007. *Peasants and production in the medieval north-east: the evidence from tithes, 1275–1536*. Woodbridge.

Domar, Evsey D. 1970. 'The causes of slavery or serfdom: a hypothesis', *Journal of Economic History*, 30 (1970).

DuBoulay, Robin. 1967. *The lordship of Canterbury: an essay in medieval society*. London.

Dunn, Andrew. 2004. *The Peasants' Revolt: England's failed revolution*. Stroud.

Dyer, Alan. 1991. *Decline and growth in English towns 1400–1640*. Basingstoke.

Dyer, Christopher. 1980. *Lords and peasants in a changing society: the estates of the bishopric of Worcester, 680–1540*. Cambridge.

Dyer, Christopher. 1984. 'The social and economic background to the rural revolts of 1381,' in Rodney H. Hilton and Trevor H. Aston, eds., *The English Rising of 1381*. Cambridge.

Dyer, Christopher. 1988. 'The Revolt of 1381 in Suffolk: its origins and participants', *Proceedings of the Suffolk Institute of Archaeology and History*, 36.

Dyer, Christopher. 1989. *Standards of living in the later Middle Ages: social change in England c.1200–1520*. Cambridge.

Dyer, Christopher. 1991. 'Occupation of the land: west Midlands', in Edward Miller, ed., *The agrarian history of England and Wales, volume III: 1348–1500*. Cambridge.

Dyer, Christopher. 1991. 'Tenant farmers and farming: west Midlands' in Edward Miller, ed., *The agrarian history of England and Wales, volume III: 1348–1500*. Cambridge.

Dyer, Christopher. 1991. 'Farming practice: west Midlands', in Edward Miller, ed., *The agrarian history of England and Wales, volume III: 1348–1500*. Cambridge.

Dyer, Christopher. 1994. *Everyday life in medieval England*. London.

Dyer, Christopher. 1996. 'Memories of freedom: attitudes towards serfdom in England, 1200–1350', in Michael L. Bush, ed., *Serfdom and slavery: studies in legal bondage*. London.

Dyer, Christopher. 2000. 'Work ethics in the fourteenth century', in James Bothwell, P. Jeremy, P. Goldberg, and W. Mark Ormrod, eds., *The problem of labour in fourteenth-century England*. Woodbridge.

Dyer, Christopher. 2000. 'Small towns', in David Palliser, ed., *The Cambridge Urban History of Britain: volume I, 600–1540*. Cambridge.

Dyer, Christopher. 2002. *Making a living in the Middle Ages: the people of Britain 850–1520*. New Haven.

Dyer, Christopher. 2005. *An age of transition?: economy and society in England in the later Middle Ages*. Oxford.

Dyer, Christopher. 2005. 'Villeins, bondsmen, neifs and serfs: new serfdom in England c.1200–1600', in Paul Freedman and Monique Bourin, eds., *Forms of servitude in north and east Europe: decline resistance and expansion*. Turnhout.

Dyer, Christopher. 2007. 'The ineffectiveness of lordship in England, 1200–1400', in Christopher Dyer, Peter Coss, and Chris Wickham, eds., *Rodney Hilton's Middle Ages: an exploration of historical themes*. Past and Present Society.

Dyer, Christopher. 2007. 'Were late medieval English villages self contained?', in Christopher Dyer, ed., *The self contained village: the social history of rural communities 1250–1900*. Hatfield.

Dyer, Christopher. 2017 'The Midland economy and society 1314–1348: insights from changes in the landscape', *Midland History*, 42.

Dyer, Christopher, and Hoyle, Richard H. 2010. 'Britain 1000–1500' in Bas van Bavel and Richard H. Hoyle, eds., *Rural economy and society in north west Europe 500–2000: social relations, property and power*. Turnhout.

Dyer, Christopher, and Slater, Terry. 2000. 'Midlands', in David Palliser, ed., *The Cambridge Urban History of Britain: volume I, 600–1540*. Cambridge.

Edwards Jeremy, and Ogilvie, Shelagh. 2018. 'Did the Black Death cause economic development by "inventing" fertility restriction?', CESifo Working Papers, no. 7016.

Edwards, Jeremy, and Ogilvie, Shelagh. 2019. 'What can we learn from a race with one runner?: a comment on Foreman Peck and Zhou', *Economic History Review*, 72.

Eiden, Herbert. 1998. 'Joint action against "bad" lordship: the peasants' revolt in Essex and Norfolk', *History*, 83, no. 269.

Eiden, Herbert. 2008. 'The social ideology of the rebels in Suffolk and Norfolk in 1381', in M.-L. Heckmann and Jens Rohrkasten, eds., *Von Novgorod bis London*. Gottingen.

Epstein, Stephan A. 1991. 'The theory and practice of the just wage', *Journal of Medieval History*, 17.

Evans, Ralph. 1996. 'Merton College's control of its tenants at Thorncroft, 1270–1349', in Zvi Razi and Richard M. Smith, eds., *Medieval society and the manor court*. Oxford.

Evans, Ralph. 2004. 'Whose was the manorial court', in Ralph Evans, ed., *Lordship and learning: studies in memory of Trevor Aston*. Woodbridge.

Faith, Ros. 1981. 'The class struggle in fourteenth-century England', in Raphael Samuel, ed., *Peoples' history and socialist theory*. London.

Faith, Ros. 1984. 'Berkshire: fourteenth and fifteenth centuries', in Paul D.A. Harvey, ed., *The peasant land market in medieval England*. Oxford.

Faith, Ros. 1984. 'The Great Rumour of 1377 and peasant ideology', in Rodney H. Hilton and Trevor H. Aston, eds., *The English Rising of 1381*. Cambridge.

Faraji-Rad, Ali, and Pham, Michel T. 2017. 'Uncertainty increases the reliance on affect in decisions', *Journal of Consumer Research*, 44.

Farmer, David L. 1977. 'Grain yields on the Winchester manors in the late Middle Ages', *Economic History Review*, 30.

Farmer, David L. 1983. 'Grain yields on Westminster abbey manors, 1271–1410', *Canadian Journal of History*, 18.

Farmer, David L. 1988. 'Prices and wages', in Hubert E. Hallam, ed., *The agrarian history of England and Wales, vol. II*. Cambridge.

Farmer, David L. 1991. 'Marketing the produce', in Edward Miller, ed., *The agrarian history of England and Wales, volume III: 1348–1500*. Cambridge.

Farmer, David. 1991. 'Prices and wages', in Edward Miller, ed., *The agrarian history of England and Wales, volume III: 1348–1500*. Cambridge.

Farmer, David L. 1995. 'Woodland and pasture sales on the Winchester manors: disposing of a surplus or producing for the market?', in Richard H. Britnell and Bruce M. S. Campbell, eds., *A commercialising economy: England 1086–1300*. Cambridge.

Feiling, Kenneth G. 1911. 'An Essex manor in the fourteenth century', *English Historical Review*, 102.

Field, R.K. 1993. 'Migration in the later Middle Ages: the case of the Hampton Lovell villeins', *Midland History*, 9.

Finberg, Herbert P.R. 1951. *Tavistock abbey: a study in the social and economic history of Devon*. Cambridge.

Firnhaber-Baker, Justine. 2016. 'Introduction', in Justine Firnhaber-Baker and Dirk Schoenaers, eds., *The Routledge handbook of medieval revolt*. Abingdon.

Fochesato, Mattia. 2018. 'Origins of Europe's north-south divide: population changes, real wages and the "little divergence" in early modern Europe', *Explorations in Economic History*, 70.

Foden, Peter, trans. 2013. *Records of the manor of Norton in the liberty of St Albans 1244–1539*, Hertfordshire Record Society, 29.

Foreman-Peck, James, and Zhou, Peng. 2018. 'Late marriage as a contributor to the industrial revolution in England', *Economic History Review*, 71.

Foreman-Peck, James, and Zhou, Peng. 2019. 'A response to Edwards and Oglivie', *Economic History Review*, 72.

Fox, Harold S.A. 1984. 'Some ecological dimensions of medieval field systems', in Kathleen Biddick, ed., *Archaeological approaches to medieval Europe*. Kalamazoo.

Fox, Harold S.A. 1991. 'Occupation of the land: Devon and Cornwall', in Edward Miller, ed., *The agrarian history of England and Wales, volume III: 1348–1500*. Cambridge.

Fox, Harold S.A. 1996. 'Exploitation of the landless by lords and tenants in early medieval England', in Zvi Razi and Richard M. Smith, eds., *Medieval society and the manor court*. Oxford.

Freedman, Paul. 1999. *Images of the medieval peasant*. Stanford.

French, Henry, and Hoyle, Richard H. 1999. 'The land market of a Pennine manor: Slaidburn, 1650–1780', *Continuity and Change*, 14.

French, Henry, and Hoyle, Richard H. 2003. 'English individualism refuted and reasserted: the land market of Earls Colne (Essex), 1550–1750', *Economic History Review*, 56.

French, Henry, and Hoyle, Richard H. 2007. *The Character of English Rural Society: Earls Colne, 1550–1750*. Manchester.

Fryde, Edmund B. 1978. 'The tenants of the bishops of Coventry and Litchfield, and of Worcester, after the plague of 1349–9' in Roy F. Hunnisett and J.B. Post, eds., *Medieval legal records: essays in memory of C.A.F. Meekings*. London.

Fryde, Edmund B. 1996. *Peasants and landlords in later medieval England*. Stroud.

Fryde, Edmund B., and Fryde, Natalie. 1991. 'Peasant rebellion and peasant discontents', in Miller, ed., *Agrarian history III*, in Edward Miller, ed., *The agrarian history of England and Wales, volume III: 1348–1500*. Cambridge.

Furber E.C., ed. 1953. *Essex sessions of the peace 1351, 1377–79*, Essex Archaeological Society, Occasional Papers, 3.

Galloway, James A. 1995. 'London's grain supply: changes in production, distribution and consumption during the fourteenth century', *Franco-British Studies*, 20.

Galloway, James A. 2000. 'One market or many?: London and the grain trade of England', in James A. Galloway, ed., *Trade, urban hinterlands and market integration c.1300–1600*. Centre for Metropolitan History, Institute of Historical Research.

Galloway, James A. 1998. 'Driven by drink?: ale consumption and the agrarian economy of the London region, c.1300–1400', in Martha Carlin and Joel L. Rosenthal, eds., *Food and feasting in medieval Europe*. London.

Galloway, James A. 2009. 'Storm flooding, coastal defence and land use around the Thames estuary and tidal river c.1250–1450', *Journal of Medieval History*, 35.

Galloway, James A. 2012. 'Metropolitan food and fuel supply in medieval England: regional and international contexts', in Piet van Cruyningen and Eric Thoen, eds., *Food supply, demand and trade: aspects of the economic relationship between town and countryside (Middle Ages to nineteenth century)*. Turnhout.

Galloway, James A., Keene, Derek, and Murphy, Margaret. 1996. 'Fuelling the city: production and distribution of firewood and fuel in London's region, 1290–1400', *Economic History Review*, 49.

Gasquet, Francis. 1908. *The Black Death of 1348 and 1349*. London.

Ghosh, Shami. 2016. 'Rural economies and transitions to capitalism: Germany and England compared (c.1200–c.1800)', *Journal of Agrarian Change*, 16.

Given-Wilson, Chris. 1983. 'Purveyance for the royal household 1362–1413', *Bulletin of the Institute of Historical Research*, 56.

Given-Wilson, Chris. 2000. 'Service, serfdom and English labour legislation, 1350–1500', in Anne Curry and Elizabeth Matthew, eds., *Concepts and patterns of service in the later Middle Ages*. Woodbridge.

Given-Wilson, Chris. 2000. 'The problem of labour in the context of English government, c.1350–1450', in James Bothwell, P. Jeremy P. Goldberg, and W. Mark Ormrod, eds., *The problem of labour in fourteenth-century England*. Woodbridge.

Goddard, Richard. 2004. *Lordship and medieval urbanisation: Coventry, 1043–1355*. London.

Goldberg, P. Jeremy P. 1986. 'Female labour, service, and marriage in the late medieval urban north', *Northern History*, 22.

Goldberg, P. Jeremy P. 1992. *Women, work and life cycle in a medieval economy: women in York and Yorkshire c.1300–1520*. Oxford.

Goldberg, P. Jeremy P. 2000. 'What was a servant?', in Anne Curry and Elizabeth Matthew, eds., *Concepts and patterns of service in the later Middle Ages*. Woodbridge.

Goldberg, P. Jeremy P. 2004. *Medieval England: a social history 1250–1550*. London.

Goldberg, P. Jeremy P. 2006. 'Life and death: the ages of man', in Rosemary Horrox and W. Mark Ormrod, eds., *A social history of England 1200–1500*. Cambridge.

Gould, David. 2017. 'The distribution of rabbit warrens in medieval England: an east–west divide', *Landscape History*, 38.

Grantham, George. 1994. 'Economic history and the history of labour markets', in George Grantham and Mary McKinnon, eds., *Labour market evolution: the economic history of market integration, wage flexibility and the employment relation*. London.

Grantham, George. 2012. 'France', in Harry Kitsikopoulos, ed., *Agrarian change and crisis in Europe, 1200–1500*. Abingdon.

Green, Monica H. 2015. 'Editor's introduction', in Monica H. Green, ed., *Pandemic disease in the medieval world: rethinking the Black Death*. Kalamazoo.

Green, Richard F. 1999. *A crisis of truth: literature and law in Ricardian England*. Philadelphia.

Greif, Avner. 2006. *Institutions and the path to the modern economy: lessons from medieval trade*. Cambridge.

Grieg, James. 1988. 'Plant resources', in Grenville Astill and Annie Grant, eds., *The countryside of medieval England*. Oxford.

Gross, Charles. 1890. *The Gild Merchant, volume I*. Oxford.

Hall, David. 2014. *The open fields of England*. Oxford.

Hanawalt, Barbara A. 1986. 'Peasant resistance to royal and seigniorial impositions', in Francis X. Newman, ed., *Social unrest in the late Middle Ages*. New York.

Harding, Alan. 1973. *The law courts of medieval England*. London.

Harding, Alan. 1984. 'The revolt against the justices', in Rodney H. Hilton and Trevor H. Aston, eds., *The English Rising of 1381*. Cambridge

Hare, John. 2011. *A prospering society: Wiltshire in the later Middle Ages*. Hatfield.

Haren, Michael. 2000. *Sin and society in fourteenth-century England: a study of the Memoriale Presbiterorum*. Oxford.

Hargreaves, Paul V. 1999. 'Seigniorial reaction and peasant responses', *Midland History*, 24.

Harriss, Gerard L. 1975. *King, parliament, and public finance in medieval England to 1369.* Oxford.

Harriss, Gerard L. 2005. *Shaping the nation: England 1360–1461.* Oxford.

Harry, David. 2019. *Constructing a civic community in late medieval London: the common profit, charity and commemoration.* Woodbridge.

Harvey, Barbara. 1977. *Westminster abbey and its estates in the Middle Ages.* Oxford.

Harvey, Barbara. 2006. 'The abbot of Westminster's demesnes and the Black Death of 1349', in M. Meek, ed., *The modern traveller to our past: festschrift in honour of Ann Hamilton.* Dublin.

Harvey, Paul D.A. 1984. 'Conclusion', in Paul D.A. Harvey, ed., *The peasant land market in medieval England.* Oxford.

Harvey, Paul D.A. 1991. 'Occupation of the land: Home Counties', in Edward Miller, ed., *The agrarian history of England and Wales, volume III: 1348–1500.* Cambridge.

Harvey, Paul D.A. 1991. 'Tenant farming: Home Counties', in Edward Miller, ed., *The agrarian history of England and Wales, volume III: 1348–1500.* Cambridge.

Harvey, Paul D.A. 1997. 'English estate records', in Richard H. Britnell, ed., *Pragmatic literacy, east and west 1200–1330.* Woodbridge.

Harwood Long, William. 1979. 'The low corn yields of medieval England', *Economic History Review,* 32.

Hatcher, John. 1970. *Rural economy and society in the Duchy of Cornwall 1300–1500.* Cambridge.

Hatcher, John. 1973. *English tin production and trade before 1550.* Oxford.

Hatcher, John. 1977. *Plague, population and the English economy 1348–1530.* London.

Hatcher, John. 1981. 'English serfdom and villeinage: towards a reassessment', *Past and Present,* 90.

Hatcher, John. 1994. 'England in the aftermath of the Black Death', *Past and Present,* 144.

Hatcher, John. 2003. 'Understanding the population history of England 1450–1750', *Past and Present,* 180.

Hatcher, John. 2008. *The Black Death: an intimate history.* London.

Hatcher, John. 2011. 'Unreal wages: long-run living standards and the "golden age" of the fifteenth century', in Ben Dodds and Christian Liddy, eds., *Commercial activity, markets, and entrepreneurs in the Middle Ages: essays in honour of Richard H. Britnell.* Woodbridge.

Hatcher, John. 2015. 'Lordship and villeinage before the Black Death: from Karl Marx to the Marxists and back again', in Maryanne Kowaleski, John Langdon, and Phillipp R. Schofield, eds., *Peasants and lords in the medieval English economy: essays in honour of Bruce M.S. Campbell.* Turnhout.

Hatcher, John. 2018. 'Seven centuries of unreal wages', in John Hatcher and Judy Z. Stephenson, eds., *Seven centuries of unreal wages: the unreliable data, sources and methods that have been used for measuring standards of living in the past.* Basingstoke.

Hatcher, John, and Bailey, Mark. 2001. *Modelling the Middle Ages: the history and theory of England's economic development.* Oxford.

Helmholz, Richard H. 2000. 'Independence and uniformity in England's manorial courts', in Lloyd Bonfield, ed., *Seigniorial jurisdiction.* Berlin.

Hettinger, Madonna J. 1986. 'The role of the Statute of Labourers in the social and economic background of the Great Revolt in East Anglia', PhD dissertation, University of Indiana.

Hilton, Rodney H. 1967. *A medieval society: the west Midlands at the end of the thirteenth century.* Cambridge.

Hilton, Rodney H. 1973. *Bondmen made free: medieval peasant movements and the English rising of 1381*. London.

Hilton, Rodney H. 1975. *The English peasantry in the later Middle Ages: the Ford Lectures and related studies*. Oxford.

Hilton, Rodney H. 1981. 'The English Rising of 1381', *Marxism Today*, June issue.

Hilton, Rodney H. 1983. *The decline of serfdom in late medieval England*. 2nd edition, London.

Hilton, Rodney H. 1984. 'Introduction', in Rodney H. Hilton and Trevor H. Aston, eds., *The English Rising of 1381*. Cambridge.

Hilton, Rodney H. 1985. 'A crisis of feudalism', Trevor H. Aston and Charles H.E. Philpin, eds., *The Brenner Debate: agrarian class structure and economic development in pre-industrial Europe*. Cambridge.

Hilton, Rodney H. 1985. 'A rare Evesham abbey estate document', in Rodney H. Hilton, *Class conflict and the crisis of feudalism*. 1st edition, London.

Hole, Jennifer. 2016. *Economic ethics in late-medieval England*. Basingstoke.

Hole, Jennifer. 2017. 'The justification of wealth and lordship versus rulers' exploitation in medieval England', *Parergon*, 27.

Holmes, Clive. 1957. *The estates of the higher nobility in fourteenth-century England*. Cambridge.

Holt, Richard. 2000. 'Society and population 600–1300', in David Palliser, ed., *The Cambridge Urban History of Britain: volume I, 600–1540*. Cambridge.

Horrox, Rosemary, ed. 1994. *The Black Death*. Manchester.

Howell, Cicely. 1976. 'Peasant inheritance customs in the Midlands, 1280–1700', in Jack Goody, Joan Thirsk and Edward P. Thompson, eds., *Family and inheritance: rural society in western Europe 1200–1800*. Cambridge.

Howell, Martha C. 2010. *Commerce before capitalism in Europe 1300–1600*. Cambridge.

Hudson, John. 1996. *The formation of English common law: law and society in England from the Norman Conquest to Magna Carta*. London.

Humphries, Jane, and Weisdorf, Jacob L. 2015. 'The wages of women in England, 1260–1850', *Journal of Economic History*, 75.

Humphries, Jane, and Weisdorf, Jacob L. 2019. 'Unreal wages?: real income and economic growth in England, 1260–1850', *The Economic Journal*, 129, issue 623.

Hunnisett, Roy F., and Post, J.B., eds. 1978. *Medieval legal records: essays in memory of C.A. F. Meekings*. London.

Hyams, Paul R. 1980. *King, lords and peasants in medieval England: the common law of villeinage in the twelfth and thirteenth centuries*. Oxford.

Hyams, Paul R. 1996. 'What did Edwardian villagers mean by law?', in Zvi Razi and Richard M. Smith, eds., *Medieval society and the manor court*. Oxford.

Hyams, Paul R. 2012. 'Notes on the transformation of the fief into the common law tenure in fee', in Susanne Jenks, Jonathan Rose, and Christopher Whittock, eds., *Laws, lawyers and texts: studies in medieval legal history in honour of Paul Brand*. Leiden.

Hybel, Nils. 1989. *Crisis or change: the concept of crisis in the light of agrarian structural reorganisation in late medieval England*. Aarhus.

Ibbotsen, David J. 1999. *An historical introduction to the law of obligations*. Oxford.

Ingram, Hannah. 2015. 'Crisis and conscious property management: reconstructing the Warwickshire land market', *Midland History*, 40.

Jacobsen, Joyce P., and Skillman, Gilbert L. 2004. 'Introduction', in Joyce P. Jacobsen and Gilbert L. Skillman, eds., *Labour markets and employment relationships: a comprehensive approach*. Oxford.

Jeffrey, R.W., ed. 1927. *The manors and advowson of Great Rollright*, Oxfordshire Records Society, 9.

Jewell, Helen. 1990. 'Piers Plowman a poem of crisis: an analysis of political instability in Langland's England', in John Taylor and Wendy R. Childs, eds., *Politics and crisis in fourteenth-century England*. Stroud.

Johnson, Tom. 2020. *Law in common: legal cultures in late-medieval England*. Oxford.

Jones, Ernie D. 1989. 'Going round in circles: some new evidence for population in the later Middle Ages', *Journal of Medieval History*, 15.

Justice, Steven. 1994. *Writing and rebellion, England in 1381*. Berkeley.

Kaeuper, Richard W. 1988. *War, justice, and public order: England and France in the later Middle Ages*. Oxford.

Kanzaka, Junichi. 2002. 'Villein rents in thirteenth-century England: an analysis of the Hundred Rolls of 1279–1280', *Economic History Review*, 55.

Kanzaka, Junichi. 2018. 'Manorialisation and demographic pressure in medieval England: an analysis of the Hundred Rolls of 1279–80', *Journal of Historical Geography*, 60.

Karakacili, Erin. 2004. 'English agrarian labour productivity rates before the Black Death: a case study', *Journal of Economic History*, 64.

Kaye, Joel. 2014. *A history of balance 1250–1375: the emergence of a new model of equilibrium and its impact on thought*. Cambridge.

Keen, Maurice H.K. 1990. *English society in the later Middle Ages 1348–1500*. London.

Keene, Derek. 2000. 'Changes in London's economic hinterland as indicated by debt cases in the Court of Common Pleas', in James A. Galloway, ed., *Trade, urban hinterlands and market integration c.1300–1600*. Centre for Metropolitan History, Institute of Historical Research.

Keene, Derek. 2012. 'Crisis management in London's food supply 1250–1500', in Piet van Cruyningen and Eric Thoen, eds., *Food supply, demand and trade: aspects of the economic relationship between town and countryside (Middle Ages to nineteenth century)*. Turnhout.

Kennedy, M.J.O. 1976. 'Resourceful villeins: the Cellarer family of Wawne in Holderness', *Yorkshire Archaeological Journal*, 48.

Kenyon, Nora. 1962. 'Labour conditions in Essex in the reign of Richard II', in Eleanor Carus-Wilson, ed., *Essays in economic history, volume II*. London.

Kettle, Ann J. 1989. '1300–1540', in G.C. Baugh, ed., *VCH Shropshire, volume IV*. London.

Kilby, Susan. 2010. 'Struggle and enterprise: the experience of servile peasants in Wellingborough, 1258–1322', *Midland History*, 35.

Kimball, Elizabeth G., ed. 1939. *Rolls of the Warwickshire and Coventry sessions of the peace 1377–1397*, Dugdale Society, 16.

King, Edmund. 1991. 'Occupation of the land: east Midlands', in Edward Miller, ed., *The agrarian history of England and Wales, volume III: 1348–1500*. Cambridge.

King, Edmund. 1991. 'Tenant farmers and farming: east Midlands', in Edward Miller, ed., *The agrarian history of England and Wales, volume III: 1348–1500*. Cambridge.

Kissane, Alan. 2017. *Civic community in late medieval Lincoln: urban society and economy in the age of the Black Death, 1289–1409*. Woodbridge.

Kitsikopoulos, Harry. 2002. 'The impact of the Black Death on peasant economy in England 1350–1500', *Journal of Peasant Studies*, 29.

Kitsikopoulos, Harry. 2008. 'Manorial estates as business firms', *Agricultural History Review*, 56.

Kitsikopoulos, Harry. 2012. 'England', in Harry Kitsikopoulos, ed., *Agrarian change and crisis in Europe, 1200–1500*. Abingdon.

Klima, Arnost. 1985. 'Agrarian class structure and economic development in pre-industrial Bohemia', in Trevor H. Aston and Charles H.E. Philpin, eds., *The Brenner Debate: agrarian class structure and economic development in pre-industrial Europe*. Cambridge.

Knapp, Ethan. 2014. 'John Gower: Balzac of the fourteenth century', in Ana Saez-Hidalgo and Robert F. Yeager, eds., *John Gower in England and Iberia: manuscripts, influences, reception*. Cambridge.

Kosminsky, Evgeny A. 1956. *Studies in the agrarian history of England in the thirteenth century*. Oxford.

Kowaleski, Maryanne. 1995. *Local markets and regional trade in medieval Exeter*. Cambridge.

Kowaleski, Maryanne. 2006. 'A consumer economy', in Rosemary Horrox and W. Mark Ormrod, eds., *A social history of England 1200–1500*. Cambridge.

Kowaleski, Maryanne. 2015. 'Peasants and the sea in medieval England', in Maryanne Kowaleski, John Langdon, and Phillipp R. Schofield, eds., *Peasants and lords in the medieval English economy: essays in honour of Bruce M.S. Campbell*. Turnhout.

La Poutre, Hugo J.P. 2015. 'The contribution of legumes to the diet of English peasants and farm servants, c.1300', *Agricultural History Review*, 63.

La Poutre, Hugo J.P. 2017. 'Fertilisation by manure: a manor model comparing English demesne and peasant land, c.1300', *Agricultural History Review*, 65.

Lacey, Helen. 2008. 'Grace for the rebels', *Journal of Medieval History*, 34.

Lambert, Bart, and Pajic, Milan. 2014. 'Drapery in exile: Edward III, Colchester and the Flemings 1351–1367', *History*, 99 no. 338.

Lambert, Bart, and Pajic, Milan. 2016. 'Immigration and the common profit: native cloth workers, Flemish exiles, and royal policy in fourteenth-century London', *Journal of British Studies*, 55.

Lander, John. 1969. *Conflict and stability in fifteenth-century England*. London.

Landsteiner, Erich. 2011. 'Demesne lordship and the early modern state in central Europe: the struggle for labour rent in lower Austria in the second half of the sixteenth century', *Agricultural History Review*, 59.

Langdon, John. 1988. 'Agricultural equipment', in Grenville Astill and Annie Grant, eds., *The countryside of medieval England*. Oxford.

Langdon, John. 2004. *Mills in the medieval economy: England 1300–1500*. Oxford.

Langdon, John. 2015. 'Bare ruined farms?: extents for debt as a source for landlord versus non-landlord agricultural performance in fourteenth-century England', in Maryanne Kowaleski, John Langdon, and Phillipp R. Schofield, eds., *Peasants and lords in the medieval English economy: essays in honour of Bruce M.S. Campbell*. Turnhout.

Langdon, John, and Masschaele, James. 2006. 'Population growth and commercial activity in medieval England', *Past and Present*, 190.

Larson, Peter L. 2006. *Conflict and compromise in the late medieval countryside: lords and peasants in Durham 1349–1400*. London.

Larson, Peter L. 2010. 'Village voice or village oligarchy?: the jurors of the Durham Halmote court, 1349 to 1424', *Law and History Review*, 28.

Lee, John S. 2011. 'Grain shortages in medieval towns', in Ben Dodds and Christian Liddy, eds., *Commercial activity, markets, and entrepreneurs in the Middle Ages: essays in honour of Richard H. Britnell*. Woodbridge.

Lee, John S. 2018. *The medieval clothier*. Woodbridge.

Letts, John B. 1999. *Smoke-blackened thatch*. Reading.

Levett, Ada E. 1916. *The Black Death on the estates of the see of Winchester*. Oxford.

Levett, Ada E. 1938. *Studies in manorial history*. Oxford.

Liddell, W. H., and Wood, R. G., eds. 1982. *Essex and the Great Revolt of 1381*. Chelmsford.

Liddy, Christian. 2003. 'Urban conflict in late fourteenth-century England: the case of York in 1380–1', *English Historical Review*, 475.

Lilley, Keith D. 2015. 'Urban planning after the Black Death: townscape transformation in later medieval England (1350–1530)', *Urban History*, 42.

Lis, Catharina, and Soly, Hugo. 2012. *Worthy efforts: attitudes to work and workers in pre-industrial Europe*. Leiden.

Little, Lester K. 2011. 'Plague historians in lab coats', *Past and Present*, 213.

Lloyd, Terrence H. 1964. 'Some documentary sidelights on the DMV of Brookend', *Oxoniensa*, 64.

Lock, Ray. 1992. 'The Black Death in Walsham-le-Willows', *Proceedings of the Suffolk Institute of Archaeology and History*, 37.

Lock, Ray, ed. 2002. *The court rolls of Walsham-le-Willows, vol. II, 1351–1399*. Suffolk Records Society, 45.

Lodge, Eleanor C. 1907. 'Economic and social history', in *Victoria County History of Berkshire, volume 2*. London.

Lomas, Richard A. 1977, 'Developments in land tenure on the Prior of Durham's estate in the later Middle Ages', *Northern History*, 13.

Lucas, Adam. 2014. *Ecclesiastical lordship: seigneurial power and the commercialization of milling in medieval England*. Farnham.

Maddicott, John R. 1975. 'The English peasantry and the demands of the Crown, 1294–1341', *Past and Present*, Supplement 1.

Maddicott, John R. 1978. 'Law and lordship: royal justices as retainers in thirteenth- and fourteenth-century England', *Past and Present*, Supplement 4.

Malanima, Paolo. 2018. 'Italy in the Renaissance: a leading economy in the European context, 1300–1550', *Economic History Review*, 71.

Martin, Janet. 2012. 'Russia', in Harry Kitsikopoulos, ed., *Agrarian change and crisis in Europe, 1200–1500*. Abingdon.

Masschaele, James. 1997. *Peasants, merchants, and markets: inland trade in medieval England, 1150–1350*. Basingstoke.

Massingberd, W.O. 1902. *Court rolls of the manor of Ingoldmells in the county of Lincoln*. London.

Mate, Mavis E. 1978. 'The role of gold coinage in the English economy, 1338–1400', *Numismatic Chronicle*, 18.

Mate, Mavis E. 1984. 'Agrarian economy after the Black Death: the manors of Canterbury Cathedral Priory', *Economic History Review*, 37.

Mate, Mavis E. 1985. 'Labour and labour services on the estates of Canterbury Cathedral Priory in the fourteenth century', *Southern History*, 7.

Mate, Mavis E. 1991. 'Occupation of the land: Kent and Sussex', in Edward Miller, ed., *The agrarian history of England and Wales, volume III: 1348–1500*. Cambridge.

Mate, Mavis E. 1998. *Daughters, wives and widows after the Black Death: women in Sussex 1350–1500*. Woodbridge.

Mate, Mavis E. 2006. 'Work and leisure', in Rosemary Horrox and W. Mark Ormrod, eds., *A social history of England 1200–1500*. Cambridge.

Mayhew, Nicholas J. 1995. 'Modelling medieval monetarisation', in Richard H. Britnell and Bruce M.S. Campbell, eds., *A commercialising economy: England 1086–1300*. Cambridge.

Mayhew, Nicholas J. 2013. 'Prices in England 1170–1750', *Past and Present*, 219.

McGibbon Smith, Erin. 2005. 'Reflections of reality in the manor court: Sutton-in-the-Isle, 1308–1391'. PhD dissertation, University of Cambridge.

McGibbon Smith, Erin. 2012. 'Court rolls as evidence for village society: Sutton-in-the-Isle in the fourteenth century', in Mark Bailey and Stephen H. Rigby, eds., *Town and countryside in the age of the Black Death: essays in honour of John Hatcher*. Turnhout.

McIntosh, Marjorie K. 1986. *Autonomy and community: the royal manor of Havering 1200–1500*. Cambridge.

McIntosh, Marjorie K. 1998. *Controlling misbehaviour in England 1370–1600*. Cambridge.

McKisack, May. 1964. *The fourteenth century 1307–1399*. Oxford.

McLoughlin, Vanessa. 2006. *Medieval Rothley, Leicestershire: manor, soke and parish*. PhD dissertation, University of Leicester.

Middleton, Anne. 1997. 'Acts of vagrancy in the C-version autobiography and the Statute of 1388', in Steven Justice and Kathryn Kerby-Fulton, eds., *Written work: Langland, labour and authorship*. Philadelphia.

Mileson, Stephen. 2017. 'Openness and closure in the later medieval village', *Past and Present*, 234.

Miller, Edward. 1951. *The abbey and bishopric of Ely*. Cambridge.

Miller, Edward. 1991. 'Occupation of the land: southern counties', in Edward Miller, ed., *The agrarian history of England and Wales, volume III: 1348–1500*. Cambridge.

Miller, Edward. 1991. 'Occupation of the land: Yorkshire and Lancashire', in Edward Miller, ed., *The agrarian history of England and Wales, volume III: 1348–1500*. Cambridge.

Miller, Edward. 1991. 'Tenant farmers and farming: Southern Counties', in Edward Miller, ed., *The agrarian history of England and Wales, volume III: 1348–1500*. Cambridge.

Miller Edward. 1991. 'Tenant farmers and farming: Yorkshire and Lancashire', in Edward Miller, ed., *The agrarian history of England and Wales, volume III: 1348–1500*. Cambridge.

Miller, Edward, and Hatcher, John. 1978. *Medieval England: rural society and economic change 1086–1349*. London.

Miller, Edward, and Hatcher, John. 1995. *Medieval England: towns, commerce and crafts, 1086–1348*. Harlow.

Millward, Robert. 1982. 'An economic analysis of the organisation of serfdom in eastern Europe', *Journal of Economic History*, 42.

Milsom, Stephen F.C. 1977. *The legal framework of English feudalism*. Cambridge.

Mollat, Michel, and Wolff, Phillipe. 1983. *Popular revolutions of the late Middle Ages*. London.

Moore, Tony K. 2016. 'War and finance in late-medieval England', paper to the Anglo-American Seminar on the Medieval Economy and Society, Stirling.

Moss, David. 1980. 'The economic development of a Middlesex village', *Agricultural History Review*, 28.

Mullan, John. 2003. 'The transfer of customary land on the estates of the bishopric of Winchester between the Black Death and the plague of 1361', in Richard H. Britnell, ed., *The Winchester pipe rolls and medieval English society*. Woodbridge.

Mullan, John, and Britnell, Richard H. 2009. *Land and family: trends and local variations in the peasant land market on the Winchester bishopric estates 1263–1415*. Hatfield.

Muller, Miriam. 1999. 'The function and evasion of marriage fines on a fourteenth-century English manor', *Continuity and Change*, 14.

Muller, Miriam. 2009. 'Peasants, lords and developments in leasing in late medieval England', in Bas van Bavel and Phillipp R. Schofield, eds., *The development of leasehold in northwestern Europe, 1200–1600*. Turnhout.

Muller, Miriam. 2012. 'Conflict and revolt: the Bishop of Ely and his peasants at the manor of Brandon in Suffolk c. 1300–81', *Rural History*, 23.

Munro, John H. 2003. 'Wage-stickiness, monetary changes and real incomes in late-medieval England and the Low Countries, 1300–1500: did money matter?', *Research in Economic History*, 21.

Munro, John H. 2012. 'The late medieval decline of English demesne agriculture: demographic, monetary and political-fiscal factors', in Mark Bailey and Stephen H. Rigby, eds., *Town and countryside in the age of the Black Death: essays in honour of John Hatcher*. Turnhout.

Munro, John H. 2015. '"Money matters": a critique of the Postan thesis on medieval population, prices and wages', in John Drendel, ed., *Crisis in the later Middle Ages: beyond the Postan-Duby paradigm*. Turnhout.

Musson, Anthony J. 2000. 'New labour laws, new remedies?: legal reaction to the Black Death crisis', in Nigel Saul, ed., *Fourteenth-century England*. Woodbridge.

Musson, Anthony J. 2001. *Medieval law in context: the growth of legal consciousness from Magna Carta to the Peasants' Revolt*. Manchester.

Musson, Anthony J. 2002. 'Sub-keepers and constables: the role of local officials in keeping the peace in fourteenth-century England', *English Historical Review*, 470.

Musson, Anthony J. 2004. 'Reconstructing English labour laws: a medieval perspective', in Kellie Robertson and Michael Uebel, eds., *The Middle Ages at work: practising labour in late medieval England*. Basingstoke.

Musson, Anthony J. 2018. 'Patterns of supplication and litigation strategies: petitioning the Crown in the fourteenth century', in Thomas W. Smith and Helen Killick, eds., *Petitions and strategies of persuasion in the Middle Ages: the English Crown and the church, c.1200–c.1550*. York.

Musson, Anthony J., and Ormrod, W. Mark. 1999. *The evolution of English justice: law, politics and society in the fourteenth century*. Basingstoke.

Myrdal, Jan. 2012. 'Scandinavia', in Harry Kitsikopoulos, ed., *Agrarian change and crisis in Europe, 1200–1500*. Abingdon.

Myrdal, Jan, and Sapoznik, Alexandra. 2017. 'Technology, labour, and productivity potential in peasant agriculture: England c.1000 to 1348', *Agricultural History Review*, 65.

Mysliwski, Grzegorz. 2012. 'Central Europe', in Harry Kitsikopoulos, ed., *Agrarian change and crisis in Europe, 1200–1500*. Abingdon.

Newman, Christine M. 2011. 'Marketing and trade networks in medieval Durham', in Ben Dodds and Christian Liddy, eds., *Commercial activity, markets, and entrepreneurs in the Middle Ages: essays in honour of Richard H. Britnell*. Woodbridge.

Newton, Kenneth C. 1960. *Thaxted in the fourteenth century*. Chelmsford.

Nightingale, Pamela. 1996. 'The growth of London in the medieval English economy', in Richard H. Britnell and John Hatcher, eds., *Progress and problems in medieval England*. Cambridge.

Nightingale, Pamela. 1995. *A medieval mercantile community: the Grocers' Company and the politics and trade of London, 1000–1485*. New Haven.

Nightingale, Pamela. 2010. 'Gold, credit, and mortality: distinguishing deflationary pressures on the late medieval English economy', *Economic History Review*, 63.

Nightingale, Pamela. 2015. 'The impact of crisis on credit in the late medieval economy', in Alex T. Brown, Andy Burn, and Rob Doherty, eds., *Crises in economic history: a comparative approach*. Woodbridge.

North, Douglas C., and Thomas, R. Paul. 1971. 'The rise and fall of the manorial system: a theoretical model', *Journal of Economic History*, 31.

North, Douglas C., and Thomas, R. Paul. 1973. *The rise of the western world: a new economic history*. Cambridge.

Noy, David, ed. 2011. *Winslow Manor Court Books, Part I: 1327–1377; Part II: 1423–1460*. Buckinghamshire Records Society Publications, 35 and 36.

Ogilvie, Shelagh. 2007. 'Whatever is, is right', *Economic History Review*, 60.

Ogilvie, Shelagh. 2014. 'Choices and constraints in the pre-industrial countryside', in Chris Briggs, Peter T. Kitson, and Stephen J. Thompson, eds., *Population, welfare and economic change in Britain, 1290–1834*. Woodbridge.

Oldland, John. 2014. 'Wool and cloth production in late medieval and early Tudor England', *Economic History Review*, 67.

Oldland, John. 2019. *The English woollen industry c.1200–c.1560*. Abingdon.

Olson, Sherri. 1991. 'Jurors of the village court: local leadership before and after the plague in Ellington, Hunts.', *Journal of British Studies*, 30.

Olson, Sherri. 1996. *A chronicle of all that happens: voices from the village court in medieval England*. Toronto.

Olson, Sherri. 2009. *A mute gospel: the people and culture of the medieval English common fields*. Toronto.

Oman, Charles. 1906. *The Great Revolt of 1381*. Oxford.

Ormrod, W. Mark. 1990. 'The Peasants' Revolt and the government of England', *Journal of British Studies*, 29.

Ormrod, W. Mark. 1990. *The reign of Edward III. Crown and political society in England*. New Haven.

Ormrod, W. Mark. 1996. 'The politics of pestilence: government in England after the Black Death', in W. Mark Ormrod and Philip Lindley, eds., *The Black Death in England*. Stamford.

Ormrod, W. Mark. 1999. 'England in the Middle Ages', in Richard J. Bonney, ed., *The rise of the fiscal state in Europe*. Oxford.

Ormrod, W. Mark, Killick, Helen, and Bradford, Phil, eds. 2017. *Early commons petitions in the English parliament c.1290–c.1470*, Camden 5th Series, 52.

Ottaway, Patrick. 2017. *Winchester: an archaeological assessment*. Oxford.

Owst, G.R. 1933. *Literature and pulpit in medieval England*. Oxford.

Page, Frances M. 1934. *The estates of Crowland abbey*. Cambridge.

Page, Mark. 2003. 'The peasant land market on the estates of the Bishop of Winchester before the Black Death', in Richard H. Britnell, ed., *The Winchester pipe rolls and medieval English society*. Woodbridge.

Page, Mark. 2012. 'The smallholders of Southampton water: the peasant land market on a Hampshire manor before the Black Death', in Sam Turner and Bob Silvester, eds., *Life in medieval landscapes: people and places in the Middle Ages*. Oxford.

Page, T. William. 1901. *The end of villeinage in England*, American Economic Association, 3rd series, I. New York.

Page, William, ed. 1906. *Victoria County History of Norfolk, volume 2*. London.

Palliser, David. 2014. *Medieval York 600–1540*. Oxford.

Palma, Numa. 2018. 'Reconstruction of money supply over the long run: the case of England, 1270–1870', *Economic History Review*, 71.

Palmer, Robert C. 1985. 'The economic and cultural impact of the origins of property: 1180–1220', *Law and History Review*, 3.

Palmer, Robert C. 1993. *English law in the age of the Black Death, 1348–1381: a transformation of governance and law*. Chapel Hill.

Palmer, Robert C. 2003. 'England: law, society and the state', in Stephen H. Rigby, ed., *A companion to Britain in the late Middle Ages*. Oxford.

Pamuk, Sevket. 2007. 'The Black Death and the origins of the Great Divergence across Europe, 1300–1600', *European Review of Economic History*, 11.

Peberdy, Robert B. 1994. 'The economy, society and government of a small town in late medieval England: a study of Henley-on-Thames c.1300 to c. 1540'. Ph.D. dissertation, University of Leicester.

Penn, Simon A.C., and Dyer, Christopher. 1994. 'Wages and earnings in late medieval England: evidence from enforcement of the labour laws', in Christopher Dyer, *Everyday life in medieval England*. London.

Persson, Karl G. 1984. 'Consumption, labour and leisure in the later Middle Ages', in D. Merijot, ed., *Manger et boire au Moyen Age*, I. Nice.

Pham, Michel T. 2007. 'Emotion and rationality: a critical review and interpretation of empirical evidence', *Review of General Psychology*, 11.

Phillips, Jennifer. 2005. 'Collaboration and litigation in two Suffolk manor courts 1289–1360'. PhD dissertation, University of Cambridge.

Platt Colin. 1996. *King Death: the Black Death and its aftermath in late-medieval England*. London.

Pollock, Frederick, and Maitland, F. William. 1896. *The history of English law before the time of Edward I, volume I*. Cambridge.

Poos, Lawrence R. 1983. 'The social context of the Statute of Labourers enforcement', *Law and History Review*, 1.

Poos, Lawrence R. 1991. *A rural society after the Black Death: Essex 1350–1525*. Cambridge.

Poos, Lawrence R. 2000. 'Medieval English manorial courts: their records and their jurisdiction', in Lloyd Bonfield, ed., *Seigniorial jurisdiction*. Berlin.

Poos, Larry R., and Bonfield, Lloyd, eds. 1997. *Select cases in manorial court 1250–1550: property and family law*, Selden Society, 114.

Post, J.B. 1973. 'Some limitations of the medieval peace rolls', *Journal of the Society of Archivists*, 4.

Postan, Michael M. 1972. *The medieval economy and society: an economic history of Britain in the later Middle Ages*. London.

Postles, David. 1989. 'Cleaning the medieval arable', *Agricultural History Review*, 37.

Postles, David. 2000. 'Migration and mobility in a less mature economy: English internal migration, c. 1200–1350', *Social History*, 23.

Powell, Edgar. 1896. *The rising in East Anglia in 1381*. Cambridge.

Prescott, Andrew. 1998. 'Writing about rebellion: using the records of the Peasants' Revolt of 1381', *History Workshop Journal*, 45.

Prescott, Andrew. 2016. '"Great and horrible rumour": shaping the English revolt of 1381', in Justine Firnhaber-Baker and Dirk Schoenaers, eds., *The Routledge handbook of medieval revolt*. Abingdon.

Prestwich, Michael. 1980. *The three Edwards: war and state in England 1272–1377*. London.

Pribyl, L. Kathleen. 2017. *Farming, famine, and plague: the impact of climate in late medieval England*. Berlin.

Putnam, Bertha H. 1908. *The enforcement of the Statutes of Labourers during the first decade after the Black Death, 1349–1359*. New York.

Putnam, Bertha H. 1938. *Proceedings before the justices of the peace in the fourteenth and fifteenth centuries*. London.

Raban, Sandra. 1993. 'Landlord return on villein rents in north Huntingdonshire in the thirteenth century', *Historical Research*, 66.

Raftis, J. Ambrose. 1957. *The estates of Ramsey abbey: a study in growth and organisation.* Toronto.

Raftis, J. Ambrose. 1964. *Tenure and mobility: studies in the social history of the medieval village.* Toronto.

Raftis, J. Ambrose. 1986. 'Social change versus revolution: new interpretations of the Peasants' Revolt of 1381', in Francis X. Newman, ed., *Social unrest in the late Middle Ages.* New York.

Raftis, J. Ambrose. 1996. *Peasant economic development within the English manorial system.* Stroud.

Raftis, J. Ambrose. 1996. 'Peasants and the collapse of the manorial economy on some Ramsey abbey estates', in Richard H. Britnell and John Hatcher, eds., *Progress and problems in medieval England.* Cambridge.

Ravensdale, Jack. 1975. *Liable to floods: village landscape on the edge of the Fens AD 450 1850.* Cambridge.

Ravensdale, Jack. 1984. 'Population changes and the transfer of customary land on a Cambridgeshire manor in the fourteenth century', in Richard M. Smith, ed., *Land, kinship and life cycle.* Cambridge.

Razi, Zvi. 1980. *Life, marriage and death in a medieval parish: economy, society and demography in Halesowen 1270–1400.* Cambridge.

Razi, Zvi. 1993. 'The myth of the immutable English family', *Past and Present*, 140.

Razi, Zvi. 1996. 'Manorial court rolls and local population: an East Anglian case study', *Economic History Review*, 49.

Razi, Zvi. 2007. 'A reply to the revisionists', in Christopher Dyer, Peter Coss, and Chris Wickham, eds., *Rodney Hilton's Middle Ages: an exploration of historical themes.* Past and Present Society.

Razi, Zvi, and Smith, Richard M. 1996. 'The origins of the English manor courts as a written record', in Zvi Razi and Richard M. Smith, eds., *Medieval society and the manor court.* Oxford.

Rees, Una. 1983. 'The leases of Haughmond abbey, Shropshire', *Midland History*, 8.

Rees Jones, Sarah. 2000. 'Household, work and the problem of mobile labour: the regulation of labour in medieval English towns', in James Bothwell, P. Jeremy P. Goldberg, and W. Mark Ormrod, eds., *The problem of labour in fourteenth-century England.* Woodbridge.

Reynolds, Susan. 1977. *An introduction to the history of English medieval towns.* Oxford.

Reynolds, Susan. 1994. *Fiefs and vassals: the medieval evidence reinterpreted.* Oxford.

Rigby, Stephen H. 1993. *Medieval Grimsby. Growth and decline.* Hull.

Rigby, Stephen H. 1995. *English society in the later Middle Ages: class, status and gender.* Basingstoke.

Rigby, Stephen H. 1995. 'Historical causation: is one thing more important than another?', *History*, 259.

Rigby, Stephen H. 2000. 'Gendering the Black Death: women in later medieval England', *Gender and History*, 12.

Rigby, Stephen H. 2003. 'Serfdom', in *The Oxford Encyclopedia of Economic History*, volume 4. Oxford.

Rigby, Stephen H. 2006. 'Introduction: social structure and economic change in late-medieval England', in Rosemary Horrox and W. Mark Ormrod, eds., *A social history of England 1200–1500.* Cambridge.

Rigby, Stephen H. 2010. 'Urban population in late medieval England: the evidence of the lay subsidies', *Economic History Review*, 63.

Rigby, Stephen H. 2015. 'Justifying inequality: peasants in medieval ideology', in Maryanne Kowaleski, John Langdon, and Phillipp R. Schofield, eds., *Peasants and lords in the medieval English economy: essays in honour of Bruce M.S. Campbell*. Turnhout.

Rio, Alice. 2017. *Slavery after Rome 500–1100*. Oxford.

Robertson, Kellie. 2006. *Labourer's two bodies: literary and legal productions in Britain 1350–1500*. Basingstoke.

Robertson, Durant W. 1986. 'Chaucer and the economic and social consequences of the plague', in Francis X. Newman, ed., *Social unrest in the late Middle Ages*. New York.

Robo, Eugene. 1929. 'The Black Death in the hundred of Farnham, *English Historical Review*, 45.

Rollison, David. 2010. *A Commonwealth of the people: popular politics and England's long social revolution, 1066–1649*. Cambridge.

Ronan, Nick. 1989. '1381. Writing in revolt: signs of confederacy in the chronicle accounts of the English rising', *Forum for Modern Language Studies*, 25.

Rosser, Gervase. 1989. *Medieval Westminster 1200–1540*. Oxford.

Rutledge, Elizabeth. 1988. 'Immigration and population growth in early fourteenth century Norwich: evidence from the tithing rolls', *Urban History Yearbook*, 15.

Russell, Josiah C. 1948. *British medieval population*. Albuquerque.

Saaler, Mary. 1991. 'The manor of Tillingdown: the changing economy of the demesne 1325–71', *Surrey Archaeological Collections*, 81.

Salisbury, Edward. 1961. *Weeds and aliens*. London.

Salter, Henry E., ed. 1908. *Cartulary of the abbey of Eynsham, volume II*. Oxford.

Sapoznik, Alexandra. 2013. 'Resource allocationand peasant decision making: Oakington, Cambridgeshire, 1360–99', *Agricultural History Review*, 61.

Sapoznik, Alexandra. 2013. 'The productivity of peasant agriculture: Oakington, Cambridgeshire, 1360–1399', *Economic History Review*, 66.

Sapoznik, Alexandra. 2019. 'Peasant agricultural productivity', paper to the Anglo-American Seminar on the Medieval Economy and Society, Worcester.

Saul, Anthony. 1982. 'English towns in the late middle ages: the case of Great Yarmouth', *Journal of Medieval History*, 8.

Saul, Nigel. 1990. 'Conflict and consensus in English local society', in John Taylor and Wendy R. Childs, eds., *Politics and crisis in fourteenth-century England*. Stroud.

Schneider, Eric B. 2014. 'Prices and production in agricultural supply response in fourteenth-century England', *Economic History Review*, 67.

Schofield, Phillipp R. 1996. 'Tenurial developments and the availability of customary land in a later medieval community', *Economic History Review*, 49.

Schofield, Phillipp R. 1997. 'Dearth, debt and the local land market in a late thirteenth-century village community', *Agricultural History Review*, 45.

Schofield, Phillipp R. 1998. 'Peasants and the manor court: gossip and litigation in a Suffolk village at the close of the thirteenth century', *Past and Present*, 159.

Schofield, Phillipp R. 2002. 'Introduction', in Phillipp R. Schofield and Nicholas Mayhew, eds., *Credit and debt in medieval England c.1180–c.1350*. Oxford.

Schofield, Phillipp R. 2007. 'Lordship and the peasant economy, c.1250–c.1400: Robert Kyng and the Abbot of Bury St Edmunds', in Christopher Dyer, Peter Coss, and Chris Wickham, eds., *Rodney Hilton's Middle Ages: an exploration of historical themes*. Past and Present Society.

Schofield, Phillipp R. 2015. 'Lordship and the early history of peasant land transfer on the estates of the abbey of Bury St Edmunds', in Maryanne Kowaleski, John Langdon, and

Phillipp R. Schofield, eds., *Peasants and lords in the medieval English economy: essays in honour of Bruce M.S. Campbell*. Turnhout.

Schofield, Phillipp R. 2016. *Peasants and historians: debating the medieval English peasantry*. Manchester.

Seabourne, Gwen. 2004. *Royal regulation of loans and sales in medieval England*. Woodbridge.

Seebohm, Frederic. 1865. 'The Black Death and its place in history: part I', *The Fortnightly Review*, 2.

Seebohm, Frederic. 1866. 'The Black Death and its place in history: part II', *The Fortnightly Review*, 4.

Sharp, Buchanan. 2013. 'Royal paternalism and the moral economy in the reign of Edward II: the response to the Great Famine', *Economic History Review*, 66.

Sharp, Buchanan. 2016. *Famine and scarcity in late medieval and early modern England: the regulation of grain marketing 1256–1631*. Cambridge.

Shaw, D. Gary. 1993. *The creation of a community: the city of Wells in the Middle Ages*. Oxford.

Shrewsbury, J.D.F. 1970. *A history of bubonic plague in the British Isles*. Cambridge.

Sillem, Rosamund, ed. 1937. *Some sessions of the peace in Lincolnshire, 1360–1375*, Lincoln Record Society, 30.

Simpson, A.W. Brian. 1975. *A history of the common law of contract: the rise of the action of assumpsit*. Oxford.

Simpson, A.W. Brian. 1986. *A history of the land law*. 2nd edition, Oxford.

Slack, Paul. 1990. *The impact of plague in Tudor and Stuart England*. Oxford.

Slavin, Philip. 2009. 'Chicken husbandry in late-medieval eastern England, 1250–1400', *Anthropozoologica*, 44.

Slavin, Philip. 2009. 'Death and survival: Norfolk cattle, c.1280–1370', *Fons Lumini*, 1.

Slavin, Philip. 2010. 'Late-medieval goose farming: evidence from eastern England, c.1250–1400', *Agricultural History Review*, 58.

Slavin, Philip. 2014. 'Market failure during the Great Famine in England and Wales (1315–1317)', *Past and Present*, 222.

Slavin, Philip. 2015. 'Peasant livestock husbandry in late thirteenth-century Suffolk: economy, environment, and society', in Maryanne Kowaleski, John Langdon, and Phillipp R. Schofield, eds., *Peasants and lords in the medieval English economy: essays in honour of Bruce M.S. Campbell*. Turnhout.

Slavin, Philip. 2019. 'The second wave: contours of the *Pestis secunda* in England and Wales 1361–2', paper to the Anglo-American Seminar on the Medieval Economy and Society, Worcester.

Slota, Leon A. 1998. 'Law, land transfer, and lordship on the estates of St Albans abbey in the thirteenth and fourteenth centuries', *Law and History Review*, 6.

Smith, Richard M. 1983. 'Some thoughts on hereditary and proprietary rights in land under customary law in thirteenth- and early fourteenth-century England', *Law and History Review*, 1.

Smith, Richard M. 1984. 'Some issues concerning peasants and their property in rural England 1250–1800', in Richard M. Smith, ed., *Land, kinship and life cycle*. Cambridge.

Smith Richard M. 1988. 'Human resources', in Grenville Astill and Annie Grant, eds., *The medieval countryside*. Oxford.

Smith, Richard M. 1996. 'A periodic market and its impact upon a manorial community: Botesdale, Suffolk and the manor of Redgrave', in Zvi Razi and Richard M. Smith, eds., *Medieval society and the manor court*. Oxford.

Smith, Richard M. 2007. 'Moving to marry among the customary tenants of late thirteenth- and early fourteenth-century England', in Peregrine Horden, ed., *Freedom of movement in the Middle Ages*. Donington.

Smith, Richard M. 2012. 'Measuring adult mortality in an age of plague', in Mark Bailey and Stephen H. Rigby, eds., *Town and countryside in the age of the Black Death: essays in honour of John Hatcher*. Turnhout.

Smith, Richard M. 2015. 'Dearth and local political responses: 1280–1325 and 1580–1596/7 compared', in Maryanne Kowaleski, John Langdon, and Phillipp R. Schofield, eds., *Peasants and lords in the medieval English economy: essays in honour of Bruce M. S. Campbell*. Turnhout.

Smith, Richard M. 2018. 'Some emerging issues in the demography of medieval England and prospects for their future investigation', *Local Population Studies*, 101.

Steinberg, Marc W. 2016. *England's great transformation: law, labour and the Industrial Revolution*. Chicago.

Stephenson, Martin. 2012. 'Risk and capital formation: seigniorial investment in an age of diversity', in Mark Bailey and Stephen H. Rigby, eds., *Town and countryside in the age of the Black Death: essays in honour of John Hatcher*. Turnhout.

Stevens, Matthew F. 2019. *The economy of medieval Wales 1067–1536*. Cardiff.

Stevenson, Abigail. 2014. 'From Domesday Book to the Hundred Rolls: lordship, landhold- ing and local society in three English hundreds, 1086 to 1280'. PhD dissertation, University of London.

Stockton, Eric, ed. 1962. *The voice of one crying: the major works of John Gower*. Seattle.

Stone, David J. 2001. 'Medieval farm management and technological mentalities: Hinderclay before the Black Death', *Economic History Review*, 54.

Stone, David J. 2003. 'The productivity and management of sheep in late medieval England', *Agricultural History Review*, 51

Stone, David J. 2005. *Decision-making in medieval agriculture*. Oxford.

Stone, David J. 2006. 'The consumption of field crops in late medieval England', in Christopher M. Woolgar, Dale Serjeantson, and Tom Waldron, eds., *Food in medieval England. Diet and nutrition*. Oxford.

Stone, David J. 2012. 'The Black Death and its immediate aftermath: crisis and change in the Fenland economy 1346–1353', in Mark Bailey and Stephen H. Rigby, eds., *Town and countryside in the age of the Black Death: essays in honour of John Hatcher*. Turnhout.

Stone, David J., ed. 2017. *The accounts for the manor of Esher in the Winchester Pipe Rolls 1235–1376*. Surrey Record Society, 46.

Stone, David J., and Sandover, Richard, eds. 2019. *Moor medieval: exploring Dartmoor in the Middle Ages*. Exeter.

Swanson, Heather. 1989. *Medieval artisans*. Oxford.

Swanson, Heather. 1999. *Medieval British towns*. Basingstoke.

Sweetinburgh, Sheila. 2010. 'Farming the Kent marshlands', in Sheila Sweetinburgh, ed., *Later medieval Kent 1220–1540*. Woodbridge.

Theilmann, John, and Cate, Frances. 2007. 'A plague of plagues: the problem of plague diagnosis in medieval England', *Journal of Interdisciplinary History*, 37.

Thomson, John A.F. 1983. *The transformation of medieval England 1370–1529*. Harlow.

Thornton, Michael J. 2004. 'Rural society in the manor courts of Northamptonshire, 1350–1500'. PhD dissertation, University of Leicester.

Titow, Jan Z. 1969. *English rural society 1200–1350*. London.

Titow, Jan Z. 1994. 'Lost rents, vacant holdings, and the contraction of peasant cultivation after the Black Death', *Agricultural History Review*, 42.

Tompkins, Matthew. 1981. 'Park, one of the St Albans manors', in *The Peasants' Revolt in Hertfordshire* (no editor). Stevenage.

Tompkins, Matthew. 2006. 'Peasant society in a Midlands manor: Great Horwood 1400 to 1600'. PhD dissertation, University of Leicester.

Tout, Thomas E. 1928. *Chapters in the administrative history of medieval England, volume III*. Manchester.

Tuck, J. Anthony. 1984. 'Nobles, commons and the Great Revolt of 1381', in Rodney H. Hilton and Trevor H. Aston, eds., *The English Rising of 1381*. Cambridge.

Tuck, J. Anthony. 1991. 'Occupation of the land: northern borders', in Edward Miller, ed., *The agrarian history of England and Wales, volume III: 1348–1500*. Cambridge.

Tuck, J. Anthony. 1991. 'Tenant farming and farmers: northern borders', in Edward Miller, ed., *The agrarian history of England and Wales, volume III: 1348–1500*. Cambridge.

Tuck, J. Anthony. 1996. 'A medieval tax haven: Berwick-upon-Tweed and the English crown, 1333–1461', in Richard H. Britnell and John Hatcher, eds., *Progress and problems in medieval England*. Cambridge.

Vinogradoff, Paul. 1892. *Villeinage in England*. Oxford.

Voigtlander, Nico, and Voth, Hans-Joachim. 2013. 'How the West "invented" fertility restriction', *American Economic Review*, 103.

Wade, J., 'Set-aside land study', http://www.setasidestudy.cu.uk/2-3-vegetation-studies-on-set-aside, accessed 14 September 2016.

Walker, John, and Andrews, David. 2018. '65–69 Bradford St, Bocking, Essex: an unusual timber framed building of the mid-14th century', *Essex Historic Buildings Group Newsletter*, 7.

Walker, Simon. 2006. 'Order and law', Rosemary Horrox and W. Mark Ormrod, eds., *A social history of England 1200–1500*. Cambridge.

Watts, John. 2009. *The making of polities. Europe 1300–1500*. Cambridge.

Watts, John. 2016. 'Conclusion' in Justine Firnhaber-Baker and Dirk Schoenaers, eds., *The Routledge handbook of medieval revolt*. Abingdon.

Waugh, Scott L. 1991. *England in the reign of Edward III*. Cambridge.

Wells Furby, Bridget. 2012. *The Berkeley estate 1281–1417: its economy and development*, Bristol and Gloucestershire Archaeological society Monographs, 1.

Whittle, Jane. 1998. 'Individualism and the family-land bond: a reassessment of land transfer patterns among the English peasantry c.1270–1580', *Past and Present*, 160.

Whittle, Jane. 2000. *The development of agrarian capitalism: land and labour in Norfolk 1440–1580*. Oxford.

Whittle, Jane. 2004. 'Tenure and landholding in England 1400-1580: a crucial period of the development of agrarian capitalism?', in Bas van Bavel and Peter Hoppenbrouwers, eds., *Landholding and land transfer in the North Sea areas (late Middle Ages–19th century)*. Turnhout.

Whittle, Jane. 2007. 'Peasant politics and class consciousness: the Norfolk rebellions of 1381 and 1549 compared', in Christopher Dyer, Peter Coss, and Chris Wickham, eds., *Rodney Hilton's Middle Ages: an exploration of historical themes*. Past and Present Society.

Whittle, Jane. 2008. 'Leasehold tenure in England c.1300–1600: its forms and incidence', in Bas van Bavel and Phillipp R. Schofield, eds., *The development of leasehold in north-western Europe, 1200–1600*. Turnhout.

Whittle, Jane. 2015. 'The food economy of lords, tenants and workers in a medieval village: Hunstanton, Norfolk, 1328–48', in Maryanne Kowaleski, John Langdon, and Phillipp R. Schofield, eds., *Peasants and lords in the medieval English economy: essays in honour of Bruce M.S. Campbell*. Turnhout.

Whittle, Jane, and Rigby, Stephen H. 2003. 'England: popular politics and social conflict', in Stephen H. Rigby, ed., *A companion to Britain in the late Middle Ages*. Oxford.

Williamson, Janet. 1985. 'Dispute in the manorial court: Lakenheath in the early fourteenth century', *Reading Medieval Studies*, 11.

Wilson, P.J. 1992. 'The natural regeneration of vegetation under set-aside in southern England', in James Clarke, ed., *Set-Aside*, British Crop Protection Council, 50.

Wilson, W.B., ed. 1992. *Mirour de l'Omme*. East Lansing.

Wood, Andy. 2013. *Memory of the people: custom and popular senses of the past in early modern England*. Cambridge.

Wood, Diana. 2002. *Medieval economic thought*. Cambridge.

Woods, Margaret. 2018. *Medieval Hadleigh*. Layham,

Wrigley, E. Tony. 1967. 'A simple model of London's importance in changing English society and economy 1650–1750', *Past and Present*, 37.

Xu, Mingjie. 2015. 'Disorder and rebellion in Cambridgeshire in 1381'. PhD dissertation, University of Cambridge.

Yates, Margaret. 2007. *Town and countryside in west Berkshire 1327–1600: social and economic change*. Woodbridge.

Yates, Margaret. 2013. 'The market in freehold land, 1300–1509: the evidence of feet of fines', *Economic History Review*, 66.

Zanden, Jan Luiten van. 2002. '"Revolt of the Early Modernists" and the "First Modern Economy": an assessment', *Economic History Review*, 55.

Index